Surviving Genocide

Surviving Genocide

NATIVE NATIONS AND
THE UNITED STATES FROM THE
AMERICAN REVOLUTION TO
BLEEDING KANSAS

Jeffrey Ostler

Yale UNIVERSITY PRESS

New Haven & London

Published with assistance from the Annie Burr Lewis Fund.

Published with assistance from the Oregon Humanities Center and the College of Arts and Sciences at the University of Oregon.

Yale University Press books may be purchased in quantity for educational, business, or promotional use. For information, please e-mail sales.press@yale.edu (U.S. office) or sales@yaleup.co.uk (U.K. office).

Set in Adobe Garamond type by Newgen North America.
Printed in the United States of America.
The maps are by Bill Nelson.

Library of Congress Control Number: 2018958482
ISBN 978-0-300-21812-1 (hardcover : alk. paper)

A catalogue record for this book is available from the British Library.

This paper meets the requirements of ANSI/NISO Z39.48-1992 (Permanence of Paper).

10 9 8 7 6 5 4 3 2 1

To University of Oregon graduate students, past and present

Contents

Note on Terminology

Native America has always included hundreds of distinct communities, often tied to other communities through kinship relations and common cultural traditions and with changing identities over time. In this book, I often refer to particular sets of communities as nations and treat them as relatively discrete and stable entities. My reason for doing so is twofold: first, to recognize the sovereignty of Native peoples, and second, to facilitate narration. My decisions, however, involve some simplifications. The Creeks, for example, are a multilingual confederacy in which local identities were often paramount. Similarly, Ojibwes, Ottawas, and Potawatomis, which I generally treat as three separate nations, formed the Three Fires, which in turn was part of a larger group known as the Anishinaabe, which included Nippisings, Mississaugas, Algonkins, and others. With a few exceptions, I have used the most current name for each Native nation and have noted alternative or earlier names in parentheses.

Introduction

AN ICY RIVER AND A RAGING SEA

In December 1831, while on the east bank of the Mississippi River at Memphis, Alexis de Tocqueville witnessed a band of Choctaws being forced west from their homelands by the United States government. In a little-known section of his otherwise famous *Democracy in America,* Tocqueville recalled that the "cold was exceptionally severe; the snow was hard on the ground, and huge masses of ice drifted on the river." The Choctaws "brought their families with them; there were among them the wounded, the sick, newborn babies, and the old men on the point of death." As the Choctaws embarked on a steamboat to cross the river, "neither sob nor complaint rose from that silent assembly." Soon, however, Tocqueville heard a "terrible howl." Left on the riverbank, the Choctaws' dogs had realized "that they were being left behind forever." Still howling, the dogs "plunged into the icy waters of the Mississippi to swim after their masters." The implicit fate of their animals forecast a similarly grim future for the Choctaws. Tocqueville predicted that they would soon cease to exist.[1]

In using Choctaw removal as an example of the destruction of Indians under American democracy, Tocqueville posed one of his characteristic paradoxes. The Spaniards, he observed, committed "unparalleled atrocities which brand them with indelible shame," but even so they "did not succeed in exterminating the Indian race" and were even forced to give Indians their rights.

On the other hand, Americans had exterminated the Indians and had done so "with wonderful ease, quietly, legally, and philanthropically, without spilling blood and without violating a single one of the great principles of morality in the eyes of the world." In sum, Tocqueville wrote, "It is impossible to destroy men with more respect to the laws of humanity."[2]

Tocqueville's contrast between an American bloodlessness that was ultimately more destructive than Spanish cruelty exposed the hypocrisy of Anglo Protestantism by standing the "Black Legend" of Spanish atrocities on its head. Nonetheless, Tocqueville seriously understated Americans' violence toward Indigenous people. Tocqueville was also mistaken in predicting that the Choctaws would disappear. Despite unfathomable suffering and terrible loss of life, the Choctaw Nation survived removal. (In fact, Tocqueville's account of the dying dogs as an omen of Choctaw disappearance was inaccurate—in a letter to his mother written at the time, Tocqueville related that the dogs actually boarded the steamship.)[3] Despite these flaws, however, Tocqueville put his finger on the undeniable fact that U.S. expansion unleashed destructive forces on American Indian nations. He also identified what may be a particular genius of the American people: their ability to inflict catastrophic destruction all the while claiming to be benevolent.

Since Tocqueville wrote about the United States' destruction of American Indians, thousands of books have been produced about Native people, U.S. Indian policy, and U.S. warfare against Native communities. Despite this, we lack a general overview of the impact of U.S. expansion on American Indian nations. This book is the first of two volumes intended to provide a comprehensive overview. This volume covers roughly the eastern half of the United States from the 1750s to 1860. As shown in Figure 1, this geography includes the territory the United States claimed when it gained independence from the British empire in 1783; Florida (part of the Spanish empire in 1783 and acquired by the United States in the late 1810s); and the eastern part of the 1803 Louisiana Purchase—Louisiana, Arkansas, Missouri, eastern Oklahoma, eastern Kansas, eastern Nebraska, Iowa, and Minnesota—a region that U.S. officials envisioned as a place to relocate Indians with homelands east of the Mississippi River, which I call the "zone of removal."[4] The second volume will focus primarily on the western half of the United States from the early 1800s to the end of the century, although it will also consider the conditions of Indian nations that remained in the East after 1860. In writing this book, I have benefited from a vast library of published materials. A good portion of this library consists of scholarly histories of individual Native nations, particular

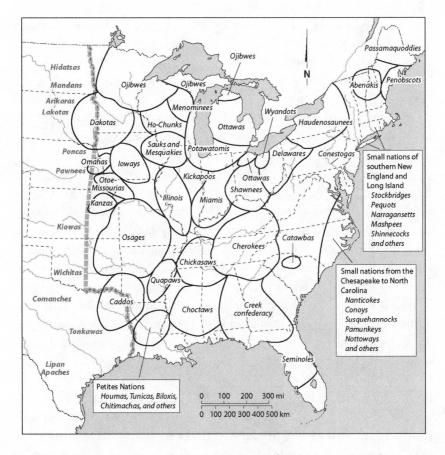

Fig. 1. Geography of the book, showing territories of Native nations around 1760
(dashed lines indicate modern state boundaries)

events, and phases of U.S. policy. I have also drawn on an array of published primary sources produced by missionaries, traders, travelers, correspondents, ethnographers, and government officials. Many of these sources contain the voices of Native people, and I have tried to bring these voices into the narrative. I have also incorporated the writings of Native people themselves.

What exactly was the impact of U.S. expansion on American Indian nations? How destructive was it? How did Indians respond to destructive forces? To what extent and how did they survive? To begin to answer these questions—the central questions of this book—we need to first recognize that one of the basic purposes of the United States was to take the lands of Native people and to make them available to speculators and settlers, including small farmers and large planters owning enslaved people. Historian Lorenzo Veracini succinctly captures the agenda of settler colonial empires, the United States included, by contrasting settler colonialism with ordinary colonialism. In colonialism (think, for example, of the British empire in South Asia), Veracini explains, the colonizer says to the colonized, "You, work for me." By contrast, in settler colonialism, the colonizer says, "You, go away." How would the United States try to make Indigenous people go away? What, in other words, were the means of elimination?[5]

The United States imagined several ways that Native people might be dispossessed. One possibility American leaders envisioned was that Indians would conveniently disappear as a result of seemingly "natural" and supposedly inevitable historical trends. This self-serving fantasy, however, did not happen. American leaders also talked a great deal about another possibility, that the United States might "civilize" Indians and assimilate them into American society. Historians have generally accepted American leaders' professions of a desire to civilize Indians at face value. In my view, however, U.S. officials were never seriously committed to a policy of civilization. As early as Thomas Jefferson's presidency (1801–1809), U.S. actions made it clear that despite talk of civilization and assimilation, the United States would ultimately pursue a third option for the elimination of Indians east of the Mississippi River: they would be moved west of the Mississippi. For practical reasons, it was not possible to implement a full-scale policy of removal until 1830 with the passage of the Indian Removal Act. In the meantime, the United States took a piecemeal approach to eliminating Indian lands and opening them to settlement by demanding that Native nations agree to treaties that ceded a portion of their lands. The preference of U.S. officials was for Native nations to willingly accept demands for their lands, but many Native leaders refused to agree to land cession treaties. These leaders regarded treaties that other leaders signed (almost always under coercive pressure) as illegitimate and often turned to militant resistance to defend their lands. When this happened, U.S. officials pursued another policy option: genocidal warfare. For several reasons, including cost, lack of capacity, and the necessity to appear to be acting according to Tocqueville's "laws of humanity," the United States did not make outright genocide its first option for elimination. But, as this book will show, U.S. officials developed a policy that "wars of extermination" against resisting Indians were not only necessary but ethical and legal.

As the United States expanded and pursued the elimination of Native people, it unleashed a variety of destructive forces on Indian communities:

war and violence, disease, material deprivation, starvation, and social stress. These forces were interrelated in complex ways. American warfare against Indians, for example, sometimes resulted in substantial loss of life from direct killing, but it also had other destructive consequences. American soldiers' rape of Native women, a phenomenon that is documented in the historical record and likely occurred far more frequently than the documents reveal, did not usually result in death. As legal scholar Sarah Deer explains, however, rape frequently "traumatized" Native women and left them unable "to contribute productively to the community."[6] Warfare also frequently resulted in the burning of Indian towns and crops, and this often led to material deprivation and starvation, conditions that favored disease. Similarly, the process of moving eastern Indians west of the Mississippi, though sometimes involving direct violence and massacre, was lethal primarily because the conditions of removal—lack of adequate food, clothing, and shelter, unfavorable environmental conditions (including weather), and social stress associated with forcible deportation—made people vulnerable to a variety of pathogens. After removal, Native nations attempting to make new homes in the West continued to suffer from social stress and poverty, which in turn increased their vulnerability to entrepreneurs seeking markets for liquor. All of this made people more vulnerable to disease, including alcoholism. Indians were not powerless in the face of forces of destruction. As we will see, they managed more often than not to avoid taking massive casualties at the hands of American military operations (and sometimes inflicted great damage on American armies) and were often able to minimize the impact of deadly disease. Indians succeeded in rebuilding their communities after wars and removals, but over time, many Indian nations, suffering from multiple assaults, experienced substantial population losses.

We know surprisingly little about general demographic trends for Indians in the eastern United States. How many Native people lived east of the Mississippi River in 1783, when the United States gained its independence and claimed control over that territory? And how many were in that same territory in 1830, when the United States fully implemented its policy of removal? Although there are no estimates in the existing scholarship, sufficient data exist for individual nations and particular regions to arrive at estimates. Remarkably, despite fifty years of aggressive American expansion, the Indigenous population east of the Mississippi actually *increased* from the 1780s to 1830. The population of some nations declined, but most either remained stable or grew, making for an overall rise. A growing Indigenous population hardly means that U.S. expansion was benign. Rather, an increasing Indigenous population is a testament to Native capacities to adapt to changing conditions and rebuild their populations after periods of warfare and destruction, in short, to their resilience. It is also a major rebuke to the central argument U.S. policymakers used to justify removal: that Indians were vanishing and needed to be moved to "save" them from total extinction.

A growing Indigenous population prior to 1830 further highlights the enormously destructive impact of removal. Historians have written a great deal about the Cherokee Trail of Tears (1838–1839) and to a lesser extent about trails of tears suffered by other Indian nations forced west during the era of removal. Some removals, such as the multiple removals of the Ho-Chunks (Winnebagos) and Sauks and Mesquakies (Foxes), however, are almost entirely unknown. We also lack a general assessment of removal's overall destructiveness and its demographic impact, not just on the trails of tears themselves but as a consequence of them. What happened to the Choctaws Tocqueville observed crossing the Mississippi when they reached their new homes? What happened to other Indian nations in similar situations? Some managed to rebuild or at least maintain reduced populations, but others, especially those forced to move multiple times, suffered from slow, steady, and largely unknown demographic catastrophes in the decades before the Civil War. Equally unclear is the impact of removal on Indian nations with homelands west of the Mississippi in the zone of removal. This area was not an empty wilderness. In order to prepare the way for removal, the United States dispossessed these nations, while allowing eastern Indians coming into the zone of removal to engage in destructive war against western nations. As a result of these factors as well as settler expansion west of the Mississippi, nations indigenous to Arkansas, Missouri, Iowa, eastern Kansas, and eastern Nebraska also suffered material deprivation that led to disease and major population losses. Without taking these losses into account, we will never appreciate the full impact of the United States policy of forcing tens of thousands of Indians West.

As they faced forces of destruction, Native leaders frequently alleged that Americans, or some portion of them, intended not only to take their lands, but to kill them all in order to do so. The title of this book, *Surviving Genocide,* recognizes this important and neglected perspective. For Native people in real historical time, all too often this was the challenge before them: to avoid what they perceived as the very real possibility that their communities, their people, their nations would be totally annihilated. That Indians believed that Americans had genocidal intentions toward them does not by itself "prove" that the United States or its citizens actually committed genocide, but it does require us to take the question of genocide in American history seriously. Debates about this question have been contentious and difficult to resolve. In addition to disputing how to define genocide and assess intent, scholars have differed over the relevant facts, such as how many Indians U.S. military forces actually killed or whether or not Americans gave smallpox-infected blankets to Indians. (For readers interested in an overview of the debate about genocide in American history, I have provided one in Appendix 1.) This book is not intended to resolve the genocide debate once and for all, but I will periodically address the question of genocide and argue that genocide was part of the history under consideration. Not only did the United States establish genocidal warfare as a policy option (as outlined above), American military forces attempted to commit acts of genocide and sometimes succeeded, government officials routinely relied on the threat of genocidal violence to secure agreement to treaties, and the policy of Indian removal had genocidal consequences. As the United States invaded Indian country, Native leaders had good reason to believe that Americans intended to destroy them all.

To write of a U.S. invasion of Indian country recalls an older historiographical moment, one signified by the title of Francis Jennings's 1976 book *The Invasion of America*. Fifteen years later, in his enormously influential work *The Middle Ground*, Richard White called for a different kind of history. "The history of Indian–white relations has not usually produced complex stories," White wrote. "Indians are the rock, European peoples are the sea, and history seems a constant storm. There have been but two outcomes: The sea wears down and dissolves the rock; or the sea erodes the rock but cannot finally absorb its battered remnant, which endures." White sought instead to tell a story of a "search for accommodation and common meaning" in a particular place and time, the *pays d'en haut* of the Great Lakes in the seventeenth and eighteenth centuries.[7] Since then, many other historians, similarly wanting to write new narratives showing Native people as active agents in history, have focused especially on times and places where Indians had substantial autonomy.[8] All of this literature has broadened and deepened our understanding of the long and complex history of North America. It is important for historians to continue work in this direction. It is also important to improve our analysis of times and places where the balance of power did not favor Indigenous people, or in other words, where Indians were subject to a raging sea.

In focusing on a situation of an escalating imbalance of power, I have tried to show that Indians were not *simply* acted upon or *entirely* victims. To do this, I have highlighted the myriad forms of individual and collective action that the historical record abundantly documents and offered explanations for the logic behind these actions. In so doing, I frequently quote Native people as they narrated visions, foretold possible futures, rallied supporters, criticized other Indians, exposed Americans' hypocrisy and racism, expressed fears and hopes, assented to treaties, recalled betrayals, protested injustice, and grieved losses. I have also tried to show not only that Native people *did* survive but *how* they did, or, in other words, to give accounts of what scholars in Indigenous studies are increasingly calling *survivance*.[9] So, this book contains stories of migration, rebuilding, adjustment, reciprocity, peacemaking, resistance, and military victory. At the same time, while Indian nations did survive, it is impossible to deny that the U.S. invasion had a destructive impact on almost all of them.

As Alexis de Tocqueville watched the Choctaws cross the icy Mississippi in late 1831, he was a witness to the "dark side" of democracy in America.[10] Since then, as the United States became a continental and then a world empire, Americans have seldom confronted the fact that their version of democracy required the dispossession of the continent's Indigenous people. Nor have Americans ever really acknowledged the costs to Native people of building the United States on Indigenous lands. At the time of this writing, it hardly seems likely that the federal government will establish a Truth and Reconciliation Commission to honestly assess the United States' impact on Native nations and propose meaningful remedies, including land return, for deep historical injustices. Perhaps, though, the current crisis of American democracy may lead to deeper questioning of democracy's foundations and a recognition of the need for a truthful accounting and a genuine reconciliation with America's first peoples.

PART ONE

Disease, War, and Dispossession

CHAPTER I

Trajectories, 1500s–1763

Sometime in mid-1776, just as the United States was declaring its independence from Great Britain, a delegation of Mohawks, Ottawas, Shawnees, Nanticokes, and Delawares traveled to the Cherokee capital of Chota on the Little Tennessee River in what is now southeastern Tennessee. Their purpose was to ask Cherokees to join a movement of Native American nations fighting to retain their independence against colonial expansion. At Chota, an unnamed Shawnee spokesman produced a war belt made of purple wampum nine feet long and spoke of a long history of injustice toward Indigenous people. According to British agent Henry Stuart, the Shawnee spokesman related that "the Virginians" (a term Indians applied to greedy settlers from all of the American colonies) had "taken away all their Lands" and "unjustly brought war upon their Nation," thus reducing the Shawnees from a "great people" to a "handful." In general, the spokesman elaborated, the "red people" had once been "Masters of the whole Country," but now they "hardly possessed ground enough to stand on." Lands where Indians had recently hunted "were thickly inhabited and covered with Forts & armed men; [and] wherever a Fort appeared in their neighbourhood, they might depend there would soon be Towns and Settlements." Historical trends combined with recent developments, the Shawnee spokesman argued, made it "plain, there was an intention to extirpate them."[1] At the very moment that the thirteen colonies imagined a future free from British tyranny, Indians feared that the colonists intended their complete and utter destruction.

The history the Shawnee spokesman related was straight as a line drawn by a ruler. Indians had once been numerous and prosperous, but Europeans had taken their lands and reduced their populations. Historians today are more aware than ever of the complexities of North American history and would want to qualify the Shawnee spokesman's account. They might point out, for example, that Native nations often formed alliances with colonizers and went to war against other Native nations, thus contesting a simple narrative of colonists versus Indians. They might also observe that Native nations were more powerful than Europeans in many parts of the continent long after 1492 and that there were "middle grounds" of mutual accommodation, facts that challenge linear accounts of Native declension.[2] Despite complexities, however, the historical trajectories the Shawnee spokesman identified were very real. Since the late sixteenth century, when Europeans began colonizing North America, the Native population of eastern North America had fallen, in many cases catastrophically. By 1776, European colonization had resulted in the dispossession of many Native nations, especially east of the Appalachians where non-Indians far outnumbered Indians. In those areas and areas just to the west where colonization had intensified in the 1750s and 1760s, Indians had ample reason to think that they faced the prospect of annihilation. Farther west, where Native nations retained their lands and still had political sovereignty and substantial economic independence, the threat from "Virginians" was not imminent. Even so, Indians everywhere had experienced—and adapted to—upheavals and forces of destruction stemming from the European invasion.

For several decades, historians have emphasized a single cause for Native depopulation: the so-called "virgin soil" epidemics that occurred when Europeans first arrived in North America. According to the virgin soil epidemic theory, Europeans brought crowd diseases, especially smallpox and measles, for which Native Americans had no immunity. The consequence was population collapses of 70 percent or more for almost every Native community that came in direct or indirect contact with Europeans. Recent scholarship, however, has shown that virgin soil epidemics did not occur everywhere and that Native populations did not inevitably crash as a result of contact. Most Indigenous communities were eventually afflicted by a variety of diseases, but in many cases this happened long after Europeans first arrived. When severe epidemics did hit, it was often less because Native bodies lacked immunity than because European colonialism disrupted Native communities and damaged their resources, making them more vulnerable to pathogens.[3]

As the Shawnee spokesman well knew, the Indigenous population generally fell during the period from the arrival of Europeans in the 1500s to the mid-1700s. By how much did it decline? What were the causes? Factors the Shawnee spokesman identified—war and loss of land—were powerful. There were also many other interrelated forces of destruction, including enslavement, disease, material deprivation, malnutrition, and social stress. As we will see, these forces of destruction hit some nations harder than others. To add to the complexity of the situation, some nations were able to rebound from population losses, while others suffered little if any decline at all.

THE SOUTH, 1539–1745

In 1539, the Spanish conquistador Hernando de Soto along with over 600 men landed at Tampa Bay (Fig. 2). Spanish explorers had earlier skirted the Atlantic and Gulf coasts, but not until de Soto did the Spanish try to conquer the chiefdoms of the American South. De Soto's expedition sowed destruction throughout the region. He and his men plundered Native food supplies, robbed graves, and raped and enslaved Native women. At Mabila, a town in present-day central Alabama, a *mico* (chief) known as Tascalusa tried to ambush de Soto, but de Soto's men killed as many as 3,000 of Tascalusa's men. The expedition also encouraged outbreaks of disease. At first glance, these outbreaks might seem to be examples of virgin soil epidemics. Recently, however, careful studies have revealed that it is highly unlikely that members of these expeditions had smallpox or measles. Instead, the disruptions caused by the expedition increased the vulnerability of Native people to diseases including syphilis and dysentery, already present in the Americas, and malaria, a disease recently introduced from the eastern hemisphere. De Soto's men likely carried the parasite that causes malaria and introduced it to anopheles mosquitoes, which in turn transferred it to southern Indians.[4]

There is little doubt that the de Soto expedition destabilized many Native chiefdoms and contributed to a decline in their populations, but it is impossible to tell the extent of this decline or its duration. For the South as a whole, studies yield an estimate of 567,000 for the region's Indigenous population before contact and 191,000 in 1685. This decline reflects the impact of the de Soto expedition and the difficulty of rebuilding populations in

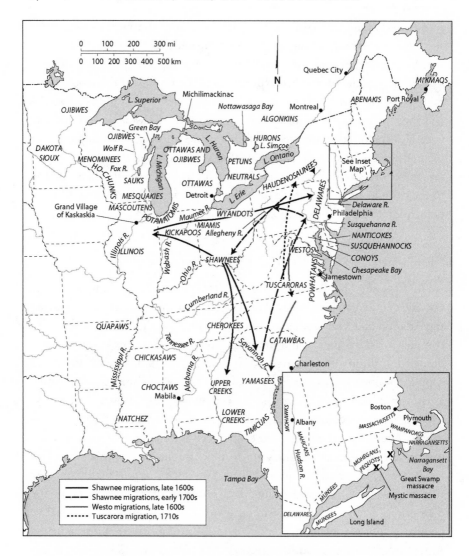

Fig. 2. Eastern North America, 1600s–1750s (dashed lines indicate modern state boundaries)

its wake, as well as many other direct and indirect consequences of European colonization throughout the South. Timucuas, for example, a people with a likely pre-Columbian population of tens of thousands in northern Florida and southeastern Georgia, were incorporated into Spanish missions in the late 1500s. There they were subject to forced labor and, because of poor living conditions and malnutrition, succumbed to wave after wave of unidentifiable diseases. By the mid-1600s, their population was only 2,500. To the north in what would become Virginia, English colonists who settled at Jamestown in 1607 steadily encroached on the lands and resources of the Powhatan chief-dom with a population of at least 13,000. There is no evidence of an epidemic until 1617, when a "great mortality" afflicted the colonists but was "far greater among the Indians." This outbreak occurred amid reports of poor harvests and so may have been related to malnutrition. As the colonists increasingly encroached on their lands, the Powhatans attacked English settlements in 1622 and again in 1644. In both instances, the English retaliated by burning crops and in 1646 imposed a treaty requiring the Indians to cede a substan-tial portion of their land. As the colonial population along Chesapeake Bay and the Potomac River increased in the 1650s and beyond, the dozens of Algonquian-speaking tribes in Virginia and Maryland suffered from a variety of diseases, including malaria, typhus, and possibly smallpox. Native vulner-ability was not simply a matter of deficient immunity. Instead, as colonists took their resources, Native communities were subject to malnutrition, star-vation, and social stress, all making people more vulnerable to pathogens. Repeated epidemics created additional trauma and population loss, which in turn disrupted the provision of health care. Populations plummeted not only because of deaths, but because fertility was reduced and repeated colonial assaults prevented populations from rebounding. By 1700, the population along the coastal plain of Virginia was estimated at only 1,450. Along the Potomac, the Indigenous population was probably even less.[5]

The first smallpox epidemic to hit the South did not arrive until 1696, a century and a half after de Soto set foot in the region. For smallpox to spread it needs repeated contact between bodies infected with the virus and bodies vulnerable to it. Conditions in the late seventeenth century were especially favorable. Since the 1650s English traders operating out of Virginia and, be-ginning in the 1670s, South Carolina promoted a growing trade in captives with the southern nations. Building on Indigenous practices of captive tak-ing, these traders encouraged Native nations to supply them with captives in exchange for clothing, tools, and especially firearms. English traders then sold captives into slavery in the Atlantic coast colonies or the West Indies. Some Native people—those that were well armed and closely connected to colonial traders—benefited from the slave trade, but even these only briefly. Take, for example, the Westos, a Native nation of about 500 that fled Haude-nosaunee (Iroquois) attacks in the Ohio Valley and migrated to Virginia in the 1640s. Armed by Virginia and later South Carolina slave traders, the Westos became formidable raiders, attacking Native communities in Georgia,

Tennessee, the Carolinas, and Florida, and gaining a monopoly over the slave trade. Eventually, however, Westo power threatened the interests of Carolina traders, who wanted competition among multiple suppliers of human bodies rather than a Westo monopoly. In 1682 Carolinians, assisted by Shawnees, went to war against the Westos, reducing their population to fifty. For most Native nations, the slave trade was disastrous from start to finish. Its destructive impact was due not only to the subtraction of the captives themselves but also to the loss of reproductive capacities (raiders frequently targeted girls and women), as well as the loss of men killed defending their towns against raids. The disruptions of the slave trade and the movement of traders and captives across a broad geography also created a favorable environment for the spread of smallpox should the virus ever arrive. It came to Virginia in 1696 on ships bearing slaves from Africa. It first struck English settlements and then spread across trade networks, reaching as far west as Arkansas, where it devastated Quapaws. By the time the epidemic burned itself out in 1700, it had taken the lives of tens of thousands of Indians. The South's Native population, estimated at 191,000 in 1685, now stood at 129,000.[6]

Similar forces of destruction continued to hammer the Native people of southeastern North America over the next half century. The slave trade depleted some communities to the point of near extinction. A variety of diseases —smallpox, malaria, typhoid, and dysentery—afflicted weakened bodies. And the region was wracked by war. In 1711 in North Carolina the Tuscaroras, fearing enslavement by the English and having seen colonists take much of their land, attacked settlements. After Carolina forces counterattacked and captured as many as 1,000 Tuscaroras, the remainder took refuge with the Five Nations Haudenosaunees in the North. Four years later Yamasees, numbering perhaps 1,200, and their allies in South Carolina rose up against colonists and were soon driven to Florida, where their population was reported at 300 in 1726. In the lower Mississippi Valley, Natchez Indians, objecting that the French in Louisiana "treat us as if we were . . . slaves," attacked French settlers in 1729. Using Choctaw and Tunica allies, the French retaliated against the Natchez, killed 100 warriors, and took 500 captives, who were sent into slavery in the Caribbean. By 1732, the number of Natchez warriors was estimated at 300, down from 4,000 in 1715. As illustrated by Choctaw and Tunica support for the French in the Natchez War, alliances frequently shifted and cut across European/Native lines. During the Yamasee War, for example, Cherokees saw an opportunity to develop a trading alliance with South Carolina and so sided with the colonists, while igniting an on-and-off war with the

Yamasee-allied Creeks that would last for close to two generations. Cherokees also suffered from a serious smallpox epidemic in 1738–1739. By 1745, the South's Native population had fallen to an estimated 59,000. In eastern Virginia and the eastern Carolinas, there were probably under 4,000. Some Nanticoke and Conoy communities remained on the eastern shore of Chesapeake Bay in Maryland, but the majority sought protection from further destruction by migrating north to the Susquehanna Valley in Pennsylvania. Most of the South's Indigenous people were in the interior and consisted of four nations: Cherokees (population 9,000), the Creek confederacy (population 12,000), Choctaws, and Chickasaws (combined population 14,500). These nations had not existed in 1540 but had been formed from the fragments of earlier chiefdoms and communities shattered by two centuries of war, disease, and slave raids.[7]

THE NORTHEAST, 1500S–1740S

In 1611 at the French colony of Port Royal in Acadia (present-day Nova Scotia) the Mi'kmaq sachem Membertou told Jesuit missionary Pierre Biard that when he was young his people had been "as thickly planted . . . as the hairs upon his head," but they had "diminished since the French have begun to frequent their country." Biard wrote that some Mi'kmaqs "think that the French poison them," while others attributed their decline to adulterated and spoiled food the French sold to them, which "corrupts the body and gives rise to the dysentery and other diseases which always attack them in Autumn." By the early 1610s, the Mi'kmaqs had been dealing with Europeans from the time French fishermen appeared in their waters close to a century earlier. They were one of the first northeastern nations to face the challenge of incorporating disruptive and greedy newcomers into a world of shared resources represented by the metaphor of the "common pot." Since the early sixteenth century, French traders had brought guns, metal and glass goods, brandy, and foodstuffs to exchange for moose hides and, beginning in the 1580s, beaver pelts. Over time, dietary change, including excessive alcohol consumption (a kind of poisoning), led to malnutrition and increasing vulnerability to disease. No major epidemics were recorded, but a variety of diseases (in addition to dysentery, Biard identified pleurisy and quinsy) steadily took lives and hindered fertility. From a pre-contact population of at least 12,000 and perhaps as high as 50,000, the Mi'kmaq population had fallen to between 3,000 and 3,500 in the early 1610s.[8]

It was not until 1616 that a major epidemic hit the coastal Northeast. It is impossible to identify the disease with certainty. Possible candidates include yellow fever, plague, typhus, leptospirosis, chicken pox, hepatitis, plague, and smallpox. Whatever it was, the epidemic was terribly deadly, taking upwards of 80 percent of the affected Nations (Abenakis, Massachusetts, and Wampanoags) before subsiding in 1619. For unknown reasons, this epidemic did not spread south of Narragansett Bay (Rhode Island) or to interior areas. The epidemic's uneven impact shaped the context for European colonization in the Northeast. Needing allies against the powerful Narragansetts, who were untouched by the epidemic, Wampanoags allied with English pilgrims who founded a colony at Plymouth, Massachusetts, in 1620. In turn, the Narragansetts began to trade with the Dutch, who in 1614 founded a trading post at Fort Orange, near present-day Albany, New York. The establishment of additional English colonies in Massachusetts Bay and Connecticut accelerated the growth of intensely competitive networks involving tribute and exchanges of European goods for furs and shell beads known as wampum. Northeastern Indians were also affected by French colonization in the St. Lawrence Valley. To develop a source of beaver pelts, in 1609 the French supplied the Montagnais, Algonkins, and Hurons with muskets so that they could attack Mohawks, the easternmost of the Five Nations Haudenosaunees (the others were the Onondagas, Oneidas, Senecas, and Cayugas). Needing a source of weapons to defend themselves, the Mohawks turned against Dutch-allied Mahicans so that they could establish commercial ties with the Dutch at Fort Orange. This link also connected Mohawks to wampum supplied by Narragansetts.[9]

Although the growth of European trade provided Native communities with momentary opportunities to increase their material well-being, the proliferation of trade networks wound up facilitating the spread of the smallpox virus when it arrived in 1633. The Pequots and tributary Mohegans in Connecticut had been spared the 1616 epidemic, but smallpox devastated them in 1633. According to one estimate, their population fell from 16,000 to 3,000. The epidemic also spread to the Haudenosaunees, and their population was cut in half from 20,000 to 10,000. This epidemic may have spread to the Hurons in 1634, or it may have been another unidentifiable disease that struck them that year. In any event, losses from the 1633 smallpox epidemic combined with another smallpox outbreak six years later contributed to a decline in the Huron population from 18,000 in the early seventeenth century to 9,000 by 1640.[10]

Colonial expansion also promoted violence. In some cases, violence took the form of intertribal war. After the Haudenosaunees obtained a reliable source of arms from the Dutch, they began attacking Hurons in the late 1630s. Their purpose was partly to obtain captives to replace people lost during the 1633 smallpox epidemic. They also plundered the Hurons for beaver pelts and to acquire new trapping territory. Haudenosaunee attacks culminated in 1649 with the destruction of several Huron villages between Nottawasaga Bay and Lake Simcoe in present-day Ontario, killing as many as 700 Hurons, taking hundreds captive, burning crops, and leaving hundreds more to starve. Their nation shattered, survivors set in motion a Huron diaspora. Some Hurons took refuge in nearby Petun and Neutral communities, although these were soon subject to Haudenosaunee assaults. Others resettled in Jesuit missions in Quebec. Many survivors were incorporated into Haudenosaunee communities, while still others migrated to the western Great Lakes, where they were taken in by Ottawas, and then to Detroit and northwestern Ohio, where they formed a descendant nation known as the Wyandots.[11]

In other cases, colonists directly instigated war. In 1634 during a trade dispute with the Dutch, Pequots mistakenly killed an English trader. Instead of accepting Pequot offers to make restitution, the Puritan leadership of Massachusetts Bay Colony insisted that the Pequots give up the killers. When the Pequots refused to relinquish their legal sovereignty and after another English trader was killed (probably by Narragansetts), the Massachusetts Bay Colony declared war on the Pequots. The Pequots posed no real threat, but the Puritans saw them as "proud and insolent" tools of Satan, who "threatened not only physical survival but the basic spiritual foundations of the Puritan commonwealth." In May 1637, English forces, along with Narragansett and Mohegan allies, set fire to a Pequot fort on the Mystic River in southeastern Connecticut, burning hundreds alive and shooting others who tried to escape—600 to 700 in all. The English, Narragansetts, and Mohegans hunted down surviving Pequots, killing some and capturing others. Narragansetts and Mohegans kept some captives. Others were sold into slavery in New England households and Caribbean plantations. Even so, some Pequots survived genocidal war. By the 1650s, they had reestablished themselves as a separate nation.[12]

Five years after the Pequot War, another colonial war erupted when William Kieft, director of the Dutch West India Company, decided to punish the Munsees for their attacks on Dutch settlers on Staten Island and western Long Island. In February 1642, when Wecquaesgeek Munsees took refuge from Mahican raids with the Dutch at New Amsterdam, Kieft ordered Dutch colonists to massacre the unsuspecting refugees. The colonists murdered many Indians in their sleep, hacked infants to pieces, and threw children to drown in the Hudson River. The death toll was 120. After further Munsee attacks, Kieft enlisted a veteran of the Pequot War, John Underhill, to annihilate Munsee communities. From late 1643 into early 1644, Underhill's mercenary army burned Munsee villages, including one near present-day Stamford, Connecticut, where as many as 700 perished, as at Mystic seven years earlier, mostly in flames.[13]

As the Pequot War was breaking out, Pequots hoped to recruit Narragansetts to an anticolonial alliance, warning that "the English were minded to destroy all Indians." At that time, the Narragansetts did not see the English as a threat and welcomed the opportunity to weaken a rival. In the early 1640s, however, Narragansett sachem Miantonomi concluded that all Indians needed to come together against the colonists. In the days of "our fathers," Miantonomi related, "our plains were full of deer," but since then the English had taken their lands, allowed their cattle to "eat up the grass" and their hogs to "spoil our beds of clams." If these trends were not stopped, "we shall starve to death!" Miantonomi was unable to unite New England's Native nations. They had too many alliances with colonists and were too much at odds with one another. But in the 1670s, as the processes Miantonomi identified accelerated, a Wampanoag sachem, Metacom (known to the English as King Philip), mobilized most of his own people as well as the Nipmucks and some Narragansetts against English colonialism. To explain the origins of King Philip's War, historians have often focused on the Plymouth Colony's trial and execution of three Wampanoags for murdering their kinsman and Christian convert John Sassamon because he supposedly warned the English at Plymouth that Metacom was planning an uprising. Recently, however, historians have pointed out that there is no hard evidence that Sassamon was murdered—his death may have been a hunting accident—and that even if he was killed, it was for other reasons. As a "praying Indian," Sassamon and others like him, who were increasingly allied with the English, threatened to undermine the authority of Metacom, the female sachem Weetamoo, and other non-Christian Indians. Moreover, Sassamon had played a key role in Plymouth Colony's taking of Wampanoag lands. Recent historians have also emphasized that Metacom, Weetamoo, and other leaders had multiple reasons for going to war. Not only did they interpret Plymouth Colony's trial and execution of the three Wampanoags as an act of oppression, if not a declaration of war, they had faced decades of environmental destruction, encroachments from settlers and their livestock, and unjust land transactions. At stake was an overwhelming "English threat to the survival of their homelands."[14]

In June 1675 the Wampanoags ambushed English settlements in southern Massachusetts. After further attacks and counterattacks, the English sent an army against neutralist Narragansetts in the Great Swamp in southern Rhode Island. The English targeted the Narragansetts in part because they were harboring Weetamoo and her warriors, but colonial officials also promised soldiers "a gratuity in [Narragansett] land." In December, at a partially completed fort, Narragansetts held off the attackers for a time, but eventually the colonists broke through and set fire to the fort, killing and burning as many as 1,000. For the next several months, Metacom and his allies had the upper hand, destroying towns throughout Rhode Island and Massachusetts. But the tide began to turn when Mohawks, allied with New York (controlled now by the English), cut off Metacom's access to guns at Albany. In late spring and summer 1676, colonial forces, supported by Mohegans and Pequots, assaulted Wampanoags, Nipmucks, and Narragansetts. In two instances—one in northwestern Massachusetts near Deerfield in May, the other at Nipsachuck Swamp in northern Rhode Island in July—these forces committed out-and-out massacres, slaughtering without regard to age or sex. Metacom was shot dead in August and his decapitated head placed on a pole at Plymouth. The war took the lives of 800 colonists, but it was far more damaging to Indians, who lost 3,000 to violence and war's other killers—starvation and disease. An additional 2,000 were taken captive and enslaved. The majority of those killed and captured belonged to communities that supported Metacom, but the war was devastating for other Native communities. In the war's early days, Massachusetts Bay Colony officials rounded up several hundred Christian Indians from the colony's "praying towns" and confined them at Deer Island in Boston Harbor. There, according to one colonial observer, they suffered "great distress for want of food." Many died before their release months later.[15]

King Philip's War was devastating in and of itself. It also opened the door to less dramatic but equally lethal forms of destruction. Without the threat of Native international armed resistance, settler colonialism accelerated. From 1680 to 1740 New England's non-Indigenous population increased from 66,000 to 290,000. In the 1720s Abenakis in northern New England and Mi'kmaqs in Nova Scotia (since 1713 an English colony) conducted guerrilla operations against English settlements and faced colonial counterattacks.

In general, however, New England's colonial expansion did not require war. Instead, it took the form of a gradual but relentless erosion of Native communities' land base and the confiscation and ruin of their hunting grounds and fisheries. In a word, dispossession meant poverty and poverty meant malnutrition, depression and stress, poor health care, low fertility, high infant mortality, and vulnerability to a host of diseases. Some diseases, like scrofula (a form of tuberculosis) and alcoholism, were ever-present scourges. Others, their precise identity unknowable, erupted periodically as epidemics. Prior to King Philip's War, New England's Native population was probably 30,000. By the 1770s, the earliest date for which an estimate is possible, the region's population had fallen to perhaps 3,500, a decline of close to 90 percent in a century. Scholars are accustomed to associate losses of this magnitude with smallpox and other crowd diseases that struck nonimmune populations in the early phase of the European invasion. Long after the first smallpox epidemic, however, the intensification of colonial settlement had produced a slow-motion demographic catastrophe that placed New England's Indian communities on the brink of extinction. As we will see, they would survive, but it would take heroic persistence and adaptation.[16]

Farther from areas of intensive settlement, Haudenosaunees in New York retained considerable power in the mid-eighteenth century. After their destruction of the Hurons in 1649, Haudenosaunees experienced losses in new wars with the French and French-allied Indians. They suffered even more from repeated outbreaks of disease between 1668 and 1679. But by continuing to incorporate captives into their communities, Haudenosaunees maintained a stable population of somewhere between 9,000 and 12,000. This changed during an imperial conflict between France and Britain known as King William's War (1689–1697), when the French and enemy Natives demolished Haudenosaunee towns. At the end of the war, the Haudenosaunee population had been reduced to between 6,000 and 7,000. After these disastrous years, in 1701 the Haudenosaunees negotiated treaties with the French and British that allowed them to pursue a policy of neutrality with these two imperial powers. At the same time, they relied on diplomacy to extend their influence over other Native nations, especially to the south in Pennsylvania and Maryland, and in the 1710s incorporated the Tuscaroras as the sixth member of their confederacy. Although Haudenosaunee communities suffered from the effects of a growing trade in rum in the early 1700s and another outbreak of smallpox in 1733, their population had reportedly rebounded to 8,800 by 1738 (this figure does not include a few hundred Haudenosaunees, often known as Mingos, who had migrated to the upper Ohio Valley). The straight downward line the Shawnee spokesman drew in 1776 was often apt, but there were many exceptions.[17]

PENNSYLVANIA, THE OHIO VALLEY, ILLINOIS, AND THE WESTERN GREAT LAKES, 1650S–1750S

The first written reference to the Shawnees dates to 1673, when Jesuit missionary Jacques Marquette, traveling down the Mississippi River, reached its confluence with the Ohio River. There he heard from his Miami guides of "a people called the Chaouanons," who lived up the Ohio "in so great numbers that in one district there are as many as 23 villages, and 15 in another." Shawnees had additional villages on the Cumberland River in Kentucky and Tennessee. It is impossible to tell how many Shawnees populated these villages. Estimates range from 2,000 to 4,000 and may be conservative. There is no evidence that the Shawnees or other Ohio Valley nations had yet been afflicted by epidemics of smallpox and measles. According to Marquette, however, the Shawnees were being hammered by the "barbarity of the Iroquois, who cruelly burn them." Indeed, it has long been thought that Haudenosaunee raids drove the Shawnees and other Native communities from the Ohio Valley in the 1660s and 1670s. Recently, however, historians have questioned this interpretation, pointing out that Jesuits propagandized Iroquois cruelty and greatly exaggerated the range, size, and impact of Haudenosaunee war parties. This new perspective recognizes that Ohio Valley nations vacated much of the region in the 1670s and 1680s, but argues that Haudenosaunee attacks were a minor factor. Instead, Ohio Valley Indians sought new opportunities in a changing world. Many nations—Miamis, Potawatomis, Mascoutens, and Kickapoos—relocated their villages to the northwest so that they could be closer to Green Bay (Wisconsin), the center of a vibrant fur trade involving the French, Ottawas, Ojibwes, Menominees, Ho-Chunks, Sauks, Mesquakies (Foxes), Crees, and Assiniboines. At the same time, to solidify ties with the French, the Illinois established a large town—the Grand Village of Kaskaskia—on the upper Illinois River. The Shawnees, described by a British trader in 1754 as the "greatest Travellers in America," chose another path and dispersed in many directions. Some Shawnees relocated to the Savannah River along the Georgia–South Carolina border, where, as we have seen, they assisted Carolina traders in crushing the Westos and then became enslavers themselves. Other Shawnees joined Tallapoosa, Abihka, and Alabama communities in Alabama (these communities would later become members of the Creek confederacy). Shawnees also moved northwest to join Miami and Illinois communities near the Grand Village of Kaskaskia before migrating yet again in the early 1690s, this time east to live among Delawares (close relatives of the Munsees) on the Delaware and upper Susquehanna rivers in Pennsylvania, where they prospered by selling furs to Pennsylvania traders. The Delawares who invited Shawnees to share their lands had earlier been displaced from Delaware and New Jersey. Unlike the Shawnees, Delawares had suffered grave losses from smallpox and other diseases in the seventeenth century. By the early 1700s, their population was perhaps 3,000, down from 10,000 or more a century earlier. The Delawares' experience led them to conclude that the English colonists "wanted to get rid of them and deliberately infected them by selling them matchcoats that had been exposed to smallpox germs." Such conclusions must have influenced Shawnee perceptions of colonial intentions, as voiced by the Shawnee spokesman visiting Chota in 1776.[18]

Shawnees who migrated east eventually encountered difficulties emanating from European colonialism. Those on the Savannah River grew powerful for a time, but in the ever-shifting brutality of the Carolina slave trade, Catawbas plundered their towns, and so in the early 1700s, many Shawnees relocated north on the lower Susquehanna River in Pennsylvania. This left a few hundred Shawnees who eventually relocated to Creek country after the Yamasee War. Shawnees who moved to the lower Susquehanna settled among communities with much to tell about colonialism's destructiveness. In addition to Delawares, there were a small number of Susquehannocks. A half century earlier Susquehannocks numbered 5,000, but disease and war with Haudenosaunees and the colonies of Maryland and Virginia had reduced their population to as few as 250 by 1698. Like Shawnees who had earlier settled in Pennsylvania, new Shawnee communities on the lower Susquehanna hoped to prosper in William Penn's "peaceable kingdom." In the 1710s, however, German and Scots-Irish settlers desiring Indian lands began to outnumber traders seeking skins, leading Shawnees on the lower Susquehanna to move again, this time west to the Allegheny and upper Ohio rivers in western Pennsylvania. By the late 1730s, some Shawnees had established villages on the Scioto River in southern Ohio, near the villages Marquette had learned of sixty years before. Shawnees who had earlier moved from the Illinois River to live on Delaware lands near the Delaware River in northeastern Pennsylvania were also forced out, along with their Delaware friends, in the late 1730s and early 1740s. The cause was a fraudulent treaty. In 1686, Delawares had sold a tract of land to Pennsylvania, but one of the boundaries remained vaguely defined as simply the distance a man "can go in one day and a half." In the Walking Purchase of 1737, Pennsylvania officials used this sale to cheat Delawares out of a much larger tract than originally envisioned. Instead of using a single walker to measure the boundary, the colony employed three "walkers" who did more running than walking, covering sixty miles instead of an expected twenty-five. By 1745, these Delawares and Shawnees relocated to the upper Ohio in western Pennsylvania, carrying with them bitter memories of what one Delaware decried as a "Fraud and great Fraud."[19]

As most Shawnees returned to the Ohio Valley (a minority remained in the South among Creek communities), they established relations with communities that had recently migrated there such as Haudenosaunees who had established villages on the Allegheny River. Consistent with a strategy of dispersal and alliance building that Shawnees had pursued for decades, they also reconnected with other nations that had left the region and had since returned. In 1696, French officials in Montreal decided to control the fur trade through Detroit and shut down western posts at Michilimackinac (between Lake Huron and Lake Michigan) and Green Bay. Miamis, Weas, and Kickapoos built new villages on the Wabash and upper Maumee rivers and forged ties, often through marriage, with independent French traders known as *coureurs du bois* who traded with English firms in Albany and Philadelphia. The Shawnees, already linked to Philadelphia traders, sought to develop new relationships with New France so that they could play one colonial entity off the other. Trade allowed Shawnees to prosper, as did the productive fields and orchards managed by Shawnee women. It is possible that the Shawnee population had declined since Marquette first heard of them in 1673. In tracking the dizzying Shawnee migrations of this period, historians have not reported significant population losses from disease, war, or any other cause. The earliest reliable estimate for the Shawnee population shows 1,800 Shawnees in 1768, which may represent a decline from unidentifiable causes over the previous century, but it is impossible to be certain. Nor is there evidence that Kickapoos or Potawatomis suffered major losses from epidemics or war. The only clearly documented disease outbreaks are for the closely related Miamis, Weas, and Piankashaws. An epidemic, variously identified as measles or smallpox, struck their town of Ouiatenon on the Wabash River in western Indiana in 1715. Seventeen years later a "mysterious illness" reportedly took 300 lives. Smallpox may have been the culprit, but one scholar has plausibly attributed the illness to the importation of brandy from the English post of Oswego on the southern shore of Lake Ontario in New York. Under this theory, traders may have intentionally poisoned the brandy to punish these communities for their recent shift toward the French or unintentionally added a poisonous substance in the course of the routine practice of diluting brandy prior to shipment. The combined Miami, Wea, Piankashaw population was reported to be 3,000 in 1736, down from an estimated pre-contact population of between 4,000 and 5,600. In general, though, Native communities in the Ohio Valley were far less affected by disease than those to the east.[20]

The largest and most powerful Native nation north of the Ohio River in the seventeenth century was the Illinois confederacy, a group that included Peorias, Kaskaskias, Cahokias, and others. Illinois prosperity rested on their exploitation of rich bison herds that populated the Illinois prairies and their development of trade networks from Louisiana into the eastern Great Lakes. As Illinois power increased, they became aggressive enslavers, undertaking raids against the Sioux and Pawnees to the west and Ho-Chunks, Menominees, and Mesquakies to the north. The Illinois incorporated some captives into their own communities and as time went on traded an increasing number to the French. By the late 1600s, the Illinois population was at least 10,500 and perhaps as high as 20,000. In 1694, however, shortly after the Shawnees and Miamis left, an unidentified disease struck the Grand Village of Kaskaskia. Because there is no record of an epidemic at this time in the histories of nearby nations, it is possible this outbreak was caused by endemic pathogens suddenly spreading in a densely populated urban area. Eight years later, as the Illinois were abandoning the Grand Village for new villages on the Mississippi south of the Missouri and beginning to establish connections with the new French colony of Louisiana, they were hit by another epidemic, probably smallpox. Reports of smallpox among the Quapaws on the Arkansas River in 1698 and Indians north of New Orleans in 1699 suggest the virus may have been transmitted up the Mississippi. Two more epidemics hit the Illinois, one in 1714 that scholars have been unable to identify and another in 1732–1733 said to be smallpox. The Illinois also lost fighting men and captives in war with the Haudenosaunees from the 1650s into the 1670s and with the Mesquakies from the 1650s to 1730. Overall, disease, occurring independently of war, was clearly the major cause of a catastrophic decline in the Illinois population from between 10,000 and 20,000 in the 1680s to 6,000 in 1700 and 2,500 in 1736—at least 75 percent in a half century.[21]

To the north in what is now Wisconsin, the Upper Peninsula of Michigan, and eastern Minnesota, Ottawas, Ojibwes, Ho-Chunks, Menominees,

Mascoutens, Sauks, and Mesquakies suffered less from disease. There are reports of smallpox and other ailments reaching the western Great Lakes in the seventeenth and early eighteenth centuries and taking many lives, but there is no evidence of a single epidemic ravaging the entire region, as in the Northeast in 1633 or the Southeast in 1696, or of repeated epidemics, as happened to the Illinois. Scholars have often asserted that the appearance of disease in this region resulted in population collapses, but such conclusions seem based on the questionable assumption of the uniformly lethal impact of so-called virgin soil epidemics. It bears repeating that conditions for the introduction, spread, and severity of disease varied considerably. Indian villages in the western Great Lakes were less densely populated and more dispersed than in other places, and this may have prevented disease from spreading. It is also conceivable that for various reasons—more efficacious medical practices, greater material well-being, better diet—the impact of disease outbreaks was not as severe as in other places, and that communities were able to recover from population losses when they occurred. Indians in this region did suffer losses in intertribal conflict, often fueled by the trade in slaves with France, but slave raiding in this region was less intense than it was in the Southeast. Disease, assisted by war and enslavement, likely reduced Ottawa, Ojibwe, Ho-Chunk, and Menominee populations from 1650 to 1750, but almost certainly not by anything close to the 70 percent or more in other places in eastern North America.[22]

If Indians in this region were largely spared catastrophic epidemics, one nation came close to being annihilated in war. This was the Mesquakies, known to the French as the Reynards and hence, in English, as the Foxes. In the 1670s most of the 2,000 or more Mesquakies were living along the Wolf River near Green Bay, while others lived in villages in Wisconsin and northern Illinois. Although allied with Mascoutens, Sauks, and occasionally Miamis, the Mesquakies were frequently at war with Ojibwes, Ottawas, Dakota Sioux, and Illinois—the latter regarded the Mesquakies as "devils on earth" with "nothing human but the shape." Mesquakie men died fighting in raids and counterraids, but over time the loss of women and children taken as captives to be sold into colonial households of Quebec City, Trois-Rivières, and Montreal probably had a greater demographic impact. To strengthen their position and to gain the return of slaves the Mesquakies secured an alliance with the French in the early 1700s. Many Mesquakies moved east to the French post of Detroit in 1711. As soon as the Mesquakies arrived, however, Ottawas, Ojibwes, Illinois, Potawatomis, and Miamis set upon them, taking

captives to add to the ranks of Mesquakies enslaved to French masters. By
1713, most Mesquakies had returned to Wisconsin. From there, they sought
a new alliance with Haudenosaunees and the British at Albany, leading the
French to negotiate a new agreement with them in 1716. For the Mesquakies,
an enduring peace with the French would require the return of Mesquakie
captives. Ultimately, however, even though French officials had a broad vision
of including the Mesquakies in an alliance of all the region's Indigenous nations, they were trapped by the dependence of French colonists on Mesquakie
slaves and repeatedly rebuffed Mesquakie demands on this crucial issue. In
1727, pressured by the Illinois, Ojibwes, and Ottawas, the French encouraged
new slave raids against the Mesquakies. In turn, the Mesquakies declared war
on their Native enemies and the French. Over the next few years, French
and Native forces repeatedly attacked the Mesquakies, including a massacre
of a reported 500, including 300 women and children, on the Grand Prairie
of Illinois in 1730. By 1732, the Mesquakie population had been reduced to
140 (not counting hundreds enslaved elsewhere). The Mesquakies might have
disappeared entirely. Fortunately, however, the Sauks, closely tied to them
through kinship, accepted the Mesquakies' request to join their village on
the Fox River. The French, determined to exterminate every last Mesquakie,
demanded that the Sauks surrender the Mesquakies, but the Sauks refused.
Knowing that the Sauks would now be targeted just the same as the Mesquakies, leaders of both nations decided that the only way to survive genocide
was to move beyond the reach of the French empire. They relocated west of
the Mississippi to Iowa. Over the next decades, the Mesquakies would rebuild
their population and with the Sauks form a powerful new nation. As we have
already seen and will see over and over in this book, Native people were nothing if not resilient. Decline was not necessarily permanent.[23]

THE SEVEN YEARS' WAR

From de Soto's invasion of the South in the 1540s through the Natchez
and Fox wars in the early eighteenth century, colonial wars were regional in
scope. None spread throughout the entirety of eastern North America. In the
early 1750s, however, when growing imperial rivalry between France and Britain ignited violent conflict in the Ohio Valley, war spread south to the Carolinas and north to upstate New York and Quebec, and its deadly consequences
were felt in the western Great Lakes. What became known as the French
and Indian War was part of the Seven Years' War, a broader imperial conflict

fought in Europe and India, and was the first transregional war in North American history. It triggered a second war in the 1760s—known variously as Pontiac's War, Pontiac's Rebellion, and Pontiac's Uprising—when several Native nations in the Ohio Valley and Great Lakes united to defend themselves against newly hegemonic British power. The Seven Years' War and Pontiac's War set in motion events that would lead to the American Revolution.

The Seven Years' War originated in 1754 when the French and British moved to construct a fort at the same strategic location, where the Monongahela and Allegheny rivers join to form the Ohio River (modern-day Pittsburgh; Fig. 3). Firing erupted in May when a Virginia militia under George Washington's command, intending to block the French construction of Fort Duquesne at the Forks of the Ohio, clashed with a French detachment in southwestern Pennsylvania. Washington's men killed nine French soldiers and wounded their commander, Joseph Coulon de Villiers de Jumonville. Soon after the fighting, Tanaghrisson, a Seneca leader allied with the British, came upon Jumonville and killed him. When the war broke out, Indians living in the Ohio Valley were fearful. Although they had profited from the ties they had cultivated with French and British traders who supplied them with guns, ammunition, cloth, and liquor, many Ohio Valley Indians were deeply suspicious of both empires. According to George Croghan, a trader with long experience in the area, many Indians "imagine . . . that ye Virginians and ye French Intend to Divide ye Land of Ohio between them." To accomplish this division, Delaware leaders Shingas, Tamaqua, Delaware George, and Pisquetomen charged, the "*French* and *English* intend to kill all the *Indians*." These allegations anticipated those the Shawnee spokesman would make two decades later against the Virginians.[24]

Despite theories of French–English collusion, most Ohio Valley nations had greater reason to fear English over French colonialism. Thus far, French designs in the Ohio Valley had been limited to trade. Indians in the region knew the English as traders, but they also had considerable knowledge of colonial settlers. Having been evicted from Pennsylvania in the late 1730s and early 1740s, Delawares and Shawnees living on the Allegheny and upper Ohio rivers had experienced settler colonialism firsthand. In the early phases of the war, then, most Ohio Valley nations leaned toward the French. When Major General Edward Braddock tried to recruit Indian fighters for a British campaign to take Fort Duquesne, he came up empty-handed. "Decades of relentless settlement expansion . . . had effectively alienated many potential allies." In sharp contrast, French officials drew on previous alliances to recruit

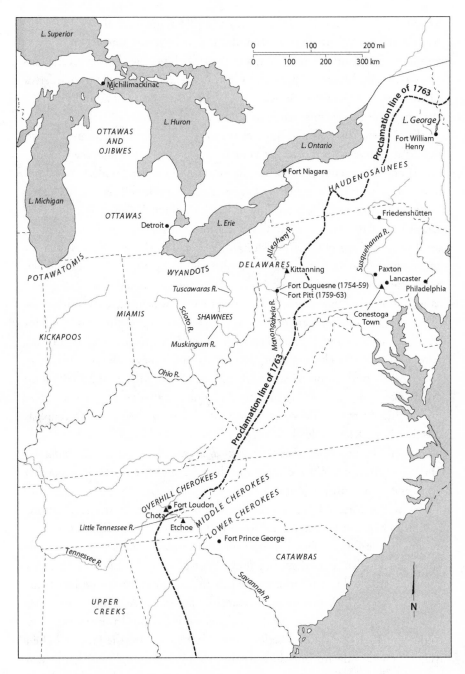

Fig. 3. The Seven Years' War, Pontiac's Uprising, and the Proclamation of 1763
(dashed lines indicate modern state boundaries)

between 600 and 700 Indian fighters, including Abenakis from the St. Lawrence River Valley, Ojibwes and Ottawas from the western Great Lakes, as
well as Delawares, Shawnees, Miamis, and Wyandots from the Ohio Valley,
to defend Fort Duquesne against Braddock's offensive. Native forces constituted the majority of the 900-man French army that in July 1755 turned back
Braddock's army of 1,400 and killed 400. On the heels of Braddock's defeat
Delawares and Shawnees declared war on the English and attacked settlements in western North Carolina, western Virginia, and eastern Pennsylvania, taking the lives of as many as 1,000 by the end of 1756.[25]

The tide soon turned. Pennsylvania, Virginia, and Maryland offered bounties for Indian scalps, thus encouraging frontiersmen to enlist in militias. In
September 1756, a Pennsylvania militia surprised the Delaware town of Kittanning on the Allegheny River in a predawn attack and shot down as many
as fifty of the town's 300 to 400 residents. Casualties would have been higher
had its armed defenders not held off the militia long enough for the majority
to flee to safety. Delawares had strong evidence that at least one of the two
European powers—the English—really did intend to kill them all. Fears of
another Kittanning or worse combined with the British naval blockade of the
French, which made it impossible for the French to supply their allies, led a
growing faction of Ohio Valley Indians to seek peace. Pennsylvania officials,
under pressure to protect settlers on their frontier, were open to the same.
Negotiations between Delawares, Haudenosaunees, and Pennsylvania culminated in October 1758 with an agreement that prohibited colonial settlement
west of the Allegheny Mountains. The following month, the French, bereft
of Indian allies and facing a British army marching on Fort Duquesne, blew
up the fort, allowing the British to erect Fort Pitt in its place (Fig. 4). For the
moment, the war for the Ohio Valley was over, but peace would hold only
as long as the British respected their agreement to halt colonial expansion.[26]

The most destructive violence of the Seven Years' War did not take place
where it erupted, but to the south in Cherokee country. For decades, Cherokees had enjoyed peaceful relations with South Carolina and the British empire. In 1730, a Cherokee delegation led by Attakullakulla (Little Carpenter)
traveled to London, where they fastened their people to a "Chain of Friendship" with King George II. Cherokees were drawn into the Seven Years' War
in early 1758, when hundreds of their men responded positively to General
John Forbes's efforts to enlist them in his campaign to take Fort Duquesne.
When Forbes's attack on the fort was delayed, the Cherokees departed, hoping to reach home in time for their annual Green Corn Ceremony. As the

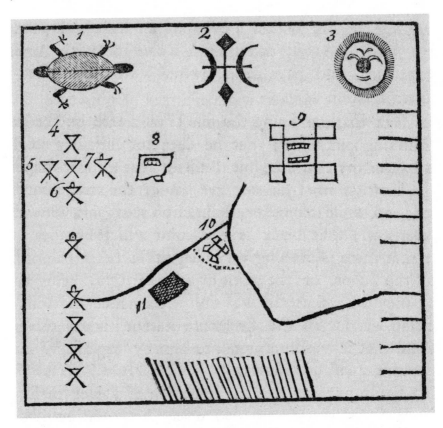

Fig. 4. In the early 1780s Wingenund, a Delaware warrior, peeled the bark off a sugar maple and used charcoal and bear's oil to paint this "map" of the Ohio country twenty years before. The map depicts the Allegheny and Monongahela rivers with Fort Pitt (#10) at the confluence. Two other forts are shown (#9 is Detroit; #8 is unidentified). A river turtle (#1) symbolizes the Delaware Nation; Wingenund's personal identification is to the right (#2). Other markings signify scalps and warriors taken prisoner (#4–7) and the number of times Wingenund went to war (the horizontal lines under #3). This sketch of Wingenund's map was published by the Society of Antiquaries of London in 1782. The sketch and its interpretation appear in Bray, "Observations," 159–62. Courtesy of the Newberry Library, Chicago.

Cherokees made their way south, Virginians and North Carolinians killed thirty of them, claiming they were hostile Shawnees or "Rogue" Cherokees. That winter, hunters from South Carolina trespassed on Cherokee lands and three military officers at Fort Prince George (in South Carolina's far north-western corner) "forcibly violated" some Cherokee women "and in the most shameless manner, at their own houses, while the husbands were away making their winter hunt." Cherokee leaders like Attakullakulla argued for restraint, but others, urging retaliation, killed as many as thirty colonials in the first months of 1759. That fall moderate Cherokee headmen, led by Oconostota (Stalking Turkey), undertook negotiations with South Carolina governor William Henry Lyttelton at Charleston, but Lyttelton seized several Cherokee negotiators and imprisoned them at Fort Prince George, where some contracted smallpox and died. Hoping to rescue the prisoners, Cherokees attacked the fort in February 1760 and killed its commanders. But before the Cherokees could seize their relatives, guards butchered them.[27]

After Cherokees continued to attack South Carolina settlements, Colonel Archibald Montgomery mobilized a punitive expedition of 2,000 men. As this force approached the Cherokee town of Etchoe in June 1760, Cherokees ambushed it, forcing Montgomery to retreat, although at significant cost. In addition to killing between sixty and eighty Cherokees and taking forty prisoners, Montgomery's men pillaged and burned five towns. By causing Cherokees from the destroyed villages to flee to more remote communities, Montgomery's expedition also fanned the flames of a simmering smallpox outbreak. Although Attakullakulla continued to counsel peace, Lyttelton's outrageous imprisoning of negotiators inclined Oconostota to war. In August Oconostota led militant Cherokees in an attack on Fort Loudon, five miles from the Cherokee capital of Chota in eastern Tennessee. After killing the commanding officer, they "stuffed earth into his mouth, and said, 'Dog, since you are so hungry for land, eat your fill.'" In the meantime, Montgomery had taken the captured prisoners to Charleston. There, according to Colonel James Grant, soldiers "daily committed . . . great abuses . . . upon the Cherokee women," strong evidence confirming that British military personnel repeatedly raped Cherokee women. By early 1761, smallpox had spread throughout Cherokee country, taking hundreds of lives in addition to those already lost in battle. A second British expedition that year was even more destructive. This one, consisting of 2,500 British and colonial soldiers commanded by Colonel Grant, reached Etchoe in June. Cherokees tried to ambush Grant's army but were unable to halt his advance. Recognizing their vulnerability against such a large army, they decided to minimize losses by abandoning their towns. Although Grant ordered his men "to put every soul to death," they were unable to kill more than few dozen Cherokees. But there were other means to inflict misery and loss of life. Grant was satisfied to report that he had driven "about 5,000 people . . . into the woods and mountains to starve." Reduced to eating "old-acorns," a food that "will barely keep hogs alive," many did starve. Others succumbed to a still-raging smallpox epidemic. Left to fend for themselves, hundreds more might have perished than actually did, but their relatives in the Overhill towns of eastern Tennessee, despite their fears of contracting smallpox, took in many of them. The Anglo-Cherokee War, a distinct conflict within the Seven Years' War, was devastating. From an estimated population of 9,000 in 1745, the Cherokee population fell to 7,000 by the mid-1760s.[28]

As the Anglo-Cherokee War revealed, pathogens thrive on war. The movement of armies and displaced people create prime conditions for viruses and other germs to spread. War's companions—famine, rape, trauma—weaken bodies, making them less able to fight off disease. Disrupted communities are less capable of providing compassion and care. In the late 1750s and early 1760s smallpox ravaged many areas of eastern North America, hitting European and African American populations in cities like Charleston, where a reported 730 died in early 1760, but wreaking far greater havoc on Native communities. The Catawbas, a nation living in the Carolina piedmont, lost more than half of their 1,500 people to the same epidemic. Smallpox was also terribly destructive for Indians in the western Great Lakes region. They had known sporadic outbreaks in the past, but it was not until the Seven Years' War that they suffered a regionwide epidemic. Ojibwes, Menominees, Potawatomis, and Ho-Chunks were probably exposed to the smallpox virus sometime in the summer of 1757 as hundreds of men from these nations traveled east to fight with the French, eventually destroying Fort William Henry, a British post at the southern end of Lake George in eastern New York. Although many historians have told a story of "viral retribution" in which Indians contracted smallpox from the very soldiers they killed and scalped at Fort William Henry, in fact the entire region around the fort was "infested with the virus," and so it is impossible to know exactly when and where it first entered the bodies of France's Native allies. Whatever its origins, when the Indians returned to their homelands, they carried with them the "seeds of a great epidemic." By early 1758, according to French reports, there was "great unrest" among Menominees, Ottawas, and Potawatomis because of "the great loss they have suffered from smallpox." Menominees lost 300 of their 1,100 people. As the epidemic spread, some Indians held the French responsible for its infliction. Others, however, attributed the "great number they lost" to the "English poisoning the Rum and giving them the Small Pox, for wh[ich] they owe them an everlasting ill will." It is impossible to estimate the number of lives taken by smallpox in 1758–1759. A report that reached Fort Niagara that the Potawatomis on the St. Joseph River in southern Michigan/northern Indiana "almost entirely perished of this epidemic" was exaggerated, but it conveyed something of the devastation. Memories of the epidemic among Ottawas decades later also revealed its catastrophic impact. "Lodge after lodge was totally vacated—nothing but the dead bodies lying here and there in their lodges—entire families being swept off by the ravages of this terrible disease."[29]

PONTIAC'S WAR AGAINST BRITISH COLONIALISM

Fighting between the British and the French in North America wound down after September 1759, when General James Wolfe defeated General Louis-Joseph de Montcalm on the Plains of Abraham and took control of Quebec. The Seven Years' War formally ended in 1763 with the signing of the Treaty of Paris. Yet, conflict between Indians and the British did not end with the French defeat. With the French gone from the Ohio Valley, the British tried to take advantage of their monopoly on colonial power to abolish the middle ground and impose a new regime on the region's Indigenous people. [30]

In 1762 Jeffrey Amherst, commander of Britain's North American army, ordered traders to curtail gift giving to Indians. For decades, this practice had served as a way to cultivate reciprocal bonds of allegiance between equals. But now, as George Croghan wrote in his journal, Indians coming into Fort Pitt were "much Displast" with the meager presents they received and wondered why the British "Sett So Little Store by thire freindshipe." To reduce the power of Native nations, Amherst also restricted the sale of arms and ammunition. Traveling from Fort Pitt to Michilimackinac, one British official discovered that Indians objected that this policy would leave them unable "to kill game Sufficient for the support of their families." Croghan reported another reason for alarm. Indians, he said, saw "stopping ye Sale of powder & Lead" as a sure sign that "we intend to make Warr on them." At stake was the very survival of Indian nations. Upon returning from negotiations with the "Western Nations" in Detroit in summer 1762, Sir William Johnson, British Superintendent of Indian Affairs, reported that the nations were "not only very uneasy, but jealous of our growing power" and fearful that "we should hem them in and in the end extirpate them."[31]

To resist dependency, subjugation, and eventual annihilation, Native leaders throughout the region organized a multinational alliance broader than anything so far seen in eastern North America. This confederation did not suddenly spring into existence. It was grounded in a religious and political revival that had been brewing for decades through the teachings of prophets like one at a Shawnee town on the Susquehanna River who in 1737 predicted that unless they stopped trading skins for rum, the Master of Life would "wipe them from the earth." The best known of these prophets was a Delaware named Neolin who resided in a village on the Tuscawaras River in eastern Ohio. In the late 1750s or early 1760s Neolin had visions in which the Master of Life instructed Indians to undertake a project of moral reformation, including the disavowal of European goods and ways of life. The Master of Life also told prophets of His opposition to the colonial takeover of Indigenous lands. To Pontiac, an Ottawa war leader, the Creator said, "As to those who come to trouble your lands,—drive them out, make war on them."[32]

We have no records documenting how Native leaders planned to drive the British east of the Appalachians, but we know this was what they had in mind in early May 1763 when Pontiac and a force of three to four hundred Ottawas, Potawatomis, and Wyandots laid siege to the British fort at Detroit. Within the next few weeks, Ottawas, Potawatomis, Wyandots, Ojibwes, Kickapoos, Miamis, and Senecas captured eight other British posts, including Fort Michilimackinac, which Indians seized by cleverly staging a game similar to lacrosse to divert the soldiers' attention. In late June Delawares began sporadic firing on Fort Pitt and a month later had it under siege. In the summer and fall, Shawnee and Delaware war parties struck colonial settlements in western Virginia, Maryland, and as far east in Pennsylvania as Berks County, only sixty miles west of Philadelphia. By the end of the year Shawnees and Delaware fighters had killed dozens of settlers, taken dozens more captive, and caused hundreds to flee for the safety of towns.[33]

Many British officials and colonists believed that Indians who attacked forts and settlements deserved to be exterminated. One way to achieve this was through biological warfare. In July 1763 General Amherst wrote Colonel Henry Bouquet, at the time in Lancaster, Pennsylvania, preparing a force to relieve Fort Pitt. "Could it not be contrived," Amherst asked, "to Send the *Small Pox* among those Disaffected tribes of Indians?" Bouquet responded that he would "try to inocculate the Indians by means of blankets." Amherst approved, adding that Bouquet should "try Every other method that can serve to Extirpate this Execreble Race." At the same time, as John Heckewelder, a Moravian missionary to Christian Indians on the upper Susquehanna River, observed, frontiersmen adopted "the doctrine . . . that the Indians were the Canaanites, who by God's commandment were to be destroyed."[34]

Bouquet himself probably never had the opportunity to "Send the *Small Pox.*" Weeks before Bouquet's response to Amherst, however, the British at Fort Pitt, acting on their own, had done precisely what Bouquet proposed. According to William Trent, a trader at the fort, in late June when two Delawares came to the fort to persuade the British to withdraw, he and the fort's commander, Captain Simeon Ecuyer, "gave them two Blankets and an Handkerchief out of the Small Pox Hospital" where several soldiers were ill with the disease. Trent hoped this would "have the desired effect." Whether it did or not is impossible to say. According to a trader named Gershom Hicks, smallpox did break out among Indians in the upper Ohio Valley, but it was in spring 1763—a few months before the Fort Pitt incident. The British distribution of items containing the smallpox virus in late June may have infected additional Indians, but there is no direct evidence of this. What is clear, however, is that the British not only contemplated but committed an act of biological warfare that was intended to kill as many Indians as possible. British officials also turned to more conventional methods for destroying Indians when they sent two armies—one commanded by Bouquet, the other by Colonel John Bradstreet—into the Ohio country in summer and fall 1764 with orders to "extirpate" Indians who refused to surrender. Bradstreet's expedition ran into logistical difficulties and was unable to reach Shawnee towns he was targeting on the Scioto River. Bouquet's expedition made it to the Muskingum River in eastern Ohio, where he secured the release of 300 white captives from Shawnees, Delawares, and Ohio Haudenosaunees. But Bouquet could not realize his ultimate goal of crushing centers of resistance farther west on the Scioto.[35]

Later the same year frontiersmen attempted to realize their genocidal aspirations. In mid-December a militia fifty strong from Paxton, a Pennsylvania town on the Susquehanna (near modern-day Harrisburg), attacked the Native community at Conestoga Town forty miles downriver. Descendants of Susquehannocks, Haudenosaunees, and others, the Conestogas had established their town in the late seventeenth century. William Penn himself had welcomed the Conestogas to Pennsylvania, pledging that they would "live in true Friendship & Amity as one People." The Paxton Boys, as they became known, killed six Conestogas, while fourteen others fled to the nearby town of Lancaster (Fig. 5). Pennsylvania officials afforded them protection, but the Paxton Boys came to Lancaster and slaughtered all fourteen, including

Fig. 5. On December 27, 1763, the Paxton Boys rode into Lancaster, Pennsylvania,
where a sheriff held fourteen Conestogas in a workhouse for protection.
This 1841 engraving has been frequently reproduced but usually without noting its
inaccuracies: formal attire, including top hats, for the perpetrators, and little clothing
for the victims. From Wimer, *Events in Indian History,* between pp. 488 and 489.
Reproduced by University of Oregon Digital Scholarship Services.

women and infants. The Paxton Boys then marched toward Philadelphia, an-
nouncing their intention to kill Indians from the Moravian mission towns in
northeastern Pennsylvania who had fled to the safety of the City of Brotherly
Love. Faced with the prospect of confronting British and colonial troops,
the Paxton Boys stopped six miles short of Philadelphia and agreed to halt
their efforts to kill Indians in exchange for an airing of their grievances that
the Quakers who controlled Pennsylvania had failed to protect frontiersmen
from Indian raids. Much has been written about the slaughter of the Conestogas, but less attention has been paid to the disaster that befell the panicked
Moravian Indians who sought refuge in Philadelphia. Pennsylvania officials
quickly dispatched them for protection under Sir William Johnson on the

Mohawk River west of Albany. But New York governor Cadwallader Colden refused to allow the refugees passage on the spurious grounds that the groups harbored "a number of rogues and thieves." Pennsylvania officials then decided to house the Moravians in Philadelphia's city barracks. Within those confines, smallpox and fevers broke out. By December 1764, when the Moravians were released to return to their town of Friedenshütten on the upper Susquehanna, fifty-six of the 140 had perished. As they traveled home, they suffered from "extreme weather . . . [and] frequent food shortages" and lost "several" additional members of their community on what has been termed an "Eighteenth-Century Trail of Tears."[36]

Some scholars in genocide studies have seen the Paxton Boys' murder of the Conestogas as an act of genocide, pointing out that the Paxton Boys "clearly explained their genocidal intent against all Indians" when they defended themselves by writing, "Who ever proclaimed War with a Part of a Nation, and not the whole?" The Paxton Boys did not kill as many Indians as they would have liked, although the fact that they were only partially successful is irrelevant to an evaluation of their intent. Moreover, the Paxton Boys' destruction went beyond those they directly killed. Although the Paxton Boys did not plan the deaths of the fifty-six Moravian Indians taken by disease in Philadelphia and in a narrow legal sense these deaths were not intentional, they cannot be characterized as accidental. Rather, these deaths (over one-third of the relevant population) were consistent with the goals of the Paxton Boys' campaign and a direct consequence of their actions. At first glance it may seem as though British and Pennsylvania officials were completely opposed to genocide. After all, they stopped the Paxton Boys from entering Philadelphia and murdering the Moravian Indians. Leading Pennsylvanians like Benjamin Franklin, who denounced the Paxton Boys as "barbarous Men who committed [an] atrocious act," were genuinely appalled by their actions. A closer look, however, reveals complicity. In August 1763, four months before the Conestoga massacre, Pennsylvania governor James Hamilton authorized a bounty of ten pounds per Indian scalp, thus providing official authorization for indiscriminate Indian killing. Pennsylvania's formal authorization of a new scalp bounty in July 1764 retroactively offered an additional measure of legitimacy for the actions of the Paxton Boys. Furthermore, British military officials who called for the extirpation of all Indians (and attempted to achieve it) established complicity on the part of the British empire itself. Defenders of the Paxton Boys' killing of the Conestogas later argued that because the Conestogas "were in Confederacy with our open Enemies," they were "justly exposed . . . to an aggravated Destruction." This was precisely the position of British officials who advocated biological warfare against Indians who resisted imperial policy. In the absence of evidence that the Conestogas were truly in league with Indians who attacked Pennsylvania settlements, British officials could not condone the slaughter of the Conestogas, but they did agree with the frontiersmen that enemy Indians should be exterminated. It was at this point that settler and imperial perspectives converged.[37]

In contrast to genocide studies scholars, most historians in the field of early America have avoided using the term *genocide* in connection with the Paxton Boys, preferring, if anything, the less severe term *ethnic cleansing*. While certainly critical of the Paxton Boys, some have been equally critical of the supporters of Pontiac, arguing that they engaged in "parallel campaigns" of racial ethnic cleansing. It is true that both groups used violence and imagined the elimination of their enemies, yet there were crucial differences. Beyond the obvious point that Pontiac's supporters were defending their land against an invasion, while the Paxton Boys represented the invaders, Pontiac's supporters did not really hope to eliminate all settlers. Shawnees and Delawares struck deep into Pennsylvania, but their primary objective, consistent with that of Pontiac and other movement leaders, was to counter British aggression and colonial expansion west of the Appalachians. Philadelphia and New York could stay. Pontiac and his supporters did have theories about race, positing separate creations for "red," "white," and "black" people. Crucially, though, they placed each "race" on a horizontal plane, maintaining that the Creator had given each race distinctive but equally valuable characteristics. In contrast, although the Paxton Boys saw themselves as innocent victims defending themselves against savages, they represented aggressive frontiersmen who believed they were entitled to hold Indian lands previously taken and acquire new lands farther west. The Paxton Boys lacked the capacity to eliminate Indians from Pennsylvania and eastern Ohio, let alone all of North America, but their ideology, extended forward in time, implied an Indian-free continent. And, although frontiersmen also classified people as red, white, and black, they conceived of these races vertically, with whites supreme.[38]

Compared to the Seven Years' War, which unleashed forces of destruction over broad swaths of eastern North America, Pontiac's War was less damaging. Native communities suffered some losses from disease from 1763 to 1765. The Moravians, who lost over a third of their people to smallpox and fever in Philadelphia after fleeing the Paxton Boys, were hit very hard. In the Ohio Valley and Great Lakes, however, the impact of disease was less severe. The

Shawnee leader Killbuck stated in early 1765 that smallpox and other un-named illnesses had taken the lives of 149 Shawnee men and an unspecified number of women and children. These were considerable losses, but smallpox did not spread as widely or cut as deeply as it had in 1758–1759. Part of the reason was that prior exposure to the virus had created greater immunity within affected populations and encouraged the development of practices to limit the disease's spread. John M'Cullough, a white captive in a Delaware community in the early 1760s, observed that as soon as smallpox broke out, the sick "were immediately moved out of town, and put under the care of one who had had the disease before."[39] Violence was also less severe in the 1763–1765 period. In a cruel irony, the only colonial Indian massacre during the time of Pontiac's War was of a group—the Conestogas—that did not support Pontiac's confederacy and was vulnerable precisely because it had chosen to accommodate to settler society. Otherwise, because British military expeditions were largely ineffective, the towns of the Ohio Valley did not ex-perience anything like those of the Cherokees a few years earlier. Confedera-tion fighters who captured and laid siege to British forts and attacked colonial settlements took few casualties.

Unable to impose surrender through military victory, the British turned to diplomacy. In summer 1764 Sir William Johnson entered negotiations at Fort Niagara with representatives of twenty nations from New York to Wiscon-sin. To some extent, Johnson was guided by the rationale behind the famous Royal Proclamation of 1763. Issued by King George III five months after the start of Pontiac's War, the proclamation established a boundary between colonial settlement and Indians at the crest of the Appalachians. London officials who devised this boundary did not expect it to be permanent. Con-cerned that unchecked expansion would make the colonies ungovernable, alienate Indians, and pull the empire into war, officials intended the 1763 Proclamation to regulate, not block, expansion. In inviting Native nations to Fort Niagara in summer 1764, Johnson assured them of the empire's commit-ment to "A Free fair & open Trade" and "That we will make no Settlements or Encroachments contrary to Treaty, or without their permission." Despite this, the majority of Pontiac's confederacy remained wary of the British and did not agree to peace. A year later, however, the confederation had become short of arms and ammunition, battles and disease had thinned their fighting forces, and their communities were increasingly weary of war. In 1765 Shaw-nee, Delaware, Ohio Seneca, Ottawa, Potawatomi, Ojibwe, and Wyandot leaders held talks with British representatives and agreed to peace. Pontiac himself "smoaked out of the pipe of Peace" and then asked that the pipe be sent to Sir William Johnson so that "he may know that I have made Peace, & taken the King for my father."[40]

Peace's implications were uncertain. Confederation leaders who had gone to war against the British empire saw peace, in the words of Shawnee chief Nimwah, as a repudiation of the British assertion that they were "Masters of this Country" and an affirmation that "it is the Property of us Indians." This interpretation, of course, meant that the boundary drawn by the Proclamation of 1763 would be permanent. British officials understood the end of war very differently. Pontiac and his supporters had taught imperial officials that there were costs to imperiousness and aggressive expansion and so, in the words of a written agreement with the Shawnees and Delawares, British officials recognized "Native Rights." But this agreement's categorization of Shawnees and Delawares as "Children of the Great King of England" who were to "pay all due submission and subjection" meant that these rights were ultimately to be determined by the empire. With Native sovereignty compromised, any boundary between the empire and Indian country could be altered and altered again.[41]

CONCLUSION: A VIRGINIAN'S PREDICTION

From his Mount Vernon plantation George Washington often contemplated the Proclamation of 1763. His hope, as he expressed it to frontiersman, surveyor, and soldier William Crawford, was that the proclamation was merely "a temporary expedient to quiet the Minds of the Indians." Washington predicted that the proclamation "must fall . . . in a few years."[42] Washington had no burning desire to hew logs for a cabin in the wilds of Ohio, but he was passionate about speculating in Ohio's Indian lands. If the proclamation remained in effect, his financial future would be at risk.

Had Washington's prediction of the proclamation's fall been accurate it is possible that the American Revolution would not have happened. Colonists' desire for independence from a tyrannical king had many sources, but one of them was that the Proclamation of 1763 did not completely fall. As we will see in the next chapter, the Crown would modify the proclamation's boundary, but imperial policy nonetheless continued to restrict the liberty of colonists to speculate in and settle on Native lands. Colonists saw themselves as victims of growing British tyranny, but from the perspective of Indians colonists hardly seemed oppressed. Indeed, as the colonists moved closer to declaring their independence, they seemed increasingly dangerous to Native nations. Although the British empire did not fully recognize Native sovereignty and would attempt to accommodate colonial interests by moving the proclamation's boundary west, the king nonetheless afforded Indians some protection. Should colonists gain their independence, Native nations would be at the mercy of Virginians. And if the Shawnee who spoke at Chota in mid-1776 was right, Virginians threatened not just the freedom of Indians but their very existence.

CHAPTER 2

⊶————◄◊◈◊►————⊷

Wars of Revolution and Independence, 1763–1783

In 1765, when Pontiac met with British officials at Detroit, he had a less cynical interpretation of the Proclamation of 1763 than George Washington. In contrast to Washington's characterization of the proclamation as a "temporary expedient to quiet the Minds of the Indians," Pontiac expected the boundary it established to be permanent. Even as Pontiac smoked the pipe of peace, however, settlers from Virginia were streaming over the Appalachians into southwestern Pennsylvania and cutting their initials into the bark of trees, thus claiming the land by "tomahawk right." Indians refrained from attacking squatters who intended to steal their lands. Instead, they turned to King George III. In May 1766, a delegation of Delawares, Shawnees, Wyandots, and Senecas informed Captain William Murray, the king's representative at Fort Pitt, that "as soon as the peace was made last year . . . , a number of our people came over the Great Mountain and settled at Redstone Creek & upon the Monongahela" south of Fort Pitt. The delegates were eager to "promote the good work of Peace," but squatters' violation of the terms of peace, coupled with the fact that "several of their People" had recently been "Murdered on the Frontiers on Several Provinces," made them fearful that war would come again. Consistent with imperial policy to deter illegal settlement, Murray ordered the squatters to leave and sent a detachment of troops to enforce his order. The troops "destroy[ed] as many Hutts as they could find," but settlers soon returned. By October 1767, as the trader George

44

Croghan reported, "there [were] double the number of Inhabitants" in the new settlements as had lived there before. A few months later a Pennsylvania settler named Frederick Stump and his servant, John Ironcutter, murdered ten Native people (four men, two women, three girls, and an infant) living in the Susquehanna Valley about ninety miles north of where the Paxton Boys had massacred the Conestogas four years before. Pennsylvania officials arrested Stump and Ironcutter and confined them in Carlisle, but local citizens stormed the jail and spirited the two away. When news of these murders reached Shawnees and Delawares in the Ohio Valley, they were outraged and held councils to consider the possibility of a new war.[1]

Nations to the south also suffered from trespassing squatters and unprovoked violence. In 1766, Cherokees protested that families from North Carolina and Virginia had recently settled on "a great deal of our best lands" on the upper Savannah and Saluda rivers in northwestern South Carolina. That same year, near Staunton, Virginia, in the Shenandoah Valley a group calling themselves the Augusta Boys, a gesture of solidarity with Pennsylvania's Paxton Boys, killed six Cherokees. The Paxton Boys, never brought to trial by Pennsylvania, reciprocated by offering their assistance to prevent the Augusta Boys from being punished, insisting as a matter of white racial privilege that "no man shall suffer for the Murder of a Savage." Adding to assaults on the Cherokees, Superintendent of Indian Affairs Sir William Johnson encouraged Haudenosaunees to send war parties against Cherokee towns. This, thought Johnson, would divide Cherokees from other nations and prevent the revival of multinational resistance to imperial authority. In September 1766 Cherokee Beloved Man Kittagusta appealed to Sir William's counterpart in the South, John Stuart, to prevent the British from aiding northern raiders. "We are tired of war," Kittagusta said, "for our enemies are too numerous." For Creeks, the problem was not colonists from Virginia or the Carolinas, but their kindred spirits from Georgia. In 1763 a Creek leader known to Anglophones as The Mortar complained that Georgians had invaded Creek lands with "People Cattle and Horses." Because of this, Creek men were unable to "supply their Women and Children with Provisions as they could do formerly, their Buffalo, Deer and Bear being drove off the Land and killed." There are no reports of settler violence against Creeks at this time, but Creeks nonetheless shared the fear, widespread among Indians during this period of North American history, that "the English entertain a settled design of extirpating the whole Indian Race, with a View to possess & enjoy their Lands." Imperial officials attributed the Creeks' adoption of this view to the work of outside agitators, in particular the French and Spanish, who had "inculculated [the] idea among the Indians." But Creeks and other Native people had ample reason to reach this conclusion on their own. They did not require European inspiration.[2]

Despite fears of English malevolence, Native leaders who appealed to imperial officials to stop colonial aggression and violence understood that the objectives of settlers and imperial officials were not necessarily identical. Indians had evidence of official machinations to divide and conquer, as when Sir William fomented intertribal war, and they saw that officials were sometimes unable (or unwilling?) to evict trespassing settlers. Nonetheless, they recognized that their best hope of retaining their lands, short of going to war on their own, was for the king to enforce the boundary he had proclaimed in 1763.

Imperial policy satisfied no one. When British officials accommodated colonial demands for Indian lands, as they had planned all along, they violated what Indians regarded as solemn agreements. At such moments, it appeared that imperial and colonial interests were aligned *against* Native interests. On the other hand, because British officials did not meet *all* colonial demands for Indian lands, colonists became alienated from empire. By 1773, the breakdown of imperial authority would allow for the eruption of a new war between Indians and settlers in the Ohio Valley. Two years later, when shots were fired at Lexington and Concord, no one heard them with greater concern than Indians. After the Seven Years' War, they knew all too well what it was like to be engulfed in a war between white adversaries. Early on, most Native communities sought to stay out of the conflict as best they could, but as the Revolutionary War developed a growing number judged that an independent United States posed a far greater threat than the British empire. As Native communities tilted toward or openly allied with the British, they became vulnerable to an American army intent not only on defeating a tyrannical king but on exercising a self-evident right to possess the continent's lands. The result was destruction on a scale that exceeded that of the Seven Years' War.

BOUNDARY PROBLEMS

Despite the expectations of Pontiac and many other Indians that the British would respect the permanence of the 1763 Proclamation line, it was only a matter of time before British officials adjusted the boundary between the colonies and Indian country. Sir William Johnson, in charge of negotiating a new boundary north of the Ohio River, approached his task with more than one idea in mind. On the one hand, since 1758 he had called for substantial regulation of settlement and was a proponent of the 1763 Proclamation. On the other hand, Johnson was allied with Philadelphia merchants who were pushing the claims of the "Suffering Traders" to lands south of Fort Pitt to compensate for losses during the conflicts of the late 1750s and early 1760s. Johnson had also invested, along with Benjamin Franklin and other Pennsylvanians, in a speculative enterprise that was eyeing Indian lands in southern Illinois. Johnson had close ties to the Haudenosaunees (he had a long-term relationship, including several children, with Molly Brant, a woman of an influential Mohawk family) and was committed to upholding the position the Haudenosaunees had long claimed as the central mediators between the British and the Delawares, Shawnees, and other nations of the upper Ohio Valley, whom the Haudenosaunees regarded as their subordinates.[3]

In October 1768 Johnson convened an intertribal council at Fort Stanwix, near present-day Rome, New York (Fig. 6). Over 3,000 Indians were present. About three-quarters were Haudenosaunee, while the remainder were from the supposedly subordinate nations—Delawares, Munsees, and Shawnees, among others. Although the lands of these nations were under threat, they were granted only observer status. The negotiations took place under the fiction that the Six Nations controlled the Ohio Valley and its peoples. Speculators, traders, and representatives of New York, New Jersey, Pennsylvania, and Virginia, all anxious to ensure a boundary that would accommodate their western interests, were also on hand. In the end, the Haudenosaunees accepted gifts and cash in the amount of £10,460, a "massive and unprecedented payment from colonists to Indians." In exchange the Haudenosaunees ceded some of their western New York lands, much of western Pennsylvania, and lands south of the Ohio River to the Tennessee River (most of present-day Kentucky, at the time claimed by both Virginia and Pennsylvania). Although the Six Nations had the right to cede lands in New York, their claim to ownership of lands in Pennsylvania, western Virginia, and Kentucky rested on a dubious theory of previous conquest. Shawnees, Delawares, and western Haudenosaunees, who saw themselves as independent of the Six Nations, vehemently rejected the idea that the Six Nations could sell their lands without their approval. Shawnee leaders called on Ohio nations to "unite and attack the Englishe."[4]

Imperial officials were also unhappy with the Fort Stanwix Treaty. The Earl of Hillsborough, secretary of state for the colonies, had instructed Johnson to negotiate a boundary that would terminate at the confluence of the

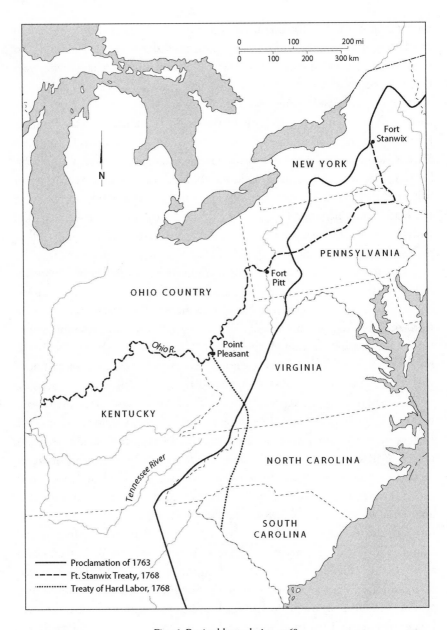

Fig. 6. Revised boundaries, 1768

Kanawha and the Ohio rivers (present-day Point Pleasant, West Virginia). At that point, it would continue along a southern boundary that John Stuart negotiated with the Cherokees at the Treaty of Hard Labor at the time of the Fort Stanwix proceedings. Had Johnson followed Hillsborough's instructions, western Virginia and Kentucky would have remained Indian country. When Hillsborough learned of the terms of the Fort Stanwix Treaty, he informed Johnson that "the deviation" from the line in his earlier instructions "is contrary to the opinion of His Majesty's servants on this side." Johnson's treaty, Hillsborough feared, would "produce jealousy and dissatisfaction amongst the Cherokee" and "throw into confusion" the line Stuart had negotiated at Hard Labor. Although Virginia speculators began surveying lands presumably opened up by the Fort Stanwix Treaty, in early 1770 Hillsborough placed a ban on settlement in Kentucky, thus keeping alive the Proclamation of 1763 and depriving speculators of secure title. Although imperial officials bent slightly to Virginia's demands and negotiated with the Cherokees for a series of moderate adjustments of the Hard Labor line, extending it west to the mouth of the Kentucky River by 1772, this fell short of Virginia's desires. Virginia's leading men objected to *any* restrictions on their activities and continued to demand the repeal of the Royal Proclamation.[5]

RENEWAL OF WAR, 1773–1774

Although imperial policies were alienating prominent colonists who wanted Indian lands as capital investments, that did not mean Indigenous approval of those same policies. To the contrary, the Treaty of Fort Stanwix angered western Indians, as did a new invasion of Kentucky inaugurated when Daniel Boone famously led a party of settlers through the Cumberland Gap in 1769. In 1770 representatives of several Ohio Valley and Great Lakes Indian communities, including Miamis, Delawares, western Senecas, Piankashaws, and Kickapoos, met with Shawnees on the Scioto River to form a new multinational confederacy, termed by British officials the Scioto confederacy, to plan ways to halt the invasion. Two years later, Lieutenant General Thomas Gage reported to London on intelligence he had received from Haudenosaunee sources about confederationist thought. "As the white people have advanced from the coast," the confederationists said, "the original natives have been destroyed, and of the numerous nations which formerly inhabited the country possessed by the English not one is now existing." Now, as they observed the English "drawing nearer and near to them," they "see it must be soon their turn also to be exterminated." This perspective, echoing similar views expressed in the 1750s and 1760s, revealed that Indians feared not only that they would lose their lands, but that they would become victims of all-out genocide.[6]

Although many Indians with experience of colonists agreed that they posed a major threat, not all agreed with the confederationists' approach. White Eyes, an influential Delaware chief, for example, maintained that the best path for survival was through cultivating peaceful relations with the colonists. Most Cherokees also rejected confederationist overtures. Cherokees were sufficiently angry at colonists, especially Virginians, to consider joining the resistance. But after the devastating blows inflicted on them by British armies in the early 1760s, Attakullakulla and other prominent leaders advocated a policy of avoiding conflict so that they could rebuild their towns and renew their farms. They were reluctant to again face troops. Most Cherokee leaders decided to maintain diplomatic relations with British officials, agreeing to relinquish their claims to some Kentucky lands, hoping that this would direct the course of settlement in a more northerly direction away from their major towns.[7]

As Indians debated how best to deal with colonial aggression, a cycle of killings and counterkillings triggered full-scale war in the upper Ohio Valley. In late 1773 Daniel Boone escorted several white families, thirty people in all, into Kentucky. With their hunting grounds under threat, militant Cherokees joined Delawares and Shawnees in an attack on Boone's party, which killed six men, including one of Boone's sons. The next spring, Isaac Crabtree, a survivor of the attack, took revenge by killing a Cherokee known as Billy, who was attending a settlers' festival in what is now eastern Tennessee. Around the same time, a notorious Indian killer named Michael Cresap led a group of southwestern Pennsylvania settlers in an attack on a Shawnee and a Delaware piloting a canoe down the Ohio from Fort Pitt. After killing both men, Cresap announced that he would "put every Indian he mett with on the River to Death." The next day Cresap and his men attacked another group of Indians who stopped at Cresap's cabin to trade. In late April another group of Virginians, led by Daniel Greathouse, lured several Shawnees and Ohio Senecas into an ambush, killing at least eight of them. Among the dead were relatives of a Cayuga war leader named Logan, who vowed revenge and led war parties on deadly raids against nearby settlements.[8]

Like the Paxton Boys a decade earlier, Cresap and Greathouse acted on their own, without official authorization. Nonetheless, it is possible to overstate the independent role of frontiersmen in fomenting violence. Metropolitan elites did not do the killing, but they contributed to it. Imperial officials were facilitators by neglect. One key policy decision, made by British officials in late 1771, was to abandon Fort Chartres (on the Mississippi) and Fort Pitt and withdraw the British military presence from the West. This move, undertaken for reasons of economy in view of the need to police growing colonial unrest in the East, underscored the weakness of the empire's commitment to halt or even regulate colonists' violation of Indian lands. It also gave free rein to local individuals and groups willing to kill. Virginia's colonial elites and public officials enabled frontier violence in more direct ways. To secure Virginians' speculative interests in lands south of the Ohio River from Fort Pitt into Kentucky, Virginia's colonial governor, John Murray, Earl of Dunmore, sent his deputy, John Connolly, to occupy the vacated Fort Pitt and declare that the surrounding area belonged to Virginia, not Pennsylvania. Dunmore also encouraged settlers to occupy Indian lands and attack their inhabitants, going so far as to thank Cresap for his bloody labor and awarding him a captain's commission in the colonial militia. Dunmore's actions also had the effect of modulating tensions between lower-class frontiersmen and upper-class gentlemen.[9]

The outbreak of violence in early 1774 provided Dunmore with a rationale for war. In June he summoned the Virginia militia to march to Shawnee towns on the Scioto (Fig. 7). Dunmore ordered militia leaders to "make as many Prisoners as they can of Women and Children" and to "reduce the Savages to sue for Peace." In early August, a militia 400 strong reached Shawnee towns on the Muskingum River in eastern Ohio, destroyed cornfields, and killed "several" of the towns' people. In the fall, Dunmore mobilized a much larger force of 2,500 volunteers, sizable enough to divide into two armies. One army, commanded by General Andrew Lewis, moved down the Kanawha River and reached the Ohio in early October. As Lewis prepared to cross the Ohio at Point Pleasant, a force of 700 Shawnees and Ohio Senecas, led by the aging Shawnee chief Cornstalk and war chiefs Black Hoof and Blue Jacket, attacked. In the bloodiest fighting between Indians and Europeans in North America since the Anglo-Cherokee War over a decade earlier, Indians killed as many as seventy-five Virginians, while suffering thirty dead of their own. After Point Pleasant Cornstalk's force returned to the Shawnee towns, where Cornstalk counseled peace as the only viable option for survival. Otherwise, he argued, the Shawnees might just as well "kill all our women and children, and go and fight till we die." A few days later, Dunmore, at the head of the

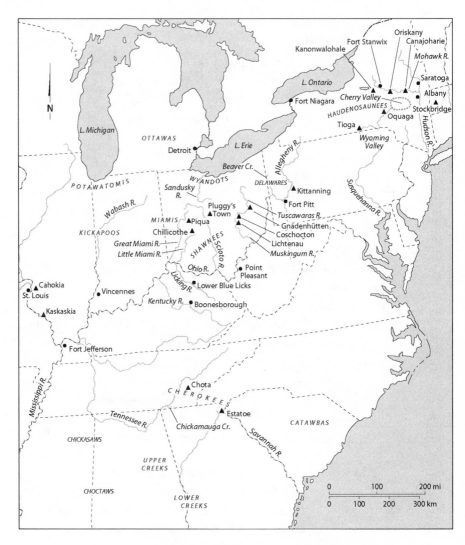

Fig. 7. Era of the Revolutionary War (dashed lines indicate modern state boundaries)

other Virginia army, entered Shawnee country. Rather than risk catastrophic violence or the burning of Shawnee towns, Cornstalk accepted Dunmore's terms: that Shawnees abandon their claim to hunting lands in Kentucky, return white captives, and send four hostages, including Cornstalk's son, to Williamsburg to guarantee peace. Dunmore's army then attacked a nearby Seneca town, which had refused these terms, killing five and taking prisoners.[10]

TOWARD REVOLUTION

Dunmore's War suggested the possibility of a consensus of frontier settlers, colonial elites, and imperial officials (Dunmore was a royal governor,
appointed by the Crown) in favor of aggressive acquisition of Native lands.
But Dunmore was acting largely on his own. Even as he went to war, imperial
planners in London took several actions to restrict colonists' access to Indian
lands. They abolished the practice of making land grants, prohibited land
bounties to veterans of the Seven Years' War (many of these had been purchased by speculators), reaffirmed the Proclamation of 1763, and arranged for
Parliament to pass the Quebec Act. Of these, the Quebec Act, seen throughout the colonies as one of the Intolerable Acts, assumed a particularly prominent place in an emerging revolutionary ideology. Colonists objected to the
Quebec Act for several reasons. Because it failed to provide Quebec with an
assembly and instead asserted royal authority, it seemed of a piece with other
acts (the closing of Boston's port and major modifications to the Massachusetts charter after the Boston Tea Party) that revealed an imperial conspiracy
to deprive colonists of their liberty. The Quebec Act's provisions for legal
protection to Catholicism, a religion colonial Protestants considered tyrannical if not satanic, added to fears of an impending despotism. For colonists
looking west, especially Virginians, the Quebec Act's provision for extending
Quebec's boundaries south to include the Ohio Valley was particularly egre-
gious. This provision, explicitly intended to halt colonial expansion, infringed
on colonists' perceived right to Indian lands and was, in the words of Richard
Henry Lee, a Virginia delegate to the First Continental Congress in fall 1774,
the "worst grievance" of all.[11]

This is not to say that all colonists who supported independence were concerned about restrictions on western expansion. There were many reasons to
believe that British tyranny required revolutionary action. Nor did all speculators and frontiersmen favor breaking with Great Britain. Washington, Jefferson, and other Virginia speculators were leading revolutionaries. In Pennsylvania, however, although speculators like Benjamin Franklin and George
Croghan favored breaking with the empire, most men with investments in
western land companies saw Virginia, which had recently claimed western
Pennsylvania, and not the king as the primary threat to their aspirations.
When the revolution broke out, many Pennsylvania speculators remained
loyal to the empire. Others sought to remain neutral or came late to the cause
of independence. Nor was there consensus among the 50,000 or so colonists

west of the Appalachians. Many were attracted to a movement that promised liberty, but others had strong connections to the empire. For squatters, the key question in 1776 was whether an independent confederation of states would create policies and provide military support to advance settler interests in maintaining and strengthening their hold on Indian lands. The answer to this question was unclear.[12]

Colonial elites who declared independence recognized the need to define a common bond between themselves and frontier settlers against the British. In the short term, they would need settler manpower to defeat the British army and its potential Native allies. In the long run, they would need to maintain settler support as they constructed a new nation. In compiling the Declaration of Independence's list of George III's "injuries and usurpations," Thomas Jefferson linked frontier hatred of Indians to republican fears of monarchical tyranny when he wrote that the king "has endeavoured to bring on the inhabitants of our frontiers, the merciless Indian Savages, whose known rule of warfare, is an undistinguished destruction of all ages, sexes and conditions." The racist proposition that Indians were savages who threatened innocent white Americans and so deserved extermination, along with the implicit assumption of unlimited settler entitlement to Indian lands, would become foundational to the nationalism forged in the violent years ahead.[13]

THE GREAT FEAR OF 1776

Even as one of Virginia's most famous men was drafting the Declaration of Independence, the Shawnee spokesman we encountered at the beginning of Chapter 1 was addressing Cherokees about the intentions of Virginians and other colonists. The history the Shawnee spokesman told of his own people—a once great nation now merely a "handful"—was not precisely accurate. Shawnee numbers had fallen since the time of European contact, but not as sharply as he suggested. Nonetheless, for two decades colonial violence had stalked Shawnees, taking the lives of many. The Shawnee spokesman could see where this might lead. He was also well aware of the histories of nations that had experienced deeper losses than his own. The Delawares, closely connected to the Shawnees, were a prime example. The Shawnee spokesman also knew that his words would resonate with his Cherokee audience. The Cherokees had not been reduced to a handful, but they had suffered population losses for decades. And, like the Shawnees, the Cherokees' experience of colonists since 1759 provided abundant evidence to support the Shawnee spokesman's contention that

Virginians possessed an "intention to extirpate them." Indeed, some Cherokees had already voiced this perspective. In March 1776, a few months before the Shawnee spokesman's address, Attakullakulla's son Dragging Canoe, unlike his father inclined toward militancy, told British agent Henry Stuart at Mobile that the Cherokee Nation "had but a small spot of ground left . . . to stand upon" and that the colonists' unrelenting demands for land indicated that it was their "Intention . . . to destroy [the Cherokees] from being a people."[14]

We know a great deal about how oppressed colonists went to war against Britain to secure their liberty, but even historians who show an awareness that Indians existed in 1776 have not fully appreciated the crisis for Native communities at the moment of American independence. If we take the words of the Shawnee spokesman and Dragging Canoe seriously, Indians faced the worst of all imaginable possibilities—that their families, their communities, their nations, their race would cease to exist. The eruption of fighting between colonists and the British amplified these fears. British agent John Cameron reported in 1776 that Cherokee men, no doubt recalling the Anglo-Cherokee War in the early 1760s, were "very uneasie About their Women and Children, saying that [if] any rupture should happen between them and white people the Women &c would run to the wood and starve." Catawbas, no strangers to war either, "were alarmed, and could not tell what to make of it," while far to the north in what is now Maine, an Abenaki woman "expressed much concern about the times." It was "strange," she said, to see "*Englishmen* kill one another. I think the world is coming to an end."[15]

WAR WITHIN WAR: CHEROKEES AND THE SOUTHERN COLONIES

When the Revolutionary War began, most Native communities tried to stay out of the conflict. Some, however, saw an opportunity to roll back recent colonial assaults on their lands. Although most Cherokee leaders were reluctant to go to war, a minority, led by Dragging Canoe, saw an opportunity to make an alliance with the British against the southern colonies. John Stuart urged the Cherokees to hold off until their attacks could be coordinated with British military operations, but Cherokees proceeded on their own timetable. In August 1776 they sent a force of 600 men against western settlements from Virginia south to Georgia, killing some settlers and destroying buildings.[16]

Many leaders of the American Revolution welcomed Cherokee resistance, as it provided a rationale to crush the Cherokees and perhaps, as Thomas

Jefferson wrote, drive them "beyond the Missisipi." In the summer of 1776, Virginia, Georgia, and the Carolinas retaliated by sending militia forces totaling over 5,000 men against Cherokee towns. At this early stage of the Revolutionary War, there was no need to have these men deployed against British forces elsewhere and so the capacity to employ massive force against Indians was high. To avoid catastrophic loss of life, Cherokees had no choice but to abandon their towns, but at the cost of losing their dwellings and cornfields. In some cases, fleeing Cherokees burned their towns themselves, thus depriving militia men of the pleasure. More often, though, Cherokees left their crops and homes to American torches. The militias killed resisting or fleeing Cherokees when they could, but militiamen expressed frustration at their lack of capacity to take lives. In a typical and revealing entry, one militiaman noted that his comrades "marched very carefully" toward the Cherokee town of Estatoe and then, once the town was in sight, "rushed in with all speed possible." This witness went on to report that "contrary to our expectation or desire, we got no Indians there, save one that escaped with being shot in his thigh." This and other reports document the frequent killing and capture of one, two, or three Cherokees, sometimes armed, often not. The largest single number of recorded deaths was sixteen. The total number of deaths might have been higher had not militiamen valued money over blood. One officer related a dispute about whether to kill three prisoners or sell them (presumably into slavery). They eventually decided to sell. The price of £242 was presumably shared among the militia's ninety-seven members.[17]

Some Cherokees sought refuge with the Creeks and the British in Florida. As in 1761, many Cherokees went to the Overhill towns in southeastern Tennessee, but this time 4,000 Virginia militiamen invaded the Overhill country. At Chota, the Cherokee capital on the Little Tennessee River, Attakullakulla, The Raven, and Nancy Ward, the nation's Beloved Woman, negotiated a peace with advancing troops, thus sparing Chota, but Cherokees at other towns, seeing that the Virginians were about to attack, "fled with their wives and children to the woods" (Fig. 8). Overall, as the ethnographer James Mooney later wrote:

> More than fifty of their towns had been burned, their orchards cut down, their fields wasted, their cattle and horses killed or driven off. . . . Hundreds of their people had been killed or had died of starvation and exposure, others were prisoners in the hands of the Americans,

and some had been sold into slavery. Those who had escaped were fugitives in the mountains, living upon acorns, chestnuts, and wild game, or were refugees with the British.[18]

The events of 1776 led many Cherokees to seek peace with the colonists. Others, however, associated with Dragging Canoe, who talked constantly of being "surrounded," built new towns along Chickamauga Creek off the Tennessee River. Calling themselves the "Real People," in contrast to other Cherokees whom they denounced as "Virginians," the Chickamauga Cherokees cultivated alliances with the British and confederationists north of the Ohio, while encouraging the immigration of white colonists and traders loyal to the king and African Americans liberating themselves from slavery. In December 1780 a Virginia–North Carolina militia moved against Chickamaugua and other Cherokee towns on the Tennessee. "There was no withstanding them," The Raven recalled a year later, "they dyed their hands in the Blood of many of our Women and Children, burnt 17 towns, destroyed all our provisions by which we & our families were almost destroyed by famine this Spring." The Americans killed a reported twenty-nine Chickamauga Cherokees. By 1781 the British had withdrawn from the West, encouraging a massive settler invasion of Cherokee lands and allowing new attacks on Chickamauga towns. Though the 1783 Treaty of Paris ended the Revolutionary War for the initial protagonists, peace did not come for the Cherokees. Even after signing the Treaty of Hopewell with the United States in 1785, in the hope, as Nancy Ward expressed it, that "we are now under the protection of Congress and [will] have no more disturbances," settlers violated Cherokee boundaries, leading to further violence. Cherokee losses would have been greater had Cherokees not been alert to avoid exposure to smallpox. In 1780, for example, when a delegation of Cherokees visited Savannah, Georgia, to plan combined military operations with the British, they said "they were willing & ready to give every assistance in their power to the Great King, . . . but that as the small pox . . . raged throughout the province," they had decided that "if only one of the party was infected the others would disperse & run into the woods." Indeed, within days, they had departed Savannah to "shun the smallpox," thus employing hard-won knowledge gained in previous epidemics.[19]

Fig. 8. Nancy Ward, the Cherokee Nation's Beloved Woman, guided her people through the turbulent years of the Seven Years' War, the American Revolution, and the early Republic. In 1817, five years before her death, she petitioned the Cherokee National Council to stand firm against removal. This statue, erected in the early twentieth century along the Clinch River in eastern Tennessee, draws on Christian symbolism to depict her as an advocate of peace. Photograph courtesy of Ray Smith.

ON THE PERIPHERY OF WAR: CREEKS, CHOCTAWS, AND CHICKASAWS

Other southern Indian nations were in a better position to avoid destructive forces during the Revolutionary War. Cherokees attempted to persuade Creeks to join their raids on settlements in 1776, but they declined. Creek resolve to avoid fighting the Americans only increased when Cherokees, fleeing American reprisals, came to Creek towns with tales of their towns aflame. As the war progressed, some Creeks conducted raids on settlements, though Creek leaders generally discouraged raiding parties lest their people be engulfed by destruction. Creeks suffered some losses when American forces under Colonel Elijah Clarke attacked British-held Augusta in 1780, where Creeks had come for a council. Two years later, when Creeks combined with Loyalists to attack Savannah, they suffered seventeen dead. Overall, though, the number of Creeks killed during these years was far less than the number of Cherokees. The war's disruption of trade caused economic hardship, but not to the extent of loss of life. Creeks were hit by smallpox in 1779–1780, but they minimized losses by dispersal and quarantine. Crucially, the Creeks were never forced to abandon their towns and see them torched.[20]

Farther west, Chickasaws and Choctaws tried to avoid being pulled into the maelstrom of the Revolutionary War. They avoided serious losses. At the war's outset, Choctaws made peace with Creeks, thus ending a destructive intertribal war. The Choctaw trade with the British brought material benefits, but it also encouraged massive consumption of rum. In 1776 one Choctaw chief reportedly said that as many as 1,000 of his people had died from alcohol-related causes (especially violence) over the previous eighteen months. While alcohol caused some deaths, this figure was undoubtedly exaggerated. Chickasaws and Choctaws fought at times with the British against the Spanish, and Chickasaws attacked a new American fort (Fort Jefferson) on the Mississippi just south of the Ohio River's mouth, but their casualties were light. Their lands were not invaded.[21]

AMERICAN INVASIONS OF THE OHIO VALLEY, 1777–1780

In the Ohio Valley a minority of Indians, like Cherokee militants, saw the moment as an opportunity to preserve their independence by driving colonists from their lands. From a base near the Scioto River in central Ohio known as Pluggy's Town, Delawares, Shawnees, Wyandots, and western Haudenosaunees raided Virginia and Kentucky settlements. In spring 1777 the Continental Congress and Virginia planned a counterattack, in the words of Virginia governor Patrick Henry, so that the Indians at Pluggy's Town might be "punished in an exemplary manner." Before these plans could be executed, however, the American agent at Fort Pitt, George Morgan, argued that a military campaign would serve only to drive neutrals to the British.[22]

Although Morgan blocked military operations, settlers' actions soon undermined his diplomatic approach. In July, western Pennsylvanians, angry at Senecas for having killed a frontiersman near Kittanning and fearing Haudenosaunee reprisals, killed several Senecas shortly after their arrival at Fort Pitt at Morgan's invitation. Four months later, another group of settlers came to Fort Randolph, which the Americans had erected at Point Pleasant a year earlier. They had heard that Indians were being held at the fort and wanted to kill them. The confined Indians were Shawnee accommodationists—Cornstalk, his son, and a few others—who had come to the fort in peace only to be taken hostage by the fort's commander on the theory that "the Shawanese are all our enemies." When the settlers reached Fort Randolph, they stormed a cabin where the hostages were being held and killed Cornstalk, his son, and another man. Not long after, yet another group of settlers killed the brother of Captain Pipe, a key advocate of Delaware neutrality, two women, and a child. News of these events encouraged many Ohio Indians to take an anti-American position. Although positions occasionally shifted, from this point to the end of the war a majority of Indians in the Ohio region were inclined toward the British.[23]

Violence in the region, though at times horrific, could have been worse, as can be seen in back-and-forth skirmishing that took place between Shawnees and Kentucky settlers. In February 1778, a Shawnee leader named Blackfish led a war party from Chillicothe on the Little Miami River, south against Boonesborough on the Kentucky River. Before reaching their target, the Shawnees encountered a party of thirty-one men, including Boone himself, gathering salt at Lower Blue Licks. To deter the Shawnees from striking his town, Boone agreed to be taken hostage along with his men, in this way averting bloodshed. Upon returning to Chillicothe, Blackfish adopted Boone to replace a son earlier killed by Kentuckians. Boone appeared to cooperate with Shawnees, going so far as to participate in discussions with British officials, but in June he escaped. In September, Blackfish held Boonesborough under siege for several days, but he was unable to take the town and returned north without major losses on either side. In May 1779 Kentuckians tried to put an end to Shawnee raids and dispatched Colonel John Bowman at the head of a militia of 300 men toward Chillicothe, where they found forty fighters prepared to defend their town. Chillicothe's civilians had been evacuated. Bowman's militia mortally wounded Blackfish and killed one other Shawnee and then burned crops, took horses, and plundered property—a destructive raid, but not a devastating one. In this case, the relative absence of bloodshed was not because of diplomacy, as at Lower Blue Licks; rather, it revealed the limited capacity of a small militia to inflict destruction, as well as Indians' abilities to avoid it.[24]

More ambitious military operations also revealed the limits of American power in the Ohio region, though even these could be cruelly destructive. The main theater of war in the East demanded most of the Continental Congress's attention and resources, but Congress was forced to respond to westerners' demand for protection lest westerners decide the king might better defend them. In February 1778 General Edward Hand, the Continental Army's commander at Fort Pitt, led a militia of 500 men from Fort Pitt toward the Sandusky River in northern Ohio to punish Indians who were receiving British aid from Detroit. Because of bad weather Hand's force never reached his destination and returned to Fort Pitt. Before arriving there, however, some of the men fell upon two small encampments on Beaver Creek in western Pennsylvania, one Delaware, one Munsee, and shot to death and then scalped six of their inhabitants—an old man, four women, and a boy. This atrocity made Hand's campaign counterproductive. Some Delaware leaders, notably White Eyes and Killbuck, though outraged by this act, continued to counsel neutrality on the grounds that a war against Americans would be catastrophic. But other Delawares abandoned neutrality; in the aftermath of Beaver Creek, sixty men went to Detroit, where they sang war songs with Ottawas, Wyandots, Potawatomis, and Miamis.[25]

From a position of weakness, Congress decided that before undertaking a new campaign against Detroit and anti-American Indians, they should secure support from the Delawares and enlist them as guides and fighters. In mid-1778, congressional commissioners met with the Delawares at Fort Pitt and produced the first written treaty between the United States and an Indian nation. In this treaty, the commissioners were forced to confront the charge that "it is the design of the [United] States . . . to extirpate the Indians and take possession of their country." Although the commissioners attributed this allegation to the "enemies of the United States" (meaning the British), Ohio

Valley Indians had been indicting various groups of Europeans with an intent to commit genocide for at least two decades. To counter the allegation, the commissioners promised not only to guarantee Delaware lands but to consider admitting the Delawares and other Indian nations as a state in the new union. While these promises may have persuaded Delawares who were inclined to think that the Americans did intend extirpation and dispossession, the treaty soon spawned mistrust. Delawares left the Fort Pitt negotiations believing that the treaty did nothing more than recognize their neutrality, but the written document not only ensured that American troops would have free passage through Delaware country on the way to Detroit, it required Delawares to "engage to join the troops of the United States aforesaid, with such a number of their best and most expert warriors as they can spare," in other words, an alliance. A year later, upon reading the articles of the treaty, Killbuck said they are "wrote down false," an allegation confirmed by George Morgan, who stated that there had never been a conference with Indians "so improperly or villainously conducted."[26]

The ensuing operation, commanded by General Lachlan McIntosh, again revealed U.S. military deficiencies. McIntosh left Fort Pitt in late 1778 with Detroit as his object. Upon reaching the Tuscarawas River in eastern Ohio, McIntosh summoned nearby Delawares and informed them that any tribe in the region that refused to submit to his authority "Should be looked upon as Enemys to the United States of America." Given the poor condition of McIntosh's men (McIntosh had to beg the Delawares for supplies), these threats seemed hollow, and his audience "Set up a General Laugh." Indeed, McIntosh's lack of provisions made him unable to proceed against Detroit and he soon retreated. As with Hand's campaign, McIntosh's revealed virulent Indian hating among ordinary militiamen when some of them murdered their guide, the Delaware chief White Eyes. Knowing this would damage any Delaware alliance, official reports tried to hide the cause of his death by attributing it to smallpox.[27]

Even the Revolutionary War's most celebrated western operation, George Rogers Clark's Illinois campaign, had some of the same characteristics of the Hand and McIntosh failures. Clark's expedition was authorized not by Congress but by the state of Virginia, partly in response to settlers' frustrations with Congress's seeming indifference to their vulnerability to Indian attacks, and partly to enhance Virginia's claims to western lands. In mid-1778, on the heels of the Hand fiasco, Clark led a small force of 200 rangers down the Ohio River with the intention of securing the Illinois country. On July 4,

Clark and his men took Kaskaskia, a town of French traders in what is now southern Illinois. Clark then sent a detachment east to the Wabash River, where they took Vincennes from the British and declared the inhabitants "citizens of the Republic of Virginia." Clark himself occupied Cahokia, centuries before the site of the largest Indian city in North America, just across the river from St. Louis. From there he sent emissaries to the region's Indian nations. Wishing to assess the Americans' intentions, delegations representing Kaskaskias, Piankashaws, Kickapoos, Ojibwes, Ottawas, Potawatomis, Ho-Chunks, Sauks, Mesquakies, Osages, Ioways, and Miamis traveled to Cahokia. Clark had a reputation as an Indian hater, once declaring that he would like to "see the whole race of Indians extirpated, that for his part he would never spare Man woman or child of them on whom he could lay his hands." Given his practical aims, however, Clark tried to use what he termed the "French mode" of negotiating with Indians, seeking to establish common ground and appearing more an "Indian lover" than hater. Yet, he was unable to fully suppress the conqueror's voice. Clark informed Indians that he "had instructions from the Great Man of the Big Knives not to ask Peace from any People but to offer Peace and War, and let them take their Choice."[28]

To counter Clark's move to take the West, Lieutenant Governor of Canada Henry Hamilton and allied Ottawas, Ojibwes, and Potawatomis recaptured Vincennes in December 1778. In February Clark successfully attacked Vincennes and captured Hamilton. During this operation, Clark (or one of his men) tomahawked six Indians and "hung the scalps of the Indians killed . . . on the tents of the surrendering British," making plain his ruthlessness. Clark reinforced this message with a written statement to "the Warriers of the different Nations." It, too, was a bloody communication. Through it, Clark offered two belts: "one for Peace, and the other for War." The one for war "has your great English fathers Scalp tied to it, and made red with his Blood." Those who took the belt of peace could return the one for war, but those who took the war belt should know that the "next thing will be the Tomahawk" with "Your Women & Children given to the Dogs to eat."[29]

In contrast to McIntosh, whose bombast was met by laughter, Indians took Clark's threats seriously. Clark expected his saber rattling to result in submission, but Indians could easily interpret Clark's talk of indiscriminate tomahawking and the bodies of women and children devoured by dogs as confirmation of a central rationale for resisting. Like other Virginians, Clark seemed intent upon "extirpating" Indians. At the same time, Clark's inability to follow through on his threats would have given Indians encouragement.

Clark hoped to attack Detroit and its Native allies, but many of his militiamen, "disgruntled with the harsh conditions of being soldiers," deserted and promised reinforcements never arrived. Clark abandoned his plans. Once again, the rhetoric of American military commanders exceeded their capacity.[30]

By 1780, American military forces operating in the Ohio Valley and Kentucky had inflicted far less destruction than those that had invaded Cherokee country in 1776. Despite this, or perhaps because of it, Indians in the West increasingly saw Americans as their greatest threat and continued to organize a confederation of western nations in alliance with the British empire. Supplied by the British at Detroit, Indians undertook successful raids against American settlements from Tennessee to Pennsylvania.[31] This, in turn, created pressure for renewed military action against Indians. In the early 1780s American operations became increasingly devastating and eventually targeted not only Indians at war with the United States but those who had hoped an alliance with Americans would bring security.

The second of George Rogers Clark's western military expeditions illustrates the tendency toward greater destructiveness. Like his 1778 operation, this one was authorized by Virginia. In January 1780 the state's governor, Thomas Jefferson, ordered Clark to summon a militia "against those tribes of Indians between the Ohio and Illinois rivers who have harrassed us with eternal hostilities." The goal, Jefferson wrote in a formulation he would repeat many times over the next three decades, "should be their extermination, or their removal beyond the lakes or Illinois river." With a force of 1,000 men, Clark marched against the Shawnees. In August, as Clark's militia approached Chillicothe, Shawnees evacuated it and then a few days later made a stand at the nearby fortified town at Piqua. There, Shawnees and their Delaware, Wyandot, and western Haudenosaunee allies held off the Virginians for several hours, but Clark turned three cannons on Piqua's blockhouse, forcing the Indians to retreat. Clark's men entered the village, where they found many dead and wounded and "bashed in the skulls" of those still living. Determining casualties is difficult, though by Clark's account his militia killed around forty Indians, while losing fourteen of its own. By depriving Shawnees of their fall harvest, Clark's burning of crops left them in a perilous situation. "Our Women & Children," Shawnees told the British, "are left now destitute of Shelter in the Woods or Food to subsist upon." Many sought refuge at Detroit, but the British, short on supplies themselves, tried to keep them away. It is unclear whether starvation or disease took additional lives, and if so how many.[32]

The following spring, Colonel Daniel Broadhead led a force of 300 men (regulars and militia) from Fort Pitt against the Delaware town of Coschocton at the confluence of the Tuscarawas and Muskingum rivers. Perhaps more than any other Ohio Valley nation, the Delawares had been pulled apart by countervailing pressures from the British and the Americans. Coschocton had been a neutral town with pro-American leanings, but anti-American Delawares had recently taken control and exiled Killbuck, still allied with the Americans despite his objections to the 1778 Treaty. As an indication of divisions deep enough to qualify as civil war, Killbuck himself guided Broadhead's expedition against his own people. In April 1781 Broadhead and his men attacked Coschocton and neighboring Lichtenau, taking several prisoners and burning both towns. After Broadhead determined that fifteen of the prisoners had raided American settlements, he had them "dispatched with tomahawks and spears, and then scalped." Later, a militiaman named Lewis Wetzel, a notorious Indian killer, came up behind a Delaware chief who was trying to negotiate peace with Broadhead. With a "tomahawk concealed in his hunting-shirt," Wetzel "struck him on the back of the head . . . , causing instant death." Some like-minded militiamen wanted to attack Christian Indians at nearby towns, but Broadhead's officers prevented this, thus revealing a settler–metropolitan tension over the legitimacy of killing all Indians or just those militantly defending their lands.[33]

THE GNADENHÜTTEN MASSACRE, MARCH 1782

Clark's and Broadhead's military operations did not end resistance. Instead, they strengthened Ohio Valley Indians' opposition to Americans and encouraged additional raids. These attacks fueled fear and hatred among settlers, especially when Native fighters targeted women and children, as they did in March 1780, killing and scalping James Roark's wife and seven of his eight children on the Clinch River in western Virginia. For many settlers, the inability of Congress to provide protection meant that they would have to act on their own. Unable to strike militant towns and inclined to think of all Indians as belonging to a single category of murderous savages, some frontiersmen in the spirit of the Paxton Boys looked toward the most vulnerable Indians in the region, those at Moravian mission towns.[34]

Since the 1760s, the Moravians had moved their towns from the upper Susquehanna to eastern Ohio. In the mid-1770s, they had a string of towns— Salem, Schönbrunn ("beautiful spring"), and Gnadenhütten ("tents of grace")—on the Tuscarawas River. The combined population of these towns was around 400. When the Revolutionary War began, the missionaries and their converts took an official position for neutrality, though they became increasingly pro-American as the war progressed. Shortly after Broadhead's attack on Coschocton, a British-allied Delaware named Buckongahelas, accompanied by eighty men, visited Gnadenhütten to persuade the Indians there to come under his protection, arguing that the "many cruel Acts" of the Americans—their encroachment on Indian lands and their "murdering" of those "who were placed for protection under the roof of their fathers' house" (a clear reference to the Paxton Boys)—meant they could not be trusted. The Moravian Indians, or perhaps the missionaries speaking for them, declined this offer, saying that "they had found no cause to mistrust the sincerity of their American Brethren." A few months later, in August 1781, a new delegation led by the Wyandot leader Pomoacan made a similar appeal to the Moravian Indians. He identified "two powerful and mighty spirits or gods" that stood with "jaws toward each other to swallow" the native converts, a reference to anti-American Ottawas and Ojibwes on the one hand and American frontiersmen on the other. Caught between these forces, Pomoacan continued, "you are in danger, from one or from the other, or even from both." Some Moravians thought they should "at once arise and go," while others said "they would rather die on the spot, for in the bush must they all perish." In the event Wyandots took the missionaries prisoner and forced their converts to accompany them to the Sandusky, 100 miles to the northwest.[35]

On the Sandusky, the Moravian Indians endured a harsh winter with little food. A group of just over 100 decided to return to their abandoned towns on the Tuscawaras River in the hope of harvesting the crops they had left behind. On March 6, 1782, as some of the Moravians were gathering corn at Gnadenhütten, 160 militiamen from Pennsylvania and Virginia under the command of David Williamson appeared. The militia "hailed" the Moravians "as friends and brothers" and said they had come to assist them "on account of their being friends to the American people." At this, the Moravians gave up guns and hatchets. Having rendered the Indians defenseless, the militiamen seized them and others who had been working the fields at nearby Salem and accused them of aiding Indians who had been raiding American settlements. As evidence, they pointed to items in the Moravians' recently abandoned cabins—pewter bowls and teakettles—as well as to the fact that their horses were branded. The militiamen were certain that the Indians had acquired these items from raids on white people; no savage could legitimately possess these appurtenances of civilization. Williamson and his men then considered whether or not to kill their captives. By most accounts, they held a vote on the matter. Recent scholarship plausibly argues that only a minority were initially inclined to participate in a mass execution and that the majority succumbed to the pressures of a vocal minority. Whatever the case, in an especially chilling manifestation of the "dark side of democracy," a large majority eventually voted in favor of slaughter.[36]

Once they had decided to kill their captives, Williamson and his men gave them time to "prepare themselves in a Christian manner" and so throughout the night of the 7th, the Moravian converts prayed and sang hymns. The next morning, the militiamen bound their captives two by two with ropes and ushered them into two houses ("slaughter-houses," the killers called them), one for the men, the other for the women and children. There, the Americans took up cooper's mallets, hatchets, swords, and knives and killed ninety-two of the ninety-four captives. Two boys lived. One, scalped and left for dead, crawled away. The other somehow slipped into the cellar of one of the houses, where he observed the blood from above as it "penetrated through the flooring, and . . . ran in streams" into his hiding place. Just before reaching Gnadenhütten, the Williamson militia had killed four other Moravians, making a total of ninety-six killed, including thirty-two women and thirty-four children (Fig. 9).[37]

After burning the two slaughterhouses, the Williamson militia returned east, though not before continuing their murderous spree by attacking a group of Delawares under U.S. protection near Fort Pitt, killing several. In June another Pennsylvania militia of about 500 men set out to the Sandusky River in northwestern Ohio hoping to strike villages sponsoring raids on American settlements. Commanding this militia was George Washington's close friend William Crawford. Since receiving Washington's prediction that the Proclamation of 1763 would fall, Crawford had surveyed Indian lands and raised a company of men for the Virginia militia during Dunmore's War. Crawford now vowed to "extermenate the whole Wiandott Tribe." When Crawford's militia reached the Sandusky, Wyandots, western Senecas, and Delawares forced them to retreat and took Crawford and some of his men prisoner. The Indians, by now fully briefed about the details of the slaughter of the Moravians, asked for "Williamson the head murderer." Upon learning

THE MORAVIAN INDIAN MARTYRS.

Fig. 9. Although this drawing of the 1782 Gnadenhütten massacre was made long after
the event (1850), it reveals facts documented in the primary sources. Women and children
in one of the two slaughterhouses are shown praying, not for deliverance but for peace
in the afterlife. A militiaman wields a mallet as an instrument of genocide, while two
others witness the horror. From Barber and Barber, *Historical, Poetical and Pictorial
American Scenes,* 77. Reproduced by University of Oregon Digital Scholarship Services.

that Williamson, in fact second in command of the militia, had not been
taken prisoner, they decided that since Crawford was the head of an expedition that planned to "do the same to us" as had been done to "the believing
Indians, and our relations in Pittsburg[h]," he was an equally worthy object
for revenge. One piece of evidence that supported the Indians' assessment of
the Crawford militia's intentions was a report from spies who had visited a
place where the militia had camped. There they saw that the bark from trees
had been peeled so that coal could be used to write the words: "*No quarters
to be given to an Indian, whether Man, Woman or Child.*" Declaring that the
Crawford militia and the colonizers it represented "are all alike!—they want

our country from us, and know of no better way of obtaining it, than by killing us first!," the Indians burned Crawford and other prisoners at the stake.[38]

Even before Gnadenhütten, Indigenous people in the Ohio Valley believed that colonizers intended not only to take their lands but to kill them
all. In 1778 at Fort Pitt U.S. commissioners had attempted to assuage these
fears by promising Natives a place in the new settler polity, but the subsequent four years had revealed that the United States was committed to elimination, not inclusion. Native people would long remember the ninety-six
slaughtered at Gnadenhütten as irrefutable proof of Americans' intentions.[39]

THE UNITED STATES' INVASION
OF IROQUOIA, 1778–1779

Among the nations hit hardest during the Revolutionary War were those
comprising the Haudenosaunees, or the Six Nations—the Mohawks, Oneidas, Onondagas, Cayugas, Tuscaroras, and Senecas spread across New York
from just west of the Hudson River to the southern shores of Lake Erie.
(There were also separate and largely independent Haudenosaunee communities in the Ohio Valley, such as the one at Pluggy's Town, noted above.)
The destruction the Haudenosaunees suffered was all the more shocking as
it came to one of the strongest Indigenous polities in eastern North America, one that had maintained relationships of peaceful coexistence with their
non-Indian neighbors and had avoided being drawn into the destruction of
the Seven Years' War. As illustrated by the strong hand they played in the
1768 Fort Stanwix negotiations, the Haudenosaunees possessed considerable
diplomatic clout. With 2,000 men capable of going to war and their homelands strategically situated between the revolting colonies and Canada, both
the British and Americans had an especially strong interest in cultivating the
people of the Longhouse.[40]

Because of the Crown's long-standing diplomatic and trading relations
with the Haudenosaunees and its support (limited as it was) for checking
colonial expansion, the British were in a stronger position than the Americans
to recruit Haudenosaunees. Some Six Nations communities, however, especially among the Oneidas and Tuscaroras to the east, had developed strong
ties with New England missionaries and so were potentially inclined toward
the Americans. Still, the existing balance of power limited Americans' initial
hopes to promoting Haudenosaunee neutrality rather than actively recruiting
them as allies. A delegation from the Second Continental Congress explained

to the Six Nations in July that this is a "family quarrel" between an imperious father and an oppressed son. As such, "You Indians are not concerned in it. ... We desire you to remain at home, and not join on either side, but keep the hatchet buried deep." By contrast, the British made an aggressive push for Six Nations support, with Colonel John Butler warning them in June 1776 that the Americans' "intention is to take all your Lands from you and destroy your people, for they are all mad, foolish, crazy, and full of deceit."[41]

At first, like most other Native people, Haudenosaunees generally tried to stay out of the "family quarrel." As Oneidas informed the governor of Connecticut in 1775, "We are unwilling to join on either side of such a contest, for we love you both—old England and new." A few Haudenosaunees, however—notably the Mohawk war leader Joseph Brant (Thayendanegea), Molly Brant's brother and protégé of the recently deceased Sir William Johnson—supported the king from the outset. After fighting with the British in the Battle of Long Island in August 1776, Brant risked a dangerous crossing through enemy territory to reach his home country, where he tirelessly rallied his people against the Americans. In early 1777 Brant raised the British flag at the town of Oquaga and then created his own military force, going so far as to recruit non-Indian Loyalists. Most Haudenosaunee leaders were less enthusiastic about committing themselves. Soon, though, they had no choice but to take sides as Haudenosaunee territory became a battleground for the contending armies.[42]

In August 1777, as part of a planned British invasion of the Hudson Valley, Colonel Barry St. Leger, with a force of 1,400 men, including 600 to 800 Native allies (mostly Haudenosaunees, though also including a large contingent of Mississaugas), laid siege to Fort Stanwix, the site of the 1768 treaty and a key U.S. position. To relieve the siege, General Nicholas Herkimer fielded an army of 1,000 men, including some sixty Oneidas. As Herkimer advanced on Fort Stanwix, Molly Brant learned of his mission and informed the British, allowing them to ambush Herkimer near the Oneida town of Oriskany. Herkimer held his ground, but at the cost of his own life, those of 200 or more Americans, and at least a few of the Oneidas. The British suffered twenty-five to thirty dead, while the Indians fighting with them lost at least thirty-three, most of them Senecas. When word of these casualties reached Seneca towns, according to Mary Jemison, a non-Native captive adopted into the Seneca Nation, the "mourning was excessive, and was expressed by the most doleful yells, shrieks, and howlings." The Battle of Oriskany has often been seen as the beginning of a civil war among the Haudenosaunees. If so, however, it was a relatively restrained type of civil war. After the battle, Oneidas raided the home of Molly Brant to punish her for tipping off St. Leger, and Mohawks burned houses and fields at Oriskany to punish Oneidas for assisting Herkimer. Yet, recognizing that they faced perilous times, Haudenosaunees were careful to limit reprisals.[43]

After defeating the British at Saratoga in October 1777, the Americans were in a much stronger position and so pressed Haudenosaunee communities to make peace. Many Haudenosaunees wavered, but others judged that the British (with their help) could defeat the colonists. In early July 1778, a force of over 400 Haudenosaunees led by the Seneca chief Sayengeraghta (Old Smoke) along with 100 British rangers ambushed American forces in the Wyoming Valley of northern Pennsylvania, killing 300 while losing only a few of their own. The Haudenosaunees then burned several hundred settler dwellings. Although Indians refrained from killing noncombatants, lurid rumors of scalping and other atrocities quickly gained the status of fact among Americans inclined to believe the worst about "merciless Indian Savages."[44]

In response to what Americans called the Wyoming Massacre, New York governor George Clinton called for the U.S. military to destroy the "Principal Place of Rendezvous for the Enemy," the Haudenosaunee town of Oquaga, north of the Wyoming Valley. Clinton persuaded General Washington to authorize an expedition. In October 1778, Lieutenant Colonel William Butler with 300 troops reached Oquaga. After residents fled and hid, Butler's men burned the town, including at least forty houses, and its cornfields. In those cornfields, one soldier recalled eleven years later, they found "several small children." The soldier boasted about "what cruel deaths they put them to, by running them through with bayonets and holding them up to see how they would twist and turn."[45]

Governor Clinton's theory that Oquaga's destruction would bring peace was quickly falsified. Haudenosaunees countered with new raids, including one in November on Cherry Valley near modern-day Cooperstown. In this attack, led by British captain Walter Butler, Joseph Brant, and the Seneca leader Cornplanter, Indians killed thirty-two settlers, many women and children, and scalped some, explaining their actions as retaliation for the indiscriminate killings of their own people. With some justification, though without acknowledging its provocations, this event became known among Americans as the Cherry Valley Massacre. Its horrors, often inflated, were widely broadcast. The massacre provided the immediate rationale for the largest United States military operation against Indians of the Revolutionary War, the Sullivan-Clinton expedition of 1779.[46]

In his May 1779 orders to Major General John Sullivan, George Washington outlined the goals of the military operation:

> The total destruction and devastation of their settlements and the capture of as many prisoners of every age and sex as possible. It will be essential to ruin their crops now in the ground and prevent their planting more. . . . Our future security will be in their inability to injure us[,] the distance to which they are driven[,] and in the terror with which the severity of the chastisement they receive will inspire them.

Washington realized that the destruction of Haudenosaunee crops would force Indians to seek supplies from the British, thus straining imperial resources, but this was a decidedly secondary consideration to the major objective of destroying the Haudenosaunees so that they could no longer block American settlement. As Washington mobilized troops against them, Haudenosaunees voiced the same fears Indians elsewhere had been expressing for at least two decades. When Sayengeraghta attempted to recruit their ancient enemies, the Hurons in Canada, he told them that the Americans wish to "extirpate us from the Earth, that they may possess our Lands."[47]

The invasion of Iroquoia began in April 1779, when Colonel Goose Van Schaick led a quick-strike force of about 500 from Fort Stanwix (recently renamed Fort Schuyler) against Onondaga towns, not far to the west. Van Schaick's men attacked three towns, burning houses and crops, slaughtering horses and cattle, killing at least twelve townspeople, and taking thirty-four prisoners, many women. General James Clinton (the governor's brother) had warned Van Schaick against allowing his troops to "violate the chastity of any women," observing that "the savages" never do so. According to an Onondaga chief, however, Van Schaick's men "put to death all the Women and children, excepting some of the Young Women, whom they carried away for the use of their Soldiers & were afterwards put to death in a more shameful manner," clear evidence of rape as a tool of colonial violence.[48]

A few months later, a much larger army assembled. One brigade commanded by Clinton moved down the Susquehanna from Canajoharie, seventy miles west of Albany, while Sullivan led three additional brigades from Pennsylvania up the Susquehanna. The 4,500 troops were to join at Tioga just north of the Pennsylvania–New York border. On July 2, as Sullivan's men approached Haudenosaunee territory, they paused in the Wyoming Valley where they viewed "bones scattered over the ground for near two miles, & several Sculls . . . that had been Scalped and inhumanly mangled with the Hatchet." With these images in mind, two days later—the third anniversary of the signing of the Declaration of Independence—Sullivan and his officers drank thirteen "Patriotic Toasts." The tenth—"Civilization or death to all American savages"—mocked the pretension that "savages" could be civilized and thus celebrated genocide's necessity. Had Joseph Brant learned of this toast, he would not have been surprised. On August 19 Brant wrote of his people's "determination to fight the Bostonians," observing that "it is their intention to exterminate the People of the Long House." The sheer size of the Clinton-Sullivan force, half of the entire Haudenosaunee population of around 9,000, suggests that Brant's perspective was not unreasonable.[49]

Ten days after Brant wrote, he helped lead a British-Haudenosaunee ambush against Sullivan's and Clinton's combined force at Newton, just north of the Pennsylvania–New York border, but they were unable to spring their trap and were forced to retreat. Sullivan and Clinton's men killed at least twelve, including one female, scalping several and skinning the legs of two men to make leggings as gifts for the officers. U.S. troops then moved against Haudenosaunee towns. On at least ten occasions, Sullivan and Clinton tried to surprise towns, but failed. Haudenosaunees, men and women alike, debated whether to fight or evacuate their towns, but they decided that the risks of fighting were too high. The costs of withdrawing from their towns was also high, as it allowed the American army to destroy forty Haudenosaunee villages along with their crops, by all accounts magnificent stands of squash, beans, potatoes, pumpkins, watermelons, and cornstalks sixteen feet high. (A smaller ancillary operation conducted by Colonel Broadhead from Fort Pitt destroyed several additional Haudenosaunee towns on the upper Allegheny River.) At the same time, the Haudenosaunees' strategy meant that they avoided massive casualties to combatants and noncombatants, as well as limiting opportunity for the capture and rape of women and girls. The U.S. army did directly kill a number of Six Nations people. A sharpshooter named Murphy killed at least thirty-three, and there were many other casualties. Still, as Sayengeraghta later explained, "We lost our Country it is true, but this was to secure our Women & Children." The greatest loss of life occurred after the armies had departed and an especially harsh winter descended on the Great Lakes. By that time, many Haudenosaunees had fled to Canada, while others took refuge with the British at Fort Niagara, where they suffered from lack of food, exposure, and poor living conditions. In all, "several hundred" died from starvation, exposure, and illness (especially dysentery) at Fort Niagara. A smaller number of American-allied Oneidas—around 406—took refuge at Fort Schuyler, where "scores" died under conditions of "abject poverty."[50]

George Washington had accomplished his goal of "total destruction and devastation of their settlements," but this did not destroy the Haudenosaunees' will to resist. For the next two years Haudenosaunee war parties with Tory and British support continued their attacks. These were directed mainly at settlements and resulted in a considerable number of American deaths, but Brant also targeted the American-allied Oneida village of Kanonwalohale, burning houses and material possessions as the inhabitants took refuge with American troops. As in the Ohio Valley, the withdrawal of British support in 1782 reduced the ability of anti-Americans to sustain operations, leaving Brant to describe himself as "between two Hells," the hell of American aggression and the hell of British betrayal. Killings and burnings ebbed, but Haudenosaunee communities would long carry memories of the Americans' invasion. In 1790, the Seneca leader Cornplanter informed President Washington that he was known among the Six Nations as "the town destroyer" and that "to this day, when that name is heard, our women look behind them and turn pale, and our children cling close to the necks of their mothers."[51] Long after the Continental Army's invasion of their homeland, Haudenosaunees continued to fear that the United States intended to destroy every last one of them. In the early nineteenth century, the Seneca prophet Handsome Lake addressed his people's "constant fear that the white race would exterminate you" by counseling them that "The Creator will care for his Oňgwë'we (real people)." The genocidal intentions of Americans might not be realized, but it would take the Creator's protection for Haudenosaunees to survive.[52]

THE "MOST DESTRUCTIVE" WAR

For Native nations of eastern North America, the "family quarrel" between a British father and his American son ended the same way it had begun, with Native leaders having no say. When representatives from the United States and Great Britain met in Paris in 1783 to sign a treaty recognizing the son's emancipation, not a single Native person was present. Although excluded from the proceedings, Native nations would be affected by the terms of this treaty, especially its provisions that within the European imperial system gave the United States control over territory from the East Coast to the Mississippi River south of Canada and north of Florida (in a separate agreement,

Britain returned Florida to Spain). Most of the territory of the new United States was in fact Indian country. Had the Treaty of Paris been theirs to draft, Indians undoubtedly would have written it differently. They also would have chosen not to have been dragged into the family quarrel in the first place, even though many Indians, once the war began, saw opportunities to advance their interests. Indians' fears at the beginning of the Revolutionary War proved to be well founded, as the war unleashed massively destructive forces.

In 1787 Samson Occom, a Mohegan Christian, wrote that the American Revolution "has been the most d[e]structive to poor Indians of any wars that ever . . . happened in my day." Indeed, by most measures the extent of destruction during the wars of 1774–1782 exceeded what occurred during those of 1754–1763. In the Anglo-Cherokee War of 1760–1761, British military forces burned close to two dozen Cherokee towns. By contrast, American forces destroyed around fifty Cherokee towns in 1776, at least seventeen more in 1780, and several others in 1781 and 1782. In the early 1760s British generals facing the resistance movement led by Pontiac wanted to destroy Indian towns in the Ohio Valley, but they were unable to reach them. Between 1779 and 1782, however, colonial militias burned at least ten towns in the Ohio Valley. In New York, Haudenosaunees were largely untouched by the conflicts of the late 1750s and early 1760s. Between 1777 and 1780, however, U.S. troops burned over fifty Haudenosaunee towns. In sum, never before had Europeans destroyed so many Indian towns over such a wide area—from the Carolinas to New York—as Americans did during their war to obtain independence from Britain, a conflict that necessarily involved war against Indians not only as British allies but as defenders of their lands against American invasions. This destruction had its most obvious impact in terms of material deprivation, but the attacks on Indian towns involved actions damaging in other ways. Haudenosaunee people at Fort Niagara during the winter of 1779–1780 were not only hungry, cold, and sick. They had seen the graves of their ancestors desecrated, false face masks (used in healing ceremonies) looted, and their sisters, daughters, and mothers violated.[53]

By another measure, Indians directly killed by non-Native military forces, destruction was also greater during the wars of 1774–1782. Reports of Cherokees directly killed in 1776 suggest that the total number was around 100, with an additional twenty-nine Chickamauga Cherokees killed by militiamen in 1780. (These were substantial losses, but probably no higher than in the early 1760s.) Haudenosaunees lost at least fifty men and perhaps as many as 100 in raids and battles against American settlements and troops. During its

destruction of Haudenosaunee towns, U.S. troops killed an additional seventy to 200 Haudenosaunee men, women, and children. In the Ohio Valley,
including Dunmore's War, at least 250 Natives were directly killed between
1774 and 1783. The Williamson militia alone killed ninety-six at Gnadenhütten and perhaps an additional thirty near Fort Pitt; Americans also killed
thirty at Point Pleasant (1774) and forty at Piqua (1780). By contrast, from
1754 to 1765, the number of Indians directly killed by colonial militias in
the Ohio Valley and Pennsylvania was probably under 100. All told, United
States forces killed between two and four times as many Indians during the
Revolutionary War as British and colonial forces did during the Seven Years'
War and Pontiac's War.

As during the 1750s and early 1760s, many Native communities were hit
by disease during the Revolutionary War years. The reason was the same: the
conditions of war encouraged the spread of pathogens. Smallpox first erupted
in and around Boston in 1774. Over the next few years, the movement of
troops and civilians transported the variola virus throughout the theater of
war, eventually infecting dozens of Indian communities. Documented cases
of smallpox broke out among Mohawks (1775–1776), Oneidas (1780–1782),
Senecas (1780–1782), Onondagas (1776–1777), Haudenosaunee refugees at
Fort Niagara (1779–1780), Shawnees (1776), Wyandots (1781), Creeks (1779–
1780), and Chickamauga Cherokees (1783). There is no way to know how
many died in these epidemics. Certainly, several hundred perished from disease during the 1774–1783 period; the number could easily be above 1,000.[54]

Two nations—the Haudenosaunees and the Cherokees—experienced a
net loss in their populations as they fought to retain their independence.
Scholars have stated that the Haudenosaunee population fell by one-third
(from 9,000 to 6,000) between 1775 and 1783. A figure of 9,000 for the 1775
Haudenosaunee population is reasonable, but scholars have failed to provide
sources for the 1783 figure of 6,000. Reports of Haudenosaunees killed at
the hands of American forces and from starvation and disease, summarized
above, suggest total losses of between 1,000 and 1,500. Taking into account
the fact that between 1,500 and 2,000 migrated to Canada after the U.S. invasion would yield an estimate of close to 6,000 Haudenosaunees in New York
in 1783. Perhaps, then, scholars have mistaken a decline within New York
for an absolute decline. In any case, the total number of Haudenosaunees in
New York and Canada in 1783 was probably between 7,500 and 8,000, marking an absolute decline of between 1,000 and 1,500. Scholars of Cherokee
demography have provided more careful estimates. One authority suggests

that the numbers of Cherokees increased from 7,200 in the early 1760s to 8,500 in 1775, and that their population fell again to 7,500 in 1790. Under the conservative assumption that the Cherokee population did not increase from 1783 to 1790, this would mean that the Cherokees endured a decline of at least 1,000 from 1776 to 1783 (higher if, as is certainly possible, the Cherokee population increased from 1783 to 1790). To put this in perspective, a loss of 1,000 from a total population of 8,500 (12 percent) would be equivalent to a loss of roughly 38 million people from the present-day United States population. Estimates for population losses among Ohio Valley Indians are lacking altogether. Delaware, Shawnee, Wyandot, Miami, and Ohio Valley Haudenosaunee populations may have fallen, though probably by a smaller percentage than among the Cherokees or New York Haudenosaunees. The population of other nations—Potawatomis, Ottawas, and Kickapoos—likely did not fall at all.[55]

Some of the most vulnerable Native communities were those that had adopted the colonists' religion and many of their ways of life. The massacre at Gnadenhütten, as we have seen, killed close to 100 Moravians. With a total population of 400, this was an immediate loss of 25 percent of their population. Within the zone of European settlement, another Christian Indian community—the Stockbridges—also experienced enormous losses. Established in the 1730s on the upper Housatonic River in western Massachusetts, the "praying town" of Stockbridge brought together Mahican and Housatonic Indians. On the eve of the Revolution, Christian Indians from Brothertown, New York, joined the Stockbridge community, as they said, "till these troubles be over." When war broke out, the Stockbridge community, surrounded by colonists, had no choice but to support the Americans. Stockbridge men enlisted in significant numbers and fought against the British and their Native allies in New York, New Jersey, and Canada. By the end of the war, forty of the Stockbridge enlistees had died. Out of total Stockbridge population of 300, this was a loss of well over 10 percent. In the meantime, Stockbridge Indians who remained at home during the war were forced to sell the town's lands to satisfy creditors. The result was that the Revolution "inflicted the coup de grâce" on Stockbridge. The last piece of Indian land in Stockbridge was sold in 1783, and while a few Stockbridge Indians remained in western Massachusetts, most migrated to Oneida lands in New York, where they reconstituted their community. Other Indian communities in New England also suffered devastating losses. Men from the praying town of Natick, another community of Christian converts near Boston that had experienced dispossession and gnawing poverty since the time their ancestors had been confined on Deer Island during King Philip's War (see Chapter 1), also enlisted in the American army. Some returned disabled and unable to help their families, while others "either died in the service or soon after their return home." Mohegans and Pequots lost men to war as well.[56]

Not all Native communities that supported the Americans in the Revolutionary War fared poorly. When the war broke out, the Catawbas in South Carolina, like other Native nations surrounded by colonists in revolt, pledged allegiance to the Americans. During the war, Catawbas served with American forces throughout the South, including against the Cherokees; they also provided cattle to American troops camped near their reservation. Some Catawba men lost their lives in combat, and in 1780 British forces burned their village, but they emerged from the war with their land base intact and with the gratitude of many South Carolinians.[57]

A QUESTION OF GENOCIDE

As the South Carolinians' momentarily favorable attitude toward the Catawbas underscores, not all Americans had genocidal attitudes toward all Native people. Nor did the United States as a matter of policy try to kill every single Indian it conceivably could have. Under a restrictive definition of genocide, the absence of an intent to kill all Native people would mean that neither the United States nor its people committed genocide during the period of the Revolutionary War. Several scholars, however, have identified the Gnadenhütten massacre as an act of genocide. As with the Paxton Boys' massacre of the Conestogas, the Williamson militia's belief that all Indians deserved extermination, the premeditation with which the militia acted, and the fact that they targeted unarmed people and spared no one, make categorizing Gnadenhütten as an act of genocide fairly straightforward. A more challenging question is the extent to which Gnadenhütten is an outlier. How different was it from other American manifestations of violence toward Indians during this period? How much did it depart from an emerging U.S. policy toward Indians?[58]

Although the Williamson militia's actions were extreme, the nature and extent of American violence against Indians during the wars of 1774–1783 make it difficult to set aside Gnadenhütten as an anomaly. As we have seen, U.S. officials, including Thomas Jefferson, George Rogers Clark, George Clinton, and George Washington, repeatedly declared an intention to extirpate, exterminate, or destroy Indians they defined as enemies. In many instances, American military operations were unable to fully realize their intentions, in part because of their lack of capacity (as in the Hand and McIntosh expeditions), but even more because Indians consistently decided not to risk massive loss of life, especially women and children, and instead evacuated otherwise vulnerable towns. Had Indians not taken this approach, had they consistently tried to defend their towns against an enemy with overwhelmingly superior numbers and firepower, American armies would undoubtedly have killed a much larger number of people, including noncombatants. American intentions are most clearly revealed when they were able to surprise Native towns. In those instances, they regularly killed women, children, and older men. They also took prisoners and used them as hostages to gain leverage for surrender, sold them into slavery, sexually assaulted them, and killed them in cold blood. To the extent that the statements of military and government officials allow for the identification of an "official" U.S. policy toward Indians, it could be stated this way: we do not intend the physical elimination of all Indians, but we do intend to exterminate Indians belonging to communities we regard as enemies, especially those we think have been engaging in "savage" warfare. In practice, the latter category was expansive and at times could include most or even all Indians.[59]

The response of U.S. military officials and metropolitan elites to the Gnadenhütten massacre further shows a degree of consensus. In the aftermath of Gnadenhütten, William Irvine, the commander at Fort Pitt, although opposed to murdering peaceful Indians, felt powerless against frontiersmen who charged him and his troops with a failure to protect them. By April 1783, Irvine had concluded that the only option was to give in to the views that animated the Williamson militia. He advised General Benjamin Lincoln that "nothing short of a total extirpation of all the western tribes of Indians, or at least driving them over the Mississippi and the lakes, will insure peace." In the East, many authorities said they were appalled by the slaughter of Christian Indians and were embarrassed by what it said about the citizens of the new republic. Yet, with few exceptions, newspapers up and down the eastern seaboard justified the Williamson militia's actions and expressed far more outrage about burning Crawford at the stake. Consistent with the general tenor of public opinion, Pennsylvania state officials did not discipline Williamson. Instead, they allowed him to continue as an officer in the state militia. Similarly, although Congress ordered an investigation into Gnadenhütten, nothing came of it, suggesting a fairly shallow disapprobation, even a degree of tacit approval. Benjamin Franklin's assessment of the massacre is also revealing. At the time ambassador to France, Franklin denounced the "'cruel' killers of 'little Children,'" but focused his anger much more on the "'single Man in England, who happens to love blood,'" for it was "'he who has furnished the savages with the Hatchets and Scalping knives, and engages them to fall upon our defenseless Farmers.'" Two decades earlier Franklin had drawn a sharp line between the Paxton Boys and their innocent victims, but he was now inclined to see the actions of Williamson and his men as an understandable, even if not fully legitimate, response to what his fellow founding father termed the "merciless Indian savages."[60]

In the end, Native leaders like the Shawnee spokesman, the Cherokee Dragging Canoe, or the Mohawk Joseph Brant had ample reason for their belief that Americans intended to "exterminate" or "extirpate" them, terms synonymous with the modern concept of genocide. To some extent, the thinking of these and other like-minded Indians was based on their understanding of a history, now more than two centuries long, in which Native nations had endured unprecedented and unrelenting forces of destruction stemming from the European invasion. Their thinking was also informed by their knowledge of recent and current events. What else could it mean when army after army, each numbering in the thousands, marched against Shawnee, Cherokee, and Haudenosaunee towns with combined populations not much more than the size of the invading armies? Native communities targeted by these armies might avoid genocide, but as Gnadenhütten revealed, the possibility of total annihilation was all too real.

CONCLUSION: THE TOWN DESTROYER'S PREDICTION REVISITED

At the close of the Revolutionary War, sixteen years had passed since George Washington wrote William Crawford that the Royal Proclamation of 1763 "must fall . . . in a few years." Although Washington's prediction was wrong, it was not completely wrong. It had taken a Revolutionary War, but by the time Americans secured their independence through the 1783 Treaty of Paris, they were no longer bound by a king who set boundaries between themselves and Indian country. When Washington became the United States' first President, he led a nation committed to the principle that its citizens had the liberty to obtain Indian lands.

How exactly would Americans dispossess Native nations? In the late 1780s and 1790s, as the United States began to consolidate itself as a postcolonial nation with its own imperial ambitions, there would be significant debates about the pace and regulation of western expansion, the terms of settler enfranchisement, and the appropriate authority and means for taking Indian lands. But these debates would take place on terrain all Americans had come to share through the experience of bloody conflict with enemies who stood in the way of self-evident truths. And how would Native nations rebuild their communities and protect their lands and people from an unfettered United States led now by the Town Destroyer himself? More than ever, Indigenous communities faced agonizing decisions about how best to survive.

CHAPTER 3

Just and Lawful Wars, 1783–1795

In 1798 the Seneca chief Farmer's Brother spoke to Americans of "the late contest between you and your father, the great king of England." The Revolutionary War, he recalled, was "like a raging whirlwind which tears up the trees." What would happen "after the whirlwind?" How would Haudenosaunees and other Native nations rebuild their communities? How would they maintain community well-being in a world that included a newly liberated United States with boundless ambition? The end of the Revolutionary War would provide war-weary Native nations with a respite from violence, but the threat of war would soon return.[1]

NATIVE COMMUNITIES AFTER THE REVOLUTIONARY WAR

In the aftermath of war's destruction, many Haudenosaunees established new settlements. One of the largest was in Canada, at Grand River in Ontario. Initially established by the Mohawk leader Joseph Brant with the encouragement of the British, Grand River quickly became a multinational community, including residents from all Six Nations as well as Mahicans, Delawares, Tutelos, and Nanticokes also seeking peace and security from the whirlwind's disruptions. Among Grand River's new residents was a Nanticoke girl named Way-Way, who had been born on the upper Susquehanna River.

After the "white man destroyed our crops and run us off in the war," she recalled, her family returned home. Increasingly surrounded by a thickening population of non-Indians, however, they soon relocated to Grand River. By 1789 Grand River's 1,200 residents lived along a forty-mile stretch of river, where they planted and harvested crops, constructed a church, a school, and new houses (including Brant's, a "genteel mansion" where guests were offered brandy, port, and Madiera). In 1792 a Scottish visitor found the Grand River Indians if not exactly prosperous, "better and more comfortably lodged than the generality of the poor farmers in my country."[2]

The largest new Haudenosaunee settlement was on the United States side of the border at Buffalo Creek, known in Haudenosaunee traditions as a place the "God of Thunder and Lightning" had designated as desirable to "raise good crops & enjoy perfect good health." Buffalo Creek's residents constructed several villages and created a viable economy—farming, hunting, gathering, fishing, and trading furs to the British at Fort Niagara for supplies and clothing. The majority of the population at Buffalo Creek, about 2,000 in 1783, were from the Six Nations, with the Senecas the largest of these groups and taking the leadership role. Like Grand River, Buffalo Creek also incorporated non-Haudenosaunees. Under the principles of the Great Law of Peace, originally given by the prophet Deganawida, Buffalo Creek functioned successfully as a multinational community.[3]

Many Haudenosaunees returned to their war-ravaged towns. When the war ended, some Oneidas went to Grand River, but most decided to rebuild Kanonwalohale. Under pressure from burgeoning New York settlements, Oneidas turned to a strategy they had earlier used of encouraging other Indians to live with them to create a buffer against outsiders. A small group of Tuscaroras responded to the Oneidas, as did the Stockbridges of Massachusetts and the Brothertowns, another community of Christian converts who had joined the Stockbridges on the eve of the Revolutionary War. Onondagas, Cayugas, and Senecas also rebuilt towns in the Finger Lakes area and the Genesee and Allegheny valleys.[4]

Cherokees, too, took diverse approaches to rebuilding after war's devastation. Some returned to the locations of destroyed towns, though others decided on new sites—deeper in the mountain valleys or farther west—as part of a strategy of "self-isolation." In these remote areas, memories of violence remained strong. In 1796, when U.S. Indian Agent Benjamin Hawkins visited the Cherokee town of Willstown in northeastern Alabama, he discovered that children, raised on stories of colonial warfare, "were exceedingly alarmed at the sight of white men." One "little boy . . . could not be kept from screaming." Most Cherokees remained suspicious of non-Indians, listened little to missionaries, and continued to pursue their traditional ways of life. In one winter ceremony, the Booger Dance, masked Cherokees imitated white intruders, mocking them as "fools ignorant of basic Cherokee civilities," and in this way used laughter to defuse the threat they posed. A minority of Cherokees, perhaps 20 percent of the total population, began to accumulate property, including a few black slaves. This minority would become increasingly important in building a new kind of Cherokee nation in the early nineteenth century. A smaller minority considered migrating west of the Mississippi and in 1788 petitioned Spanish officials for permission to take refuge "in the territory of the great king of Spain." Esteban Miró, governor of Louisiana, granted permission for six Cherokee villages to live under Spanish authority in Missouri and Arkansas. This marked the beginning of a steady stream of Cherokee migration west. By 1804, there were perhaps as many as 1,000 Cherokees living west of the Mississippi.[5]

In the Ohio Valley, Americans' repeated attacks led many Native communities to seek safer places. For the Moravian Indians, any possibility of returning to their towns in eastern Ohio ended after the slaughter at Gnadenhütten. A month after the massacre missionary David Zeisberger wrote in his diary that "from the white people, or so-called Christians, we can hope for no protection." About half of the Moravians found refuge with Delawares and Shawnees on the Great Miami River in western Ohio. The other half, under Zeisberger's guidance, established a new community called New Gnadenhütten near Detroit on Ojibwe land. After four years, however, Ojibwes asked the Moravians to leave and so they established a new mission, New Salem, on the Huron River in north-central Ohio. The Delawares of Coschocton and Lichtenau, who had been attacked by Colonel Broadhead in 1781, also relocated from eastern to western Ohio. Similarly, Shawnees withdrew from the Scioto, Little Miami and lower Mad rivers to the upper Mad River and Loramie Creek, in some cases establishing new villages, in others joining those already existing.[6]

Many Native nations were relatively untouched by destructive forces during the Revolutionary War, but they too faced challenging new circumstances. For Creeks, Chickasaws, and Choctaws, the departure of British traders made it critical to find new sources of European products—guns, ammunition, rum, agricultural implements, domestic tools, clothing, and blankets. There were two possibilities for trade: the Americans and the Spanish. Many Choctaw, Chickasaw, and Creek communities negotiated with Spain to secure trade relations with Panton, Leslie, and Company, a firm of Scottish traders operating out of Pensacola under Spanish license. For Creeks, the emerging leader Alexander McGillivray, son of a Creek mother and Scots father and educated in Charleston, played a crucial role in securing and brokering this trade as a partner in the Panton and Leslie firm. Other southeastern Indians took a different approach. Creeks and Choctaws oriented toward Americans negotiated with Georgia and South Carolina for access to traders based in Augusta and Savannah, while similarly inclined Chickasaws discussed a trading post in their country with representatives of Virginia, North Carolina, and the unrecognized state of Franklin (proclaimed in 1784 by settlers in present-day Tennessee, then western North Carolina).[7]

PLANNING AN EMPIRE OF LIBERTY, 1783

In contrast to Indian nations, who were in a largely defensive position, newly independent Americans took a far more aggressive stance, rapidly acting upon an assumed liberty to possess Indigenous lands. After the Treaty of Paris, settlers poured into the Mohawk River Valley of New York and the upper Susquehanna in Pennsylvania. In western Pennsylvania, contested ground for decades, the non-Indian population increased from 33,000 in 1783 to 95,000 by 1800. The population of Kentucky (still part of Virginia) soared from 12,000 in 1783 to 74,000 in 1790, while the population of Tennessee (still within North Carolina) increased from under 10,000 to 36,000 over the same period. In lesser numbers, settlers also pushed into northern Vermont, southern Ohio, western Virginia, and west of the Savannah River into Georgia. Speculators also exercised their newly won freedom to capitalize on western lands. In 1784 George Washington observed that the "rage for speculating" in lands north of the Ohio River was sufficient "that scarce a valuable spot within any tolerable distance of it, is left without a claimant." The "most successful land speculator of his time," Washington knew what he was talking about.[8]

To notice a rage for speculation might suggest that U.S. expansion was fueled by simple greed. There was no shortage of greed, but we must also recognize that expansion was central to America's political identity as a unique experiment in republican liberty. American political theorists were acutely aware of the historical tendency of republics to degenerate into despotic empires. Looking west, they saw a solution to the fragility of republics. Not only

would a theoretically infinite supply of land meet the economic demands of
a growing population of speculators, slave owners, and small farmers, by allowing for the continual reproduction of widespread property holding among
white men, it would allow the United States to escape the tendency, inherent
to polities with finite amounts of land (such as England and France), to develop a small landed aristocracy with a much larger class of unfree tenants and
laborers incapable of exercising political independence. The United States
would be an expansionist empire, but it would be an empire of a different
sort than the world had ever known. In Thomas Jefferson's phrase, it would
be an "empire for liberty." Widespread property ownership among white men
would also ameliorate social class divisions and reinforce a common identity
among free whites of racial superiority in relation both to African Americans,
conceived of as inherently inferior, and Native Americans, sometimes granted
the capacity to advance beyond their current ostensibly primitive stage of human development but often thought of as irredeemable savages.[9]

While all Americans agreed that they were entitled to Indian lands, they
differed about how these lands should be acquired. In 1783 some U.S. leaders
advocated continuing to prosecute war against Indians. George Rogers Clark
proposed that Virginia authorize an army of 2,000 men against Ohio Valley
Indians. Sooner or later, Clark argued, it would be necessary to demonstrate
"that we are always able to crush them at pleasure." Rather than wait, it would
be best to seize the "present moment" to "Reduce them to Obedience." The
commander of the Continental Army, George Washington, did not advocate
dispossession by conquest and instead proposed intimidation. Washington's
scheme was to settle the West with settler-soldiers. The "appearance of so
formidable a Settlement" in Indian country, Washington imagined, would
"enable us to purchase upon equitable terms of the Aborigines their right of
preoccupancy; and to induce them to . . . remove into the illimitable regions
of the West."[10]

Both of these schemes ran into a major obstacle. As Virginia governor
Benjamin Harrison wrote Clark in rejecting his appeal for military action:
"the distress'd situation of the State with respect to its Finances, call on us to
adopt the most prudent Oconomy." With similar concerns in mind, Washington gave up his idea of settler-soldiers along with any notion of a war of
conquest. This was not because Indians did not deserve to "be compelled to
retire . . . beyond the Lakes," as he put it to Congress. Rather, "policy and
oeconomy point very strongly to the expediency of being upon good terms

with the Indians, and the propriety of purchasing their Lands in preference to attempting to drive them by force of arms out of their Country."[11]

In October Congress outlined a plan to obtain Indian lands. Following Washington's lead, Congress asserted that the United States would be justified in using military force to expel Indians from territory it claimed, but rejected that approach as impractical and costly. Unlike Washington, however, Congress did not propose to purchase Indian lands and instead ordered a commission to simply demand a land cession from Ohio Valley Indians. This commission was instructed to inform its Indigenous audience that their "acts of hostility and wanton devastation" meant that the United States had the perfect right to force them "to retire beyond the lakes." The commissioners would then state that because Americans "are disposed to be kind to them," the United States "would draw a veil over what is passed." Having established American generosity, the commissioners would then inform Indians that they must accept "a boundary line between them and us" running from the mouth of the Great Miami northeast to Lake Erie. Although this new boundary would require them to vacate most of the present-day state of Ohio, Indians would presumably accept the kindness of partial, rather than total, dispossession.[12]

IMPOSING LAND CESSIONS, 1783–1786

Before setting out for the Ohio country, the congressional commission turned its attention to the Haudenosaunees in New York. Contending that the Articles of Confederation granted states authority over Indians within their boundaries, the state of New York had announced its intention to make a treaty with the Six Nations. To assert federal authority, the commissioners preempted New York by summoning Six Nations representatives to Fort Stanwix, the site of the 1768 treaty (see Chapter 2). In October 1784 the commissioners declared that the United States, not New York, had authority to make peace with Indians and then insisted that the Haudenosaunees (with the exception of America's erstwhile allies, the Oneidas) cede lands in western New York and northwestern Pennsylvania. When Mohawk chief Aaron Hill (Kanonraron) rejected this demand, Arthur Lee, one of the U.S. commissioners, rebuked the Haudenosaunees for claiming to be "a free and independent nation." "It is not so," he declared. "You are a subdued people." Coming on the heels of the Continental Army's destruction of their homelands,

Haudenosaunee leaders felt they had no choice but to accept U.S. demands. As they later protested to Congress, the commissioners told them that "you could crush us to nothing" and so "they therefore gave up that country." As for the Oneidas, the commissioners assured them that the United States would reward their wartime support by protecting their lands. Despite this, a year later New York insisted that the Oneidas sell a portion of their lands to the state. Oneidas felt that their assistance in the cause of American independence should protect them from dispossession, but New York rejected their argument and the Oneidas consented to sell 460,000 acres to New York for $11,500. Within two years, New York completed its betrayal of an ally in America's war for independence when it sold three-quarters of these lands for over $125,000.[13]

After Fort Stanwix, U.S. commissioners traveled west. In January 1785 they met with a limited representation of Ohio Valley Indians—mainly Wyandots and Delawares with a few Ottawas and Ojibwes on hand—at Fort McIntosh, northwest of Fort Pitt (Fig. 10). Despite Congress's assumption that Indians would be grateful that the United States had decided against compelling them to "retire beyond the lakes" and so willingly part with much of eastern and southern Ohio, Native leaders rejected any land cession. Their kindness spurned, the commissioners bluntly replied: "we claim the country by conquest; and are to *give* not to receive." Some leaders signed the Fort McIntosh Treaty, fearing they would lose even more of their land if they did not, but at least as many refused to sign. This itself rendered the treaty illegitimate according to any standard of meaningful consent. Furthermore, many Ohio Valley nations declined to participate in the proceedings in the first place and so had not agreed to anything. After the treaty, Shawnees, who were entirely unrepresented, made it known that they regarded the Ohio River as the boundary between Indian country and the United States. Should Americans cross that boundary, Kekewepellethe (also known as Captain Johnny) said in May 1785, they would "take up a Rod and whip them back to your side."[14]

Although the United States regarded the Fort McIntosh Treaty as legitimate, widespread Native resistance forced American leaders to seek some degree of Shawnee acquiescence. In January 1786 at Fort Finney at the mouth of the Great Miami River, two commissioners, Richard Butler and George Rogers Clark, met a minority of Shawnees, most from the Mekoche division of the Shawnees under the leadership of Moluntha. Acting on their historical role as healers and diplomats, Mekoches were willing to meet with the Ameri-

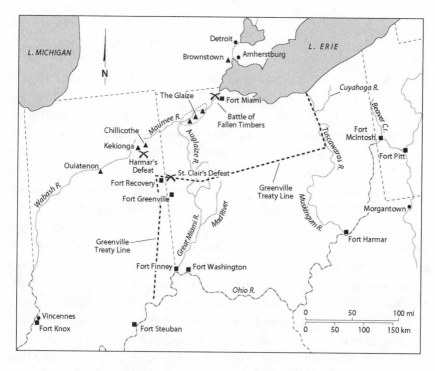

Fig. 10. War for the West in the Ohio Valley, 1785–1795
(dashed lines indicate modern state boundaries)

cans to "go on with the good work of peace," but they did not intend to "enter into any Engagements respecting Lands." Although Butler, a trader among the Shawnees, was familiar with diplomatic protocol and allowed ceremonial speeches and the smoking of peace pipes, he and Clark imperiously insulted the Shawnees by demanding that they provide hostages as a guarantee of peace and that they "acknowledge the United States have the sole and absolute sovereignty of the whole country ceded by the King of Great Britain." Kekewepellethe, a militant spokesman from another Shawnee division, rejected both demands. Hostages, he said, were unnecessary, since "when we say a thing we stand to it, we are Shawnese." As for assertions of U.S. sovereignty, "God gave us this country, we do not understand measuring out the lands, it is all ours." When Kekewepellethe reinforced his words by giving the commissioners a string of black wampum, signifying rejection if not war, Butler rebuked the Shawnees as an "obstinate nation," threatened "the destruction of your women and children," and took up the black string of wampum and "dashed it on the table." He and Clark then threw down a black-and-white string of wampum to indicate that the Indians could choose between peace (on U.S. terms) or genocidal war. The Shawnees took this threat seriously. Only six years had elapsed since Clark himself had assaulted the Shawnee town of Piqua, killing men, women, and children alike. After discussions among themselves, Moluntha and other Shawnee leaders presented another belt, this one white, asking the commissioners "to take pity on our women and children" and agreeing to swallow U.S. demands. Even so, the majority of Shawnees had stayed away from Fort Finney. For good reason, they continued to regard the original Fort McIntosh Treaty as illegitimate.[15]

Native nations in the South also faced serious threats to their lands. Through three treaties negotiated with a minority of Creek leaders in 1783, 1785, and 1786, Georgia doubled the amount of land within its boundaries open to white settlement. North Carolina, which until 1789 claimed territory west to the Mississippi, did not even bother with the pretense of treaty making and simply "confiscated" most Indian lands within the state. The self-proclaimed and nonrecognized state of Franklin (carved from what would eventually become eastern Tennessee) got into the act as well, negotiating land cessions with a limited number of Cherokees in June 1785 and July 1786. With state governments the aggressors, many Native leaders saw federal authorities as offering some protection. In fall 1785 U.S. commissioners met with Cherokees at Hopewell, South Carolina. Cherokees ceded some of their lands, but the Treaty of Hopewell recognized their core territory and contained a provision for Congress to investigate evicting North Carolina/Franklin squatters in east Tennessee. Cherokees saw these terms as preferable to what they had been hearing from North Carolina and Franklin. Choctaws, however, were less satisfied. They had traveled to Hopewell to secure trade relations with the United States as part of a peace agreement between equals. As Taboca, a senior negotiator, explained to the commissioners, "You see our women are painted white—an emblem of peace and of their hopes of being able to raise up their Children in peace." The commissioners, however, offered a different vision of peace, with the Choctaws subordinate to the United States and under its protection. Under the treaty, the United States agreed to establish trading posts, but only if the Choctaws agreed to cede tracts of land around them. These tracts were small—only six square miles—but Choctaws complained after the treaty that they had been deceived into signing a document containing this provision, indicating their unwillingness to give up any land at all.[16]

THE UNITED INDIAN NATIONS, 1783–1786

The aggressiveness of the United States, including its member states, in demanding land cessions increased support for a multinational Native confederation that had been organized immediately after the United States secured its independence. In September 1783, "to defend their country against all invaders," Shawnees, Wyandots, Delawares, Ottawas, Ojibwes, Potawatomis, Creeks, Chickamauga Cherokees, and Haudenosaunees met on the Sandusky River in northwestern Ohio. There, taking the advice of the Mohawk Joseph Brant that "our Interests are alike" and that nothing should "ever be done but by the voice of the whole," the assembled delegates agreed to act in concert to prevent settlers from "encroaching upon our Lands." Should Americans attempt to take Indian lands by force, this latest incarnation of previous multinational confederacies would respond by coordinated self-defense. Should Americans try to coerce individual nations—or portions of individual nations—to cede lands, the confederacy would insist on the illegitimacy of such cessions.[17]

Building on the 1783 Sandusky conference, Indians from Lake Erie south to the Cumberland, Tennessee, Coosa, Alabama, Tallapoosa, and Chattahoochee valleys sponsored attacks on settlers and met among themselves, as Shawnees said, to "make everything straight and strong." At the Wyandot town of Brownstown south of Detroit in December 1786, Mohawks, Wyandots, Delawares, Shawnees, Ottawas, Ojibwes, Potawatomis, Chickamauga Cherokees, Miamis, Weas, and Piankashaws, calling themselves the United Indian Nations and so placing themselves on an equal plane with their adversary, "solemnly renewed . . . the Indian union of 1783." In an especially powerful oration, one speaker, likely Brant, recounted a history of Indian dispossession from "before Christian Nations Visited this Continent" and "we were the Sole Lords of the Soil" to the present. Why, he asked, were Indians "not Still in possession of our forefathers birth Rights?" The reason was that they had lacked "that Unanimity which we now So Strongly and Repeatedly recommend to you. . . . The Interests of Any One Nation Should be the Interests of us all." The United Indian Nations issued a statement to the Congress of the United States outlining a proposal for "a lasting reconciliation" with "a set of people born on the same continent with ourselves." The statement criticized the United States for "having managed everything respecting us your own way" and informed Congress that "partial treaties" (i.e., the Fort McIntosh and Fort Finney treaties made with only select groups of Indians) were "void and of no effect." Any "cession of our lands should be made . . . by the united voice of the confederacy." To establish "peace and tranquillity" the confederationists proposed a conference in the spring and requested Congress "to order your surveyors . . . to cease from crossing the Ohio." Should the United States reject this plan, the United Indian Nations would be "obliged to defend those rights and privileges which have been transmitted to us by our ancestors," a clear assertion of sovereignty and the right of self defense.[18]

John Heckewelder, a Moravian missionary with long experience in the Ohio country, provided an unusually thorough account of the historical perspective informing the United Indian Nations. According to Heckewelder, confederationists found the treaties the United States had recently imposed on them to be "highly offensive." They objected that commissioners "spake to us, as if we had been a conquered people; and who *must*, whether willing or not, submit to the dictates of a proud Conquerer." Indians also indicted Americans for the Gnadenhütten massacre, where "they did kill upwards of one hundred of our People, who never took up a single Weapon against them but remained quiet at home, planting Corn and Vegetables." Confederationists did not see Gnadenhütten as an outlier but rather as revealing the means Americans intended to use to gain Indian lands. As evidence, they pointed to the fact that Americans were beginning to create farms on the very lands where the Moravians had been killed. Furthermore, they argued, the designs of Europeans in America had been apparent for several centuries. "Our forefathers received the White People with kindness," confederationists said. "They gave them Land to live, and plant upon," but Europeans had never been "satisfied with this," always saying they "must have more Land; and if we are not quick in giving it to them, they take it, saying we *will* have it." Given this historical tendency, Indians alleged, Americans would not rest until "they have extirpated us entirely; and have the *whole* of our Land!" At stake, by this account, was not just avoiding dispossession but preventing genocide.[19]

THE NORTHWEST ORDINANCE AND U.S. INDIAN POLICY

The message from the United Indian Nations reached Congress on July 18, 1787. This was a crucial moment in United States history. After six years under the Articles of Confederation, delegates from twelve of the thirteen states were secretly meeting in Philadelphia to amend the Articles or scrap them altogether in favor of a stronger Constitution. At the same time, on July 13 in New York City Congress passed a key piece of legislation, the Northwest

Ordinance. The Northwest Ordinance is best known for creating a frame-work for the orderly creation of territories in the area north of the Ohio River into the Great Lakes and their eventual admission to the Union on an "equal footing" with existing states. In this way, the ordinance balanced the priority of U.S. leaders to regulate the pace of expansion with the priority of frontiers-men to resist the reestablishment of tyrannical colonial rule from which they had just freed themselves. The Northwest Ordinance also contained an often overlooked expression of Indian policy:

> The utmost good faith shall always be observed toward the Indians, their lands and property shall never be taken from them without their consent; and in their property, rights and liberty, they never shall be invaded or disturbed, unless in just and lawful wars authorised by Congress; but laws founded in justice and humanity shall from time to time be made, for preventing wrongs being done to them, and for preserving peace and friendship with them.[20]

Consistent with the "utmost good faith" clause, Secretary at War Henry Knox recommended to Congress that it respond to the message of the United Indian Nations by authorizing a commission to negotiate a "general treaty . . . with the tribes of [I]ndians, within the limits of the United States, inhabiting the country northward of the Ohio, and about Lake Erie." In making this recommendation, Knox considered the alternative—war—and rejected it for two reasons. First, to fail to respond to the Native confederacy's appeal for a treaty would make it "appear that we preferred War to Peace" and the "United States may have the verdict of mankind against them." The consequence would be to "fix a stain on the national reputation of America." Second, "the finances of the United States are such at present as to render them utterly un-able to maintain an Indian war with any dignity or prospect of success." For a "small sum of money" it would be possible to purchase land from Indians, whereas a war "may cost much blood and infinitely more money." In August a congressional committee accepted Knox's recommendation and further ad-vised that the commissioners negotiating a treaty should reject a "language of superiority and command" and instead "treat with the Indians more on a footing of equality" and "convince them of the Justice and humanity as well as the power of the United States."[21]

Consistent with a general tendency to take statements of policy at face value, many historians have seen the Northwest Ordinance's profession of "utmost good faith . . . toward the Indians" and Congress's acceptance of

Knox's recommendations as a repudiation of a policy of claiming Indian lands by right of conquest in favor of a new policy recognizing that Native nations owned their lands and so requiring the United States to purchase them. Despite the adoption of an ostensibly new policy, however, basic premises were unaltered. The United States might begin with gentler tones when asking Indians to give up their lands and would provide compensation, thus recognizing what Knox called "the Indian right of the soil." It is mistaken, however, to equate acknowledgment of a "right of the soil" with anything close to an actual recognition of Indigenous sovereignty. Not only would the United States claim a right of preemption and so deny Indians the right to sell lands to parties other than the federal government; more important, the United States would not recognize an Indigenous right to refuse to sell when presented with reasonable terms as unilaterally defined by the United States. One influential study of Native dispossession argues that a treaty General Rufus Putnam negotiated with Wea, Kickapoo, Piankashaw, Potawatomi, Peoria, and Kaskaskia leaders in 1792 that guaranteed their "right to refuse to sell" confirms an "official recognition by the government of the United States that Indians owned their land," but this argument fails to reckon with the fact that the Senate chose not to ratify this treaty precisely because the Senate opposed acknowledging any such right. Arguments for a major policy shift in 1787 also fail to interrogate the Northwest Ordinance's provision for "just and lawful wars." For historians inclined to take policy pronouncements on their own terms, a commitment to "just and lawful wars," especially when preceded by an expression of "utmost good faith," manifests an enlightened humanitarianism. But what did "just and lawful wars" actually mean? Although the ordinance did not specify the conditions under which the United States would be justified in going to war against Indians, Knox had outlined these conditions in a separate report to Congress dated July 10 in which he observed that "if after proper efforts a peace with the [I]ndians could not be obtained by reason of their wicked and blood thirsty dispositions, the commanding officer should endevor by force to expel them from their towns or extirpate them." In other words, should Indians refuse to give up their lands on terms the United States dictated, it would be just and lawful for the United States to inflict catastrophic violence on them.[22]

WEIGHING WAR, 1787–1789

In October 1787, three months after the passage of the Northwest Ordinance, Congress instructed Arthur St. Clair, recently appointed governor of the Northwest Territory, to negotiate a treaty with the nations north of the Ohio. St. Clair then sent word to the United Indian Nations of his intention to meet with them at Fort Harmar at the mouth of the Muskingum. Before formal negotiations began, St. Clair made clear their parameters when he rejected a proposal floated by Joseph Brant and other moderate confederationists for a boundary on the Muskingum (giving the United States only the eastern quarter of Ohio). Instead, St. Clair insisted that Indians must accept the boundary established under the Fort McIntosh and Fort Finney treaties, which also ceded the southern half of Ohio. Any departure from the earlier conquest policy would not entail a reconsideration of treaties dictated under that policy. Not surprisingly, many Indians saw in St. Clair yet another in a line of "proud Conquerors" that, as Heckewelder had learned, they found "highly offensive." Some, notably Mohawks, Shawnees, Kickapoos, and Miamis, refused to meet with St. Clair. As an indication of their deep suspicions of Americans' intentions, they feared that when they reached Fort Harmar, soldiers planned to "kill them all, either by putting poison in the spirits . . . or communicating the small-pox with the blankets." Some Native leaders, however, decided to meet with St. Clair. When discussions began in late December 1788, delegates like Shendata, a Wyandot who opened the proceedings by asking the Americans "to have pity and compassion" and "let the Ohio be the boundary line," evidently thought St. Clair might be open to persuasion. After days of discussion, however, it became clear that St. Clair, displaying a supposedly repudiated spirit of "superiority and command," was unwilling to give an inch. "The United States . . . were much inclined to be at peace with all the Indians," St. Clair said, "but if the Indians wanted war they should have war." Utmost good faith had been shown. The consequence of rejecting U.S. generosity was clear.[23]

Many leaders at Fort Harmar signed a treaty confirming the boundary established by the Fort McIntosh Treaty. In exchange they received goods valued at $6,000. Their reasons for signing were complex. St. Clair's threats of war were undoubtedly a factor, as were the material benefits the treaty offered. The majority of the United Indian Nations, however, rejected the legitimacy of these treaties, which they denounced as "pen and ink witchcraft" able to "speak things we never intended," and continued to defend the Ohio River boundary. To counter a massive migration of non-Indians into the Ohio region, in 1789 militant Miamis, Weas, Kickapoos, Shawnees, Wyandots, Delawares, and Chickamauga Cherokees stepped up military operations, targeting forts and settlements along the Ohio River as far east as present-day Morgantown, West Virginia. To the west, Indians harassed military convoys between recently establish forts Steuben (across the Ohio from Louisville) and Knox at Vincennes, forcing the army to detail troops to accompany them. All along the Ohio, confederationists harried boats conveying supplies and emigrants intending to create farms and hunt on Indian lands. Native war parties also ranged south of the Ohio River. They did not intend to reclaim Kentucky, but they sought to avenge Kentucky militia attacks and deter Kentuckians from settling north of the Ohio. In one three-month period, Kentuckians reported that Indians had killed twenty settlers and taken over 100 horses.[24]

Federal officials continued to see disadvantages in war. In June 1789 Knox repeated his preference for "forming treaties of peace with them." The alternative, "raising an army, and extirpating the refractory tribes entirely," was costly and risked damaging America's effort to "establish . . . its character on the broad basis of justice." Knox further articulated what he saw as a humanitarian vision for the future of Indians. Instead of "exterminating a part of the human race by our modes of population," he asked, would it not be better if we "imparted our knowledge of cultivation and the arts to the aboriginals of the country"? Knox admitted that "the civilization of the Indians would be an operation of complicated difficulty," but he rejected the idea that "the human character" was "incapable of melioration or change." Drawing on Enlightenment theories of stages of development, Knox saw this supposition as "entirely contradicted by the progress of society, from the barbarous ages to its present degree of perfection."[25]

As much as Knox preferred to gain Indigenous lands without war, and as much as he hoped that dispossessed Indians might embrace the gift of civilization, thus making dispossession all the more honorable, he and other federal officials eventually decided upon extirpation. At the most obvious level, their decision was a response to settlers' demands for protection, as evidenced by dozens of petitions, in the words of one from Harrison County, Virginia, beseeching the President "to take our distressed situation under your parental care, and grant us such relief as you in your wisdom shall think proper." But federal officials were not dragged into war by westerners' demands in some triumph of frontier democracy. National leaders did not have to respond to western grievances and in fact often resisted them. Most metropolitan elites resolutely opposed Shays' Rebellion, a movement of farmers demanding debt relief in western Massachusetts in 1786–1787. Their fear of what James Madison described in Federalist 10 as "improper or wicked projects" like Shays' Rebellion led them to seek a stronger federal government through a new Constitution. Similarly, metropolitan elites opposed the so-called Whiskey Rebellion, a frontier movement of the early 1790s that opposed a federal excise tax on distilled spirits, seeing it as enriching the already wealthy and an affront to liberties secured by the blood of revolution. President Washington had no hesitation in raising an army of 13,000 men to crush the rebellion. Unlike these cases of class-related economic conflict, however, metropolitan officials eventually supported frontier demands for military action against Indians. Metropolitan elites often looked upon frontiersmen as "white savages" and frequently denounced them for provoking conflict by attacking peaceful Indians or squatting on lands that Indians had yet to give up through the treaty process. The army even tried at times to evict squatters, as for example in 1787 when a detachment of 160 troops burned a dozen squatter cabins at Mingo Bottom up the Ohio River from Fort Harmar. But federal officials did not devote anything near as many resources to evicting squatters as they did to subduing whiskey rebels, and they were unable to prevent the number of squatters from increasing over time. Despite tensions with frontiersmen over the pace and process of expansion, Americans in charge of the national government were as deeply committed as frontiersmen to western expansion and to the eventual elimination of Indians. As guardians of the nation's purse and trustees of its reputation within the civilized world (as they defined it), eastern elites wished to cultivate expansion "with honor" and so did not advocate rushing to war. But they were willing to take this step once alternatives had been exhausted and they could claim to have demonstrated "utmost good faith."[26]

THE U.S. CONSTITUTION AND NATIVE NATIONS

The willingness of federal officials to use military force against the United Indian Nations was strengthened by the ratification of the new Constitution in 1789. Historians of the Constitution have seldom paid attention to Indians, but recent scholarship demonstrates that the Constitution's drafters and advocates saw the need to create an orderly and effective process for obtaining lands from Indians and recognized that meeting this objective might require war. Two lines of thought about United States–Indian relations informed the Constitution's making. One line of thought sought to curb what James Madison saw as "state encroachments on federal authority" such as the "wars and Treaties of Georgia with the Indians" and to establish the federal government's authority to regulate commercial relations with Indian nations and make treaties with them. A second line of thought emphasized the need for a strong central government that could support robust military operations to subdue, in Alexander Hamilton's words, "the savage tribes on our Western frontier [who] ought to be regarded as our natural enemies." To accomplish this, Hamiltonians successfully advocated for a standing army, a strong executive with powers of military command, and a Congress with powers of taxation to "provide for the common Defence." In September 1787, as the Constitutional Convention was completing its work, Knox expressed his hope that the "majority of the people" would decide to ratify the Constitution, since "without money & without credit," the United States would continue to be unable to "chastise the despicable bands of murdering savages on the frontiers." A year later, when General Josiah Harmer, commander of a weak western army, learned of the Constitution's ratification, he rejoiced that "the wheels of government will now soon be put in motion, in order that we may be enabled to extirpate these perfidious savages if they continue committing hostilities."[27]

JUST AND LAWFUL WAR AS GENOCIDAL WAR

With U.S. military capacity on a firmer foundation, in late 1789 President Washington ordered St. Clair to negotiate peace with the United Indian Nations, but peace could take place only if the confederation agreed to U.S. conditions. If Indians rejected what Washington thought of as "reasonable terms" and "continue their incursions," it would be necessary for the United States "to punish them with severity." To convey this message, St. Clair arranged for a French trader, Antoine Gamelin, to visit several villages along the Wabash and Maumee rivers. When Gamelin met the Kickapoos, he informed them of St. Clair's words that "I do now make you the offer of peace; accept it or reject it, as you please." Kickapoos were "displeased" and found St. Clair's words "menacing." Because of the "bad effect" of St. Clair's words, Gamelin "took upon myself to exclude them" as he continued his errand among other nations. Even so, confederationists like the Shawnee war leader Blue Jacket, who entertained Gamelin for supper at his home on the evening of April 29, expressed "doubt in the sincerity of the Big-knives, . . . having been already deceived by them," and observed that peace could never come until the Americans ceased settling north of the Ohio.[28]

In late May 1790, as U.S. officials continued to receive reports of "depredations of the Indians," Knox began to plan a military expedition against "the banditti Shawanese and Cherokees, and some of the Wabash Indians." Washington approved these plans, and in June Knox ordered General Josiah Harmar and Governor St. Clair to make plans to "extirpate, utterly, if possible, the said banditti."[29] Knox's call for the extirpation of resisting Indians was not idle rhetoric. Three years after the adoption of the Northwest Ordinance, Knox's orders to Harmar and St. Clair provided an official interpretation of the phrase "just and lawful wars" to mean wars of extirpation.

As we have seen, U.S. officials frequently spoke of the extirpation of Indians. What exactly did they mean by this term? One leading authority observes that *extirpation* was used interchangeably with the word *extermination* in the late eighteenth century and meant "utter destruction." Given this meaning, both terms expressed the modern "concept of genocide."[30] To be clear, Knox and other U.S. officials who called for the extirpation of Indians did not target all Native communities, only those that had sponsored "depredations," or to put it another way, that exercised a right of self-defense against a U.S. invasion. Nor did officials intend to kill every last member of the communities they targeted. But they did intend to surprise communities of men, women, and children of all ages and use overwhelming military force against the inhabitants. U.S. forces would capture some members of these communities, especially women who would be used as leverage in subsequent negotiations. But if they were successful, U.S. forces would also inevitably kill a large number of people, including noncombatants. Under a common-sense definition of genocide—the physical killing of a substantial portion of a group—the kind of warfare Knox ordered was intended to be exactly that. This was a far different species of war than the "total war" the United States conducted against non-Indians. In the late stages of the Civil War, the United States devastated the economy and resources of the rebellious southern states, but as General William Tecumseh Sherman marched to the sea, he did not try to surprise communities of Georgians in the hope of killing large numbers of their inhabitants.[31]

On what basis did Knox consider genocidal war against "banditti" Indians to be "just and lawful"? Knox did not provide a rationale, evidence that the legitimacy of extirpative war against Jefferson's "merciless Indian savages" or Hamilton's "savage tribes" and "natural enemies" of the United States was self-evident. Had Knox been asked to cite a legal authority, he would have turned to the Swiss jurist Emmerich de Vattel, author of *Law of Nations,* published in 1758, and widely regarded by U.S. founders as the world's preeminent authority on law and war. In the tradition of John Locke, whose 1690 *Second Treatise of Government* contrasted the "wild Woods and uncultivated waste of *America* left to Nature without any improvements, tillage, or husbandry" with England's "well Cultivated" lands, Vattel made a strong distinction between agricultural/civilized peoples who cultivated and improved the land and "savage" peoples who ostensibly did not. In writing about North America, Vattel argued that the "people of Europe, too closely pent up at home, finding land of which the savages stood in no particular need, and of which they made no actual and constant use, were lawfully entitled to take possession of it, and settle it with colonies." From this legal grounding in the "doctrine of discovery," Vattel further contended that "those nations . . . who inhabit fertile countries but disdain to cultivate their lands and chuse rather to live by plunder . . . deserve to be extirpated as savage and pernicious beasts" and that civilized nations had a "right to join a confederacy for the purpose of punishing and even exterminating . . . savage nations . . . who seem to delight in the ravages of war." These formulations did not allow for extermination of all Indians under all conditions, but they did provide legal basis for extermination under those Knox stipulated: against "banditti" engaged in "depredations."[32]

U.S. MILITARY OPERATIONS IN THE OHIO VALLEY, 1790–1791

To extirpate the "banditti" Indians, Knox and St. Clair ordered Josiah Harmar to lead a force of 1,100 militiamen and 300 federal troops against Native towns on the upper Maumee. His force departed Fort Washington in late September 1790. Proceeding, in the words of one historian, like a "herd of elephants trampling through the underbrush," it was poorly suited to achieve surprise. Indeed, as Harmar approached his target in mid-October, he received intelligence that Indians were preparing to abandon their towns. Obviously intending to kill people before they could find safety, he sent a detachment "to endeavor to surprise" the Shawnee and Miami village of Kekionga, but by the time these troops arrived, its residents, easily able to monitor Harmar's approach, had departed. Harmar ordered another detachment to "reconnoitre the country" and then proceeded to the nearby town of Chillicothe. It, too, had been evacuated and so, as one of the officers re-corded, "the army all engaged [in] burning and destroying everything that could be of use: corn, beans, pumpkins, stacks of hay, fencing and cabins, etc." The army burned four other towns. Harmar was not content with ma-terial destruction and so ordered another detachment to "surprise any par-ties" that might return to Kekionga. But rather than catching Indians off guard, Harmar's detachments provided targets for otherwise outnumbered Miamis, Potawatomis, and Shawnees. On terrain they knew well, confedera-tion fighters, led by Blue Jacket and the Miami Little Turtle, ambushed and overwhelmed a portion of Harmar's army, killing 178 U.S. soldiers and mili-tiamen. Most of the remaining militiamen panicked and took flight, leaving Harmar no choice but to march his troops back to Fort Washington. From there, Harmar reported that his expedition had burned five towns and that his men had killed over 100 Indians, allowing St. Clair to proclaim that "the savages have got a most terrible stroke." In actuality, though, Harmar in-flated the number of Native casualties. More reliable reports indicate that it was between ten and forty, significant losses for small communities, but not large enough to compromise the confederation's ability to sustain continuing resistance. When accurate reports reached the East, Washington denounced Harmar as a drunkard. Harmar soon resigned.[33]

Although the United States had suffered a significant defeat, its leaders never entertained the possibility of retreating from their ambitions to take the Ohio Valley. Immediately on the heels of Harmar's resignation, St. Clair be-gan planning a new expedition, but it would take months for him to assemble the necessary men and supplies. Under pressure to take immediate action, Washington and Knox authorized a quick-strike force of 750 Kentucky mili-tiamen to attack Indian towns north of the Ohio. Knox ordered the militia's commander, Brigadier General Charles Scott, to "assault the said towns, and the Indians therein, . . . sparing all who may cease to resist, and capturing as many as possible, particularly women and children." Taking women captive had two purposes. First, they would be used as hostages to ensure that Indians submitted to the terms Knox wished to impose. Second, because they would be unable to plant, cultivate, and harvest crops, their communities would suffer pain. But this did not mean that Scott's operation would avoid killing noncombatants. In June 1791, when Scott's militia reached its destination, the Wea town of Ouiatenon and satellite Wea and Kickapoo villages on the Wabash, he "discovered the enemy in great confusion, endeavoring to make their escape over the river in canoes." The detachment he ordered to pursue them "destroyed all the savages with which five canoes were crowded." Scott did not specify the age and sex of those killed, but almost certainly the canoes contained women, children, and older men. In all, Scott burned several towns—mostly evacuated—and reported killing thirty-two Indians and taking fifty-eight prisoners, mostly women, who had likely stayed behind to care for sick family members, and their children. Scott congratulated himself that "no act of inhumanity has marked the conduct of the volunteers of Kentucky on this occasion," citing as evidence that his men had not engaged in the "inveterate habit of scalping the dead," though a British agent on the scene three weeks later reported that militiamen had killed and "literally skinned" a Wea chief. Of course, from the perspective of the local residents, scalping and flaying were only one aspect of an assessment of the "humaneness" of Scott's expedition. Scott's firing on canoes filled with people taking flight would have supported longstanding Indigenous beliefs of Americans' malevolent intentions.[34]

Indian people would also have questioned the humanity of Scott's taking of prisoners. A few months after the prisoners were confined at Fort Washington, their relatives came to plead for their release (Fig. 11). Military officers replied that the prisoners would be held until all the Wabash nations sued for peace. The following summer, the Weas came again to Fort Washington to obtain their relatives' freedom, fearing, as their spokesman said, that they "will all die if they remain here much longer." In September 1792, after more than a year in captivity, General Rufus Putnam finally returned the prisoners to their homes as part of an initiative to cleave some of the more moderately inclined confederationists away from militancy. Miraculously, few of the prisoners perished, although they may well have been subject to sexual assault and undoubtedly endured untold mental and physical suffering. Most available documents do not include the voices of these prisoners of a "just and lawful" war, although an officer at Fort Washington did record the personal names the prisoners chose to give. As a recent study points out, these names—Green Willows, Soft Corn, Clear Sky, Deep Moss, White Stalk, Trod Ground, Roasting Ears, Swift Waves, Speckled Loon, Proper and Tall—spoke of close connections between Native women and the lands they desperately hoped to retain.[35]

St. Clair initiated his military operation in October 1791. As his force of 2,000 moved north from Fort Washington toward the town of Kekionga and nearby Miami, Shawnee, and Delaware towns, confederation scouts had little difficulty monitoring an army even larger and louder than Harmar's. St. Clair

Fig. 11. Fort Washington (modern-day Cincinnati) was one of several forts the United States constructed after the Revolutionary War to assert power in Indian country. Not only was Fort Washington a base from which U.S. military forces attacked Native communities, but its walls served as a prison for several dozen Wea women and children, taken from their homes and held hostage for over a year. Library of Congress Prints and Photographs Division.

had little respect for his adversaries, believing that Indians fought for personal glory and so lacked the capacity for disciplined coordination. He was wrong. Although Native war leaders did not organize their men as systematically as European or American armies, they were better able to take advantage of the terrain and to respond flexibly to opportunity and danger. In this instance, the United Indian Nations army had advantages of experience and confidence. Having prepared themselves by fasting and religious rituals, confederation fighters, British agent Simon Girty reported, "were never in greater Heart to meet their Enemy, nor more sure of Success." By contrast, many of St. Clair's men were raw recruits. As St. Clair slowly marched his men north in bad weather with insufficient rations, many deserted. On November 3, when he camped fifty miles short of his target, his fighting force had declined to 1,100, close to the size of the confederation army that had decided on a bold plan for an all-out assault on St. Clair's army. The Native attack came at daybreak on the 4th. Catching the Americans entirely by surprise, confederation fighters easily surrounded St. Clair's encampment, methodically picked off his men, and repelled a series of bayonet charges. Within three hours, the confederation army killed over 600 of St. Clair's men before those remaining fled, mostly in panic. This was the largest number of Americans killed by Indians in any single battle, far exceeding the 268 fatalities in the much better known 1876 Battle of the Little Bighorn. In achieving this victory, confederation forces lost far fewer men, probably between 20 and 50.[36]

THE HEADQUARTERS OF THE
UNITED INDIAN NATIONS, 1792

Although they had destroyed St. Clair's army, leaders of the United Indian Nations recognized that they had not yet won the war for Ohio. A month after the confederacy's victory over St. Clair, the Ottawa war chief Egushawa urged confederationists to remain united and applauded their efforts to "send deputations from each tribe, to other nations, to present to them the scalps of your enemies, and to invite them to unite with you in the war!" Several months later, in September 1792, hundreds of delegates, representing Indigenous communities from large portions of eastern North America, gathered at the confederacy's new headquarters at a place called The Glaize, near the confluence of the Auglaize and Maumee rivers (fifty miles southwest of modern-day Toledo). The population of The Glaize was around 2,000, mostly Shawnees, Delawares, and Miamis, along with a smattering of British traders. Delegates came from all the nations of the Ohio Valley. There were also Creeks and Chickamauga Cherokees from the South, Senecas and Mahicans from the East, and Sacs and Mesquakies from the West.[37]

The confederacy's principal spokesman, a Shawnee leader named Painted Pole, exhorted Indians to unity, arguing that "the Americans wanted . . . to divide us." But not all delegates were in agreement. An aspiring young Seneca leader from Buffalo Creek, Red Jacket, counseled confederacy leaders to consider selling some of their lands. A year earlier, at Philadelphia, federal officials had made a deal with him: in exchange for an annuity to the Haudenosaunees and a promise to halt New York settlers from claiming preemption rights to unceded lands, Red Jacket had agreed to lead a Haudenosaunee delegation west to persuade the United Indian Nations to accept a compromise boundary. When Red Jacket proposed that the confederacy sell some Ohio lands, Painted Pole insisted: "We do not want compensation. We want restitution of our country." Confederation leaders said they would meet with U.S. officials on the lower Sandusky, but only if the Americans agreed to remove forts they had recently constructed and restore the Ohio River boundary.[38]

The path to survival articulated at The Glaize—unity and armed resistance—depended on material resources, both external (from the British and Spanish) and local (The Glaize supported extensive cornfields and was close to good hunting grounds and rich fisheries). Like its predecessor in the early 1760s, the confederacy of the early 1790s also looked to spiritual power. Militant communities revived traditional ceremonies and ritually consumed and vomited the "black drink," thus purifying themselves. They also appealed to prophets for success in war. On one occasion in late 1792, several Shawnees, thinking of joining an expedition against a U.S. convoy, called on Coocoochee, a Mohawk prophet living at The Glaize. Using powers of divination, she forecast success: "Many scalps, many prisoners, and much plunder." Coocoochee also drew on historical analysis to make predictions about the future. She spoke of the "first landing of the 'pale-faces' from their monstrous canoes with their great white wings, as seen by her ancestors," of their "increasing strength and power, their insatiable avarice, and their continued encroachments on the red men." From this reading of history, she predicted that the "Long-knives . . . would not be satisfied until they had crowded the Indians to the extreme north to perish on the great ice lake; or to the far west until, pushing those who should escape from their rifles into the great waters, all would at length be exterminated."[39]

Here again, we see that the United Indian Nations was fighting for nothing less than the survival of Indian people. The pervasiveness of an Indigenous consciousness of genocide at The Glaize was confirmed by a Mahican visitor from the mission town of Stockbridge, Massachusetts, by the name of Hendrick Aupaumut. Sent as an emissary in advance of Red Jacket and other Haudenosaunees, Aupaumut reported that confederationists feared, as had Indians in the Ohio Valley for decades, that Americans were planning to poison them. Residents of The Glaize told Aupaumut that they had recently received intelligence that Americans "have brought a large quantity of Goods and Liquors in the forts, which they will send with the army, and that before they will come to battle against the Indians they will put a Poison in the Goods and Liquors." Aupaumut further related that confederationists made the general argument "that the white people are deceitful in their dealings with us the Indians" and "have taken all our lands from us." Even the colonists' efforts to "Civilize" Indians were duplicitous. According to Aupaumut, the Indians he spoke with contended that after "the Big Knives . . .

Christianize number[s] of them so as to gain their attention, then they would [kill] them, and have killed of such 96 in one day," a clear reference to the unforgotten massacre at Gnadenhütten ten years before.[40]

CULTIVATING PEACE WITH WAR IN MIND

After the United Indian Nations' annihilation of St. Clair's army, U.S. government officials did not consider retreating from their objective of destroying Native resistance. Secretary Knox was prepared to argue for renewed military action, but before doing so, he wanted to cultivate a sense that the United States had acted in a manner consistent with the "utmost good faith" clause of the Northwest Ordinance. Had the United States been justified in going to war against the Indian confederacy? His answer was an emphatic yes. In a statement to President Washington reviewing the events leading up to what he described as "the late disasters," Knox insisted that earlier treaties with Indians had been fairly conducted. The "Miami and Wabash Indians" had been invited to come to Fort Harmar, but they had rejected the invitation. Instead, with other "banditti," they "continued their depredations." The United States had made further peace overtures, but these "were treated . . . with neglect" and "outrages were renewed with still greater violence than ever." It therefore "became necessary to make an experiment of the effect of coercion." The experiment, of course, had failed. This meant that the confederation would likely gain strength and that the United Indian Nations would be even more certain to reject "offers of peace on reasonable terms." Knox therefore proposed that an "adequate military force should be raised as soon as possible," one better trained and more disciplined than the army recently routed.[41]

With a new Constitution ratified, U.S. officials were now in a position to field a substantially stronger military force than before. Rather than relying on poorly trained volunteer militia forces, officials proceeded to build a regular army. In 1792 Knox sought—and Congress funded—an increase in the number of regiments from one to four, allowing for an army of over 5,000. In addition, new funds were available for training and supplies. Prior to this buildup, from 1789 to 1791 the U.S. War Department spent a total of $632,000, 15 percent of total federal expenditures. By 1794, military spending had increased to $2,639,000 and represented 38 percent of all expenditures.[42]

Two years would elapse before the United States would ready an army to resume the war for Ohio. In the meantime, U.S. officials sponsored several diplomatic initiatives. Characteristically, historians have uncritically evaluated U.S. policymakers' statements of intent and have characterized these initiatives as a sincere and humanitarian "peace offensive." Given that U.S. policymakers had already decreed that the western confederacy's position lacked the slightest legitimacy (by this time, officials had even dropped their earlier suggestions that settlers were partly to blame for frontier violence) and that they were predicting that the United Indian Nations would reject U.S. conditions for peace, U.S. diplomacy was not intended to avoid war. Diplomacy might draw some of the softer support away from the militants' orbit, but its main purpose was to create the appearance that a war to dispossess Indians was consistent with principles of justice. A summary of discussions among President Washington and the members of his cabinet by Secretary of State Thomas Jefferson makes the government's objectives crystal clear. Meeting in February 1793, cabinet members easily concurred that the United States should send a commission to council with the Indian confederacy in the West, though "merely to gratify the public opinion" and "not from an expectation of success."[43]

The major diplomatic initiative was undertaken by commissioners Benjamin Lincoln, Timothy Pickering, and Beverley Randolph. In April 1793, when Knox briefed the commissioners, he did not inform them of the cabinet's cynical view of their mission. Presumably, Knox thought that the commissioners would perform credibly only if they were under the illusion that higher officials thought they might succeed. Knox authorized the commissioners to offer a onetime payment of $50,000 along with a $10,000 annuity in exchange for the United Indian Nations' recognition of the Fort Harmar boundary line. As a fallback, Knox informed the commissioners that they could propose modifying the Fort Harmar boundary to allow Indians to retain some lands east of it that the federal government had not already granted to speculative land companies. This, however, was a very modest concession and a rejection not only of the confederation's position but of the compromise floated a few years earlier by Joseph Brant and still on the table for a revised boundary at the Muskingum River.[44]

In late July and August the U.S. commissioners engaged Wyandots, Delawares, Shawnees, Miamis, western Haudenosaunees, Potawatomis, Ottawas, and Ojibwes in talks at Amherstburg on the east bank of the Detroit River in Upper Canada. In face-to-face meetings with the commissioners and in a subsequent message, confederation spokesmen explained their position that previous treaties had been forced on them by a minority of chiefs "through fear" and that they had no intention of accepting an illegitimate boundary. "Money, to us, is of no value," they explained, and "no consideration whatever can induce us to sell our lands, on which we get sustenance for our women and children." The United Indian Nations would be happy to make peace, but only if the Americans would "agree that the Ohio shall remain the boundary line between us." The commissioners, of course, countered that this would be impossible, though they offered what they characterized as major concessions. First, they raised the possibility of modest revisions in the Fort Harmar line, and second, they stated that U.S. officials had previously erred in claiming that all territory south of the Great Lakes belonged to the United States through the Treaty of Paris. The king had not conveyed these lands to the United States (since he had never purchased them from the Indians) and had only granted the United States the right to purchase them, the commissioners said. From the confederacy's perspective, however, there was no point in modest adjustment to the Fort Harmar boundary. The Ohio River boundary, they insisted, had been established by the British and illegitimate treaties since then had not altered that fact. They also failed to see any difference between the United States taking their lands through conquest or purchase. They wondered, with some incredulity, that the commissioners "seem to expect that because you have at last acknowledged our independence, we should for such a favor surrender to you our country." On August 16, the commissioners sent a message to the Indians saying that "the negotiation . . . is at an end." Thomas Jefferson was not surprised by this outcome. He wrote Thomas Pinckney, ambassador to Great Britain, that "we expected nothing else, and had gone into the negociations only to prove to all our citizens that peace was unattainable on terms which any of them would admit."[45]

THE BLACK SNAKE, 1794

Even as the United States was sending emissaries west under the banner of peace, General Anthony Wayne, St. Clair's replacement, was busy preparing for the war policymakers had viewed as inevitable all along. By September 1794, Wayne had assembled an army of 2,000 regular troops and 1,500 militiamen and scouts to strike the "audacious savages," as Knox termed them. After Harmar and St. Clair, U.S. officials desperately wanted to avoid a third humiliating defeat. With caution always in mind, Wayne erected a series of posts along his route north from the Ohio River and used rangers and Indian scouts (Chickasaws and Choctaws) to closely monitor confederation movements and so avoid the fate of his predecessors. The first preference of U.S. officials was for Wayne's army to overawe Indians and cause them to surrender without a fight. Should defenders of The Glaize resist, however, Wayne's army would attempt to inflict, in Knox's words, "severe strokes to make them sensible how necessary a solid and permanent peace would be to prevent their utter extirpation." What if the defenders continued to fight? Knox did not explicitly say, but the logic was obvious: sustained resistance would eventually mandate total annihilation.[46]

Native leaders at The Glaize carefully monitored the slow progress of Wayne's massive army. In late June 1794, Blue Jacket saw an opportunity to ambush a pack train carrying supplies to Fort Recovery, a post Wayne had constructed at the site of St. Clair's defeat. Blue Jacket, Little Turtle, and a force of over 1,000 Potawatomis, Ottawas, Ojibwes, and western Haudeno-saunees succeeded in taking several hundred animals and killing perhaps forty soldiers, but they were unable to capture the fort and retreated. Having failed to deliver a major blow, many Ojibwes, Ottawas, and Potawatomis decided to return to their homes, leaving the confederation army with only half its fighting men.[47]

A month later, Wayne's army began moving toward The Glaize. As he drew near, village leaders hastily evacuated women and children. An Ottawa named Kin-jo-i-no (Chief of the Open Heart) later recalled:

All was consternation and fright throughout the villages. They fled from the cornfields on the fertile bottom lands. Canoes were loaded to descend the river; ponies were laden with packs and the smaller children were hastily conducted over the trails leading down the river. Old women, burdened with immense packs strapped to their shoulders, followed their retreating families with all the haste their aged limbs would permit.

A few days later, as Wayne's men moved down the Maumee, confederation leaders debated whether to fight or not. Blue Jacket favored making a stand. Little Turtle expressed doubt. On August 20 confederation leaders attacked Wayne at a place called Fallen Timbers, twenty miles upriver from Lake Erie. Weaker than it had been a few years earlier and facing a stronger, more disciplined force, the confederation army was unable to turn back Wayne's. Confederation casualties were significant (forty to sixty killed) but not overwhelming. Their inability to block the U.S. army, however, gave the troops a free hand to continue an American practice of town destruction, burning cabins and cornfields, uprooting gardens, and despoiling graves along a fifty-mile stretch of the Auglaize and Maumee rivers.[48]

After Fallen Timbers, confederation forces retreated to Fort Miami, a nearby British post. Fort Miami was one of several western forts within U.S. territory that the British were supposed to have relinquished after 1783 but had retained as leverage to secure American debts to British creditors. When Native fighters reached Fort Miami, they had every reason to expect the British to aid them. They were stunned to find the gates closed in their faces. Although British officials had provided the United Indian Nations with arms and supplies, by 1794 London officials were deeply concerned that continued assistance might drag the empire into war at a time when Britain was fighting revolutionary France. A few months later, the prospect for any renewal of British support disappeared altogether when Britain signed Jay's Treaty, agreeing to abandon the western posts. Confederationists were bitter about what Blue Jacket later recalled as the moment when "we saw the British dealt treacherously with us." Delawares complained that British officials had urged the confederation to "fight for your land," but all along they had been saying this only "so that we may all be blotted out."[49]

After Fallen Timbers and the closed gates of Fort Miami, some United Indian Nations leaders wanted to fight on, but most eventually decided that their best chance for survival was to negotiate with General Wayne. This was not an easy decision. For a generation, confederationists had committed to armed resistance to prevent Americans from annihilating them and taking their lands. The name confederationists bestowed on Wayne—Black Snake—reflected their deep suspicions of Americans. According to John Heckewelder, they gave Wayne this name because "he had all the cunning of this animal, who . . . hides himself in the grass with his head only above it, watching all around to see where the birds are building their nests, that he may know where to find the young ones when they hatched." In meeting with Black Snake in June 1795 at Fort Greenville, Blue Jacket informed him of rumors that the Americans intended "the massacre and destruction" of Ohio Valley Indians and in this way invited Wayne to rebut them as a condition for peace. Wayne assured Blue Jacket and other leaders that "we have now buried the hatchet," thus disavowing any intention of further warfare. At the same time, he forced the United Indian Nations to accept a massive land cession—25,000 square miles in eastern and southern Ohio (more than half of the state). The Greenville Treaty also required Indians to cede other lands—a tract Virginia had granted to George Rogers Clark as well as strategic tracts along the Maumee,

Fig. 12. Little Turtle (Miami) helped plan major victories over U.S. forces in the early 1790s. After signing the 1795 Treaty of Greenville, Little Turtle frequently visited Philadelphia. Benjamin Rush inoculated him against smallpox, and he sat for this portrait by Gilbert Stuart. A few months after his death in summer 1812, U.S. troops destroyed his village in Indiana. Drawing based on Stuart's painting (destroyed in 1814), in Wood, *Lives of Famous Indian Chiefs*, 289. Reproduced by University of Oregon Digital Scholarship Services.

Wabash, and Illinois, where permanent military posts could be maintained, unambiguous signs of Americans' future intentions. The treaty provided a onetime payment of $20,000 and annuities of no more than $1,000 to each signatory nation. It also guaranteed that Indians had the right "quietly to enjoy" their remaining lands "without any molestation from the United States," though by affirming that the United States had the sole right to purchase, the treaty clearly implied that Native nations would eventually be requested to sell additional lands. Under these conditions, Indians would continue to have cause to fear for their survival (Fig. 12).[50]

RESISTANCE AND WAR IN THE SOUTH, 1788–1794

In contrast to the Ohio Valley, where the federal government took the lead in seizing Native lands, the states played a larger role in parallel initiatives in the South. As we have seen, states aggressively negotiated and in some instances simply imposed land cessions on Cherokees and Creeks. The federal government was less aggressive, and in some cases Native leaders saw federal treaties as protection against rapacious settlers, but federal treaties, too, involved land cessions many tribal leaders found illegitimate. Under these conditions, some Cherokees and Creeks supported the United Indian Nations. Few traveled across the Ohio River to fight with confederation forces, but they were aware of the situation in the North and were prepared to take up arms in defense of their own lands in the South.

Chickamauga Cherokees, led by Dragging Canoe, had been engaged in their own war against American settlers for several years. In May 1788 Cherokees killed John Kirk and his family, who were squatting on Cherokee land in violation of the 1785 Hopewell Treaty near the nation's capital of Chota (Fig. 13), where twelve years earlier the Shawnee spokesman we met in Chapter 1 had indicted colonists for an insatiable greed for Indian lands. To retaliate, an unofficial settler militia, led by John Sevier, governor of Franklin, attacked Chota and the nearby town of Chilhowee in June. At Chilhowee militiamen killed several Cherokees under a flag of truce, including Old Tassel, a peace chief who had said a few months earlier that he was trying to "stand up like a wall between Bad people [Chickamaugas] and my Brothers, the Virginians." Chota had survived the horrors of the Revolutionary War period, but this latest attack caused many residents to abandon the town and settle with relatives in western South Carolina, seeking to live in "peace where it is light & clear." Others from Chota and Chilhowee decided to join the Chickamau-

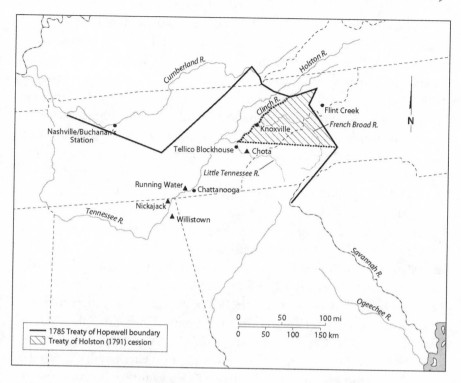

Fig. 13. War for the West in the South, 1785–1794
(dashed lines indicate modern state boundaries)

gas, thus adding strength to the resistance. After Cherokees targeted several settlements, including Gillespie's Station near Knoxville, where they killed twenty-eight settlers, Sevier set out again for Cherokee country.[51]

In January 1789, Sevier and his militia reached a temporary village associated with the Cherokee leader Young Tassel (John Watts), the old chief's nephew, on Flint Creek in the Appalachian foothills of northeastern Tennessee. According to Sevier's report, using "grasshopper guns"—a light cannon carried on horseback—his men pinned down the Cherokees and eventually engaged them in hand-to-hand combat. Sevier reported that he had "buried 145 of their dead." Because the evidence for this event rests on a single letter from Sevier that appeared in Georgia and South Carolina newspapers, it is possible that Sevier exaggerated the number killed or even fabricated the event altogether. If not, however, the slaughter at Flint Creek was the deadliest single event in the by now long history of European warfare against Cherokees.[52]

Although the Chickamauga Cherokees gained strength in the late 1780s, most Cherokees remained wary of militancy. In July 1791, they negotiated the Treaty of Holston with William Blount, governor of the newly created Southwest Territory (what would become the state of Tennessee in 1796) at White's Fort (Knoxville). This treaty was hardly favorable to the Cherokees, as it ceded lands along the Holston and French Broad rivers that had been settled in violation of the Hopewell Treaty, and many signers protested that they had agreed only under duress. A few months later, when a delegation of Cherokees journeyed to Philadelphia to contest the treaty, Secretary Knox increased the annuity in the original treaty and pledged to speak with the President about evicting illegal settlers. Knowing well the hardships of war, most Cherokees chose to place their hope in federal assurances to protect their remaining lands and provide assistance.[53]

Many Creeks also contested a settler invasion. During the first four months of 1788, Creeks reportedly killed forty Georgia settlers who had encroached on their lands west of the Ogeechee River, causing many others to abandon settlements and seek safety nearer the coast. Unable to field a militia against the Creeks, Georgia governor George Handley called on U.S. commissioners to negotiate a truce. The most prominent Creek leader, Alexander McGillivray, had considered making an alliance with the Chickamaugas in response to Dragging Canoe's appeal to "forever banish the American from our hunting grounds." Nonetheless, he agreed to attend talks with U.S. officials. Like Cherokees who signed at Hopewell in 1785, a significant number of Creeks—even those inclined toward militancy like McGillivray—hoped that the United States would be able to prevent Georgians from overrunning their lands. At the same time, however, McGillivray expressed suspicions of all Americans when he informed federal treaty commissioners that Cherokees "are taking refuge in our territory" from "acts of hostility committed in the most barbarous manner by the Americans." Coming at a time when Congress was making "professions of the most friendly nature," McGillivray continued, it seemed that such professions were only "deceitful snares to lull [Indians] into a security, whereby the Americans may the more easily destroy them."[54]

U.S. officials feared that McGillivray had the inclination and talent to create, as one American agent put it, "a dangerous confederacy between the several Indian nations, [and] the Spaniards and British agents." At the same time, with their hands full in the Ohio Valley, federal officials were reluctant to do anything to provoke the Creeks to war on the southern frontier. With these considerations in mind, U.S. officials made extraordinary efforts to cultivate McGillivray. In 1790, McGillivray accepted U.S. overtures to visit the capital city of New York to negotiate a treaty. In exchange for an annuity and guarantees of Creek sovereignty, McGillivray and other Creeks agreed to sell some, but not all, of the lands supposedly ceded in previous treaties negotiated with Georgia. Secretary Knox, who personally conducted the negotiations, quite literally purchased McGillivray's allegiance through secret articles making him an honorary brigadier general with a handsome annual stipend. Bribery of this sort had not been used in previous treaties, but it would become more common in treaty negotiations in the early nineteenth century. What appeared to be a diplomatic coup in prying McGillivray (and hence the Creeks) from Spain and the Ohio Valley confederationists, however, did not eliminate conflict. Reflecting ongoing tensions between a federal government wanting to control Indian affairs and state governments that asserted states' rights in this area, Georgia officials rejected the Treaty of New York and openly encouraged their citizens to violate the boundary it established. Many Creeks from towns unrepresented at New York also denounced the treaty for ceding any land at all.[55]

Despite federal treaties with the Cherokees and Creeks, violence continued on the southern frontier. The reasons were simple and familiar. Squatters paid no attention to treaty boundaries and established settlements on Native lands. When they did, some Native leaders exercised a right of self-defense and used violent means to remove them. Settlers then formed militias to counterattack.

In late summer 1792, a force of a few hundred Chickamauga Cherokees, Creeks, and Shawnees who had lived among the Creeks for decades decided to undertake a military operation against Nashville and other settlements on the Cumberland River. A few months before, the Chickamaugas had secured arms from the Spanish at Pensacola, Florida, and the militants were confident in their mission. Before setting out from Willstown, a Cherokee leader known as Bloody Fellow tried to dissuade the fighters. Not long before, Bloody Fellow had supported armed resistance, but he had signed the Treaty of Holston and recently visited the U.S. capital of Philadelphia to meet American leaders. There Bloody Fellow agreed to peace and returned with an American flag and placed it in Willstown's town square. Bloody Fellow asked his compatriots to look the flag and asked, "Don't you see the stars in it? They are not towns, they are nations; there are thirteen of them. These are people who are very strong, and are the same as one man." Because of this, Bloody Fellow urged his kinsmen to "stay at home and mind your women and children." Refusing this advice, Young Tassel, the Chickamaugas' main leader since the death of Dragging Canoe a few months earlier, and the other warriors painted themselves black, performed a war dance, and "fired balls through the flag." A few days later they set out for Buchanan's Station, a post guarding Nashville, where on September 30 they launched a midnight raid. But as Young Tassel's force approached, they frightened the post's cattle herd, allowing settlers within the post to repel the attack.[56]

Native losses at Buchanan's Station were not high—they suffered three killed and seven wounded—though the failure of their mission was discouraging. Nonetheless, support for armed resistance did not evaporate. As confederationists continued to raid settlements on the Cumberland and French Broad rivers (from 1792 to 1794 they killed over 100 settlers), residents of the Southwest Territory demanded "the protection of permanent troops" against "repeated depredations . . . from large bodies of savages." But federal officials were unable to answer the call. The reason, as Knox wrote to Washington in April 1794, was that all available troops were tied up in "the operations in which General Wayne is engaged." Knox authorized Southwest Territory governor William Blount to call a militia into service, but only to defend settlements and not for "direct offensive expeditions."[57]

In September 1794 James Robertson, commander of the Southwest Territory militia, ordered Major James Ore to lead a force of Tennessee and Kentucky militiamen against two Chickamauga Cherokee towns, Nickajack and Running Water along the Tennessee River, west of present-day Chattanooga. Although unauthorized by higher officials, Governor Blount, a federal government appointee, tacitly supported the operation by allowing Ore and his men access to supplies and arms from the federal arsenal at Knoxville. After surrounding and surprising Nickajack, Ore later reported, "the slaughter was great" but the number killed could not be "accurately reported, as many were killed in the Tennessee." Overall, Ore estimated that at both towns the militia had killed fifty Chickamaugas. Although the details are hazy, the attack on Nickajack in particular may have been more a massacre than a battle, as those shot in the river were probably trying to escape and likely included women and children. Fallen Timbers, the climax of a highly visible federally sponsored expedition, is far better known than the contemporaneous militia operation in Tennessee. Yet, since the combined population of Nickajack and Running Water was much smaller than the population of The Glaize, these attacks were proportionally more devastating.[58]

After learning of Ore's attacks at Nickajack and Running Water, Secretary Knox immediately objected to Blount that the attacks were offensive and therefore "not authorized." Nonetheless, Knox had a difficult time maintaining a bright line between the presumably "just and lawful war" the U.S. army had been conducting north of the Ohio and the "unauthorized" war undertaken by Ore's militia in the South. Robertson's rationale for ordering Ore's militia into action was that he had received "information that a large body of Creeks, with the Cherokees of the Lower towns, were . . . determin[ed] to invade" Nashville and other settlements along the Cumberland River. By this rationale, Ore's preemptive strike was more of a defensive than an offensive operation. Presented with Robertson's rationale, Knox was unable to sustain his objections. Instead of disciplining Robertson, he promised that the federal government would provide "all reasonable defensive protection." Although Knox did not directly say so, he had more or less conceded that Ore's operation was, if not technically "lawful," certainly "just" by the standard Knox had applied north of the Ohio River. Knox's operations, too, were in a sense "offensive" in that they targeted communities distant from American settlements, but the rationale he offered was essentially the same as Robertson's: to defend against "banditti" engaged in "depredations." The issue, then, was federal authority and not a rejection of "frontier warfare" as a fundamentally different kind of war.[59]

THE DIRT CAPTAIN, 1794

Like Anthony Wayne after Fallen Timbers, William Blount moved to take advantage of the attacks on Nickajack and Running Water by summoning Cherokee leaders to Tellico Blockhouse on the Little Tennessee River not far from Chota. The circumstances Young Tassel and other Cherokee leaders confronted as they prepared to meet Blount in November paralleled those Blue Jacket faced when he agreed to talk with Wayne around the same time: declining external support (Spain, stretched thin by war with revolutionary France, had restricted aid) and the prospect of the complete destruction of their people at the hands of American armies, a threat Blount made plain enough when he informed Cherokee leaders that "war will cost the United States much money, and some lives, but it will destroy the existence of your people, as a nation, forever." Unlike Wayne, Blount had not led an army to dispossess Indians, but he had pushed hard to take Cherokee lands in the

1791 Treaty of Holston. Since then, he had tacitly supported Tennessee militias seeking to secure a settler invasion and was now threatening genocide to end resistance. Perceiving Blount to be the leader of a movement to take their lands, Cherokees gave him the name "Dirt Captain." Like Native leaders who counseled with Wayne at Fort Greenville, those who met Blount at Tellico Blockhouse faced agonizing choices. For Cherokee leaders who had been counseling against militancy, Nickajack and Running Water were proof that continued resistance would only bring catastrophe. They urged Chickamaugas to "walk together in the paths of peace," not just for the sake of

Fig. 14. Dragging Canoe, born around 1738, was a major figure in the Chickamauga Cherokee resistance against settler colonialism. He died in 1792, two years before devastating militia attacks at Nickajack and Running Water. Although there is no known likeness of Dragging Canoe, this 1991 drawing gives a compelling interpretation. Drawing by Mike Smith. Courtesy of Ray Smith.

Chickamauga communities but because all Cherokees were subject to violent retribution from settler militias. Like their counterparts in the Ohio Valley, Chickamauga militants had fought heroically. Now, though, they heeded the call of their kinsmen by accepting the 1791 Treaty of Holston and laying down their arms (Fig. 14). Somehow they might persuade the Dirt Captain and other American leaders to protect what lands they had left.[60]

CONCLUSION: CONQUEST AND BENEVOLENCE

The Greenville Treaty and the Tellico Blockhouse agreement marked the end of a crucial phase in what has been called the "Long War for the West."[61] Twenty years before, on the eve of their war for independence, American colonists had invaded portions of Indian country west of the Appalachians, but nowhere was their presence uncontested. By 1795, the United States had established control over western Pennsylvania, most of Ohio, western Virginia, the western Carolinas, Kentucky, and most of Tennessee. Kentucky had already become a state in 1792; Tennessee would follow in 1796 and Ohio in 1803.

U.S. success did not come about because of superiority in battle. In the Ohio Valley in the early 1790s, U.S. military forces killed perhaps 150 Native fighters, whereas confederation forces killed close to 800 Americans. By that measure, the United Indian Nations clearly won this phase of the war. But despite the fact that confederation forces' knowledge of terrain and their flexible methods of fighting allowed them to inflict massive casualties on two U.S. armies, their adversary had overriding long-term advantages. Unlike the Indian confederation, which possessed a limited supply of fighting men and economic resources, the United States, especially once organized under a Constitution with mechanisms to fund large armies, was able to take advantage of its greater population and economic resources to continually mobilize new military operations. As it did, the federal government gained westerners' often tenuous allegiance, thus reinforcing its capacities.[62] The U.S. government took a less direct role in combating Native resistance in the South, leaving the work to local militias (partially supported by federal funds). Given more or less constant warfare between settlers and Indians, it is difficult to arrive at figures for total casualties in the South from 1787 to 1795. Native casualties were almost certainly higher in the South than the North, even without including the 145 Cherokees Sevier reportedly killed at Flint Creek in 1789. Despite these differences, though, the logic of the situation on the southern frontier was similar to that in Ohio. American settlements in Kentucky and Tennessee, growing in population each year and linked, albeit tenuously, to broader networks of economic support, were able to sustain aggressive warfare against smaller Indigenous communities with finite resources that could not afford sustained losses over time.

In the end, Native decisions were perhaps guided less by the actual amount of destruction they suffered than by the threat that they might suffer much greater destruction if they continued to fight. Many U.S. military operations (regular and militia) inflicted substantial damage on targeted communities as measured by lives lost through direct killing, destruction of crops and buildings, plundering of graves, taking of prisoners, and likely sexual violence. Overall, however, American military operations of the late 1780s and early 1790s were less destructive than those during the Revolutionary War. In part this was because of American incompetence, as seen, especially, in the spectacular failure of St. Clair's expedition. But Native competence was an equally important factor. Yes, St. Clair was a fool, but the United Indian Nations' killing of over 600 of his men with few losses of their own is evidence of their abilities to plan and carry out sophisticated operations. Confederation leaders also minimized the potential for massacre by monitoring American forces and, when necessary, evacuating towns in advance of their arrival. As always, the decision to abandon towns meant material losses and increased the chances of starvation and disease. Compared to the period 1774–1783, however, when Haudenosaunees and Cherokees suffered significant population losses from the intersecting factors of material deprivation and disease, communities that saw their towns and fields torched in the early 1790s managed to avoid serious losses from famine or sickness. Nonetheless, Indians were very much aware that American armies were willing and able to inflict horrific destruction. It might be possible to defeat them once or twice and to deflect the brunt of their destructive potential, but by 1795 most Native leaders had reached the painful conclusion that continued resistance against relentlessly aggressive Americans risked catastrophe.

Judging by their results, U.S. military operations in the Ohio Valley in the late 1780s and early 1790s hardly seem genocidal. Two of the three major expeditions (Harmar's and St. Clair's), although killing some confederation fighters and destroying a few towns, were routed by confederation armies. The third expedition (Wayne's) killed a larger number of confederation fighters and razed the fields of a major population center, but it did not slaughter noncombatants. Nonetheless, an assessment based solely on results fails to recognize that these and other military operations in the region carried the possibility of surprising Native villages and killing large numbers of their inhabitants, including noncombatants. Indians could avoid catastrophe by ambushing or evading U.S. troops or submitting to U.S. terms for peace. Otherwise, however, they were subject to what Americans called extirpation. That extirpation did not occur (or was only partial, as in Scott's attack on Ouiatenon) was not because of an inherent restraint on the part of commanders and the troops they led. Rather, it was because Indians were able to avoid becoming the victims of genocidal killing. Ironically, then, U.S. incompetence and Native competence combined to camouflage the genocidal potential of U.S. military operations in the Ohio Valley during this period. South of the Ohio, settler militias, operating from positions closer to Native communities and able to achieve surprise, realized an intention to inflict massive destruction, as at Nickajack and Running Water in 1794 and (possibly) Flint Creek in 1789. But this did not mean that militias were inherently more inclined to extirpative warfare than U.S. regular forces; the variable was capacity, not intention.[63]

A recognition that U.S. military operations were potentially genocidal, or to put it another way, that the United States authorized genocidal warfare against resisting Indians (regarding it as just and lawful), calls into question easy dismissals of the issue of genocide during this period of U.S. history. The United States did not consistently commit genocide, but it was willing to do so, and its officials repeatedly communicated that willingness. When the Mohawk prophet Coocoochee foresaw that the "Long-knives . . . would not be satisfied until . . . all would at length be exterminated," she was doing no more than stating what U.S. officials frequently said themselves. Extermination might be avoided, but it was a stated goal under some conditions and a very real possibility.

U.S. officials preferred to achieve their major objective—obtaining the lands of Indigenous people—without having to kill large numbers of the people those lands supported. A better option was for Indians to "voluntarily" cede substantial portions of their lands. To some extent, this preference was a matter of convenience. It was cheaper to dispossess Indians without having to raise armies. It was also a matter of perception. Officials wanted to see themselves—and they wanted observers to see them—as acting honorably, or, to put it in terms of the Northwest Ordinance, acting with utmost good faith. Officials were concerned to cultivate the right impression among three groups. Two of these groups consisted of their peers. One, signified by Jefferson's reference to the need to "gratify the public opinion" through peace initiatives all but foreordained to fail, was an elite public in metropolitan centers consisting of respectable men of learning, affairs, and God, who, devoted to principles of the Enlightenment and Christianity, wished to create a nation that exemplified the highest principles of civilization. The other group, indicated by Knox's concerns about the "verdict of mankind" and the "national reputation of America," consisted of arbiters of civilization in Europe. Scholars have pointed out that the United States was the "first example" within European imperialism of a "successful settler revolt against metropolitan rule." From this fragile position, one that required that America not only equal Europe's civilization but develop an even higher version, U.S. policymakers felt the need to avoid the appearance of inhumanity.[64]

U.S. officials also hoped to secure recognition of their commitment to utmost good faith from Indians themselves. This desire was particularly evident in the negotiations Wayne conducted with United Indian Nations leaders at Fort Greenville in 1795. During those proceedings, which consumed a full two months, Wayne took pains to create "an atmosphere of mutual respect and friendship," adhering to Indian protocols and attempting to persuade Indian leaders of his (and America's) "sincerity" and "good faith." In presenting themselves this way, Wayne and officials in Washington who guided his approach hoped to obtain acknowledgment of America's lawfulness and justice from Native nations. This does not mean that Indigenous leaders who signed the treaty were deceived by this "façade of civility." One scholar's characterization of those who signed the Greenville Treaty as "browbeaten peoples who were leery of the accord they had just struck" captures the reality of the situation. At some level, Americans were uneasy about their position as conquerors who had secured assent only through the threat of using extreme violence, and so it was not so much that Americans were naturally "sincere" about their benevolence, as that they needed to cultivate a sense of it. To do this required obtaining gestures of consent from the dispossessed.[65]

CHAPTER 4

Survival and New Threats, 1795–1810

When Blue Jacket left the treaty grounds at Fort Greenville in August 1795, he traveled to a village he had recently established on the upper Maumee River.[1] This village was near another military post, Fort Wayne, constructed by Wayne himself a year before. Blue Jacket's decision to live near this extension of United States power into Indian country indicated a major shift in his evaluation of how his people could survive. For over twenty years Blue Jacket and other Native leaders had fought to hold a colonial invasion at bay. Although they were unable to do so, they had at least avoided the very real possibility of catastrophic destruction. Because continued armed resistance risked annihilation, Blue Jacket now judged that his people's best hope for survival would be to accept an imbalance of power and insist that Americans live up to their professions of honorable intentions.

Blue Jacket's decision marked a significant transition from a period of militant resistance and war to a period of relative peace. Blue Jacket's signing of the Greenville Treaty highlighted the agonizing choices Native people were forced to make with their very existence at stake. Survival was a challenge for all Native communities, whether they decided to fight the American advance or not, whether they were in the path of an expanding settler empire or colonized within it. What decisions did Native communities make about how best to survive in the late eighteenth and early nineteenth centuries? What strategies did they pursue? What projects did they undertake? How were they able to avoid, minimize, and recover from the impact of destructive forces?

SURVIVING WAR

To live in peace, Native communities had to survive war. Under constant threat from U.S. military forces, Native communities developed and improvised evacuation plans to ensure the protection of vulnerable people and material items critical to personal and family well-being and religious practice. Although the details of these practices are poorly documented, the Ottawa Kin-jo-i-no's account of the evacuation of The Glaize in 1794 (noted in the previous chapter) provides a glimpse of an orderly process that required careful planning: "Canoes were loaded to descend the river; ponies were laden with packs and the smaller children were hastily conducted over the trails leading down the river." Most of the historical sources, written by invaders, document only the efficiency of evacuation procedures, as when Major John Hamtramck, part of Harmar's 1790 operation, arrived at a Piankashaw town at the mouth of the Vermillion River in western Indiana and reported his disappointment at finding "nothing but empty houses."[2]

Decisions to evacuate towns and fields risked starvation and exposure, but Native people were able to rely on their own resourcefulness and ties of kinship and alliance to survive. The Cherokees, whose towns were destroyed more frequently than those of any other Native nation in the late eighteenth century, regularly sought refuge in undamaged Cherokee villages until they were able to rebuild. In the Ohio country, a landscape with diverse and abundant resources, communities that lost crops to American torches avoided starvation by temporarily increasing their reliance on hunting, fishing, and gathering shellfish and plant foods. Ohio Valley Indians could also expect to find an ethic of reciprocity and shared sacrifice among relatives in the region's multiethnic communities. To avoid draining the resources of allied communities, however, it was also useful to seek assistance from the British. In mid-1791, for example, Miamis, Delawares, and Shawnees in a cluster of towns on the upper Maumee and upper Wabash, having been hit by Harmar's expedition several months before, decided to relocate their villages to The Glaize to find safety in numbers. To minimize their impact on the resources of The Glaize, they requested British agent Alexander McKee to supply them with "a sufficient quantity of Corn . . . for the support of their Families."[3]

MAINTAINING POPULATIONS

Although Native communities suffered some losses during the wars of the late 1780s and early 1790s, there is little evidence of a permanent population decline among most of the nations most heavily involved in the conflicts of this period—Shawnees, Wyandots, Potawatomis, and Chickamauga Cherokees. The closely related Miamis and Weas may have been an exception. Their population fell from 4,000 in 1768 to 1,400 in the early 1820s; some of this decline may have resulted from the conflicts and hardships from the 1770s through the 1790s. Indians maintained their populations not only through internal reproduction but by incorporating outsiders into their communities. There were two sources of outsiders. One was captives. In the late 1780s and early 1790s Indians undertook fewer raids than earlier, so the opportunity for taking captives declined. Still, there were several captives living at The Glaize in 1792, some of whom had been adopted only recently. A number of captives, including blacks taken from Carolina and Tennessee slave owners, were living in Chickamauga Cherokee towns. As evidence of the success of Native assimilation, during negotiations with Cherokees in 1795 U.S. officials secured the release of three recently captured children, but one taken when he was twelve years old and now a "man in the Nation"—a husband and father—was "unwilling to return to the white People." Communities also increased their numbers and reproductive capacity through marriage with non-captive outsiders. For decades, Native women in the Great Lakes region had married French traders. Such marriages were primarily motivated by a desire to cement trading alliances, but they also helped small communities subject to disease and hunger maintain their numbers. Even after the Seven Years' War brought an end to France's imperial presence, many French continued to live in the region. Among the Miamis and Weas, especially, a sizable number had some French ancestry, with intermarriage and sexual relations continuing into the 1790s. The nations of the South—Creeks, Cherokees, Choctaws, and Chickasaws—also intermarried with Europeans, particularly Scots Highlanders, who worked as traders and British imperial officials. European fathers often lived a good part of their time in Indian towns, adopting some Native ways, though they were generally not regarded as actual community members. Their children, however, were just as fully Cherokee, Creek, Shawnee, or Wyandot as anyone else.[4]

Native communities also frequently incorporated African Americans escaping slavery and free blacks seeking a better life in Indian country. A handful of escapees lived among Native communities in the Ohio country. Information about most was never recorded, but a few like Pompey appear in the historical record. Also known as the Black Shawnee, Pompey was a translator and fighter for his adopted people, giving his life in the September 1778 siege of Boonesborough. Far more former slaves could be found in southern Indian communities. One community in Louisiana, categorized by whites as a black community and called by the disparaging term Red Bones, in actuality included people with mixed ancestry—African, but also Westo, Biloxi, and Choctaw. The largest number of escapees could be found among the Creeks. Runaways started to arrive in Creek towns in the 1760s and most were eventually adopted into Creek clans. Two decades later, an emerging Creek elite, represented by Alexander McGillivray, began enslaving blacks, yet many enslaved people from colonial settlements, sometimes encouraged by Afro-Creeks, continued to look to Creek country for freedom. In many cases, blacks became fully assimilated as Creeks, though they sometimes formed separate settlements within a Creek world.[5]

Indians in southern New England (Connecticut, Rhode Island, and Massachusetts), with a total population of around 2,000 in 1783, also incorporated African Americans into their communities. These were not escapees from slavery, but free blacks, some free from birth and others freed as New England states began to allow emancipation in the late eighteenth century. In New England's Indian communities, women generally outnumbered men, as a large number of men had died while fighting for the Americans during the Revolutionary War and working at sea as whalers and fishers. Native women in southern New England sometimes married men of European ancestry, but more frequently they married African Americans. Black men in the region outnumbered black women; shared experiences of racial prejudice and similar economic status also encouraged Indian–black marriages and sexual relations. Although some Indians objected to African Americans and their children as community members, they generally welcomed these newcomers.[6]

MIGRATION

While most Native communities tried to survive where they were, some decided to put distance between themselves and American settlers and armies. In the late 1700s, some Shawnees, Delawares, and Miamis relocated from villages on the Maumee and upper Wabash rivers in western Ohio and eastern Indiana to the White and lower Wabash rivers in western Indiana. Kickapoos pioneered new towns along the Vermillion River in western Indiana and eastern Illinois. Some communities wanted even greater distance from Americans and moved beyond the territory claimed by the United States. In 1793, as the United States army was invading Ohio, Baron de Carondelet, the governor of Spanish Louisiana, granted Shawnees and Delawares land near Cape Girardeau to create a buffer between Louisiana and the powerful Osages. Over the next several years, Shawnees from the Ohio Valley along with others who had earlier taken up residence among the Creeks joined this new community. By 1810 a majority of Shawnees lived west of the Mississippi. Cherokees, too, migrated west. In the early 1790s, as violence engulfed Cherokee communities in eastern Tennessee, a chief known as The Bowl led a group of Chickamauga Cherokees west to the St. Francis River in what is now southeastern Missouri, where a few Cherokees had migrated a decade earlier (see Chapter 3). These communities west of the Mississippi would face many challenges, but for the moment creating new homes in the West seemed the most secure path.[7]

ECONOMIC STRATEGIES

The majority of Indian communities east of the Mississippi River chose to remain within territory claimed by the United States. All faced significant problems that were in one way or another related to American expansion.

A major problem was declining game. By 1795, Americans had taken significant hunting lands from Indians, especially those of Kentucky. Even so, in the Ohio Valley and lower Great Lakes, game animals remained fairly abundant and hunting remained an important part of Native economic strategies, supplying meat for subsistence and pelts for trade. After 1795, however, game decreased in this region. In part, this was because Natives were able to hunt in more areas than before. The end of war with the United States in 1795 allowed men to spend more time hunting instead of defending against American troops and enhanced the safety of traveling. Growing horse herds also allowed hunters to travel farther than before. A more significant factor, however, was that expanding American settlement reduced game populations. Settlers were voracious hunters, killing buffalo, deer, bear, and elk in great numbers. Their new farms destroyed habitat.[8]

Similar trends occurred in other regions. In Creek country, deer had become a rare sight by the late 1790s. Cherokee hunters in Tennessee in the first years of the new century were able to find only small game (raccoons, foxes, and wildcats). When Choctaws and Chickasaws experienced scarcity in the 1780s and 1790s, they temporarily relieved pressure on resources in their own country by undertaking "long hunts" west of the Mississippi, but this only delayed the decline of game on their own lands. To the north, the expansion of settlement in Pennsylvania, New York, and Vermont also led to scarcity. In the early 1800s, Seneca and Oneida men continued to hunt, but they generally found fewer animals than before. Fish were also becoming scarcer, as settlers dammed rivers for mills and caught salmon and whitefish for commercial markets. During the same years, western Abenakis were reportedly in an "almost starving condition," the result of settlers hunting moose and deer.[9]

One way Indians compensated for declining game was by raising livestock. Even before 1795, many communities had incorporated cattle and hogs into their economies. Aided by federal and missionary "civilization" programs, Native communities increased the number of these and other farm animals in the late 1790s and early 1800s. Consider, for example, a Shawnee community led by a chief named Black Hoof. After the Greenville Treaty, these Shawnees remained at their town of Wapakoneta on a small reserve in northwestern Ohio, hoping to survive in a place where settlers were becoming more numerous. Black Hoof's people did not want to convert to Christianity, but they took the advice of Quaker missionaries and purchased breeder stock of hogs and cattle. By the 1810s, most families at Wapakoneta kept at least some livestock; several owned more than 200 head of cattle, hogs, and horses. In Chickasaw country, too, as Rush Nutt, a Philadelphia physician, observed in 1805, there were "plenty of hogs & cattle." Tellingly, an American who attended a Choctaw feast in 1813 dined on beef and pork rather than wild game. Cherokees, too, followed a similar path. Most of their increased production of livestock was for their own consumption (including cows for milk, butter, and cheese), but in the early 1800s they regularly brought cattle, horses, hogs, and geese to nearby American settlements for sale or barter. They also found a market for cattle hides as a partial replacement for a diminishing one in deer skins. Even more than Cherokees, Creeks began to specialize in raising cattle with an eye to the market. As an example of their enterprise, in 1802 Creeks from the town of Coweta drove 2,000 head for sale in Georgia. It was relatively easy for Native men to make a transition from hunting to stock raising, as the work patterns were similar. Cherokees, for example, allowed their cattle free range, and so when it came time to kill them, they had to be pursued and shot. Indian nations' growing reliance on livestock was undoubtedly a constructive adaptation to the decline in hunting, though it created new problems. Among Creeks, for example, Micco Thlucco, who had been to New York and "seen much of the ways of white people," established a new town oriented toward growing corn to feed hogs and cattle. Many women, however, continued to raise crops at the older town. This was one of many examples illustrating growing divisions between men and women within Creek society and a transition away from matrilocal towns (husbands living in their wives' communities) toward patriarchy. Increasing numbers of livestock also had the effect of decreasing habitat for game, thus accelerating trends already under way. Creeks complained that non-Indian livestock was damaging deer browse; their own livestock did the same.[10]

Growing crops continued to be central to Native economies. In the early 1800s Potawatomi women maintained fields near their villages along the St. Joseph River in southern Michigan/northern Indiana. Non-Indians did not want to recognize Indians as farmers and so described these fields as small gardens. To recognize them for what they were—large fenced fields of 100 acres or more filled with corn, beans, pumpkins, and wheat—would undermine the idea that Indians were wasteful hunters and undercut a central argument for eliminating them. The St. Joseph River was beyond the reach of American military operations in the 1790s and so Potawatomis did not have to abandon and replant their fields. Indians who did have to flee invading armies were able to establish productive economies based on agriculture at new villages (Fig. 15). On the Wabash and its tributaries in Indiana, Miamis supplemented crops with fish, waterfowl, mink, otter, beaver, and muskrats. At the same time, Native communities continued to rely on noncultivated plants, especially in times when crops failed. In 1807, for example, drought struck Creek fields. In that "hungry year," Creeks subsisted largely on wild foods.[11]

In most Indian communities, farming remained largely women's work, as it had always been. In some communities, however, especially those near areas of American settlement and in regular contact with federal officials or missionaries, a handful of Native men began to farm. Though Cherokees, in the words of federal agent Return Meigs, generally thought "it was disgraceful for a young man to be seen with a hoe in his hand," a few chiefs accepted government offers to provide plows and began to farm in the late 1790s and early 1800s. Other men followed the example of their leaders, and by 1811 one in every four Cherokee families had a plow. This did not mean, however, that farming had become entirely men's work. Rather, men did some plowing and harvesting, while women continued to care for the crops as they grew. At the same time, a handful of well-off Cherokees were becoming more reliant on

Fig. 15. This 1839 painting by George Winter shows the home of Deaf Man, a Miami
Indian, and his wife, Frances Slocum, who became a Miami after being taken
captive from a Pennsylvania settlement as a young girl in the early 1780s. The main
dwelling, fences, outbuildings, and livestock reveal the success of economic strategies
that Native people of the Ohio Valley pursued in the early nineteenth century.
Courtesy of Tippecanoe County Historical Association, Lafayette, Indiana.

slaves to work their fields. By 1808, this class of Cherokees held over 500 enslaved blacks. Some Creeks, too, were using enslaved labor to grow cotton
and corn on commercially oriented farms.[12]

Beyond core economic activities, Indigenous communities took advantage of an array of other opportunities to minimize hard times and improve
their well-being. In New York, Oneidas sold fish and leased some of their
lands to non-Indian settlers. Senecas logged pines, turned them into boards
and shingles at their sawmill, and then floated them down the Allegheny to
Pittsburgh for sale. Creek women harvested hickory nuts and made oil, earn-
ing $1,200 from that source in 1800, while Creek men stole horses and sold
them on the black market. Creek men also found sporadic work as couriers,
guides, wranglers, and loggers, though wage labor remained supplementary
rather than fundamental. Cherokee men became blacksmiths, wheelwrights,
millers, and coopers. By the turn of the century, as southern nations began
growing cotton, they also acquired spinning wheels, cotton cards, and looms.
In 1799, federal agent Benjamin Hawkins reported that 300 Creek women

Fig. 16. This photograph from the early 1900s in Oklahoma of a Cherokee woman with
a child at a spinning wheel shows a major adaptation Cherokees had made a century
earlier. After two devastating wars with colonial armies, Cherokees embarked on a program
of economic development and changed gender roles. Men plowed and some managed
enslaved labor, while women focused on new forms of domestic labor, including spinning
yarn. Courtesy of the Museum of the Cherokee Indian, Cherokee, North Carolina.

and children were regularly wearing homespun, while by 1809 Cherokees reportedly had 1,600 spinning wheels and 467 looms (Fig. 16). Farther west,
Choctaw women, according to one U.S. agent, had taken up spinning with
"considerable spirit"; eight years later Choctaw leader Mingo Homastubbee
requested assistance to "learn our women to spin and weave." North of cotton
country, Indians used other materials—flax and wool—to produce cloth. In
1811, Quaker missionaries in Seneca country reported that fifty women had
recently learned to spin. A problem, however, was that few of them had time
to make yarn except during the winter months, when they were less burdened
by agricultural labor.[13]

Wage labor was far more prevalent among Indians east of the Appalachians. On the few small reservations in southern New England, Indians
were able to survive economically through a "mixed subsistence economy,"

consisting of small-scale agriculture, raising livestock, fishing, and hunting, along with regular seasonal wage work. By the late eighteenth century, however, many Indians in this region had been driven into debt and deprived of their lands. While some dispossessed Indians joined reservation communities like Mashpee on Cape Cod and Gay Head on Martha's Vineyard, many labored outside Native communities. Since the 1720s, Mashpees, Chappaquiddicks, Wampanoags, and others in the region had been found on whaling and fishing vessels. By the early nineteenth century, whaling crews typically included one or more Native people. In a world of limited economic options, whaling offered men a way to support their families. It also presented an opportunity to escape discrimination on land for a less racially exclusive world at sea, where Native men were judged more by their experience and abilities than by presumed racial characteristics. Although work at sea offered unique advantages, it was dangerous and required long absences from home. Because of this, some Native men preferred laboring in port towns or on farms. Even so, men's work was insufficient to meet the needs of most families and communities, and so women also labored to acquire needed resources. Native women bartered cranberries, wood, butter, and cheese, and traveled throughout the region with baskets and brooms strapped to their backs in search of customers. Poverty and debt also forced parents to send their children into indentured servitude in non-Native households. Such labor had some advantages, reducing debt and providing an opportunity to acquire skills such as spinning and weaving, but children frequently endured oppressive conditions. The Mohegan minister Samson Occom wrote of a servant who told him that a "young man . . . whipt and Beat him allmost every Day." The reason: "because I am an Indian." Such occurrences were more common than not.[14]

ALCOHOL AND DEBT

Even as Native communities creatively responded to possibilities within the European commercial economy, they were forced to contend with two interrelated problems: growing exposure to alcohol and increased indebtedness.

No one recognized the damage from alcohol more than Indians themselves, and they took steps to curb its destructive consequences. Some of these involved devising ways to reduce the violence that frequently accompanied drinking. Oliver Spencer, a captive who lived among Ohio Valley Indians, wrote that "before deliberately commencing a drunken revel," Indians would "select some one to remain sober, to whose charge they commit their knives, tomahawks, and other dangerous weapons." The use of designated weapons-keepers meant that injuries were limited to "bruised eyes or bloody noses." Spencer also observed that an inebriated man might sing loudly upon his return home, a way to warn family members to "keep out of his way."[15]

Native leaders also appealed to U.S. officials to stop the flow of liquor into their communities. Miami chief Little Turtle, himself a moderate drinker who enjoyed the pleasures of French wine with his evening meal, traveled to Washington, D.C., during the winter of 1801–1802. There he called on a fellow connoisseur, President Thomas Jefferson, to halt what he termed the "fatal poison"—rye from western Pennsylvania and bourbon from Kentucky—that was keeping his people poor. Already, a series of federal laws under the heading of "Trade and Intercourse" acts contained provisions to regulate the liquor trade. In 1802, at Jefferson's urging, Congress attempted to strengthen enforcement by authorizing the president to "prevent or restrain the vending or distributing of spirituous liquors among all of any of the said Indian tribes." Such laws, however, were no match for the enterprise of American businessmen, who devised countless ways to evade weak mechanisms of enforcement.[16]

Indians, too, were unable to regulate capitalism, but they took steps of their own to prevent its products from reaching consumers. In one instance, related by naturalist William Bartram, Creeks came upon two smugglers transporting forty kegs of Jamaican rum. Taking their tomahawks to this cargo, they gave "the liquor to the thirsty sand, not tasting a drop of it themselves." More formally, Cherokees made efforts to ban outsiders from selling spirits and criminalized alcohol consumption in the late 1700s and early 1800s. Native communities also created temperance movements. The Seneca prophet Handsome Lake, described by Seneca historian Arthur C. Parker as a "dissolute person and a miserable victim of the drink habit," had a vision of hell. In the vision, a habitual drunkard was punished by having to drink from a cup of molten metal, causing him to fall to the ground "with vapor steaming from his throat." Handsome Lake became a teetotaler and urged his people to take a temperance pledge: "I will use it nevermore."[17]

The sale of a highly addictive substance like alcohol contributed to the mounting indebtedness of many Indian nations. As traders plied Indians with whiskey and rum and sold them ammunition, tools, and clothing, Native nations required commensurate purchasing power to avoid a trade deficit. With the decline of game, however, these nations often lacked the means to purchase the commodities traders offered outright. Traders increasingly extended credit. By the early 1800s, Choctaws owed the firm of Panton and Leslie $48,000 and were incurring additional debt at a new U.S. factory (trading house) on the Tombigbee River in western Alabama. Creek debt to the same company was about three times as high. Creeks also incurred debt to the United States at a factory at Fort Wilkinson on the Oconee River in Georgia.[18] As we will see, U.S. officials used these debts as a tool to leverage land cessions in the early 1800s. Indians in the Ohio Valley and New York do not seem to have become indebted to the extent of those to the South, yet their need for income to support purchases of liquor and other trade goods also created pressures for them to accept annuities that accompanied government demands for land cessions.

JEFFERSON'S PLANS FOR AGGRESSIVE DISPOSSESSION OF NATIVE NATIONS

Indian nations struggling to survive within territory claimed by the United States hoped that Americans would not insist that they give up additional lands. At times, U.S. officials sounded as if they might allow Indian nations the option of retaining their lands. In July 1801, a few months after becoming President, Thomas Jefferson assured a delegation of Cherokees (through Secretary of War Henry Dearborn) of "the friendship of the United States and that all our proceedings towards you shall be directed by justice and a sacred regard to our Treaties." Because the "White people are very numerous," Jefferson continued, the United States "should therefore be desirous to buy land," but "we never wish to buy, except when you are perfectly disposed to sell."[19]

Although we do not know exactly how Cherokees understood Jefferson's assurances, it would have been perfectly reasonable for them to have taken the President's words as a recognition of their right to refuse to sell their lands. Despite this commonsense interpretation of his message to the Cherokees, however, Jefferson did not intend to depart from the policies that Henry Knox and George Washington had established in the late 1780s and early 1790s. Like Knox and Washington, Jefferson was committed to displaying the Northwest Ordinance's "utmost good faith . . . toward the Indians" and to cultivating a sense that U.S. expansion was proceeding honorably. But, like his predecessors, Jefferson did not believe that Native nations had full ownership of their lands or that these nations could legitimately say no when presented with terms the United States defined as reasonable. Should Indians be indisposed to sell, their disposition would have to change. Jefferson was much more honest about his intentions before non-Native audiences. In his first address to Congress, he announced that "a spirit of peace and friendship generally prevails" with "our Indian neighbors," yet in commenting on the growing U.S. population in the same speech, Jefferson remarked on the "extensive country still remaining vacant within our limits." Jefferson had not literally forgotten America's Indian neighbors, but since Native nations had no permanent right to their lands, these were for all intents and purposes empty and available for settlement. This was not news to Congress; its members assumed a future of thoroughgoing dispossession.[20]

In the early years of his presidency, some westerners worried that Jefferson was insufficiently committed to the rapid acquisition of Native lands. In responding to one such westerner, a Tennessee judge, slave owner, merchant, and speculator named Andrew Jackson, Jefferson affirmed his intention of "obtaining lands from the Indians," while adding that this should be done "by all *honest* and *peaceable means.*" During his eight years in the White House, Jefferson did not disappoint frontier expectations for aggressive dispossession. Through thirty-two treaties, Jefferson gained around 200,000 square miles of land, an area 20 percent larger than the future state of California. The primary impetus behind these acquisitions was to make land available for speculators, small farmers, and slave owners. Jefferson was also concerned about strategic issues and so he focused on securing territory along the Ohio and Mississippi rivers, near Detroit, and along the southern border. This was to sever possible connections between Indians and the Spanish or British and to compress Indians into an interior region where they would be easier to control.[21]

JEFFERSONIAN DISPOSSESSION IN THE SOUTH

One of the first targets of Jeffersonian dispossession was the Creek Nation. In this instance, the federal government was under pressure from the state of Georgia. Under the 1802 Georgia Compact, Georgia had agreed to relinquish its claims to western lands (what would eventually become Alabama and Mississippi). In exchange, the United States pledged to "extinguish the Indian title to all the other Lands within the state of Georgia." Much of this land was under Creek ownership. To begin extinguishing Creek title, the Jefferson administration authorized a federal commission led by Benjamin Hawkins and the controversial James Wilkinson, soon to become governor of the territory created from the Louisiana Purchase and perhaps involved in a conspiracy to establish an independent southwest empire.[22] A close look at the negotiations with the Creeks reveals Jefferson's "honest and peaceable means" in action.

In May 1802 Hawkins and Wilkinson arrived at a Georgia fort named after Wilkinson himself (Fig. 17). Their goal was to persuade Creek leaders to sell lands south of the Altamaha River and between the Oconee and Ocmulgee. Some Creek leaders, especially from the Upper Towns in Alabama, refused to attend altogether. Those from the Lower Towns, closer to American settlement in western Georgia, were more amenable to making modest concessions. Even so, they were reluctant to part with their lands, not only because of their economic importance but because they feared ceding them would encourage further illegal encroachment into the heart of their country. The Creeks' principal spokesman, Efau Haujo (Mad Dog), objected that "it is like splitting us in two, and giving away half of us." Nonetheless, so that they could pay debts they owed to Panton and Leslie, the Creeks agreed to cede a small portion of the requested lands. Rather than accepting the Creeks' indisposition to sell additional land, Wilkinson began turning the screws. He sharply scolded the Creeks for "shut[ting] your ears against us" and "offer[ing] to your Father a small strip, which will hardly enable us to pay your debts." Should the Creeks listen to the President's advice, Wilkinson continued, "he will never forsake or deceive you." But what, he asked, would happen when a child "turns a deaf ear to the voice of his father"? Though unstated, the answer was clear enough: without any hope of federal protection, Georgians would continue to encroach on Creek lands and Creeks would eventually lose them without receiving a penny in return. With this sword above their heads, Creek leaders met privately and decided to sell more land, not as much as the commissioners had initially proposed (only about a third of the territory between the Oconee and Ocmulgee, and nothing below the Altamaha), but enough to result in a treaty. Wilkinson's threats were subtle but very real.[23]

It took only a year for Hawkins and Wilkinson to propose a new land cession. Creeks successfully resisted this initiative, but Hawkins returned in 1804 and this time obtained additional land. When the treaty was sent to the Senate, however, that body refused to ratify it on the grounds that the price the United States offered was too high. With the legislative branch insisting on parsimony, officials in the executive branch summoned the Creeks to Washington. Hopoie Micco, the Creek national speaker, refused to go to Washington for fear that a land cession would take place and that antitreaty Creeks would blame him for it. But a small Creek delegation, including William McIntosh, who had emerged as a key Creek leader since the death of

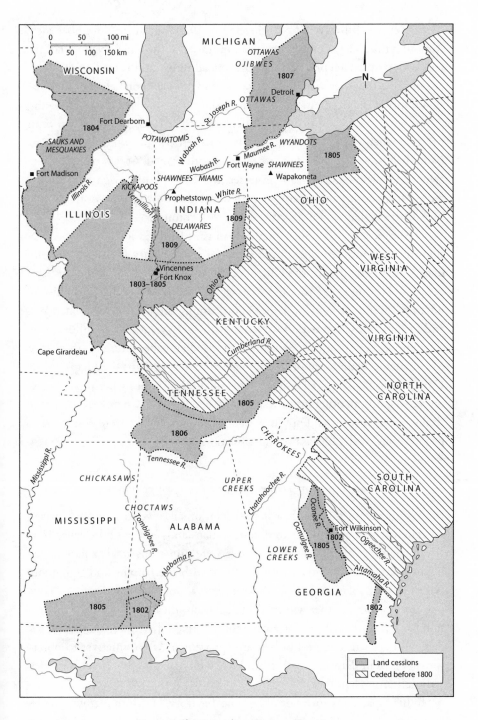

Fig. 17. Jeffersonian dispossession, 1801–1809

Alexander McGillivray in 1793, traveled to Washington in November 1805. Although this delegation represented a minority of the Creek Nation, consistent with past federal practice, the Jefferson administration acted on the dubious premise that they were fully authorized to cede land on behalf of their nation. During the negotiations, McIntosh skillfully contested the treaty terms, pointing out that the price being offered for their lands was only two cents per acre when the government sold land to settlers for two dollars an acre. Nonetheless, he and the other leaders eventually signed. At this point, bribery came into play. U.S. officials promised the Creek leaders rights to operate ferries, toll booths, and taverns along a new federal road from Washington to New Orleans that would pass through Creek country.[24]

U.S. officials used similar methods to gain land cessions from other nations in the South. In May 1803 Secretary of War Henry Dearborn contemplated how best to have the Cherokees "brought to reason" and grant land cessions. He suggested to Cherokee agent Return Meigs the possibility of offering "an inducement" to James Vann, among the wealthiest of Cherokees and in Dearborn's estimation someone with "very great private influence on the nation." A year later, Dearborn authorized an expenditure of up to $300 to encourage Vann's support. Although Vann was perhaps the biggest prize, U.S. officials made special arrangements, including granting personal reserves on ceded lands, to other influential Cherokees. By 1806, Cherokees had ceded sizable tracts in central Tennessee. Such dishonest tactics were employed in negotiations with Chickasaws and Choctaws as well.[25]

JEFFERSONIAN DISPOSSESSION IN THE NORTH

In contrast to the South, where federal officials worked on each nation separately, those attempting to obtain Indian lands in the Ohio Valley took advantage of a situation in which there were numerous smaller nations living in relatively close proximity, sometimes with overlapping and ambiguous claims to particular territories. This meant that not only could officials favor one faction over another within a single nation, they could cultivate one nation (or a faction within it) against another. These dynamics, along with the deployment of threats and bribes, are apparent in U.S. initiatives to obtain Indian lands undertaken by William Henry Harrison—aptly characterized as "Mr. Jefferson's hammer."[26]

In his capacity as governor of Indiana Territory, Harrison met with representatives of several nations—Weas, Potawatomis, Piankashaws, Kickapoos, and Eel Rivers (a Miami subgroup recognized as a distinct nation in the 1795 Greenville Treaty)—at Vincennes in August 1802. After distributing annuities due the tribes through the Greenville Treaty, Harrison informed his audience of President Jefferson's "ardent wish to see you prosperous and happy." Harrison also asked them to agree to his interpretation of an ambiguously defined tract of land ceded in the Greenville Treaty along the southern Wabash River in Indiana known as the Vincennes tract. Harrison argued that the Vincennes tract was quite large (over one million acres), but tribal leaders claimed it was only 8,000 acres and refused to agree to Harrison's boundaries. A Kickapoo spokesman said that "the Land was made for our fathers and us—We wish not to Provoke the [Great] Spirit by selling any now." To help his cause, Harrison enlisted Little Turtle, the former Miami militant who was now receiving a personal payment of $150 per annum from the U.S. government. Harrison also cultivated William Wells, Little Turtle's son-in-law, and Jean Baptiste Ducoigne, a Kaskaskia leader who twenty years earlier had traveled to Virginia and befriended its governor, now the president. Little Turtle, Wells, and Ducoigne persuaded the other leaders to allow them to draw up a treaty specifying the dimensions of the Vincennes tract.[27]

This arrangement provoked significant opposition within the nations whose leaders had agreed to it. It also inspired protests from Delawares whom Harrison had not included in the negotiations. Wanting the appearance of widespread consent, Harrison called for a new council to be held at Fort Wayne in June 1803, but few of the region's leaders agreed to attend. A few months earlier, in writing to Harrison on Indian policy, Jefferson had observed that it would be useful to encourage Ohio Valley Indians to increase their indebtedness to traders. Once "run in debt," Indians "become willing to lop them off by a cession of lands." Unfortunately for Harrison, the relevant nations did not have significant debts, but the Greenville Treaty gave him another potent—and blunter—instrument. Harrison notified the Indians that he would withhold annuities from any nation that failed to send representatives to Fort Wayne. This threat was powerful not simply because of its impact on material well-being, but also because annuities were distributed by tribal leaders and these leaders needed them to demonstrate generosity, a central obligation of leadership. Harrison's decision to distribute annuities only to those nations who met him at Fort Wayne was enough to cause most nations to rethink their rejection of his invitation. But that did not mean capitulation to his demands. Once at Fort Wayne, Delawares and Shawnees made plain their objections to Harrison's interpretation of the size of the Vincennes tract. Eventually, Harrison, again relying on Little Turtle, persuaded the Shawnees and the others present—Delawares, Potawatomis, Miamis, Weas, Piankashaws, and Kaskaskias—to accept his expansive interpretation of the Vincennes tract. Since Harrison considered this tract to be included in the Greenville Treaty cession, the United States paid nothing for it except an annual distribution of a "quantity of salt not exceeding one hundred and fifty bushels" to compensate for a salt lick within the tract. Shortly after, Harrison also secured a large land cession in southern Illinois from the Kaskaskias, a relatively weak nation that had recently suffered attacks from Potawatomis and Shawnees. They were willing to sign the 1803 Fort Wayne Treaty in exchange for U.S. protection.[28]

Harrison next turned his attention to lands between Vincennes and the Ohio River. Delawares were living on these lands, but only because the recognized owners, Miamis and Piankashaws, had granted them permission when they moved west after Wayne's invasion a decade earlier. Although Harrison realized this, he chose to negotiate directly with the Delawares. At Fort Wayne in August 1804, he got them to make their marks on a treaty ceding the southwestern corner of Indiana in exchange for a ten-year annuity of $3,000. A year later, Delaware leaders Buckongahelas, Hockingpomskon, and Tetapachsit contended that the document they had signed was actually a peace treaty and not an agreement to cede land. Throughout the region Native leaders, including even Little Turtle, joined the Delawares in denouncing the treaty. Jefferson decided that Harrison should call a new council to insist that "the transaction was not only open and fair, but such as they have no right to object to." Jefferson further suggested to Harrison that the United States had possibly been "defective in our kindnesses" to Little Turtle and that it might be wise to provide him with a "liberality" (adding to an expanding lexicon of euphemisms for bribery). At Vincennes in August 1805, Harrison gained the Delawares' explicit acknowledgment of the treaty the year before, as well as an additional cession from the Miamis, Eel Rivers, and Weas in southeastern Indiana. In exchange, Harrison guaranteed Miami claims to lands on the Wabash. These lands were contested with the Kickapoos, who were perceived to be less open to persuasion and thus had not been invited to the council. Harrison also provided the Potawatomis an annuity. Ostensibly, this was a payment for ceded lands, but since the Potawatomis had never lived on the lands in question, this annuity was a means of binding them to colonial power. Behind the scenes, Harrison remedied any previous deficiency in kindness toward Little Turtle by providing him with an additional $50 annuity and a black slave purchased from a Kentucky plantation.[29]

A NEW NATIVE CONFEDERACY, 1805–1808

The United States' assault on Native lands under the Jefferson administration led to a revival of a new multinational Native resistance movement. It originated at a Shawnee town on the White River in Indiana in spring 1805 when a disreputable, boastful, and frequently inebriated Shawnee known by the disparaging nickname Lalawethika (Noisemaker) fell to the earth as if dead. At first, Lalawethika's people assumed he had passed out from drunkenness, but when he did not awake, they thought he had succumbed to a sickness that had been afflicting them throughout the winter. As Lalawethika's family made funeral preparations, however, he suddenly awoke. He later related that while unconscious the Master of Life had showed him two pathways, one leading to a place "abounding in game, fish, pleasant hunting grounds and fine cornfields," the other a place where the wicked were tormented according to their sins. Drunks like Lalawethika were condemned to drink "liquor resembling melted lead" that caused their bowels to be "seized with an exquisite burning."[30]

After this vision Lalawethika began exhorting Indians to undertake a program of moral reformation: abstinence from alcohol, the selective rejection of European trade goods and technology, a disavowal of acquisitiveness, renewed respect for game animals, and a return to pre-contact modes of dress and consumption. He also set forth a new set of religious practices based to some extent on Catholic ritual, though operating according to a Native logic of using spiritual power for this-worldly survival. Implicit in Lalawethika's initial message of moral and religious reform was a critique of U.S. colonialism, one he expressed more openly as his teachings developed. In November while visiting Wapakoneta, he informed Shawnees along with visiting Ottawas, Wyandots, and Senecas that unlike the British, Spanish, and French, who were friends, the Master of Life did not create the Americans. "They are not my children, but the children of the Evil Spirit," he said. In another vision, Lalawethika saw a "great ugly crab that had crawled from the sea, its claws full of mud and seaweed," an image that drew on myths common to many Indian nations of an "earth diver" that brought the land into being from the sea. This crab, the Master of Life explained, "comes from Boston and brings with it part of the land in that vicinity. If you Indians do everything which

I have told you, I will overturn the land, so that all the white people will be covered and you alone shall inhabit the land." By the end of 1805, Lalawethika moved his village to Greenville, implicitly contesting the treaty written there ten years earlier.[31]

Soon after his initial visions, Lalawethika took a new name, Tenskwatawa (Open Door), signifying that he "opened the sky for men to go up to the Great Spirit." Often he is known as the Shawnee Prophet, or simply The Prophet (Fig. 18). Although the best known, Tenskwatawa was not the only prophet to emerge in the early 1800s. Another was a Delaware woman named Beata. Once baptized by the Moravian missionaries, Beata had since rejected Christianity. She now related a vision in which two spirits told her that "Indians must continue to live as before." If they did not, "a storm-wind will come and tear up all the trees in the forest, and all Indians will die." An Ottawa called The Trout and a Potawatomi whose name, Main Poc, referred to his crippled hand, a sign of a close connection to spiritual power, also related millennial visions and preached the need for moral reformation and Indian unity. Tenskwatawa's older brother Tecumseh also joined. As the movement developed, Tecumseh became its most prominent leader.[32]

Although the prophecies of Tenskwatawa, Beata, The Trout, and Main Poc carried powerful critiques of Americans, the movement did not initially oppose the United States either politically or militarily. Rather, supporters of Tenskwatawa's prophecies targeted Indians in the Ohio Valley who had made accommodations with the children of the Evil Spirit. In early 1806 Delawares on the White River charged seven community members with using witchcraft to inflict disease and summoned Tenskwatawa to hear the evidence and make a judgment. Most of the alleged witches were Christian Indians who had relocated to a new Moravian mission on the White River in 1801. Since the mission's founding, many Delawares had denounced it for having a genocidal agenda. The mission's purpose, they said, was "to make the Indians tame, so as to have them killed by the white people, as had been done in Gnadenhütten." The accused were also implicated in recent land cessions. In the end, six of the seven charged were sentenced to death, though two were released before being burned.[33]

Tenskwatawa also presided over witchcraft trials among the Wyandots, but the identification of witches proved to be a passing phase. By mid-1806, Tenskwatawa was devoting his energies to recruiting new followers rather than purging Native enemies. Tenskwatawa successfully recruited Blue Jacket, now in his early sixties and retaining substantial influence from his home

Fig. 18. At one time known as Lalawethika (Noisemaker), the Shawnee prophet
Tenskwatawa (Open Door) inspired thousands of Native people in the early 1800s
to envision a future in which Americans no longer threatened Native lands and ways
of life. After U.S. military forces twice burned his headquarters in the early 1810s,
Tenskwatawa retreated to Canada and eventually tried to persuade Shawnees to relocate
west of the Mississippi. George Catlin, *Ten-squát-a-way, The Open Door, Known as
the Prophet, Brother of Tecumseh,* 1830. Smithsonian American Art Museum. Photo
credit: Smithsonian American Art Museum, Washington, D.C./Art Resource, N.Y.

on the Detroit River. He also also received vital assistance from The Trout, Main Poc, and other prophets. By the end of 1807, the movement had adherents among Shawnees, Delawares, Wyandots, Menominees, Ho-Chunks, Ottawas, Ojibwes, and Potawatomis. Growth, however, created problems. So many people came to hear Tenskwatawa at Greenville during the winter of 1807–1808 that there wasn't enough food. Growth also led to opposition from settlers in Ohio, U.S. officials, and nearby villages, especially Wapakoneta, where Black Hoof and like-minded leaders feared the new movement would be disastrous for their policy of selective cooperation with Americans. In spring 1808, Tenskwatawa relocated his headquarters to the Wabash River near Tippecanoe Creek in western Indiana, closer to his supporters and farther from his opponents. This town became known as Prophetstown.[34]

The movement led by Tenskwatawa, Tecumseh, and their associates can be seen as another in a long line of anticolonial confederation movements stretching back to the 1760s. Conditions for opposing U.S. expansion were quite different in the new century, however. By 1808, the United States had established several permanent military posts in the West: Fort Wayne on the upper Maumee, Fort Detroit, Fort Dearborn near the southern end of Lake Michigan, Fort Knox at Vincennes, and Fort Madison on the western bank of the Mississippi in southeastern Iowa. Settlers were no longer on the fringes of the Ohio Valley. With a non-Indian population of 45,000 in 1800, Ohio had become a state in 1803; the settler population of Indiana Territory, organized in 1800, reached 25,000 in 1810. Given these conditions, Tenskwatawa and Tecumseh were wary about directly confronting U.S. power and took a more defensive posture than earlier movements.[35]

PREPARING FOR WAR, CONTINUING DISPOSSESSION, 1807–1809

Since the Fort Greenville Treaty, U.S. officials had hoped to eliminate Indians from the Ohio Valley without the expense of another war. When he first learned of Tenskwatawa's prophecies, President Jefferson took some comfort in the theory that it was "a transient enthusiasm, which, if let alone, would evaporate innocently of itself." By 1807, however, information Jefferson had received indicated that "we should immediately prepare for war in that quarter." In addition to instructing the state of Ohio and the territories of Indiana and Michigan to raise militias, Jefferson ordered Michigan territorial governor William Hull to meet with "the chiefs of the several tribes." Hull was to assure tribal leaders that "we have no intention ever to strike them or to do them an injury of any sort, unless first attacked or threatened." There was, however, a caveat. If "we are constrained to lift the hatchet against any tribe," Jefferson instructed Hull to inform the chiefs, "we will never lay it down till that tribe is exterminated, or driven beyond the Mississippi." In the event of war "they will kill some of us; we shall destroy all of them." Jefferson's declaration of the possibility of genocidal war was more than idle musing, as though the Great Father was in a bad mood that day. It was an official statement of a policy for dealing with Indians who refused to accept U.S. terms for dispossession.[36]

The United States was not yet ready to wage war, but it was deeply committed to the ongoing work of dispossession. In summer 1809 Harrison summoned a carefully chosen group of Miamis, Potawatomis, Eel Rivers, and Delawares to Fort Wayne for a series of September meetings. Leaders from these and other nations most likely to oppose a treaty were excluded. During the council, Harrison threatened to withhold annuities, pitted the leaders present against each other (getting the Potawatomis and Delawares, with no real claim to the lands in question, to pressure the Miamis into signing), and made liberal distributions of whiskey (government documents record the issue of 218 gallons). Eventually, Harrison managed to secure what can only be described as a highly coerced form of consent to the cession of two tracts, one north of Vincennes, the other in eastern Indiana. To minimize opposition, Harrison further offered Miamis additional annuities provided they convinced Kickapoos, intentionally left out of the negotiations, to accept the treaty now that it was becoming a fact. Some Kickapoo leaders agreed to receive a onetime issue of goods and an annuity for agreeing to the Fort Wayne Treaty.[37]

Although Harrison had not directly threatened to kill Indians in order to take their lands, confederation leaders saw U.S. aggressiveness, as manifested in the 1809 Fort Wayne Treaty and many other acts, as evidence, in Moravian missionary John Heckwelder's summary of Tenskwatawa's teachings, that the "white people . . . sought nothing short of their utter destruction, in order to get their whole country to themselves." The persuasiveness of this critique led to greater support for the new confederacy. A growing number of Miamis questioned the accommodationist approach of their kinsman Little Turtle and took up residence at Prophetstown. They were joined by an influx of Sauks, Mesquakies, Ho-Chunks, Ioways, Kickapoos, Potawatomis, and Wyandots. The treaty also led Tenskwatawa and Tecumseh to take a more confrontational stance toward the United States. They did not plan military action, but they were more willing than before to assert their opposition to U.S. actions and policies.[38]

TECUMSEH'S ALLEGATIONS

In June 1810, Tenskwatawa sent a message to Harrison warning that "his people should not come any nearer to him," that "he smelt them too strongly already." With this and other protests arriving in Vincennes along with rumors of war, Harrison invited Tenskwatawa to visit him, saying that if the prophet could prove that the "17 fires" had "purchased land from those who had no right to sell" that the lands would "instantly be restored." Harrison also offered to arrange for Tenskwatawa and three chiefs of his choosing to "carry your complaints before your great Father" in Washington. Though the invitation was addressed to his brother, it was Tecumseh, now assuming a more prominent leadership role, who responded to it. Along with several other Indians, he traveled to the governor's headquarters in August. Over the next few days, the two men had lengthy discussions. Tecumseh insisted that Indian lands belonged to Indians collectively and could not be signed away by illegitimate chiefs, while Harrison vigorously defended the treaties he had negotiated. Neither yielded an inch on the issues at hand.[39]

On August 20, perhaps in frustration and anger, perhaps hoping a forceful speech might break the impasse, perhaps to rally his supporters, Tecumseh delivered a blunt and extensive critique of Americans. He first asked Harrison to "recollect that the time the Delawares lived near the white people (Americans) . . . and yet one of their town[s] was surprised and the men women and children murdered." This, of course, was a reference to the Gnadenhütten massacre, an event still very much on the minds of Ohio Valley Indians. Tecumseh further cited the killing of the Shawnee peace chief Moluntha in 1786. Americans had given the Shawnees flags, telling them that if they held them, "no harm will be done you," but "the person bearing the flag [Moluntha] was murdered with others in their village." Given these actions, Tecumseh asked Harrison, how "can you blame me for placing little confidence in the promises of our fathers the Americans"? Later in his speech, Tecumseh added another event to his list of reasons for Indians' lack of confidence in "the white people," one much farther away in time and space: "when Jesus Christ came upon the earth and you kill'd and nail'd him on a cross."

In addition to issuing a broad indictment of Americans, Tecumseh directly criticized the actions of Harrison himself, saying that "you have taken our lands from us" by making "distinctions of Indian tribes in allotting to each a particular track of land to make them to war with each other." This identified a divide-and-conquer strategy that involved not only taking lands but promoting physical destruction. Harrison's use of annuities, too, revealed darkly destructive purposes. Americans always presented annuities for land as a mutually beneficial exchange, but, Tecumseh alleged, when Harrison issued goods to the Kickapoos after they agreed to the Fort Wayne Treaty, "you kill'd many." The goods carried "small pox by which many died."[40]

Historians have noted some of the allegations in Tecumseh's speech to Harrison, but they have done so in passing and often in the passive voice, without revealing the full force of his critique.[41] At Vincennes, however, Tecumseh charged that Americans had consistently murdered defenseless Indians. Not only that, he accused Harrison personally of intentionally infecting Indians with smallpox. Although Tecumseh did not articulate his views of Americans in general terms, his specific indictments amounted to an overarching argument that the United States consistently and intentionally pursued the genocidal destruction of Indians.

In making these allegations, Tecumseh was giving voice to a line of argument Indians had articulated for decades. In earlier chapters, we have seen substantial evidence for an Indigenous consciousness of genocide, beginning in the Seven Years' War when Delawares stated that the French and British intended to "kill all the Indians and then divide the land among themselves." In 1776, the Shawnee spokesman identified an "intention to exterminate them." At the close of the Revolutionary War, the Seneca chief Old Smoke said that the Patriots desired to "extirpate us from the Earth, that they may possess our Lands." And in the early 1790s the Mohawk prophet Coocoochee predicted that the "Long Knives" would push the Indians north to "perish on the great ice lake" or west "into the great waters" and that "all would at length be exterminated." We have also observed several instances of Indians accusing Europeans and Americans of intentionally spreading disease, as when Indians refused Arthur St. Clair's invitation to meet with him at Fort Harmar in 1787 for fear that the Americans would "poison the spirits" or "communicate the smallpox by the blankets." Even Native leaders oriented toward accommodation with the United States did so because they thought this was the best—perhaps the only—way to avoid being completely destroyed. The leader of the Stockbridge Indian Christian community, Hendrick Aupaumut, tried to convince non-Christian Natives to convert by arguing that if they did not, "your villages will be desolated or possessed by a people who will cultivate your lands. . . . and finally, you will be extinct from the earth."[42]

One response to Tecumseh's allegations and the general line of thought they represented would be to say that they overstated Americans' genocidal intentions and leave it at that. It would be a mistake, however, to simply dismiss this Indigenous perspective. First, the perspective itself is a vital part of the history we are considering and provides a crucial context for understanding the decisions Indians made. To support a movement of resistance, to sign a treaty, to move to a safer place, to make accommodations: all of these decisions were matters of life and death not just for individuals but for entire communities. Second, although the United States did not establish a policy of exterminating every single Indian, it was certainly reasonable for Native people, given their history and experiences, to conclude that Americans had genocidal intentions toward them. Finally, from an objective standpoint, a Native perspective that Americans intended to destroy them all was closer to the mark than some might think. When U.S. officials repeatedly threatened to annihilate Native communities and confederations who resisted American demands to give up their land, and when U.S. military operations repeatedly targeted communities that included noncombatants, they revealed genocide as an all-too-real possibility.

CONCLUSION: TOWARD WAR AGAIN

When Tecumseh finished his speech, Harrison began to defend the United States. According to Harrison, Tecumseh then stood up and "with the most violent gesticulations . . . began to contradict what I said in the most indecent manner." Harrison also reported that several of Tecumseh's men quickly "sprung up, arm'd with war clubs, tom[a]hawks, and spears," although historians have noted they did so only after a Potawatomi named Winamac, a supporter of Harrison, loaded his weapon. Harrison summoned a detachment of soldiers and adjourned the council, possibly averting bloodshed (Fig. 19). When the council resumed a day later, Tecumseh continued to hold firm. He was more conciliatory, but he nonetheless warned Harrison that should Americans begin surveying lands ceded at Fort Wayne, "it will be productive of bad consequences." By this time it was clear that neither Tecumseh nor

Fig. 19. In August 1810 Tecumseh, the Shawnee leader of the western confederacy, conversed
for several days with Indiana territorial governor William Henry Harrison. This drawing
erroneously depicts Tecumseh raising a hatchet against Harrison. In fact, Tecumseh attacked
Harrison with words, accusing him and the U.S. government of an intent to commit
what would today be called genocide against Native people. John Reuben Chapin, *Genl.
Harrison & Tecumseh,* 1810s. New York Public Library, Art and Picture Collection.

Harrison would budge on the immediate question of the legitimacy of the
1809 Fort Wayne Treaty, and so the conference adjourned.[43]

Although Harrison reported to Secretary of War William Eustis that he
was "far from believing that an Indian war is inevitable," in a sense the United
States was already at war with Indians of the trans-Appalachian West.[44] Every
year hundreds of squatters illegally occupied Native lands. Every year U.S.
officials demanded that some Native nation give up lands they did not want
to give up. Every time Native leaders said no, officials did not allow that response to stand. Instead they employed tactics ranging from bribery to with-
holding annuities, the former further dividing already divided communities,
the latter a form of economic warfare. Knowing of the United States' capacity
and will to inflict catastrophic violence, Indians were reluctant to turn to violence to halt the American invasion. But many felt they needed to organize

collectively across tribal lines to somehow block ongoing dispossession. For the moment, the confederacy of Tenskwatawa and Tecumseh had avoided raiding settlements or attacking U.S. forts, but their very efforts to mobilize a new confederacy and their arguments that recent treaties were illegitimate threatened the overriding American goal of obtaining Native lands. After the meeting between Tecumseh and Harrison at Vincennes in August 1810, the outbreak of violent conflict was perhaps not inevitable, but it was closer than it had been for many years.

CHAPTER 5

Wars of 1812

On June 1, 1812, President James Madison asked Congress to declare war on Great Britain. The bulk of his address indicted the British for violating America's right to freedom of the seas and impressing American citizens into service in the British military. For these reasons, the War of 1812 is often seen as a "Second War for Independence." But Madison mentioned an additional cause for war: British support for "the savages on . . . our extensive frontiers," who practiced "a warfare which is known to spare neither age nor sex and to be distinguished by features peculiarly shocking to humanity."[1] Madison's words, of course, echoed the Declaration of Independence's grievance against George III for inciting the "merciless Indian savages." They revealed that, just as they had in 1776, Americans were going to war against Britain in 1812 to eliminate Native resistance so that they could possess Indian lands. Like the Revolutionary War, the War of 1812 was not simply a war against Great Britain. Within the War of 1812 were other wars against Native nations.

BARRIERS TO WAR

When Tecumseh met William Henry Harrison in Vincennes in August 1810, he made clear the Indian confederacy's opposition to U.S. initiatives to take their lands. But this did not mean that Tecumseh wanted war. Sensing that the confederacy needed to be strengthened and that the United States

151

would not strike anytime soon, Tecumseh redoubled his organizational efforts. Not long after leaving Vincennes, he went west, visiting Potawatomis and Kickapoos on the Illinois River, Ho-Chunks on the Rock River, and Menominees as far north as Green Bay (Fig. 20). He then turned south to Saukenuk, a Sac and Mesquakie (Fox) town of several thousand near Rock River on the Mississippi, and went on to Missouri to mobilize Shawnees and Delawares who had moved there some years earlier. Later in the fall, Tecumseh briefly returned to Prophetstown and then paid a visit to Fort Amherstburg, a British post on the Canada side of the Detroit River, to seek British aid in the form of arms, ammunition, and food. The following spring, Tecumseh traveled northeast to Ohio Indian communities. He hoped to recruit the so-far impervious Shawnees at Wapakoneta, as well as to increase confederacy support among Senecas and Wyandots on the Sandusky. Already some Wyandots had moved to Prophetstown, bringing to Tenskwatawa the "Great Belt which was the Symbol of Union between the Tribes in their late war with the United States." Tecumseh further organized a delegation of Ohio Valley Haudenosaunees, who traveled to Buffalo Creek (New York), where representatives of all Six Nations assembled to hear a message about the imperative for Indian unity. In 1812, Tecumseh would embark on a journey to the South (discussed below).[2]

Tecumseh's efforts bore some fruit, but the barriers the confederation faced were high. Many of the people he contacted were wary of antagonizing the United States, a concern that was often reinforced by a lack of trust in British assistance. And, although Tecumseh tried to persuade Indians to reject treaty annuities, it was difficult for leaders of communities who had become dependent on them to do so. Some agreed not to accept annuities, but in the fall of 1810, as they anticipated the need to feed and clothe their people over the coming winter, most leaders with a claim to annuities eventually came to Fort Wayne or Vincennes to receive them. Then, too, many Native leaders genuinely believed that adapting to the Americans rather than resisting them was the most hopeful path. Aware of divisions among Indians, U.S. officials moved aggressively to leverage these to maximize advantage. At councils with Indians near Detroit and at Fort Wayne, Michigan territorial governor William Hull and U.S. agent John Johnston provided liberal provisions (including annuities), reminded accommodationist chiefs of Tenskwatawa's and Tecumseh's denunciations of them, and worked to secure declarations of neutrality should war again break out between the United States and Great Britain.[3]

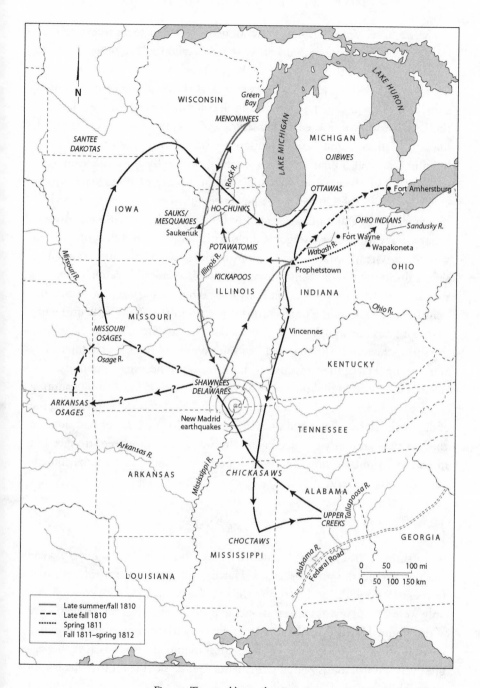

Fig. 20. Tecumseh's travels, 1810–1812

As we have seen, U.S. policy sanctioned the use of force to exterminate Indians who resisted U.S. authority. If policy allowed for military action, however, it did not require it. In late 1810 and early 1811 there were significant limits on U.S. willingness to wage war against the confederacy of Tecumseh and Tenskwatawa. One factor affecting decisionmakers was the weakness of the U.S. army. Committed to low taxes and deeply suspicious of a standing army, Jefferson and James Madison (President since 1809) had not made building national military strength a great priority. By 1810, the army consisted of fewer than 7,000 men stationed at a score of posts across half a continent. Still, the United States possessed sufficient manpower, especially if augmented by state militias, to go to war against the confederacy. A more immediate constraint was ongoing diplomatic conflict—and the potential for war—with Great Britain over freedom of the seas and the impressment of sailors during the Napoleonic Wars. The Madison administration's preoccupation with these issues inclined it against taking military action against the confederacy. Besides, the official on the ground in the West, William Henry Harrison, was not arguing for military action. In late 1810 and into the following spring, he repeatedly reported that the strength of the Indian confederacy was waning. Harrison was willing to argue for war if necessary, but at the moment it seemed that diplomacy could secure his immediate goal of resuming the process of land acquisition so that Indiana could become a state. Had the Indian confederacy been raiding settlements, as its predecessor had done in the late 1780s and early 1790s, demands for war would have been stronger, but in an indication of a more cautious disposition, leaders of the 1810s confederacy discouraged raids.[4]

TOWARD WAR: PROPHETSTOWN

In spring 1811, Harrison dispatched a party to survey the 1809 Fort Wayne cession. Should the survey succeed, Harrison planned to proceed with new treaties. In a rebuke to Harrison's theory of a weakening confederacy, not only were the surveyors turned away, the Indians who challenged them were Weas whom Harrison had thought to be cool to Tecumseh and Tenskwatawa. Around the same time, confederation members began to act more aggressively. Potawatomis raided settlements near Kaskaskia on the Mississippi River; although the Indians killed very few, settlers in the recently organized Illinois Territory panicked and fled toward the safety of Kentucky. In June

Tenskwatawa seized a shipment of salt on its way to tribes that had agreed to the Vincennes tract in 1803, saying he needed it to meet the needs of the 2,000 warriors soon to arrive in Prophetstown. These events led Harrison to argue for military action. "If some decisive measures are not speedily adopted we shall have a general combination of all the Tribes against us," he wrote Secretary of War William Eustis in July. Harrison's insistence, along with petitions from Illinois, Indiana, and Michigan, led Eustis to dispatch regular troops from Pittsburgh and authorize Harrison to supplement them with state and territorial militias. At the same time, Eustis informed Harrison of Madison's "earnest desire that peace may, if possible, be preserved with the Indians, and that to this end every proper means may be adopted." In all likelihood, this was an accurate expression of the Madison administration's position, rather than a charade to create moral cover, as with the Washington administration's promotion of peace negotiations in 1793.[5]

In the meantime, in late July 1811 Harrison and Tecumseh agreed to meet once more at Vincennes. It is difficult to know the thinking of either man. Perhaps, as some scholars have suggested, Harrison was determined on war and decided to negotiate to create the appearance of exhausting all avenues for peace. On the other hand, Harrison had been talking with Tenskwatawa and Tecumseh for years and would have had some cause to believe that negotiations could succeed in avoiding war. Although he had served as aide-de-camp to Anthony Wayne in 1794, Harrison had little military experience. Should he go to war, he would try his best to become a second Wayne, but he was also aware of what Tecumseh's and Tenskwatawa's predecessors had done to St. Clair. Tecumseh's motivations in meeting with Harrison are also difficult to discern, though a clue may be found in something new he said to Harrison when they met. A year earlier, Tecumseh had rebuffed Harrison's offer to have him travel to Washington to discuss issues directly with President Madison. Now, however, Tecumseh told Harrison that he planned to travel south for several months and then "go and see the President and settle everything with him." This suggests that Tecumseh was opening a new path to prolong negotiations.[6]

Harrison might have waited for negotiations between Tecumseh and Madison to play out, but he decided that the departure of Tecumseh and several warriors for the South left Prophetstown vulnerable to attack. In August Harrison assembled a force of 400 regulars and 600 Indiana and Kentucky militiamen and in late September began the 150-mile march from

Vincennes to Prophetstown at the confluence of the Wabash and Tippecanoe rivers (Fig. 21). On November 6, with Harrison's army within a mile of
Prophetstown, Tenskwatawa and Harrison agreed to negotiate the next day.
But before a council could occur, firing broke out in the predawn darkness on
the 7th. There are conflicting accounts of the initial shooting. One interpretation is that Tenskwatawa decided on a surprise attack and prophesied that the
spirits would deliver a great victory. Another perspective, however, contends

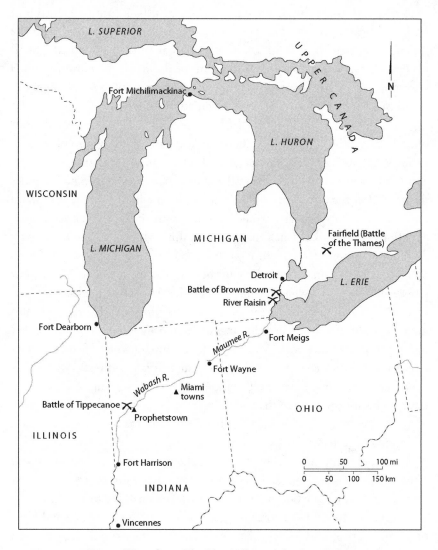

Fig. 21. Wars of 1812: The Ohio Valley and the Great Lakes

that Tenskwatawa was committed to peace and made no plans to attack. Instead, when U.S. sentinels killed two Ho-Chunks, some of the Indians, acting on their own, sought revenge by attacking Harrison's camp.[7]

Whatever the case, Harrison's army was thrown on its heels by the initial attack but was able to regroup and mount a counterattack against a much weaker force of only 400 men short on powder and lead. Harrison forced the Indians to abandon Prophetstown, allowing his men a free hand to torch crops and buildings and desecrate graves. With over 100 wounded and sixty-eight killed and his men shaken, however, this destruction did not last long. Harrison quickly returned to Vincennes. The number of Indians killed was smaller (around fifty), though in percentage terms significantly higher. There were few, if any, noncombatant casualties, as the fighting occurred at some distance from the village.[8]

The Battle of Tippecanoe is one of the best-known events in U.S.–Indian warfare, in no small part thanks to the memorably alliterative campaign slogan ("Tippecanoe and Tyler, too") that propelled Harrison and his running mate John Tyler into the White House twenty-nine years later. Yet, even though Tippecanoe's fame has misled some historians to argue that Harrison's attack sent a crippling message of American resolve that damaged Tenskwatawa's credibility among his followers, the battle was not a decisive U.S. victory. Not only did Tenskwatawa's reputation remain high, Harrison's attack encouraged the confederacy to take a more militant position. Prior to Tippecanoe, the confederacy's leaders had emphasized building the movement's strength and discouraged raids, but by "cleaving the hornet's nest with his sword," Harrison freed Ho-Chunks, Potawatomis, and Kickapoos to attack frontier settlements as never before. Before Tippecanoe, Indians linked to the confederacy had killed fewer than ten settlers; in the first six months of 1812, they struck down as many as forty-six.[9]

"THEY WOULD EVEN KILL OUR OLD MEN, WOMEN, AND LITTLE ONES"

If many confederationists remained optimistic after Tippecanoe, for the movement to succeed it would need to mobilize additional support. At the farthest reach of their hopes, Tecumseh and Tenskwatawa envisioned Indians from the Gulf of Mexico to the Great Lakes united and able to hold off U.S. colonialism. It was with this vision in mind that Tecumseh left Prophetstown in August 1811 and traveled south with a delegation of Ho-Chunks,

Kickapoos, and Shawnees. Tecumseh and his party first visited Chickasaws (northern Mississippi), though, unable to convince them to turn away from their orientation toward the Americans, he stayed only briefly. He then went on to Choctaw country (central Mississippi), calling on leaders of several villages. But a Choctaw national assembly, urged by the influential accommodationist leader Pushmataha, rejected his invitation to join the confederacy.[10]

All along, Tecumseh had been more optimistic about his next destination—the towns of the Upper Creeks in what is now central Alabama. As we have seen, some Creeks had supported the confederacy in its previous incarnation in the late 1780s and early 1790s. Many had shown interest in the confederacy's revival and a Creek delegation visited Prophetstown in 1810. Kinship ties stemming from the eighteenth century, when Shawnees established settlements on the Tallapoosa River, facilitated Shawnee-Creek collaboration. Tecumseh himself likely had some Creek ancestry, as did another member of his delegation, a Shawnee prophet named Seekaboo, who was fluent in Muskogee, the dominant language among Creek communities. The immediate conditions facing Creeks were also conducive to organizing. Creeks, thus far on the fringes of U.S. expansion, were increasingly angry about the growing number of non-Indians traveling through their territory on the Federal Road from Georgia through Mississippi Territory. Although some Creek leaders had agreed to allow this road in 1805, many Creeks had always rejected its legitimacy. To add to their distress, even as Tecumseh arrived, U.S. superintendent Benjamin Hawkins was demanding permission for another road through their country. Tecumseh's three-month-long visit triggered a vibrant religious and political movement centered in Upper Creek towns on the Alabama and Tallapoosa rivers. During much of Tecumseh's stay, a comet burned in the night sky, and shortly after he left, a series of earthquakes centered in northeastern Arkansas and southeastern Missouri (known as the New Madrid earthquakes) were felt in Creek country. Perhaps Creeks interpreted these events as spiritual confirmation of Tecumseh's message, although there were more mundane causes for Creek mobilization (like opposition to settler expansion).[11]

After leaving Creek country, Tecumseh traveled west, crossing the Mississippi to try once more to recruit Shawnees and Delawares in Missouri. Sometime during this portion of his journey, the New Madrid earthquakes struck. Though some Indians near the epicenter evidently believed that "the Shawanoe Prophet has caused the earthquake to destroy the whites," Missouri Shawnees attributed the shaking of the earth to their neglect of traditional ceremonies and did not necessarily interpret it as affirmation of Tecumseh's message.

The record does not provide direct evidence of their thinking, but the premise behind their move to Missouri in the first place—to escape conflict in the East—likely argued against joining the confederacy, as did their cultivation of peaceful relations with United States.[12] Tecumseh also visited Osage villages either along the Arkansas River (northeastern Oklahoma) or the Osage River (western Missouri). According to John D. Hunter, a white captive who heard Tecumseh address the Osages, he spoke "in long, eloquent, and pathetic strains," explaining that Indians "are threatened with a great evil; nothing will pacify [the white men] but the destruction of all the red men. . . . The white men want more than our hunting grounds—they wish to kill our warriors; they would even kill our old men, women, and little ones." Hunter stated that the Osage chiefs seriously considered Tecumseh's message for several days before ultimately rejecting it. This suggests that they found Tecumseh's account of America's genocidal intentions plausible but were unpersuaded that direct resistance was the best path.[13] Tecumseh had more success on the final leg of his journey, where he traveled through parts of Iowa, Minnesota, and Illinois on his way back to Indiana, visiting Ioways, Sauks and Mesquakies, Santee Dakotas, Kickapoos, Potawatomis, Ojibwes, and Ottawas. Some among these nations had already supported the confederacy. His discussions shored up this support and expanded the number of recruits.[14]

When Tecumseh returned to a partially rebuilt Prophetstown sometime before spring 1812, he heard news that U.S. officials had invited him, Tenskwatawa, and other confederation leaders to visit Washington. By this time, "war hawks" in Congress were agitating for war against Great Britain and the Madison administration was concerned to discourage an alliance between the Indian confederacy and the British. As we have seen, Tecumseh had expressed interest in a proposal of this sort, informing Harrison that he would travel to Washington after his return from the South. In this case, however, he and other confederation leaders would have been part of a much larger delegation of western Indians, many opponents of the confederacy. Perhaps Tecumseh suspected that U.S. officials would allow the voices of accommodationist leaders to drown his own.[15]

WAR WITHIN WAR: THE OHIO VALLEY
AND THE LOWER GREAT LAKES

Any hope for diplomacy evaporated on June 18, when the United States declared war on Great Britain. Some of the reasons for this declaration—

British restrictions on freedom of the seas and its impressment of sailors—were remote from the frontier, but U.S. war hawks also argued for the necessity of seizing Canada in order to prevent the British from continuing to prop up Indian resistance in the Ohio Valley and Great Lakes. Invoking a conspiracy theory born at the time of the American Revolution, one congressman announced that "we shall drive the British from our Continent—they will no longer have an opportunity of intriguing with our Indian neighbors, and setting on the ruthless savage to tomahawk our women and children."[16] From the outset, then, the War of 1812 was linked to a national agenda of subjugating Indians and obtaining their lands. And, although the United States' war aims were, first, to invade Canada, and then when this failed, to prevent a British victory, fighting the British necessarily involved fighting Indians, not only those allied with the British but those resisting U.S. expansion in general. Within the War of 1812, then, can be seen the continuation of a war the United States had been fighting against western Indians since its inception.

The months prior to the outbreak of war between the United States and Britain had been devoted to hedging bets and playing for time. With war now in motion, protagonists quickly committed. The British had earlier worried that providing aid to the Indian confederacy might provoke war with the Americans. Once the war began, British officials in Upper Canada could aggressively pursue an Indian alliance. Indeed, with few troops and at the end of a tenuous line of supply, the British desperately needed such an alliance and so sent to the western nations a wampum belt called "the King's Great Broad Axe." This belt signified the capacity of a British–Indian alliance "to cut down all before it." In turn, despite memories of the betrayal of 1794, when the British had denied aid to the Indian confederacy after the Battle of Fallen Timbers, the 1810s confederacy gravitated toward the British. Already at Fort Amherstburg to seek food, ammunition, and arms when war broke out, Tecumseh pledged to support British military efforts and recruited Wyandots to join him. After skirmishing with U.S. troops in July, the following month Tecumseh led twenty-four men in a stunning ambush of 150 American troops near Brownstown (see Fig. 21), killing nineteen and wounding twelve. By mid-August Tecumseh and General Isaac Brock had repelled William Hull's attempt to capture Upper Canada and had taken Detroit. The British–Indian alliance scored two other significant victories in the war's early months. In July, testifying to the efficacy of Tecumseh's recruiting efforts, Dakotas, Menominees, Ho-Chunks, Ottawas, and Ojibwes joined British troops to capture Fort Michilimackinac at the straits between Lake Huron and Lake Michigan. On the southern end of Lake Michigan (the future site of Chicago) Potawatomis captured Fort Dearborn and killed several dozen of the soldiers and noncombatants stationed there without serious losses of their own (only about fifteen were killed). These victories strengthened the hand of the confederacy, with many Indians who had previously pledged friendship to U.S. officials now willing to take up arms in the cause—now suddenly possible—of ridding their lands of American settlers.[17]

The confederacy's summer victories were significant, but they were achieved against outposts of U.S. empire. For the confederacy to realize its goal of permanently rolling back American settlement, it would need to achieve military success in the central zone of contestation—Indiana and eastern Ohio. In September confederation forces laid siege to Fort Wayne but, lacking artillery, they were unable to capture the fort and were forced to withdraw when Harrison led an army of 2,000 men in relief. Discouraged by this defeat and failed attempts to take Fort Harrison on the Wabash and Fort Madison on the Mississippi, many Indians returned to their villages. Americans proceeded to take the offensive, burning Indian towns in Indiana and leading Tenskwatawa to evacuate Prophetstown in anticipation of another attack. On November 22, 1,000 Kentucky militiamen reached Prophetstown. Although confederation forces ambushed a patrol, they judged that it would be impossible to hold off the Kentuckians and so abandoned their capital. Once more, Americans took their torches to Prophetstown. Americans continued their destruction into December. By the close of 1812, regular and militia forces had attacked twenty towns in eastern Ohio, Indiana, and central Illinois, killing a few dozen of their inhabitants, burning homes, crops, food supplies, shooting cattle and horses, and in at least a few instances plundering graves. Most of these towns had aligned with the confederacy, but Harrison also ordered attacks on Miami towns where few supported Tenskwatawa and Tecumseh. Among the villages burned was that of the recently deceased Little Turtle, for almost twenty years a leading spokesman for accommodation with the Americans.[18]

U.S. military operations against Indian towns in late 1812 were far more significant than the better-known Battle of Tippecanoe. These attacks marked the close of sixty years of intertribal militant defense of the Ohio country. Although some confederationists regrouped at locations in Indiana and Ohio, the Americans' destruction forced most resisting Indians to follow Tenskwatawa and seek assistance at British posts on the periphery of the homelands they had fought so hard to defend.[19]

In some ways, Harrison's burning campaign of late 1812 reprised Wayne's much better known destruction of The Glaize in 1794. But Harrison's campaign revealed something more consequential, if less dramatic, than Wayne's. Because Wayne's target was deep in Indian country, at considerable distance from American settlements, he required months to assemble a large force and establish a series of posts to secure supply lines. By 1812, however, settlement had advanced much closer to the heart of Ohio Valley Indians' territory. This meant that Harrison was able to strike more quickly, and he was able to draw on a reservoir of westerners (Kentuckians, Indianans, Ohioans, Pennsylvanians) to serve in the federal army and state militias. This helps explain the effectiveness of his campaign; it also highlights the consequences of a growing U.S. population, not just because of its impact on Native lands and resources, but as a source of military power. Not only was the United States as relentless as it had been in 1794, it was now stronger.

For the remainder of the war, Ohio Valley confederationists fought on the periphery of their homelands. They achieved some significant victories, though mainly in defense, as they battled U.S. forces trying to retake Detroit. In January 1813 Indians led by the Wyandot leader Roundhead combined with British forces to defeat Kentucky militiamen at River Raisin on the eastern shore of Lake Erie in southern Michigan, killing close to 200 in battle with minimal casualties of their own. A day later, Indians slaughtered between thirty and sixty prisoners, causing American commanders thereafter to exhort their troops to "remember the Raisin." Three months later, while laying siege to Fort Meigs, a new post Harrison established on the Maumee River in northeastern Ohio (near modern-day Toledo), the Indians and British again inflicted significant casualties, killing as many as 160 Kentuckians. Once again, Indians began killing prisoners, though Tecumseh intervened to halt the slaughter. In theory, these victories might have allowed the British–Indian alliance to go on the offensive in Ohio, Indiana, and Illinois, but the British and Indians lacked sufficient supplies and manpower to do more than hold their position. Soon enough they were unable to do even that. In September American ships commanded by Commodore Oliver Perry destroyed a British fleet on Lake Erie, severing their supply line. With Harrison leading a new army against them, the British withdrew into Upper Canada. Most of the Indians returned to their homes, but about a third, including Tecumseh and Tenskwatawa, agreed to honor their alliance with the British. In October, Harrison with a force of 3,500 overwhelmed British-Indian forces on the Thames River near Fairfield (also known as Moraviantown), founded a generation earlier by Moravian missionaries and Christian Indians hoping to find sanctuary from American militias and armies. The British and the Indians did not suffer a great many casualties (only a few dozen were killed), though among the dead was Tecumseh himself, shot down while exhorting his men to take courage. After the Battle of the Thames, as it became known, some Kentucky militiamen flayed the corpse of an Indian thought to be Tecumseh and fashioned razor strops from the skin.[20]

As the fighting was ending, some American soldiers set out for nearby Fairfield. They hoped to find Indians, but only missionaries were there. Terrified of another Gnadenhütten, the Moravian Indians had "disappeared in the bush." Over the protests of the missionaries, Americans pillaged the town and set it aflame, later spreading stories that the women of Moraviantown had "thrown their children into the Thames, to prevent their being butchered by the Americans!" These stories, false by all evidence, may have testified to an American awareness of the terror Indian women would have experienced at the thought of American soldiers; they also were calculated by a racist agenda to undermine Indian humanity by proving that even Christian Indians could not become truly civilized.[21]

The circumstances and place of Tecumseh's death—fighting with retreating British troops far from the center of the confederacy he had helped build —more than his death itself underscore the waning of Native resistance in the Ohio Valley. Earlier in the year, Indians had raided settlements in Indiana, but Indiana rangers counterattacked, burning several more towns (most abandoned before they were hit). Guerrilla war continued in Illinois into 1815 as the United States consolidated its position in the West, but Americans' relentless destruction of villages in the confederacy's heartland in 1812–1813 had fatally weakened the Native resistence movement. Tellingly, Prophetstown, twice destroyed, was never rebuilt. After the Battle of the Thames, some of Tenskwatawa's followers urged him to return to the Wabash to build a new Prophetstown. Fearful of American reprisals, however, The Prophet decided to remain in Canada.[22]

In assessing the extent of destruction of Indian nations in the Ohio Valley from 1811 through 1814, the emphasis should be placed on the destruction of towns and its consequences more than on the number of Indians directly killed in battle. In fact, if the outcome of the War of 1812 in the Ohio Valley and Great Lakes region had been determined by casualty figures, the Indians would have won easily. The largest number of Indians killed in any engagement was at Prophetstown/Tippecanoe in 1811. That number—around fifty—

was much lower than the 200 Americans killed at River Raisin (not counting the prisoners massacred after) or the 160 killed at Fort Meigs. The Battle of the Thames was a climactic defeat for Tecumseh and his British allies, not because of the casualties, rather because it marked the end of any realistic hope for the confederacy to achieve its aspirations. This meant that the United States was now in a considerably stronger position to consolidate its power in the Ohio Valley. In their attacks on Indian towns, Americans killed some, but not a large number. In most instances, Indians turned to the time-honored tactic of abandoning their villages when they became aware that U.S. military forces were approaching. When they could, Indians attacked Americans, as in December 1812, when Miamis killed ten Americans and wounded forty-eight others out of a force that had just burned three of their towns. The Americans' destruction of towns, crops, and livestock, of course, caused material hardship (as intended), though the evidence suggests loss of life was not as high as in some similar situations. British reports from Upper Canada after the Battle of the Thames, for example, indicate that over 1,000 Indians, two-thirds women and children, suffered through the winter of 1813–1814 eating only one meal a day, but it appears that famine did not occur.[23]

WAR WITHIN WAR: THE CREEK RED STICKS

As confederationists fought with the British north of the Ohio River, their Creek allies undertook a separate war to blunt U.S. power in the South. From the start, Creek militants, known as Red Sticks for the red war clubs they carried,[24] were far more willing to take militant action against Americans than confederationists in the Ohio Valley.

In spring 1812, not long after Tecumseh's departure, Red Sticks attacked travelers on the Federal Road. They also raided a white settlement near the confluence of the Duck and Tennessee rivers (Fig. 22) in central Tennessee, killing two children and taking captive a woman named Martha Crawley, who became a symbol of "the virtuous mother menaced by savages." Enraged by these actions, the *Nashville Clarion* called for a military expedition against the Red Sticks not only "to exact a terrible vengeance for the blood they have spilt among us" but to hasten the day "when all the southern [I]ndians shall be pushed across the Mississippi." For the moment, however, federal officials favored other approaches. Creek agent Benjamin Hawkins turned to the Creek National Council, a body increasingly functioning as a mechanism for U.S. indirect rule of the Creek nation, and pressured its

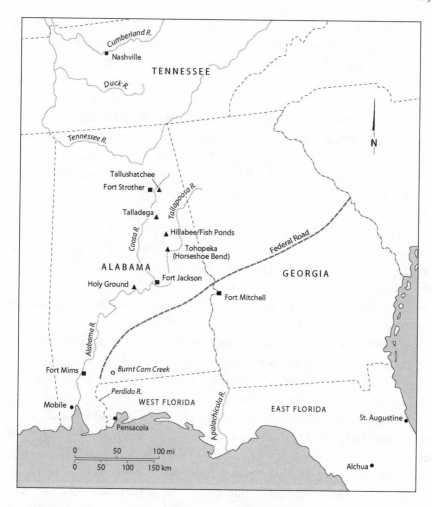

Fig. 22. Wars of 1812: The Southeast

accommodationist leaders to punish Red Sticks. Accordingly, the National Council ordered that those involved in these raids and attacks be executed. Council-sanctioned war parties killed eight Red Sticks. This led to what many scholars have described as a Creek civil war. Red Sticks killed several members of the National Council and their allies and burned houses and other property, especially targeting conspicuous signs of the new order like spinning wheels and cattle. As in the early phases of the prophetic movement north of the Ohio, there were also accusations of witchcraft.[25]

Like other confederationists, Red Stick leaders were aware of the importance of extending their movement to other nations. Despite the Choctaws' rebuff of Tecumseh, Red Sticks appealed to them once more and recruited a few. The situation looked more promising in Cherokee country, where Cherokee prophets had begun calling for greater attention to the Green Corn Ceremony and rejection of American technologies, while criticizing Cherokee leaders for selling land and cooperating with U.S. officials and missionaries who promoted civilization. Despite considerable affinities with Red Sticks, however, Cherokee dissidents rejected Red Stick overtures for a military alliance. Much more than the Creeks, who had been on the periphery of the wars of the 1760s through the 1790s, Cherokees bore searing memories of their people cut down and their towns set aflame by colonial and American armies.[26]

Only in Florida among the Seminoles and closely related communities of blacks who had escaped slavery did the Red Stick message find fertile ground. Originally from Lower Creek towns, Seminoles had migrated south into Florida in the early and mid-eighteenth century. Over time, they became largely independent of the authority of Creek towns and fiercely protective of their own autonomy. Some blacks lived in Seminole communities. Some were slaves of Seminoles (though slavery in Seminole society was much less oppressive than on southern plantations) and others were kin. Many more blacks lived in communities founded by maroons, who had escaped slavery in South Carolina, Georgia, and the French colony of St. Domingue. Though distinct, these maroon communities had close political and cultural ties to Seminoles and so their people are known as Black Seminoles. At the time of Tecumseh's visit to Creek country, Seminoles and Black Seminoles were more suspicious than ever of U.S. intentions to eliminate Florida as Indian country, a place of freedom from plantation slavery and a possible center for inciting slave revolts such as the one that occurred in St. Domingue in 1791 and led to the creation of the independent black nation of Haiti in 1804. Their suspicions were sound. In October 1810, President Madison issued a proclamation annexing the portion of the Spanish colony of West Florida east of the Perdido River, advancing the fallacious contention that West Florida was part of the Louisiana Purchase. A few months later, U.S. agents began encouraging Anglo planters near St. Augustine in East Florida to revolt.[27]

In March 1812, acting without formal authorization, U.S. troops invaded East Florida. Their goal was to take St. Augustine. With Spanish support and inspired by Tecumseh's teachings as transmitted through Red Stick Creeks, Seminoles and their black allies harried American supply lines and in September repelled a U.S. army marching on the town of Alchua (near modern-day Gainesville). This victory caused Georgia governor David Mitchell to fear that his state would be subject to "the very worst evils imaginable," no doubt a reference to the slave revolt in Haiti two decades earlier. A combined army of Tennessee militiamen and U.S. regulars reached Alchua in February 1813, where they reported killing thirty-eight Seminoles, burning 386 houses, destroying 5,000 bushels of corn, and taking 800 cattle and horses. By this time, however, Federalists in the Senate, who had opposed war with Britain and objected to expanding it to a war against Spain, one that would extend the power of slave states, defeated a formal authorization for an invasion of East Florida. American forces withdrew from Seminole country, though only a few years would pass before they returned (see Chapter 8).[28]

As conflict waned in Florida, it escalated in Mississippi Territory (which included present-day Alabama). In July 1813 Mississippi Territory militia leaders became alarmed when they heard reports that Red Stick Creeks were on their way to Pensacola to obtain arms and ammunition from the Spanish. With a few guns, gunpowder, lead balls, flour, and corn, the 300 Red Sticks returned home, splitting into smaller groups to avoid detection. Eighty miles northeast of Mobile, near Burnt Corn Creek, a territorial militia of about 180 men, including thirty Creeks, intercepted one of the Red Stick parties of between sixty and 100. Although few were killed on either side, the outnumbered Red Sticks took heart in holding off the Americans and Creeks they detested as collaborationists. Emboldened by Burnt Corn Creek and angry at Creeks who had taken up arms against them, Red Sticks decided to attack Fort Mims, forty miles west of Burnt Corn Creek. At Fort Mims somewhere on the order of 250 non-Indian settlers and pro-American Creeks (including a few slaves) were under the protection of 140 U.S. volunteers and militiamen. The Red Stick army, consisting of about 700 men and led by Far Off Warrior and William Weatherford, surprised Fort Mims on August 30. Through several hours of fighting, the fort's defenders held off the attackers, but Red Sticks regrouped, renewed their assault, set fire to the fort, and began massacring civilians who had not been burned to death. In all, Red Sticks killed somewhere between 250 and 300 of those within the fort. Estimates of Red Stick losses range widely, from thirty to 200.[29]

The situation after Fort Mims was similar to the one following the Haudenosaunees' attack on Cherry Valley in late 1778 (see Chapter 2). As at Cherry Valley, Indians at Fort Mims had killed noncombatants, including women and children, and scalped many of their victims. After both events, Americans were understandably horrified by the loss of life and accounts of atrocities, but at the same time they inflated the number killed and the extent of atrocities, circulating lurid accounts of women "butchered, then stripped and subjected to every brutal indignity that the savages could think of," while overlooking the provocations that led Indians to these actions and forgetting times when they had done the same—or worse.[30] Both events, too, occurred in the context of American war with Great Britain. As in 1779 against the Haudenosaunees, the United States conducted a punitive and massively destructive military campaign against the Red Sticks, one that became a war of its own, though it dovetailed with larger national aims of securing economic and political independence vis-à-vis the British empire and establishing control over new swaths of Indian territory.

Fort Mims strengthened regional and federal support for military action. Citizens of Nashville immediately demanded a war to "exterminate the Creek Nation and Abettors." In early September, a committee of the Tennessee General Assembly recommended a military force sufficient in size "to carry a campaign into the heart of the Creek nation and exterminate them." Accordingly, the legislature authorized Andrew Jackson, commander of the state's militia, to mobilize a force of 3,500 men to "repel the invasion of the state of Tennessee by [the Creeks] and their allies." Fort Mims was a good 250 miles south of the Tennessee border and the theory of a Creek invasion far-fetched, but the legality of mobilizing the militia depended on an argument for self-defense. President Madison approved Tennessee's actions and placed the Tennessee militia under the formal command of the U.S. army, thus officially endorsing a military expedition organized for the purpose of exterminating the Creek nation. Federal officials also authorized two additional forces, a Mississippi territorial militia commanded by General Ferdinand L. Claiborne and a Georgia state militia commanded by General John Floyd. Together the three militias constituted a force of between 4,000 and 6,000 men.[31]

In responding to Fort Mims, Madison did not use the language of extermination, but his predecessor did. Three months after Fort Mims, Jefferson observed to the German geographer and naturalist Alexander von Humboldt that the "cruel massacres" Indians had "committed on the women and children of our frontiers . . . will oblige us now to pursue them to extermination, or drive them to new seats beyond our reach." Jefferson's formulation—extermination or removal of resisting Indians—was one he had often made and reflected widely held views among American leaders. There were, though, some dissenters. Despite the "tale of terror" at Fort Mims, *Niles' Weekly Reg-*

ister was unable to "reconcile ourselves to the extermination" of the Creeks or to banish them "to the wilds of the Mississippi," where they would likely "become extinct through their wars with the tribes" already there. Instead, the journal proposed, the Creeks, after their inevitable defeat, should be dispersed on small tracts of land so that they would be "compelled . . . to attend to husbandry."[32]

On the heels of Tennessee's authorization of military action against the Red Sticks, Andrew Jackson appealed to "Brave Tennesseans" to defend their state from "the savage foe . . . advanc[ing] towards your frontier with their scalping knifes unsheathed, to butcher your wives, your children, and your helpless babes." Within weeks, he had mobilized an army and moved into Creek country. On November 3, one of his brigades, commanded by Brigadier General John Coffee, surrounded Red Sticks at Tallushatchee on the Coosa River, killing a reported 186 and taking eighty prisoners. "We have retaliated for the destruction of Fort Mimms," Jackson reported, though he evidently did not mean that he had *fully* retaliated. Six days later, Jackson's forces trapped a Red Stick army of 1,000 men at Talladega, forty miles south of Tallushatchee. Firing at close range against the poorly armed Red Sticks (lacking gunpowder, many were forced to use bows and arrows), the Americans killed at least 300. Jackson regretted that the number killed was not higher. "Not an Indian could have escaped," he said to Tennessee governor Willie Blount (William Blount's half brother), had it not been for a break in his line.[33]

These losses were extraordinary. In just a week's time the Red Sticks had seen close to 500 of their fighting men cut down. At the sister towns of Hillabee and Fish Ponds, Red Sticks were "panic struck" and sent a flag of peace to Jackson along with a message expressing their willingness to accept any terms he offered. On November 17 Jackson sent word that he would negotiate with the Red Sticks, while being sure to let them know that the peace he planned to impose would cause them to "remember Ft. Mims in bitterness & tears." The next day, one of Jackson's generals, John Cocke, by all accounts unaware of Jackson's overtures, ordered troops under General James White to assault Creek towns on the Tallapoosa River. White and his men destroyed several towns; at the largest one, they reportedly killed "64 warriors & took 256 prisoners," mostly women and children. Although many of Jackson's biographers have their subject expressing "grief and rage" upon learning of White's action, there is no evidence for this in Jackson's correspondence. The Creeks who survived these attacks were certain not only that Jackson felt little regret over White's attack but that he had intentionally betrayed them.[34]

Jackson wished to press on, but his troops were poorly supplied. Many preferred to return home rather than starve in the cause of destroying Indians, a reminder that ordinary men enlisted in missions of mass killing are not necessarily wholly dedicated to the cause. Though Jackson fought mightily to prevent desertion, the strength of his army dwindled. It was not until reinforcements arrived in early 1814 that he was able to resume offensive operations. In the meantime, other American armies took up the slack. In late November Floyd's Georgia militia, supplemented by anti–Red Stick Creeks, attacked two more Red Stick towns on the Tallapoosa and reportedly killed upwards of 200. In December Mississippians led by Claiborne marched on a town Red Sticks had established on the upper Alabama River (thirty miles west of present-day Montgomery) called the Holy Ground. Red Stick prophets believed that Holy Ground was "a spot made sacred by the great spirit" and encircled by a "destructive barrier . . . which a white man could not pass over alive." As Claiborne's troops approached, the Red Sticks, aware of the prophecy's provisional character, took the precaution of evacuating the town's women and children. When the Americans breached the barrier, most Red Stick fighters fled. The Americans killed thirty Indians and burned the town.[35]

Despite truly staggering losses, the Red Sticks remained committed to fending off the American armies. In part, this was because they were still confident in their prophets' predictions that they could ultimately prevail. Red Stick calculations were also influenced by their assessment that they had a reasonable chance of securing additional arms and ammunition from Spanish and British sources. Even without new supplies, however, Red Sticks twice engaged Jackson's army in late January on the Coosa River. Although they killed twenty of Jackson's men and forced him to withdraw north to Fort Strother, the cost was an additional 200 dead of their own. Still, the Red Sticks pressed on. Just days after tangling with Jackson, a force of 1,300 Red Sticks—the largest contingent they had so far assembled—ambushed Floyd's Georgians and allied Creeks, inflicting dozens of casualties before artillery fire ended their offensive. Floyd reported killing forty-nine, though he, too, was unable to remain in the field and returned to Fort Mitchell near the Georgia border.[36]

All along, Red Sticks had relied on a combination of spiritual and material power. Although Holy Ground had fallen, Red Sticks believed they could hold off Americans at a recently founded town on the Tallapoosa River named Tohopeka (fifty miles northeast of present-day Montgomery). Prophets had advised that this site, never before occupied, would be a fortuitous place to make a new beginning. The location also afforded tactical advantages. Surrounded on three sides by the river (hence the Americans' name for the place, Horseshoe Bend), the town could be attacked from only one direction, and this could be blocked by a well-constructed breastwork, or "wooden fence" (the meaning of Tohopeka). Under the leadership of the prophet Monahee and war leaders William Weatherford and Menawa, the Red Sticks used timber and trees to build a breastwork between five and eight feet high. They also made plans for using canoes to escape downriver should it become necessary. It would be difficult to defeat the Americans in open battle, as aid from the Spanish or British had failed to materialize. Probably only one in three fighting men had a gun. The rest would have to fight with war clubs, bows and arrows, or spears.[37]

Jackson, his army again reinforced and now at 3,300, including 500 Cherokees and 100 Creeks, departed Fort Strother on March 14 and reached Tohopeka thirteen days later. At first, Jackson judged that the town would be difficult to take. "It is impossible to conceive a situation more eligible for defence than the one they had chosen," he later wrote, adding that "the skill which they have manifested in their breast work, was really astonishing." After further thought, however, Jackson began to see the town as a potential slaughter pen. The key was to block off possible escape routes. "Determining to exterminate them," Jackson dispatched a portion of his army, including the Cherokee and Creek auxiliaries, to the other side of the river and then trained his artillery on the breastworks. After two hours, the Cherokees and Creeks, acting on their own, crossed the river and set fire to some of the town's buildings. This diversion allowed Jackson's troops to overwhelm the barricade and enter Tohopeka. Lacking anything close to the firepower of the Americans, the Red Sticks were unable to prevent the Americans from annihilating them. After the carnage had ended, Jackson's troops counted 557 Red Stick fighters dead. Claiming the necessity of ensuring an accurate body count, they cut the nose from each corpse. Some took other trophies. According to one of Jackson's men, "the Tennessee soldiers cut long strips of skin from the bodies of the dead Indians and with these made bridle reins." Many Red Sticks—250 to 300—tried to escape, but were unable to reach their canoes and so tried to swim across the river. Captain William Bradford reported that "the river ran red with blood" as the Americans fired without restraint. According to U.S. reports, most of the 350 women and children in the town were taken prisoner and turned over to the Indian auxiliaries. In contrast to the over 800 Red Sticks killed, the Cherokees lost eighteen men and the Americans twenty-six (Fig. 23).[38]

Fig. 23. Menawa (the Great Warrior), born around 1765, was one of the preeminent leaders of the Red Stick Creeks. Likely an architect of the breastworks at Tohopeka (Horseshoe Bend), Menawa escaped being killed in Andrew Jackson's March 1814 attack, probably by slipping down the Tallapoosa River in a canoe. Menawa opposed removal in the 1830s, but he and his family were forced to go to Oklahoma in 1836, where he died not long after. Courtesy of the Alabama Department of Archives and History, Montgomery.

The U.S. assault on Tohopeka ended sustained Red Stick resistance in Alabama. A handful of Red Sticks continued attacking settlers, but most lacked the will and the capacity to continue. In surrendering to Andrew Jackson in April, Weatherford spoke of devastating facts. "Once I could animate my warriors to battle," he said, "but I cannot animate the dead. My warriors can no longer hear my voice: their bones are at Talladega, Tallushatchee, Emuckfaw, and Tohopeka."[39] In a little more than five months, American armies, augmented by Native allies, had killed somewhere between 1,880 and 2,050 Creeks. Assuming a total population of between 15,000 and 17,000 for the entire Creek Nation, this would be a loss of 11–14 percent, over twice that if figured as a percentage of Red Stick supporters.[40] These totals and percentages reveal a far larger number directly killed than in any other British or U.S. military operation so far considered in this book.

According to U.S. reports, the Red Sticks killed were almost entirely armed men. After Tohopeka, Jackson "lament[ed] that two or three women and children were killed by accident," but beyond this, his and other reports indicate that almost all women and children either escaped or were taken captive—but almost never killed. U.S. commanders did have an incentive to spare noncombatants, both to blunt accusations of inhumanity and to provide captives to Native auxiliaries as a form of compensation. Nonetheless, there is little doubt that American forces killed more than just one or two noncombatants here and there, and that some of these were killed intentionally. One soldier recalled that during the fighting at Tohopeka a militiaman fatally struck a young boy in the head with the butt of his musket. When an officer reproached the militiaman "for barbarity in killing so young a child," he replied that "the boy would have become an Indian some day." Even when American soldiers and Native auxiliaries refrained from close-quarter killing of noncombatants, attacks on towns by their very nature placed women and children in harm's way.[41] Red Sticks took precautions to limit civilian casualties. At Holy Ground, for example, upon learning of Claiborne's approach, women and children were able to escape to safety, probably according to a prearranged plan. Similarly, the fact that the sex ratio at Tohopeka was weighted toward men suggests that Red Stick leaders placed many noncombatants in towns they judged to be less vulnerable to an American attack. Nonetheless, it is impossible to believe that every one of the 250 to 300 people reportedly shot to death as they swam across the Tallapoosa to escape annihilation at Tohopeka was a male of fighting age.

Direct killing was the most destructive aspect of America's war of extermination against the Red Stick Creeks, but the war was damaging in other ways. Americans destroyed forty-eight Upper Creek towns and the Creeks abandoned twelve others. (Creeks opposed to the Red Sticks also experienced some destruction in early 1813, including loss of houses, crops, and livestock.) With their towns and crops in ruins, it is not surprising, as a Georgia newspaper reported, that many Red Sticks "have been reduced by famine to mere

skeletons." Over 2,000, mostly women and children, sought food and supplies at three camps the Americans established in the region, lest, in Jackson's
words, they "embrace the proffered friendship of the British." Another 2,000
Red Sticks took refuge in Spanish West Florida between the Apalachicola
River and Pensacola. At first they were living, in the words of one report,
"on the spontaneous produce of the earth," but in July 1814 many Red Sticks
found relief at Pensacola when the British arrived there with supplies. Once at
Pensacola, Red Sticks joined with Seminoles and African Americans in con-
templating further military action against Americans, but Jackson attacked in
November and forced them to retreat to the Apalachicola. The signing of the
Treaty of Ghent in December and Jackson's victory over the British at New
Orleans the following month brought an end to the War of 1812 and led the
British to withdraw from Florida. By this time, Seminoles reported that "famine is now devouring up our ourselves and our children." The Seminoles were
suffering, but they did not hold the Red Sticks responsible, since they "have
seen their children dying in the woods for want and who can blame them
when pressed by such cruel necessity." All told, although many Red Sticks
died from starvation and disease in 1814–1815, the evidence does not permit
even rough estimates. Probably their losses from these causes were not as great
as those of the Cherokees in the early 1760s or the Haudenosaunees in the late
1770s from similar causes, but it is impossible to say for sure.[42]

Another consequence of the war was the further loss of Creek land. At
first, U.S. officials proposed fairly lenient terms. Red Stick leaders would surrender and the Creeks as a whole would cede some land to satisfy the U.S.
demand for an indemnity for war costs, but Creeks who had supported the
government would be given individual grants of land. When Jackson heard
about these terms, he was furious and maneuvered to be appointed head of
a treaty commission to impose a punitive peace. In July 1814, Jackson summoned the leaders of the Creek Nation to a new fort (unsurprisingly named
for himself) at the confluence of the Coosa and Tallapoosa rivers, right in the
heart of Creek country. Almost all of the Creeks who arrived at Fort Jackson
on August 1 had supported the United States against the Red Sticks. When
Jackson read his treaty terms, the Creeks were stunned. Instead of rewarding
them for their service, Jackson proposed to punish all Creeks by requiring
them to cede about a third of their land in Georgia and over half of their land
in present-day Alabama, approximately 36,000 square miles, the second largest land cession the United States had demanded of an Indian nation to date
(the largest was the 1808 Osage cession, discussed in Chapter 7). Nothing was

said about individual grants of land to U.S.-allied Creeks. When Big Warrior (Tustanagee Thlucco), a leading supporter of the Americans, objected
to the injustice of punishing all Creeks, the general was ready with a reply.
When Tecumseh, an enemy of the United States, came to Creek country in
1811, Jackson said, the Creek chiefs should have sent him to the British, delivered him to U.S. authorities, or shot him then and there. Their failure to act
proved their disloyalty. Jackson then informed the Creeks that they had two
choices: be driven into the sea or sign the treaty. Later, Big Warrior explained
that he and the thirty-four others who signed did so because Jackson "threatened us and made us comply with his talk. . . . I found the General had great
power to destroy me."[43] To survive genocide, it was necessary to sign.

WAR OF EXTERMINATION

Why was the United States' war against the Creeks so much more destructive than the one it carried out against Indians north of the Ohio? One
possible answer is Andrew Jackson. Whether lauded as national hero for defeating the Red Sticks (then) or vilified as one of America's most notorious
Indian haters (now), Jackson has typically been seen as a singular figure mag-
nifying America's best or worst attributes. There is no question that Jackson
prosecuted what he characterized as a war of extermination with uncommon
ruthlessness. By contrast, Harrison was more oriented toward diplomacy and
was cautious about using military force against Tecumseh and Tenskwatawa.
When he did attack Prophetstown it was with mixed results. It is also revealing that Harrison took a less punitive attitude toward Indians after the fighting had ended. In treaties with Ohio Valley Indians at Fort Wayne in 1814 and
Detroit a year later, Harrison's primary concern was to secure peace rather
than gain land. Imposing a land cession, he thought, would prolong the war,
an expensive proposition. Land acquisition could resume in due time.[44]

Still, too much can be made of differences between Jackson and Harrison,
or for that matter between Jackson the crass frontiersman and a cosmopolitan
figure like Thomas Jefferson, who, although gesturing toward grand theories about humanely incorporating Indians within American civilization, also
countenanced wars of extermination. A more salient factor was the Creeks'
willingness to confront U.S. military power. In the north, Tenskwatawa and
Tecumseh's confederacy revived a movement that had ebbed and flowed
among several Native nations for half a century. During that time, Ohio Valley Indians had accumulated substantial experience dealing with European

and U.S. military forces. As Tenskwatawa and Tecumseh contemplated that history, it gave them serious pause about militarily challenging the United States. Tecumseh and other war leaders in the North were capable of bold action, as when they defeated Hull's invasion of Upper Canada and took Detroit or when they seized forts Michilimackinac and Dearborn. In the Ohio Valley, though, they generally chose not to risk fighting American armies, instead allowing their towns to be torched. By contrast, although some Creeks had joined the western confederacy in the late 1780s and early 1790s and had fought with Chickamauga Cherokees, Creeks had relatively little experience with American military forces. None had ever invaded Creek country. In the early 1810s, the Creeks were one of the two largest Indian nations east of the Mississippi, and though not all Creeks supported the Red Stick movement, a majority did. With as many as 3,000 fighting men, Red Sticks thought they could hold off the Americans in their home country, even if it meant absorbing considerable losses.

Another important difference was that in most of the military engagements north of the Ohio, Indians fought with British forces. This meant that Indians in that region had ample supplies and fought with well-armed allies; it also meant that when Americans encountered Indians in battle they adhered more closely to codes of conduct governing war with Europeans than those operating in war with Indians. At the Battle of the Thames, Harrison dealt with Indian and British combatants similarly, taking almost all of them prisoner, a necessity given the American argument that they treated Indians better than the British, who manipulated them and encouraged their savage instincts. On the other hand, the Red Sticks did not fight with the British or Spanish and, despite their efforts to obtain material support in Florida, were poorly armed when they encountered American armies. Even Andrew Jackson would have been more reluctant to engage in wholesale slaughter of Creeks had Europeans been fighting alongside them.

The United States' war against the Red Sticks, more than any other officially sanctioned action against Indians from 1783 to 1814, revealed the contours of a war of extermination. In contrast to many U.S. military operations,[45] war against the Red Sticks combined two conditions necessary for the full realization of a war of extermination. First, despite some problems of supply and personnel, the United States prosecuted the war with relative competence and efficiency. Second, a poorly armed targeted group was willing to repeatedly resist U.S. forces (rather than, as we have often seen, avoid engagement as a strategy of self-preservation). Under these conditions, where the on-the-ground balance of power decisively favored the United States, there were few constraints on the exercise of violence. Because American forces attacked Red Stick fighters, who were able to fight back (at least at first), the engagements of the U.S. war against the Red Sticks are usually referred to as battles. Yet, many of these battles took on the characteristics of massacres. Since U.S. forces had such an overwhelming firepower advantage, as engagements progressed it became increasingly likely that Indians being killed no longer had ammunition and were essentially defenseless. U.S. commanders might have offered opportunities for surrender earlier, but it was not until more or less all Indian fighters had been killed or had escaped that they did.[46] Furthermore, with varying degrees of intention, American soldiers killed at least some women and children. Losses of noncombatants would have been higher had Creeks not taken action to protect them, especially by sequestering them.

A war of extermination, then, meant mass slaughter, though it did not require the killing of every individual who conceivably could have been killed. To accomplish the settler colonial goal of subjugating resisting Indians with a view to eventually taking their lands, the United States could afford to stop short of total possible annihilation and at the same time gain significant advantages by taking some prisoners. In contrast to some other situations we considered earlier in this book, Jackson and other commanders were not interested in using prisoners as hostages. Instead, they turned the prisoners over to Creek and Cherokee auxiliaries as a portion of their compensation. Taking prisoners (rather than killing them) as well as feeding refugees (rather than letting them starve) also allowed Americans to make a war of extermination appear—to themselves and observers in the "civilized" world—consistent with principles of Christian humanitarianism. No U.S. leader mastered the art of reconciling catastrophic destruction and paternalistic benevolence better than Andrew Jackson. In addition to taking prisoners, while lamenting the supposedly accidental deaths of a very small number of women and children, Jackson also "rescued" a ten-month-old Creek infant, taken from his mother who lay dead at Tallushatchee. Claiming that Creek women allied with Americans wanted to kill the child, Jackson and his wife Rachel adopted the boy, named Lyncoya, and raised him until his death from tuberculosis at the age of sixteen. On a personal/psychological level, Jackson, himself an orphan, evidently identified with the child, but his rescue also dramatized his own investment in a national ideology of paternalism. In the same way that Jackson assumed the role of father to Lyncoya, while at the same time destroying his people, so did Americans think of themselves as good parents to their Indian children even as they declared the necessity of Native extinction.[47]

Was the U.S. war against the Red Stick Creeks genocidal? Neither scholarship on the Creek War nor works in genocide studies have addressed this question. This is surprising, since the total number of Red Sticks killed (at least 2,000) exceeded those killed in many other events, such as the massacre of ninety-six Moravian Indians at Gnadenhütten in 1782 or the slaughter of between 100 and 200 Cheyennes at Sand Creek (Colorado Territory) in 1864, that have often been treated as instances of genocide. One reason that the U.S. war against the Red Sticks has not been considered as a possible instance of genocide is that the war has usually been narrated as a series of battles. As noted above, however, many of war's conflicts had some of the characteristics of massacres, both because Red Sticks were poorly armed and suffered far more casualties than the Americans and their Native allies, and because Red Stick casualties included noncombatants. Does a war of this sort qualify as genocide? Under a restrictive definition of genocide requiring an intent to kill every single member of a targeted group, the answer would be no, since the United States' primary objective was not to kill all Red Sticks but to end their resistance. Leaving it there, however, fails to see that to achieve this objective, the United States as a matter of policy was willing, if necessary, to kill more or less every single Red Stick. In this case, as in others, U.S. officials' preference was for dispossession to proceed without provoking militant resistance. When such resistance did emerge, however, officials were prepared to undertake what they characterized as a war of extermination. The extent to which such a war would actually result in genocide was contingent on a number of factors, including the commitment of the Red Sticks to sustain resistance over time. Had the Red Sticks quickly abandoned militant resistance once U.S. forces mobilized against them, their losses would have been relatively light and the genocidal potential of war largely unrealized, but the Red Sticks' willingness to continue to engage U.S. forces despite taking substantial casualties meant that the Creek War became increasingly genocidal over time. To prevent total genocide, Red Stick leaders eventually decided to cease armed resistance. If, however, the Red Sticks had continued to resist, a more complete genocide would have occurred. The U.S. war against the Creeks, then, was not a clear-cut case of total genocide, but the possibility of total genocide was present at the outset and was partially realized.

CONCLUSION: SIXTY YEARS OF WAR

The War of 1812, when remembered at all, usually brings to mind the British burning of Washington in August 1814, Francis Scott Key's witnessing of bombs bursting in air above a fort guarding Baltimore's harbor a month later, or Andrew Jackson's victory at New Orleans in January 1815. The memorialization of these events emphasizes the war as a Second War of Independence and loses sight of one of the most important consequences of the events of 1812–1815: the end of sixty years of war for the Indian lands between the Appalachians and the Mississippi. This did not mean that Indian nations in the East had been destroyed. But the U.S. defeat of confederationists north and south accelerated the process of western settlement and encouraged ever more aggressive designs on the territory of Native nations. Not only would Indians be subject to demands that they cede portions of their remaining lands, but the United States would begin to implement a policy, long fantasized about but thus far impractical, to remove every last Indian from the eastern United States.

PART TWO

Preparing for Removal

CHAPTER 6

Nonvanishing Indians on the
Eve of Removal, 1815–1830

Although the United States did not formally adopt a policy of Indian removal until 1830, momentum to force eastern Indians west of the Mississippi grew after the War of 1812. U.S. officials did not argue that removal was necessary simply for the sake of national development regardless of its impact on Native people. Instead, they crafted elaborate justifications for removal as the only humane way to save eastern Indians from an otherwise inevitable destiny to become extinct. The humanitarian argument for removal rested on a reading of North American history in which Indian nations had repeatedly disappeared in the face of colonial expansion. In one of thousands of examples of the mythology of the vanishing Indian, Speaker of the House Henry Clay declared in 1819:

> The poor children of the forest have been driven by the great wave which has flowed in from the Atlantic ocean to almost the base of the Rocky Mountains, and overwhelming them in its terrible progress, has left no other remains of hundreds of tribes, now extinct, than those which indicate the remote existence of their former companion, the mammoth of the new World![1]

As with many myths, there was some truth in the idea that European American colonization had caused the disappearance (or near disappearance) of many Indian nations. Certainly, it had an incredibly damaging impact on most. But myths often prey upon grains of truth for self-serving purposes, and sometimes they are simply wrong. Scholars have exposed how the discourse of the vanishing Indian was an ideology that made declining Native populations seem to be an inevitable consequence of natural processes and so allowed Americans to evade moral responsibility for their destructive choices. Yet scholars have neglected to ask a basic question about the empirical underpinning of the myth: How many Indians were living in the area the United States claimed at its inception in the 1770s and 1780s, and how many were living in that same area in 1830? Was the Indigenous population in fact declining? An analysis of the available information shows that the population of some Indian nations fell over these decades, but this did not mean they were doomed to continue on a road to extinction. More damaging to the myth, however, is that the population of many nations east of the Mississippi remained stable or even increased. All told, there were actually *more* Indians east of the Mississippi in 1830 than there had been at the time of the American Revolution or the adoption of the U.S. Constitution. Juxtaposing Indigenous demography with the U.S. insistence that Indians were disappearing makes clear that the policy of removal was built on a false premise.

EAST OF THE APPALACHIANS

On the eve of the American Revolution, as we saw in Chapter 1, New England's Native population was somewhere around 3,500 to 4,000. By the 1820s, this number had dropped to perhaps 2,500. The population of a few nations such as the Penobscots and Passamaquoddies in Maine, where non-Indian settlement was fairly light and Native communities retained access to fishing and hunting resources, increased slightly from the 1780s into the 1820s. Otherwise, however, the population of many New England Indian nations fell. Some of the decline was due to migration out of the region, but some was because of an absolute decline in tribal populations.[2]

Several factors contributed to falling populations. Southern New England Indian communities were hit hard during the Revolutionary War (see Chapter 2). They lost men killed while fighting alongside the colonists and suffered further dispossession when, for example, creditors sought satisfaction for debts. Afterward, a shrinking—in some cases, nonexistent—land base made it ever more difficult for Indians to support themselves solely through hunting, fishing, stock raising, and farming, though these activities remained a vital component of their economic strategies. New England Indians were no longer being enslaved as they had been in the seventeenth century. But because of land loss, Natives dispersed from their communities and labored for outsiders as indentured servants or wage workers, primarily as whalers and day laborers, though in a few instances in occupations such as carpenters, barbers, or mill operatives. Servitude and wage labor in the early nineteenth century, along with the production and sale of craft items, formed another key dimension of Indians' strategies for survival, yet they also indicated persistent poverty and generally provided an inadequate means for escaping it. Some communities tried to compensate for downward demographic pressures by an open immigration policy for Indians from particularly beleaguered communities. Native people also married non-Natives, white and black, and incorporated them and their children into their communities.[3]

In an increasingly constricted world, some community leaders decided that their best hope was to seek new homes outside New England. Before the Revolution the Mohegan minister Samson Occom had encouraged Christian Indians from Connecticut, Rhode Island, Massachusetts, and Long Island to form a new settlement to be called Brothertown, among the Oneidas in central New York (twenty miles south of modern-day Utica). Although the outbreak of war temporarily delayed these plans, in the early 1780s, a small number of Mohegans, Pequots, Narragansetts, Tunxis, and Montauks migrated to Brothertown. The Stockbridge Indians of Massachusetts also established a new home in Oneida country in the 1780s and 1790s. The upheavals of the revolutionary period and the subsequent northern expansion of American settlement also led many western Abenakis to relocate to the mission settlement of St. Francis in Quebec, though several hundred, increasingly intermarried with non-Indians (primarily French-speakers), continued to live within the United States.[4]

Native communities along the eastern seaboard to the south also experienced population declines in the decades after the American Revolution. In the mid-1770s, there were around 400 Indians living in eastern Virginia. By 1790, this number had been halved, and a count taken in 1825 showed only forty-seven. This figure was undoubtedly too low, as many Indians with mixed African ancestry were classified by Virginia law as "free negroes," but it indicated an unmistakable trend. Estimates of North Carolina Native populations also show a decline from 500 in 1775 and 300 in 1790. Surveys in the early 1820s reported not a single Indian living in that state. As in Virginia, this was because the largest Native community in North Carolina, the Lumbees, descendants of various Indian groups who had intermarried with African Americans (as well as European Americans), were considered "free persons of color." In South Carolina Catawbas had a population of perhaps 400 to 500 in the late eighteenth century. Catawba numbers suddenly fell to a reported 110 in 1825, probably an undercount though still indicative of major losses. The reason for this drop is unclear. Nothing fundamental had changed for the Catawbas. They retained a small reservation and did not suffer from any major outbreak of disease or famine, leaving us to surmise that something finally broke under the cumulative impact of years of oppression.[5]

UPSTATE NEW YORK, WESTERN PENNSYLVANIA, AND OHIO

In contrast to the heavily Europeanized zone of the eastern seaboard, Indians in upstate New York, western Pennsylvania, and Ohio were living in an area that had been only partially colonized at the time of the creation of the United States. At the start of the Revolutionary War, most Native communities in this region continued to hold enough land to sustain viable economies and retain a measure of autonomy. By the 1820s, however, an intensification of colonial pressures had led to a decline of the Indigenous population.

The largest nation in this transitional zone in 1775 was the Haudenosaunees, with a population of 8,000 to 9,000. Fifty years later, the Haudenosaunee population within U.S. borders had declined to around 4,300 (with an additional 1,000 or so Brothertowns, Stockbridges, Montauks, and Delawares living among them). The major reason for this decline was the decision of many Haudenosaunees to move to Canada after the 1779 U.S. army invasion. In 1830 an estimated 2,500 were living in Canada. Still, adding this figure to the number in the United States gives a total population in 1830 of 6,800, marking an absolute decline of more than 1,000 since 1775. By this time, the state of New York and the federal government had dispossessed the Haudenosaunees of approximately 95 percent of their land base at the time of the American Revolution. They were living on increasingly smaller reservations surrounded by a much larger and growing settler population. Land loss meant a decline in access to game and less productive agriculture. There is no record of any major outbreak of disease or further population decline after the catastrophe of the 1770s. The Haudenosaunees' population was not falling further, but they were unable to rebuild their numbers to earlier levels.[6]

The number of Indians (Shawnees, Delawares, Wyandots, Ottawas, Senecas, Cayugas) in western Pennsylvania and Ohio showed an even sharper drop, falling from 7,000 or so in 1775 to only 2,500 in the early 1820s, almost all of whom were in northwestern Ohio. The main reason for this decline was that many people within these nations decided to migrate west to escape encroaching colonization. Historically an especially mobile and versatile people, the Delawares chose multiple destinations. By the early 1800s, some had established multiethnic communities on the White River in Indiana. Others, including those in Moravian communities, had established new homes in Canada, while still others joined Delaware communities already west of the Mississippi in Missouri. Many Shawnees, a people with a similar history of fragmentation and migration, followed a similar path. By the early 1820s, as many as 1,500 Shawnees were living west of the Mississippi, some near Cape Girardeau in southeastern Missouri and others in southwestern Missouri and northwestern Arkansas. A strategy of dispersal was successful. In the late 1810s, just prior to the time the main body of Delawares on the White River in Indiana moved to Missouri (see below), the total Delaware population was between 3,600 and 3,900, slightly larger than it had been (3,500) in 1768. On the eve of the Indian Removal Act, Delawares were not vanishing. Nor were Shawnees. The total Shawnee population—east and west of the Mississippi—increased from 1,800 in 1768 to around 2,100 in the early 1820s.[7]

But what of Wyandots, Senecas, Ottawas, and Shawnees who decided to stay in northwestern Ohio? Were they disappearing? These communities were increasingly outnumbered by American settlers, their land base was small, and the numbers of some had fallen. But they retained enough land to allow them to pursue a viable economic strategy of incorporating elements of settler society, including raising livestock, growing fruit trees, diversifying farming, and producing cloth. To some extent, they were dependent on treaty annuities, which would not last forever, and on missionaries, who supplied livestock and spinning wheels and whose continued support was not guaranteed. Nonetheless, there was no inherent reason why Native communities in northwestern Ohio could not continue to maintain stable populations—provided Americans decided not to take the rest of their lands.[8]

THE NORTHWEST

At the time of the American Revolution, the combined population of the nations of what was then the Northwest—Illinois, Kickapoos (including the closely related Mascoutens), Menominees, Sauks and Mesquakies (Foxes), Miamis, Weas, Piankashaws, Ojibwes, Ottawas, Potawatomis, and Ho-Chunks (Winnebagos)—was somewhere around 28,000, probably at or near a historic low. Remarkably, however, by the 1820s the population in this region had rebounded to between 40,000 and 45,000. The population of some nations had fallen during this period. The Illinois confederacy, consisting of Peorias, Kaskaskias, and Cahokias, had seen its population decrease from a height of over 10,000 in the late seventeenth century to 2,500 in 1736 (see Chapter 1). Because of disease and violent conflict with other nations and European settlers, their population continued a sharp decline in the late eighteenth century. Some dispersed and joined other tribal communities, but even so, by the early 1820s, their population was estimated to be only thirty-six. As noted in Chapter 4, the Miamis, Weas, and Piankashaws, with a combined population of 4,000 in 1768, also suffered a substantial drop in numbers to 1,400 by the early 1820s. No single event (massacre or disease outbreak) explained a loss of this magnitude. The fact that Wea and Miami towns were repeatedly targeted by U.S. military forces (particularly in the early 1790s and again during the War of 1812) must be part of the explanation. U.S. attacks did not result in massive casualties, but even small losses, combined with material deprivation following the burning of villages, undoubtedly took a toll. Most nations in this region, however, either maintained stable populations or saw their numbers increase. What conditions made this possible? Potawatomis in southern Michigan and Illinois and Kickapoos in Illinois benefited from annuity payments and retained sufficient land to sustain permanent villages with productive farmlands and ample livestock. There and in upper Michigan, Wisconsin, and eastern Minnesota, Indians pursued a still-viable trade in furs and deer skins, as well as selling grain, maple sugar, dried meat, corn, craft goods, and feathers (used in mattresses). In northwestern Illinois, Sauk, Mesquakie, and Ho-Chunk women mined lead for exchange with traders (an astonishing 400,000 pounds exchanged hands in 1811 alone) and nearby Indian communities. Thus, despite recurrent disease, seasons of hardship, alcoholism, and sporadic intertribal conflict, economic conditions in the Northwest were favorable for demographic stability or expansion, particularly in a situation where exchange networks encouraged sexual relations with outsiders. For the most part, the children of traders became part of Native communities, adding to their numbers and reproductive capacities.[9]

THE SOUTH

At the time of the American Revolution, the combined population of the five major nations in the South—the Cherokees, Chickasaws, Choctaws,

Creeks, and Seminoles, known as the "Five Civilized Tribes"—was around 40,000. According to the mythology of the vanishing Indian, these numbers should have fallen over the next few decades, but they did not. From 1775 to the early 1820s, some Cherokees, Chickasaws, and Choctaws relocated west of the Mississippi and some Creeks moved to Florida, but the majority of Indians within these nations continued to live in their homelands. The Cherokee population, about 8,500 in 1775, dropped to 7,500 by 1790, but then rose to between 18,000 and 20,000 (including between 4,000 and 6,000 west of the Mississippi) by the early 1820s. Over the same period, the Choctaw population increased from 14,000 to 21,000; Chickasaws from 2,300 to 3,600; Creeks from 14,000 to 20,000; and Seminoles from 1,500 to 5,000. The growth of the Creek population is particularly striking, as it occurred despite the substantial number killed during the 1813–1814 Creek War. The combined population for the five nations, including those in the West, in the early 1820s was between 70,000 and 74,000, an increase of at least 75 percent.[10]

As in the Northwest, the growth of Native populations in the South rested on land retention. A diminished but still adequate land base allowed Indians to continue to develop the mixed economies they had begun pioneering in the late eighteenth century: combining hunting (for subsistence and exchange), farming, orchard cultivation, gathering berries and plant foods, raising livestock, producing craft items for the market and cloth for domestic use, and managing treaty annuities. A recent study of Cherokee demography and medicine identifies additional factors, many of which are applicable to other Indian nations: the introduction of smallpox vaccination, peace with other Native nations and with the United States, incorporation of (mostly male) European American Loyalists, who fled to Cherokee country during the Revolutionary War and became marriage partners, and growing fertility stemming from the replacement of a hunting economy with one based on livestock, thus keeping men closer to home and providing both men and women with a more reliable source of protein. The southern nations, or at least an elite minority within them, also exploited a growing number of enslaved people of African descent in order to produce surpluses of cotton and other products for the market.[11]

SUMMARY OF POPULATION TRENDS
IN THE EASTERN UNITED STATES

This overview of population trends east of the Mississippi River establishes a crucial fact that has been entirely overlooked in histories of Indian removal: there were *more* Indians living east of the Mississippi in the early 1820s than there had been at the time of American independence (1776–1783). There were between 88,000 and 95,000 Indians living within that territory on the eve of the American Revolution. By the early 1820s, this number had increased to between 112,000 and 121,000 (not including groups of Shawnees, Delawares, and Cherokees, who had migrated west of the Mississippi). These figures, it bears emphasizing, are only estimates, but there are strong grounds for confidence in the general trends they reveal. For our purposes, the important point is that they clearly show an increase over time.[12]

Even if Native populations had been on a downward trajectory, the policy of Indian removal would not have been justified. But realizing that Native populations were actually increasing underscores that the removal policy was built on a falsehood. Indians were not vanishing. Perhaps the relatively small populations of Native people along the Atlantic seaboard forecast a future in which all the nations east of the Mississippi were destined to suffer massive population losses and so needed to be removed to prevent them from suffering total extinction. But although Native people along the Atlantic seaboard had been repeatedly hammered by colonial forces of destruction, this does not mean that their populations were preordained to continue on a downward trend to some final extinction. In fact, precisely because most of these nations were small and held little land, planners of removal did not bother forcing them to move (an indication that the goal of the policy was not to "save" vanishing Indians but to get Native lands). Ironically, then, communities that looked most like they were disappearing were protected from removal. As we will see toward the end of this book, these communities proved resilient in the 1840s and 1850s and did not disappear. Furthermore, there was no necessary reason for Indian nations with stable or growing populations to experience population declines in the future. Advocates of the mythology of the vanishing Indian posited that as Native Americans experienced greater contact with whites, they were inevitably destined to experience population declines to the eventual point of complete disappearance. But, as we have seen, the many Indian nations with stable or growing populations from the 1770s into the 1820s had long histories of interaction with European Americans. They had successfully adapted to new conditions and had overcome disease, war, and dispossession. There was every reason to think that they could survive—even thrive—within the United States provided they were allowed to retain viable land bases.

DEEP ROOTS OF REMOVAL

For good reason, the United States policy of Indian removal is associated with Andrew Jackson and his signing of the Indian Removal Act in 1830. But a singular focus on Jackson obscures the fact that he did not invent the idea of removal. Nor, as has often been argued, did removal suddenly emerge in the late 1820s as an alternative to a supposedly "failed" civilization policy. Jackson himself understood the deep roots of the policy he championed. Months after the passage of the Removal Act, Jackson described the legislation as the "happy consummation" of a policy "pursued for nearly 30 years."[13] Indeed, Jackson's predecessors and their subordinates had long imagined the removal of eastern Indians. As early as 1783, George Washington articulated the possibility that an army of settler-soldiers would cause Indians to cede their lands and "remove into the illimitable regions of the West." A decade later, Timothy Pickering, at the time in charge of federal negotiations with the Six Nations, proposed relocating all eastern Indians beyond the Mississippi River as an "alternative to extinction."[14] Removal entered the realm of geopolitical possibility ten years later when Jefferson arranged for the United States to purchase Louisiana from France and envisioned the new territory as space for the eventual relocation of eastern nations.

U.S. officials not only talked about removal well before 1830, they took concrete steps to make it happen. One of these was to prepare the grounds for removal by dispossessing Indians west of the Mississippi, a project to be discussed in the next chapter. The United States also tried to persuade many eastern nations to move beyond the Mississippi.

EARLY ATTEMPTS TO REMOVE SOUTHERN NATIONS

The Louisiana Purchase was only five years old when the United States raised the possibility of removal with the Cherokees. In early 1808 U.S. agent to the Cherokees Return J. Meigs informed Henry Dearborn, Jefferson's Secretary of War, that "there never will be quietness on any of these frontiers until the Indians are removed over the Mississippi." Dearborn immediately authorized Meigs to pursue this possibility. The result was that in May a small delegation of Cherokees visited Washington, where Jefferson advised the Cherokees to "settle on our lands beyond the Mississippi." This group of Cherokees had some genuine interest in moving west, but, in a forecast of a future of substantial Cherokee opposition to removal, the majority of the

Cherokees wished to remain where they were. At a subsequent meeting in December, many Cherokee leaders protested to Jefferson that removal contradicted the government's earlier advice for them to take up "farming and Industrey." Why, they asked, having followed that advice, would the government now want them to "throw away the wimmen's Spining wheles?" At first, Cherokee opponents of removal did not argue for trying to stop those Cherokees who wished to emigrate, though they strongly objected to government proposals to "exchange" their treaty lands in the east for a new tract of land in Arkansas for western Cherokees. Over the next two years, James Madison's administration continued to promote Cherokee removal. If anything, Cherokee opposition hardened. In late 1809 and early 1810, a newly unified Cherokee National Council strongly opposed exchanging eastern for western lands, going so far as to declare that Cherokees who moved west were "committing treason against the motherland." Led by chiefs Tolluntuskee and The Bowl, who traveled from Missouri to promote western migration, about 800 Cherokees relocated to Arkansas in 1810. But this was far less than the 2,000 Meigs had predicted would depart.[15]

The prospect of removal reappeared in Cherokee country when Andrew Jackson, heading a U.S. commission, arrived at the Cherokee Agency in June 1817 to present the Cherokees with two choices. They could either move to Arkansas or become citizens of the United States. Both involved relinquishing their eastern lands. A month before Jackson's visit, thirteen Cherokee women, including Beloved Woman Nancy Ward, petitioned the National Council to hold firm against removal. The petitioners drew upon "the power of motherhood" within traditional Cherokee culture to remind the councilmen that agreeing to move west, in the words of the petition, "would be like destroying your mothers." This argument strengthened the spines of members of the Cherokee National Council, but in persuading U.S. officials to leave them alone they took a different tack and attempted to turn the American discourse of civilization to their advantage. Cherokees, the council wrote, were "not yet civilized enough to become citizens of the United States." On the other hand, to go west would result in "return[ing] to the same savage state of life that we were in before . . . our white brothers . . . extended their fostering care towards us." The only alternative was to remain in their homelands, where they could continue to advance. To some extent arguments that accepted U.S. premises about civilization reflected sincere beliefs held by an emerging Cherokee elite, although they were also calculated to undermine the paternalistic certainty of U.S. officials. Talking about civilization also served to cultivate an important alliance with the American Board of Commissioners for Foreign Missions, which had recently established missions among the Cherokees and other southern nations. At the end of the negotiations, Cherokee leaders signed a treaty that ceded some lands in Georgia and Tennessee, but they did not believe the treaty required individual Cherokees to choose between removal or U.S. citizenship (the government's interpretation). Instead, they saw the treaty as allowing a third choice of retaining Cherokee citizenship on Cherokee lands. When Return Meigs began enrolling Cherokees for removal, the Cherokee National Council sent a delegation to Washington to oppose the treaty's ratification. Cherokees were unable to prevent ratification, but their opposition slowed down Meigs's efforts and allowed space for further diplomacy.[16]

As before, Cherokee women counseled against removal. In a January 1818 letter to U.S. officials, Margaret Ann Scott, a relative of Nancy Ward and bilingual graduate of a mission school, wrote that "our neighboring white people seem to aim at our destruction" and implored them "for the sake of the dear crucified Savior, who shed his blood for the red, as well as the white people" to protect Cherokees from being "driven away from the land of our fathers." Scott also authored a second women's petition to the Cherokee National Council. More than the first, this petition relied on the external yardstick of civilization, stating that "the thought of being compelled to remove [to] the other side of the Mississippi is dreadful to us" because removal would bring Cherokees "to a savage state again." In February 1819 the National Council sent another delegation to Washington, where Secretary of War John C. Calhoun backed away from insisting on removal. Cherokees could remain in the East, Calhoun said, but they would have to part with all of their lands except those "necessary for their wants and conveniences." In the Treaty of Washington Cherokees agreed to cede additional lands in Georgia, Tennessee, and Alabama, though with the belief—or at least the hope—that this treaty would finally put a stop to U.S. demands for Cherokee lands. Nonetheless, during the 1820s Americans continued to try to push Cherokees west. The state of Georgia played an increasingly prominent role, citing the 1802 Georgia Compact, which in exchange for Georgia giving up its claims to western lands obligated the federal government to obtain the cession of Indian lands within Georgia as early as possible on "reasonable terms." Even so, Cherokees consistently frustrated the efforts of U.S. commissioners to persuade, bribe, and divide them. It would take until the mid-1830s for the United States to finally force the Cherokees west.[17]

Although the United States initially focused on convincing Cherokees to move, most southern nations came under similar pressure in the 1820s. The only exception was the Seminoles in Florida, who did not face demands for expulsion until the early 1830s. The Choctaws first learned of U.S. schemes to relocate them in late 1820, when Andrew Jackson and Thomas Hinds, a Mississippian who had fought alongside Jackson at New Orleans, called upon them to accept the offer of the Great Father's "friendly assistance." As if the Choctaws were ignorant of their own lives, the two Americans informed them that they "are in a distressed condition." To save them, "your father and friend," President James Monroe, wanted to move his "Choctaw children" to "a country beyond the Mississippi," a place were they "may live and be happy." And if they did not go? The mythology of the vanishing Indian provided the answer: "Without a change in your situation," Jackson and Hinds declared, "the Choctaw nation must dwindle to nothing." When Choctaw leader Apuckshunubbee consented to only a small cession, the commissioners applied more pressure, warning that "the patience of your father the President may be exhausted" and that should the Choctaws listen to "evil counsel . . . your nation must be discarded from the friendship and protection of their white brothers." Rejection, they reiterated, "may be a measure fatal to your nation." Although the precise content of this threat was vague, that was the point, as it left open the possibility of anything from withdrawing economic assistance, to unilateral confiscation of all Choctaw lands (without providing any lands in the West), to military reprisal. Faced with these threats, Choctaw leaders signed the 1820 Treaty of Doak's Stand, which exchanged about one-third of Choctaw lands within the state of Mississippi for a larger area in Arkansas. Still, the treaty did not require Choctaws to move. Only a few relocated to Arkansas. In the late 1820s, the government made additional attempts to convince the Choctaws to give up their Mississippi lands, but to no avail. Choctaws were united in favor of retaining their homelands and refused to concede that government officials knew what was best for them.[18]

Chickasaws were even more successful in frustrating U.S. efforts. Chickasaws had been aware of the possibility of removal since 1805, when Thomas Jefferson told a Chickasaw delegation that the United States had recently obtained Louisiana and that "we would prefer giving you lands there" in exchange for all or part of their present lands. But it was not until two decades later that removal became a serious possibility. In fall 1826, Thomas Hinds and John Coffee, a veteran of the Red Stick War, spent several days in the Chickasaw nation trying to convince its leaders to sign a treaty to relocate across the Mississippi. If they refused, the commissioners predicted, the Chickasaws would "see your nation gradually diminish, and your people dwindle away, until the very name and language of a Chickasaw is forever lost." Perhaps Chickasaws had already heard the argument that Indian nations were on the road to extinction and that the only way to avoid this fate was to agree to removal. Perhaps they had never heard it before. Either way, Chickasaw leaders knew it was false and responded that "industry is spreading amongst us; population is increasing." All that was needed for them to continue to "bring forth good fruit" was the continued "assistance of our father the President." The commissioners, however, were impervious to the fact of nonvanishing and so fell to castigating their "red brothers" for their "headstrong obstinacy." Eventually, Chickasaw resistance left Hinds and Coffee no choice but to depart. But before leaving, Hinds issued the Chickasaws a veiled threat: "If calamity shall hereafter fall upon this people, let the blame also fall upon their own heads."[19]

The Creeks also heard from U.S. officials claiming to know what was best for them. In 1824, two federal commissioners, Duncan Campbell and James Meriwether, assured Creeks that the President "has not sent us here to make offers or propose schemes for your injury or destruction." On the contrary, "the most earnest wish of his heart is, that you should be preserved." To this end, the Creeks should exchange their lands for new lands beyond the Mississippi where you "would secure a safe and permanent resting place, . . . free from interruption and disturbance." Did the Creeks have a choice to decide for themselves where they might best survive? No, said the commissioners, since under the 1802 Georgia Compact, the United States must obtain all Indian lands within Georgia's boundaries. Big Warrior, Little Prince, and other Creek leaders countered this reading of the Georgia Compact by citing previous treaties and official promises assuring them that they would never be forced to part with their lands without their consent. And this they would never give: "The proposal to remove beyond the Mississippi, we cannot for a moment listen to." A decade before Creeks had been torn apart by civil war, but now most Creeks were united against removal. Nonetheless, a small minority of Creek leaders, notably William McIntosh, were willing to accept Campbell's overtures for a new treaty at Indian Springs that exchanged all of the Creeks' remaining lands in Georgia as well as two-thirds of their Alabama lands for new lands in the West. Although the Senate ratified this treaty, the Creek National Council challenged its legitimacy on two fronts. Internally, the council found McIntosh guilty of treason for selling lands without national authorization and then executed him. Externally, the council sent a delegation, led by Big Warrior's successor, Opothle Yaholo, and Menawa, by now an aging warrior, to Washington to point out that the treaty had been signed by unauthorized leaders who had been bribed. After a full five months of negotiations, this delegation achieved the remarkable feat of securing a new treaty, the 1826 Treaty of Washington, that declared the previous year's Indian Springs treaty null and void, preserved Creek lands in Alabama (though at the cost of giving up any claim to their Georgia lands), and guaranteed U.S. protection of these lands. The majority of Creeks were determined to stay in the East, though a few thousand, mostly followers of McIntosh, moved west to what is now Oklahoma in the late 1820s.[20]

EARLY ATTEMPTS TO REMOVE NORTHERN NATIONS

By far the majority of books about removal focus on Native nations south of the Ohio River—especially the Cherokees. Because of this, it is often forgotten that the United States spent considerable energy trying to convince Indians north of the Ohio to go west. Even less known is that these efforts began well before the 1830 Indian Removal Act.

One target was the Haudenosaunees in New York. Although the 1794 Treaty of Canandaigua assured the Haudenosaunees that the United States would "never claim" their reservations or prevent them from the "free use and enjoyment" of their lands, in 1818 a U.S. official apprised distressed Senecas on the Buffalo Creek reservation (modern-day Buffalo) of Secretary of War Calhoun's advice that they move west of the Mississippi. Oneidas, too, were dismayed to learn that New York governor DeWitt Clinton had reported to the state legislature that he wished to see all New York Indians emigrate "to an extensive territory remote from the white population." Oneidas protested to the state legislature and President James Monroe against efforts by "sundry individuals to poison the minds of [the Indians] and to make them discontented with their present residence and desirous of removal to the west." To strengthen their position, the Oneidas reminded Monroe of their alliance with the United States in its struggle to achieve independence and of America's consequent debt to them. A leading proponent of Haudenosaunee removal was the Ogden Land Company, owners of the preemption right to purchase Seneca lands at Buffalo Creek and three other New York reservations should the Senecas cede them. With the anticipated completion of the Erie Canal, Seneca lands stood to become very valuable if the Ogden Company was able to convert them into commodities for purchase by American settlers. David A. Ogden, the company's chief spokesman, urged President Monroe to support the removal of Senecas, since they were "retarding the progress of cultivation and improvements and detracting from the public resources and prosperity." Federal officials evidently decided not to try to convince Senecas to move west, at least not yet. Instead, in 1826 a federal commission used the threat of removal to convince Senecas to accept a treaty ceding close to three-quarters of their New York lands: if Senecas did not comply, "your great Father the President will drive you off, and you will not get a cent for your lands." With this threat hanging over them, Red Jacket and other Seneca leaders signed. Within a year, however, Red Jacket was leading a movement to overturn the treaty, claiming in petitions to various officials, including President John Quincy Adams, that the treaty had been secured only through coercion and bribery. Because of the efforts of Red Jacket and other leaders, the Senate refused to ratify the treaty and a federal investigation concluded that the Senecas had signed the 1826 treaty only because "the terrors of a removal enchained their minds in duress." During the 1820s, a few Oneidas moved to Green Bay (present-day Wisconsin) with Brothertowns and Stockbridges, but most Haudenosaunees successfully resisted removal.[21]

The specter of removal also appeared in northwestern Ohio. By 1815, Ohio had been a state for over a decade and had a non-Indian population in excess of 300,000. Nonetheless, in the northwestern part of the state, 2,500 Wyandots, Shawnees, Ottawas, Delawares, Senecas, and Cayugas lived in villages on the Sandusky River, the upper reaches of the Great Miami River, and the Maumee River and its tributaries. The 1795 Greenville Treaty and the 1805 Fort Industry Treaty had greatly reduced Indian lands in Ohio. Even so, Ohio Indians retained treaty rights to a fairly large area (approximately one-sixth of the state) still valuable for hunting, fishing, and plant procurement to augment their core agricultural economies. A new wave of settlement after the end of the War of 1812 led the United States to seek additional lands. In the 1817 Treaty of Fort Meigs, a U.S. commission headed by Michigan territorial governor Lewis Cass convinced the Ohio nations to sell all their Ohio lands (and some in Indiana and Michigan), except for small tracts of between ten and forty-eight square miles, in return for annuity payments. To gain the assent of key leaders, cement leaders' allegiance to the United States, and enhance leaders' authority over potentially recalcitrant tribal members, Cass wrote provisions into the treaty providing chiefs individual land grants along with control over the distribution of annuities and reservation lands.

Although the Fort Meigs Treaty did not stipulate anything about removal, some federal officials saw removal as the next logical step. A year after the treaty, Secretary of War Calhoun wrote Cass that the "great object is to remove, altogether, these tribes [in Ohio] beyond the Mississippi" and authorized him to offer the Ohio nations an increase in their annuity payments and equivalent lands in the West if they agreed.[22]

Ohio Indian leaders did not view the Fort Meigs Treaty as a point on the road to removal. Consistent with their policy of economic and cultural adaptation, they saw it as a way to strengthen an already existing treaty-based alliance with the federal government and an affirmation of their intention to remain where they were. For Wyandots the treaty promised that the "President would make a strong fence around them, and maintain them in the peaceable and quiet possession of that spot for ever." Black Hoof, the Shawnee leader at Wapakoneta, planned to use annuities from this treaty, as he had in the past, to enhance economic development, including purchasing livestock to raise for an emerging market in Cincinnati. He also intended to send Shawnee children to American schools and obtain economic and political assistance from Quaker missionaries, despite the fact that most Shawnees rejected the Christian message of universalism, arguing that the Creator had given one religion to Indians and another to whites. Black Hoof, close to eighty years old in 1817, had fought for decades to preserve a homeland for his people—at first trying to block U.S. settlement, then trying to stake a position within it—and was not about to abandon that commitment (Fig. 24). Nor were other Ohio Indians. In September 1818 at St. Mary's, Ohio, when Cass presented Wyandots, Shawnees, Senecas, Cayugas, and Ottawas with the "proposition to remove to the west of the Mississippi," it was "received by them with such strong symptoms of disapprobation, that we did not think it proper to urge them too far upon the subject."[23]

Though rebuffed, Cass was not about to abandon the idea of ridding Ohio of Indians. In the early 1820s, he came up with the surprising idea of enlisting none other than one of the great resisters in American Indian history, the Shawnee prophet Tenskwatawa, in the service of his scheme. Since the 1813 Battle of the Thames, Tenskwatawa had remained north of the border, but as settlement advanced into Upper Canada, he became alienated from the British. Aware of The Prophet's discontent, Cass invited him to Detroit in 1824 and persuaded him to establish a village in southern Michigan and advocate for removal. Although Tenskwatawa was unable to convince Black Hoof to change his mind, in 1826 he led 250 Shawnees from

Fig. 24. Born around 1740, the Shawnee leader Black Hoof fought against colonial and U.S.
forces from his teens into his fifties. After signing the 1795 Fort Greenville Treaty, Black Hoof
built a strong community at Wapakoneta in northwestern Ohio. Shortly after his death
in 1831, the U.S. government expelled his people to Kansas. *Ca-Ta-He-Cas-Sa-Black Hoof,*
Principal Chief of the Shawnees, 1838. Library of Congress Prints and Photographs Division.

Wapakoneta to join Shawnees already in the West on a new reservation in
Kansas. Other Ohio Shawnee leaders, notably one known as Captain Lewis,
also encouraged migration and led other groups to Kansas. The willingness
of many Shawnees to leave Ohio for the West (a semivoluntary removal)
might suggest that these Shawnees gave up too quickly and are somehow
less admirable than their relatives who steadfastly resisted removal. Yet, there
are many ways to resist and many possible paths for survival. This was especially so for a people like the Shawnees with a long history of dispersal and
migration.[24]

Despite Cass's limited success promoting Shawnee removal, other Ohio nations blocked it. Wyandots, for example, were well aware of pressures on the Shawnees to migrate, and so they persuaded James Finley, a Methodist missionary working with them, to recommend that they remain on the upper Sandusky. Similarly, Wyandots wrote Secretary of War Calhoun in 1824 that "it was not their wish to remove" and reminded him that at the 1817 Fort Meigs treaty "they were told, and most sacredly promised, that if they would cede all their lands, except the present reservations, they would never again be spoken to on this subject."[25]

U.S. officials had an easier time with the Delawares on the White River in Indiana and two Kickapoo communities, one on the Wabash in Indiana, the other in central Illinois. In the late 1810s, both nations agreed to treaties providing annuities and equivalent lands in Missouri in exchange for ceding all of their lands east of the Mississippi. By 1821, about 1,300 Delawares and 1,600 Kickapoos had moved west to Missouri, along the way suffering from "sickness, hunger, and illness." Delaware leaders signed the 1818 removal treaty with "much reluctance," and two chiefs, Anderson and Lapahnihe, signed only because the U.S. commissioners gave them lifetime annuities in a separate written agreement. For the "personal safety" of these leaders, this agreement was kept secret from other Delawares. Kickapoos' acceptance of removal was apparently more "voluntary," although it was nonetheless influenced by colonial pressures. Kickapoo leaders spent considerable time with relatives already in Missouri in 1817 discussing the question of removal before agreeing to do so. One consideration was their recognition that they were unable to "raise a warrior force strong enough to block American settlement." For Kickapoos, migration seemed the best way to retain their autonomy.[26]

Not all nations in Indiana and Illinois were so inclined. The Miamis agreed to a substantial land cession in 1818 (enough to create twenty-two Indiana counties), but it was not until 1826 that Lewis Cass informed them and nearby Potawatomis, "You must remove or perish." A Miami leader known as Le Gros responded that his ancestors told him "that we should stay on the land which the Great Spirit gave us, from generation to generation, and not to leave it" and rebuked the commissioners' contention that removal was the only way for the Miamis to avoiding perishing. "It is yourselves destroying us," Le Gros said, "for you make the spirituous liquor. You speak to us with deceitful lips, and not from your hearts." Unable to convince the Miamis and Potawatomis to move, the commissioners fell back on the next-best plan and secured key pieces of land along the Wabash in exchange for annuities, livestock, and houses, as well as individual land grants to selected chiefs. For now, the Miamis and Potawatomis had fended off removal, but the United States was nothing if not relentless. It was only a matter of time before another commission would visit the Miamis and Potawatomis to inform them once more that to save themselves from certain extinction they must establish new homes somewhere in the West.[27]

CIVILIZATION OR REMOVAL?

At the same time U.S. officials were telling Indians that the only alternative to disappearance was removal, officials also had much to say about a very different plan for Indians: "civilizing" them and incorporating them into an expanding America. Like removal discourse, civilization discourse also drew on the mythology of the vanishing Indian, though it charted a different path to salvation. Instead of rescuing Indians by separating them from American society, Indians would be saved by absorbing them into American society. Historians of U.S. Indian policy have often argued that a policy of removal replaced a policy of civilization in the mid- to late 1820s, when policymakers decided that the policy of civilization had "failed."[28] Already we have seen a major problem with this interpretation. Long before the mid-1820s, government officials were constantly trying to persuade Indians to move west, and as we will see in the next chapter, they were taking concrete steps to dispossess Native nations west of the Mississippi to prepare the way for the removal of eastern Indians. Two very different policies were being articulated at the same time. How can this contradiction be resolved? Some clues emerge from a close reading of what historians have frequently cited as a classic expression of an early republic civilization policy: a speech by Thomas Jefferson to a delegation of Indians from New Stockbridge, New York, in 1808.

Led by Hendrick Aupaumut, the Mahican whom the U.S. had enlisted as an emissary to the United Indian Nations at The Glaize sixteen years before (see Chapter 3), the Stockbridge delegates traveled to Washington, D.C., to seek Jefferson's guarantee to a small tract of land on the White River in Indiana. Moving to Indiana, Aupaumut thought, would protect his small community from rapacious land companies and allow him to convert non-Christian Delawares and other Indians in the White River area. Jefferson supported the delegates' request, but not before lecturing them on the reasons for "the increase of our numbers and the decrease of yours." The main cause of Indians' supposed decline, Jefferson explained, was that they had "lived by hunting the deer and buffalo." Now that these were gone, "you have been a part of every year without food," which had led to "diseases and death among your children." In addition, "wars . . . and the abuse of spirituous liquors, have assisted in lessening your numbers." Extinction could be avoided, however, if Indian men were to "learn to cultivate the earth." This would free women to "spin and weave and to clothe their families." Such changes would allow Indians to "raise many children" and so "double your numbers every twenty years," with the result that "your children will never be tempted to sell the spot on which they have been born, raised, have labored, and called their own." Once this had occurred, Jefferson continued, Aupaumut's descendants would appreciate the value of property and would then desire to "live under . . . our laws" and "unite yourselves with us." At that time, "you will mix with us by marriage, your blood will run in our veins, and will spread with us over this great island."[29]

Taken at face value, Jefferson's speech suggests a sincere desire to save Indians from an otherwise inevitable extinction, a desire grounded in a view of Indians as capable of advancing to the level of whites. Despite historians' fondness for quoting this speech, however, they have failed to notice, let alone explore, the irony that this particular audience already met Jefferson's definition of civilization. Not only were the Stockbridge Indians Christians, many were literate, they knew how to "cultivate the earth," and they had adopted the gendered division of labor Jefferson prescribed. They did not need Jefferson's fatherly advice. In fact, Aupaumut was offering similar counsel (cast in fraternal, not paternal, terms) to non-Christian Indians in Indiana, saying that if they followed the Stockbridges' example, "the great and good spirit will bless you that . . . you shall increase, both in number and substance."[30] Despite Jefferson's profession of Indians' ultimate racial equality as measured by their ability to "advance" toward civilization, he was unable to recognize that the Indians standing before him actually conformed to his criteria for civilization, a failure that revealed a powerful, though unarticulated, operating assumption of an innate racial inferiority.[31] Instead, Jefferson deferred the moment of possible Stockbridge "civilization" to a distant future. Only after the community had adopted a new gendered division of labor, only after at least one generation and probably more had increased in number and learned to value private property, could the alchemy of marriage provide a route to the final civilization of Stockbridge Indians. However, the policies that Jefferson was actually pursuing—dispossession and removal— would not allow the Stockbridges, or any other eastern nation, to remain in place long enough to obtain the gift he offered. On the terms Jefferson offered it, civilization was structurally impossible.

But what about the fact that in the 1810s and 1820s Congress regularly appropriated funds to provide tribes with plows, livestock, spinning wheels, blacksmitheries, grist mills, and schools in the name of civilizing them? Or that Christian missionary societies, with government encouragement, provided additional financial and human resources to support the same agenda? Or that the federal government sponsored an institution of higher learning like the Choctaw Academy in Kentucky, where students from dozens of Indian nations, north and south, studied moral philosophy, trigonometry, grammar, geography, and history?[32] This does not mean that programs to civilize Indians were undertaken for the cynical purpose of hiding an actual agenda of removal. It simply means that people are capable of sincerely advocating conflicting agendas without acknowledging or fully reckoning with their fundamentally contradictory nature. Policymakers were undoubtedly sincere when they talked of the possibility of civilizing Indians. At the same time, though, in the decades before the advent of a formal policy of removal in 1830, U.S. officials undertook a series of initiatives to convince eastern Indians to move west, these initiatives steadily gained strength, and they eventually overwhelmed any residual commitment to civilization. Jefferson's failure to acknowledge the "civilized" Stockbridge Indians standing right in front of him along with concrete actions he took to promote removal strongly suggest that "civilization" was the weaker of the two priorities all along.

JUSTIFYING REMOVAL

The policy the United States adopted in 1830 of uprooting tens of thousands of people from their homelands and relocating them hundreds of miles away did not just happen with the stroke of a pen. A policy of removal took time to mature and involved substantial effort even before its formal adoption. We have already seen U.S. officials working hard to convince Native people to go west in the decades before 1830. At the same time, officials also needed to construct arguments justifying removal. This work was particularly laborious for Americans because the act of taking Indian lands and forcing Indians to do something against their will so clearly ran counter to American ideals of freedom, honor, and Christian brotherhood.

One step in the justification of removal was to undermine the sovereignty of Native nations. Attacks on Native sovereignty were nothing new, but they

accelerated after the end of the War of 1812. Andrew Jackson led the way. After dictating the 1814 Treaty of Fort Jackson to the Creeks, Jackson turned his
attention to other southern nations. Working within the treaty system, Jackson and other officials secured modest cessions from Chickasaws, Cherokees,
and Choctaws in fall 1816. By this time, Jackson had wearied of tiresome negotiations to procure cessions, and so in March 1817 he urged President-elect
James Monroe to consider a new approach. The federal government, Jackson
advised, should abandon the "absurdity" of negotiating treaties with Indians
as if they were "independent nation[s]" and instead recognize them as subject
to U.S. sovereignty with only a "possessory right to the soil." In a precocious
assertion of what would become known as the plenary power doctrine, Jackson argued that Congress should "regulate all the concerns of the Indians,"
including taking their lands as a way to accelerate their adoption of American
civilization, something he characterized as being in their own interest. The
argument here was not directly connected to removal, but to the extent that
it sanctioned dispossession, it established a crucial precondition.[33]

Most U.S. leaders, including President Monroe, were unwilling to abandon the treaty-making process. Respect for the laws of humanity, as Tocqueville put it in *Democracy in America,* required obtaining (or creating an illusion of) Indian consent to dispossession. Nonetheless, there was considerable
agreement among American leaders about Jackson's underlying assertion that
Indians did not own their lands. Indeed, Chief Justice John Marshall, often
considered an antagonist to Jackson, gave legal authority to precisely this view
in his 1823 decision in *Johnson v. M'Intosh.* In this decision, considered by one
legal authority to be one of the "ten worst Indian law cases ever decided," Marshall drew on the "doctrine of discovery" to argue that European governments
(including the United States) had "ultimate dominion" over the land and "an
exclusive right to extinguish the Indian title of occupancy, either by purchase
or by conquest." Indians, characterized in racist language as "fierce savages
whose occupation was war," were not the full owners of the land and instead
had only a "right of occupancy." There was nothing fundamentally new in
Marshall's decision, but by giving judicial authority to the long-standing view
that Indians did not have full ownership of their land, *Johnson v. M'Intosh*
contributed to a mounting assault on Native sovereignty.[34]

Although the argument that Indians did not have full ownership rights
to their lands did not necessarily mandate removal, it and other attacks on
Native sovereignty coincided with official assertions that removal would soon
be necessary. In addressing the "condition of the aborigines within our limits"

in his 1824 message to Congress, President Monroe observed that "unless the tribes be civilized they can never be incorporated into our system in any form whatever." Rather than pause to consider whether or not civilization projects had been or could be successful, however, Monroe, apparently assuming that they had not and could not, drew on the mythology of the vanishing Indian and pronounced that "with the extension of our settlements, their situation will become deplorable if their extinction is not menaced." It was therefore necessary to move them far from "our settlements." To complete the work of reconciling removal with the United States' commitment to humane ideals, Monroe then considered how removal should be accomplished. One possibility was to send Indians west by force, but Monroe rejected this as "revolting to humanity and utterly unjustifiable." Having repudiated inhumanity, Monroe then articulated the only presumably humanitarian course of action: the U.S. should provide "inducements" for Indians to move into the "vast territory" between the Mississippi and the Rocky Mountains/Mexico, where they would be provided with "schools for every branch of instruction in literature and the arts of civilized life."[35]

Monroe's argument for removal established the basic template for future arguments: since Indians could not survive in the East, the only humane option was to move them. Both of these premises were deeply flawed. First, eastern Indians were not vanishing, they were not predestined to vanish in the future, and they could have survived (and even prospered) indefinitely in their homelands with sufficient support and protection from the federal government. Second, by Monroe's own logic, removal was not a humane option. Setting aside commonsense concerns about moving large numbers of people great distances to new places, Monroe's contention that settlement had an inherently deleterious impact on Indians meant that removed Indians would eventually be subject to the same forces that threatened their extinction in the East. Even as Monroe spoke, it was plain enough that the process of settlement was already well under way in areas that had earlier been designated for Indian removal. Missouri, once imagined as a permanent home for relocated Indian nations, had become a state three years before. Arkansas, organized as a territory in 1819, was moving along the same path.

As an indication of the Monroe administration's commitment to a comprehensive policy, in early 1825 Secretary of War John C. Calhoun outlined a plan for removal. Calhoun did not recommend moving every single Indian from the East. The "small remnants of tribes" along the eastern seaboard from Maine to South Carolina would not be forced west. Evidently, they controlled such a small amount of land and were so far from the West that it would not be worth the trouble. Recognizing that by this time there was a shortage of lands west of the Mississippi for the relocation of eastern Indians, Calhoun further advised against moving the much larger Indian populations in the upper Great Lakes (northern Michigan and Wisconsin). In fact, Calhoun thought that there were sufficient lands in the upper Great Lakes region to accommodate Indian nations from the lower Great Lakes and New York. Rather than moving these nations west of the Mississippi, it would be better to relocate them to the upper Great Lakes, where the "climate and nature of the country are much more favorable to their habits." Moreover, Indians from the lower Great Lakes and New York could be "collected" with "greater facility" to the upper Great Lakes than to places like Iowa, Missouri, or Kansas. With these exceptions, however, the large majority of eastern Indians would be moved west of the Mississippi, where they would find a "permanent home for themselves and their posterity, without being disturbed by the encroachments of our citizens." Calhoun, like Monroe, was also well aware of the acceleration of U.S. expansion since 1815 and so had ample basis to realize that the promise of a permanent and undisturbed home was bound to be chimerical. Whether in self-deception or outright deceit, however, Calhoun's assurance of a benevolent removal was fast becoming official dogma.[36]

CHEROKEE RESISTANCE TO REMOVAL
AND THE U.S. RESPONSE

Although momentum for a comprehensive removal policy gained strength in the late 1820s, there was significant opposition. A major source of resistance came from the Cherokee Nation. To defend themselves and their lands, Cherokees, or more precisely a smaller subgroup consisting of fairly wealthy people with Cherokee and European ancestry, had undertaken a major project of strengthening the Cherokee Nation in the 1820s. Cherokee leaders centralized executive decisionmaking and judicial authority, established a legal regime oriented toward paternalism and individual property rights (including rights to own black slaves), and promoted Euroamerican education, Christianity, and literacy in English and Cherokee. (Cherokee became a written language based on the Cherokee linguist Sequoyah's invention of a Cherokee syllabary in the late 1810s; Fig. 25.) In 1825 the Cherokees established a new capital city at New Echota (in northwestern Georgia) complete with legislative hall, courthouse, and printing press, which published a national

Fig. 25. The Cherokee linguist Sequoyah was born around 1770 in Tennessee. He fought with the United States against the Red Stick Creeks in 1814. Not long after, he completed his work on a syllabary for the Cherokee language. While in Washington in 1828, he sat for a portrait by Charles Bird King, and a year later he moved to Oklahoma. He died sometime in the early 1840s while on a journey to Mexico to visit Cherokees there. Museum of the Cherokee Indian, Cherokee, North Carolina. Photo credit: Mireille Vautier/Art Resource, N.Y.

bilingual newspaper, the *Cherokee Phoenix*. Two years later, the Cherokees held a constitutional convention. The resulting document, modeled on the U.S. Constitution, was ratified, not coincidentally, on July 4. In becoming a "mirror of the republic," Cherokees remained culturally distinct, but they had made themselves legible to the United States as a civilized and sovereign nation and thus demanding recognition. Cherokee nation building was also designed to strengthen internal unity, understood as a vital condition for national defense.[37]

The Cherokees' adoption of a constitution in 1827 offered a serious test of the U.S. commitment to a policy of civilization. If that commitment was more than simply rhetorical, the United States would be obligated to accept the Cherokee Constitution and allow for the permanent presence of a civilized Cherokee Nation on Cherokee lands. When confronted with an actual rather than a theoretical case of Indians conforming to the criteria Americans had established for civilization, however, federal and state government officials did not celebrate this achievement. Instead, they denied the legitimacy of the Cherokee Constitution and insisted that Cherokees go west.

Historians have often focused on the state of Georgia's leading role in the assault on the Cherokee Nation that followed the Cherokee adoption of a constitution. Indeed, it would be difficult to overstate the aggressiveness with which Georgia moved to counter the Cherokee Nation's claims to sovereignty. In December 1827 the Georgia Senate "solemnly warn[ed]" the Cherokees that "the lands in question *belong* to Georgia—She *must* and she *will* have them." The Georgia legislature followed up on this declaration by passing legislation declaring all Cherokee laws null and void effective June 1, 1830. It is important to note, however, that even before the longtime enemy of Native sovereignty, Andrew Jackson, became President, Georgia's stance had the full support of the executive branch. In late 1827 Superintendent of Indian Affairs Thomas McKenney reported to Congress that Cherokees "ought not to be encouraged in forming a constitution and government *within* a state of the republic, to exist and operate independently of our laws." A year later, in his last annual address to Congress, President John Quincy Adams observed that the United States had "unexpectedly found [Indians] forming in the midst of ourselves communities claiming to be independent of ours, and rivals of sovereignty within the territories of the members of our Union" (i.e., Georgia). Although Adams had shown some ambivalence about removal, he now endorsed this project. In so doing, he gestured to the standard paternalistic argument that removal would "do justice to those unfortunate children of nature." For Adams, however, there was a more fundamental issue requiring removal: the necessity of securing for states "their rights of sovereignty and of soil."[38]

Had Andrew Jackson not been elected President in 1828, the federal government likely would have adopted a formal policy of removal anyway. The executive branch was clearly moving in that direction, and although Congress had yet to act, momentum was building for legislation. Nonetheless, Jackson's election brought to the presidency someone far more devoted to Indian removal than any previous president. Removal had been Jackson's "major policy aim" for a quarter century. Having Andrew Jackson in the White House meant that the United States would pursue removal more relentlessly—and with more destructive consequences—than it might have done otherwise. The new President did not bring novel arguments to bear on the issue. In his first message to Congress in December 1829 Jackson repeated familiar phrases about the humanitarian imperative to protect Indians from disappearing. When "surrounded by whites" Indians were "doom[ed] . . . to weakness and decay," he declared, and so "humanity and national honor demand that every effort should be made to avert so great a calamity." In addition, Jackson asserted the impossibility of recognizing "a foreign and independent government" within existing states' boundaries. Jackson's contribution was an unprecedented determination to make Indian removal a reality.[39]

The new President's intentions were no secret to the Cherokees. Anticipating that Jackson would move aggressively against them by supporting Georgia's attack on their sovereignty and in this way pressure them to abandon their homeland, Cherokees began a campaign of their own. In February 1829, they submitted a memorial to Congress, protesting Georgia's assertion of legal jurisdiction and citing the United States' historic commitment, inscribed in numerous treaties, to recognize their national sovereignty and promote their civilization. Cherokees also enlisted the support of missionary allies. While in Washington to present the Cherokee memorial, Principal Chief John Ross paid a visit to Jeremiah Evarts, corresponding secretary of the American Board of Commissioners for Foreign Missions. Ross told Evarts that should Georgia try to execute its laws, Cherokees would resist, "preferring death to subjugation or exile."[40]

Over the next several months, Evarts and other missionaries, inspired by Cherokee appeals as well as Christian duty, orchestrated a remarkable campaign to uphold Cherokee treaty rights and block removal legislation. The key text opposing removal was a series of essays Evarts wrote under the pen name "William Penn." These were initially published in the *National Intelligencer,* widely copied by other journals, and republished as pamphlets. The William Penn essays provided a comprehensive overview of Cherokee treaties with Great Britain, the colony of Georgia, and the United States to establish the merits of the Cherokee position that "the title to the soil and sovereignty over [Cherokee] territory have been repeatedly *guaranteed to the Cherokees, as a nation,* by the United States, in treaties which are now binding on both parties." From this position, Georgia's use of the discovery doctrine to deny Cherokee land title was tantamount to the claim that *"force becomes right."* In addition to establishing the illegality and immorality of violating treaties, Evarts also considered the destructive consequences of moving "60,000 souls, men, women, and children, most of them in circumstances of deep poverty." Removal, he forecast, would "be attended with much suffering."[41]

Evarts's writings inspired dozens of local Christian organizations to send antiremoval petitions to Congress. Evarts also influenced Catharine Beecher, the daughter of Lyman Beecher, a prominent figure in a religious revival sweeping New England known as the Second Great Awakening. After hearing Evarts speak in Boston, Catharine Beecher published an anonymous circular calling on U.S. women to petition Congress to protect the Cherokees and other Indian nations, "as by solemn and oft-repeated treaties they are bound to do." To allow states to take "such measures as will speedily drive them from their country" was sure to lead to their "final extinction." Beecher's circular influenced many like-minded white women in the North. Seeing themselves as guardians of Christian and American morality, they launched the "first national petition drive by [U.S.] women," inundating Congress with dozens of petitions, each signed by hundreds of women (the largest was from Pittsburgh, with 670 signers). Although this expression of women's activism has usually been seen as arising solely from non-Native women, it was inspired by Cherokee activism. In 1818–1819, Margaret Ann Scott, a leading Cherokee opponent of removal, had corresponded with the non-Native poet Lydia Sigourney to "impress" on her "the urgency of the Cherokee case." Ten years later, Sigourney, a close associate of Beecher, called Beecher's attention to the moral outrage of Cherokee removal.[42]

Even before the emergence of the antiremoval movement, the Jackson administration had begun cultivating allies of its own. Superintendent of Indian Affairs McKenney secured support from Dutch Reformed, Presbyterian, and Episcopalian churches, while influential proremoval Baptist missionary Isaac McCoy spent several months speaking on behalf of removal in eastern cities. The Jacksonians also commissioned Lewis Cass to write an essay on removal, which appeared in the January 1830 issue of the widely read *North American Review.* Drawing on the authority of his experience with Indians as governor of Michigan Territory and federal treaty commissioner, Cass voiced the usual humanitarian position that "the only means of preserving the Indians from that utter extinction which threatens them, is to remove them" and pledged that the United States would guarantee Indian lands in the West "'as long as the grass grows or the water runs.'" Such sentiments were combined with a relentless attack on the continent's original inhabitants. Ignoring millennia of Indigenous success in North America, Cass described Indians as "rude and barbarous," incapable of true nationhood, and possessing no more than a temporary right of occupancy in their lands. Though predating the emergence of formal racial theories grounded in biology, often mistakenly seen as a necessary feature of racist ideologies, Cass's argument clearly characterized Indians as a racial group inherently inferior to Europeans.[43]

In early 1830 Jackson's allies introduced removal legislation in the House and Senate. The opposition's primary leader was New Jersey senator Theodore Frelinghuysen, a devout temperance man who had long taken an interest in Indian missions. For three days Frelinghuysen spoke on the Senate floor in support of the Cherokee position and offered an amendment guaranteeing federal protection of Cherokees until such time as they chose voluntarily to move. Georgia senator John Forsyth took the lead in rebutting Frelinghuysen, arguing that the truly humane position was Georgia's: that "the Indians in the United States would be benefitted by their removal beyond the states, to a country appropriated for their exclusive residence, cannot be doubted by any dispassionate man who knows their condition." Other supporters of removal indicted opponents of the current removal bill for their hypocrisy, pointing out that there had been little objection when outgoing President Adams had endorsed removal only months before. Thus, they said with some degree of truth, the current opposition was patently partisan.[44]

The Removal Bill passed the Senate by a vote of 28 to 19. It was even closer in the House, with 102 in favor and 97 against. Because representatives from the southern states voted heavily for the legislation, it would have failed except that the Constitution's clause counting enslaved people as three-fifths of a person for the purposes of representation increased the South's voting power. President Jackson signed the bill into law on May 28, 1830. The United States was now formally committed to a policy of relocating eastern Indians west of the Mississippi.[45] The intensity of the removal debate and the fact that opponents of removal came close to blocking removal legislation suggests that this was a rare moment when the United States came close to taking a significantly different path in its relations to Indian nations than the one it chose. Perhaps the defeat of removal legislation in 1830 would have allowed Cherokees and other Native nations to remain permanently in their eastern homelands. Yet, even if federal removal legislation had failed in 1830, there are reasons to doubt that most eastern nations could have avoided being forced west. For one thing, the Jackson administration would have continued to press for removal legislation and done little to protect Cherokees from Georgia's 1829 legislation, scheduled to take effect on June 1, 1830. More important, although the removal debate in Congress highlighted significant divisions, there was considerable consensus about removal's ultimate necessity. Those who spoke against removal in 1830 did not oppose removal altogether. Rather, they objected to the process by which it was being accomplished. The central outrage Frelinghuysen identified in his Senate speech was not removal itself, but the "unwarrantable pretensions of Georgia, in her late violent legislation." Although he defended Cherokee sovereignty and appeared to support the possibility of Cherokees permanently retaining their lands, Frelinghuysen's amendment for federal protection of the Cherokees called for this only until such time as the Cherokees voluntarily signed a removal treaty. Even the most celebrated antagonist to removal, Jeremiah Evarts, admitted (in a conversation with Georgia congressman Wilson Lumpkin in early 1829) that eastern Indians would eventually have to relocate west. Differences of opinion were more about process and timing and less about the ultimate end.[46]

NOTHING BUT RUIN

In any event, the Indian Removal Act did pass. Three days later, in an assertion of "perfect settler sovereignty," the state of Georgia claimed full jurisdiction over the Cherokee Nation, denying its very existence. By Georgia's reckoning, the Cherokee Nation did not own its lands, its constitution and laws were meaningless, and its claims to legal jurisdiction within its territory spurious.[47] Georgia could not pass legislation compelling the Cherokee Nation to relocate west of the Mississippi. But by the reckoning of Georgia officials, legislating the Cherokee Nation out of existence would allow Georgians to make life so miserable for the Cherokees that they would eventually agree to depart.

The immediate source of immiseration for the Cherokees took the form of an invasion of Georgia settlers. Even before 1830, hundreds of Georgians, spurred by the discovery of gold on Cherokee territory in 1829, had illegally squatted on Cherokee lands. On the heels of the Removal Act, Georgia began surveying Cherokee lands in preparation for a lottery that would allocate these lands to Georgia's eager white citizens. By summer 1830, as the Cherokees wrote in a statement of grievances addressed to the U.S. Congress,

Georgians had "flocked in thousands to our gold mines" and "by violence" had "forced the natives out of their houses, and taken possession." In one instance, a relatively prosperous Cherokee couple provided supper to two Georgians. Later that night, when their hosts were temporarily away, the Georgians returned the couple's hospitality by burning down their house. Under their most recent treaty with the Cherokee Nation, signed in 1819, the federal government was bound to protect the Cherokees from "white people who . . . may . . . intrude on the lands reserved for the Cherokees." The federal government made some pretense of fulfilling this obligation when the War Department dispatched troops to evict a few Georgia squatters, but the few who were evicted quickly returned. By the time they did, the troops had withdrawn, in the words of the Cherokees' statement of grievances, leaving "our country again exposed to the ravages of intruders." Without federal protection, Cherokees were at the mercy of Georgia and its citizens. The Cherokees cited several examples. In one, squatters attacked "peaceable" Cherokees. "One was cruelly murdered, another wounded, and a third . . . thrown into jail." In another example, a party of ten armed men "forced an Indian from his horse . . . and cruelly abused the persons of two aged Cherokees, one a female, causing a flow of blood, because they did not quietly suffer themselves to be robbed of their property." In addition to supporting white miners, the state of Georgia actively worked to stop Cherokees from mining their own gold. At one point, Governor George R. Gilmer secured an injunction from a court in Hall County, Georgia, to "stop [Cherokees] from digging and searching for gold within the limits of their own nation." The county sheriff dispatched thirty or forty state militiamen into Cherokee country, where they "proceeded to destroy tools and machinery for gleaning gold" and then arrested three Cherokee miners for ignoring the injunction.[48]

Cherokees were also deeply alarmed by attacks Georgia made on their national sovereignty. Sometime in the summer of 1830, a Cherokee named George Tassel killed another Cherokee man. The murder took place within the Cherokee Nation and under existing treaties should have been left to the Cherokee judicial system to resolve. But Georgia officials saw the killing as an opportunity to apply Georgia's recently passed laws asserting criminal jurisdiction over the Cherokees and so they arrested Tassel, found him guilty of murder, and sentenced him to death. Tassel's attorney appealed to the U.S. Supreme Court, which issued an injunction against Tassel's execution pending a hearing. But before the Supreme Court could consider the case, the Georgia legislature asserted "the right to punish crimes" as essential to state sovereignty and Governor Gilmer ordered Tassel to the gallows. For Cherokees, the actions of Georgia's legislature and the state's governor "breathe a spirit towards our nation of which we will not permit ourselves to speak."[49]

Cherokees faced a desperate situation, but the majority were determined to fight Georgia's efforts to force their removal. Consistent with the resistance strategy they had adopted over the previous decade, the Cherokee leadership decided to maneuver within the institutions of American civilization. Advised by former U.S. Attorney General William Wirt, the Cherokee leadership decided that the Supreme Court might be persuaded to rule that Georgia's assertions of sovereignty over the Cherokee Nation violated treaties between the Cherokees and the federal government and were therefore unconstitutional. Should that occur, the Cherokee leadership believed they could block removal. Otherwise, "if we are compelled to leave our country, we see nothing but ruin before us."[50]

CONCLUSION: DESTROY TO SAVE

As word reached them of the Indian Removal Act, other Indigenous nations shared Cherokee fears of ruin. In April 1831, Creek leaders pleaded with Andrew Jackson to listen to the voices of their nation's elders: "Our aged fathers and mothers beseech us to remain upon the land that gave us birth, where the bones of their kindred are buried." Removal, the elders said, was "the worst evil that can befall them." In Ohio, Shawnees had "dreaded" removal for years. Quaker missionaries had assured the Shawnees that "if they would improve their lands and be at peace, that they never should be asked for their land." But when "intimations" of the Indian Removal Act reached the Shawnees, "alas," they feared, "what a mistake!"[51] And in New York the Tonawanda Senecas informed the President of their hope that the "white man will not wish us far away but will take us by the hand as friends and neighbors." Since the advent of the United States, these and other Native American communities had survived genocidal violence and the theft of much of their land. They had rebuilt war-torn communities and adjusted to new economic realities. They were not vanishing, nor was it predestined that they would. A truly humane America would have protected Native communities in place, but under the guise of saving them, the United States now threatened their destruction.

CHAPTER 7

West of the Mississippi, 1803–1835

In 1803, when President Thomas Jefferson purchased Louisiana from France, the territory claimed by the United States almost doubled in size from 890,000 to 1.7 million square miles. Jefferson immediately declared that one of the advantages of the Louisiana Purchase would be to "give establishments in it to the Indians on the east side of Mississippi, in exchange for their present country."[1] Twenty-seven years before the Indian Removal Act, Jefferson could go beyond fantasizing about eliminating Indians from the eastern United States. He had a place to put them.

In proposing the Louisiana Purchase as a location for eastern Indians, Jefferson said nothing about the Native nations—Osages, Otoe-Missourias, Caddos, Quapaws, Kanzas, Ioways, Omahas, and others—who actually owned those lands. If eastern Indians were to be moved west, nations indigenous to what I have termed the "zone of removal" would either have to give up some of their lands to accommodate newcomers or be moved someplace else. Historians have seldom considered the impact of removal on nations west of the Mississippi. Obviously, though, removal was bound to affect these nations. Immediately after the Louisiana Purchase—long before the Indian Removal Act—western nations began to be affected by an incipient policy of removal. As they anticipated moving eastern Indians west, U.S. officials took steps to reduce the lands of western nations. They then began to pressure eastern Indians to move onto the lands of these dispossessed nations. In the 1810s and 1820s, when a growing number of eastern Indians crossed the Mississippi, western nations saw them as invaders.

Jefferson's vision of the Louisiana Purchase as a new home for eastern Indians assumed that the yeomen farmers he idealized and his own class of enslavers would not desire lands west of the Mississippi. In his first inaugural address in 1801, Jefferson rhapsodized that east of the Mississippi there was "room enough for our descendants to the hundredth and thousandth generation."[2] It took less than a single generation for this prediction to prove false. Even before the War of 1812 Americans were taking up lands west of St. Louis, and the non-Native population west of the Mississippi exploded after 1815. Increasing settlement subjected western Indian nations to forces of destruction long familiar to eastern nations. It also meant that the zone of removal steadily shrank. In 1803 Jefferson imagined a fairly large zone of removal encompassing roughly the present-day states of Arkansas and Missouri, the eastern parts of Oklahoma and Kansas, and possibly Iowa and eastern Nebraska. As settlement increased, however, Native people arriving from the East and those indigenous to the West would have to be squeezed into an ever-smaller space. This dynamic would cause problems from the 1810s into the 1830s. As we will see in later chapters, it would prove catastrophic in the 1840s and 1850s.

PREPARING FOR REMOVAL
(AND FUTURE SETTLEMENT), 1803–1808

To prepare for removal, the Jefferson administration first turned its attention to the Osages, a people Jefferson accurately perceived as the "great Nation south of the Missouri" (Fig. 26). A century earlier, the Osages had established a trading alliance with the French as the French moved down the Mississippi River from the Great Lakes. The Osages exchanged corn, bison products, horses, and captives for French guns and ammunition. By blocking Native nations to the west from obtaining munitions, the Osages used their military superiority to raid nations to the west—Wichitas, Pawnees, Apaches, and Caddos—for fresh supplies of horses and captives to be enslaved in French and English colonies. Although circumstances changed when the French lost Louisiana to Spain in 1763, the Osages continued to rely on alliances with Europeans, including building new connections with British traders in the Ohio Valley, and war with Native nations to maintain their hegemony. Epidemic diseases occasionally erupted west of the Mississippi, as when smallpox spread

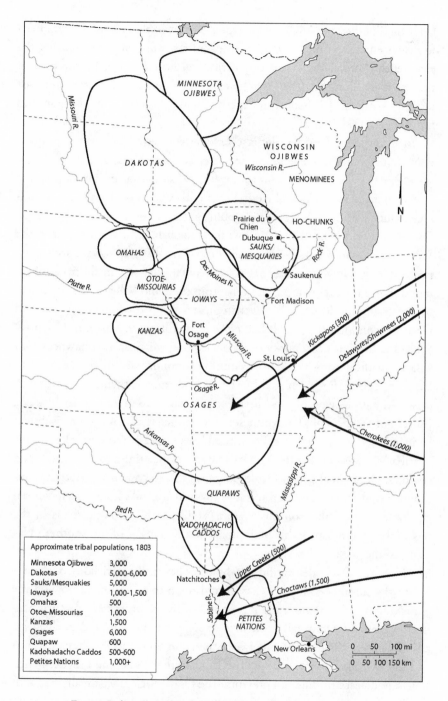

Fig. 26. Indian nations in the eastern Louisiana Purchase, 1803–1815
(dashed lines indicate modern state boundaries)

from the Southeast in 1696 (see Chapter 1). But likely because Osages lived in dispersed communities, they were spared the worst of them. During the eighteenth century, the Osage population fell little if at all. By the time of the Louisiana Purchase, they numbered at least 6,000 and controlled a vast territory—much of Missouri, northern Arkansas, southeastern Kansas, and northeastern Oklahoma.[3]

In spring 1804, President Jefferson requested Pierre Chouteau, a member of St. Louis's leading French family with close connections to the Osages, to arrange for an Osage delegation to travel to Washington. In summoning the Osages, Jefferson had two objectives in mind. One was to establish a trading alliance with the Osages. This would undercut connections between the Osages and Spain and Britain and weaken Spanish and British power in the West. Jefferson also saw an Osage alliance as the first step toward securing a peace among Native nations that were frequently at war in the zone of removal. Since the 1780s eastern nations from the Ohio Valley and Illinois had been crossing the Mississippi River in greater numbers. Some Shawnee and Delaware communities established permanent villages in Missouri. Others—Sauks and Mesquakies, Potawatomis, Kickapoos, Miamis, and Shawnees with villages in the East—sought new hunting grounds west of the Mississippi River to replace those depleted by settlers and Indians themselves. Not surprisingly, nations west of the Mississippi—Osages, Ioways, and the Dakotas (eastern or Santee Sioux) in Minnesota—defended their lands. The result was an increase in intertribal war. From the U.S. perspective, the problem of intertribal war was not that it took Native lives. Rather, unless the United States could end intertribal war, it would be impossible to convince eastern nations to move west. No one wanted to move to a war zone. As Louisiana territorial governor James Wilkinson observed, a "solid peace" among Indians in the region was "an indispensable preliminary to the transfer of the Southern Nations, to the West of the Mississippi."[4]

When the Osage delegation, led by chief Pawhuska, arrived in Washington in the summer of 1804, Jefferson told them that "we are all now of one family, born in the same land, and bound to live as brothers." He then outlined a plan for a mutually beneficial trading relationship and pledged his assistance in healing a breach between the main body of Osages in Missouri and the Arkansas Osages who had split off in the 1780s. The President then distributed peace medals and presents. The Osages welcomed an alliance with the United States, as it gave them access to a new supply of goods that would enable them to maintain their dominant position.[5]

Having established an alliance with the Osages, Jefferson administration officials called on several nations on both sides of the Mississippi—Osages, Sauks and Mesquakies, Delawares, Miamis, Potawatomis, Kickapoos, Kaskaskias, Dakotas, and Iowas—to assemble at St. Louis, where they agreed to a "firm peace" in October 1805. This peace was ephemeral. Shortly after the St. Louis conference, a Potawatomi war party led by Main Poc attacked an Osage village near modern-day Jefferson City, Missouri, killing a reported thirty-four women and children and taking sixty prisoners. Some Osage leaders looked to the United States to enforce the St. Louis accords, but others turned against the Americans. One source of their anger stemmed from Captain Zebulon Pike's expedition to explore the southern Louisiana Purchase. When 200 adult Osages and "a large number of children" died from "an unknown fever" in 1806, many Osages concluded that "this evil . . . was drawn upon them by Capt. Pike." Evidently discerning a general American malevolence, over the next two years some Osages proceeded to attack settlers west of St. Louis.[6]

The breakdown of relations with the Osages led U.S. officials to take a different approach to managing the zone of removal. After the Osages attacked American settlers, Meriwether Lewis, Louisiana's territorial governor, imposed a trade embargo on the Osages and urged Kickapoos, Shawnees, Delawares, Ioways, and Dakotas to attack Osage villages. He then dispatched William Clark to construct a new post, Fort Osage, on Osage lands in western Missouri, just east of present-day Kansas City. After this assertion of U.S. domination, in late 1808 Clark summoned Osage leaders to meet him at the new fort to settle recent disputes. What looked to the Osages to be a forum to restore peace was actually intended by Clark to be a mechanism to seize land. According to Clark's report, the Osages "chearfully approved" of a treaty that included a massive land cession—almost all of Missouri south of the Missouri River and almost all of Arkansas north of the Arkansas River—50,000 square miles in all. This was the largest land cession to this point in United States–Native American history. From the perspective of U.S. planners, the treaty opened up a vast territory that would accommodate the eventual removal of eastern Indians. From an Osage perspective, however, the treaty did not contain a land cession at all. Upon learning of the treaty's provisions, Osages who had signed alleged that Clark had deceived them and that they had agreed only to allow Americans hunting privileges in Osage territory. At the time Clark defended the treaty, but years later developed a bad conscience about the transaction, saying that "if he was to be damned hereafter it would be for making that treaty." This was rare admission by a U.S. official of having acted dishonorably in negotiating with Indians.[7]

U.S. officials also secured a major land cession from the Sauks and Mesquakies (Foxes). Since the Fox Wars of the 1730s, when the Sauks saved the Mesquakies from annihilation at the hands of the French and the two nations migrated west of the Mississippi into Iowa (see Chapter 1), the Sauks and Mesquakies had built themselves into a formidable nation with a population of around 6,000 in 1800. Over the course of the late eighteenth century, they had established several towns on both sides of the Mississippi, including Saukenuk, described by Jonathan Carver, a Massachusetts explorer hoping to find the Northwest Passage, as the "Great Town of the Saukies." Situated near the confluence of the Rock River and the Mississippi in western Illinois, Saukenuk's residents fished the Rock and Mississippi, kept horses on nearby prairies, raised bounteous crops, and gathered berries, nuts, and wild vegetables. From these and their other towns, the Sauks and Mesquakies controlled hunting territory in southwestern Wisconsin, eastern Iowa, and northeastern Missouri, and exchanged skins with French, British, and Spanish traders for weapons and other European manufactures. Because the Sauks and Mesquakies straddled the Mississippi River, they were both an eastern nation that from a U.S. perspective would eventually need to be moved west to accommodate American settlers, and a western nation with lands in the zone of removal that would need to be reduced to make room for eastern Indians.[8]

Just as they had with the Osages, U.S. officials seized upon a minor episode to impose a treaty on the Sauks and Mesquakies. The pretext for a council occurred in August 1804, when Sauk hunters killed four Americans in eastern Missouri. Indiana territorial governor William Henry Harrison threatened war and invited Sauk leaders to meet with him in St. Louis. The Sauks thought the purpose of this meeting was simply to negotiate a settlement for the killing of the four Americans, but Harrison asked for their assent to a treaty that ceded Sauk and Mesquakie lands on the eastern side of the Mississippi (southwestern Wisconsin, northwestern Illinois) and on the western side of the river in eastern Missouri. For the time being, Sauks and Mesquakies would be allowed to remain in Saukenuk and their other towns in western Illinois, but they would have to vacate them when the federal government sold the lands to settlers. Likely, Sauk and Mesquakie leaders who signed the treaty did so from fear of war and without realizing that the document contained a massive land cession. In any event, the majority of Sauks and Mesquakies did not regard the leaders who signed as authorized to cede tribal lands. This treaty's illegitimacy would be a source of grievance for decades.[9]

WESTERN NATIONS AND THE WAR OF 1812

The conflict between Indians and the United States that escalated in the early 1810s and folded into the War of 1812 had the potential to spread west across the Mississippi. One possibility was that Indians west of the Mississippi would join Tecumseh's resistance movement. As we saw in Chapter 5, Tecumseh attempted to enlist Osages in late 1811 or early 1812. The United States' dispossession of the Osages in 1808 created a potential basis for Osages to support Tecumseh's confederacy. But although Osages listened hard to his message, they ultimately rejected it. Likely, they perceived the United States as a potentially seriously threat down the road, but as of yet, they had not experienced the kinds of assaults that motivated Indians in the Ohio Valley and lower Great Lakes to undertake radical action. American settlers already had begun edging up the Missouri River from St. Louis, drawing nearer to Osage villages. But unlike the nations of the Ohio Valley, the Osages were not yet surrounded.[10]

Elsewhere in the region, Native nations had little experience with Americans as settlers. In the early 1810s Red Stick Creeks tried to recruit one such nation, the Kadohadacho Caddos along the Red River in southwestern Arkansas and northwestern Louisiana. The Red Sticks' failure reveals how the uneven impact of colonialism hindered the possibilities of multinational unity. The Kadohadachos were a division of the larger Caddo nation, whose territory included much of eastern Texas and southeastern Oklahoma. By the 1810s the Caddos had a long history of interaction with Europeans. In 1542, when the de Soto expedition approached their territory, the Caddos used a sophisticated system of defensive perimeters and border patrols to turn back the Spanish and avoid the destruction de Soto had visited on the southeast chiefdoms (see Chapter 1). Over the next century the Caddos developed profitable trade networks and maintained a population of at least 8,000 and probably more. From the 1690s into the early nineteenth century, however, the Caddos suffered from an average of one epidemic every fifteen years. As time went on, weakened Caddo communities were increasingly vulnerable to attacks from Wichitas, Choctaws, and Osages. Unlike the Osages, who had a reliable supply of weapons, the Caddos were frequently cut off from European suppliers. Intermarriage with Native communities and French and Spanish traders helped slow demographic decline, but the Caddos had difficulty rebuilding their numbers. By 1803, the Kadohadachos had a population of between 500 and 600; the total Caddo population was no more than 1,000.[11]

As they faced new challenges, the Caddos maintained a tradition of strong leadership. Guided by their chief Dehahuit, who impressed U.S. agent John Sibley as both "shrewd" and "sensible," the Kadohadachos seized the opportunity provided by the Louisiana Purchase to negotiate a new alliance with the United States. In 1806, as Spain and the United States tested the uncertain boundary of the Louisiana Purchase and war threatened to break out between the two empires, Dehahuit skillfully executed a series of complex negotiations. He convinced Wichitas and Comanches to join him in breaking with Spain and agreeing to a trade alliance with the United States, thus weakening Spain and putting pressure on Spain to agree with the United States to establish a neutral ground between Texas and Louisiana. Dehahuit also established relations with American traders operating out of Natchitoches on the Red River in western Louisiana. This allowed the Caddos something the Spanish had never provided: a steady supply of relatively inexpensive munitions and other European goods. When Red Stick Creeks visited the Kadohadachos in the early 1810s, they found a nation that regarded Americans as allies.[12]

Although there was little support for Tecumseh's confederation west of the Mississippi, the outbreak of war between the United States and Great Britain in 1812 encouraged some Native nations to attack U.S. positions and American settlements west of the Mississippi. In summer 1813, Sauks and Ho-Chunks laid siege to Fort Madison on the Iowa bank of the Mississippi, forcing Americans to abandon it. Indians also raided settlements in the Boone's Lick area in central Missouri, killing some settlers and causing many to seek safety within the walls of newly constructed blockhouses or by fleeing back east. Stretched thin militarily, officials in Washington, D.C., rejected Missourians' pleas for troops to augment the small number of regulars in Missouri Territory and instead authorized local militias and rangers. When Missouri officials were unable to raise a strong militia, William Clark urged Osages to "wage war on the Mississippi Indians" and used the promise of American goods to relocate several hundred Sauks and Mesquakies leery of Sauk militants to central Missouri as a buffer against ongoing raids. This community would eventually become known as the Sauk and Mesquakies of Missouri.[13]

As Indians continued to threaten Missouri settlements, Clark tried new approaches. In spring 1814, he attempted to choke off the supply of British weapons by taking control of the strategic point of Prairie du Chien near the confluence of the Mississippi and Wisconsin rivers in present-day southern

Wisconsin. Clark briefly captured Prairie du Chien, but the British soon drove U.S. forces back to St. Louis. After the signing of the Treaty of Ghent between the United States and Great Britain in December, ending the War of 1812, Indians had reduced access to British arms, but they nonetheless continued to attack vulnerable American settlements well into 1815. In April Clark summoned representatives from several Indian nations of the upper Mississippi to meet him at Portage des Sioux just north of St. Louis that summer. In a rarely noted example of U.S. gunboat diplomacy, Clark arranged for the presence of 200 troops and two gunboats, thus reinforcing the message he conveyed to the assembled leaders: "say you wish for war, and we are ready; say you wish for peace and it shall be so." Most leaders in attendance signed treaties of peace and friendship. These treaties did not cede land, but they required acknowledgment of previous land cessions and bound Indians to a U.S. alliance, which would be defined on American terms in future years. Clark was particularly concerned about Black Hawk's continued opposition to the legitimacy of the 1804 treaty. When Black Hawk and other Sauks refused to visit Portage des Sioux, Clark took some Sauks at the council hostage to use as leverage and began to construct a new fort—Fort Armstrong—near the Sauks' main village of Saukenuk on the Rock River. In May 1816 Black Hawk traveled to St. Louis and signed a treaty that confirmed the land cession of 1804. Even so, Black Hawk later claimed that when he "touched the goose quill" he did so "not knowing . . . that . . . I consented to give away my village. Had that been explained to me, I should have opposed it." Did Clark deceive Black Hawk by concealing the terms of the 1816 treaty? The documentary record does not say. At the very least, Clark used strong-arm tactics to secure compliance.[14]

Indians who contested American settlement in Missouri during the War of 1812 did not suffer major losses. Unlike confederationists in the Ohio Valley or Red Sticks in the South, anti-American Indians west of the Mississippi often had the upper hand and probably experienced fewer casualties than American settlers and soldiers.[15] Western Indians controlled significant territory, allowing them freedom to conduct military operations and to hunt for subsistence and trade. They were able to obtain arms and ammunition without being overly dependent on external aid. More significant, they operated in an environment of U.S. weakness as measured by a relatively small settler population and limited military resources. Not one of their villages was burned, nor did they lose territory.

Nor did other Indians west of the Mississippi experience serious losses during these years. In Minnesota, Dakotas and Ojibwes had strong ties to

British traders, but they tried to stay out of the fighting. When British agents sent wampum belts to recruit a band of northern Minnesota Ojibwes at Leech Lake, known as The Pillagers for their fierceness in war, their leader, Flat Mouth, returned the belts with the message: "When I go [to] war against my enemies, I do not call on the whites to join my warriors. The white people have quarrelled among themselves, and I do not wish to meddle in their quarrels." Similarly, only a few Dakotas were willing to take up arms for the British. At times during the War of 1812, British traders were unable to supply Indians in the Minnesota area and caused some hardship. Lacking ammunition and powder to hunt, Dakotas were reportedly "dying with hunger" in the winter of 1814–1815. Nonetheless, the impact of the War of 1812 on Dakotas and Ojibwes was relatively light. To the south in Arkansas and Louisiana, Indians were far from British trade and diplomatic networks and so largely unaffected by the war. In 1814, when the prospect of a British invasion of New Orleans arose, Caddos offered military assistance to the Americans. But before Caddos could be mobilized, the United States defeated British forces in the Battle of New Orleans in January.[16]

AN INVASION OF AMERICAN SETTLERS AND EASTERN INDIANS

From 1815 to 1819 more people crossed the Mississippi River than during any other half decade to that point in human history. The War of 1812 had acted as a brake on American settlement west of the Mississippi, but the war's end allowed for an unprecedented population boom, part of the larger settler explosion throughout the trans-Appalachian West. In 1812, the non-Indian population (including enslaved people) of Missouri Territory was around 20,000. By 1820, this number had more than tripled, leading to the creation of a separate Arkansas Territory in 1819 and Missouri statehood two years later.[17]

A significant number of eastern Indians also moved west after 1815. The largest group of Native immigrants were Cherokees. In the early 1810s, there were approximately 1,000 Cherokees in Missouri Territory, most living near the St. Francis River in northeastern Arkansas and Missouri. After 1815, the number of western Cherokees rose considerably. By the early 1820s, there were between 4,000 and 6,000 Cherokees west of the Mississippi, almost all of them living on lands in Arkansas reserved through treaties in 1817 and 1819 (Fig. 27). These new Cherokee lands were carved from those the Osages

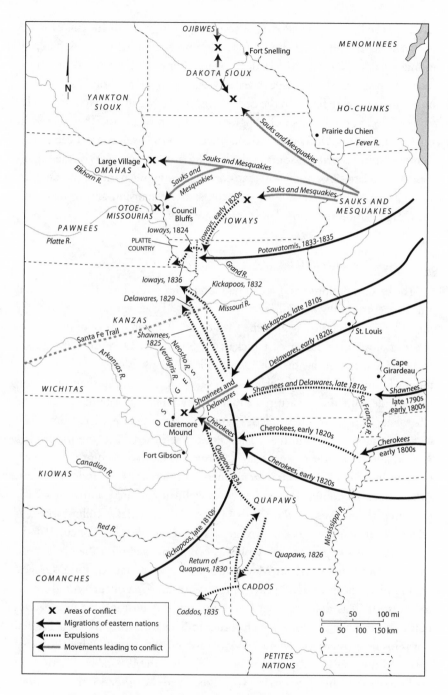

Fig. 27. Migrations, conflicts, and expulsions in the eastern Louisiana Purchase, 1815–1830s (dashed lines indicate modern state boundaries)

had supposedly ceded in 1808. The second largest group of Indians crossing
the Mississippi were Kickapoos. After signing a removal treaty in 1818, an
estimated 1,600 Kickapoos left Indiana and Illinois. Most settled on a new
reservation south of the Osage River in western Missouri, though some went
on to Arkansas and Texas. In the early 1820s, the arrival of close to 1,300 Delawares added to the number of emigrant Indians in Missouri. They settled in
the Ozarks among Delawares and Shawnees who themselves had been forced
to move from eastern Missouri in the late 1810s as white settlers pushed them
west. In the late 1810s and early 1820s, eastern emigrant nations, over 10,000
strong, formed an alliance both to check settler expansion and to drive out
the Osage Nation on whose lands they were living.[18]

THE DECLINE OF OSAGE POWER

The eastern nations and Osages had fought for years, but violence reached
a new level in 1817, when Cherokees organized a large war party (small army
might be a better term) against the Osages. In October, a force of 600 Cherokees, along with Choctaws, Chickasaws, Shawnees, Delawares, Quapaws,
and Caddos, moved against an Osage village led by Clermont II at Claremore Mound (present-day northeastern Oklahoma). Timing their operation
to coincide with the departure of many Osage men for a buffalo hunt, the
Cherokees and their allies killed a reported thirty-eight Osages, almost all
women, children, and old men. They also burned the village and its supplies
of food and took over 100 captives. Cherokees followed up on this massacre
by appealing to U.S. officials to grant them additional Osage lands in western
Arkansas. In so doing, they argued for a right of conquest and strategically
presented themselves, in the words of one of their chiefs, Tolluntuskee, as
"civilized" in contrast to the "savage," "barbarous," "rude," "uncultivated,"
and "childish" Osages. Secretary of War Calhoun sided with the Cherokees,
advising Governor Clark in May 1818 that "it seems fair that the Osages,
who . . . have been beaten in the contest" with the Cherokees, cede the contested lands. It is doubtful that Calhoun took this position because he was
persuaded that the Cherokees or any other Indians were truly civilized. Rather,
it was his investment in making the West attractive to eastern Cherokees that
governed his decision. As he explained to Clark, "the President is anxious to
hold out every inducement to the Cherokees, and the other Southern nations
of Indians, to emigrate to the West of the Mississippi."[19]

To counter Cherokee aggression, in the summer of 1818 Osages invited Shawnees, Delawares, Quapaws, Kanzas, and Mesquakies to join an anti-Cherokee alliance, making a gift of 100 horses. But the Osages had been at odds with these nations for decades or more. In the words of a historian of the region, "the gift of 100 horses could not erase 100 years of Osage aggression." Later that year, at a meeting with U.S. officials and Cherokee representatives in St. Louis, Osages and Cherokees agreed to peace, but clashes resumed. Most of these resulted in minimal casualties, but in late 1821 a Cherokee attack on an Osage hunting camp resulted in the deaths of a reported forty-one Osages, including twenty-nine women and children—the second Cherokee massacre of Osages in five years. Osages also suffered losses on the Plains to the west, where for decades they had hunted buffalo and contended with Comanches, Kiowas, Wichitas, and Pawnees. In April 1818, Pawnees annihilated forty-eight Osage hunters; five years later, Comanches reportedly killed "Twenty or Twenty five Osage Warriors."[20]

U.S. officials did little to halt violence between the Osages and other Indigenous peoples. It was another matter when Americans were involved, as became clear in 1823 when Osages targeted a party of white hunters trespassing on Osage lands. The Osages "rushed upon them and butchered them, cutting off their heads & Sticking them on poles on the prairie." In response, the government established a post (eventually named Fort Gibson) in the heart of Osage country near the Three Forks of the Arkansas River (present-day eastern Oklahoma). With U.S. troops now entrenched in their lands, in 1825 Osage leaders Clermont II and Pawhuska agreed to cede all of their remaining lands in Arkansas and Missouri as well as lands in Oklahoma. In exchange, the U.S. granted them a fifty-mile-wide strip of land in southern Kansas. In just seventeen years one of the midcontinent's most powerful Indian nations had been dispossessed of almost all of their lands.[21]

According to U.S. planners, the Osages were supposed to move immediately to Kansas. This would free up their northeastern Oklahoma lands so that Arkansas Cherokees could move there. But the Osages refused to move to Kansas, and so when the Arkansas Cherokees took up residence in northeastern Oklahoma, Osages clashed with them. Hemmed in from the east, the Osages increasingly looked to the hunting grounds of the Plains. This meant new confrontations with Pawnees and other Plains nations. Osage women continued to plant and harvest crops along the rivers, though they increasingly traveled with male hunting parties to avoid being slaughtered by

their enemies in unprotected villages. Although generally at odds with eastern
Indians, Osages cultivated new allies when possible, as when Clermont II arranged to have one of his daughters marry into a community of Creeks who
settled near his village in the late 1820s.[22]

Despite their efforts to retain a position of strength, basic dynamics at
work for years took their toll on Osage fortunes. The number of eastern Indians continued to increase; the number of white settlers continued to increase;
competition for land and game remained intense; sporadic violence between
Osages and other tribes persisted; and peace efforts continued to fail. During
the winter of 1830–1831—just months after President Andrew Jackson signed
the Indian Removal Act—Osages were unable to find enough game to support themselves and were forced to kill cattle and hogs belonging to Cherokees and Creeks in nearby villages.[23] It would be another eight years before
Osages, finding themselves at the end of the Cherokee Trail of Tears, would
finally abandon their villages in northeastern Oklahoma and rebuild them
in Kansas. Already, though, they had experienced destructive impacts from
U.S. policies and actions that promoted the migration of eastern Indians and
American settlers.

THE QUAPAW TRAIL OF TEARS

Most Indian nations west of the Mississippi in the path of eastern Indians
did not take the Osage approach of aggressively defending their lands. Like
the Caddos, the Quapaws had lost a substantial portion of their population
since the late seventeenth century. Located on the lower Arkansas River, the
Quapaws were within reach of Chickasaws to the east, who raided Quapaws
for captives to be sold to English enslavers operating out of South Carolina
(see Chapter 1). This had a negative impact on the Quapaw population, but
it was the smallpox virus, which in 1698 reached the Quapaws from the east
across networks of violence and disruption created by the slave trade, that
was so devastating. In 1700 the Quapaws numbered 2,000, down from 5,000
twenty years before. Over the next century, Quapaws cultivated an alliance
with the French and tried to do the same with the Spanish after 1763, before
establishing peace with Chickasaws and so facilitating better relationships
with English traders. The Quapaws also added to their numbers and reproductive capacities by incorporating indentured servants, accused criminals,
and African slaves escaping from French Louisiana. Nonetheless, the Qua-

paws suffered additional epidemics in 1747 and 1751. Osage raids, which increased in the late 1700s, also took lives. By 1805, the Quapaw population had fallen to around 600.[24]

Given their relatively small numbers (one-tenth the Osage population), the Quapaws saw immigrant Indians as a potential source of strength. To rebuild their numbers, Quapaws intermarried with newly arrived Choctaws in the 1790s. In the first decade of the nineteenth century, Quapaws invited Cherokees moving west to settle among them to provide a buffer against the Osages. As western Cherokee numbers increased, Quapaws solidified an alliance with them, providing support for military expeditions against the Osages. Quapaws took a similar accommodating stance toward American settlement. Just after the Louisiana Purchase Quapaws proposed selling some of their lands to the United States in exchange for a promise "that the powerful arm of the U.S. will defend us their children in the possession of the remainder of our hunting grounds." Although nothing came of this, Quapaws continued to be willing to negotiate with the United States. In 1816, when William Clark invited Quapaws and Cherokees to St. Louis, Quapaws expressed willingness to allow non-Indians to settle on a portion of their lands in exchange for livestock and farm equipment. This would allow them to make a modest economic transition on the model of their Cherokee neighbors.[25]

Under most circumstances, Clark would have eagerly embraced the Quapaws' offer. In this case, however, he was trapped by contradictions in U.S. policy. Since accepting a Quapaw land cession meant encouraging permanent white settlement in Arkansas (at this point still part of Missouri Territory), and since this was at odds with the government's desire to reserve these lands for southern Indians, Clark could not accept the Quapaw proposal. Under pressure from the Missouri territorial legislature, however, federal officials soon decided they would have to tolerate American settlement in some areas in Arkansas while proceeding with plans to relocate Indians from the Southeast to other areas of Arkansas. In the meantime, in July 1818, Clark again summoned Quapaws to St. Louis. This time the negotiations resulted in a treaty by which the Quapaws ceded much of present-day southern Oklahoma and almost all of present-day Arkansas south of the Arkansas River—a total of 47,000 square miles—while retaining hunting rights throughout the ceded territory and a small reservation south of the Arkansas River. By all accounts, the Quapaws regarded the 1818 treaty favorably. Not only had they retained their hunting rights to the ceded lands and reserved the lands around their villages, the treaty's provision of an annuity in the amount of $1,000 was considerable. In comparison, the annuity in the 1808 Osage Treaty was $1,500, but this went to a nation of several thousand, not several hundred.[26]

As word of this treaty reached Arkansas citizens, they immediately protested to Congress against "unnecessarily lavishing large Portions of Public and Private property on Savages." Once Arkansas Territory was organized in 1819, the territorial legislature notified President James Monroe that the people it represented believed the Quapaws must relinquish all but twelve of the 3,100 square miles they had reserved in the 1818 treaty. For the next few years territorial officials waged a deceitful campaign to create the impression that Quapaws were eager to depart Arkansas and live among the Kadohadacho Caddos in northwestern Louisiana. But in 1824, when the United States attempted to negotiate a new treaty, Quapaws made it clear that they had never expressed a desire to move to Caddo country and wished to remain near the burial grounds of their ancestors. "Since you have expressed a desire for us to remove," chief Hecaton told Acting Governor Robert Crittenden, "the tears have flowed copiously from my aged eyes." Nonetheless, Crittenden insisted the Quapaws sign a treaty obligating them to relocate to Caddo country and so they did. In early January 1826 a reported 455 Quapaws left for the Red River in northwestern Louisiana, arriving there by mid-February.[27]

Four years before the Indian Removal Act, the Quapaws embarked on what would become known as the Quapaw Trail of Tears. Although few died during their journey, within months of their arrival on the Red River, Quapaws were mourning the loss of sixty who reportedly starved when floods wiped out newly planted crops. Soon after, a portion of the Quapaws returned to Arkansas, where they cultivated small fields and picked cotton on nearby plantations. Although poor and, according to U.S. law, squatters on their own lands, they at least were home, and their situation was better than that of tribal members who remained in Louisiana, where Red River floods continued to destroy their crops. By late 1830, all of the Quapaws had returned to Arkansas. In December Hecaton traveled to Washington to appeal to President Jackson and Secretary of War John Eaton to allow the Quapaws to take up a small tract of land in Arkansas. But Arkansas' burgeoning settler population opposed allowing Quapaws even a sliver of their homeland. If the sovereign states of Georgia and Alabama had the right to be free of Indians, should not the soon-to-be sovereign state of Arkansas have the same right? Although Quapaws battled a second removal, by 1834 they had again been forced out. Most eventually resettled on a small reservation in the northeastern corner of Oklahoma. A few sought to remake their lives outside U.S. borders among Cherokees in Texas.[28]

THE CADDO EXPULSION AND THE PETITES NATIONS

The Kadohadacho Caddos, a small nation like the Quapaws took a similar approach toward eastern Indians. When Choctaws, Kickapoos, Delawares, Shawnees, and Cherokees began arriving in the Louisiana-Texas-Arkansas borderlands in the 1810s, Caddos generally welcomed them as allies against the Osages. In turn, the newcomers considered the Caddos of the Red River "the mother nation of the country," according them "a general superintendence over all the tribes in the vicinity." As the number of immigrant Indians grew, however, tensions arose. Cherokees increasingly asserted their authority as the leading Indian nation in a region in flux as Mexico became independent from Spain in 1821. There were also sporadic raids between Caddos and nearby Choctaw and Cherokee communities. The greatest threat to Caddos, however, was from a growing number of American planters and small farmers attracted by the promise of fertile lands along the Red River. Caddos also suffered from a scourge of unlicensed traders bringing liquor to exchange for skins in violation of U.S. trade and intercourse laws. The Caddos' chief, Dehahuit, tried to combat these twin evils. He authorized raids against settlers' horses and hogs and requested the U.S. agent at Natchitoches to arrest whiskey traders. Although U.S. officials occasionally authorized force to remove squatters from Caddo land and tried to check the flow of alcohol, the resources devoted to such efforts fell well short of what was needed.[29]

By the early 1830s, the autonomy the Caddos had possessed at the time of the Neutral Ground agreement a generation earlier had seriously eroded. Historians of the Caddos have noted that the death of their longtime chief Dehahuit in 1833 left them with weak leadership. But even Dehahuit probably could not have preserved Caddo communities in Louisiana. In the same year he died, the U.S. Army Corps of Engineers began using a steamboat to remove logs from the Red River Raft, an enormous logjam dozens of miles long that blocked navigation of the river, thus promising speculators, small farmers, and large planters greater access to Caddo lands. Two years later, a U.S. commission informed Caddos that they had no choice but to sell their lands; otherwise, they would be at the mercy of squatters. Although many Caddos were reluctant to sign a treaty, one of their new leaders, Tarshar, urged his people, since they were "starving in the midst of this land," to "get all we can for [our land], and not wait till the white man steals it away, little by little, and then gives us nothing." He and twenty-four other headmen signed the treaty. A few months later, Caddos relocated west of the Louisiana–Texas border. But even as they left the United States, the forces that had compelled the Caddos' expulsion were already operating in Texas as Anglo Americans were about to win independence from Mexico. Not for the last time had Americans asked Caddo people to go away.[30]

Perhaps surprisingly, the Caddos were the only Indian nation removed from Louisiana. Although Secretary of War Calhoun predicted in 1825 that all Louisiana Indians would be relocated, neither the federal government nor the state of Louisiana made much of an effort to drive Indians from the state. The reason, it seems, is that because the bulk of Louisiana's Native population—called by the French the *petites nations,* with a total population of around 1,000—lived in small communities in isolated areas with little land, they were in a sense invisible to the much larger non-Native population. The demographic disparity between non-Indians and Indians in Louisiana, in other words, paradoxically afforded some protection for Indians there. Although not forced from their homes, Louisiana Indians faced a loss of resources and increasing restrictions on their freedom of movement in the first decades of the nineteenth century. Even the limited land they possessed was threatened. In 1826, for example, when Tunicas protested against a squatter who claimed title to a tract of their land, Louisiana's land office ruled against them on the grounds that they "have not been reclaimed from their savage mode of life." Despite such setbacks, through a strategy of economic flexibility and diversification—planting crops, hunting when they could for trade and subsistence, picking cotton, driving cattle, and making baskets for sale in New Orleans markets—Louisiana's Indian people have been able to continue living in their homelands to the present day.[31]

INTERTRIBAL WAR IN THE NORTH

In the northeastern areas of the Louisiana Purchase (what would become Iowa and Minnesota), Native communities were not in the path of Indians immigrating from the East. Most eastern Indians who moved west voluntarily in the late 1700s and early 1800s chose locations south of the Missouri River, partly because of Spanish encouragement, partly because of proximity, and partly because the climate was better for growing crops. When U.S. officials began encouraging individual nations to move west and envisioning wholesale removal in the future, they generally focused on lands south of Iowa. This meant that Ioways, Sauks and Mesquakies, Dakotas, and Ojibwes did not experience conflict with immigrant nations. Nor, with a few exceptions, were they in the way of American settlers. Nonetheless, U.S. expansion after 1815 affected people indigenous to this area in two related ways. First, the population explosion in Ohio, Indiana, and Illinois reduced Indian hunting grounds in the Ohio Valley and so led Sauks and Mesquakies to continue an earlier reorientation of their commercial horizons toward the West and Northwest. Sauk and Mesquakie hunters regularly traveled as far as 300 miles in search of pelts. As they did, they intruded on hunting grounds claimed by other nations. Second, the development of a highly competitive American fur trade in the upper Mississippi aggravated the already existing problem of overhunting and increased the flow of alcohol into the region. All told, as Native people in this region competed for diminishing resources, the result was an increase in intertribal war. War was fueled by cycles of revenge, though its underlying logic involved control of territory and resources.[32]

Sauk and Mesquakie expansion was a particularly potent source of conflict. Smaller nations to the west were particularly vulnerable. In the 1820s the Ioways had a population of between 1,000 and 1,500, about the same as it had been in the mid-1760s. Sauks and Mesquakies had generally been at peace with the Ioways, but Sauk and Mesquakie raids forced the Ioways to relocate their villages to the west along the Missouri River near Council Bluffs and south from there into the Grand River area of northwest Missouri. Seeking to enter the bison-robe trade on the Great Plains, Sauk and Mesquakie fighters also struck Omahas in northeastern Nebraska. The Omahas numbered as many as 2,800 in the 1770s, but smallpox epidemics, one in the early 1780s, the other in 1800–1801, reduced their population to an estimated 900 in 1803. In the first two decades of the nineteenth century, the Omahas rebuilt their population to as many as 2,000. But they were vulnerable to the larger Sauks and Mesquakies, who in 1820 destroyed their major town, known as Large Village. This was the first of many Sauk and Mesquakie attacks on Omahas during the 1820s. Sauks and Mesquakies also fought with the Dakotas (eastern or Santee Sioux), a nation similar in size to their own with a population of at least 6,000 in the 1820s. Warfare between these nations was particularly intense in northern Iowa and southern Minnesota, an area where game was more plentiful than elsewhere. Every year, Black Hawk recalled, when the corn was "about knee-high, all our young men would start in a direction towards sun-down, to hunt deer and buffalo—being prepared, also, to kill [Dakota] Sioux, if any are found on our hunting grounds." In 1822 alone there were a reported 100 casualties in fighting between Sauks and Mesquakies and Dakotas.[33]

Against a backdrop of increasing intertribal warfare, in 1825 Lewis Cass, governor of Michigan Territory (which at the time included Wisconsin), and William Clark summoned the nations of the upper Mississippi and western Great Lakes to a peace conference at Prairie du Chien. U.S. treaty commissioners did not ask for land cessions. Rather, they required the nations to sign a treaty defining tribal territories on the theory that this would eliminate conflict. After the conference, U.S. officials trumpeted its success. The resulting treaties, Superintendent of Indian Affairs Thomas McKenney reported, would bring to an end their "long and bloody wars." Indians, however, were less sanguine. Noodin, an Ojibwe leader, whose people were often at war with Dakotas, assured the treaty commissioners that he, too, desired peace but that "in running marks around our country . . . it may make new disturbances or breed new wars." Other Indians attributed dark motives to the treaty commissioners. As they returned home from Prairie du Chien, some Dakotas and Menominees fell ill and died, leading them to conclude that the Americans had "poisoned" them. Such an interpretation reflected deep unease about what had transpired on the treaty grounds.[34]

In writing about this council two years later, Cass advanced a humanitarian interpretation of U.S. intentions. Cass began by arguing that the only reason for warfare between Indians in the region was "the thirst of revenge, and the necessity of having some enemy, from whom trophies of victory might be won." From this premise—that intertribal warfare was the product of a savage mentality that locked Indians into an endless cycle of purposeless violence—civilization had a clear duty to intervene. Unless the United States was able to "conclude a peace among them," the contending nations were sure to "vanish as the snow melts before the sunbeam," Cass wrote. Perhaps Cass was sincere in his expression of concern for Indians, though his concern's dependence on the construction of its object as a racial inferior—bloodthirsty and irrational—should caution against simply accepting his evaluation of himself as motivated by humanitarianism. The treaty Cass negotiated at Prairie du Chien was more than a peace treaty. In addition to setting firm territorial boundaries, the treaty required Indians to "acknowledge the general controlling power of the United States," a clear assertion of U.S. sovereignty over Native nations that established a basis for their eventual dispossession.[35]

It quickly became apparent that the Prairie du Chien Treaty did not address the underlying cause of war: increasing competition for shrinking hunting areas that were becoming less productive. This dynamic was exacerbated by the abolition of a system of government-run trading posts (known at the time as factories) in 1822, largely as a result of lobbying from John Jacob Astor's American Fur Company. The company intended to replace a government monopoly with its own private monopoly, but instead it opened the door for multiple American traders and firms, all cajoling Indian hunters to supply pelts. At one level, of course, Indians wanted traders, but they were aware, as the Dakota Black Eagle put it, that in order to "get skins," the traders "wish to push us into the Jaws of our enemies." So, violence continued in the form of retaliatory raids and murders. Two years after the Prairie du Chien Treaty, Dakotas fired into an encampment of Ojibwes just outside Fort Snelling (present-day Minneapolis). Two years later, Sauks and Mesquakies decapitated a Dakota woman, igniting a new round of attacks lasting throughout the summer and leaving many dead. In May of the following year, a party of Dakotas, Menominees, and Ho-Chunks fell upon seventeen Mesquakies and took the lives of all but one. To avenge this attack, Mesquakies and Sauks attacked a party of Dakotas, killing twelve, including women and children. In the midst of this violence, in 1830 William Clark called upon the region's Indians to gather once again at Prairie du Chien. To end conflict, Clark gained Sauk/Mesquakie and Dakota assent to land cessions in northeastern Iowa that would create a neutral ground as a buffer between those two nations. Clark also took the occasion to ask Sauks and Mesquakies to cede additional territory having nothing to do with the main agenda of ending the cycle of war. These were lands containing valuable lead deposits on the west side of the Mississippi near present-day Dubuque, Iowa. Although Clark backed off in the face of Sauk and Mesquakie insistence for a higher price than Clark was authorized to pay, this reprieve was only temporary. Two years later, in the aftermath of the Black Hawk War (to be discussed in Chapter 9), Sauks and Mesquakies would be dispossessed of these and other eastern Iowa lands.[36]

EXPULSIONS FROM MISSOURI: IOWAYS, SHAWNEES, DELAWARES, AND KICKAPOOS

As Sauks and Mesquakies sought to hold their lands, the Ioways they had forced into the Grand River area of northwestern Missouri were struggling to find a permanent home. This time, the main threat to the Ioways was from American settlers. In the early 1820s Missouri citizens began agitating for the removal of all Indians from their newly established state. Against this background, Ioway leaders White Cloud and Hard Heart signed a treaty in 1824 relinquishing their claims to lands in Missouri north of the Missouri River and agreeing to relocate along with the small Sauk and Mesquakie community that had moved to Missouri during the War of 1812. Their destination was an area known as the Platte country, just west of Grand River. The Platte country today forms the northwestern corner of Missouri but was not part of the state in 1824. Predictably enough, squatters showed little regard for lines drawn in Washington and so began taking up Platte country lands. Equally predictably, Missouri politicians agitated to redraw the state's boundaries to include the Platte country and send the Ioways elsewhere. In 1830, at Prairie du Chien, Ioways and the Sauks and Mesquakies of Missouri agreed to cede claims to the Platte country along with a good chunk of western Iowa, though they were not required to move until new lands were set aside for them. By this time, Ioways were impoverished. Game in the region had declined, making it impossible for Ioways to adequately feed themselves and purchase needed manufactured goods. The Ioways had an annuity from the 1824 treaty, but most of it went into the coffers of the American Fur Company to satisfy that company's claims to Ioway debt. At the same time, what furs Ioways could obtain were increasingly exchanged for alcohol.[37]

To add to the Ioways' problems, as we will see in Chapter 9, several hundred Potawatomis, removed from their homes in the lower Great Lakes region, arrived in the Platte country between 1833 and 1835. For the Ioways, the arrival of 250 additional Potawatomis meant a drain on already scarce resources. Because of this, and to replenish their annuity, in 1836 Ioways agreed to relocate to the Great Nemaha reservation, a small tract just on the other side of the Missouri River in the southeastern corner of present-day Nebraska. Although relocating to the Great Nehama reservation would require traveling only a few dozen miles at most, Ioways had grown weary of constantly building new communities only to have to abandon them. Hoping against hope, in late December 1836 they petitioned President Andrew Jackson to allow them to return to their village on the Des Moines River in Iowa, where lay the "bones of their fathers." In the end, however, officials ignored their appeal. Since the time of Thomas Jefferson, Americans who envisioned and planned policies for U.S. expansion had seen the Ioway Nation, when they saw them at all, as little more than an inconvenient nuisance, a problem to manage. Anticipating the creation of new state named after the dispossessed Ioway Nation, they were not about to allow them to live there, and so by the late 1830s, the Ioways had been squeezed into southeastern Nebraska. In less than two decades, indirect and direct consequences of U.S. expansion had forced them to uproot their communities at least three times (Fig. 28).[38]

Fig. 28. How would Ioways survive after multiple removals had impoverished them? In the early 1840s, Strutting Pigeon and her husband traveled to Europe with other Ioways to perform for audiences willing to pay to see exotic American Indians before they disappeared. While in London in 1844, Strutting Pigeon and her child sat for this portrait by American artist George Catlin, who accompanied the Ioways during a portion of their travels. *Strutting Pigeon, Wife of White Cloud.* Smithsonian American Art Museum. Photo credit: Smithsonian American Art Museum, Washington, D.C./Art Resource, N.Y.

Even as Missourians attempted to expel Ioways from within their boundaries, they also demanded the elimination of Shawnees, Delawares, and Kickapoos who had earlier migrated to the southwestern part of the state. In 1825, scarcely two decades after Jefferson imagined Missouri as part of the zone of removal, William Clark convinced Shawnees to sign a treaty moving them to a small reservation along the Kansas River in eastern Kansas. This treaty also envisioned that Shawnees still in the East would eventually relocate to this reservation. Four years later, Delawares, plagued by poor hunting and their crops destroyed by floods, accepted a new reservation in eastern Kansas just north of the new Shawnee reserve. Kickapoos held out until 1832 when they, too, signed a treaty moving them to a reservation in eastern Kansas just north of the Delaware reserve (although most went to Texas).[39] For decades, with varying degrees of consent, these communities had been moving west in advance of European American expansion. Would they ever have a permanent home?

REVERBERATIONS: KANZAS AND OMAHAS

The new Ioway, Shawnee, Delaware, and Kickapoo reservations in eastern Nebraska and Kansas were not created from empty wilderness. Like everywhere in North America, what would eventually become Nebraska and Kansas was Indian country, too.

One of the nations the federal government targeted to accommodate Indians being shoved out of Missouri was the Kanzas. Since the mid-1700s, the Kanzas had maintained a stable population of around 1,500. By the mid-1820s, they were experiencing a set of problems common to many Native communities in the region: competitive conflict with other Indians (Sauks and Mesquakies from the northeast and Pawnees to the west), declining game, and incursions from settlers coming up the Missouri (Fig. 29). In 1825, for an annuity of $3,500 for twenty years, the Kanza Nation relinquished its claims to lands in northwestern Missouri and a portion of its Kansas lands. The Kanzas had not been asked to leave their homeland but they were losing their political autonomy, their leaders were quarreling over annuity distributions, they were being gouged by traders, and they were suffering from disease and material deprivation. In 1827 Kanzas lost a reported 180 to an unidentified "malignant disease." Another 300 died when smallpox broke out along the Missouri River in 1831–1832. Remarkably, the Kanza population recovered from these losses and was reported to be 1,471 in 1837. Even so, the

Kanzas were on the precipice of crisis. A government agent reported in 1835 that the Kanzas "had less than twenty bushels of corn and were begging at the settlements or trying to trade a few lengths of elk string for food." Although the forces of destruction affecting the Kanzas were not directly related to American settlement on their actual lands, they were clearly related to indirect effects of settlement elsewhere, as declining hunting grounds and settler pressures forced eastern nations west into their territory. Their situation again reveals how U.S. expansion in the East reverberated far to the west.[40]

Up the Missouri River Valley, Omahas also suffered a decline in their conditions of life in the 1820s and early 1830s. In this area, there was especially intense cutthroat competition among Jacksonian-era "expectant capitalists" to use cheap, addictive whiskey to acquire pelts. The center of trade in the area,

Fig. 29. Sometime before 1820 a party of Kanzas attempted to raid a Pawnee village (likely in central Nebraska). Pawnees intercepted the Kanzas and, according to Parks, *Darkest Period,* 27, killed the eighteen raiders. This sketch of a Pawnee bison robe documents this event and illustrates intertribal violence in the borderlands between the Missouri River and the Great Lakes. The watercolor by Samuel Seymour II was painted in 1819–1820. Beinecke Rare Book and Manuscript Library, Yale University.

Council Bluffs , became known as the "whiskey capital of the West." Alcohol abuse fueled violence (including domestic violence), discouraged constructive labor, and contributed to malnutrition. At the same time, Omahas were losing their economic self-sufficiency. After Sauks and Mesquakies destroyed Large Village in 1820 (see above), Omahas established a new town about fifty miles to the southwest on the Elkhorn River, but this area was marginal for farming. The Omahas tried to take advantage of productive hunting grounds on the plains to the northwest, but the more powerful Yankton Sioux and Sicangu Lakota Sioux blocked them. The result was that Omahas were "stalked by the specter of famine" and, like the Kanzas, were vulnerable when the smallpox virus appeared in 1831–1832. Omahas had not been conquered by a U.S. army, nor had they been forced into signing a treaty ceding their lands. Nonetheless, by pushing other Indian nations west and facilitating a destructive trade in alcohol, U.S. expansion had inflicted great damage.[41]

INDIANS WEST OF THE MISSISSIPPI AROUND 1830

Well before 1830, when the United States adopted a formal policy of moving eastern Indians west, Indians west of the Mississippi had already experienced substantial impacts from U.S. expansion. Delawares, Shawnees, Kickapoos, and Cherokees, who had migrated to Missouri and Arkansas, had been kicked west to Kansas and Oklahoma to make room for white settlers and the enslaved people many brought with them. In turn, Native nations indigenous to the eastern Louisiana Purchase had experienced intertribal violence, dispossession, an erosion of political independence, and a decline in material conditions.

A few nations in the region suffered significant population losses during this period. Through a combination of material deprivation and smallpox and other diseases (including alcoholism), the Omaha population, around 2,000 in 1820, fell to 1,400 in the early 1830s. For similar reasons, the Otoe-Missourias, a nation of around 1,200 people in the 1820s living south of the Omahas on the Missouri River, were reduced to a reported 964 in 1835. Much of the destruction visited on the Omahas and Otoe-Missourias might be attributed solely to the agency of microbes and so explained as a tragic "accident." Against such a view, Isaac McCoy, a Baptist missionary at the time, contended that the smallpox epidemic that afflicted the Omahas and Otoe-Missourias in 1831–1832 was caused by American traders who wanted to destroy Comanches and Pawnees who had been attacking caravans on the

Santa Fe Trail. According to McCoy, an unnamed "man of veracity" told him that traders "brought from the white settlements the virus of smallpox; that they designed to communicate it on a present of tobacco to Indians . . . or an infected article of clothing might be left on the prairies, in a situation to be found by an Indian." Although there is no reason to think that McCoy made up this story, it seems unlikely that the means of infection he outlined would have been effective. But even if this epidemic was not intentionally caused, the outbreak was nonetheless related to social conditions. Both the Omahas and Otoe-Missourias had been exposed to smallpox earlier, and so the 1831–1832 epidemic was not a virgin soil epidemic. Rather, because they were experiencing severe social stress and material deprivation, the bodies of Omahas and Otoe-Missourias were especially vulnerable to the virus. As such, the severity of the 1831–1832 epidemic can be traced to indirect effects of U.S. expansion.[42]

Most nations with lands west of the Mississippi did not suffer serious population losses during this period. Given the hardships many endured, this is perhaps surprising and testifies to the resiliency of Native communities. The Quapaws were shoved from their lands and lost people to starvation in a precarious environment, but their population remained stable at just under 500 from the early 1800s into the 1830s. Nor did the Osages see their population fall. Although they lost 200 or more to disease in 1806 and suffered from dysentery, influenza, and smallpox in the late 1820s, they were unscathed by the smallpox epidemic of 1831–1832 (probably because they were not exposed). In fact, given the intensity of Osage war with other Indian nations, it is quite possible that the death toll from intertribal conflict (well into the hundreds) exceeded that from disease during this period. Whatever the ratio, Osage losses in war and from disease were not high enough to prevent them from maintaining a stable population of 5,000–6,000 from 1803 into the 1830s. Indeed, according to the naturalist Thomas Nuttall, Osages prided themselves on "hav[ing] maintained their usual population" even though they were "surrounded by so many enemies." The available evidence indicates that the Kadohadacho Caddo population also remained stable at around 500. We lack data for the *petites nations* of Louisiana, though their very survival suggests that any decline was not precipitous.[43]

Three of the nations discussed in this chapter—the Ojibwes, the Dakotas, and the Sauks and Mesquakies—continued to have substantial power. It was no coincidence that all three were in the northern parts of the Louisiana Purchase and so insulated from forces impinging on Indians to the south.

Because U.S. officials did not anticipate moving eastern Indians to Minnesota and because the lands of Minnesota Indians were not yet the object of speculators, farmers, and logging companies, they were not asked to cede lands until late in the 1830s and beyond. The United States had begun to assert authority over the western Great Lakes and upper Mississippi by establishing new forts (Fort Crawford at Prairie du Chien in 1816, Fort Snelling at the confluence of the Minnesota and Mississippi rivers in 1819–1820) and asking Dakotas and Ojibwes to sign documents acknowledging U.S. authority. Practically speaking, however, Minnesota's Indian communities retained their political independence. Despite problems from the fur trade (alcohol, mounting debt, and conflict over hunting grounds), Dakotas and Ojibwes gained significant material benefits from their commercial relations with American traders. They also effectively used the wealth of resources in their homelands. Ojibwes in northern Minnesota regularly harvested maple sugar, wild rice, fish, and berries, and could count on corn and potatoes from small gardens. Despite losses in intertribal conflicts, the Minnesota Ojibwe population, 3,800 in 1830, was at the very least stable and may actually have increased over the previous few decades. The Dakota population, estimated at 6,700 in 1830, was almost certainly higher than it had been at the turn of the century.[44]

The other powerful nation, the Sauks and Mesquakies, had signed U.S. documents that registered assent to land cessions, although Sauk and Mesquakie leaders maintained that they had not agreed to the actual content of these documents. In practical terms, the territory they controlled was somewhat larger than it had been in 1803 and allowed them to maintain a remarkably diverse and productive economy. Although game had declined in their main hunting areas (Iowa, southern Minnesota, eastern Nebraska, and eastern Kansas), the sheer size of this area allowed Sauks and Mesquakies to undertake successful hunting expeditions throughout the 1820s. At the same time, their villages consistently produced impressive crops of corn, beans, pumpkins, and melons. They also gained significant economic benefits from lead mining in northwestern Illinois and southwestern Wisconsin, selling some to the outside market and keeping supplies for themselves, thus limiting expenditures on ammunition. Sauks and Mesquakies had become increasingly divided over questions of policy toward the United States. A majority identified with the Sauk leader Keokuk favored accommodation, while the minority supporters of Black Hawk remained committed to an oppositional stance. Nonetheless, factionalism had not become debilitating, and the various Sauk and Mesquakie communities cooperated on many issues. Alcohol was making some inroads in the 1820s, though tribal leaders found ways to limit its consumption. On one occasion Black Hawk led a "party of my young men" to a trader's house where they "took out his barrel and broke in the head and turned out the whisky," an act presumably intended both to deter other traders and to invest young men in temperance activism. Overall, despite losses in conflict with other Indians, relative economic prosperity allowed for high fertility rates and growing numbers. With a combined population of 6,500 in 1830, there were more Sauks and Mesquakies than at any time since the two peoples had united to survive genocide a century before.[45]

In contrast to the Dakotas and Ojibwes, however, the Sauks and Mesquakies were under serious threat. Its most visible manifestation came in the form of non-Indians mining lead in the Fever (Galena) River area in the far northwestern corner of Illinois. In 1822, when miners first appeared, there were only a few dozen of them, but by 1828 there were 4,000 "lead rushers" in the area. Farmers soon followed. From the perspective of Illinois and U.S. officials, the time had come to implement the 1804 treaty, as they interpreted it, and compel the Sauks and Mesquakies to vacate their villages on the east side of the Mississippi. The Sauks and Mesquakies had thus far avoided removal, but the forces that had already uprooted nations like the Quapaws and Caddos from their lands were close at hand.[46]

CONCLUSION: TOWARD CATASTROPHE

By 1830, much had changed in the eastern Louisiana Purchase. Only three decades before, Thomas Jefferson had declared that these lands would become a new home for eastern Indians. At first, his plans appeared to be working. During his administration, U.S. officials acquired territory from two major landowners in the midcontinent, the Osages and the Sauks and Mesquakies, thus making vast tracts available for eastern Indians. And many eastern Indians migrated to these lands, especially after 1815. But in 1803 when Jefferson imagined a large zone of removal west of the Mississippi as a permanent home for eastern Indians, he failed to seriously analyze the history of American settlement since 1783. Had he done so, he would have had to reckon with the fact that it would not be long before Americans would covet western lands and demand that Indian people be eliminated from them.

Well before the passage of the Indian Removal Act in 1830, then, a major flaw in the policy was plain to anyone willing to see. Americans would continue to cross the Mississippi and take Native nations' lands for themselves. Lands available for the removal of eastern Indians would continue to shrink, and the lands of Indians indigenous to the region would continue to shrink, too. The zone of removal would have to be adjusted and readjusted. Native communities, having already relocated once, twice, or more, would be required to relocate yet again and with little hope of ever building permanent homes. The result, as we will see later in this book, would be a slowly unfolding catastrophe in America's heartland. By 1860, many nations—impoverished, starving, and afflicted by multiple diseases—were on a trajectory toward complete and total extinction.

PART THREE

Removal

CHAPTER 8

❧━━━━◄❀✿❀►━━━━❧

Removal and the Southern
Indian Nations, 1830–1840s

With the passage of the 1830 Indian Removal Act, the United States was officially committed to relocating an estimated 123,000 Indian people living east of the Mississippi—75,000 in the South and 48,000 in the North.[1] But although the United States had a policy, it lacked a comprehensive plan. One major problem was where to put the removed nations. By 1830 the zone of removal, as imagined by Thomas Jefferson when he acquired Louisiana in 1803, had already shrunk. The state of Missouri and the Arkansas Territory were off limits. U.S. officials envisioned the zone of removal to include what would become eastern Oklahoma (for the southern nations) and eastern Kansas, eastern Nebraska, western Iowa, and northern Wisconsin (for the northern nations). Most of this area was officially designated as "Indian Territory" in 1834. Beyond that, however, although officials had a fairly clear idea about where they wanted to relocate some of the more prominent nations (like the Cherokees), they had given little thought to exactly where many nations would be sent. Moreover, the zone of removal did not stop shrinking in 1830. This meant that relocated eastern Indians as well as Indians indigenous to the region would endure further dispossession and additional removals.

Nor did officials have a clear sense of how the removals should be conducted. Their two guiding principles were, first, to ensure that once a given removal was scheduled to begin it be completed regardless of other considerations, such as insufficient clothing, outbreaks of disease, and bad weather; and second, to avoid spending too much money. In some cases, officials allowed Indians to oversee their removals, using government and/or tribal funds to procure supplies and arrange travel. In most cases, removals were overseen by government agents, who used government and sometimes tribal funds to contract for supplies and transportation. This, of course, created opportunities for skimming funds and taking bribes, but the problems with removal far exceeded corruption. Nor were insufficient funds or government incompetence major factors. The problem, inherent to the project, was that moving entire communities, most impoverished and distressed to begin with, was bound to produce suffering and death. People leaving in the fall could harvest crops and avoid the fevers associated with summer travel through mosquito-infested swamps, only to be stalled by heavy rains and stuck on the road as a vicious winter descended. People leaving in the summer could arrive before snow and ice, but they would travel under a broiling sun in environments thriving with pathogens and conducive to their spread.

Southern political leaders, Andrew Jackson included, were determined to remove every single Native American from their region. Their passion was directly tied to their commitment to build the slave labor empire that South Carolina senator James Henry Hammond celebrated in his "King Cotton" speech on the eve of the Civil War. By 1830, the southern states had gained control of a substantial portion of Indian lands. This had enabled a spectacular boom in cotton production, from 85 million pounds in 1810 to 331 million pounds in 1830. Nonetheless, at the time of the Indian Removal Act, Cherokees retained over a tenth of the lands in Georgia, Creeks one-sixth of the lands of Alabama, and Choctaws and Chickasaws half the lands of Mississippi. These remaining Native lands, once cleared of their inhabitants, would allow planters to use enslaved people to produce cotton for global markets. The policy would also expand markets for slave owners on the eastern seaboard to sell slaves (often their most valuable form of property) to labor on new plantations in Alabama and Mississippi. But if southern political leaders were optimistic that new lands would accelerate the region's economic and political power, they were equally fearful that the human beings they held in chains would turn against them. Always looming was the example of St. Domingue in 1791, where slaves had risen up against French planters and established the black republic of Haiti in 1804. Gabriel's revolt in Virginia (1800), the German Coast slave rebellion in Louisiana (1811), the Denmark Vesey "conspiracy" in Charleston (1822), and the Nat Turner revolt in Virginia

(1831) all reinforced the nightmare possibility of a "second Haitian Revolution" in the American South.[2] White southerners' fears of slave rebellions gave them a particular reason to eliminate Seminoles and the Black Seminoles who lived among them. For decades, slaves had escaped plantations (especially in southern Georgia) and found freedom in Florida. Southern leaders did not want unceded Seminole lands in central Florida for plantation agriculture, but they did want to eliminate Florida as a place of freedom for Black Seminoles and destroy the potential of Florida to become a staging ground for another slave rebellion.

Andrew Jackson intended to apply the Indian Removal Act to all eastern Indian nations, but as a southerner he was especially determined to relocate those in his home region. He delegated the work of moving northern Indians to subordinates, but he personally took the lead in the South. Soon after signing the new removal law in May 1830, Jackson invited Chickasaws, Choctaws, Cherokees, and Creeks to meet with him in Franklin, Tennessee, not far from the Hermitage, his plantation home. Not long after, however, he was dismayed to find out that only the Chickasaws were willing to meet their Great Father. In a forecast of resistance to come, the other nations refused his invitation. And the Chickasaws, although willing to talk, did not want to move.[3]

CHICKASAW RESISTANCE

In August when Jackson met with Chickasaw leaders he informed them that he had no authority under the U.S. Constitution to prevent states from extending their laws over them (Mississippi, emulating Georgia, had recently done just that). The Chickasaws' only hope, said Jackson, was to move to a "country beyond the Mississippi" that the United States had provided "for the happiness of our red friends." The Chickasaws had a different interpretation of the Constitution the president was sworn to uphold. Levi Colbert and other Chickasaw leaders told Jackson that any attempt by Mississippi to assert state law over them would be "an act of usurpation on their part, unwarranted by the Constitution of the United States, and the treaties that now exist." Faced with Jackson's insistence that they move, Chickasaw leaders felt they had to sign a treaty, but they skillfully negotiated for a crucial condition. The treaty they signed gave them the right to send a delegation west. Should this delegation be unable to find "a country suitable to their wants and condition," the treaty would be considered "null and void." It is unclear whether the Chickasaws who secured the right to a delegation with veto power did so as part of a plan to have the delegation feign objectivity but ultimately reject any lands they saw. In the event, in October a delegation headed by Colbert departed for the West. Upon their return several months later, Colbert informed the Great Father that much of the country they had visited was undesirable. The only acceptable lands they had seen were those designated for Choctaw removal in eastern Oklahoma, but should the Choctaws ever be forced to move, they did not want to sell any of the lands set aside for them. The Colbert delegation's "inability" to locate acceptable western lands nullified the 1830 treaty.[4] For the time being, the Chickasaws were safe, but Jackson's representatives would soon return.

CHOCTAW REMOVAL TO A "LAND OF DEATH"

Although the Choctaws rebuffed Jackson's invitation to meet him in August 1830, this was not because Choctaw leaders were completely opposed to negotiations. Fearing that they might not be able to resist removal forever, many Choctaw leaders were willing to consider removal provided the terms were acceptable. So, even as Jackson was meeting with the Chickasaws, Greenwood LeFlore and other Choctaw leaders requested the President to send "some good men" to discuss removal with them. In turn, Jackson dispatched his close friend John Coffee and Secretary of War John Eaton to Choctaw country. In mid-September 1830 the commissioners arrived at the treaty grounds on Dancing Rabbit Creek (central-eastern Mississippi; Fig. 30), where they encountered an assembly of 6,000 of the Choctaws' population of around 20,000. The commissioners had been expecting a receptive audience, but the mood of the gathering was dark. Very few Choctaws spoke publicly in favor of removal. One who did, Killihota, faced the wrath of seven elderly women seated in the center of the council, who "gave vent to their indignation in bitter exclamations." Most speakers opposed removal, reminding the commissioners that the Choctaws had supported the United States in its war against the Creeks and informing them, in the words of Little Leader, that "we love our hunting grounds more than the white man loves his country, and we do not wish to be driven away from them." Behind such expressions were deep cultural attachments to the land as the source of all life and to the bones of relatives buried there. The Choctaws' most fundamental religious beliefs made it impossible for them to contemplate moving, especially if it was to the West, a region seen in Choctaw cosmology as the "Land of Death."[5]

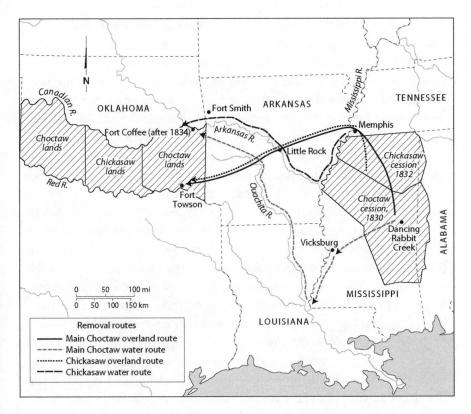

Fig. 30. Choctaw and Chickasaw removal

Confronted by massive Choctaw opposition, the commissioners issued threats. Secretary Eaton told the Choctaws with "brutal bluntness" that they "had no choice in the matter." Should they reject a removal treaty, Eaton promised that "the President, in twenty days, would march an army into their country—build forts in all parts of their hunting grounds, [and] extend the authority and laws of the United States over the Choctaw territory." If Choctaws tried to fight the U.S. army, it would "be the ruin of the tribe." The council soon disbanded and most Choctaws returned to their homes. But Choctaw leaders remained for further discussion. Perhaps because these leaders feared military reprisal, perhaps because the treaty contained provisions (bribes) granting them land and pensions, or perhaps because of both, they signed a treaty requiring them to move to new lands between the Arkansas and Red rivers in what is now southeastern Oklahoma. Ordinary Choctaws had returned to their homes under the impression that they had fought off removal. When they received news of the Treaty of Dancing Rabbit Creek, "shock and despair spread throughout the nation."[6]

Anticipating that it would be impossible to move upwards of 20,000 Choctaws (including 500 black slaves)[7] to Oklahoma all at once, the 1830 treaty called for removal to take place in stages over three years. The first stage was set for fall 1831. Beginning the journey west at this time of the year had two advantages. The first, from the government's perspective, was that Choctaws could harvest their crops, thus reducing the costs of provisioning them and their horses along the journey. The second, from the Choctaws' perspective, was that the first frost marked the onset of a season that was less sickly. (In fact, frost kills mosquitoes carrying the parasite that causes malaria.) In October, about 5,000 Choctaws gathered on the Mississippi River, some at Vicksburg, others at Memphis. Those at Vicksburg took steamboats down the Mississippi and proceeded overland or up the Ouachita River through Louisiana and Arkansas. Those at Memphis traveled overland via Little Rock, Arkansas. As they left, one emigrant, George Harkins, wrote from the steamboat *Huron* that "we go forth sorrowful, knowing that wrong has been done."[8]

It was an unusually severe winter. The migrating Choctaws endured brutal storms with heavy snows, subzero temperatures, and periods of drenching rains, all without sufficient food, clothing, and shelter. At Memphis in late December, a twenty-six-year-old Frenchman named Alexis de Tocqueville observed a party of Choctaws boarding a steamboat. In a letter to his mother, Tocqueville described an old woman "naked save for a covering which left visible, at a thousand places, the most emaciated figure imaginable" and a "young girl who had broken her arm a week before; for want of care the arm had been frozen below the fracture." After the vessel was loaded, Tocqueville further related, the Choctaws' "dogs approached the banks; but they refused to enter the vessel and began howling frightfully." When he later wrote about this incident in *Democracy in America,* Tocqueville rendered the Choctaws unable to prevent their dogs from plunging into the deadly icy waters, an image that foreshadowed Choctaw extinction. In the undoubtedly more factual account to his mother, however, Tocqueville observed that the Choctaws brought their dogs on board "by force" and so recorded an act of Choctaw survival. Choctaws would need their dogs to hunt and to accompany those who might pass away to the spirit world.[9]

After the Choctaws crossed the Mississippi, their ordeal only worsened. Captain Jacob Brown, the head removal agent, reported that 2,500 Choctaws in Arkansas had been delayed by bad weather. With temperatures near

Fig. 31. In this 1966 watercolor by Choctaw artist Valjean Hessing, Choctaws bear
burdens, care for children, and comfort one another as they walk west through the snow.
There is suffering, but there is also resolve and hope. The watercolor suggests a different
view of Choctaw removal from the one presented in Alexis de Toqueville's *Democracy in
America,* where the Choctaws' dogs plunge into the icy water of the Mississippi to forecast
the nation's disappearance. Here it seems that the Choctaws—and their animals—will
survive. Valjean McCarty Hessing, *Choctaw Removal,* 1966. Watercolor, 8¾ × 21½ in.
(22.2 × 54.6 cm). Philbrook Museum of Art, Tulsa, Oklahoma. Museum purchase, 1967.24.

zero, Brown feared that "our poor emigrants, many of them quite naked, and
without much shelter, must suffer." Brown later informed Washington officials that the emigrants made it to Little Rock without getting "frosted," but
funds to purchase food for them had not arrived and it would be impossible
for the emigrants to "sustain themselves . . . much longer." Most Choctaws
reached Oklahoma by January. How many died along the way is unclear.
It was certainly in the dozens, and more likely in the low hundreds. What
is clear is that suffering was universal. Instead of planning for a worst-case
scenario and ensuring that the Choctaws had sufficient food, clothing, and
shelter for a longer-than-anticipated journey in a worse-than-average winter,
a parsimonious and impatient government provided insufficient resources. In
many cases, Choctaws were issued only one blanket per family, and no shoes
or moccasins (Fig. 31).[10]

As they anticipated the second stage of Choctaw removal in 1832, government officials wanted the Choctaws to start in September to avoid a repeat
of the previous year's catastrophe. Nonetheless, for reasons the record does
not make clear, it was not until October that another 6,000 began leaving

their homes. As they approached the Mississippi, Choctaws heard rumors of the outbreak of cholera. Previously unknown in North America, cholera had appeared in Canada in June and soon spread to New York and other eastern cities and towns. By fall, probably by way of Chicago, the disease reached the Mississippi. Federal officials anticipated that Choctaws slated for removal would contract cholera, though none proposed reversing course and allowing Choctaws to go back to their homes. Whether traveling by land or water, all Choctaw parties suffered significant losses from cholera and other afflictions. The best figures we have are from Alfred Wright, a missionary who accompanied the Choctaws west. In early 1833 Wright reported on the deaths in four separate Choctaw parties numbering 3,200 altogether. About 150–60 in these parties had died. Many deaths were from cholera, though Wright observed that "a considerable portion of them were small children and aged and infirm persons, who could not endure the fatigue of traveling." If Wright's figures were accurate, and assuming a similar toll for other Choctaw parties, the total number who died along the route in 1832–1833 would have been around 300.[11]

Although cholera subsided after the Choctaws' arrival in Oklahoma, disease struck again that summer in the aftermath of severe flooding along the Arkansas and Canadian rivers. These floods destroyed springs, which meant that Choctaws had to drink from unsanitary ponds and rivers. Floods also wiped out recently planted crops and government storehouses and so led to undernourishment. In October 1833 the disbursement agent for the Choctaws reported that in a district along the Arkansas River 165 had died over the previous two months from "diseases . . . of a bilious nature." "Bilious" fever, along with "inflammatory" and "intermittent" fever and the general term "ague," described a variety of diseases, including malaria, typhoid fever, and yellow fever. Cholera or other bacterial diseases may also have been at work. Disease claimed many elsewhere in the Land of Death. A missionary stationed near the Red River reported in December that "not a single child is left under a year old" in that district. On the nearby Little River "the mortality has been greater among adults." Some Choctaws, especially members of wealthier families, decided to escape the Land of Death and return to Mississippi.[12]

In September 1833, as the time approached for the third and final stage of Choctaw removal, several leaders "announced . . . their unalterable determination to remain." Many, no doubt, were deterred by stories of hardship and death filtering in from the West. In October only 1,000 of the remaining 7,000 Choctaws moved west. These emigrants encountered relatively favorable conditions and reached their destination in December without enduring the hardships and loss of life experienced by previous emigrants.[13]

Four years later, the removed Choctaws were hit by another killer. In early summer 1837 a major smallpox epidemic erupted on the upper Missouri River, devastating Mandans, Arikaras, Hidatsas, Blackfeet, Crows, Assiniboines, and Pawnees. By the winter of 1837–1838, smallpox had spread south into the Choctaws' new country. Evidence that would allow a solid estimate for the death toll is lacking; scholars have suggested a range of 500–1,000.[14] Whatever the number, almost certainly it would have been lower had the Choctaws been vaccinated under a federal program established by the Indian Vaccination Act of 1832. The vaccination program initially focused on Plains Indians, who had been ravaged by an epidemic in 1831. Anticipating that smallpox might spread east, the government expanded vaccination to include the eastern nations, if only to protect whites in places like Indiana or Mississippi from catching smallpox from infected Indians. In late 1832, removal agents considered vaccinating the Choctaws slated to leave Mississippi, but, probably as a cost-saving measure, decided to delay vaccination until the Indians arrived in Oklahoma. Some Choctaws were vaccinated after relocation, but the vaccination program was never sufficiently robust to keep smallpox at bay when it arrived in 1837. The impetus for the 1832 vaccination legislation was at least partly humanitarian. Its major proponent, the Baptist missionary Isaac McCoy, witnessed the effects of the 1831 epidemic on Plains tribes and was appalled. But humanitarian shock quickly faded. Over time, the federal vaccination program was underfunded and haphazardly implemented.[15]

By the late 1830s, most Choctaws were in the West, but a few thousand remained in their homelands. The Treaty of Dancing Rabbit Creek contained a provision to allow Choctaws to give up their tribal affiliation and subject themselves to state law. Should they do so, they could obtain fee simple patents to the lands they farmed. But settlers saw Choctaws as illegal squatters who ought to have gone west and so subjected them to all manner of harassment. A Choctaw petition from 1849 provided details: "We have had our habitations torn down and burned, our fences destroyed, cattle turned into our fields and we ourselves have been scourged, manacled, fettered and otherwise personally abused, until by such treatment some of our best men have died." Some eastern Choctaws joined those in the West. But others retreated to relatively isolated areas—hills and swamps—where they worked marginal lands, foraged, hunted, and fished. By 1855, over 2,000 Choctaws remained in Alabama, Mississippi, and Louisiana.[16]

Scholars have offered a range of figures for the number of Choctaws who died as they were being moved or shortly thereafter. The highest is 6,000, a number originally provided by Cyrus Byington, a missionary to the Choctaws. Byington, however, also said that there were 40,000 Choctaws at the time of removal, when in fact the population was slightly more than half that. Other scholars have provided a figure of 2,500. The existing sources establish a death toll of between 1,200 and 1,800, but because many deaths were not reported, especially those occurring after removal, a figure of 2,500 is realistic.[17]

CHICKASAW JOURNEY TO SMALLPOX

In 1838, as the newly removed Choctaws were suffering from smallpox, the Chickasaw Nation—4,000 strong, with several hundred black slaves—arrived to take up new lands that had recently been carved from the Choctaw reservation. Chickasaws had fended off removal earlier in the decade, but in 1832 they ceded their eastern lands and agreed to move provided they could find suitable lands west of the Mississippi. As conditions deteriorated in Mississippi, Chickasaw leaders agreed in 1837 to purchase a portion of the Choctaws' western lands. Beginning in January 1838 several groups crossed the Mississippi for the West. Some traveled overland through Arkansas to Fort Towson, north of the Red River. Others took steamships down the Mississippi and then up the Arkansas to Fort Coffee. The last of these reached their destination in December. Most suffered along the way from cold or heat, lack of food, and demoralization, but Chickasaw removal would probably have occurred without great loss of life had their path west not taken them into the teeth of a major smallpox epidemic. Many Chickasaws had been vaccinated in 1832, but an insufficient number were immune to prevent the disease from spreading among them on the journey and after their arrival in Oklahoma. A new round of vaccination slowed the epidemic, but not before 500–600 had died, well over 10 percent of the entire Chickasaw Nation. Although government officials may not have known about the epidemic when Chickasaw removal commenced, in June 1838 removal agent Arthur Upshaw reported that Chickasaws still in the East had heard rumors of smallpox in the West and refused to leave. U.S. officials could have listened to the Chickasaws and saved lives by halting their removal, but they were determined to press forward and so pressured reluctant Chickasaws to go west despite their fears.[18]

PORTENTS OF CREEK EXTINCTION

The United States also could have saved lives by listening to Creeks. In the early 1830s, as over 22,000 Creeks, including close to 1,000 black slaves, faced the prospect of removal, their leaders warned government officials that their people would be subject to "starvation on the route" and, once in the West, to an unhealthy climate. Creek forecasts of suffering and death were well founded. In the late 1820s and early 1830s approximately 3,000 Creeks had "voluntarily" moved to Oklahoma, where they were hit hard by unidentified diseases. By 1833, the population of the western Creeks had declined to 2,500, a loss of 17 percent. In April 1831 Nehah Micco and other Creek chiefs notified Secretary of War Eaton that they were "compelled to refuse" the wishes of "our Father, the President" that they vacate "the land that gave us birth." Beyond wanting to remain where "the bones of [our] kindred are buried," eastern Creeks objected to removal because western Creeks had apprised them of "the unhealthiness of the country, [and] the many deaths that have taken place among them. . . . From the accounts that we have received, it is a grave yard."[19]

Federal officials did not heed Creek appeals. Instead, they decided that by making the Creeks more and more miserable where they were, the Indians would eventually give up resisting removal and go west. The primary instrument of immiseration was the state of Alabama. In 1827, the same year that Georgia asserted sovereignty over the Cherokee Nation, Alabama passed legislation extending its civil and criminal jurisdiction over the Creek Nation. This and other acts of "legislative harassment" subjected Creeks to a prejudicial legal system and opened the door to a variety of intruders. No gold miners invaded Creek territory, but there were plenty of cattle thieves, whiskey dealers, land speculators, and squatters. In 1832, as the vice tightened, Creek leaders journeyed to Washington to negotiate a treaty in the hope of staving off removal and gaining federal protection from total destruction in their homelands. Federal officials decided not to force the Creeks to accept a treaty mandating removal. Instead the treaty merely expressed the government's wish for the Creeks to move, but the treaty did dissolve the Creek Nation in the East and confirmed the Creeks' subjection to Alabama. There would be no more tribal lands in the East, but Creeks who wished to stay in their homelands could take up individual tracts of land. From the Creeks' perspective, this was far from an ideal treaty, but it did afford the slim hope that by converting tribal lands to private property the Creeks' lands might not be completely overrun. From the perspective of the federal government, however, the treaty

was a de facto removal treaty, since the privatization of Creek lands commodi-
fied them and so made them available to non-Natives through sale or swindle.
Landless Creeks would either starve to death or go west.[20]

Of the southern nations, the Creeks were the only one to try to avoid
removal by converting tribal lands to private property. As we will see in the
next chapter, some of the northern nations took a similar approach, but it was
a risky one. It threatened to undercut a key basis (collectively held lands) for
community cohesiveness, left fractionalized and privatized lands vulnerable
to acquisition by non-Indians, and subjected tribal members to non-Indian
criminal jurisdiction. It worked in a couple of cases involving communities
with relatively low populations that required a correspondingly small amount
of land, which was less likely to be targeted by squatters and speculators.
More often, it was not a permanent shield against removal.

For the 1832 treaty to work the way the Creeks wanted, the federal government would have to fulfill its obligation—written into the treaty—to protect their lands from squatters swarming onto Creek property. Secretary of
War Lewis Cass directed the eviction of a few trespassers, but once Alabama
politicians began protesting non-Indian removal, the Jackson administration,
never intending sustained enforcement of the treaty anyway, dropped its efforts. Soon, land companies began defrauding Creeks. One mechanism was
to pay Creeks to impersonate other Creeks and sell their privatized holdings. Another was to trick Creeks into signing a document as if it guaranteed
protection against fraud when it was actually a bill of sale. Another was to
threaten lawsuits and imprisonment. Whiskey was also put to use.[21]

Conditions for Creeks rapidly deteriorated. A federal attorney named
Francis Scott Key (yes, the author of the lyrics for America's national anthem)
reported in November 1833 that the Creeks "are already almost starving: very
few of them have made any corn; almost all of them have sold their land
two or three times over." Some were in despair and reportedly went into the
woods and found vines to hang themselves. Others cut down fruit trees so
that settlers about to steal their lands would at least be deprived of this benefit. A generation after the New Madrid earthquakes and three years after a
total solar eclipse, Opothle Yoholo gave voice to what must have been a widespread sense of impending doom when he told a U.S. official that "the earthquakes, the eclipses of the sun and moon, and stars of unusual appearance . . .
portended the gradual declension and final extinction of the Creeks."[22]

Destitute and dispossessed in their homelands, some Creeks considered taking their chances in the West. To encourage "voluntary" removal,

the federal government appointed agents and provided funds for provisions and transportation. In summer 1834, these agents attempted to enroll 2,000 Creeks for a fall removal. By December, however, only 630 Creeks had agreed to move. Government agents knew that proceeding with removal so late in the year was risky, but having spent a considerable portion of their funds and not wanting their efforts to fail altogether, they went ahead anyway. The Creeks traveled overland to Memphis. From there, some took steamships down the Mississippi and up the Arkansas to Little Rock and on to Fort Gibson, while others took an overland route via Little Rock (Fig. 32). Although

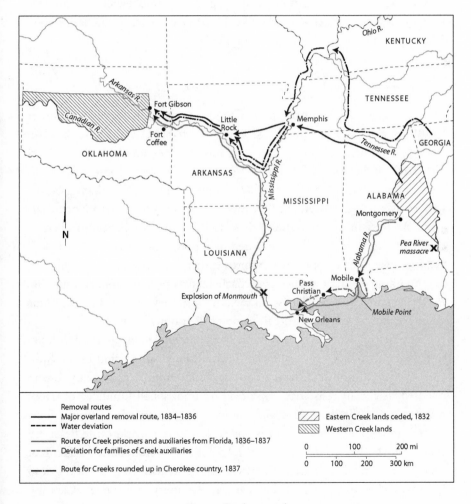

Fig. 32. Creek removal

the winter was not as severe as the one that had descended on emigrating Choctaws three years earlier, the Creeks endured snowstorms, rainstorms, and freezing temperatures. All of this caused delays, which in turn meant that provisions came up short and people went hungry. Toward the end of their ordeal, influenza struck. The U.S. official who supervised this party recorded ten deaths, though only 469 of the original 630 were reported as having arrived in Oklahoma in March. Taking into account the desertion of twenty Creeks to the Chickasaw Nation along the way, the death toll would have been close to 150. The Creeks would have suffered less had they been better equipped for a winter journey, but the very poverty that drove them from their homes left them "destitute of clothing." Government agents might have issued footwear, blankets, and the like, but they prioritized purchasing food and wagon teams and paying ferry companies.[23]

WAR AND THE ACCELERATION OF CREEK REMOVAL

The next winter, another group of 500 made the journey west with fewer hardships. But even though Creeks continued to suffer various outrages (in late 1835 and early 1836 the radical white supremacist craniologist Josiah Nott raided Creek graveyards for skulls to measure), the vast majority of Creeks were determined to resist removal. A minority of these—perhaps 1,000— took refuge with the Cherokees in eastern Tennessee and western North Carolina. A larger number, in the spirit of the Red Sticks a generation before, decided to fight. In May 1836, inspired by reports from Florida of Seminole victories over U.S. troops a few months earlier (see below), Creek militants began raiding plantations and stage coaches, appropriating food and supplies for their deprived communities. In the long run, they intended to "whip the white people" and roll back the invasion of their homelands.[24]

Secretary of War Lewis Cass immediately ordered General Thomas Jesup to command an army to secure the "unconditional submission of the Indians." Within a month, federal troops and state militia, assisted by Creeks opposed to violent resistance, captured and imprisoned hundreds of Creek militants and sent them in chains, along with their relatives, from Montgomery to Oklahoma by way of Mobile, New Orleans, and Little Rock. Of the 2,500 who began the journey in July 1836, 339 were reported missing or dead by the time they arrived at Fort Gibson in September. Most of the dead had succumbed to fever (probably malaria), dysentery, and cholera. Cass also seized the opportunity provided by what has become known as the Second

Creek War to accelerate wholesale Creek removal, arguing that since it was impossible to "determine . . . who are hostile and who are friendly," it would be necessary to remove all Creeks, using military force if necessary. Any pretense of "voluntary" removal had evaporated.[25]

In August government agents rounded up an additional 12,000 nonmilitant Creeks and divided them into five detachments for removal. Although Creeks did not want to depart their ancestral homelands, now that they were forced to go, they made preparations vital for their survival in the West. After extinguishing the sacred fires that burned in the center of their towns, community leaders designated "fire carriers" to carry embers from the fires, light fires from them at campsites along the way, and then bear the embers again the next day. In this way, the sacred fires would be kept alive so that they could continue to "represent . . . the entire community and the people's connection to their ancestors and the Maker of Breath." The five detachments traveled overland to Memphis. From there they intended to take an overland route to Little Rock, but that year swamps west of Memphis were "impossible to pass through with loaded wagons." Government officials wanted the Creeks to take steamboats down the Mississippi and up the Arkansas. Some Creeks did this, but many refused, fearing that the corpses of those who died en route would be thrown overboard and "denied a proper Creek burial." Whatever the route, the hardships the Creeks experienced were not unlike those of previous emigrants. When snows fell and the ground froze in December, many walked barefoot, "leaving bloody footprints in the snow." Various illnesses took their toll. By the time the last detachment reached Oklahoma in January, a reported 188 had died.[26]

Federal officials now moved to finalize Creek removal. In late 1836, the War Department ordered General John E. Wool to pursue Creeks who had taken refuge in Cherokee country over the past few years. Notwithstanding Wool's objection that "humanity revolts" at the prospect of Creeks being "hunted and dragged like so many beasts to the emigrating camp," he complied with his orders and pursued the Creeks into the forests, where they were subsisting on no more than the "sap of the timber." By May 1837 over 500 Creeks had been captured (several hundred remained in Cherokee country and were later moved west with the Cherokees), many destitute and sick with dysentery. Loaded on flatboats, they traveled down the Tennessee River to the Ohio, where they were transferred to steamboats, which took them down the Mississippi and up the Arkansas to Little Rock and then overland to Fort Coffee. Reports indicate that seventy-one escaped and nine died along the way. Later that year, government agents also rooted out a few hundred Creeks, many in a "sick and helpless condition," who had fled to Chickasaw country in Mississippi.[27]

By 1837, about 4,000 Creeks remained in Alabama. In contrast to those who had taken up arms to resist removal, these Creeks were from nonmilitant communities. Many of their men had enlisted the previous fall to fight with U.S. forces against Seminoles in Florida. By the terms of their enlistment, these auxiliaries were supposed to be released in February 1837, reunited with their families, and then moved west, but the army held them in service until the summer and early fall. Creeks waiting for their male relatives to return from Florida were particularly vulnerable. Alabama citizens raided Creek homes, taking livestock, corn, guns, and equipment. Alabama militiamen killed a ninety-year-old Creek man. He was found with "his head litterally stove in, with . . . butts of muskets." The militiamen also raped several women and girls. One fifteen-year-old girl escaped and later stated that "the men wished to ravish her; she refused, and ran towards a thicket which was near by, when she was fired at." When Creeks protested this and other violations of government officials' assurances of protection, the officer in charge decided to separate the Creeks from Alabama citizens by sending the Creeks to Mobile Point on the Gulf Coast to await the arrival of their relatives from Florida. While there, hundreds of Creeks fell ill with dysentery and fever, and a reported ninety-three died. The situation was dire enough that agents moved the Creeks to Pass Christian near the Mississippi Gulf Coast, a healthier place with several springs. An additional eighty-four Creeks, most ill before their arrival, died there.[28]

With the return of the discharged Creek auxiliaries from Florida in mid-October, forced migration recommenced. Most of the parties traveled by steamship up the Mississippi and Arkansas rivers and then by land to Fort Gibson without suffering major loss of life. But on October 31, the *Monmouth*, a steamship carrying 611 Creeks, passed Profit Island (just north of Baton Rouge). Instead of taking the side of the island designated for northbound travel, the *Monmouth* took the wrong route and collided with a steamboat traveling downriver. About 300 of the 611 Creeks aboard the vessel perished. Some critics faulted the "avaricious disposition" of the Alabama Emigrating Company for chartering "rotten, old, and unseaworthy boats." The company responded that the *Monmouth* was only twelve months old and that the collision was an accident that occurred under conditions of poor visibility (at night in a drizzle). A Creek leader, Jim Boy, who survived the disaster, identified a broader context for the tragedy. A year later Jim Boy petitioned the United States for compensation for property lost on the *Monmouth* (the government was unwilling to consider compensation for lives lost). In so doing, he indicted the federal government. If the Creek auxiliaries had been discharged from service in Florida in a timely fashion, Jim Boy pointed out, they would have reached Alabama in time to travel overland instead of by steamship.[29]

Although the federal government was having some success moving Creeks, several hundred had established encampments in remote areas of southern Alabama and western Florida. Most of these were militants who had avoided capture. Others had fled south to escape removal camps. In early 1837 the War Department tried to round them up and send them west. To do so, federal officials relied on Alabama and Florida militias. Many militiamen were less interested in removing Indians than in killing them. In March 1837, while undertaking a "search-and-destroy mission," an Alabama militia broke through Creek forces defending an encampment on the Pea River (fifty miles southeast of Montgomery) and slaughtered "men, women, and children alike"—at least fifty in all. Over the next several months, Florida volunteers attacked similar encampments in the Florida panhandle, killing a few dozen, including ten who had been taken prisoner (nine of these were women or children). Some Creeks were captured and sent west, though many evaded troops. Some remained in southern Alabama and the Florida panhandle, while others joined Seminole communities on the Florida peninsula.[30]

By 1838, the large majority of the Creek confederacy had been sent west. Official reports indicate that perhaps 1,000 Creeks perished as they traveled. Even more died after they reached their unwanted destination. According to a government official who conducted censuses of the Creeks in Oklahoma in 1836 and 1838, no fewer than 3,500 Creeks succumbed to "bilious fevers" shortly after their arrival in Oklahoma during the winter of 1836–1837. This is a truly staggering figure, well in excess of the 1,800–2,000 who perished during the 1813–1814 Red Stick War. All told, from a preremoval population of around 24,000 (including enslaved blacks), the Creek population had fallen to somewhere between 17,000 and 19,000, a decline of 20–30 percent over the course of a decade. The Creeks had rebuilt their population after 1814. But in the West, living on lands the government had promised for their salvation, they would continue to lose population in the decades following removal.[31]

CHEROKEES AND THE U.S. SUPREME COURT

Of all the southern Indian nations, the Cherokees went the farthest in using the U.S. legal and political system to defend themselves against removal. As we saw in Chapter 6, after the passage of the Indian Removal Act, the state of Georgia asserted criminal and civil jurisdiction over Cherokees. In late December 1830, following the arrest and execution of Corn Tassel, the Cherokees' attorney William Wirt filed a suit asking the U.S. Supreme Court to rule unconstitutional Georgia's extension of its laws into Cherokee territory.

In March 1831 the Supreme Court issued its ruling in *Cherokee Nation v. Georgia.* The decision was ambiguous. On one hand, the court found that Indian tribes within the United States "cannot be denominated foreign nations," but were instead "domestic dependent nations." This meant that the Cherokee Nation had no standing in court. On the other hand, although characterizing the Cherokee Nation as a "domestic dependent nation" diminished Cherokee sovereignty, the Court's recognition of a partial, if ill-defined, sovereignty contested Georgia's claim of "perfect settler sovereignty" and left the door open to further legal challenges. Although Cherokees were disappointed by the Court's ruling that they had no standing in court, Principal Chief John Ross took heart in reading the decision as "conclusively adverse" to Georgia's pretensions.[32]

To test Ross's reading of *Cherokee Nation v. Georgia* as "adverse" to Georgia, the Cherokees needed to bring forward a case in which the plaintiff (or plaintiffs) would have standing. They found one in March 1831 when Georgia arrested two missionaries, Samuel Worcester and Elizur Butler, who had refused to comply with a new Georgia law that required missionaries in Cherokee country to take an oath of allegiance to the state of Georgia. In September, after Worcester and Butler were found guilty and sentenced to prison, Wirt filed a new suit. As U.S. citizens, Worcester and Butler had standing in court and so the Supreme Court would now be able to overturn Georgia's legislative aggressions. As this suit went forward, Cherokees tried to persuade U.S. officials and the general public of the justness of their cause. In late 1831, a delegation traveled to Washington to submit a memorial appealing for relief to the secretary of war. After meeting a stone wall on that front, two of the delegates, John Ridge and Elias Boudinot, proceeded to New York, Philadelphia, and Boston, where they attempted to educate the American public about how the treaties the Cherokees had signed with the United States ought to protect them from Georgia's assertions of sovereignty.[33]

The Supreme Court issued its decision in *Worcester v. Georgia* in March 1832. The *Worcester* decision did not revise Marshall's formulation of "domestic dependent nations" in the *Cherokee Nation* case, nor did it overturn the decision nine years earlier in *Johnson v. M'Intosh* that Indians had only an occupancy right to their lands. Nonetheless, in *Worcester v. Georgia* Marshall, writing for the majority, found that the "laws of Georgia . . . are repugnant to the treaties, and unconstitutional and void."[34] The decision affirmed the validity of Cherokee treaties with the United States and held Georgia's legislation over the Cherokees unconstitutional in ways that mattered at the time and remain important today. To the extent that *Worcester* represented a shift in Marshall's thinking about Native nationhood since the time of the *Johnson* decision, this was a consequence of Cherokee political action. For years, Cherokees had been defending their sovereignty and had taken steps to make their nationhood visible to Americans (think, for example, of the Cherokees' adoption of a constitution based on the U.S. Constitution). *Worcester v. Georgia* was a consequence of the Cherokees' fight for national survival.[35]

Cherokees were jubilant about the *Worcester* decision. John Ridge, declared it "a great triumph on the part of the Cherokees," while ordinary Cherokees celebrated with "Rejoicings Dances and Meetings." But could the Supreme Court change the terms of a battle that pitted the executive branch of the federal government and the state of Georgia against the Cherokee Nation? Tellingly, Andrew Jackson greeted news of the *Worcester* decision by saying that "the decision of the supreme court has fell still born, and they find that they cannot coerce Georgia to yield to its mandate." Years later, the newspaperman Horace Greeley distilled Jackson's statement into the oft-quoted "John Marshall has made his decision; now let him enforce it!"[36]

Despite the Cherokees' initial elation, it soon became clear that the existing balance of power was unchanged. Concluding that *Worcester v. Georgia* was a hollow victory in the face of the President's continued support for Georgia, a minority faction within the Cherokee leadership reached the painful decision to abandon the fight and seek the best terms for a removal treaty. By mid-1832 John Ridge, his father Major Ridge, and Elias Boudinot, soon to be known as the Treaty Party, were trying to persuade John Ross to accept removal. Ross held out some hope that the Whig candidate for President, Henry Clay, more sympathetic to the Cherokees than Jackson, would defeat the incumbent that fall. When Clay lost, Ross and his allies, known as the National Party, tightened his control over the Cherokee National Council to prevent the Treaty Party from negotiating for removal and continued his approach of lobbying Congress and potential allies. Some of the Cherokees' non-Indian friends remained supportive of Ross's position, though most began to counsel against further resistance. Even the two missionaries who had suffered imprisonment for the Cherokee cause, Worcester and Butler, eventually changed their minds. After being released from prison in January 1833, they counseled Cherokees to accept what they now believed was the Cherokees' inevitable fate to be forced west.[37]

"A FRAUD UPON THE CHEROKEE PEOPLE"

For years, Cherokees had worked to build national unity and cultivate influential outsiders. Now they were divided and had few allies. The facts on the ground were also increasingly unfavorable. By late 1832, Georgia had completed its survey of Cherokee lands and held lotteries for them. Thousands of lottery winners were taking possession of Cherokee farms and pastures. Although these "fortunate drawers" were obligated by Georgia law to respect Cherokee improvements, they appropriated livestock and burned fences and houses. Some felt entitled not only to Cherokee lands but to Cherokee women. In one instance, a Georgia sheriff stopped at the home of two married Cherokee women and "called for a drink of water." Finding the women alone, he tried to rape one of them, but the other "laid hold of him." The sheriff left, but not before lashing the two with his horsewhip. The two women went to a local magistrate for justice, only to be told that "no Indian testimony could be received." Under Georgia law, they were without rights. Overall, the condition of ordinary Cherokees was deteriorating. Missionaries reported that until the "past two or three years" the people had been "obtaining the various necessaries and comforts," but that "anxiety and despondency respecting their national affairs have manifestly exerted an unfavorable influence; and . . . a dark cloud hangs over them." Besides this, as a government agent observed, "their suffering from poverty is great."[38]

Despite dreadful conditions, a clear majority of Cherokees wished to stay. Supported by this majority, Ross continued to oppose removal, going so far as to propose an "amalgamation" plan. Similar to the approach taken by the Creeks in their 1832 treaty, Cherokees would sell most of their land in exchange for a promise to be allowed to become citizens and obtain patents to tracts of private property. Major Ridge feared that under this plan the Cherokee people would be "cheated, oppressed, reduced to beggary, become miserable outcasts, and as a body dwindle to nothing." It would be much better to reconstitute the nation in the West, far from its oppressors. John Ridge tried to convince Ross to support removal, but he refused. Ridge attacked Ross as a dictator, Ross called Ridge a traitor, and the two factions became ever more polarized. In fall 1834 Elijah Hicks of the National Party moved to impeach the Ridges from the National Council. Not long after, two Ross supporters, acting on their own, assassinated a member of the Treaty Party.[39]

In early 1835 the Jackson administration attempted to exploit the Cherokees' internal divisions by negotiating a treaty with the Treaty Party and then using it to leverage Ross's agreement. Although it was illegal under Cherokee law for any group other than the National Council to agree to a land sale, Boudinot and the two Ridges made known their willingness to negotiate (Fig. 33). Accordingly, U.S. commissioner John Schermerhorn (known to the Cherokees as the "Devil's Horn," a term with more than one connotation) convened a council with Cherokees at New Echota in December. The National Party refused to attend, and so, although a majority in attendance signed a treaty agreeing to sell their eastern lands and move west, this was not a majority of the nation. Schermerhorn and the Treaty Party thought they might win over Ross and thus have a clear majority, but Ross protested that the document signed at New Echota was "deceptive to the world, and a fraud upon the Cherokee people." The National Party obtained 16,000 signatures on a petition against the treaty. Confronted with the fact of majority Cherokee opinion, Schermerhorn resorted to the classic colonial move of depicting Ross as an authoritarian dictator who manipulated his people against their best interest. Andrew Jackson submitted the Treaty of New Echota to the Senate in March 1836. After weeks of intensive debate and maneuvering, the opposition came very close to preventing ratification. The final vote was thirty-one in favor and fifteen against, only one more than the required two-thirds.[40]

"THE CRUELEST WORK": ROUNDING UP THE CHEROKEES, 1838

The New Echota Treaty required the Cherokees to leave their homes no later than May 23, 1838. Because the majority of Cherokees regarded the treaty as illegitimate, U.S. officials anticipated the possibility of mass resistance and so issued preemptive threats. While marching through Cherokee country to root out refugee Creeks in late 1836 and early 1837 (see above), General John Wool announced to Cherokees that they must prepare to depart. Any

Fig. 33. John Ridge was thirty-three years old when he signed the Treaty of New
Echota in 1835. Educated at a mission school in Connecticut, Ridge was a staunch
opponent of Cherokee removal until he realized that the Supreme Court's 1832
decision in *Worcester v. Georgia* would provide little protection against Georgia's
assault on Cherokee sovereignty. In 1839, just after the Cherokees' removal to
Oklahoma, allies of John Ross assassinated Ridge, his father, Major Ridge, and Elias
Boudinot for the crime of selling the nation's land. This lithograph by John T. Bowen
was published in 1838. Library of Congress Prints and Photographs Division.

resistance to complying with the treaty "would be their destruction," a clear
signal of the United States' willingness to use military force if necessary. Wool
also assessed Cherokee military capacities, looking for signs of any recent importation of arms and ammunition, and moved to break the power of antiremoval leaders, arresting and briefly detaining Ross and others.[41] In early May

1838, two weeks before the deadline for removal, General Winfield Scott re-iterated Wool's threats. The "President of the United States," Scott informed the Cherokee Nation, "has sent me with a powerful army. . . . [T]housands and thousands" of troops "are approaching from every quarter." Not only would it be "hopeless" to "render resistance," even flight would ignite "a general war and carnage." The result would surely be the "destruction of the Cherokees."[42]

We should pause here to register exactly what was going on. The words of General Wool and General Scott were not those of random individuals. Both were authorized representatives of the U.S. government with the full force of the army behind them. The message they conveyed was not some idle threat but an official statement of intent to use overwhelming—indeed, genocidal—violence against the Cherokees should they resist or flee. Cherokees knew exactly what Wool and Scott meant. Although it had been almost sixty years since colonial militias desolated the heart of their country, Cherokees had not forgotten the overwhelmingly destructive potential of American military operations.

Cherokees' historical knowledge argued against overt resistance, but compliance was also a terrifying prospect. Eight years earlier, just after the passage of the Indian Removal Act, Cherokees had informed Congress of deep reservations:

> The removal of families to a new country, even under the most favorable auspices, and when the spirits are sustained by pleasing visions of the future, is attended with much depression of mind and sinking of heart. This is the case, when the removal is a matter of decided preference, and when the persons concerned are in early youth or vigorous manhood. Judge, then, what must be the circumstances of a removal, when a whole community, embracing persons of all classes and every description, from the infant to the man of extreme old age, the sick, the blind, the lame, the improvident, the reckless, the desperate, as well as the prudent, the considerate, the industrious, are compelled to move by odious and intolerable vexations and persecutions.[43]

Since then, five groups of Cherokees (totaling about 2,200) had migrated west, the most recent making the journey in early 1838. Although four of those groups completed their ordeal without massive loss of life, the experience of one of them, a party of 524 that departed in March 1834, confirmed forecasts of ruin. This party lost a reported eighty-four to disease (mostly from cholera)

as they traveled west and an additional 170 or so from other unidentified afflictions in the months after their arrival—a death toll of close to 50 percent.
Cherokees, of course, knew about this. They were also aware of the facts of
the Choctaw and Creek removals, if from no other source than Choctaw and
Creek delegates in Washington in early 1838, who informed John Ross—also
visiting the capital—of the massive loss of life they had sustained.[44]

The death toll from prior removals did not lead U.S. officials to reconsider
their plans to move the Cherokees west. This was not because officials were
ignorant. Removal agents and missionaries reported the number of deaths
for particular parties, and these provided the basis for a general picture in
Washington. Perhaps officials refused to look at this information. Perhaps
they gave it a glance—maybe even more than a glance—but then shoved
it from their minds. Whatever the case, they had ample cause to know that
moving something on the order of 19,000 Cherokees west was almost certain
to be deadly.[45]

Immediately after the May 23 deadline, U.S. troops began rounding up
the Cherokee Nation for removal. Although General Scott ordered his troops
to proceed "in a humane and merciful manner," their actions revealed a disposition to punish and inflict pain. A woman named Ooloocha later recalled
that "soldiers came and took us from home. They first surrounded our house
and they took the mare while we were at work in the fields and they drove
us out of doors and did not permit us to take anything with us not even a
second change of clothes." Evan Jones, a Baptist missionary, confirmed that
Ooloocha's testimony was typical when he reported that "multitudes were allowed no time to take any thing with them, except the clothes they had on."
The roundup, Jones further observed, created opportunities for "plunderers,
who, like hungry wolves, follow in the train of the captors." Thieves rifled
Cherokee houses, took possession of their livestock, and, as the ethnologist
James Mooney later learned, robbed their graves of the "silver pendants and
other valuables deposited with the dead." Once the troops captured Cherokees, they concentrated them in camps to await removal. As they did, missionary Daniel Butrick recorded, the soldiers "use[d] the same language as if
driving hogs, and goad[ed] them forward with their bayonets." One man,
"seeing his children thus goaded on, picked up a stone and struck a soldier."
For this he was handcuffed and "whipped a hundred lashes." Many years later,
a soldier who participated in the roundup said that although he had "fought
through the civil war and seen men shot to pieces and slaughtered by the
thousands, the Cherokee removal was the cruelest work I ever knew."[46]

The army was unable to collect every single Cherokee. Many fled to the woods, where hundreds died and others "subsisted on roots and wild berries." A few hundred survivors eventually joined a small group of Cherokees whose homes were in the mountains of southwestern North Carolina and who were exempt from the Treaty of New Echota's removal requirements. The large majority of Cherokees, however, could not evade the dragnet. By mid-June, as missionary Elizur Butler wrote, Georgia had been "completely . . . swept of Cherokees," a metaphor anticipating modern historians' indictment of Cherokee removal as ethnic cleansing.[47]

DEATH CAMPS AND THE CHEROKEE TRAIL OF TEARS

Three parties totaling 2,740 (including slaves) departed for the West in June 1838, traveling most of the way by water—down the Tennessee River to the Ohio, then to the Mississippi and up the Arkansas to Little Rock and on to Fort Gibson (Fig. 34). By the end of September when their journeys were over, the three parties numbered only 1,900–2,000. Some of the decline was due to the desertion of perhaps 300, but most of it was because people succumbed to disease. Government agents did not provide a full account of the death toll, though a report on the second party documented the deaths of seventy Cherokees in three weeks. An observer in Arkansas who witnessed all three parties reported that they were "suffering very much with measles and fever." A reasonable estimate would be that between 500 and 700 perished along the way.[48]

Several additional parties were slated to follow these three, but as reports of high mortality trickled east, the Cherokee National Council petitioned General Scott to delay their departure "till the sickly time is over." Otherwise, they said, "the whole nation will die." Although it provoked the wrath of contractors who had been anticipating profiting from the sale of food, supplies, and transportation, Secretary of War Joel Poinsett did not want to alienate the Cherokee leadership further and so assented to their plea to delay until fall.[49]

Tragically, this apparent reprieve left the remaining 16,000 Cherokees in a death trap. Throughout the summer, Cherokees remained confined in internment camps. The two largest were at Ross's Landing (near Chattanooga, Tennessee) and the old Cherokee Agency in eastern Tennessee. Conditions were abysmal (insufficient food, little or no shelter, unclean water, and unsanitary conditions), and they were made worse by an extraordinarily hot summer with very little rain. On July 12, missionary Elizur Butler wrote that dysentery

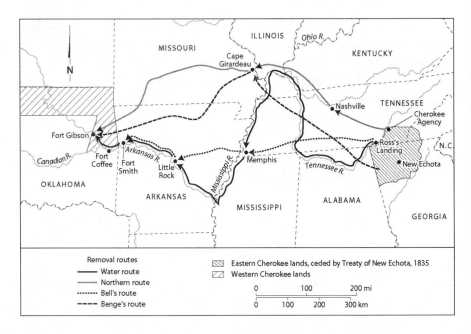

Fig. 34. Cherokee removal

was rampant and that measles had also appeared. Appointed as a physician at one of the camps, Butler tried his best to treat the sick, but his efforts and those of Cherokees themselves could do no more than ease the sufferings of the dying. By early August, Butler reported that several hundred "infant children have been removed by death." A month later, Butler added whooping cough and "remitting fevers" to the catalog of diseases destroying Cherokee bodies. Butler's fellow missionary Daniel Butrick also documented a mounting catastrophe, writing in late July that twenty were dying daily in the largest of the camps, with five additional per day in the others. The Cherokee Nation was further attacked by white men who raped Cherokee girls and women. In one instance, Butrick wrote in his diary, soldiers came upon a "young married woman, a member of the Methodist society." Through "fear or other causes" they induced her to drink liquor and "yield to their seduction, so that she is now an outcast." In another case, two men from a nearby settlement followed a grandmother and her grandson and granddaughter. One of the men seized the granddaughter, took her away, and "abus[ed] her in the most shameful manner" while the other "was fighting away her almost frantic grandmother & brother." These and other cases of rape were not just attacks on individuals; they were part and parcel of an ongoing assault on the well-being of the Cherokee Nation.[50]

By the time removal resumed in early October 1838, around 2,000 of the 16,000 Cherokees in the camps had perished.[51] Those who remained alive (many ill and malnourished) were divided into fourteen parties. Because of the lateness of the season, the rivers were too low for navigation, and so all went by land. Twelve parties took the "northern route" through Tennessee, Kentucky, and southern Illinois to the Mississippi, and then through Missouri and Arkansas to Fort Gibson in Oklahoma. Two groups took different routes, one following "Bell's route" directly west to Memphis and Little Rock and up the Arkansas River to Fort Smith, the other taking "Benge's route" northwest through northeastern Alabama, Tennessee, and Kentucky to Cape Girardeau, Missouri, and west to Fort Gibson. The first parties completed their journeys in early January, though bad weather and ice on the Mississippi delayed many emigrants, and the last did not arrive until March. One newspaper reported that many Cherokees in a party traveling through Alabama were "destitute of shoes and other necessary articles of clothing." Already, "50 of them have died." Evan Jones, traveling with another party through Missouri, wrote in late December that it had been "exceedingly cold." Those who were "thinly clad" were "very uncomfortable," and it seemed likely that "great numbers of the young, and the infirm will inevitably be sacrificed." The "fact that the removal is effected by coercion," Jones added, "makes it the more galling to the feelings of the survivors." The official reports state that there were 13,948 people in all fourteen parties at the beginning of the journey and 12,129 at the end, a decline of over 1,800. Extrapolating from an incomplete record of deaths along the way suggests that at least 700 died, but the number was probably higher, since it is unlikely that over 1,000 deserted. Whatever the exact number, disease, exposure, fatigue, malnutrition, and despair had taken a terrible toll.[52]

There are few reports on the conditions for these fourteen parties after their arrival in Oklahoma. Given the prevalence of disease on the trail, losses undoubtedly continued, though had they been anything close to those of the Choctaws and Creeks immediately after their removals, reports would have found their way into the historical record. Even without considering possible mortality in Oklahoma in 1839, the death toll for the main phase of Cherokee removal (1838–1839) was close to 4,000. In addition, as many as 400–500 Cherokees may have perished while avoiding capture in North Carolina in 1838–1839. Taking into account that number along with the 250 or more who died in the 1834 removal and the additional number who reportedly died shortly after their arrival in Oklahoma in mid-1838 suggests a total approaching 5,000 out of an eastern Cherokee population of 22,000–23,000 prior to the first removal in 1834.[53] American "benevolence" had resulted in a Cherokee population decline of at least 20 percent.

PRELUDE TO SEMINOLE REMOVAL, 1816–1832

Unlike the other southern nations, the Seminoles in Florida did not possess territory the United States desired for settlement. Nonetheless, as early as the 1810s, with Florida still a colony of Spain, Americans began to eye Seminole lands because a Seminole Florida offered a place of freedom for people desiring to escape enslavement on southern plantations, especially in Georgia. Not only did slave owners wish to retain their human property, they feared that a growing population of self-liberated blacks might provide fertile ground for fomenting slave revolts, possibly leading the entire Southeast to follow the path of Haiti, the world's first independent black republic.

U.S. aggression against the Seminoles began in July 1816, when American soldiers and sailors, along with Creek auxiliaries, attacked Negro Fort, a fortified town of Black Seminoles, Seminoles, and Creek Red Sticks on the Apalachicola River, about 150 miles east of Pensacola (Fig. 35). When a gunboat fired on the fort, a cannonball landed in a powder magazine, causing a massive explosion that killed several dozen inside the fort. This triggered what is known as the First Seminole War. After Seminoles attacked a naval vessel on the Apalachicola in November 1817, killing forty, U.S. forces, commanded by Andrew Jackson, marched against several Seminole towns in northern Florida. Most were deserted, but in April U.S. troops killed a reported forty Seminole men defending a village on Econfina Creek, near modern-day Panama City. Besides fighting Seminoles and Black Seminoles, Jackson captured Spanish posts at St. Marks and Pensacola. This pressured Spain to cede Florida to the United States a year later in the Adams-Onís Treaty.[54]

With the United States now claiming Florida within the European imperial system, federal officials began to dispossess the Seminoles as a prelude to their eventual removal. The first step in this process occurred at Moultrie Creek (near St. Augustine) in 1823, when U.S. commissioner James Gadsden offered the Seminoles an annuity of $5,000 for twenty years and a reservation in central Florida in exchange for ceding two-thirds of their lands. To con-

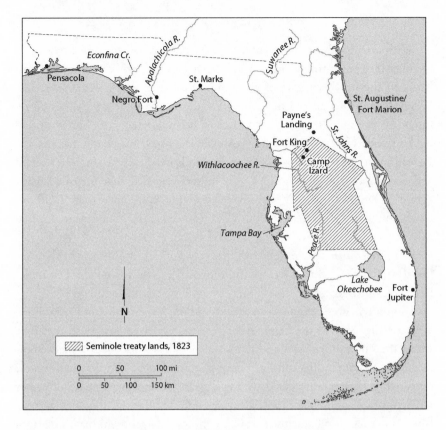

Fig. 35. First and Second Seminole wars

vince Seminole leaders to sign, Gadsden reminded them that Andrew Jackson had "subdued" the Red Sticks in 1814, and in 1817 could have "driven you into the ocean" if he had wished. Gadsden did not need to tell his audience what would happen if they rejected the treaty. The message was clear enough. In 1832 the same James Gadsden met with Seminoles at Payne's Landing south of modern-day Gainesville to demand their agreement to a new treaty. This one required them to be incorporated into the Creek Nation and relocate to the Creeks' western lands. In the absence of any record of the proceedings at Payne's Landing, there is no direct evidence that Gadsden repeated the threats he had issued in 1823 or used other means of coercion and deceit. Soon, however, Seminole leaders would protest that they had not freely agreed to the Payne's Landing Treaty.[55]

THE SECOND SEMINOLE WAR

With a removal treaty in hand, U.S. officials moved to implement it. In October 1834 government agent Wiley Thompson met with Seminoles at Fort King, in the northern part of the Seminole reservation in central Florida. When Thompson ordered the Seminoles to prepare for removal, they all refused. An emerging leader named Osceola had migrated as a child with Red Stick Creeks. Now close to thirty years old, he urged his people to obey the "Great Spirit" by not departing "from the lands which we live on, our homes, and the graves of our fathers." Other leaders objected that they had never agreed to the 1832 treaty. Micanopy, for example, contended that "I did not touch the pen; I only reached over and pointed to it." Thompson accused Micanopy of lying, but Charley Emathla countered by saying, "At Payne's Landing the white people forced us into a treaty" and pointing out that unlike Thompson, "I was there." An unmoved Thompson told the Seminoles that "you must go; and if not willing, you will be compelled to go."[56]

Soon after, President Jackson authorized an increase in troops stationed at Fort King. Should the Seminoles refuse the Great Father's wish that they vacate their homes, Jackson told them (through Thompson), "I have then directed the Commanding officer to remove you by force." Rather than submit to this threat, Seminoles decided to fight. On December 28, 1835, a force of 180 Seminoles led by Micanopy, Jumper, Hulbutta Harjo (Alligator), and the Black Seminole Abraham attacked a U.S. military detachment marching from Tampa Bay to reinforce Fort King, killing all 110, including its commander, Major Francis Dade. The same day, Osceola and other Seminoles raided Fort King and killed Agent Thompson. Not since the western confederacy's destruction of St. Clair's army in 1791 had Indians killed as many Americans.[57]

These attacks were not rash acts taken on the spur of the moment. The Seminoles' decision to go to war was as carefully calculated as the Cherokees' decision to take Georgia to court. Why were Seminoles, more than the other southeastern nations, willing to fight? Like all other Indian nations, they loved their land. One of their chiefs, known in the sources by his English name, John Hicks, explained it this way: "Here our navel strings were first cut, and the blood from them sunk into the earth and made the country dear to us." But Seminoles were a relatively small nation. Including Black Seminoles, they numbered between 5,000 and 6,000, only a quarter the size of the Creeks or the Cherokees. How could they hope to prevail against the United States?[58] One possible explanation is that Seminoles had no choice. Black

Seminoles, in particular, felt their only alternative was to fight to preserve their freedom. It was either war or a return to former chains somewhere in the South or enslavement by wealthy Creeks. But, although Black Seminoles had influence, they did not control Seminole decisionmaking.[59] Why would the Seminoles themselves decide on war? Seminoles had a strong tradition of militant resistance to the United States. Many had been part of the Red Stick movement a generation before. Yet, the Red Stick experience might well counsel *against* war. Andrew Jackson and other American war leaders had killed as many as 2,000 Red Stick Creeks in 1814. What would prevent something as catastrophic or worse?

Although we do not have access to records of Seminole decisionmaking, two important considerations can be identified. First, the Seminoles in 1835 were better armed than the Red Sticks had been. At Horseshoe Bend a generation earlier, only one in three men had a gun. After the First Seminole War Seminoles began stockpiling guns and ammunition. Not only did they use annuities from the 1823 treaty to purchase arms from American traders, they halted an earlier cultural practice of placing arms and ammunition in graves to accompany the deceased into the afterlife. This does not mean that Seminoles had ceased to rely on spiritual power. Prophets such as Otulke Thlacco were able to "make known the approach of troops, find game, and control the seasons." Still, guns mattered. Second, in contrast to other southern nations surrounded by very large settler populations and an infrastructure of roads and forts, Seminoles controlled a sizable area (not only their central Florida reservation, but the otherwise uninhabited areas to the south) and were at some distance from a relatively thin zone of settlement. In 1830, the non-Native population of Florida was only 35,000, with the large majority in the panhandle. (By comparison, Georgia's population was 517,000, Alabama's 310,000, and Mississippi's 137,000.) Seminoles realized that U.S. armies would have serious difficulties operating against them in central and southern Florida, a land laced with swamps and heavily wooded hammocks that would provide cover to those who knew its terrain and thwart those who did not. For good reason, then, the majority of Seminoles judged that they could succeed in countering a U.S. invasion. They would undoubtedly suffer disruption, material deprivation, and loss of life, but they could inflict enough damage on American forces to leverage a settlement and avoid removal.[60]

The Second Seminole War lasted seven long years. At first, Seminoles had the upper hand. After what Americans termed the "Dade massacre," the

U.S. army quickly mobilized against the Seminoles, sending its "most distinguished officer," General Winfield Scott, to raise militia forces and take command. Acting on his own, another general, Edmund P. Gaines, brought 1,000 troops from New Orleans to Florida. In February 1836, a force of Seminoles led by Osceola, Jumper, and Hulbutta Harjo attacked Gaines and his men, pinning them down at Camp Izard, just southwest of Fort King, for several days and forcing them to eat their horses and mules. The following month, as Scott's forces moved through the Florida peninsula, Seminoles harassed them, losing a few fighters, but avoiding being trapped by Scott's men. Having failed to crush the Seminoles, America's top general offered his resignation. That summer, the "sickly season" in Florida, hundreds of soldiers fell ill from diarrhea, dysentery, and fever. Many died. Troops withdrew from the field and the army abandoned Fort King and other posts in central Florida, allowing Seminoles an opening to raid plantations in northern Florida.[61]

Despite their successes, some Seminoles decided that conditions would be better outside a war zone and so agreed to removal. In April 1836, a party of 407 Seminoles led by Holahte Emathla and Black Dirt departed from Tampa Bay. They traveled by schooner to New Orleans and then ascended the Mississippi by steamboat. By the time they reached Little Rock twenty-five had perished from unspecified diseases. As they proceeded, measles broke out and overland progress was hindered by heavy rains. On May 15, Lieutenant Jefferson Van Horne recorded that the party started at 11:00 a.m., "though with great difficulty on account of the great number of sick and dying." That day, they traveled only six miles and the next day not at all. When the Seminoles resumed their march on the 25th, Van Horne wrote: "Every soul soaked with rain. . . . The whole country one Quagmire." Two days later: "Numbers very low and dying, several died." When the party finally reached the end of their journey at Fort Smith, only 320 of the original 407 had survived. Once the Seminoles were settled among the Creeks along the Canadian River, unidentified diseases continued to destroy them. A year after removal, only half of the original 407 were alive. In retrospect, Holahte Emathla's people might have been better off resisting removal. But staying in Florida was perilous, too. Catastrophe loomed everywhere.[62]

In early 1837 the army, now commanded by General Thomas Jesup (fresh off his assignment rounding up Creek dissidents), planned for a massive winter campaign to avoid the "sickly season." Nine thousand troops, including several hundred Shawnee, Delaware, Kickapoo, Sauk and Mesquakie, and Choctaw auxiliaries, would eventually be mobilized—well over twice the size of Anthony Wayne's force in 1794. In the meantime, Jesup ordered small forces to attack Seminole villages, burn their houses and stored food, kill their cattle and horses, and take prisoners, including women and children, to be used to pressure Seminoles to move. Jesup also negotiated an agreement with Jumper and Micanopy to give up the fight and move to Oklahoma. By the end of May, several hundred Seminoles were in a detention camp near Tampa Bay awaiting transport to the West. On June 2, however, a party of Seminoles led by Osceola and Coacoochee (Wildcat) entered the unfortified camp and spirited the potential emigrants away.[63]

Jesup responded to this setback by doubling down on the tactic of securing Seminole prisoners to use as bargaining chips. His methods were devious. In September 1837, when a Florida militia captured Coacoochee's father, King Philip, Jesup invited Coacoochee to talk in St. Augustine. Although Coacoochee arrived carrying a white flag, Jesup confined him and others with him in St. Augustine's Fort Marion. Jesup pulled a similar stunt a few weeks later when Osceola and Coa Hadjo sent word that they wanted to negotiate. Jesup replied that he was willing to talk, but it was a lie. As Osceola and Coa Hadjo approached St. Augustine, Jesup ordered a military detachment to intercept them. They, too, carried a white flag, but Jesup had instructed the detachment to ignore such emblems and so Jesup's men seized the Seminoles and sent them to Fort Marion. With key Seminole leaders within the supposedly impregnable walls of Fort Marion and with a huge army on the move, Jesup was confident that the war would soon end. But he seriously underestimated Seminole resolve and ingenuity. Over the course of several weeks, some of the Fort Marion prisoners stopped eating so that they could lose weight. On November 29, they squeezed through a narrow opening and used knotted blankets to allow the escape of Coacoochee, a Black Seminole named John Cavallo, and eighteen others. King Philip and Osceola, weak from hunger and sickness, decided not to follow. Officials sent Osceola to South Carolina's Fort Moultrie, where he died not long after. King Philip perished en route to Oklahoma the following year.[64]

Even as Seminoles were escaping Fort Marion, Jesup's army was marching on their strongholds in central and south Florida. Given that the Seminoles had a fighting force barely more than a tenth the size of the Americans', it is remarkable that they weren't annihilated. Seminoles were unable to ambush U.S. troops, but they were able to fend them off. In the largest battle of this phase of the conflict—on Christmas Day near Lake Okeechobee—400 Seminole fighters held their ground against a force twice as large under the command of future President Zachary Taylor. After more than two hours of fierce firing, the Seminoles retreated, but not before killing twenty-six and wounding 112 of Taylor's men. Their own reported losses were eleven killed and fourteen wounded. Over the next month, Seminoles faced additional attacks without allowing U.S. forces to inflict major casualties or take prisoners. Three factors allowed the Seminoles to avoid catastrophe. First, Seminoles were on their home terrain and so could evade troops seeking to destroy them. Second, even after two years of war, Seminoles had been able to replenish their arsenal. U.S. troops sometimes abandoned powder kegs as they retreated from Seminole forces, and the corpses of soldiers killed in battle yielded guns. Seminoles also obtained munitions by raiding American plantations and trading hides and jerked meat with Cubans and Bahamians. U.S. officials grudgingly recognized a third factor. As one lieutenant put it, these "rude sons of the forest" possessed "a courage in attacking." But it was not just Seminole fighters who were brave. All community members endured privation, the loss of loved ones, and the fear of death in the hope of continuing to live in their lands.[65]

Still, war was taking its toll. By early 1838, probably about 100 Seminole and Black Seminole men had lost their lives while fighting or in prison. War also damaged the Seminole economy. Some of this was direct (Americans burned towns and killed cattle), but some was through the disruption of normal economic activities. Seminoles tried their best to adapt to wartime conditions by replanting some of the fields U.S. military forces destroyed, planting new fields in concealed areas, and continuing to rely on cattle raising (and raiding), hunting, fishing, and gathering plants, especially the roots of coontie, a vital source of carbohydrates. Nonetheless, reports indicate that many Seminoles were close to starvation and that children were dying in large numbers. In February 1838 Seminole leaders Tuskegee and Halleck Hadjo made known their willingness to cease fighting provided they could be left alone in southern Florida. With the failures of the previous months in mind, General Jesup recommended to Secretary of War Joel Poinsett that the government abandon its attempt to force the Seminoles to move west. "My decided opinion," Jesup wrote, "is that unless *immediate* emigration be abandoned, the war will continue for years to come, and at constantly accumulating expense." While waiting for Poinsett's response, 500 Seminoles camped near Jesup's temporary headquarters at Fort Jupiter on the Atlantic coast (just north of modern-day Palm Beach).[66]

A few weeks later, Poinsett's reply arrived. Indian removal, he curtly informed Jesup, was the "settled policy of the country." Poinsett commanded

Jesup to "put it out of the power of these Indians to do any further mis-chief. They ought to be captured, or destroyed." Two days after receiving Poinsett's letter, Jesup returned to his old tricks and seized the 500 Semi-noles camped nearby who had been awaiting a negotiated settlement. Jesup dispatched them across the peninsula to Tampa Bay, where they would be transported by ship west. A month later, when word of Jesup's capture of the 500 reached Seminoles at Lake Okeechobee, Hulbutta Harjo and Yahol-achee's (Cloud's) people, numbering 360, decided to surrender and added to the number at Tampa Bay.[67]

As they awaited expulsion, Seminole women and girls were vulnerable to American officers and enlisted men. Evidence of rape comes from two sources. One is Seminole oral history. According to Betty Mae Tiger Jumper, elected chief of the Florida Seminoles in 1967, her great-grandmother grew "more and more worried, because the soldiers had begun using the younger women. She was concerned for her daughters. Then, she and her oldest daughter were raped." The second source is the diary of a private stationed at Tampa Bay named Bartholemew Lynch. Lynch made several references to sexual assault, including this entry of October 6, 1838: "If the officers in Tampa would be half as mad to fight Buck Indians as they are to buck Indian Squaws, they would unquestionably be the bravest and gallantest officers in the world. The way they pitch into the squaws is a sin."[68]

In summer 1838 the government shipped a reported 1,300 Seminoles and Black Seminoles from Tampa Bay. Schooners conveyed them to New Orleans, and steamboats transported them up the Mississippi and Arkansas rivers to Fort Gibson (Fig. 36). The government agent in charge of one party of 674 reported fifty-four deaths from unidentified causes. Other parties evidently suffered fewer losses. Another group of 300 Seminoles and thirty-four Creeks from the Apalachicola area sailed for New Orleans from Pensacola in late October. As they made their way up the Mississippi, their agent reported that they had "suffered very much from sickness" and that six had died. Within months of their arrival, these people were hit by the same smallpox epidemic that struck the Choctaws. In February 1839, another 200 Seminoles and Black Seminoles, including the interpreter, negotiator, and war leader Abraham, left Tampa Bay. Somewhere north of Natchez the boiler of their steamboat exploded, killing "a number."[69]

Three years into the Second Seminole War, the U.S. government had managed to remove fewer than half of the Seminoles and Black Seminoles from Florida. Those who remained had retreated to the swamp lands in the

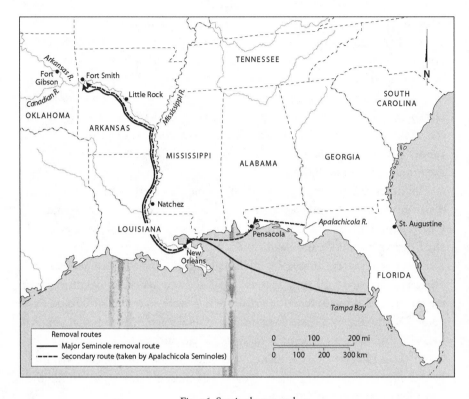

Fig. 36. Seminole removal

southern half of the peninsula, where they would be even harder to find. How to get at them? One possibility was to enlist bloodhounds. Florida territorial governor Richard Call took the initiative in early 1840, when he acquired thirty-three bloodhounds from Cubans for the army's use. Their purpose, according to the *Tallahassee Floridian,* was to "worry," "hunt," "bite," and "tear to pieces all the red devils they can catch." Northern moralists were outraged by the importation of bloodhounds from the Spanish empire. Protestant adherents to the "Black Legend" of Spanish atrocities, they saw turning bloodhounds on Indians as emblematic of Spanish/papal depravity. If the practice was not stopped, northerners petitioned Congress, it would result in a "deep and lasting disgrace . . . upon the national character."[70]

As it turned out, the bloodhounds were ineffective in the Florida wetlands. A new commanding officer, General Walter Armistead, turned to the more banal approach of using armed men to search for Seminole villages, destroy them, and kill and capture their inhabitants. This, apparently, was less disgraceful to the national character, as these tactics provoked little outcry. Between June and December 1840, U.S. forces attacked various Seminole positions, killing a few and burning crops. Though often on the defensive, Seminoles had the capacity for offensive action. In May a force of 100 led by Coacoochee ambushed U.S. troops near the site of the Payne's Landing Treaty, killing six. To the south, Chakaika organized an attack on a settlement on one of the Florida Keys. Coming by canoe at night, they destroyed most of the settlement's buildings and killed as many as thirteen. The following year, William Worth—the sixth U.S. commander in as many years—attempted to break Seminole resistance by moving against them during the summer, a time when Seminoles had counted on the sickly invaders to retreat. Worth ordered his officers to "find the enemy" and "capture, or exterminate" them. To defend themselves, Seminoles agreed to execute any messenger sent to their country, to remain in compact groups to protect their families, and to organize groups of scouts to gather intelligence on troop movements. These measures succeeded in preventing disaster, though in the second half of 1841 Worth's operations were successful in harrying Seminoles, killing and capturing some, and destroying material resources.[71]

Six years of war caused even the fiercest opponents of removal to reconsider. In July 1841 Coacoochee, the most prominent leader of Seminole resistance since his escape from Fort Marion in 1837, decided to take his chances in the West. To some extent, his thinking must have been influenced by a rope at his neck. In May government officials had seized Coacoochee during negotiations and shipped him to New Orleans, but higher officials ordered him back to Florida so that they could threaten to hang him if his people did not agree to removal. Yet Coacoochee's larger consideration was his people. In a message to them conveyed through his brother, Coacoochee underscored the priority of women and children. "I can live like a wolf, a dog," he said, but "the whites are too strong; they go by land and in boats: why should our women and children suffer?" Fortunately for Coacoochee's people and other groups of Seminoles who made the journey to Oklahoma that year (about 800 in total), they were spared substantial loss of life.[72]

By the winter of 1841–1842, approximately 1,000–1,100 Seminoles remained in Florida. The U.S. army continued to try to uproot them. In April near Lake Apopka (south of a rebuilt Fort King), forty Seminoles under the leadership of Halleck held off 400 of Worth's soldiers before disappearing into dense vegetation, an impressive military achievement. But Halleck's people were unable to hold off starvation, and so ten days later Halleck approached

Worth to discuss an end to hostilities. Taking a page from General Jesup, Worth escorted Halleck to Fort King under the pretense of pursuing diplomacy while ordering a subordinate to give Halleck's people a feast and, once their guard was down, seize them. These methods allowed the army to secure about 400 Seminoles for removal in the spring and summer. By the fall, they had completed the journey west. With only a few hundred Seminoles left in Florida, in August the United States declared the war over (Fig. 37).[73]

Had the Second Seminole War been a struggle between two groups of people with roughly the same population, Seminoles easily would have prevailed. Their knowledge of the land, their relative immunity to local pathogens, and their intelligence and fierceness in war gave them decisive advantages. But the United States' numerical advantage was overwhelming. At its height the army had 9,000 men in Florida, far more than the maximum of 1,000 Seminoles and Black Seminoles fighters. More to the point, the United States had the capacity to continuously produce fresh bodies for war. Even though over 1,500 regulars and volunteers perished in Florida from 1837 through 1842 (20 percent in combat, the remainder from disease), the United States was able to summon replacements from a vast reservoir of young men willing or persuadable to fight. Seminoles did not lose as many fighting men as the Americans, but it was much harder to replace those they lost. When the war broke out, several hundred blacks who had been enslaved on Florida and Georgia plantations escaped to Seminole country. Creeks fleeing removal from Alabama also joined Seminoles.[74] This added to the ranks of fighting men, but was not enough to offset the slow but constant drain of those killed while defending villages or in prison after capture. And, of course, the number of men capable of bearing arms declined each time a Seminole community went west. Another critical variable was that Seminole women and children were subject to severe hardship and the constant threat of violence. American women and children living in settlements that had been planted in and near Seminole territory also had reason for fear. But U.S. attacks on Seminole communities were far more frequent than Seminole attacks on American settlements, and they threatened the entire Seminole population. In sharp contrast, the bulk of the U.S. population was far from danger. Seminoles made no plans against Charleston, Philadelphia, or Boston.

Historians have characterized the Second Seminole War as a "moral failure," "an embarrassing affair," and an "idiotic war."[75] Although these descriptors are apt in themselves, they err in rendering the Second Seminole War an aberration. In fact, the war was entirely consistent with the United States'

GROUP OF OSCEOLA'S WARRIORS.

1—MICKENOPAH.   2—KING PHILIP.
3—WILDCAT.   4—CLOUD.
5—ALLIGATOR.   6—ABRAHAM.

Fig. 37. This collection of leaders of the Seminole resistance was assembled from portraits made by several artists, including George Catlin and John Casey. All six of these leaders eventually agreed to board vessels bound for New Orleans and from there go up the Mississippi and on to Oklahoma. With the exception of King Philip and Abraham, who died en route, all of them reached the West, where they labored to rebuild their communities. From Coe, *Red Patriots*, between pp. 27 and 28. Reproduced by University of Oregon Digital Scholarship Services.

policy of Indian removal. U.S. officials would have preferred that Seminoles go west "voluntarily," or, to put it another way, that the Seminoles yield to threats without Americans actually having to go to war. Because the Seminoles did not yield, however, war became necessary, and because Seminoles were hard to defeat, U.S. commanders took actions that were immoral, embarrassing, and idiotic. But these actions did not occur because the decision to go to war departed from established policy or because an unusually bad set of generals conducted the war. They flowed directly from the imperatives of the removal policy.

Focusing on the war's supposed uniqueness also has the perverse effect of understating the destruction of which it was a part. The war itself was certainly destructive. Seminoles lost men killed in battle, and community members perished under increasingly dire conditions as the war wore on. But the majority of Seminole losses between 1835 and 1842 occurred under conditions common to other removals—in detention camps waiting transportation, while en route, or shortly after arrival in the West. Jesup's capturing of Seminoles under white flags is deplorable, Call's unleashing of bloodhounds reprehensible, but it was not these actions, but the removal policy they served, that proved so deadly.

How many Seminoles perished from 1835 to 1842? According to a census of Seminoles in Oklahoma in March 1842, the population was 2,833. Adding the 1,000–1,100 remaining in Florida at that time and an additional 150 in Texas yields an estimate of 4,000–4,100 for the total postremoval Seminole population. From a preremoval population of between 5,000 and 6,000, this would mean a decline of at least 900 and perhaps as many as 2,000 (more actually died, since births partially offset deaths).[76] To put this in perspective, the 1,500 U.S. troops who died in Florida constituted one in every 8,670 of the United States' 13 million people in 1830 (0.0011 percent). By contrast, Seminole losses were at least one in six (18 percent), and perhaps as high as one in three (33 percent).

CONCLUSION: DESTRUCTION AND EVASION

Between 1830 and the early 1840s, the United States moved the large majority of the American South's Native people. At any given time, year in and year out, Indians were being forced from their homes, waiting and dying and being raped in detention camps, starving or freezing along trails of tears, or trying to rebuild their communities in disease-ridden new homes. As Native people were being expelled, slave traffickers ripped African Americans from family members in older slave states, put them in chains, and drove them along a Second Middle Passage (its own trail of tears) to clear formerly Indigenous lands and plant them to white gold. In 1850, the South produced 1 billion pounds of cotton, triple its production in the year of the Indian Removal Act.[77] The removal of Cherokees, Choctaws, Chickasaws, and Creeks was vital to King Cotton's rise. Enslaved people continued to seek their freedom and so escaped their owners, but Florida was no longer a viable destination. Most followed the North Star. From the standpoint of southern power and security, removal had been a great success, but for nations indigenous to the South it was catastrophic.

In 1830, when policymakers began implementing removal, they may have genuinely believed that their policy was a humane alternative to Indians' otherwise inevitable extinction, although even then they had to ignore the fact that eastern Indians were *not* vanishing. They also had to shut their ears to the voices of Native leaders who predicted that removal would be a disaster. But as fatalities mounted year after year, the evidence became ever more clear that the policy of removal was leading to extinction—the very thing it was supposed to prevent. Faced with the fact of massive destruction, how could American leaders continue to declare their good intentions? Perhaps advocates of removal were self-conscious hypocrites, aware that their professions of benevolence were a figleaf for naked greed. The truth, however, may be that American leaders had mastered the art of evasion.

CHAPTER 9

Removal and the Northern Indian Nations, 1830–1850s

In his annual address to Congress in December 1830, Andrew Jackson identified three beneficiaries of the government's "benevolent policy" of removal. One was the Indians. Once in the West, they would be able to "pursue happiness in their own way, and under their own rude institutions." The other two beneficiaries were the states of Alabama and Mississippi. They would "advance rapidly in population, wealth, and power." Jackson did not say anything about what his new policy might do for states north of the Ohio River, an oversight that revealed a priority to promote the interests of his home region. Nonetheless, Jackson intended the Indian Removal Act to apply just as much to the North as to the South. In applauding removal's progress before Congress a year later, Jackson observed that "the time is not distant . . . when Ohio will be no longer embarrassed by the Indian population." He then offered a grand vision of removal's potential. Ultimately, the policy would "extinguish the Indian title to all lands lying within the states composing our federal union, and remove beyond their limits every Indian who is not willing to submit to their laws."[1] With the exception of New England, where small Indian populations would be allowed to remain, Indians everywhere east of the Mississippi would be gone, he said.

Jackson's prediction that almost all northern Indians would be removed west was wrong. Removal continued for a longer time in the North than in the

South (some Indians in the Great Lakes region were being asked to relocate in the 1850s), but fewer northern Indians were actually forced from their homes. Of an estimated population of 48,000 Indians north of the Ohio River in 1830, only about 24,000 were moved. Northern political leaders were just as capable as their counterparts in the South of vigorously pursuing removal, but they were not as relentless everywhere north of the Ohio. To build the free labor empire that New York senator William Seward defended in his rebuttal to South Carolina senator James Henry Hammond's 1858 King Cotton speech, new lands had to be made available when speculators, canal developers, miners, and farmers demanded them. An ever-expanding supply of land was also thought necessary to provide a "safety valve" for discontented urban workers.[2] In areas of high demand—northwestern Ohio, southern Michigan, Indiana, Illinois, and southern Wisconsin—Native nations faced as much pressure to relocate west of the Mississippi as any of the southern nations. Most were eventually removed. In the upper Great Lakes and upper Mississippi Valley, however, where settlement was relatively light into the 1840s, there was less demand for Indian lands and resources and correspondingly less pressure to force Indians out. In contrast to Florida, where Seminoles and Black Seminoles posed an existential threat to the cotton empire and so needed to be eliminated, in northern Michigan Ottawas and Ojibwes, off the main paths of western economic development, did not harbor proletarians who had escaped Massachusetts cotton mills and might foment revolution. In upstate New York, where settlement was much heavier, speculators spearheaded a sustained effort to remove the Haudenosaunees, but they eventually yielded to fierce Haudenosaunee opposition. Eventually, some New York political leaders decided they could tolerate the presence of Indians within their state provided their land base was reduced to next to nothing and they could be taxed. In general, then, distinct varieties of settler colonialism (one based on enslaved labor, the other on free labor) had different on-the-ground consequences.

REMOVALS FROM OHIO AND INDIANA

Andrew Jackson often took the lead in pursuing removal in the South, as when he invited the southern nations to meet with him personally in Tennessee in 1830. In the North, however, he delegated the work of removal to subordinates. Foremost among them was Lewis Cass, Michigan territorial governor and after August 1831 secretary of war. As we have seen, Cass had been devoted to the cause since at least 1818, when he broached the possibility of removal with Ohio Indian leaders. In the early years of Jackson's presidency, Cass was one of the removal policy's chief ideologues.

In March 1830, Cass wrote Superintendent of Indian Affairs Thomas L. McKenney with plans for the immediate removal of most Ohio Valley Indians. Cass thought that the Ohio Senecas, already on record as willing to relocate, would be the easiest to deal with. Wyandots, Shawnees, Ottawas, Potawatomis, and Miamis opposed removal, but Cass was confident that "active discreet men acquainted with the Indians" could eliminate Indians from Ohio, Indiana, and southern Michigan, areas where demands for land and economic development were strongest. Although most Whig politicians in the region voted against the Indian Removal Act, this was due more to political partisanship and a distaste for Georgia's bullying methods than because they wished Indian nations to remain within their territories and states. After the passage of the Indian Removal Act, there was an overwhelming consensus among Ohio Valley politicians and settlers in favor of removal provided it occurred in a way that was "voluntary."[3]

Although Cass characterized the Ohio Senecas on the lower Sandusky River as willing to move, they were in fact deeply ambivalent about the possibility. It is true that Seneca spokesmen informed "Our Great Father" in 1830 that his "red children . . . wish to go away beyond the Mississippi" because "the game is destroyed around their lands in Ohio, and their young people are daily learning bad habits from the white people." Yet, as the time grew near for the Senecas to sign a removal treaty, the government's agent, John McElvain, reported that they were "restless and unsettled in their minds." Some wanted to move *east* to live with their relatives in New York, others looked *north* to Canada as a possible sanctuary, while still others thought of relocating *northwest* to Green Bay, Wisconsin, to live among Oneidas who had moved there from New York some years before. Nonetheless, in February 1831 Ohio Seneca leaders signed a treaty exchanging their Ohio reservation for new lands along the Neosho River in the northwestern corner of what is now Oklahoma. By the time arrangements for Seneca removal had been made, fall had arrived. The Senecas wanted to wait until the following spring to move, likely because they feared they would suffer from winter conditions if they left late in the year. But McElvain had other things than Seneca well-being on his mind. Concerned that delaying Seneca removal might "operate to the prejudice of the Wyandots, and might prevent them from disposing of their lands," McElvain pressed the Senecas to depart.[4]

Three hundred and forty Senecas, along with fifty-eight Delawares, left Ohio in late 1831. About two-thirds departed in mid-October. They were to travel south to Cincinnati, via water to St. Louis, and then overland to Oklahoma. The remainder, slated to take an overland route the entire way, left in early November (Fig. 38). The first of the two parties traveled quickly, reaching St. Louis within two weeks. This party proceeded west, but the same cold weather that we saw descend on Choctaw migrants in the previous chapter set in and unidentified sickness broke out. By mid-December, the official

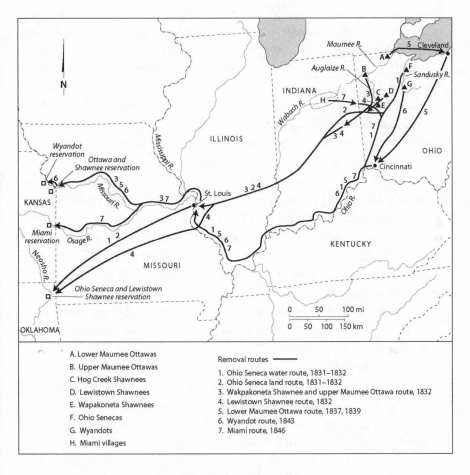

Fig. 38. Removals from Ohio and Indiana

in charge of their removal reported that several children "had their feet and hands frozen." A few of the party had died and "nearly the whole number became more or less unwell." Because of dreadful conditions and the inability to cross swollen rivers in the spring, this group remained camped for months fifty miles from St. Louis. When they finally resumed their journey in mid-May, they had to leave behind six people who were "too ill to be moved, and will no doubt die in a short time." In the meantime, the smaller party, traveling by land, made it only to Indiana before being forced to stop for the winter. When spring came, this party resumed its journey and joined the larger party in Missouri as they were breaking their winter camp. Together, the two groups traveled the last leg of their ordeal in slow misery. Swollen rivers delayed their progress and measles broke out among the children. Several perished before they reached the Neosho in early July, close to nine months after their departure. Although the existing documents do not provide a figure for the death toll during the removal of the Ohio Senecas, scattered reports indicate that a reasonable estimate would be around thirty.[5] Neither Agent McElvain nor the federal government had intended to cause the loss of close to 10 percent of the Ohio Seneca population. Nor did they know that a particularly bad winter was coming. But to describe these losses as "unintended" or "accidental" absolves the United States of its responsibility for loss of life that it would not have tolerated for its own citizens. Officials did not know in advance how deadly a particular removal might be, but it was clear that the process risked exactly what happened during the Seneca removal.

As the Senecas were being rounded up for removal, another government agent, James Gardiner, embarked upon the task of persuading Shawnees at Wapakoneta to vacate their village for western lands. Although Gardiner's primary qualification for this work was his service in the cause of securing Ohio's sixteen electoral votes for Andrew Jackson in 1828, he quickly adopted the tried and true approach of more experienced U.S. officials and told the Wapakoneta Shawnees that he knew what was best for them. The Shawnees' current condition, Gardiner said, was "deplorable." The "white people were now selling them whisky which was ruining them" and the "game was nearly gone." Shawnees, of course, knew all about whiskey's destructiveness and the scarcity of game. They had implemented a successful temperance program and had developed an economy based on farming and livestock as an alternative to one dependent on hunting. But they may not have known another piece of information (or was it a threat?) Gardiner provided them. The state of Ohio, he explained, "would soon extend her laws over them" and so Ohio would treat the Shawnees just as "Georgia had treated the Cherokees."[6]

Gardiner's overture to the Shawnees at Wapakoneta came at a perilous time. Under the leadership of Black Hoof they had built a strong community as a shield against removal. But Black Hoof, whose memory stretched back to the days when all of Ohio and a good part of western Pennsylvania were Indian country, died shortly after the passage of the Indian Removal Act. Perhaps not even their great chief could have held his people together to stave off removal, but in his absence the Wapakoneta Shawnees were "much divided about selling." Eventually, a majority of the Shawnees at Wapakoneta and its sister village of Hog Creek agreed to a treaty that ceded their Ohio lands and required them to join Shawnees in eastern Kansas. Even as they signed, however, their spokesman, Wewellipu, registered a sharp protest about the assumptions of white supremacy that underlay Gardiner's paternalistic arguments for removal. In contrast to his own belief "that the Great Spirit made all men alike," Wewellipu said, "my friend [Gardiner] thinks He made three distinct classes of men." To the "white man he gave a white skin and a great deal of sense; to the Indian a red skin, and a little less sense; and to the negro, a black skin, and very little sense."[7] Had Americans not been racists, had they treated Indians equally, they would have allowed them to stay.

To avoid a repeat of the disastrous Seneca removal, U.S. officials planned to move close to 450 Wapakoneta and Hog Creek Shawnees in summer 1832 so that they could complete their journey before winter's arrival. Other communities Gardiner had convinced to sign removal treaties would travel with them: 100 or so from small Ottawa communities on the upper Maumee and Auglaize rivers, slated to join the Shawnees in eastern Kansas, and 250 Lewistown Shawnees (a community that included many Senecas), whose destination was with Ohio Senecas on the Neosho River in Oklahoma (for their routes, see Fig. 38). The government wanted these communities to travel by water, as it was cheaper and faster, but tribal members opposed this plan. Besides the fact that "their native modesty revolts at the use of the only convenience on board a boat to obey the calls of nature," they feared that "some of their little children might be drowned" or that they would be "scalded 'like the white man cleans his hog'" in the event of an explosion. If they could not travel overland on horseback, many women said they would "remain here and die, and be buried with our relatives." By the time Gardiner gained permission for a land route and by the time supplies arrived, it was late September before the three groups were able to begin their journey. All departed except eighty-four Hog Creek Shawnees who insisted on delaying and traveled to Kansas the following spring.[8]

As they approached the Mississippi, the Shawnees and Ottawas heard "fearful accounts" of cholera ahead in St. Louis and crossed the Mississippi just north of the city. Reports document only one death among the 250 or so Lewistown Shawnees (including Senecas living among them) before they reached Oklahoma in mid-December, and only six deaths from cholera among the Wapakoneta Shawnees and Ottawas before their arrival in Kansas in late November. Nonetheless, there are reasons to believe the death toll was substantially higher, at least for the Wapakoneta Shawnees and Ottawas. There are no reports allowing for a comparison of the Lewistown Shawnees' population before and after removal, but counts of the Wapakoneta Shawnees and the Ottawas show a decline in the two groups' combined populations from 466 when they began their journey to 408 when it was over. If these figures are accurate, and assuming there were no desertions, the death toll (whether from cholera alone or cholera in combination with other diseases) would have been over 12 percent, much higher than the 5 percent estimated for the Choctaws afflicted by cholera at the same time (see Chapter 8). Perhaps because these were such small communities and the absolute number of deaths may seem unremarkable, historians have paid little attention to their sufferings. Yet, it may have been as deadly as many of the well-known trails of tears.[9]

The remaining Ottawas in Ohio, about 400 on the lower Maumee River near modern-day Toledo, attempted to avoid removal by negotiating for a treaty in 1833 that ceded most of their lands, but reserved several small tracts, totaling about 2,200 acres. Why the Ohio nations who had signed removal treaties earlier did not propose this approach is unclear. Perhaps it did not occur to them, or perhaps they judged that it would leave them with an insufficient and insecure land base. In any case, what hope the Ottawas had that this approach would keep them in Ohio soon disappeared when it became apparent that the tracts they reserved in 1833 were too small to support the entire community. So, in 1837 most Ottawas agreed to join their relatives who had earlier been sent to eastern Kansas. In August about 200 Ottawas traveled to Cleveland and from there by canal boats to Cincinnati and then by steamship to St. Louis and up the Missouri to their destination. The documentary record for this removal does not report deaths, although we do know that officials counted 200 Ottawas upon their departure and only 170 when they arrived. Assuming that the counts were accurate, it is possible that some or all of this decline was due to death, but undocumented desertions along the way may have been a significant factor. Already, many Ottawas from the lower Maumee had evaded removal by joining Ojibwe and Potawatomi communities at Manatoulin and Walpole islands in Canada, and so we know that Canada was on Ottawa people's mind as a possible destination. Not all Ottawas were forced from their homes. One hundred were removed to Kansas in 1839, but another 100 managed to stay in Ohio on lands reserved in 1833.[10]

Although Andrew Jackson had confidently predicted that Ohio would no longer be "embarrassed" by Indians, many of Ohio's Native residents refused to follow the script. In late May 1831, when Gardiner first met with the 500–600 Wyandots on the upper Sandusky and "urged them to remove to the west," their leaders were "mortified and surprised" and asked for time to consult with their people. In subsequent discussions, Wyandots expressed doubts about the quality of the western lands the government had designated for them—the Platte country in the northwestern corner of present-day Missouri (though at the time not yet part of the state). They requested "a delegation of four or five of their nation to see the country." Gardiner supported this request, naively confident that the delegates would like what they saw and that the Wyandots would happily go where they were supposed to.[11]

Once approved, the Wyandot delegation departed Cincinnati in late October 1831. When the delegates returned in January, Gardiner was dismayed to learn that their report was negative. The Wyandots stated that the lands in question had little timber and game was scarce. Although the soil was fertile, the hills were so steep that the soil was sure to wash away once plowed. Beyond this, Wyandots would be vulnerable to attacks by Sauks and Mesquakies and to incursions from the "most abandoned, dissolute and wicked class of people we ever saw; fugitives from justice from the States of Virginia, Kentucky, Tennessee and other southern States." Gardiner contended that the delegation's leader, William Walker, had secretly opposed removal all along and only pretended to be willing to consider it. Walker may well have been duplicitous just as Gardiner claimed. Why not? His strategy worked to frustrate the government's plan for the Wyandots to leave the Sandusky.[12]

Wyandots successfully thwarted removal for over a decade. Anticipating a new effort to get them to sign a removal treaty, the Wyandots used funds of their own to send another delegation to Kansas in 1834. In September, just as Ohio governor Robert Lucas opened a council with the Wyandot Nation, the delegates returned with—hardly surprising—another negative report. As negotiations proceeded, they and other Wyandot opponents of removal used this report to maintain unity and so prevent Lucas from creating momentum for signing. In theory, Lucas and other officials like Secretary of War Cass could have turned to troops, but they decided to keep chipping away at Wyandot opposition and Wyandot land. In a treaty negotiated in 1836, the Wyandots ceded a valuable strip of their reservation in exchange for funds sufficient to promote economic development and education. Finally, as federal and local officials continued to insist that Wyandots vacate the upper Sandusky, Wyandots leveraged the very thing that was forcing them out—increasing demand for their lands—to their advantage by arguing that the increasing value of lands in Ohio should entitle them to a permanent annuity of $17,500 (higher than the government initially proposed) in exchange for selling their lands and moving to a reservation near the mouth of the Kansas River (present-day Kansas City, Kansas). This provision was included in a treaty finalized in 1842.[13]

In July 1843, after "mark[ing] the graves of . . . loved ones with stone or marble tablets," a reported 664 Wyandots (including some from the Huron River area in Michigan) left for Kansas, arriving in the fall. Although there had been little loss of life during the journey west, the government agent for the Wyandots reported in fall 1844 that "about one hundred had died" since their arrival, a figure corroborated by a count of 555 Wyandots in 1845, down by 100 from the preremoval number. This agent attributed these deaths to "fatigue in removing, a change of climate, and intemperance, together with the exhalations of the low ground on which they encamped." These "exhalations" referred to "miasmas" or "bad air," commonly understood to be the cause of "fever" and "ague" and now known to be associated with swamps and other damp places that are breeding grounds for mosquitoes carrying parasites that cause malaria. Once again, relatively small absolute numbers should not obscure the disaster that befell the Wyandots. Their population had fallen by 16 percent.[14]

The Miamis in the Wabash region of northeastern Indiana, numbering around 1,000 in 1830, adopted similar tactics to those of the lower Maumee Ottawas. Under the leadership of their influential chief Jean Baptiste Richardville, a resourceful merchant and land owner fluent in Miami, French, and English, the Miamis agreed in two treaties (1834 and 1838) to sell some of their lands to satisfy debts and increase their annuities, while retaining small tracts for individuals to provide a permanent land base. But demands for Miami removal continued and Miamis were falling prey to alcoholism and internal violence. By 1839, their population had fallen to 700. Richardville decided that the consequence of the Miamis staying in their homelands would be their "total extinction." In 1840 Richardville signed a treaty requiring the Miamis to relocate to a reservation in eastern Kansas along the Osage River within five years. Even so, as the time approached, Miamis were reluctant to depart. In 1845, hoping the government might relent, Francis LaFontaine, the Miamis' principal chief after Richardville's death, turned to the tactic Wyandots had earlier employed and requested a delegation to visit lands designated for them in Kansas. Not surprisingly, this delegation returned with news that Kansas was a "miserable despicable country." LaFontaine followed up by traveling to Washington to request an extension, but in August 1846 the government's agent for the Miamis called on troops to round up his charges. Many Miamis "had to be hunted down like wild animals, some were actually found in the tops of trees, others secreted themselves in swamps." In early October, around 337 Miamis set out for the West, many carrying a "clod of dirt or small stone that they had picked off the graves . . . of their loved ones." When they arrived in Kansas several weeks later, a reported sixteen had died and two-thirds were ill. Sixteen years after the Indian Removal Act, the government had finally pried some Miamis from the Wabash, but at least 300 remained in Indiana, where they insisted on the right to remain on individual holdings granted in previous treaties. As they did, they adopted a strategy of "hiding in plain view," living and acting like their white neighbors, while retaining their sense of themselves as a distinct people.[15]

THE BLACK HAWK WAR

In early 1830, when Lewis Cass outlined his plan for relocating the region's Indians, he did not mention two nations with villages east of the Mississippi directly in the path of a mining rush—the Sauks and Mesquakies and the Ho-Chunks. Cass's omission was perhaps because they were already supposed to be west of the Mississippi. From a U.S. perspective, although the treaty William Henry Harrison convinced Sauks and Mesquakies to sign in 1804 allowed the tribes to remain east of the Mississippi, they were required to move west once Americans were ready to settle on their lands. The appearance of thousands of lead miners in the late 1820s meant that the 2,000 of the total 6,500 Sauk and Mesquakie population living in villages on the east bank of the Mississippi (Quashquame, Wapello, and Saukenuk; Fig. 39) were obligated to quietly relocate west of the river. Some of them did, but those

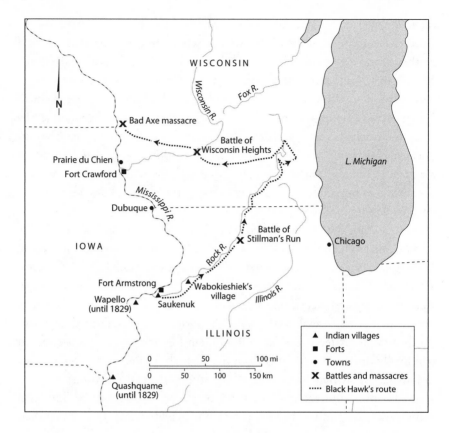

Fig. 39. Black Hawk War

under the leadership of Black Hawk continued to reside at Saukenuk. Illinois'
700 Ho-Chunks were also supposed to have moved, in this case north to
Wisconsin, home to the bulk of the nation's 5,000 people. After the so-called
Winnebago Uprising in 1827, when a portion of the Ho-Chunks, under the
leadership of Red Bird, took up arms to resist the lead miner invasion, the
United States imposed a treaty requiring Ho-Chunks living in Illinois to relocate to lands north of the Wisconsin River. Some did, although others, notably those affiliated with Wabokieshiek (White Cloud), called by non-Indians
the Winnebago Prophet, remained in their villages along the Rock River.[16]

Black Hawk and other like-minded Indians believed they had every right
to retain their villages east of the Mississippi. In May 1828 when Indian agent
Thomas Forsyth called on Sauks and Mesquakies to move west, Black Hawk
replied that "they had never sold the land higher up the Mississippi river
than the mouth of the Rocky River." By this interpretation, they had ceded

Quashquame and Wapello, but not Saukenuk, the capital of the Sauk nation located just north of the Rock River. A year later, when Forsyth again ordered the Sauks and Mesquakies to leave, Black Hawk repeated his earlier position that his people had never agreed to sell their lands. Forsyth "reminded the Black Hawk of the Treaty of 1816," in which Black Hawk had supposedly agreed to the terms of the 1804 treaty, but Black Hawk "denied that any mention was made to him about land" in the 1816 negotiations and contended that the lead American negotiator "must have inserted in the Treaty what was not explained to him & friends."[17]

Although Black Hawk tried to persuade his people to resist removal, only about one in six Sauks and Mesquakies joined him. This was not because they accepted the U.S. position that they had actually consented to vacate their Illinois villages. In 1829 Keokuk, the leader of the majority faction, bluntly informed U.S. officials that his people had been "cheated" during the 1804 treaty negotiations. Rather, Keokuk and like-minded leaders were committed to maintain diplomatic relations with Americans to protect their interests in a world of fierce intertribal competition for scarce resources. As we saw in Chapter 7, as game declined east of the Mississippi in the early nineteenth century, Sauks and Mesquakies shifted their hunting areas west and north. This meant that they clashed with Dakotas and Menominees over hunting grounds. After the 1825 Treaty of Prairie du Chien, Keokuk recognized the importance of cultivating U.S. officials in their self-appointed role as regulators of intertribal conflict. In 1830, for example, when Dakotas and Menominees killed sixteen Mesquakies as they arrived for a council at Prairie du Chien (thus avenging earlier attacks), Keokuk held U.S. officials responsible for not preventing the attack and requested that they arrange compensation from the Dakotas. Keokuk also thought that Black Hawk's resistance would provoke U.S. military action and that his people could not prevail in a war with the United States.[18]

Black Hawk's refusal to abandon Saukenuk caused U.S. officials to consider military action. In the fall of 1830 Forsyth's successor, a new agent, Felix St. Vrain, having learned that Black Hawk intended to return to Saukenuk after the upcoming winter hunt, wrote Clark that "a sufficient number of Troops should be ordered to prevent them from taking possession in the spring." In the meantime, settlers who had taken up lands near Saukenuk began complaining to Illinois governor John Reynolds that Indians were stealing their hogs and cattle and making murderous threats. When Black Hawk's band—1,600 strong, counting a few hundred Potawatomis, Kickapoos, and

Ho-Chunks who had joined—returned to Saukenuk in spring 1831, Governor Reynolds, citing the need "to protect the Citizens of this State . . . from Indian invasion, and depredation," called up a force of 700 militiamen to "remove [Black Hawk's band] *dead,* or *alive* over to the west side of the Missisippi." Likely, U.S. military officials would have taken action against Black Hawk anyway, but Reynolds's decision to activate a state militia forced their hand. To assert federal authority, General Edmund P. Gaines authorized U.S. troops to "repel" what he characterized, in a classic colonial move of reversal, as Black Hawk's "invasion" of Illinois. Gaines admonished Reynolds that mobilizing the Illinois militia was neither "necessary" nor "proper" and immediately led 225 troops from St. Louis to Fort Armstrong a few miles from Saukenuk.[19]

When Gaines arrived in early June, he informed Black Hawk and his people that although the 1804 treaty required the Sauks to relinquish their lands east of the Mississippi, "the humane disposition of the United States" had caused "your great Father" to allow you to "remain on the lands you sold, till the present time." Now, however, "you must . . . without delay move to the west side of the Mississippi." Black Hawk replied that "his Braves and People were unanimous in their desire to remain in their old fields." Three days later, Black Hawk, accompanied by several Sauk women, explained to Gaines that "the Great Spirit" had never told the women to sell their land and "that if their Chiefs had sold it," the women "had not sanctioned the sale."[20] A Sauk woman, the daughter of a chief named Mat-ta-tas, reinforced this message. Earlier instructed by Wabokieshiek to "take a stick in her hand," likely a digging stick or hoe and so a sign of women's authority over Saukenuk's fields, she "rose & said that the land was theirs & had never been sold." Unmoved by these appeals, Gaines threatened that Black Hawk's band "must move in three days, or they would be forced across the river." At the moment, however, Gaines had no more than 300 men (those he had brought from St. Louis augmented by two companies at Fort Armstrong) and so could not force the issue.[21]

By the end of June Gaines had mobilized a more formidable force. In addition to the 300 troops already at Fort Armstrong, Gaines now had 1,500 Illinois mounted militiamen and a steamship fitted with artillery pieces named the *Winnebago* (not for the last time would this misnomer for the Ho-Chunk Nation be applied to large means of transportation). Black Hawk later recalled that he would have "remained and been taken prisoner by the *regulars,*" but he feared the "multitude of *pale faces,* who were on horseback [the Illinois militiamen] as they were under no restraint of their chiefs." To prevent a massacre, Black Hawk led his people across the Mississippi on the night of June 25. Unable to kill live Indians, some militiamen unleashed their genocidal urges on Saukenuk's unprotected graveyard. As St. Vrain later reported, "fifteen or twenty graves had been uncovered, and one entire corpse taken out from the grave, and put into the fire and burned." Five days later, Gaines demanded that Black Hawk and other leaders sign a document titled "Articles of Agreement and Capitulation between the United States and the Sauk and Fox" requiring them never to reoccupy Saukenuk. Black Hawk consented, but when he made his x-mark with "a force which rendered *that* pen forever unfit for further use," his reluctance was plain for all to see.[22]

Gaines believed he had obtained the permanent removal of Black Hawk's people west of the Mississippi. But in April 1832, after several months in Iowa, Black Hawk's people, along with some Potawatomis, Kickapoos, and Ho-Chunks, over 1,000 in all, returned to Illinois. Perhaps because Black Hawk did not want to provoke the United States by directly violating the pledge Gaines had imposed, he did not return to Saukenuk. Instead, he and his people went to Wabokieshiek's village up the Rock River. Black Hawk later explained that his decision to return to Illinois resulted from intelligence brought by one of his advisors, Neapope, who had visited the British post of Fort Malden on the Canadian side of the Detroit River. According to Neapope, British officials informed him that the Americans had no right to take Saukenuk and that "in the event of *war,* we should have nothing to *fear!* as they would stand by and *assist* us!"[23]

In fact, the British had no plans to support Black Hawk in a war with the United States. This suggests the possibility that Neapope fabricated the information he provided Black Hawk, though he may simply have misinterpreted what British officials told him. In either case, Black Hawk had reason to think that Neapope's intelligence was credible. After allying with the British during the War of 1812, Black Hawk had maintained close ties with the British, so much so that Americans referred to his community as the British Band. Throughout the 1820s Black Hawk's people, as well as other Native communities in the Great Lakes and upper Mississippi Valley, regularly visited Fort Malden and other British posts to receive presents that British officials offered as a way of maintaining close ties with Indians within U.S. territory. Should the United States decide to repeat its 1812 invasion of Upper Canada (always possible), the British would need Native allies. In the late 1820s and early 1830s, when U.S. officials began demanding that the Sauks, Mesquakies, and

Ho-Chunks vacate Illinois, Wabokieshiek repeatedly pointed out that when the British and Americans made peace in 1814, "the British required . . . that [the United States] should never interrupt any nation of Indians that was at peace," a plausible interpretation of provisions in the Treaty of Ghent. For the British Band, the continued presence of British posts in the region signaled an ongoing commitment to support Indians who were peaceably resisting U.S. aggression.[24]

General Henry Atkinson, by this time in charge of U.S. military operations in the area, quickly made it clear that the United States would not tolerate Black Hawk's return to Illinois. In a conference with Keokuk and other nonmilitant Sauk and Mesquakie leaders at Fort Armstrong on April 13, Atkinson declared that "the band of the Black Hawk . . . can be easily crushed as a piece of dirt." Should they "strike . . . one white man in a short time they will cease to exist." Atkinson knew that this threat—one transparently geno-cidal—would be communicated to Black Hawk. At the same time, Atkinson began inflating the danger Black Hawk posed to settlers. On April 18 Atkinson advised higher authorities that individuals in the area whose "acquaintance with the Indians should have some weight" were sure that Black Hawk's band would "strike as soon as they secure their women and children." By the end of the month, Atkinson had adopted this view as his own, flatly telling General of the Army Alexander Macomb that Black Hawk's band "must be checked at once, or the whole frontier will be in a flame." Atkinson's intelligence did not support this interpretation. Henry Gratiot, an agent to neutral Ho-Chunks on the Illinois–Wisconsin border, visited Wabokieshiek's village and reported that Black Hawk told him that "his heart is bad—that he intends to go farther up the Rock river" and that if Atkinson sent troops after him, he "will fight them." This indicated that Black Hawk was determined to resist U.S. demands that he leave Illinois and that he may have been willing to fight should troops act against him, but this was very different from the contention that Black Hawk would take offensive action against settlers.[25]

Historians have argued that Atkinson's alarmist correspondence was out of character for a general with a reputation for caution, sobriety, and the "temperament of a peacemaker." To explain this apparent enigma, they have asserted that Atkinson "exaggerated the danger posed by the British Band in order to provoke Reynolds into mustering the militia." It is true that four days after Atkinson wrote Reynolds about the danger to the frontier, the governor notified Secretary of War Cass that he had begun mobilizing the Illinois militia.[26] But Reynolds hardly needed Atkinson to prod him to action; a year before, Reynolds had called up volunteers without federal authorization. In fact, Atkinson's categorization of Black Hawk as a dangerous threat was consistent with a widespread tendency among U.S. military officials—no matter how level-headed and peace-loving—to demonize and threaten to annihilate Indians who defied their will.

By the end of April, Reynolds's plan to mobilize an Illinois militia was well under way (Abraham Lincoln volunteered and was chosen captain of one company, though his company was mustered out without seeing combat). At the same time, Atkinson was recruiting additional volunteers from Michigan Territory as well as gathering regular army troops from nearby posts.[27] Aware of these developments, Black Hawk moved up the Rock River from Wabokieshiek's village. As he did, he received disappointing news that potential allies in the region (Ho-Chunks and Potawatomis) were reluctant to stand with him. Worse, no British support was forthcoming. At this point, he decided that self-defense was too risky and that it would be best to recross the Mississippi to Iowa.[28]

Before Black Hawk could reverse course, Illinois militiamen commanded by Major Isaiah Stillman discovered his encampment. On May 14, Black Hawk sent emissaries to Stillman with word of his intention to leave Illinois, but Stillman took three of the emissaries prisoner and then fired on a party backing them up, killing three. Stillman's main force then advanced on Black Hawk's encampment. Sauks repelled them, killing twelve of Stillman's men. Upon learning of what became known as the Battle of Stillman's Run (Stillman's men had "run" in panic), Secretary of War Cass informed Atkinson that the "commencement of hostilities, together with the previous conduct of the Black Hawk and his party, calls for the most prompt and efficient measures to chastise these Indians." Black Hawk called on his young men to "avenge the murder of our three braves!"[29]

In the early weeks of the Black Hawk War, members of Black Hawk's band and other Indians in the region who had previously cultivated neutrality conducted several attacks on settlements and military posts, killing perhaps sixty civilians and militiamen. Some of these attacks were responses to Black Hawk's call for vengeance, but some were directed at settlers who had aggrieved Indians. A party of fifty Potawatomis (sympathizers with Black Hawk, but not members of his band) attacked the farm of one William Davis who had dammed a creek and blocked fish from swimming upriver to a Potawatomi village and then flogged a Potawatomi man who tried to destroy the dam. Another purpose for raiding, indicated by accounts of Indians taking livestock, wheat, and flour from military outposts and settlements, was that it yielded badly needed resources.[30]

Indian attacks after Stillman's Run confirmed conclusions officials had already made about Black Hawk's intentions. With blood on the ground, Atkinson assured Macomb on June 15 that should "the Sacs elude us and recross the Mississippi, I will pursue them forthwith and never cease till they are anihilated or fully and severely punnished and subdued." Observing the situation from St. Louis, William Clark advised Lewis Cass that a "War of *Extermination* should be waged against them." These examples of genocidal rhetoric were not idiosyncratic. They reconfirmed a policy—in place since the nation's founding—that resisting Indians were subject to extermination.[31]

By the end of June, Atkinson had assembled a force of 450 regular troops and 2,000 volunteers. He also recruited a few hundred Menominees, Potawatomis, Dakotas, and Ho-Chunks, whose knowledge of the country would provide valuable intelligence. These auxiliaries had various motives. Menominees and Dakotas saw the U.S. war against Black Hawk as an opportunity to gain an advantage in an ongoing intertribal conflict and avenge previous losses. Only a year earlier, 100 Sauks and Mesquakies had descended on a Menominee encampment and killed twenty-five, including at least four women and nine children. On the other hand, Potawatomis and Ho-Chunks feared that if they did not support the United States, troops and militiamen would destroy their communities.[32]

The first task of Atkinson's army was to try to find Black Hawk's people as they fled north into Wisconsin and then west toward the Mississippi. On July 21, Illinois and Michigan territorial militiamen commanded by Henry Dodge and James Henry and assisted by intelligence from Ho-Chunks caught up with Black Hawk's band on the Wisconsin River. In what became known as the Battle of Wisconsin Heights, Black Hawk's soldiers held off the Americans long enough to allow women and children "sufficient time to reach the island in the Ouisconsin," but the Americans killed between forty and seventy of Black Hawk's fighters. By this time, Black Hawk's people had depleted their supplies of food and for weeks had been "forced to dig *roots* and *bark trees*." Some were dying of hunger. Most continued overland to the Mississippi, but a few hundred, mainly women and children, decided their best hope to survive was to build canoes and descend the Wisconsin River to the Mississippi and cross from there. As this smaller group traveled downriver, several died when their hastily built vessels sank. Not long after, as they neared the mouth of the Wisconsin, U.S. troops and Menominee and Ho-

Chunk auxiliaries discovered them. In a massacre with no name, they killed as many as fifty, mostly women and children.[33]

The main group, still led by Black Hawk, reached the Mississippi near the mouth of the Bad Axe River on August 1. By this time, Black Hawk's band numbered around 560, about half its size four months earlier. Some of the attrition was because of departures, but a good portion was due to starvation. As Black Hawk's people prepared to cross the Mississippi, an armed U.S. steamboat, bearing the name *Warrior*, appeared. Black Hawk knew the *Warrior*'s captain, Joseph Throckmorton, and so raised a white flag, hoping to "save our women and children." But Throckmorton thought the white flag was a "decoy" to trick him into bringing his vessel into range of Black Hawk's weapons. Throckmorton opened cannon fire on Black Hawk's people, killing twenty-three, before departing to refuel.[34]

That night, for reasons that remain unclear, Black Hawk and Wabokie-shiek with about sixty followers abandoned the main group and fled north to Ojibwe country. The next morning, as the remaining 500 people began crossing the Mississippi (some used makeshift rafts, others swam alone or with horses), Atkinson, Dodge, and Henry marched in from the east and attacked. The men tried to hold off the Americans and so allow women and children to cross the river. Some made it, but after a few hours the *Warrior* returned and, along with Menominees, fired at people as they swam the river or sought cover on two islands in the main channel (Fig. 40). By nightfall, U.S. forces and Indian auxiliaries had killed about 260 Indians, while taking forty women and children prisoner. Many of the casualties were noncombatants. One mother arose from a hiding place in the grass, holding an infant aloft in a plea for mercy, but troops instantly cut her down. The fate of her infant is unknown. Another woman tried to save her baby by fastening it to an improvised raft of cottonwood bark, hoping that the currents would take it to some desperately imagined safety. A volunteer named John House, "taking deliberate aim, shot the babe dead." When a comrade objected, House replied, "'kill the nits, and you'll have no lice.'" Illinois militiamen did some of the killing, although it would be a mistake to conclude that they were more inclined than regular troops to fire indiscriminately at Black Hawk's people. According to a laudatory report by future President Zachary Taylor, the Sixth Regiment "killed every Indian that presented himself on land, or who endeavored to seek safety by swiming the river."[35]

After Bad Axe, U.S. forces did not pursue survivors as they made their way west into Iowa. Instead, Atkinson encouraged Ho-Chunks, Menominees, and

BATTLE OF BAD AXE.   SCHLACHT VON BAD AXE.

Fig. 40. Toward the end of the 1832 Black Hawk War, a cannon aboard the U.S. steamship
Warrior fired on Sauks and Mesquakies trying to escape U.S. troops by crossing the
Mississippi River. What the image shows is clearly a massacre, but in an especially
striking example of colonial evasion, the caption refers to the event as a battle. H. Lewis,
Battle of Bad Axe on the Mississippi. Wisconsin Historical Society, image WHi-2466.

Santee Dakotas to continue the work of extermination. By late August, they
had presented U.S. officials with several dozen prisoners and over 100 scalps,
evidence of as many deaths. Black Hawk and Wabokieshiek surrendered at
Prairie du Chien on August 27 and were soon imprisoned. All told, of the
more than 1,000 who crossed the Mississippi with Black Hawk in April,
about 500 had perished by the end of the summer.[36]

Many historians of the Black Hawk War have seen it as accidental. They
identify "misunderstandings," the actions of "rash members on both sides,"
or "blunders" like Atkinson's reliance on Stillman's poorly disciplined militiamen. As with all wars, the outbreak of the Black Hawk War and the way it
unfolded were not inevitable, but an emphasis on contingency can obscure
larger contexts. One historian of the war identifies part of the context for the
war in attributing the murderous acts of the Illinois militia's "citizen-soldiers"
at Bad Axe to the "revolutionary rage that created the nation" and that re-

sulted in "a love of freedom and a glorification of violence." But focusing solely on the militiamen and a frontier tradition of "Indian hating" overlooks the congruity of metropolitan and frontier intentions and the expression of these intentions in policy.[37]

There is no question that frontiersmen had genocidal intentions toward Black Hawk's people, but it is equally true that U.S. officials did as well, especially after Black Hawk crossed the Mississippi River in April 1832. U.S. officials did not intend to destroy all Indians, as evidenced by their recruitment of Ho-Chunks, Menominees, and Dakotas, as well as their nonviolence toward nonresisting Sauks and Mesquakies. Once they categorized Black Hawk as deserving of punishment and a threat to the frontier, however, they fully intended to destroy his people. In so doing, officials were not improvising. They were executing a longstanding policy option. When they stated a capacity to crush Black Hawk's people like a piece of dirt and cause them to cease to exist or when they called for their extermination, government and military officials did not cite the 1787 Northwest Ordinance's authorization of "just and lawful wars." Nonetheless, officials were clearly operating on the assumption, embedded in that foundational legislation, that it was legal and just to prosecute genocidal war against "savages" who resisted "civilization's" demands.

Even before the Black Hawk War was over, Secretary of War Cass anticipated that its conclusion would provide valuable opportunities. He wrote to General Winfield Scott that it would be "very desirable, that the whole country between Lake Michigan & the Mississippi & south of the Ouisconsin, should be freed from Indians."[38] After the Bad Axe massacre, federal officials seized the moment to separate Indians from their lands. Whether they had supported Black Hawk, remained neutral, or assisted the United States government made no difference.

On September 19, 1832, General Scott and Governor Reynolds met with Keokuk and other nonmilitant Sauks and Mesquakies at Fort Armstrong. Despite the fact that they had refused Black Hawk's entreaties to join his movement, "partly as an indemnity . . . , and partly to secure the future safety and tranquility of the invaded frontier," Scott and Reynolds ordered them to give up a fifty-mile strip in Iowa along the western bank of the Mississippi. Keokuk asserted his past faithfulness to the United States to negotiate for a modest reduction in the size of the proposed cession and to obtain federal government recognition as "head chief." Nonetheless, as Scott and Reynolds wrote Cass, in making the Fort Armstrong Treaty "the power to dictate was very much in our hands." After an early release from prison and a tour of the East, Black Hawk settled on the Iowa River near Keokuk's village.[39] The government's removal of the Sauks and Mesquakies from their lands east of the Mississippi was complete, though it would not be the last time the United States would ask them to go someplace else.

MULTIPLE HO-CHUNK REMOVALS

Ho-Chunks in Illinois and southern Wisconsin (around two-thirds of the nation's population of 5,000) were also forced to move. In September 1832, Scott and Reynolds informed them that they must cede their lands south of the Wisconsin River. They were to relocate to an area of northeastern Iowa earlier established as a neutral ground between Sauks and Mesquakies and Dakotas (see Chapter 7). Although Ho-Chunk leaders protested about being caught between these warring enemies, they reluctantly agreed to vacate their villages the following summer. When the time came, however, Ho-Chunks refused to go. To compel compliance, officials withheld treaty annuities and mobilized troops under Henry Dodge. Undoubtedly with Bad Axe in mind, Ho-Chunks feared that Dodge's army had "been organized purposely for their extermination" and so many departed for the Neutral Ground Reservation in Iowa. Others tried to avoid Dodge, but, as an unidentified Ho-Chunk later related, Dodge "hunted us from Lake to Lake like Deer—we could not hide from him." By late 1833, most Ho-Chunks south of the Wisconsin had relocated to the Neutral Ground Reservation (Fig. 41), though some joined relatives in villages north of the Wisconsin. In 1836 smallpox struck Ho-Chunks near Prairie du Chien. Moses Paquette, of Ho-Chunk and French ancestry, later recalled that the "survivors simply fled before it like a herd of stricken deer, leaving their dead and dying behind them, unburied."[40]

A few years later the United States demanded that Ho-Chunks living in villages north of the Wisconsin River accept a treaty ceding their lands and move to the Neutral Ground Reservation. In yet another instance of the United States' use of genocidal threats, Ho-Chunk leader Dandy said that a government official told them that "if they did not sign the treaty, he would . . . kill them." Those who signed in 1837 did so "under duress," but with the understanding that the treaty said they would not have to leave Wisconsin for "eight years." In fact, however, the treaty read "eight months." In 1840, when Ho-Chunks refused to depart for Iowa, U.S. officials authorized troops to force them out. During this process, three Ho-Chunk women approached

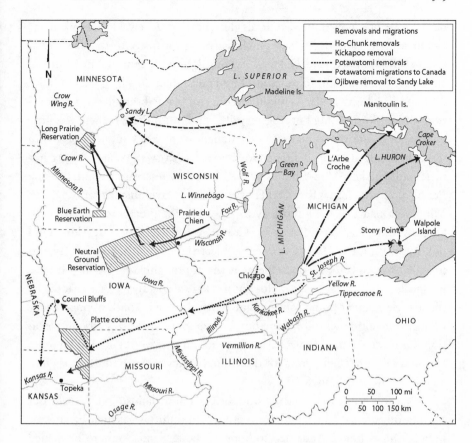

Fig. 41. Illinois and the western Great Lakes during removal

Captain Edwin V. Sumner and made plain their distress. "Throwing themselves on their knees," they cried and pled with Sumner "to kill them; that they were old, and would rather die, and be buried with their fathers mothers and children, than be taken away; and that they were ready to receive their death blows." Rather than beating three women to death, Sumner "had pity on them, and permitted them to stay." This moment of mercy, however, did not lead him to rethink the justice of his operation. Sumner's troops forced many Ho-Chunks to Iowa, though others avoided the dragnet and remained in Wisconsin, where they led a "fugitive existence."[41]

Conditions for the Ho-Chunks in Iowa were miserable. In the early 1840s government agents reported "dysentery," "considerable sickness," "bloodshed and murder" (stemming from traders selling alcohol), and "want of food." Many Ho-Chunks returned to Wisconsin. Knowing that Iowa would soon become a state, government officials decided that a new Ho-Chunk reservation must be found. In 1846 officials arranged a treaty to purchase lands for the Ho-Chunks from Dakotas at Long Prairie in central Minnesota. If anything, conditions were worse at Long Prairie than they had been in Iowa. In 1849 Ho-Chunk leader Waukon Decora complained that the new reservation was "fit for nothing but frogs, reptiles, and musquitoes." There was little game and, as the government agent assigned to the Ho-Chunks reported in 1852, the lands at Long Prairie were "covered with swamps and almost impenetrable thickets." Ho-Chunks pressed for a new reservation south of Long Prairie along the Crow River, where the land was favorable for farming. But Minnesota had become a territory in 1849. For the precise reason that Ho-Chunks wanted a reservation on the Crow River, the territory's developers did not. In St. Paul, the *Minnesota Pioneer* objected that giving these fertile lands to Indians would "retard the settlement and thoroughly destroy the business prospects" in the area. In 1854, Ho-Chunks agreed to a treaty that guaranteed them a "permanent home" on the Blue Earth River just south of present-day Mankato in south-central Minnesota. For the moment, this particular location was off the path of projected settlement, but that would not last for long. It would take only eight years for the United States to demand that they find a new "permanent home."[42]

What was it like to be evicted from beloved homelands? To try to eke out a living on inferior lands and to see one's community weakened by chronic hunger and sickness? And then to hope for better lands, only to be denied them? To be promised permanence and evicted yet again? It is impossible for most of us to fathom the answers to these questions. Because Ho-Chunks could not be fully contained on any single reservation and many continued to live in Wisconsin, it is also impossible to provide anything more than a rough estimate of the demographic impact of the upheavals the Ho-Chunks endured from 1830 to 1860. A good estimate is that in 1860 the Ho-Chunk population numbered no more than 3,500, down from 5,000 thirty years before.[43]

REMOVALS OF THE KICKAPOOS AND POTAWATOMIS

Federal officials also moved against the 750 or so Kickapoos in Illinois. In late August 1832 William Clark advised the Kickapoo religious leader Kenekuk that his community of 350 people should depart their home along the Vermillion River in eastern Illinois because "you will shortly be treated as enemies." Four years earlier, the same William Clark had attempted to persuade Kenekuk to move west, but Kenekuk told Clark that to abandon his village would be to "disobey the directions of the Great Spirit." Now, however, with Bad Axe offering an unspoken example of what it meant to be treated as an enemy of the United States, Kenekuk decided that community survival required compliance. So, he signed a treaty (also signed by Kickapoos who had migrated to Missouri years before) that designated lands in northeastern Kansas as the Kickapoos' "permanent residence." By all accounts, Kenekuk's community was especially cohesive and so was able to manage the removal process and begin rebuilding a successful agricultural economy without great damage. Around 400 Kickapoos at a nearby village under the leadership of Kishko also moved to Kansas without serious difficulty, but they soon informed government officials that they wished a separate reservation along the Osage River in eastern Kansas. When government officials refused this request, Kishko and many of his people departed, eventually settling with Kickapoos who had earlier moved to modern-day Oklahoma, Texas, and Mexico.[44]

Most Potawatomis had sided with the United States during the Black Hawk War, but their support was "ignored or forgotten." In fall 1832 a U.S. commission summoned leaders from dozens of Potawatomi communities in Wisconsin, Illinois, Michigan, and Indiana (representing over 10,000 people) to meet on the Tippecanoe River. In three treaties, the commissioners secured significant cessions of Potawatomi lands. Eager to complete a deal, the commissioners did not want to provoke Potawatomi resistance and so did not place language in these treaties requiring removal. Instead, they allowed the Potawatomis to retain no less than 120 small reservations for villages and individuals. This outcome was not quite what Cass had in mind when he said that the country should be "freed from Indians," nor was it acceptable to settlers in the region. Hence, a year later at Chicago, a new commission, headed by Michigan territorial governor George Porter, demanded that Potawatomis, Ojibwes, and Ottawas cede their remaining lands in Michigan, Indiana, Illinois, and Wisconsin and move west. When one leader, Leopold Pokagon, objected that he did not understand the treaty terms, Porter was quick to issue threats. Reminding the assembly that the Great Father had recently "treated with [Black Hawk's people] at the Cannon's mouth," he instructed them that the only way to avoid the same fate was to ignore "wicked and designing men" around them. The resulting two treaties accorded with Porter's demands for the cession of all lands (with the exception of some of the small reservations from the Tippecanoe treaties). In exchange, the Potawatomis were granted lands in western Iowa and the Platte country west of Missouri. Citizens of

Illinois welcomed this treaty, but citizens of Missouri did not, since (as shown in Chapter 7) they hoped to annex the Platte country. Missouri's senators, including the powerful Thomas Hart Benton, ensured that the Senate added an amendment eliminating the Platte country from the treaty before ratifying it. Missouri was now satisfied, but not the Potawatomis, who, if they had to move, preferred the Platte country to Iowa. Defying the will of the United States Senate, many Potawatomis traveled to the Platte country; by the end of 1836 there were 1,600 Potawatomis there. The government had finally secured the removal of a substantial portion of the Potawatomis, but they had not gone where they were supposed to.[45]

To force the Potawatomis out of the Platte country, in 1837 federal officials ceased providing them with rations. Perversely, government agents had discouraged Potawatomis from planting gardens, lest they think of the Platte country as their new home. Potawatomis now faced starvation. After a time, General Gaines ordered the resumption of rations while making clear that only a move to Iowa would prevent another shutoff. Under these circumstances, a few hundred of the Potawatomis in the Platte country under the leadership of Kikito decided to move to eastern Kansas, while the majority, led by Caldwell, accepted the government's request to make Iowa their home. But even as the majority traveled up the Missouri toward Council Bluffs, it occurred to government planners that western Iowa was becoming subject to the same process of U.S. expansion that since 1783 had driven Indians west and west again. Hence they decreed that a reservation south of the Osage River in eastern Kansas should be the permanent home of all Potawatomis (as if this same process would never extend to Kansas). Nonetheless, when the Potawatomis arrived in Council Bluffs, they defied government intentions and stayed put. Despite repeated entreaties that they relocate, the Council Bluff Potawatomis hung on until the eve of Iowa statehood in 1846 before being consolidated with Potawatomis already in Kansas on a new reservation along the Kansas River just west of Topeka.[46]

Although most Potawatomi communities forced west did not experience the loss of life commonly associated with the trail of tears metaphor, the eviction of one community from the Yellow River in northern Indiana became known as the Potawatomi Trail of Death. This community's leader, Menominee, was among those who were guaranteed a small reservation in his homeland through the 1832 Tippecanoe treaties. As pressures for removal escalated, Menominee and other leaders traveled to Washington in early 1836 and obtained Lewis Cass's assurance that his people could remain on their reservation until they sold it. Menominee interpreted Cass's words to mean that the government would cease agitating for his people's lands, but Cass offered them more as a temporary expedient, leaving the work of twisting arms to Abel Pepper, the government's agent in northern Indiana. Only months after Menominee's return home, Pepper obtained the marks of three community leaders to sell the reservation and move west by August 1838. Menominee refused to sign, but Pepper declared the transaction complete. For the next two years, assisted by Catholic missionaries who believed removal would hinder the Potawatomis' Christianization, Menominee protested that the 1836 treaty was illegitimate. When the date stipulated in the treaty for removal arrived and Pepper demanded that Menominee uproot his people, Menominee stated that if President Martin Van Buren knew the truth he would "leave me to my own" and insisted that "I have not sold my lands." As Indiana citizens continued to swarm onto their reservation, angry Potawatomis threatened the life of one squatter and chopped down the door of his dwelling. Squatters retaliated by torching several Potawatomi cabins.[47]

The eruption of violence provided Pepper with an opening to call for the militia, a request Indiana governor David Wallace quickly granted. In late August 1838, militiamen surrounded Menominee's village. A Potawatomi woman named Ko-bun-da later recalled that when she heard about the militia, she "gathered up what few clothes I had and left our home, never to return." As Ko-bun-da fled, a man named Go-bo told her that "the whole country was alive with white warriors catching Au-nish-naw-bay-og [Indians] to kill or drive them toward the setting sun." Fearing for her life and the life of her unborn daughter, Ko-bun-da spent a week hiding in a swamp before giving birth and then taking refuge with an "old trapper." From him Ko-bun-da learned that her people had been "trapped" and "driven far westward." Indeed, the militia had rounded up 850 Potawatomis from Menominee's and other nearby villages and hastened them toward the Osage River in Kansas. It took just a few days for the Potawatomis to contract typhoid fever, then spreading throughout the region. By the time they reached their destination in late October and early November, they had buried forty-two of their people. Another fifty or so slipped back to Potawatomi communities still remaining in southern Michigan and northern Indiana.[48]

By 1845, between 4,000 and 5,000 Potawatomis had been moved west of the Mississippi, but even more remained in the East. Some Potawatomis avoided removal altogether. Along the St. Joseph River in northern Indiana and southern Michigan Potawatomi communities had developed alliances with

Catholic missionaries and incorporated Catholic beliefs and practices into their religious traditions. Although their adoption of Catholicism was not strictly instrumental, presenting themselves as "Catholic Indians" gave the St. Joseph Potawatomis important allies in their fight against removal. At Chicago in 1833, the St. Joseph Potawatomis could not prevent a removal treaty, but they did secure an agreement allowing them to move north within Michigan to Ottawa and Ojibwe lands, a destination they much preferred to Kansas. In 1836, the appointed time for the St. Joseph Potawatomis to move north, their resourceful leader, Leopold Pokagon, used funds saved from earlier land sales to purchase 874 acres from the public land office. This was a slim land base, but a relatively secure one, and Pokagon's people were able to use it to remain on the St. Joseph. In 1840, the United States authorized troops to round up Pokagon's and other remaining St. Joseph River Potawatomis. When troops arrived, Pokagon handed their commanding officer a letter from a justice of the Michigan State Supreme Court stating that the Potawatomis had the legal right to remain. A Catholic priest ministering to the Potawatomis had assisted Pokagon in obtaining this document, and the troops went away. To this day, Pokagon's descendants continue to live on that same land in southern Michigan (Fig. 42).[49]

Other Potawatomis avoided being forced to Kansas by taking refuge with Ottawa and Ojibwe communities—communities with a substantial history of intermarriage with Potawatomis—in northern Michigan and Wisconsin. A much larger number, at least 3,000 and probably more, migrated into Upper Canada, settling on Manitoulin Island, Cape Croker, Stony Point, and Walpole Island. We lack detailed accounts of these migrations and conditions in Canada, though historians have not noted adverse demographic consequences. Overall, migration to Canada reveals Potawatomi determination and resourcefulness, as well as an "adaptive strategy" of mobility that they had pursued for centuries. But characterizing these migrations as "voluntary," as some scholars have done, draws a veil over colonial coercion. Andrew Jackson and Lewis Cass did not succeed in putting all Potawatomis exactly where they wanted them, but they did require Potawatomi communities to make agonizing decisions they would have preferred not to make. By the end of the 1840s, most Potawatomis—against their will—had been evicted from their homes.[50]

MICHIGAN OTTAWAS AND OJIBWES

Thus far in this chapter, we have considered Indian communities that were in the direct path of settlement and economic development in the 1830s

Fig. 42. Leopold Pokagon (Potawatomi) was born a year before the Declaration of Independence and became the leader of his community in the 1820s. By building alliances with non-Natives and saving funds to purchase lands, Pokagon and his people avoided removal. Close to 180 years after his death, his descendants, the Pokagon Band of Potawatomi Indians, continue to live in southern Michigan. Courtesy Northern Indiana Historical Society, South Bend, Indiana.

and into the 1840s. In many areas of the upper Great Lakes and upper Mississippi Valley, however, non-Native demand for Native lands was weaker. U.S. commissioners requested/demanded that Native nations in this region cede some of their lands and pressured them to move west. Like Native nations everywhere, those in this region were tenacious in fighting the dreaded prospect of being uprooted from their lands. Fortunately, because settlement was relatively light, officials were more willing to accommodate to Native resistance.

Ottawas in the northern half of Michigan's lower peninsula, with a population of approximately 4,000, watched warily as the process of removal unfolded to the south in the early 1830s. To preempt removal, their leaders informed Secretary of War Cass in 1835 that it is a "heart-rending thought . . . to think of leaving our native country forever." They proposed to Cass that they sell some of their lands in exchange for being allowed to remain "where the bones of our forefathers lay thick in the earth." Like the Cherokees, who had contended that removal would reverse their "progress" toward "civilization," the Ottawas appealed to Cass that they would continue to "advance" if allowed to remain in their home. A year later the Michigan Ottawas, along with representatives from allied Ojibwe communities, traveled to Washington in the hope of securing a treaty that would protect them from removal. The treaty was not what the Ottawas envisioned. The U.S. negotiator, Henry Rowe Schoolcraft, a man the Ottawas knew and mistrusted from his time as U.S. agent in the region, demanded that the Ottawas and Ojibwes cede more land than they had initially proposed. Eventually, the Ottawas and Ojibwes agreed to Schoolcraft's demands in exchange for several reservations, which they understood to be permanent. But before ratifying the treaty, the Senate specified that the reservations would last for only five years. After that, Michigan Ottawas and Ojibwes would have to send a delegation to "select a suitable place . . . southwest of the Missouri River" (presumably eastern Kansas) for their "final settlement."[51]

Fortunately for the Michigan Ottawas, one of capitalism's frequent crises —the financial panic of 1837—intervened. The economic downturn following the panic discouraged further settlement of Michigan's lower peninsula and bought the Ottawas time to fend off removal. In the late 1830s and into the 1840s, communities from the Grand River area north to L'Arbe Croche used annuity funds to purchase private lands, secured the support of missionaries in the area, and exchanged furs, berries, and maple sugar with newly arrived Yankee traders to sustain their communities. Over time, the threat of eviction gradually receded, as Michigan's settlers and political leaders became willing to tolerate Indian communities in areas with comparatively low settler populations. Similar dynamics worked in favor of Ojibwe communities (with a population of between 7,000 and 8,000) in the central and eastern parts of Michigan's lower peninsula. According to one government official, in the early 1850s Ojibwes were "paralyzed" by "fear of being driven from their homes" and so sought some measure of security through additional treaty negotiations. The treaty they and Michigan Ottawas signed in 1855 said nothing about removal and instead made provisions for Indians to own land as citizens. Whether this would protect Ottawas and Ojibwes from further dispossession remained to be seen, but for now the treaty was a great relief. "Instead of darkness," an Ojibwe leader named Paybahmesay said, "we find a bright light."[52]

BROTHERTOWNS, STOCKBRIDGES, ONEIDAS, AND MENOMINEES IN WISCONSIN

Most Indian nations elsewhere in the upper Great Lakes also avoided expulsion. In September 1836, a year after obtaining the New Echota Treaty from a minority of Cherokees, John Schermerhorn paid a visit to the approximately 900 Stockbridges, Brothertowns, and Oneidas who had migrated from New York (some by way of Indiana) in the 1820s and early 1830s and established communities in the Green Bay area and southwest along the Fox River to Lake Winnebago in Wisconsin. Although federal officials had assured these nations (often referred to as the New York Indians) that their new Wisconsin home would be permanent, speculators (including Schermerhorn himself) had begun eyeing lands in this area. Federal officials now wanted to dispatch the Stockbridges, Brothertowns, and Oneidas to Kansas. There they would join New York Haudenosaunees, whom Schermerhorn was also trying to force west (see below). Daniel Bread, an Oneida leader, objected to Schermerhorn's scheme, saying that "we have hardly laid down our packs or cleared land enough to live on, when word comes for us to go on." And the Oneidas had only moved once. The Brothertowns and Stockbridges had been forced west *five* times. They "no longer had any reason to believe white promises . . . since 'forever' usually meant just a few years."[53]

To avoid a sixth removal, the Brothertowns successfully petitioned the government to allow them to convert their reservation into private property and became citizens. As we have seen, this strategy did not work for the Creeks, the Ohio Ottawas, or the Miamis. But it was effective for the Brothertowns. As settlement increased in the 1850s and whites "bought lots and settled among them," Brothertowns had to leave their homes to find work in logging camps and elsewhere, but they retained enough land to keep their community anchored at Lake Winnebago. The circumstances that allowed this to work were unusual. As with Pokagon's Potawatomi community, the Brothertowns had a relatively small and cohesive population that required only a modest land base. Their Christianity, though it did not fully protect them against outsiders' racism and greed, made them tolerable to some segments of the settler population.[54]

A minority of Stockbridges opted for Kansas, but when some of them returned in 1839 with reports of "murder and drunkenness," it stiffened the resolve of the majority to avoid this fate. But how? Some Stockbridges (the Citizen Party) advocated the Brothertown strategy, while others (the Indian Party) sought to retain communal lands. Bitterly divided by colonial pressures, the Indian Party accused the Citizen Party of making "good white men" but "faithless and bad, Indians," and the Citizen Party accused the Indian Party of hypocrisy because some had bought and sold land. Nonetheless, although divided, the Stockbridges continued to fight against removal. As Wisconsin moved from territory to state, its officials requested a federal treaty to eliminate the Stockbridges. By this time, many Stockbridges expressed willingness to depart, but only on the condition that they could choose lands in Minnesota. When Stockbridges went to Minnesota and selected lands suitable for farming (they were, after all, good Christian agriculturalists), Minnesota interests blocked removal. On the eve of the Civil War, Stockbridges moved, but only fifty miles north to a reservation along the Wolf River. They had not avoided removal altogether, but their resistance had shaped the outcome in positive ways. Oneidas, too, thwarted repeated efforts by territorial and federal officials to make it seem as though an Oneida majority desired to inhabit Kansas. These efforts reached a climax in 1845, when territorial governor Henry Dodge and federal commissioners tried to obtain Oneida consent to a removal treaty. For years, Oneida leaders had worked hard to cultivate unity. Dodge and his colleagues tried hard to crack them, but only a small minority broke ranks and signed. From then on, officials decided it was no longer worth the effort to rid Wisconsin of Oneidas.[55]

The Menominees, with a population of around 2,500 in the early 1840s, did not face demands to go away until 1848, the year of Wisconsin's statehood. Already they had ceded the majority of their lands in three treaties (1831, 1832, and 1836). The 1848 treaty took their last acre and called for their removal. But to gain Menominee consent, government officials had to make some concessions. They did not insist that Menominees relocate to unfamiliar country in Kansas. Instead, they said, Menominees could move to an area recently ceded by Ojibwes along the Crow Wing River in Minnesota, lands closer and similar to their own. Officials also agreed to the Menominees' request to visit their proposed new home before moving. As if informed by a well-worn manual on tactics to resist removal, a Menominee delegation returned from Minnesota with a report disparaging the Crow Wing country. This allowed Menominees to reopen negotiations. The result was that in 1852 worn-down officials conceded that the Menominees could remain in Wisconsin on a greatly reduced reservation between the Wolf and Oconto rivers, just west of Green Bay. By this time, the Menominee population had fallen from between 3,000 and 4,000 in 1830 to only 2,000. A smallpox epidemic in 1834 had taken several hundred, and the slow erosion of Menominee lands and depletion of their hunting grounds had led to malnutrition, disease, and starvation. The removal of the Menominees to their new reservation in 1852 was less an unprecedented upheaval than yet another in a long line of cruel blows.[56]

OJIBWES IN THE NORTHWEST: THE SANDY LAKE TRAGEDY

Farther north, in the Upper Peninsula of Michigan, northern Wisconsin, and eastern Minnesota, home to approximately 8,000 Ojibwes, non-Indians desired Native lands not for their agricultural potential but because they supported vast pine forests and contained rich deposits of copper ore. In treaties of 1836, 1837, and 1842, the United States attempted to secure these resources. Although these treaties contained provisions for the cession of significant portions of Ojibwe lands in the Upper Peninsula of Michigan, northern Wisconsin, and eastern Minnesota, accounts written by Ojibwes in their language show that Ojibwes consented only to lease these lands for the purpose of timber harvesting and mining, while retaining rights to hunt, fish, and gather wild rice on them. During this time, Ojibwe leaders were deeply concerned that the government might force removal on them. In negotiations leading to the third of these treaties in 1842, Ojibwe leaders were careful to obtain officials' assurances that they could continue to live where they were. Ojibwe leaders who agreed to this treaty did so with the understanding that removal would not be considered "until the very distant future, perhaps in fifty or even a hundred years."[57]

It took only eight years for the threat of removal to appear in Ojibwe country. Removal's chief instigator was not Andrew Jackson. Deceased since 1845, the chief architect of removal could no longer dictate federal policy. Nor was it Zachary Taylor, onetime commander of troops in the Black Hawk and Second Seminole wars and now the White House's occupant. Nor was it the governments of Wisconsin or Michigan, nor timber or mining conglomerates. Surprisingly, it was the governor of Minnesota Territory (organized in 1849), Alexander Ramsey. Few territorial governors in U.S. history have ever devoted energy to moving Indians *into* their jurisdiction, but in a strange reversal of settler colonialism's typical logic of elimination, Ramsey wanted more Indians in Minnesota. An augmented Indian population, especially one owed treaty annuities, would put money in the pockets of traders, thus promoting the territory's economic development. Ramsey's control of annuities and related government contracts would also provide him with opportunities to dispense political patronage. Responding to Ramsey's lobbying, in February 1850 President Taylor, otherwise not a zealot for Indian removal, ordered Ojibwes in the Upper Peninsula of Michigan and in Wisconsin to vacate their homelands. Knowing that it would be difficult to convince these Ojibwes to obey Taylor's order, Ramsey and other officials decided to lure them to Minnesota by distributing annuity goods and payments not at the usual place—Madeline Island in Lake Superior—but at Sandy Lake in Minnesota. This would be done in the fall. During that season, Ojibwes could journey by canoe to Sandy Lake, but they would be unable to return on waterways certain to freeze in this region's early winter. Trapped at Sandy Lake, they would have no choice but to stay.[58]

In fall 1850, between 2,500 and 3,000 Wisconsin and Michigan Ojibwes made their way to Sandy Lake, where they met an additional 1,500 from northern Minnesota. All expected that annuities would be available on the announced date of October 25. Once in Sandy Lake, however, there were no annuities and little food. Over the next several weeks, many Ojibwes perished. According to one leader, Hole in the Day, his people were "fed on spoilt provisions" that "made them sick, and a great number died." Inadequate food combined with other factors—no shelter, lack of clean water, and the close proximity of so many people—to cause a severe outbreak of dysentery and measles. It was not until November 10 that Congress appropriated the funds to fulfill U.S. treaty obligations, and it was not until two weeks later that annuities reached Sandy Lake. Official expectations that Ojibwes would remain in what had become a death trap were soon dashed. Even though the waterways were already freezing, Ojibwes broke up their otherwise useless canoes for fuel and proceeded overland back to homes they had never wished to leave. At Sandy Lake, an estimated 170 of the 2,500–3,000 Wisconsin and Michigan Ojibwes perished. Even more—230—died on the return journey.

Many of these were adults, otherwise healthy and in the prime of their lives, their bodies unable to endure the multiple assaults of starvation, distress, sickness, and exposure.[59]

Government officials attempted to obscure their responsibility for the 400 dead in what became known among Ojibwes as the Sandy Lake Tragedy. Governor Ramsey contended that reports of suffering and deaths were "highly exaggerated" and that what suffering and deaths had occurred were due to the "low diet to which these people are subject at least nine months of every year," thus blaming the victims. Ojibwes knew otherwise. Flat Mouth held "our Great Father the Governor" responsible for "the children we have lost, for the sickness we have suffered and for the hunger we have endured." For Ojibwes, it was not just that the government had been negligent. They believed that the United States intended to "poison them, to hurry their removal from Wisconsin." Ojibwe experience had shown that America was not above genocide.[60]

Two years after Sandy Lake, an Ojibwe delegation, led by a nonagenarian named Bizhiki (Chief Buffalo) and a younger chief named Oshoge, traveled to Washington to visit President Millard Fillmore. As they set out, the delegates stopped at non-Indian settlements in the upper Great Lakes to secure statements against Ojibwe removal. Newcomers willingly gave their support. Similar to the situation in the northern portion of the lower peninsula of Michigan, where Ottawas and a relatively small settler population engaged in mutually beneficial relations of exchange, recently arrived miners purchased wild rice, berries, maple syrup, clothing, and moccasins harvested and produced by Ojibwe women. When the delegates arrived in Washington, they presented their "Great Grand Father" with the petitions they had gathered, along with a memorial protesting prior attempts to remove them. Observing that when "white men . . . have selected a spot to dwell at," they "cut away the underbrush and bad trees" but do not cut down the "good trees," the memorial asked the President to allow "the good trees" (i.e., the Ojibwes) to "stand and live in your domain." Two years later, Michigan and Wisconsin Ojibwes gained security against removal by signing a treaty establishing nine reservations in their home territory. When Bizhiki died on September 7, 1855, at his home on Madeline Island, he might have suspected that Ojibwes he left behind would face renewed assaults on their lands and ways of life in the years to come. At least they would do so with the graves of their ancestors close at hand.[61]

INDIANS IN NEW ENGLAND AND NEW YORK

In most cases, Native nations in areas of intense settlement were unable to resist removal, but there were some exceptions. Indians in New England, with a population of between 2,500 and 3,000, were never subject to demands that they move west. To some extent, the very ideology that justified the policy of removal—that Indians in prolonged contact with a stronger race were inevitably destined to vanish—protected New England's Native communities. If, as Harvard professor Edward Everett wrote in 1823, the Pequots were "extinguished" and the Naticks and Narragansetts had "vanished," there was no need to remove them.[62]

The 4,000 Haudenosaunees in upstate New York also avoided removal, but in this case it was because they successfully resisted. Living within the boundaries of the self-described Empire State, and with their remaining lands coveted by the aggressive Ogden Land Company, the Haudenosaunees were a prime candidate for removal. It took a long, "heroic battle," but by the end of the removal period most Haudenosaunees were still in their homelands.[63]

The battle began in 1836, when the federal government appointed John Schermerhorn treaty commissioner. In addition to his record of employing the deceptive tactic of using minority factions to approve treaties ceding tribal lands (evidenced in the New Echota Treaty with the Cherokees), Schermerhorn had family connections to the Ogden Land Company. Not long after his appointment as commissioner, mounting criticism of Schermerhorn's role in the New Echota Treaty led nervous officials to replace him. Nevertheless, paid by the Ogden Land Company, Schermerhorn remained active behind the scenes. On January 15, 1838, at Buffalo Creek (Fig. 43) a minority of Haudenosaunees signed a treaty requiring them to liquidate their lands in New York. It looked as though the federal government, the state of New York, and the Ogden Land Company had obtained their objective of Haudenosaunee elimination.[64]

Some Haudenosaunees were willing to move to Kansas, but the majority were strongly opposed. Within weeks of the conclusion of the 1838 Buffalo Creek Treaty, Haudenosaunee spokesmen argued that the treaty was illegitimate since only a minority of leaders—bribed, intimidated, and inebriated—had signed. Three years later, Minerva Black, Widow Little Beard, Susan Black Smith, and five other Haudenosaunee clan mothers, representing 207 women, petitioned President John Tyler. "We think much of our homes," they wrote, "and are strongly attached to the places which the great

Haudenosaunee Reservations, 1800

Haudenosaunee Reservations, 1860

Fig. 43. Haudenosaunee reservations, 1800 and 1860

Spirit gave to us Red children." Appealing to the Treaty of Canandaigua that George Washington had made with their nation in 1794, they asked that the freedom which Washington had obtained for his people be extended to them and their children. Supported by Quaker allies, the Haudenosaunees gained the government's concession to reopen negotiations. Although some New Yorkers remained committed to total Haudenosaunee removal, the state's Whig politicians began to see the value of an alternative approach. All along, Whigs had argued that the Jackson Democrats' relentless pursuit of removal was costly and inhumane, a contention more easily sustained as the Second Seminole War dragged on. Rather than try to force all Haudenosaunees west, it made more sense to reduce their already greatly diminished land base and make them into taxpaying citizens subject to state control. This approach would give Whigs a claim to humanitarianism and enable them to turn New York's influential Quakers into allies instead of critics. These politicians arranged a new treaty in 1842 that allowed the Senecas, the largest of the Haudenosaunee Six Nations within New York, to retain two of their reservations (the Allegany and Cattaraugus).[65]

Although the 1842 treaty protected Senecas on the Allegany and Cattaraugus reservations, its failure to restore the other two Seneca reservations liquidated in 1838 (Tonawanda and Buffalo Creek) meant uncertainty for people there. Without a guarantee of land, they might yet be forced to Kansas. Under the leadership of John Blacksmith and his successor, Ely S. Parker, Tonawanda Senecas protested that they had not consented to the 1842 treaty. Eventually, the organization of Kansas Territory under the 1854 Kansas-Nebraska Act provided Tonawandas an opening to eliminate the specter of removal once and for all. Arguing that the Kansas-Nebraska Act violated the 1838 Buffalo Creek Treaty's provision for a reservation that "shall never be included in any State or Territory of this Union," in 1857 they secured a new treaty that allowed for the repurchase of some of the Tonawanda Reservation lands that the Ogden Land Company had acquired.[66]

Senecas and other Haudenosaunees in the community of Buffalo Creek were more vulnerable. As the rapidly growing city of Buffalo devoured their lands, people from Buffalo Creek dispersed. Some moved to other Haudenosaunee communities in New York and Canada, while a few joined a small group of Haudenosaunees that a federal agent named Abraham Hogeboom induced to move west in the spring of 1846. U.S. officials had authorized Hogeboom to recruit Haudenosaunees for removal, but only if he could round up a group of at least 250 (otherwise, they calculated, the expense of removal was unwarranted). As it turned out, Hogeboom could convince only 216 to set out for Kansas. The agent proceeded with the removal even though it was unauthorized. (The record is unclear, but Hogeboom probably thought he could get away with this and still be compensated.) This meant that officials in Kansas had no knowledge that over 200 Haudenosaunees were on their way (the route they took is unclear) and so had not made any preparations. In turn, this meant that when the emigrants arrived, they spent the next several months in unsanitary conditions without sufficient food and shelter. By early 1847, a reported eighty-two had died from unspecified diseases. Rather than stay in Kansas, the survivors, under the care of a Cayuga physician named Peter Wilson, retraced their steps to New York. In August 1847, steamships deposited the ninety-four remaining Haudenosaunees in Buffalo. Destitute and sick, they were taken in by Tuscaroras and Cattaraugus Senecas. With a death toll of at least 40 percent, this little-known removal was one of the most deadly of all.[67]

Most Haudenosaunees did not endure the ordeal of forced removal. By 1860, on seven reservations—Allegany, Cattaraugus, Oneida, Onondaga, St. Regis (Akwesasne Mohawks), Tonawanda, and Tuscarora—close to 4,000 Haudenosaunees continued to live within the confines of New York state.[68] With the exception of the St. Regis Reservation (on the St. Lawrence River just south of Canada), these reservations were all in areas of dense American settlement. Haudenosaunees were the only eastern nation with a sizable population surrounded by a large settler population that was able successfully to resist removal. Why? One possible answer is that they fought harder (and more heroically). Another is that they were more unified. A comparison with the Cherokees suggests that the intensity of Haudenosaunee resistance was probably not decisive. No one can deny that the Cherokees were as determined to resist removal as any other Indian nation, or that they possessed the political imagination and resources to mount a serious challenge. On the other hand, by the time of the 1835 New Echota Treaty, Cherokees were probably more divided than Haudenosaunees at the time of the 1838 Buffalo Creek Treaty. In both cases, a minority was willing to accept a removal treaty, though in the Haudenosaunee case, this minority was probably weaker, which meant that the Buffalo Creek Treaty was ultimately less credible and so could be reopened. A more decisive factor was the external environment. Although Cherokees had some non-Indian allies after 1835, these allies were on the periphery of the fight (largely in the North). Close to home, Cherokees faced unified colonial power in the form of the combined opposition of Georgia and the executive branch of the federal government. In New York, however, Whig politicians saw advantages in allowing Haudenosaunees to stay (they could tax them), while at the same time reducing their already diminished land base. Although federal officials, New York Democrats, and the Ogden Land Company continued to seek Haudenosaunee removal after 1838, colonial power was divided.

CONCLUSION: HOPES AND FEARS

Even after the Bad Axe massacre, Black Hawk was able to find hope for the future. Following his surrender, he spent several months in prison before U.S. officials sent him on a tour of eastern cities. While in Baltimore in June 1833, Black Hawk met with President Jackson, who told the Sauk leader that he was satisfied he "would not try to do any more injury" and could return to "your own country." Black Hawk replied that he would not "go to war again" and would instead "live in peace."[69] Black Hawk's people would never again inhabit their beloved Saukenuk, but Black Hawk believed they could retain permanent homes on the west side of the Mississippi.

Weeks later, however, as Black Hawk was returning to his home country, he witnessed an alarming sight. While on board a steamboat descending the Mississippi from Prairie du Chien, Black Hawk "discovered a large collection of people in the mining country, on the west side of the river" at a place known as Dubuque (see Fig. 39). Black Hawk was "surprised at this," as he had "understood from our Great Father, that the Mississippi was to be the dividing line between his red and white children." As he continued down the river and saw that the country along the west bank of the Mississippi was "much settled by the whites," he became "very much afraid, that in a few years, they will begin to drive and abuse our people, as they have formerly done."[70]

What would the future hold for Black Hawk's people and other nations forced to leave their eastern homes in the 1830s and 1840s? Would they be able to rebuild their communities? Would their new lands be as productive as those they had left behind? Would the Great Father protect them from whiskey traders and hostile nations already in the West? Would they have enough to eat and be free from the diseases that had taken so many lives on journeys west? Would new waves of settlers force them out yet again, and if so, where would they go? Histories of Indian removal usually end with trails of tears and so don't address these questions. Nor do they consider how shoving tens of thousands of eastern Indians west of the Mississippi affected nations already there. To provide a full account of the impact of removal, we need to understand what happened in what Black Hawk accurately feared would be an ever-shrinking zone of removal.

CHAPTER 10

Destruction and Survival in the Zone of Removal, 1840s–1860

When Alexis de Tocqueville observed the Choctaws crossing the Mississippi River at Memphis in the winter of 1831–1832, he predicted a grim future for them and other removed nations. Like their howling dogs, who "plunged into the icy waters of the Mississippi to swim after their masters," the Choctaws would soon be destroyed. Tocqueville identified two sources of Choctaw destruction. One was war with other Indian nations in the West. It was not that these enemies would slaughter the Choctaws and other southern nations. Rather, to avoid war, the Choctaws would scatter. Families would dissolve and people would soon forget their language and history. Choctaws might remain as individuals, but "the nation has ceased to exist." The other was from continued settler expansion. The "same white population which is now pressing around them," Tocqueville presciently wrote, "will again be on their tracks . . . ; then they will suffer again from the same ills without the same remedies; and because sooner or later there will be no land left for them, their only refuge will be the grave."[1]

Tocqueville's forecast got some of the details wrong, but it made the crucial, if often overlooked, point that the consequences of Indian removal were felt long after its completion. The two previous chapters have documented losses from disease in the first few years after removal. A complete analysis of removal, however, requires a longer look at removed nations as they sought to rebuild their communities and survive in the West in the decades prior to the Civil War. It also requires reversing Tocqueville's vantage point and looking at the process from the perspective of Native nations indigenous to the zone of removal. As we saw in Chapter 7, nations west of the Mississippi experienced adverse consequences from an influx of eastern Indians well before the 1830 Indian Removal Act. The arrival of a much larger number of eastern Indians in the 1830s and 1840s would have even graver consequences.

CREATING PEACE

The Choctaws Tocqueville observed at Memphis were well aware of the dangers of conflict with western nations. Unlike Tocqueville, who had only a dim knowledge of the West's social geography, the Choctaws, sent against their will to a "land of death," knew exactly what they were getting into. Not only were Choctaws concerned about the still formidable Osages, they had reason to fear the nations to the west of the zone of removal on the southern Great Plains—the Comanches, Kiowas, and Wichitas (Fig. 44). Of these three nations, the Comanches were by far the most powerful. More than a century earlier, the Comanches had begun to build what has been termed a "nomadic empire" on the southern Plains. This empire stretched from the southern Rocky Mountains on the west to central Texas and central Oklahoma on the east. Through raiding and trading with Native nations and Europeans along their vast periphery, Comanches secured a steady supply of horses and captives for trade. Over time, they increasingly enslaved some of these captives to process bison robes to trade for weapons. Largely because of disease, the Comanche population fell from perhaps 40,000 in the late eighteenth century to 20,000–30,000 by the 1830s. Nonetheless, the Comanches had the military capacity not only to block Choctaws from hunting in their territory but to devastate new Choctaw towns. Although Kiowas numbered only 1,000 and Wichitas only 2,000, both nations were at peace with the Comanches and were also well prepared to defend their lands from what they saw as a Choctaw invasion.[2]

Even as removed Choctaws were trying to recover from a traumatic journey west and the sicknesses that continued to afflict them after their arrival, a young Choctaw leader named Peter Pitchlynn took steps to create a safe future for his people (Fig. 45). In 1834, he took a three-month trip onto the Plains to hunt buffalo and make peace with Comanches and Kiowas. Although Pitchlynn's trip did not bear immediate fruit, the following

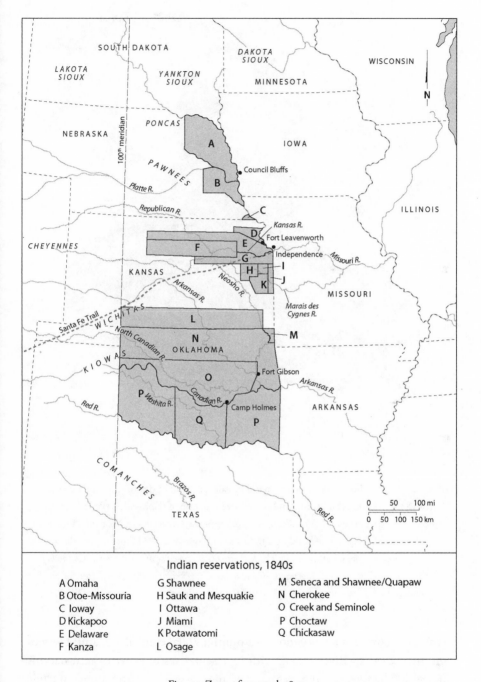

Fig. 44. Zone of removal, 1840s

Indian reservations, 1840s

A Omaha
B Otoe-Missouria
C Ioway
D Kickapoo
E Delaware
F Kanza
G Shawnee
H Sauk and Mesquakie
I Ottawa
J Miami
K Potawatomi
L Osage
M Seneca and Shawnee/Quapaw
N Cherokee
O Creek and Seminole
P Choctaw
Q Chickasaw

Fig. 45. When Choctaws arrived in what they called a "land of death," they took concrete
steps to survive and rebuild. To avoid destructive war, one of their leaders, Peter Pitchlynn,
entered negotiations with Plains tribes. A graduate of the University of Nashville, Pitchlynn
also played a key role in building a robust school system as the Choctaws sought to
make a new home. Charles Fenderich, *P. P. Pitchlynn, Speaker of the National Council of
the Choctaw Nation and Choctaw Delegate to the Government of the United States,* from
Fenderich, *Life on Stone* (1842). Library of Congress Prints and Photographs Division.

year Choctaws sent a delegation to a multinational council at Camp Holmes
on the Canadian River. Along with representatives of other eastern nations
(Creeks, Cherokees, and Senecas), they met several western nations, including Comanches, Kiowas, Wichitas, Osages, and Quapaws. The council was
sponsored by the United States, but the voluntary attendance of several thou-

sand Indians testified to the effectiveness of previous intertribal diplomacy and a general interest in minimizing destructive conflict. After signing the peace treaty, Choctaw chief Mushalatubbe gave tobacco to his "brothers who live in the West" and expressed his hope that "if there be any killing, let it be by the falling of the limbs of trees."[3]

In addition to wanting to end intertribal war, the Choctaws and other Native nations who agreed to this treaty were motivated by the prospect of commerce between newly relocated eastern Indians and Indians of the Plains. In the mid-1830s and beyond, Cherokees, Creeks, Chickasaws, Choctaws, and Seminoles exchanged agricultural products and munitions to Comanches for buffalo products and horses. The eastern nations also traded for captives, which Comanches were acquiring by raiding Mexican settlements as far south as Zacatecas and San Luis Potosí and the growing Anglo settlements of Texas. Cherokees, Creeks, Chickasaws, Choctaws, and Seminoles incorporated some of these captives into their communities and sold or ransomed others.[4]

Maintaining peaceful trading relationships required continuous cultivation. In 1845, for example, a party of Wichitas attempted to raid the horse herd of a Creek town on the western part of the Creek Reservation. Before the Wichitas could strike, the Creeks drove off the raiders and then tracked them, cornered them, and killed between four and six. Creeks feared that raiding might escalate and called for a council with all the region's nations. Because the Comanches had substantial influence over the smaller Wichitas, Creek diplomats were particularly eager for Comanches to attend the council. When a Creek delegation arrived with the invitation in Comanche country, the recipients declined in no uncertain terms. By one account, the Comanches held four of the delegates in a ring and would have shot them except that an elderly Comanche woman pleaded for their lives. The Creeks escaped only by giving up "all their effects," including their clothing and horses. Comanches then set about arranging their own council with Kiowas, Wichitas, Caddos, Cheyennes, and others. Creeks feared that this rival council's purpose was to make an alliance against them. What had gone wrong? The documents do not reveal the thinking of everyone, but it is noteworthy that one of the reasons the Comanches gave the Creek delegation for rejecting their invitation to attend the Creek council was that the buffalo "had got too far from them by smelling the cattle, hogs, etc., of the Creeks." By the mid-1840s, the southern Plains bison herds were starting to diminish. Historians have identified Comanche overhunting and increasing pressure on grasslands from their vast horse herds as the primary causes, but it was also reasonable for Comanches to identify Creek livestock as a threat to their hunting territory. Scarcity encouraged suspicion and rumor, and suspicion and rumor could lead to war.[5]

Although their efforts had yet to bear fruit, Creek diplomats persisted. Their next move was to prevail upon Caddos to carry tobacco and white beads (a symbol of peace) to the Comanches. Soon after, Creeks and other southeastern nations took advantage of a U.S. initiative to promote peace between the southern Plains nations and the state of Texas, admitted to the Union in December 1845. Creeks and others recognized that U.S. officials would have a hard time convincing Plains nations to make peace with Anglo Texans, a group that since the Texas Revolution of 1836 had manifested an intention to exterminate Plains Indians. Accordingly, a delegation of Cherokees, Creeks, Chickasaws, and Seminoles volunteered to assist the U.S. commission tasked with negotiating a treaty on the Brazos River near present-day Waco. Although the treaty was to be between the United States and the southern Plains tribes, delegates from the southeastern nations played a crucial role in securing the agreement. Cooacoochee, one of the main leaders of Seminole resistance in Florida, urged his "red brothers of the West" to listen to the "good talk" of the U.S. "chiefs," and expressed his hope that "they would all unite and make a good treaty for all parties." Elijah Hicks, a Cherokee delegate who had helped lead Cherokee resistance to removal, assured the Plains people that "the words [sic] of the President was true and was always good." Hicks knew a great deal about the mendacity of U.S. presidents and perhaps meant his words to apply only to the current one (James K. Polk), but it could be that the moment required some fibbing of his own. In any case, diplomacy worked. The 1846 treaty called for an exchange of captives between Plains people and Texas and an end to horse stealing, so often the trigger for fighting.[6]

Diplomacy and trade continued to prevent conflict from escalating, although changing conditions in the late 1850s presented new challenges. Between 1847 and 1860, the population of Texas more than quadrupled, increasing from 140,000 to 600,000. As Texans pushed west, they constantly provoked conflict with Comanches and Kiowas. In turn, Texas rangers and U.S. troops repeatedly struck Indians on the southern Plains. For a time, the federal government offered Indians small reservations within Texas, but Texans soon demanded the expulsion, if not extermination, of Wichitas, Comanches, and Caddos living in what one historian describes as "concentration camps." Increasingly, southern Plains communities looked to western Oklahoma and southern Kansas as places beyond the reach of the Texas Rangers.

As more and more people were pushed into a smaller area, intertribal conflict increased. Comanches fought with Sauks and Mesquakies in western Kansas in 1854; four years later, Comanches attacked Delawares and Kickapoos in south-central Oklahoma. Comanches and Wichitas repeatedly targeted Choctaw and Chickasaw horse herds. None of these clashes, however, resulted in significant loss of life. As before, diplomacy worked to limit violence. In an 1855 treaty, Choctaws leased the western portion of their Oklahoma lands so that Comanches and Wichitas could have a permanent reservation. Choctaw leaders hoped that this would encourage Comanches and Wichitas to take up farming and become less dependent on raiding their livestock. This treaty also called for the United States to move Delaware, Kickapoo, and Shawnee communities living on Choctaw/Chickasaw lands to already established reservations for these nations in Kansas. For years, Choctaws and Chickasaws had complained of Delaware, Kickapoo, and Shawnee raids; their removal to Kansas eliminated another source of tension. Contrary to Tocqueville's prediction that fear of enemies would lead to Choctaw disintegration, then, it had encouraged successful initiatives to secure peace.[7]

PATTERNS OF INTERTRIBAL CONFLICT

As seen in Chapter 7, eastern Indians moving into the zone of removal prior to 1830 frequently clashed with nations already there, especially the Osages. After crushing losses at the hands of Cherokees and their Indigenous allies, notably in massacres of 1817 and 1821, Osages vacated their Arkansas villages in the 1820s. According to a treaty of 1825, the Osages were supposed to move to a tract of land in southern Kansas, but they chose to locate their villages in northeastern Oklahoma, lands the United States had designated for the Cherokees. Given the history of Cherokee–Osage conflict, the arrival of several thousand Cherokees in the late 1830s might have precipitated a new and even more deadly war between those two nations, but by this time conditions had changed. Unlike the earlier situation, when a small number of newly arrived Cherokees sought to establish dominance in the region, the Cherokees now had clear control over their Oklahoma reservation and so had no need to renew war with the Osages. In the late 1830s, the Osages still had a population of between 5,000 and 6,000 (close to what it had been for the previous few decades), but they were now surrounded by a much larger Cherokee population. Under these circumstances, the Osages decided not to challenge the Cherokees and instead relocated north to Kansas.[8]

Though unwilling to contest Cherokees, once in Kansas, Osages clashed with other nations. In cooperation with Kanza Indians, Osages fought Pawnees to control territory in central Kansas and south-central Nebraska valuable for hunting buffalo. According to one government agent, Osages were "constantly at war with Pawnees," but reports of Osage–Pawnee hostilities suggest relatively low-level conflict. Osages also occasionally fought Sauks and Mesquakies and Comanches, but compared to Osage losses from Cherokee attacks in earlier decades, casualties were light. Overall, peaceful commerce rather than deadly war characterized relations between the Osages and the southern Plains nations. Throughout the 1840s and into the late 1850s, Osages used funds from treaty annuities to acquire arms, ammunition, blankets, sugar, and coffee from American traders and exchanged them with Comanches and Kiowas for mules and horses, which Osages in turn sold to settlers and whiskey traders in Missouri and Kansas. This trade was sufficiently lucrative that when U.S. officials sent presents to Comanches and Kiowas in 1854, thus threatening to undercut the Osage position, Osages tried to convince Comanches and Kiowas that "*bad medicine* had been put in the goods to kill them off."[9]

Ioways, Sauks and Mesquakies, Omahas, and Otoe-Missourias continued to depend on hunting and so clashed with one another as well as with Plains nations to the west—Arapahoes, Cheyennes, Dakota and Lakota Sioux, and Pawnees.[10] Ioways and Sauks and Mesquakies did not suffer greatly from intertribal war, but Omahas and Otoe-Missourias took substantial losses at the hands of Plains tribes. Situated just to the west of the Missouri River, the Omahas and Otoe-Missourias inhabited an area with sufficient rainfall to support crops, but to avoid starvation they also needed to hunt on the Plains to the west. As we observed in Chapter 7, Omahas and Otoe-Missourias had small populations of just over 1,000 and were vulnerable to raids from the east (Sauks and Mesquakies) and the west and northwest (Pawnees and Sioux). The destructiveness of these raids increased in the 1840s. The Yankton Sioux and Sicangu Lakota Sioux were particularly aggressive. These two groups, members of the larger Sioux nation, possessed a large hunting territory west of the Missouri River on the plains of South Dakota and Nebraska, which they were determined to protect and even expand. As on the southern plains in Comanche territory, bison in the central Plains were becoming scarcer in the 1840s. In addition, unlike the Comanches, whose population had fallen, the populations of western Sioux communities were generally increasing in the 1830s, 1840s, and 1850s, in part because of the migration of Dakotas from Minnesota who wanted to join more prosperous western communities. To exclude Omahas and Otoe-Missourias from hunting in central and western Nebraska, Yank-tons and Sicangus went beyond simply attacking Omaha and Otoe-Missouria hunting parties. They waited until these parties had left their villages and then set upon defenseless people left behind. In 1843 a government agent reported that Omahas "lost some thirty of their nation" to Sioux war parties attacking their villages. Three years later, Yanktons massacred a reported seventy-three women and children. Omahas were "frantic with fear" at the prospect of Sioux violence and had no good option. If Omaha men stayed home to guard vil-lages, the people would starve. On the other hand, continuing to send hunters onto the Plains left villages vulnerable, and the hunting parties themselves were at risk of Sioux attacks. A brief peace with the Sioux and Pawnees in the mid-1850s brought some relief, but in 1859 a party of Arapahoes, Cheyennes, and Oglala and Sicangu Lakotas struck seventy Omahas on a buffalo hunt, killing seventeen, "principally of the aged and infirm." The Otoe-Missourias were in a similar situation. Pawnees and Arapahoes killed thirty in 1845, and a Sioux attack two years later took the lives of twenty-eight. Sioux and Chey-ennes repeatedly threatened them over the next several years.[11]

Of all the nations in the zone of removal, those from the Ohio Valley and lower Great Lakes—Delawares, Kickapoos, Miamis, Ottawas, Potawatomis, Senecas, Shawnees, and Wyandots—experienced the least conflict with other Indians. Some of these nations, particularly Delawares and Potawatomis, sought buffalo on the Plains and occasionally clashed with Plains nations. As well, Kickapoos, Delawares, and Shawnees who had migrated west of the Mississippi prior to 1830 and established communities in Texas and western Oklahoma frequently fought with relocated southern nations and Plains na-tions. But the northeastern nations relocated to Kansas in the 1830s and 1840s pursued farming as the best route for economic development. They relied less on hunting than nations indigenous to the region and so were less likely to become involved in conflict over hunting grounds.[12]

RESOLVING INTERNAL CONFLICTS

For some relocated nations, the threat of internal conflict and violence equaled or exceeded dangers from intertribal war. The means the United States used to force nations west—signing removal agreements with mi-nority factions and providing favors to particular tribal leaders, to cite two common practices—were inherently divisive. The sufferings along trails of tears understandably aggravated factionalism and set the stage for possible conflict in the West.

In June 1839, just months after the last Cherokees arrived in Oklahoma, supporters of Principal Chief John Ross killed three Cherokees who had signed the 1835 Treaty of New Echota, Major Ridge, John Ridge, and Elias Boudinot. Since signing the treaty, these men had lived in fear for their lives, knowing that it was a capital offense under Cherokee law to sell tribal land without proper authority. After putting pen to paper at New Echota, Major Ridge predicted what would happen, saying, "I have signed my death warrant." Although the killing of the Ridges and Boudinot had legal sanction, the Treaty Party and their allies, the Old Settlers (those who had emigrated west before the 1830s), saw the acts as murder. To avenge the deaths, Stand Watie fatally stabbed a Ross supporter in 1842. Violence escalated over the next few years and verged on full-scale civil war. Over a ten-month period beginning in November 1845, thirty-three Cherokees were killed. To put a stop to the escalating violence, leaders from the Ross faction, the Treaty Party, and the Old Settlers reached an agreement. Formalized by treaty with the United States, the agreement settled controversies over the distribution of funds from previous treaties and declared a "general amnesty" for previous "offenses and crimes," thus blocking the cycle of revenge killings.[13]

Creeks were also deeply divided. During the removal process, Upper Creeks had assisted U.S. troops in subduing Lower Creeks who were resisting. No wonder, then, that once in Oklahoma the two factions "rival[ed] the other in animosity and bitter hatred." Unlike the Cherokees, however, Creeks settled their differences without bloodshed. In February 1839, a council attended by a reported 500 Upper Creeks and 1,000 Lower Creeks agreed to establish a single general council composed of representatives of both factions. The general council was given legal and judicial authority and authorized to meet annually.[14]

Although the establishment of this council brought a degree of unity to the Creeks, it did not represent Seminoles. By the reckoning of the U.S. government and the Creek Nation, Seminoles were simply renegade Creeks who were supposed to live under Creek authority after removal. Despite the fact that a treaty in 1845 afforded the Seminoles some autonomy, they continued to protest being "compelled to merge their tribal organization into that of the Creeks." Seminoles also objected to Creek claims that many Black Seminoles were escaped slaves of Creek masters. They also objected to Creeks attempts, often successful, to kidnap Black Seminoles. Some Seminoles sought to establish homes among the Cherokees, while others, including some Black Seminoles, migrated to Mexico in the early 1850s. Most Seminoles, however, remained on Creek lands. In 1856, arguing that the Creek council damaged the "vital interests of their feeble nation," Seminoles secured Creek agreement to a treaty that recognized the Seminoles as a separate nation and provided them with a portion of the Creek reservation.[15]

Factionalism also plagued some of the relocated northeastern nations. For Shawnees, the process of removal resulted in the merger of communities that had been dispersed from Ohio to Missouri to Texas. Now on a single reservation in Kansas, leaders of previously separated communities jockeyed for position, including control over annuities due from previous treaties. As they did, they made alliances with competing groups of Methodist, Baptist, and Quaker missionaries. According to one Baptist missionary, the Shawnees "are more divided among themselves than any other tribe in this region." To protect tribal sovereignty, Shawnee leaders created for the first time in their history a national council, but many Shawnees objected to the centralization of authority in fewer hands. Kickapoos were also divided between supporters of two rival leaders: Kenekuk, who pursued a policy of accommodation with the United States, and Kishko, who opposed cooperation and was willing to stay in Kansas only if he could have a separate reservation from Kenekuk's. When the government denied this request, Kishko led disaffected Kickapoos to Texas and Mexico. From there, they returned annually to collect their share of treaty annuities. Whether persistent factionalism in one place (as with the Shawnees) or factionalism resulting in diaspora (as with the Kickapoos) was more damaging is difficult to say. In neither case, however, did internal divisions lead to politically motivated violence.[16]

CONFRONTING THE SCOURGE OF ALCOHOL

A more significant source of violence was alcohol abuse. Relocated eastern Indians had battled the destructive effects of alcohol for generations. Had they believed U.S. officials who assured them that removal would protect them from whiskey, they might well have been more sympathetic to complying. But as Wyandots reported after visiting eastern Kansas in 1831, rather than being "removed from the temptations to intemperance, . . . we shall have a more worthless and corrupt class of whites to deal and associate with than is to be found in this part of Ohio." Although it is impossible to quantify levels of alcohol consumption for specific nations over time, consumption may well have increased after removal. Certainly, there was no shortage of liquor west of the Mississippi. Federal legislation passed in 1832 made it illegal to introduce "ardent spirits" into Indian country. Nonetheless, the area between the Platte River in Nebraska and the Red River, a distance of 500 miles, was "inundated with whiskey dispensed by prominent merchants and small-time hucksters whose principal customers were Indians." In the 1830s, such outlets were concentrated on the eastern edge of the zone of removal. At the "whiskey capital" of the West—the sister cities of Council Bluffs, Iowa, and Bellevue, Nebraska, both on the Missouri River—liquor reportedly flowed "as freely" as the river itself. To the south, as many as seventy "whiskey shops" on the western boundary of Arkansas alone were selling to Indians. Supply expanded west in the 1840s. The growth of traffic on the Santa Fe Trail through Kansas created a "whiskey pipeline" consisting of whiskey ranches and cheap saloons known as "doggeries." Similar establishments—and even a distillery—sprang up on the Texas side of the Red River in the 1840s. Small-time entrepreneurs brought whiskey onto Indian reservations "in jugs, bottles, flasks, vials, and gum elastic snakes or belts, to different parts of the country." These "prairie bars" were "concealed in the woods, on the prairies, or about their persons," and their contents distributed as opportunity allowed.[17]

U.S. officials were aware that free-flowing liquor west of the Mississippi contradicted a key premise of Indian removal—as Lewis Cass expressed it to the Creeks, that removal was necessary to protect Indians from "bad white men" using "ardent spirits" to "tempt or debauch" them. Yet if the federal government could not prevent white men from doing bad things east of the Mississippi River, what magic would allow the government to stop wickedness in the West? Congress did strengthen penalties for violating federal prohibition law and provided new mechanisms for enforcing the law, but these measures were completely ineffective. Even when officials brought charges for illegal vending, the judicial system, composed of judges and juries with much greater sympathy for free enterprise than Indian welfare, often failed to deliver convictions. When guilty verdicts were rendered, penalties were insufficient to deter further crime. One Samuel C. Roby, found guilty in 1848 of selling alcohol to Ottawas in Kansas, received a fine of $1.00. Seven years after Roby's conviction, the Ottawa reservation was "surrounded by white squatters, most of whom were running whiskey shops on the very boundaries of the reservation." Another problem was that federal law applied only to Indian reservations. This meant that vendors residing in Iowa, Missouri, Arkansas, and Texas could legally sell alcohol to Indians who came to them from nearby reservations. Although some scholars have concluded that this legal limitation on federal authority absolves the federal government of responsibility, this interpretation too easily gets the architects of removal off the hook for the removal policy's failure to separate Indians from the corrosive influence of alcohol. Officials who advocated for removal did not acknowledge it, but they knew enough about American history to realize that new states were sure to be created in the West and that purveyors of alcohol would find their way to them.[18]

As with other addictive substances, the simple availability of alcohol created its own demand. The sufferings and trauma of removal provided an additional stimulus. In postremoval Choctaw communities, a sense of despair contributed to alcohol consumption and triggered a cycle of further abuse and deeper despair. Before removal, Choctaw kinship networks and practices—hunting and warfare—had socialized young men and given purpose to their lives. But these systems were eroding and could no longer provide a check on destructive behavior. Similar processes undoubtedly operated for other relocated nations.[19]

Documentation of alcohol abuse and its connections to domestic violence and conflict between men is incomplete. Government agents frequently reported that drunkenness among Indians led to "rows," broils," and murders, but agents seldom provided numbers. When they did, they usually lumped violent deaths related to alcohol together with deaths from other causes. The agent for the Delawares stated in 1851 that thirty-two had died from "drunkenness and other diseases" over the previous year, suggesting that these deaths had not resulted from alcohol-induced violence but from alcoholism or related disease. Clearly, though, alcohol-related violence was a significant force of destruction throughout the zone of removal.[20]

Excessive drinking was damaging in other ways. By the 1840s, many nations had access to significant funds from treaty annuities. When used to purchase whiskey, as often happened, income from annuities was unavailable for basic needs like food and clothing, let alone investments in equipment or livestock. Government agents frequently explained alcohol abuse in ways that drew upon widespread allegations of Indians' innate racial inferiority. One agent, for example, attributed their "indolence and drunkenness" to their status as "children of nature, easily led astray and seduced into bad habits."[21] Although attributing alcohol abuse to Indians' status as "children of nature" was racist, it is true enough that drunkenness discouraged productive labor. It is also true that chronic drinking and its association with a deficient diet weakened bodies, making them more vulnerable to pathogens.

Indians were well aware that alcohol was a scourge, although they did not agree that the problem stemmed from their alleged status as primitives. Instead, they cited the history of their encounter with alcohol. In 1834, a Delaware leader agreed with a U.S. official that "whiskey is bad for our people," but he pointed out that "the whites first gave us whiskey. We did not . . . love it. The white man said it was good and our young men took it." Indians were also more confident than their overseers that the problem could be addressed. In contrast to one government agent who lamented that the "whiskey trade" was "gradually wearing away the substance of the Indians, and effecting slowly, but certainly, their ruin, and the extirpation of their race," leaders of Native communities did not believe decline was inevitable. In 1844, as political hatred and violence (fueled partly by liquor) threatened to rip apart their nation, Cherokees organized a temperance society. After creating a new governmental structure the following year, Cherokees strengthened legislation prohibiting alcohol on Cherokee lands. Cherokees also demanded that non-Indians accept their responsibility for the problem. They petitioned federal authorities to abandon Fort Gibson, where whiskey peddlers sold to soldiers and Indians alike. They also demanded that the Arkansas legislature close down the "fountains of deadly evil to the Indians on your border." It was harder for Cherokees to convince outsiders to take constructive action than it was to persuade their own people. Although liquor continued to flow unabated into Cherokee country, numerous local temperance societies thriving in Cherokee country by 1852 revealed a determination to eliminate its use.[22] Other Native nations, including Choctaws, Miamis, Senecas, and Wyandots, organized temperance societies. Several nations acted against tribal members who violated laws prohibiting the sale and consumption of liquor. The southern nations used their police forces, known as Light Horses, to "destroy . . . whiskey wherever they find it." Potawatomis took a different tack, "punishing, by fine and imprisonment, any Indian known to be guilty of bringing liquor onto the reservation, or of being drunk." Among the Kickapoos in Kansas, the "old men" punished those introducing liquor "with stripes and public whippings," while Shawnees shaved the heads of women who drank excessively. It is impossible to document the effectiveness of these measures, but they undoubtedly reduced alcohol abuse from what it would have been otherwise. Even more, robust temperance programs reveal that although removal had damaged the fabric of community and nation, Native communities had the fortitude to confront a problem not of their own making.[23]

EDUCATION

If much of the work of the removed Native nations was to deal with immediate threats, they also looked to the future. Many tribal leaders promoted education. Of all the removed nations, the Choctaws and Cherokees established the most extensive school systems. In the early 1840s, the Choctaws used their education funds, guaranteed to them in previous treaties, to create enough schools to educate all the nation's children and many of its adults. The system they established had two tiers. The first consisted of six academies, three male and three female, that taught moral philosophy, mathematics, history and geography, and Latin. To staff the academies the Choctaw General Council contracted with the Methodist Episcopal Church and the American Board of Commissioners for Foreign Missions. Although some children from poorer families enrolled in these academies, they primarily served the children of the Choctaw elite. Most Choctaw children, along with some adults, attended local schools that taught the three Rs—reading, writing, and arithmetic. Cherokees also invested funds in creating local schools, although their system was less robust than the Choctaws' and relied heavily on mission schools sponsored by Baptists, Congregationalists, and Methodists. Cherokees also established two seminaries, one for girls, one for boys, to train their own teachers who could provide bilingual instruction, although these closed for lack of funds in 1856. Elsewhere in eastern Oklahoma and eastern Kansas, Native nations generally lacked the resources to fund education and so the only schools were run by missionaries. These provided potentially valuable knowledge and could serve as a way to alleviate economic hardship (a child enrolled in a mission school was one less mouth to feed), but Native people often resisted sending their children to mission schools because they objected to efforts to convert them to Christianity. Among the Shawnees, for example, a community led by Wawahche-paekar "were opposed to the Education of their children or of receiving any religious instruction and also opposed [to] the adoptions of the habits of the white man."[24]

REBUILDING ECONOMIES

Perhaps the most crucial challenge for Indians in the zone of removal was to build new economies. Without economic self-sufficiency, people would suffer from hunger and be more vulnerable to disease. Relocated eastern nations—

all with extensive experience with crops and livestock—attempted to repro-
duce familiar practices and adapt according to necessity and opportunity.

The hardships and losses during removal created obstacles to economic re-
construction. When the Chickasaws arrived in Oklahoma, for example, many
were sick and malnourished. For several months, they remained confined in
camps, where they received poor rations and lost horses and cattle to creditors
preying on their misery. Gradually, however, Chickasaws began to spread out
on the Chickasaw District (earlier purchased from Choctaws) and establish
farms. Wealthier families who owned the large majority of the nation's 1,000
black slaves fared best. Once in the West, Chickasaws' slaves cleared the land
to create plantations and then did the bulk of the work to make them productive. The Chickasaw plantations ranged in size from 100 to 1,000 acres
and produced cotton, corn, wheat, oats, and rye. Surrounding grazing lands
supported growing herds of horses, cattle, sheep, and goats. Chickasaw commercial farmers found markets close at hand, selling grain and meat to nearby
military posts and supplying overlanders traversing their lands on their way
to Texas or California with horses, cows, and oxen. They also turned to more
distant markets, shipping cotton and grain down the Mississippi and driving cattle and horses to buyers in Missouri, Arkansas, and Louisiana. The
large majority of Chickasaws were subsistence farmers. They cultivated fields
of at most ten acres, growing corn, potatoes, yams, melons, and pumpkins.
Most families raised chickens, milk cows, and hogs, and some planted small
orchards. In addition to working in the fields, women and girls spun yarn and
wove cloth. While farming and stock raising were the core of their economy,
Chickasaws engaged in numerous supplemental enterprises. On their own
lands, they hunted small animals for pelts, and they occasionally ventured
onto the Plains for buffalo. Chickasaws ran lumber and grist mills, cotton
gins, and small stores, traded with the Plains nations, and established ferry
services for Anglos wishing to cross the Red River. At places where oil seeped
from the ground, Chickasaw entrepreneurs opened spas for settlers from Texas
and Arkansas seeking a remedy for rheumatism and other chronic afflictions.[25]

Choctaws, Creeks, and Cherokees developed similar economies. Within
these nations, a small elite (2–3 percent of the total population) exploited
the labor of people they held as slaves to reestablish plantations producing
surpluses of grain to sell to nearby settlers and cotton for the world market.
These plantations were sufficiently productive to allow the slave population
to increase through natural reproduction. Planters also purchased slaves from
non-Native enslavers. The Choctaws' slave population increased from 500

before removal to 2,300 in 1860; the Cherokees' rose from 1,600 to 2,500; and the Creeks' from 900 to 1,500. But if elites were successful, the large majority of the Choctaws, Creeks, and Cherokees often struggled to get by. Unlike the other southern nations, the Seminoles had never engaged in commercial farming. Faced with having to build a new economy in Oklahoma, they chose to pursue a combination of subsistence agriculture and hunting. Even if Seminoles had wanted to establish plantations, most Black Seminoles enjoyed substantial autonomy and could not have been exploited this way.[26]

Nations removed from the Ohio Valley and Great Lakes, with a few exceptions, such as a handful of the "more opulent" Shawnees, did not use enslaved people to labor for them. Otherwise, their economies had characteristics similar to those of the nations from the South. A relatively wealthy minority relied on family labor to produce occasional surpluses of grain and livestock for sale in local markets—travelers needing provisions on their way through Kansas, missionaries requiring wheat and oats, military post commanders looking for a source of beef. Most families practiced subsistence farming on communal lands and shared what the land offered across extended networks of kin. To supplement agricultural production, Delawares and Potawatomis conducted buffalo hunts on the Plains to the west, but most of the nations from the Ohio Valley and Great Lakes wanted to avoid conflict with the Plains nations. Treaty annuities were of some benefit, although traders often claimed annuities as payment for tribal debts. In 1846, after satisfying traders, Delawares received only $5.74 per capita, enough to buy a cloth blanket and a couple of pair of shoes, but little else. To do more than simply survive, Indians had to pursue any opportunity they could. Many citizens of the Ohio Valley and Great Lakes nations had valuable skills and were able to find employment as translators, interpreters, carpenters, blacksmiths, and shoemakers. Others without specialized skills occasionally worked for Missouri farmers or at local Christian missions. Another possibility was to charge non-Indians a toll to use bridges or ferries to cross rivers. Wyandots had a sufficient number of ferries on the Kansas River that their tribal government created an official position to oversee their operation. Senecas built a grist mill and collected fees from local settlers who brought their grain for grinding. Indians had been industrious before removal and continued to be industrious after. The sheer range of their economic pursuits should be appreciated for its own sake. It also exposes the racist views of American leaders like Albert Gallatin, the founder of the American Ethnological Society, who asserted in 1836 that "the Indian disappears before the white man, simply because he will not work."[27]

In many years enough rain fell at the right times to allow crops to mature. The 1840s, in fact, was a decade of above-average rainfall in the zone of
removal. Many Native communities relocated from the East suffered from
farm-destroying floods. In general, though, the climate of eastern Kansas and
eastern Oklahoma—on the edge of the arid Great Plains—is drier than east
of the Mississippi. During the 1850s, Native agriculturalists saw a return to
a more normal climate and experienced crop failures. Dry seasons were reported for eastern Oklahoma in 1851, 1853, 1854, 1855, and 1860. Drought did
not hit Kansas until 1854; including that year, dry, hot summers were reported
in five of the next seven years. In these years, government agents reported that
Indians might "perish from famine," but they provided few details. At the
very least, the impact of drought forced Indians to take desperate measures.
In 1860, after several seasons of poor crops, Kickapoos in Kansas decided to
winter with their southern relatives, "where game can be found to supply
their wants." This was an extraordinary reversal of the usual practice of Kickapoos in western Oklahoma annually visiting Kansas to collect their portion
of treaty annuities.[28]

THE ZONE OF REMOVAL SHRINKS AGAIN:
THE KANSAS-NEBRASKA ACT OF 1854

Even as drought came upon their lands, Native communities in one area
of the zone of removal faced the prospect of losing their lands altogether
when the United States organized Kansas as a territory under the 1854
Kansas-Nebraska Act. Removal treaties with the northeastern nations guaranteed them reservations as a "permanent residence," a "home forever" or for
"as long as they shall exist as a nation." The creation of Kansas Territory did
not by itself liquidate Indian lands, but it meant that the United States would
demand that Indians accept new treaties that would reduce or eliminate reservations that had been promised them in perpetuity. Even before treaties were
signed, squatters invaded Indian reserves in eastern Kansas. Many squatters,
such as army officers who occupied Delaware lands in 1854, were engaging in
the by-now traditional American activity of claiming cheap land for speculative purposes. Others had political goals in mind. Some crossed the border
from slave-state Missouri with the intention of organizing Kansas as a territory open to slavery, the first step on the road to ensuring Kansas would eventually enter the Union as a slave state. Others from New England, the Middle
Atlantic states, and the Ohio Valley came with the opposite goal of organizing

Kansas as a free territory so that it could become a free state. Though bitterly divided over the question of the extension of slavery into new territories, those who were invading Kansas agreed on one thing: Indians must go.[29]

Could policymakers have foreseen the invasion of Kansas when they promised Indians permanent homes there? Writing in 1830, Lewis Cass conceded that it was possible that "in the course of ages, our population should press upon that barrier" (the barrier between U.S. settlement and the lands guaranteed to removed Indians), but by that time Indians either would have "acquired new habits" and so welcome U.S. expansion, "yielded to their fate and passed the Rocky Mountains," or simply "disappeared." In any case, Cass wrote, "these are events too remote to influence any just view of the subject," as if centuries would pass before U.S. citizens showed the slightest interest in the lands of Kansas, Nebraska, or Oklahoma. Basic facts roundly contradicted Cass's assessment. Missouri had become a state nine years before the 1830 Indian Removal Act, and Arkansas was well on its way to statehood. Why would western expansion stop there?[30]

Some historians have tried to get the architects of removal off the hook by arguing that policymakers mistakenly believed that eastern Kansas and eastern Oklahoma were part of what was known at the time as the "Great American Desert" (the arid Plains west of the 100th meridian). According to this line of thought, placing Indians on what were thought to be arid lands unsuitable for white settlement absolves policymakers of making a false promise to Indians when they pledged them permanent homes. Other historians, however, have pointed to a serious problem with this basis for acquittal, as it leaves policymakers open to a different indictment, that they simply "dump[ed] the Indians into . . . desolate wastes." These historians defend policymakers by correctly showing that U.S. officials knew that the lands designated for removed Indians (eastern Kansas and Oklahoma) were not far enough west to be in the truly arid Plains and so had sufficient rainfall to support agriculture. But this defense revives the initial indictment: policymakers promised relocated Indians permanent homes in lands they had every reason to know would soon be coveted by U.S. citizens. Either way, the policy is indefensible.[31]

Less than three generations after the Louisiana Purchase, Americans had arrived in Kansas. What would the United States do about Native people living there? One possibility was to move them yet again, but space, at one time seemingly limitless, was fast closing in. As New York senator William Seward asked of Indians in Kansas, "Where shall they go? . . . back again across the

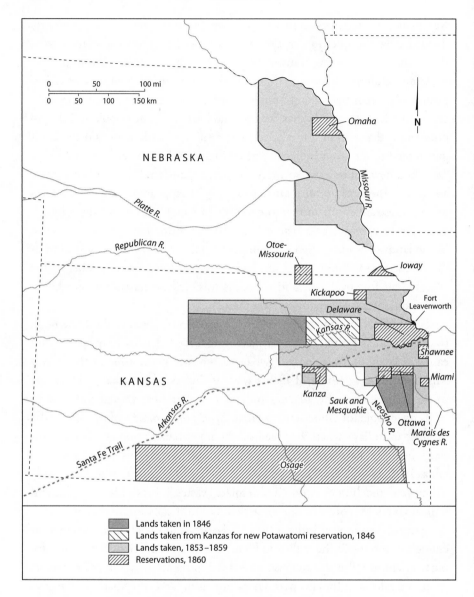

Fig. 46. Dispossession in eastern Nebraska and eastern Kansas, 1846–1860

Mississippi? . . . over the Rocky Mountains?" Most Native nations in eastern Kansas would eventually be squeezed into Oklahoma, but for the time being the government's plan was to keep them where they were while shrinking their lands. In fall 1853, anticipating the passage of the Kansas-Nebraska Act, Commissioner of Indian Affairs George Manypenny began requesting

Native nations to sign treaties ceding the majority of their lands. According to Quaker missionary Henry Harvey, Shawnees were "thrown . . . into great commotion." They were "fearful that the United States will ultimately have all their country, and only have to refer back to past events to justify that fear." In other words, Shawnees knew their history. At first, Manypenny's requests met with steadfast refusal. But in spring 1854 Manypenny summoned leaders of most of the nations of eastern Kansas and eastern Nebraska to Washington. Once there, Delawares, Ioways, Kaskaskias, Kickapoos, Miamis, Omahas, Otoe-Missourias, Peorias, Shawnees, Weas, and Wyandots agreed to treaties ceding most of their lands and calling for what remained to be allotted to individuals and held as private rather than communal property. Over the next few years, the United States secured similar treaties from the Kanzas, Potawatomis, and Sauks and Mesquakies. On the eve of the Civil War, when Kansas became a state, most of the lands Indians held in eastern Kansas prior to 1854 had been taken away by the U.S. government (Fig. 46).[32]

DISEASE IN THE ZONE OF REMOVAL

Throughout the zone of removal in the 1840s and 1850s, Native communities were hit by deadly disease. Although it is impossible to specify the precise weight of the factors that made Indians in eastern Nebraska, eastern Kansas, and eastern Oklahoma susceptible to pathogens, it is clear enough that material deprivation, malnutrition, and alcoholism (itself a disease) all contributed. Beyond this, the psychological stress resulting from being ripped from homelands and suffering losses along trails of tears undoubtedly interacted with material factors not only to weaken bodies but to limit communities' capacities to provide therapeutic care.[33]

Scholarship on disease and Native Americans frequently emphasizes the horrific impact of major epidemics, especially smallpox and measles. These diseases hit some of the nations in the zone of removal, although they never engulfed the entire region. When smallpox broke out among Sauks and Mesquakies in 1851, it killed close to 500 and would have taken more except for an emergency vaccination initiative. Officials also vaccinated Ioways, Otoe-Missourias, and Omahas. No deaths were reported for Ioways, but smallpox "made some ravages" among the Otoe-Missourias and Omahas. One year later, measles broke out in Osage communities, and as this epidemic raged, typhoid fever added to the misery. Reports state that between 800 and 1,000 Osages died that year. In 1855, Osages and Kanzas contracted smallpox, probably through exposure to travelers from New Mexico along the Santa Fe Trail. As soon as a government physician "could procure fresh virus, he vaccinated all [the Osages] he could find," but despite these efforts, 400 Osages died. The Kanzas, apparently unvaccinated, lost a similar number—according to reports, over 400. Smallpox also appeared among the Kickapoos in 1857 and took twenty-four lives. The relocated southeastern nations in Oklahoma did not suffer as much from smallpox. The "dreadful scourge . . . committed its ravages" among the Cherokees in the winter of 1851–1852, but it is doubtful that more than a few hundred perished. Otherwise, smallpox evidently did not afflict Creeks, Choctaws, Chickasaws, or Seminoles.[34]

Although some Indians in the zone of removal escaped smallpox and measles, almost all communities were hit with varying frequency by an assortment of diseases. Some of these were identified specifically, if not necessarily always accurately, as cholera, measles, dysentery, consumption, scrofula, and typhus. Others were identified generally as fever (in most cases, probably malaria) or simply "sickness." These diseases did not usually produce high death tolls at a single stroke, but they had a cumulative effect that in some cases prevented tribal populations from growing and in others contributed to declining populations. For some nations, the evidence does not allow a clear picture of demographic trajectories. But for many, the sources document catastrophic losses that have been almost entirely neglected as a part of U.S. history.

DEMOGRAPHY OF THE REMOVED SOUTHERN NATIONS

For good reason, scholars of the Cherokees have emphasized the suffering and loss of life on the Trail of Tears, but it is also important to realize that the Cherokee population continued to fall in the 1840s and 1850s. Around 16,000 Cherokees survived removal. Assuming an Old Settler population of between 4,000 and 6,000, the total Cherokee population west of the Mississippi in 1840 would have been between 20,000 and 22,000. A federal census taken of all five southeastern nations in 1860 counted only 16,332 Cherokees (including 2,511 enslaved people). This count did not include the few hundred Treaty Party Cherokees who had never reconciled with the Cherokee national government and moved to Arkansas, or the handful of others who had sought fortunes in the California gold fields in the 1850s. Even so, the Cherokee population fell by at least 20 percent. At first glance, a decrease of this magnitude may seem unlikely. Although Cherokees had to deal with violence, alcohol, drought, and disease, neither government reports nor Cherokee sources document catastrophic events that might explain such a loss. Reports, although vague, indicate that the smallpox outbreak that affected Cherokees in 1851–1852 did not take anything close to thousands of lives. Government agents reported "fevers and other diseases" causing "deaths among the children" in 1857. The following year brought disease of a "malarious character," with some fatalities "among the more advanced in years." Again, though, these events did not result in a sudden population collapse. Nonetheless, spread over twenty years, a decline from 20,000 to 16,000 could have occurred through high infant mortality combined with low fertility and life expectancy. All it would have taken would have been an average annual loss of less than 2 percent, losses that may not even have been perceptible. The wealthiest Cherokees were exempt from these conditions. For them, compared to the traumas of removal and its violent aftermath, the 1850s seemed to be a "golden age." But the situation was different for the impoverished majority, who were struck by constant low-level assaults in the form of malnutrition, exposure, alcohol, and pathogens.[35]

The 1860 census also shows a decline in Chickasaw, Creek, and Seminole populations. The Chickasaw population fell from 5,000 in 1842 (not including enslaved people) to 4,260 in 1860 (with an additional 975 slaves), about 15 percent. The Creek decline was sharper: from 20,000 in 1842 to only 15,082 (including 1,532 slaves) in 1860, close to 25 percent. The Seminoles also lost a significant portion of their population. The best estimate for the 1843 population of Seminoles in Oklahoma is 3,500–3,600, a figure that probably includes Black Seminoles. The 1860 census showed 2,630, but this census did not count Black Seminoles. The absence of Black Seminoles from the 1860 count indicates that the overall population decline since 1843 was not as steep as might appear at first glance, but the 1860 figure also reflects the recent arrival of several hundred Seminoles from Florida as a result of yet another war—the Third Seminole War—when the United States tried to eliminate every last Seminole from Florida so that speculators might pursue a bizarre fantasy of draining the Everglades for plantations. All of this makes it difficult to compare the 1843 and 1860 figures, but it is clear that there was a substantial decline in the Oklahoma Seminole population. Only the Choctaws seem to have avoided a postremoval population loss. The 1860 census revealed a Choctaw population of 13,666 plus 2,349 slaves (16,015 total), a slight increase from the immediate postremoval number of 15,500.[36]

DEMOGRAPHY OF THE REMOVED NORTHERN NATIONS

The northern nations suffered even greater population losses after removal. Let us first consider nations that began moving west of the Mississippi
in the 1790s and early 1800s—the Delawares, Shawnees, and Kickapoos. In
1829, a few years after the departure of the Indiana Delawares to Missouri (see
Chapter 6), there were a reported 3,000 Delawares west of the Mississippi.
By 1845, however, the number of Delawares in the West was only 1,059. The
Delaware population then stabilized and was reported at 1,008 in 1860. Even
if, as seems possible, the 3,000 figure for 1829 is too high, the Delawares had
endured a major decline in the 1830s and early 1840s. The Shawnee population also fell. In the early 1820s, the Shawnees numbered about 2,200. Several
small communities remained in Ohio, but the majority had moved to Missouri. Soon after 1825, the government ordered Shawnees out of Missouri to
Kansas. Most complied and went to Kansas, but several hundred decided
they had had enough of the United States and relocated to Texas (still part
of Mexico). In the early 1830s most remaining Shawnees were forced out of
Ohio and joined those already in Kansas. We lack population figures for the
Shawnees in Kansas until 1853, when they reportedly numbered 930. After
adding 100 or so Lewistown Shawnees who had amalgamated with Senecas
on the Neosho, and perhaps 700 who moved from Texas to the Canadian
River in Oklahoma after the Anglo invasion of Texas in the 1830s, the total
Shawnee population was 1,750, a decrease of close to 20 percent. Kickapoo
numbers also declined. In the early 1820s, the total Kickapoo population was
probably around 2,200, with the majority (1,600) already west of the Mississippi in Missouri. A decade later, on the eve of their removal, the eastern
Kickapoo population was an estimated 750, while the population west of the
Mississippi (by now mostly in Oklahoma and Texas) had fallen to 1,200, for
a total of 1,950. Thereafter, the only reports are for the Kickapoo population
in Kansas. These range from a high of 516 in 1845 to a low of 325 in 1860. Assuming a stable population of what became known as the southern Kickapoos
(living at various times in Texas, Mexico, and Oklahoma) of around 1,200,
the Kickapoo population on the eve of the Civil War would have been around
1,500, a decline of close to a third over a forty-year span.[37]

With one exception—the Wyandots on the Neosho Reservation in northeastern Oklahoma, who maintained a stable population of around 550—the
nations removed after 1830 were also demographically weakened. The Ohio
Senecas' numbers declined from around 500 in the early 1830s to 300 in 1840.

Their population stabilized over the next two decades, but it never recovered. Although many Potawatomis escaped removal, several thousand were forced west, with some going to Missouri and others to Iowa before being consolidated in Kansas in 1848, with a reported population of 3,235. This was a decline from an estimated 4,000–5,000 Potawatomis who were moved west during the 1830s and 1840s (see Chapter 9). A decade later, in 1859, the government agent stated that the Potawatomis had "suffered more from sickness and there have been more deaths amongst them during the past year than for any year during my agency, and there can be no doubt but the tribe is fast on the decline." A census in 1860 counted only 2,405 Potawatomis, a drop of 25 percent in twelve years (Fig. 47). Losses for other nations were larger. The Ottawa population fell from a reported 340 in 1840 to 207 in 1860, around 40 percent. The Miami population, a little over 300 after removal in 1846, had been cut in half to 166 by 1859. Of all the nations removed from north of the Mississippi, the Sauks and Mesquakies experienced the most catastrophic decline. At the close of the Black Hawk War, the Sauk and Mesquakie population was around 6,000. By 1860, it had collapsed to 1,280, a full 80 percent. These are shocking numbers. Even the least severe decline (that of

Fig. 47. Taken around 1865, this photograph of a Potawatomi family
outside their home in Kansas testifies to the resilience of Native people in
the aftermath of removal. Kansas State Historical Society, Topeka.

the Potawatomis, with a loss of 25 percent) was equivalent to the worst that occurred through the removal process. The sufferings of the trails of tears are unfathomable. Those in this part of the zone of removal were even worse.[38]

THE SAUK AND MESQUAKIE CATASTROPHE

The problems described earlier in this chapter—alcohol, poor crops, on-going dispossession, and disease—suggest some of the factors behind these demographic collapses. A sharper picture emerges from considering the nation hit the hardest, the Sauks and Mesquakies. Many books have been written on the Black Hawk War, and so there is some knowledge of Sauk and Mesquakie losses at that time. Their history after 1832, however, is almost entirely unknown.

For a time, Sauks and Mesquakies lived on the Iowa, Des Moines, and Skunk rivers in central Iowa. These areas had been part of their hunting grounds for decades, but they had never established villages there. Not long after their arrival, in 1838, Iowa became a territory, which meant that, like Missouri and Arkansas, this part of the zone of removal was no longer available for removed Indians. In 1840 government officials declared that because the Sauks and Mesquakies were "fast progressing towards extermination," the only way to save them was to move them "south of Missouri." Apparently realizing that there was no obvious place "south of Missouri" to put the Sauks and Mesquakies, in 1841 a U.S. commission headed by Iowa territorial governor John Chambers proposed a different destination: north to the headwaters of the Des Moines River in southern Minnesota. When Sauks and Mesquakies objected to that location as a "country of distress" and "the poorest I ever saw," officials backed off. But not for long. A year later, Chambers returned and obtained the reluctant consent of Sauk and Mesquakie leaders to move to a "tract of land . . . upon the Missouri river, or some of its waters." But the same problem arose. In a shrinking zone of removal, there was no space to squeeze them along the Missouri or its tributaries. Until they figured out where to put them, officials ordered the Sauks and Mesquakies to make a temporary move to western Iowa.[39]

Once in this way station, Sauk and Mesquakie women, the nation's farmers, were unable to find decent soil for planting. Because there were few stands of timber, there were no sheltered locations for their winter lodges. Mosquitoes thrived in the area's lakes and marshes, and they carried a parasite that causes malaria. After three years, officials gave the Sauks and Mesquakies the "choice" of two tracts in eastern Kansas for "a permanent and perpetual residence." The tract they selected on the Marais des Cygnes River was apparently better than the one they rejected. Even so, once they arrived on their new reservation in 1845–1846, the Sauks and Mesquakies found themselves on a sandy prairie that proved hard to farm. The only game was to the west in areas controlled by dangerous Plains nations that, unlike the Sauks and Mesquakies, had yet to experience a decline in their power. By this time, the Sauk and Mesquakie population had fallen precipitously. In 1838, a government agent stated that their population was 4,546, down from 6,000 six years before. A decade after that, while still in western Iowa, another agent reported that their population was 3,000. Sauks and Mesquakies realized what was happening. At a council in 1841, Wapello, a Sauk leader, called upon U.S. officials to "have pity on us; we are but few, and are fast melting away." A century earlier, the French and their allies had almost exterminated the Mesquakies in the Fox Wars. The Sauks had taken them in, saving them from total annihilation. Now, destruction from a different source threatened the extinction of these two allied nations.[40]

Had the Sauks and Mesquakies been sent to Kansas right after the Black Hawk War, their losses might not have been quite as high. Multiple removals created a situation of virtual homelessness, making it impossible for people to adjust to new environments and adding to social stress. Even so, the forces of destruction for the Sauks and Mesquakies were similar to those operating against most removed nations. The sources make clear that the Sauks and Mesquakies did not have enough food (and so were certainly suffering from malnutrition), were under constant pressure from traders to consume alcohol (which would have aggravated malnutrition and contributed to violence), lacked adequate clothing and shelter, and for all of these reasons were vulnerable to deadly illness. After their removal to Kansas, Sauk and Mesquakie numbers continued to plummet. Government agents counted 2,153 in 1853, 1,367 in 1857, and 1,280 in 1860. The Sauk and Mesquakie Nation—already reduced by as much as 50 percent before their removal to Kansas—had been halved yet again. The smallpox outbreak of 1851 was the single most lethal event, taking around 500 lives (see above), but it was the more or less constant presence of multiple diseases in an environment of poverty and extreme social stress that was so destructive.[41]

THE DEMOGRAPHY OF NATIONS INDIGENOUS
TO THE ZONE OF REMOVAL

By the 1840s, most nations with homelands in Arkansas, Missouri, and Iowa had been concentrated in a small area that included a tiny corner of northeastern Oklahoma, parts of eastern Kansas, and southeastern Nebraska. With the exception of the Quapaws on the Kansas–Oklahoma border, who maintained a stable population of around 400, all of these nations experienced terrible losses from 1840 to 1860.[42]

Already these nations had been weakened by multiple forces of destruction: intertribal warfare, the whiskey trade, and loss of land and resources. The Omaha population, reduced from 2,000 in 1820 to 1,400 in the early 1830s, stabilized over the next decade, but it then resumed a downward trend, falling from 1,300 in 1844 to 800 in 1855, close to 40 percent. The Otoe-Missourias, with 943 people in 1840, lost a similar proportion of their numbers. In 1860, they had only 500 people. For decades, Osages had maintained a population of between 5,000 and 6,000 despite warfare with the eastern nations and substantial dispossession. After they were forced into Kansas in the late 1830s, however, the Osages were increasingly impoverished and vulnerable not only to smallpox outbreaks in 1852 and 1855, but to multiple diseases (typhus, malaria, dysentery, cholera, whooping cough, scurvy) that constantly preyed on weakened bodies. Osages tried to counter disease by dispersing their villages, thus limiting the potential for contagion. Some Osages blamed the missionaries for intentionally inflicting them with disease and relied on traditional Osage medicine, but others asked the missionaries to baptize them or their sick relatives, thinking that baptism was not a means for saving souls in the next world but a way to restore health in this one. Despite all they could do, however, the Osage population fell to 4,500 by 1850. Seven years later, it was down to 3,500, a loss of between 30 and 40 percent in two decades. The Kanzas and Ioways were hit even harder. The Kanza population fell from 1,606 in 1841 to 803 in 1860 (50 percent). The Ioway population collapsed from a reported 669 people in 1848 to only 305 in 1861, a loss of close to 60 percent in just thirteen years.[43]

THE KANZA CATASTROPHE IN BLEEDING KANSAS

One of the indispensable subjects in U.S. history textbooks is "Bleeding Kansas," where proslavery and antislavery settlers violently clashed from 1856 to 1861. The story of Bleeding Kansas is important, as it both forecast the Civil War and accelerated its coming. In relating this story, however, historians almost never acknowledge that the blood of settlers fell on Indian lands and that these lands were fast filling with the graves of Native people. There were fifty-six documented political killings in Kansas during the time of Bleeding Kansas. In 1855 alone, the Kanza Nation lost 400 of its citizens to smallpox. That year, John Montgomery, the government agent for the Kanzas, reported to his superiors in Washington that "the Kan[z]as are a poor, degraded, superstitious, indigent tribe of Indians; their tendency is downward, and in my opinion, they must soon become extinct, and the sooner they arrive at this period, the better it will be for the rest of mankind." As appalling as we may find Montgomery's wish for Kanza extinction, our ignorance of the Kanza catastrophe testifies to powerful legacies of the myth of the vanishing Indian. Montgomery at least acknowledged Kanza people; standard narratives assume that they had already disappeared or had never existed at all.[44]

Once we realize that Bleeding Kansas takes its name from an actually existing Native nation, how do we explain the catastrophe that befell them? U.S. officials and American citizens who advocated for the removal of eastern Indians gave absolutely no thought to the Kanza Nation. Historians since have seldom recognized that the Kanzas were casualties of the policy of Indian removal. Clearly, though, shoving eastern nations onto the lands of western nations was bound to create hardship. The situation would have been less catastrophic had the United States blocked settlement at the Mississippi River and so reserved a larger space for the removed nations and those indigenous to the west. Even so, removal played a crucial role in creating the conditions for the Kanza catastrophe. As removal's consequences unfolded in the 1840s and 1850s, U.S. officials regarded the Kanza Nation as nothing more than a nuisance, occupying space needed for other purposes (Fig. 48). In 1825, the Kanzas had agreed to a treaty that ceded the majority of their lands except for a tract of land along the Kansas River. A generation later (1846), federal officials asked the Kanzas to vacate this reservation. The purpose was to make room for the consolidation of the much larger Potawatomi Nation—driven from Missouri and Iowa—on a single reservation in Kansas. But just as the government had no place to put the Sauks and Mesquakies when they ordered them out of Iowa in 1842, officials had no plans for a substitute reservation for the Kanzas. Without a home, the Kanzas were unable to plant crops and were reduced to begging for relief at Fort Leavenworth and calling on the generosity of nearby tribes. Two years later, government officials established

Fig. 48. In 1857 leaders of the Kanza (Kaw) Nation were summoned to Washington by
U.S. Commissioner of Indian Affairs George Manypenny to cede yet more of their land.
Although this drawing in a London newspaper shows the central (unidentified) figure in
the "noble savage" tradition of a natural orator, it gives him and the other figures dignity
at a time when their people were suffering unfathomable losses. *Illustrated London News,*
April 25, 1857. Reproduced by University of Oregon Digital Scholarship Services.

an agency for the Kanzas, but the place they chose, along the upper Neosho
River, was smack in the middle of the Santa Fe Trail. Over the next several
years, the Kanza reservation was an open house to U.S. troops on their way to
fight in the Mexican War, Forty-Niners on their way to California, proslavery
border ruffians from Missouri, Fifty-Niners rushing to Colorado for Pike's
Peak gold, and an assortment of scoundrels and thieves. Whiskey, cholera,
and smallpox were the gifts they brought.[45]

COULD DESTRUCTION HAVE BEEN PREVENTED?

Were there alternatives that might have prevented the massive loss of life
that occurred in the zone of removal before the Civil War? Because most

agents in charge of western reservations were political appointees, turnover was high and corruption was rampant. Perhaps federal investment in creating a professional corps of agents could have secured the vision Commissioner of Indian Affairs George Manypenny articulated in 1854—that Kansas would become a place for the "complete and thorough civilization of the red man."[46] But apart from the fact that a more robust civilization program would have entailed damaging assaults on the religions and cultures of Native communities, it is difficult to see how even the most competent and devoted government agents could have overcome the problems inherent to removal. Similarly, instead of improvising emergency vaccination efforts when smallpox appeared, the federal government could have developed a more robust program to ensure that all nations were vaccinated. At most, however, this would have minimized only one disease (smallpox); the more prevalent bacterial and parasitic diseases would have continued to flourish under frequently wretched conditions. This and other conceivable patches, such as trying harder to stop the alcohol trade, ramping up efforts to deter squatters, or establishing a program for distribution of food to relieve hunger in times of poor crops, would not have addressed the root problems—dispossession, deracination, social stress, and chronic poverty—that were afflicting Indian communities.

Perhaps a broader structural protection, such as the creation of an Indian state within the zone of removal equal to the other states of the Union, would have promoted the well-being of Native people. In the 1830s the proremoval Baptist missionary Isaac McCoy promoted such a plan, including a provision to prohibit white settlement, and Congress entertained it. A bill to establish an Indian state made its way to the floor of the House of Representatives in 1834, but objections that the proposal was unconstitutional and would establish a "military despotism" in the West were strong enough that the bill died before a vote could be taken. Efforts to revive the idea over the next several years met a similar fate. Had this proposal succeeded, it is possible that conditions for Indians would not have been as dreadful, but the objections Indians made at the time—that an Indian state would destroy tribal sovereignty and, as the Choctaw Peter Pitchlynn said, "introduce discord, dissensions, and strife among them"—identify serious weaknesses.[47]

In the end, though, the overwhelming rejection of proposals for an Indian state revealed the strength of a national consensus for elimination. This or any other effective alternative would have required a United States founded on radically different principles: one that would have protected the land bases of Indian nations and respected their sovereignty instead of assuming settler entitlement to all Indian lands; one, in other words, that would not have shoved Indians west and then allowed settlers to follow them. Eighty years after the Declaration of Independence and half a continent west, the destruction that occurred in the zone of removal was a logical consequence of America's founding purpose.

CHAPTER 11

The Name of Removal

In the early 1850s, Hiram G. Thorpe, a blacksmith on the Sauk and Mesquakie Reservation in Kansas, found extra work making cheap coffins for Sauks and Mesquakies who were dying from smallpox and other diseases. Around that time, he married a Sauk woman named No-ten-o-quah (Wind Woman). The three children Wind Woman bore and raised helped ensure that, despite the real danger of annihilation, the Sauk and Mesquakie Nation would endure. One of Hiram and Wind Woman's grandsons was Jim Thorpe, born in 1887 in Oklahoma, a generation after the final removal of the Sauks and Mesquakies after the Civil War. Representing the United States in the 1912 Stockholm Olympics, Thorpe won gold medals in the decathlon and the pentathlon. When he returned to the United States, thousands cheered as he and the other athletes paraded down Fifth Avenue to New York's City Hall, honoring him as the "greatest athlete in the world" (Fig. 49).[1]

What should we call what Hiram Thorpe witnessed as he nailed coffins on the Kansas frontier? What is the name for what Wind Woman helped prevent when she and Hiram brought children into a world where a whole nation was dying? How, in the final analysis, should we assess the policy of Indian removal?

Fig. 49. On August 24, 1912, after a tickertape parade, twenty-five-year-old Olympic champion Jim Thorpe stood before the Stars and Stripes. From the platform above, he was honored by dignitaries, including New York City mayor William Gaynor. As Americans celebrated "the greatest athlete in the world," they knew nothing about what Thorpe's Sauk ancestors had survived in the era of removal. New York World-Telegram and the Sun Newspaper Photograph Collection, Library of Congress Prints and Photographs Division.

THE COSTS OF REMOVAL

To begin, recall that from 1830 into the 1850s the United States forcibly evicted an estimated 88,000 Indians from their homelands east of the Mississippi River. Another 35,000 came under substantial pressure to move but remained in their homelands or relocated outside the United States. Recall, too, that removal was more thorough in the South than in the North. Somewhere around 64,000 of the estimated 75,000 Indians in the South who were subject to removal were forced to move west of the Mississippi. By contrast, only 24,000 of the 48,000 Indians subject to removal in the North were sent west.[2] To a significant extent, as discussed earlier, the difference between slave-based and free-labor settler colonialism explains why a higher percentage of southern Indians were removed. Slaveholders had greater need to eliminate all Indians from their region in order to guarantee the security of their regime, while northern farmers, speculators, and industrialists could tolerate the existence of Indian communities under some conditions. A secondary factor was the proximity to Canada as an escape hatch for many Native communities north of the Ohio River. Some southern Indians sought to evade eviction by moving beyond the zone of removal (to Texas and Mexico), but this was a long jump and not widely available. By contrast, it was relatively easy for Potawatomis and Ottawas to relocate to Upper Canada and so avoid removal to Kansas.

How many people died during the removal process? Of the 88,000 Indians sent west (this figure includes Ojibwes and Haudenosaunees who soon returned to their homelands), an estimated 12,000–17,000 perished (14–19 percent). This number includes deaths resulting from wars to force Indians to comply with removal as well as those occurring during roundups, detention prior to removal, the journeys themselves, and the first few years after removal. Significantly, the death rate from removal was substantially higher than for the best-known migration of the nineteenth century—the overland trails to Oregon and California. Of the 253,000 migrants who traveled on the Oregon and California trails between 1840 and 1860, an estimated 10,000 died along the way (4 percent), the vast majority from disease.[3] The removal of the southern Indian nations was more deadly than the removal of those from the North. Of the 64,000 Indians removed from the South, an estimated 11,000–14,000 (17–22 percent) died during the removal process or shortly after. By contrast, of the approximately 24,000 northeastern Indians who were moved west, firm documentation exists for only 1,200 deaths

(6 percent) during the removal process or shortly after. Because the record is incomplete, however, a reasonable estimate would be more on the order of 3,000 (12.5 percent).[4]

The reasons for the difference in the mortality rate for southern and northern removals are difficult to pin down. To some extent, chance was a significant factor affecting removals. Some groups moving west suffered from bad weather or entered areas containing contagious disease, while others escaped these perils. Decisions of government officials and Native community leaders also had consequences. When would journeys begin? What preparations would be made? What routes would be taken? Would the group be vaccinated? What resources would be made available during the journeys and in the first years after removal? In what western lands would people try to make new homes? In ways not fully foreseeable when they were made, these decisions could make a difference between life and death. Nonetheless, it is doubtful that southern Indians had worse luck or that decisionmakers made poorer choices.

Two factors are likely salient. One concerns various forms of malaria, the disease most often identified in contemporary reports as fever or ague. The deadliest form of malaria, caused by the parasite *falciparum*, requires relatively high temperatures to mature within the bodies of anopheles mosquitoes and so was restricted to areas south of the Ohio River and central Missouri. This form of malaria, with a mortality rate of 20–40 percent, would have affected the southern nations as they were being moved and after their arrival. In contrast, the northern nations would have been exposed to a less virulent form of malaria caused by the *vivax* parasite, with a mortality rate of around 5 percent.[5] The other factor is that the process of removal for the more populous southeastern nations often involved concentrating large groups of people in temporary encampments either before they left for the West or after they arrived. As we saw in Chapter 8, more Cherokees died in internment camps during summer 1838 than on the subsequent trail west. Similarly, Creeks and Choctaws suffered their greatest losses in the first few years after arriving in Oklahoma. In all of these instances, large numbers of destitute people were forced to live in confined areas where they lacked clean water, adequate food, and shelter. Under these conditions, they were acutely vulnerable to bacterial diseases—dysentery, cholera, and typhoid fever. The smallpox virus, once introduced into a community, would also have spread more rapidly among people packed into close quarters. By contrast, although many of the removals of the northern nations resulted in shocking death tolls, the number of people in any given removal was generally smaller.

Although many northern nations were spared the loss of life of most southern nations during removal, as we saw in Chapter 10, almost all of the northern nations suffered serious population declines—in some cases, outright collapses—after their arrival west of the Mississippi. To put this in perspective, the combined population of the Wyandots, Ottawas, Ohio Senecas, Potawatomis, Miamis, Sauks and Mesquakies, and Ho-Chunks just after their removals was between 16,600 and 17,600. By 1860, the western population of these nations was between 7,900 and 8,400, a decline of over one-half. Nations indigenous to the zone of removal were also hit hard. Although the Quapaw population apparently did not fall, reports show a drop in the population of the others—Omahas, Oto-Missourias, Osages, Ioways, and Kanzas. At their highest in the 1840s, the combined population of these nations was around 9,000. By 1860, this figure had fallen to 6,000, marking a loss of one-third. With the exception of the Choctaws, the southern nations also experienced further population losses after removal. The postremoval population of the Cherokees, Choctaws, Chickasaws, Creeks, and Seminoles was between 62,000 and 66,500. By 1860, this number had fallen to 54,000, a loss of 13–19 percent.[6]

NAMING REMOVAL

When the Indian Removal Act was passed in 1830, U.S. officials did not know precisely how many Indians would die as a result of removal. It was clear at the time, however, that removal would be dangerous. U.S. officials rarely acknowledged this. Toward the end of his sixty-page brief for removal published in January 1830, Secretary of War Lewis Cass did concede that "some mental and corporeal sufferings await the emigrants," but even this euphemistically phrased contingency could be mitigated by "an appropriation liberally made, and prudently applied." Six months later, as we saw in Chapter 6, Cherokees warned that "if we are compelled to leave our country, we see nothing but ruin before us." Had Cass listened to the Cherokees he might have changed his mind. But Cass had made his opinion of the Cherokees clear enough when he expressed doubt that anywhere "upon the face of the globe" could be found "a more wretched race than the Cherokees." The opinions of a people the secretary of war so clearly despised deserved little heed.[7]

Once removal became official federal policy and expulsions began, the
scale of Cass's "mental and corporeal sufferings" soon became clear as parties of
Choctaws and Senecas making their way west between 1830 and 1832 endured
dreadful conditions, suffered greatly, and lost many lives. The self-professed
humanitarianism of removal's advocates might have suggested a public recognition of these losses and a commitment to more liberal or prudently applied
resources, perhaps even a reevaluation of removal's supposed "benevolence."
Local agents in charge of particular removals sometimes worried that reports
of death and suffering would diminish public support for removal, but at a
national level, neither Cass nor Jackson nor any of removal's other leading
proponents had a word to say about death and suffering resulting from these
early removals. As the death toll mounted in the mid-1830s, federal officials
remained silent about their policy's destructive consequences, while repeating well-rehearsed claims about their devotion to the welfare of American
Indians. Even as they pursued the most publicized of all removals, that of the
Cherokees in 1838–1839, those responsible took no account of the destructiveness of previous removals and the likelihood of destruction's recurrence.
Disavowal persisted in the 1840s. Even when advocates of removal backed off
from schemes to move particular communities west, they made their calculations in terms of costs to themselves—the costs of continuing to spend time
and moral capital to uproot the Haudenosaunees, for example, compared to
the economic benefits of making Haudenosaunees into tax-paying citizens.
The well-being of Haudenosaunees was of no real concern.

Although in retrospect U.S. officials' silence about removal's devastating
mortality clearly undermines claims they made about their humanitarianism, there is always the question of the sincerity of historical actors and the
need to evaluate them, as the cliché goes, by the standards of their times.[8]
Because the lies associated with removal are so glaring—not only the refusal
to admit the policy's destructiveness but the fictions that Indians were vanishing, that removals would be entirely voluntary, and that Indians would
be guaranteed permanent homes in the West—professions of benevolence
can seem nothing more than a figleaf to cover naked greed. This perspective,
however, underestimates the capacity of ideologues to convince themselves
of the truth of what they want to believe and to hold inconvenient facts
and troubling doubts at bay. Officials' constant repetition of their arguments
about the benevolence of removal seems to have been intended as much to
reassure themselves as to convince skeptics. As for the standards of the times,
any argument that removal's proponents were merely reflecting consensual

values collapses under the weight of their own self-professed Christian humanitarianism as well as contemporary criticisms of the policy, to some degree by non-Indians but much more by Indigenous critics like the Creek leaders who in 1831 told Andrew Jackson that removal would be "the worst evil that can befall them."[9]

Historians have begun to characterize Indian removal as ethnic cleansing.[10] This label, essentially a synonym for the policy's stated goal, should be noncontroversial. But what kind of ethnic cleansing? In theory, involuntary population transfers can occur with very little loss of life, although they generally result in a substantial number of deaths from various causes, including disease, starvation, and direct killing, the latter to compel relocation and/or as an integral part of the process of relocation. The spectrum of ethnic cleansing, then, presents a wide range of actions and outcomes. One historian of ethnic cleansing in twentieth-century Europe observes that "forced deportation often becomes genocidal, as people are violently ripped from their native towns and villages and killed when they try to stay." Furthermore, even if the intent of such forced removals is not the killing of the targeted population, "it is often genocidal in its effects."[11]

Did Indian removal have genocidal consequences? On this question, it is instructive to compare the per capita death toll from Indian removal to the per capita death toll for a well-known recent case of ethnic cleansing that many scholars and legal authorities consider to fall under the category of "partial genocide" if not genocide altogether. In Bosnia and Herzogovina from 1992 to 1995, of a total population of 1.9 million, at least 68,000 Bosniaks (Bosnian Muslims) died, including 7,000 slaughtered by Bosnian Serb forces at Srebrenica. The death rate (3.6 percent) was substantially lower than that of Native Americans during removal, even without including the postremoval demographic declines.[12] By the standards of what happened in Bosnia, Indian removal clearly had genocidal consequences.

But are removal's consequences sufficient grounds to characterize the policy as genocidal? Many scholars would argue that it is. Others, however, would respond that there must be both genocidal consequences and genocidal intent, and that since the architects of removal did not intend their policy to kill Indians, the policy cannot be categorized as genocidal. But if writers who argue that consequences alone are sufficient to establish genocide give insufficient attention to the issue of intentionality, those who object to characterizing removal as genocidal on the grounds of absence of intent overlook crucial dimensions of the policy.[13]

One overlooked dimension is the duration of Indian removal. In 1830, when removal gained federal sanction, it was perhaps possible for policymakers to reasonably imagine, as Lewis Cass claimed, that removal would proceed without substantial loss of life. If asked to state their intention in 1830, officials could have replied, "We intend to move Indians west with minimal loss of life." To say this, policymakers would have had to ignore a great deal, including commonsense, the warnings of Indian people, and rapid settlement west of the Mississippi, all of which raised grave doubts that the policy could proceed without substantial loss of life. But even if we give policymakers the benefit of the doubt and take their statements of intention at face value, removal was not a one-off event. The major removals took a decade to complete, and removals continued to take place in the 1840s. This means that an assessment of policymakers' intentions must take into account their response to the unfolding disaster of removal once the policy was actually implemented. As the death toll mounted, American leaders had a choice. They could halt removal to save lives or they could continue the policy knowing that loss of life would occur. (The fact that they never admitted they had a choice does not make it any less real.) As early as the mid-1830s, if asked about their intention, officials could no longer honestly say, "We intend to relocate Indians with minimal loss of life." They would have had to respond, "We intend to continue relocating Indians knowing that substantial numbers will die." This is not precisely the same as saying, "We intend to relocate Indians *so that* substantial numbers will die," but acquitting U.S. officials of genocide for continuing to pursue a policy with genocidal consequences on the grounds that they did not formulate the policy for the explicit purpose of killing people gets them off on a technicality. In the end, the burden of proof is on American leaders. They could have escaped any allegation of an intent to destroy by stopping a policy that was destroying Indian nations, but they did not.

The second overlooked dimension of Indian removal is the policy's fundamental reliance on the threat of genocidal violence. Consistent with earlier phases of the United States' dispossession of Indians, officials' preference was for Indians to comply voluntarily with U.S. wishes—and even to express gratitude for America's generosity! When, as always happened, Indians refused to conform to this paternalistic script, officials' next option was to deploy a well-practiced array of techniques to convince them to comply: fomenting divisions, negotiating treaties with minorities and representing them as majorities, misrepresenting the provisions of proposed treaties, making promises that could not be kept, offering bribes, distributing intoxicants, predicting dire consequences from refusal while disclaiming direct responsibility for these consequences, and threatening destruction (and reinforcing these threats by displaying troops). If Indians refused to sign removal treaties or to comply with treaties they regarded as illegitimate, officials acted on their threats and turned to the next option: potentially genocidal war.

Despite the fact that the documentary record includes only a portion of what U.S. officials communicated to Indians at treaty councils and in other relevant situations, available evidence makes clear that officials routinely issued genocidal threats. To recapitulate information presented in earlier chapters, they did so at Dancing Rabbit Creek in 1830 (if the Choctaws refused a removal treaty, Jackson "would march an army into their country," and if the Choctaws fought, it would be the "ruin of their tribe"); at Fort Armstrong two years later (if Black Hawk's people did not vacate Illinois, they would be "crushed as a piece of dirt"); at Kenekuk's Kickapoo village weeks after the Bad Axe massacre (if they refused to go west, they would be "treated as enemies"); at Fort King in Seminole country in 1833 (they would be "compelled" to leave); and in 1838 in Cherokee country (compliance was the only way to prevent "destruction"). The presence of troops in other situations (e.g., to secure removals of Ho-Chunks in 1833 and Potawatomis in 1838) communicated similar existentially threatening messages.

In most cases, threats of unrestrained, overwhelming violence were sufficient to achieve the desired result. But not always. A minority of Sauks and Mesquakies (along with allies from other nations) and a majority of Seminoles continued to resist. When this happened, U.S. officials authorized the use of exterminatory violence—meaning overwhelming attacks on all members of Native communities, including noncombatants—to force compliance. This does not mean that U.S. military forces always achieved genocidal violence. Seminoles in Florida skillfully used their knowledge of the terrain to thwart U.S. forces trying to surprise or hunt them down in large numbers, and so full-scale massacre did not occur. But in some cases, as when U.S. forces intercepted fleeing Sauks and Mesquakies at the mouth of the Bad Axe River, they succeeded in committing a massacre. What happened at Bad Axe was not incidental to removal. It revealed an intention, inherent within the policy's structure, to use genocidal violence to enforce compliance when necessary. That events like the Bad Axe massacre were not more common says more about Native decisionmaking and lack of U.S. capacity than it does about U.S. intentions.

Overall, then, although the U.S. policy of removal was not intended to kill as many Indians as possible, answering the question of genocide for this particular phase of United States–Indian relations with an absolute "no" too easily dismisses the matter. First, the policy resulted in massive loss of life, which, although not its primary purpose, was a known and tolerated result of a policy sustained over two decades. Second, the policy included the option for genocidal killing and its success rested on the ability to make credible threats to engage in such killing. In its outcome and in the means used to gain compliance, the policy had genocidal dimensions.

NONREMOVED NATIONS

The costs of removal are clear enough on their own terms. They are sharpened by a comparison with the conditions of Indians who avoided removal and remained east of the Mississippi and in Louisiana on the eve of the Civil War. Although they suffered losses and experienced oppressive economic and political conditions, nonremoved nations were generally better able to fend off or avoid forces of destruction than the eastern nations forced west and those indigenous to the zone of removal. The only major exception was the Menominees, who lost most of their land from the 1830s into the 1850s and suffered from poverty, malnutrition, and incessant disease. By 1855, the Menominee population was only 1,900, down from at least 3,000 and perhaps as many as 4,000 in the 1820s.[14] Otherwise, however, Native nations east of the Mississippi did not experience population losses. Some in fact grew.

The largest populations of Indians who avoided removal and remained east of the Mississippi were found in the upper Great Lakes region, where in the mid-1850s between 18,000 and 20,000 Ojibwes and Ottawas pursued a wide range of economic activities, including fishing, hunting, farming, and harvesting wild rice and maple sugar. In this region—once described by U.S. officials frustrated by their inability to control Indians as an "interminable swamp"—it was not until after the Civil War that intensive settlement occurred. These Native communities maintained stable populations.[15]

Another sizable Indian population was in New York, where the Haudenosaunees had defeated the very real threat of removal. As we know, the Haudenosaunees suffered a significant population loss during the era of the American Revolution. In 1830, there were about 4,300 Haudenosaunees in New York (with an additional 600 in Ohio and 2,500 in Canada), down from a pre-1776 population of 9,000. Had all Haudenosaunees been forced from New York to Wisconsin or Kansas in the 1840s, it is very likely that they would have experienced another major loss. Yet because they were able to avoid removal, even at the cost of losing an additional portion of their already much-reduced land base (see Chapter 9), their population did not fall by much. According to a New York State census taken in 1855, Haudenosaunee numbers were just under 4,000. Like Indians in the upper Great Lakes, Haudenosaunees pursued diverse economic activities, though they did so on the margins of a largely non-Indian world. Their main source of subsistence was the crops they planted and harvested; a minority raised a surplus for the market. Access to already limited game resources was increasingly restricted, but it was still possible to hunt for food and pelts for exchange. Casual labor, such as chopping wood, brought in some income, as did the production and sale of beadwork and baskets. Proximity to a large postfrontier population provided additional economic opportunities. Before audiences of non-Indians curious about a supposedly vanishing race, Oneidas, for example, participated in an "INDIAN WAR DANCE" at Saratoga Springs and traveled to New York City as the "Indian Minstrel Company."[16]

The next-largest Native population in the eastern United States, Cherokees who avoided the Trail of Tears, lived under very different conditions. Instead of being surrounded by non-Indians, the mountains of southwestern North Carolina provided relative isolation. In the early 1840s, approximately 1,100 Cherokees lived in North Carolina. Some of these people had lived in North Carolina prior to removal; others had taken refuge there to avoid the army's dragnet in 1838. Over the next several years, U.S. and North Carolina officials sponsored various initiatives to convince the eastern Cherokees to relocate to Oklahoma, but according to ethnologist James Mooney, Yonaguska, a prophet and peace chief, "firmly resisted every persuasion, declaring that the Indians were safer from aggression among their rocks and mountains than they could ever be in a land which the white man could find profitable."[17] In theory the United States could have turned to miliary force, but it would not be easy for troops to go into the mountains and corner every last Cherokee. Besides, by the early 1840s, the army was exhausted by its long campaign to tear Seminoles from the swamps and hammocks of southern Florida.

Eastern Cherokees were not wealthy, but they had sufficient resources to do more than simply survive. Along rivers and creeks, fertile soil allowed for productive fields that sometimes yielded modest surpluses for sale to non-Indians. Cherokees carded and spun cotton and wool to produce their clothing, they raised livestock, they planted peach and apple orchards, and they hunted for deer, bears, wolves, panthers, and other animals, birds, and fish. Few Cherokees in North Carolina owned enslaved African Americans or were commercial farmers and so there was far less social stratification than among Cherokees in Oklahoma. Although they lived apart from non-Indians, several North Carolina Cherokees exchanged their specialized skills as shoemakers, blacksmiths, gunsmiths, coopers, chair makers, wheelwrights, and carpenters to outsiders. One man named Squirrel, for example, "manufactured a number of very superior rifles and pistols" and built several grist mills. Over time, the Cherokee population in North Carolina grew, in part by drawing in the 300 or so Cherokees who remained in Georgia, Tennessee, and Alabama after removal, and in part through natural increase. Some Cherokees traveled to visit their western relatives and a few stayed, but there was little population drain. By 1855 the population of the Cherokees in the East had risen from 1,400 shortly after removal to around 2,200. In contrast to almost all removed nations, including their own relatives in Oklahoma, the eastern Cherokee population actually grew.[18]

There was also a sizable community of Indians in eastern North Carolina, where Lumbees lived among the larger non-Indian population in Robeson County. Descendants of several different Indian nations that had migrated into the area and coalesced in the eighteenth century, Lumbees had since intermarried with non-Natives, black and white. North Carolina had generally classified the Lumbees as "free people of color," and their land base consisted of private holdings. While this made the Lumbees invisible to federal officials planning removal, it did not protect them from growing racial discrimination and abuse in antebellum North Carolina. Decades later, Lumbees recalled "'tied mule' incidents" when a "white farmer tied his mule on an Indian's land, freed several cows in the Indian's pasture, and put a hog or two in this pen. Then, the white farmer would arrive with the authorities and claim that the Indian had stolen his animals." Knowing that he would be unable to obtain justice in the courts, the Lumbee would "give up a portion of his land as a settlement." By 1860, some families retained some of their property, but most were "completely landless." The Lumbee population in 1860 was around 1,400, but there is insufficient information to tell whether their numbers had been growing or not.[19]

Dozens of Native communities could be found elsewhere in the eastern United States. Many of these communities, similar to the Cherokees in North Carolina, belonged to larger nations that had been forced west. In addition to the few hundred Miamis and Potawatomis still in Indiana and southern

Michigan on the eve of the Civil War (see Chapter 9), as many as 1,000 Choctaws resided in Mississippi. At the time of removal, these Choctaws had staked
their future to provisions allowing for private "reserves" in the 1830 Treaty of
Dancing Rabbit Creek. But settlers and speculators eventually cheated Mississippi Choctaws out of most of these reserves, leaving them "forced to eke
out an existence as squatters or as itinerant agricultural workers." Nonetheless, over 1,000 Choctaws remained in Mississippi in the 1850s. In Louisiana,
where they had established communities for decades, another 1,000 or more
Choctaws were given the option of joining their relatives in Oklahoma. But,
according to Dominique Rouquette, who had grown up near Choctaw communities in the vicinity of Lake Pontchartrain, Choctaws "refuse to abandon
the different parishes of Louisiana, where they are grouped in small family
tribes." On small tracts of land, they raised corn, pumpkins, potatoes, and
chickens, hunted to supply nearby plantations, and traveled to New Orleans
to find temporary wage work and sell medicinal plants, cane baskets, and
ground turtles. The Choctaws who frequented New Orleans "illustrate that
city streets were as useful as backcountry forests or remote swamplands in the
day-to-day struggle for survival."[20]

Many Native communities in the East were never subject to U.S. removal
policy. In 1825, when Secretary of War John C. Calhoun outlined a plan to
move the eastern nations, he noted that his scheme was "not intended to
comprehend the small remnants of tribes in Maine, Massachusetts, Connecticut, Rhode Island, Virginia, and South Carolina." Local officials occasionally
raised the possibility of applying removal to these communities. In 1843, for
example, a committee of Rhode Island legislators informed Narragansetts that
"the land in Wisconsin was excellent," but nothing came of this. Calhoun did
imagine moving the *petites nations* of Louisiana, and in 1851 Commissioner of
Indian Affairs Luke Lea suggested that it would be desirable if Louisiana were
"relieved from the annoyance of an Indian population." Again, though, there
was little impetus to extract Indian communities from Louisiana.[21]

The result was that Biloxis, Tunicas, and Houmas persisted in Louisiana;
Catawbas in the Carolinas; Pamunkeys, Chickahominys, and Nottoways in
Virginia; Montauks and Shinnecocks on New York's Long Island; Mohegans
and Pequots in Connecticut; Mashpees, Narragansetts, and Chappaquiddicks
in Massachusetts; and Passamaquoddies and Penobscots in Maine. Many of
these communities numbered under 100. Only the Houmas, with a population of around 900 in the early twentieth century, had more than a few hundred.[22] Although economic strategies varied, the most common pattern was

to engage in subsistence activities (farming, hunting, procuring wild plants) to the extent possible while exploiting available niches within the capitalist world. For Houmas, this meant fishing and hunting in a landscape of bayous and lakes while taking advantage of opportunities for peddling and casual labor in New Orleans. In southern New England, as their already slender land base continued to shrink, Indians increasingly left reservations to support themselves. They worked by day for white farmers, traveled from town to town with brooms and baskets to trade for food or a few coins, and joined the crews of whaling ships.[23]

Many communities suffered from racial discrimination, sometimes because of white supremacy toward Indians, sometimes because Indians' intermarriage with people of African ancestry allowed white supremacists to categorize them under the even more subordinate category of black. Louisiana Indians were commonly denigrated by the slur "redbone," a term implying mongrel degeneracy.[24] Native communities also suffered from assaults on their already limited economic resources and political status. The Mashpees, for example, a Wampanoag community on Cape Cod, were subject to guardians appointed by the Commonwealth of Massachusetts with power to lease lands on the Mashpees' 10,000-acre reserve, place children into indentured servitude, and appoint Christian ministers. In 1833, led by William Apess, a Pequot preacher and writer adopted into the community, Mashpees announced that they would prevent outsiders from cutting wood on their reserve and henceforth "will rule our own tribe." In what became known as the Mashpee Revolt, Apess and others enlisted William Lloyd Garrison to publish sympathetic articles in his abolitionist newspaper *The Liberator*. They traveled to Boston to address the state's legislative assembly and inform general audiences of their grievances, pointing out the hypocrisy of Massachusetts's support for the Cherokees against Georgia while at the same time oppressing Indians within its own borders. In addition to making plain to the citizens and officials of Massachusetts that Indians were very much present, the Mashpee Revolt resulted in the end of guardianship and the empowerment of the community to choose its own officials.[25]

Population trends for many Indian communities along the Atlantic seaboard and in Louisiana are difficult to discern. Since these communities generally lived under precarious conditions, it would hardly be surprising if some of them struggled to maintain their numbers. Figures for the Catawbas suggest that their population was just over 100 from the 1820s to 1850. The absence of commentary on demographic decline in the scholarship on other small communities is probably indicative of stability. Because Indians in Connecticut and Massachusetts were under state supervision, however, there is enough information to detect trends over time for them. Although the Native population within those two states had declined from 1,447 in 1825 to 1,020 in 1835, it increased to a reported 1,212 in 1850 and 1,829 in 1865. Despite the pseudoprecision of these figures, they make clear that Indians were defying predictions of their disappearance.[26]

CONCLUSION: SURVIVAL IN NEW ENGLAND

A growing Indian population in southern New England was particularly ironic in view of the attitudes of white New Englanders. If anything, New Englanders were more obsessed than other Americans with the idea that Indians had disappeared. Authors of nineteenth-century New England local histories consistently wrote of the "last Indian" to inhabit particular locales. There was Papahana, "the last" of a "considerable settlement of Indians" in Bradford, Massachusetts. Or there was the "last male of unmixed blood," buried on December 21, 1820, near Farmington, Connecticut, while the "only surviving female stood trembling by the grave." Such obsessions were not unique to New England and to some extent participated in a broader national fixation on the idea of the vanishing Indian, most famously manifest in James Fenimore Cooper's *Last of the Mohicans*. But despite their criticism of Andrew Jackson's policy of Indian removal, it was New Englanders, the self-appointed guardians of America's history and culture, who took the lead in "writing Indians out of existence" even as in their very midst Native people refused to go away. In so doing, New Englanders rhetorically completed—while also obscuring—countless acts of destruction that Native people had for centuries survived.[27]

Conclusion

HISTORIANS AND PROPHETS

Throughout the century of history covered in this book, Native Americans had more compelling reasons than anyone to analyze the forces that threatened to destroy them. Alexis de Tocqueville was briefly moved as he watched Choctaws suffer while being forced across the Mississippi River in December 1831, and he penned a trenchant critique of the United States and its citizens. But like other non-Indians, Tocqueville did not have to experience the consequences of removal and so his interest was not a matter of life and death, as it was for Native people. Although the documentary record captures only a fraction of Native analyses of settler colonialism's forces of destruction, it occasionally provides glimpses. As we saw in Chapter 2, for example, in the early 1770s when Native confederationists expressed the view that "it must be soon their turn also to be exterminated," they turned to history and cited the fact that "as the white people have advanced from the coast the original natives have been destroyed, and of the numerous nations which formerly inhabited the country possessed by the English not one is now existing."

A more detailed analysis of the history of destruction was provided by the Ottawa war chief Egushawa in 1791. At a council concerned with how best to confront the U.S. invasion of Ohio country (see Chapter 3), Egushawa began his historical overview at the moment of the creation of humans. When "God first made man," Egushawa stated, "he did it from white clay,

375

and placing him on the other side of the great salt waters, there he ought to have remained; for God gave him peculiar laws and customs, and put a book in his hands." Drawing on well-developed Indigenous theories of multiple creations, Egushawa further observed that God "then made us out of red clay, and placed us on this side [of] the great salt water, and put into our hands the bow and arrow." Egushawa expressed uncertainty about the reasons why the "white people" had "cross[ed] the great salt water." Perhaps God "drove them out of their own land, on account of their evil works," he suggested, or perhaps it was "to punish us for ours." Whatever the case, Egushawa continued, one thing was certain: whites had "introduced among us every evil and vice, and not a single virtue!"

In support of this proposition, Egushawa cited the actions of four groups of Europeans. In an apparent reference to Spanish colonists, he noted that one party of "white people . . . came to the south side of this great island; and nothing would satisfy these, but silver and gold." To acquire these metals, "they massacred whole nations; and made DOGS of those whose lives they spared!" Another party, which landed "on the sea coast of Carolina[,] . . . abused the women, and forced from them, the provisions which had been laid up from them and their children, by their absent husbands and fathers." This was perhaps a reference to the so-called "Lost Colony of Roanoke," as by Egushawa's account, when the men returned, they "destroyed . . . their white enemy . . . at one blow." A third party "landed in Virginia . . . and soon became so numerous as to justify every evil, because they had the means to commit it with impunity!" The evidence could be found in "the total extinction of the numerous nations and tribes, who inhabited the country watered by the Chesapeak[e] and its rivers!" Finally, a fourth party "arrived, among our eastern relations, who are in like manner swept off the face of the earth; and whose very names are now lost to us!" Later, as settlement advanced west, some white people, such as the Dutch, Swedes, and Quakers, were "kind and friendly," and some Indian nations, like the Delawares, lived "happily together" with them. Eventually, however, "other people of different sentiments . . . became most numerous [and] the troubles of our relations, the Lenoppi [Delawares], began!—*Frauds, murders, and massacres.*"

As if this historical account was insufficiently persuasive, Egushawa then asked his audience to "look around you! View the country which your deceased massacred relations occupied in peace, so many ages before arrival of the *whites.* . . . Do you see a single nation of your color?" With the exception of a "few Iroquois, and still a lesser number of their nephews, the Lenoppi, we know not the name of a single red man, nor the descendant of a red man, who resided on the lands watered by the rivers emptying into the great sea." Greed, rape, murders, and massacres had led to the systematic destruction of most Indian people to Egushawa's east and south. What was behind it all? "Many of these white people," Egushawa answered, "have an opinion, *called religion,* which they inculcate on the minds of their children, that they please God by exterminating us *red men.*"[1]

Sixty-three years later, a Christian Mahican, John W. Quinney, provided another extended analysis of the forces that had destroyed Indian communities. Unlike Egushawa, who addressed a Native assembly, Quinney spoke to non-Indians. Born in New Stockbridge, New York, Quinney had migrated to Wisconsin in the 1820s and had led the Stockbridge Mahicans' fight against removal to Kansas in the late 1830s and early 1840s. In the 1850s, he returned to New York to seek compensation for lands lost there. On July 4, 1854, Quinney addressed an audience at a Fourth of July celebration in Reidsville, New York, twenty miles southwest of Albany. Quinney began his historical overview "before the advent of the Europeans," when "wise men" among his ancestors "foretold the coming of a strange race, from the sunrise, as numerous as the leaves upon the trees, who would eventually crowd them from their fair possessions." This prophecy, Quinney went on to say, had been fulfilled in the early 1600s when the Mahicans "for the first time, beheld the 'pale face.'" Because these visitors were white, Quinney's ancestors thought they "must be sick. . . . They were strangers, and we took them in—naked, and we clothed them."

Quinney recognized that his non-Indian audience had some knowledge of the history of the European settlement of North America. "Your written accounts of events at this period are familiar to you, my friends," he said, "your children read them every day in their school books." But, he continued, American children "do not read" and in fact "no mind at this time can conceive, and no pen record, the terrible story of recompense for kindness, which for two hundred years has been the simple, trusting, guileless Muh-he-con-new [Mahicans]." Promises were "freely given" but were "ruthlessly—intentionally broken," as colonizers, claiming a "right of discovery," demanded of the Indians' kings "assistance to assert and maintain your hold." The consequences for the Mahicans had been catastrophic. Reduced from a population of 25,000 in 1604, "they have been victims to vice and disease, which the white man imported. The small-pox, measles, and 'strong waters' have done the work of annihilation." Not only this, "divisions and feuds were insidiously promoted between the several bands" and "they were induced to abandon their territory at intervals, and retire further to the inland." The very spot where Quinney stood, in fact, "has never been purchased or rightly obtained." His people had abandoned it "in the tortures of starvation." What was true of the Mahicans was true for "all the red men . . . made by the Great Spirit from red clay." In a rebuke to the Declaration his audience had gathered to celebrate, Quinney continued that "the Indian is left to rot and die, before the humanities of this model *Republic!* . . . One removal follows another, and thus your sympathies and justice are evinced in speedily *fulfilling the terrible destinies of our race.*" The "extinction . . . of my tribe," Quinney solemnly predicted, "is inevitable."[2]

Quinney's prophecy of his people's inevitable extinction may have revealed an inner certainty of this outcome. More likely, he was trying to elicit his audience's sympathy for his efforts to gain compensation for lands lost when the Stockbridges moved from New York to Wisconsin. Whatever the case, Quinney, like Egushawa, believed that his people had been—and continued to be—subject to forces of destruction that had historically resulted in the extermination/extinction of Indian nations throughout eastern North America. In explaining Indian decline, the two leaders emphasized different causes. Egushawa spoke more about violence than Quinney, who highlighted disease and material deprivation. Egushawa directly criticized Christianity, while Quinney called out the hypocrisies of an ostensibly Christian republic. At the same time, their respective analyses led to powerful indictments of whites' greed, mendacity, arrogance, and cruelty. Both saw the disappearance of Indians as the result of consistent and intentional actions undertaken by Europeans since the time of their arrival in the Americas. They were not wrong.

Non-Native Americans also remarked on the disappearance of Indians. In so doing, they frequently expressed feelings of melancholy, a passive emotion that supported a position that disappearance was a tragic but inevitable result of forces beyond anyone's control. The metaphors American writers crafted enhanced a sense that the destruction of Indian nations was simply an act of nature. Indians were "as certain doomed to destruction as the summer leaf is to fall under the perishing effects of the winter's frost." Or they had "melted away before the approaching whites like snow beneath the beams of the sun." To the extent that Americans identified specific causes for Native disappearance, they focused primarily on disease and alcohol and contended that inherent racial deficiencies made Indians vulnerable to these forces. Sometimes U.S. leaders recognized the wrongdoing of their predecessors. In 1823 Har-

vard professor Edward Everett conceded that the early colonists had committed acts of "injustice and cruelty." But in the next breath, Everett asserted that
Indians had committed equivalent acts of injustice and cruelty, so that the
"score of oppression, cruelty, and guilt is nearly balanced." Few non-Native
Americans developed a critical analysis of the European invasion.[3]

The vast gulf between Indigenous and settler views of history can be seen
with particular clarity through a remarkable conversation that took place in
1794 in northwestern Pennsylvania. This conversation occurred when John
Adlum, a surveyor who had been working along the upper Allegheny River,
traveled to "pay my respects" to an Indian named Logan. Adlum identified
Logan as the nephew of the famous orator of the same name who is supposed
to have delivered a speech known as "Logan's Lament," made famous by its
inclusion in Thomas Jefferson's *Notes on the State of Virginia*. When Adlum
came upon Logan, he saw that Logan "looked sorrowful" and through an interpreter asked "if it was not an improper question I should like to know the
cause of it." Logan replied that "the chiefs and most of the young men of our
Nations are going mad, they want to make war with you, without considering
what the [result] may be." Logan then observed that "it appears to me that the
great Spirit above is determined on our destruction." Logan, of course, was
referring to confederation resistance in Ohio and Anthony Wayne's military
operation to crush it. Logan's fear was that war would spread east and that he
and his people would be destroyed. To these worries, Adlum responded by
suggesting that if Logan was truly afraid, he should seek protection from U.S.
forces at a nearby fort. Logan rejected this idea, explaining that should general war break out, his country "will soon be overrun by your troops. And you
will have to kill us as we will fight desperately, and in revenge you will send
our wives and children after us." Adlum objected that "we were not so savage, that we killed so long as we found resistance—But whenever a man was
disarmed, he was considered as under our protection—And as to woemen
[sic] and children we never injured them." Logan replied that Adlum might
"think so," but "I know that it is otherwise." Logan then listed several facts:
the "account of several wars handed down to us by those who lived before
us"; violations of agreements requiring prisoners to be given up at the end of
these wars; and the Americans' destruction of "our towns and sometimes by
surprise, and you never spared any." Evidently feeling defensive, Adlum asked
for an example. At this, Logan gave Adlum "a look of surprise and indignation, and said if you do not know I will tell you of one." He then proceeded to
relate what happened at "a town on the Muskingum river, settled by some of

your good white people amongst the Indians," who had persuaded "a number of [I]ndians to cease going to war, to cultivate the ground, and to worship the Great Spirit, after the manner of these good white men." These people "were peaceable and never went to war—And what became of them?" With "great energy," Logan then told Adlum of "the horrible massacre of those innocent people." As soon as Logan began to speak of this massacre (the 1782 Gnadenhütten massacre recounted in Chapter 2), Adlum instantly realized what he was talking about. Adlum commented to his readers that he regarded that massacre as a "disgrace to our Country" and regretted that he had given Logan "an oppertunity to give me such a rebuke."[4]

From Adlum's perspective, Gnadenhütten was anomalous, and though perhaps a cause for momentary shame, not indicative of U.S. policy or actions. Although he recalled the massacre when Logan referenced it, Gnadenhütten was seldom on his mind, an event more forgotten than remembered. For Logan, however, the slaughter at Gnadenhütten weighed heavily and was always present in memory. What's more, it was one of many examples of betrayal and violence that were ultimately systemic and prophetic of the worst imaginable future.

It has been well over two centuries since Logan rebuked Adlum for his ignorance about the history of the American destruction of Indian nations. Since then, and especially over the past forty years, scholars have given us a much better understanding of the history that people like Logan, Egushawa, and John Quinney lived through. Many historical accounts support their perspective that the European invasion constituted a series of intentional, systematic actions that threatened the utter destruction of Indian nations throughout eastern North America. Nonetheless, the forgetfulness of Adlum persists, not only within the general public but among academic and popular historians. No one can complain about a shortage of books on the Founding Fathers, but it is possible to read stacks of them without learning a thing about the Gnadenhütten massacre, let alone being asked to consider it as an event revealing basic tendencies in early American history. Of course, not all historians ignore Gnadenhütten. Nor do all ignore Horseshoe Bend, Bad Axe, the Cherokee Trail of Tears, or other destructive events discussed in this book. Nonetheless, many historians continue to see destructive acts and episodes as outliers rather than as manifestations of basic tendencies. There remains a disposition to soften recognition of consistent patterns of destructive action by insisting on the ultimate goodness of America, or at least the humanitarian intentions of many of its leaders and citizens. Even critically

minded scholars are apt to inadvertently deflect attention from general metropolitan responsibility for violence by focusing on a singularly pernicious
Andrew Jackson or the frontiersmen he embodied. There is almost no recognition that U.S. officials established a policy of exterminating Indians who
opposed their will, that the "just and lawful war" clause of the Northwest
Ordinance meant genocidal war. We have also yet to come to grips with how
U.S. expansion created conditions that made Native communities acutely
vulnerable to pathogens and how severely disease impacted them. Scholars
no longer attribute Indigenous deaths from disease to the inevitable outwork-
ing of "laws of nature" grounded in racial theories of the supremacy of the
"Anglo-Saxon race." Nonetheless, Native depopulation is still often seen primarily as the result of a tragically accidental collision of European pathogens
with Native bodies lacking immunity. Historians continue to ignore the catastrophic impact of disease and its relationship to U.S. policy and action even
when it is right before their eyes. Bleeding Kansas remains a central chapter
in U.S. history, but not because Indians were dying there.

In 1854, when the Mahican John Quinney spoke about the elimination
of eastern Indians, more Native communities than ever before were subject
to forces of destruction that he, Egushawa, Logan, and many other Indians
knew all too well. By this time, most Native communities east of the Mississippi no longer faced the threat of massacre, but Americans continued to
gnaw at their lands, take their resources, murder them, deny them justice in
their courts, violate treaties, and profit from selling them alcohol. Poverty,
malnutrition, disease, and poor health care remained major problems.

In areas farther west—to be considered in the second volume of this
study—many Indian nations had already experienced devastating losses by
the mid-1850s. The Anglo invasion of Texas that began in the 1830s had resulted in the violent removal of most Indians from the state's boundaries. The
most powerful nation on the southern Plains—the Comanches—had seen its
population cut in half, from 20,000 in the late 1840s to 10,000 by the mid-
1850s. In the Pacific Northwest, Native people had been hit by epidemic upon
epidemic in the 1830s and 1840s, and even as Quinney addressed New Yorkers
about the history of Indian disappearance, settlers in southern Oregon were
passing resolutions demanding the "Extermination of the Indian race" and
forming militias to do precisely that. In California, five years into the Gold
Rush, the U.S. army and state-supported militias had slaughtered thousands
of Native people. Thousands more California Indians were perishing from
starvation and disease. As settlers made their way to California or Oregon,

U.S. soldiers mobilized to protect them as they trespassed on Indian lands in the Great Plains. In 1855, General William S. Harney, a veteran of sowing terror among the Seminoles in Florida in 1840, led a contingent of dragoons up the Platte River to punish the Lakota Sioux for killing soldiers who had broken a peace treaty the year before. When he found a camp of Lakotas in western Nebraska, Harney and his men slaughtered as many people as they could—close to 100, more than half of them women and children.[5]

Had Egushawa been able to see into the future, he would not have been surprised by what was happening in the western United States in the 1850s. Similarly, had Quinney turned toward the Pacific, he would have found additional grounds to support his exposure of the hypocrisy of the American republic, but he would not have seen anything unexpected. Surveying the continent in the mid-1850s, it might well have seemed that the western acceleration of America's empire would lead to the extermination of every last Indian.

Fortunately, this did not happen. Today, Egushawa's descendants live in Ottawa communities in Ontario, Michigan, and Oklahoma, and Quinney's form part of the Stockbridge-Munsee Nation in Wisconsin. Non-Native Americans might attribute the survival of these and hundreds of other Indian nations to an American benevolence that rejected total extermination, as if Indians ought to be grateful to Americans for allowing some of them to live. In the final analysis, however, as the United States and its citizens pursued the elimination of Indian lands and tribal communities, their actions were sufficiently destructive to justify the fears of Egushawa, Quinney, and countless other unknown Indigenous historians and prophets that their people might someday disappear. That this did not happen testifies to the resilience of their own generations and the generations since.

Appendix 1
The Question of Genocide in U.S. History

Although Raphaël Lemkin coined the term *genocide* in 1944, it was not until almost fifty years later that the question of genocide in the Americas became a matter of scholarly and public debate.[1] The debate began at the time of the Columbus Quincentennial in 1992, when activists and writers challenged a celebratory narrative of the "discovery of the New World" by arguing that the European invasion of the Western Hemisphere was consistently genocidal. Two works were particularly influential: David Stannard's *American Holocaust: The Conquest of the New World* (1992) and Ward Churchill's *A Little Matter of Genocide: Holocaust and Denial in the Americas, 1492 to the Present* (1997). As their titles announced, Stannard and Churchill made their case by arguing for an equivalence with the Holocaust. Their narrative strategy was to relate horrific event after horrific event (massacres, enslavements, epidemics), indict Europeans and European Americans for their greed, racism, and bloodlust, and link these to statistics underscoring the drastic decline of Indigenous populations in the Americas. In this way, they created the impression of an unrelenting, intentioned, and unambiguously evil process that resembled as closely as possible the Nazis' systematic annihilation of the Jews. Theirs was a story of genocide, genocide, and genocide, and there was little room for anything else.[2]

Since 1992, the argument for a total, relentless, and pervasive genocide in the Americas has become accepted in some areas of Indigenous studies and genocide studies. For the most part, however, this argument has had little impact on mainstream scholarship in U.S. history or American Indian history. Scholars are more inclined than they once were to gesture to particular actions, events, impulses, and effects as genocidal, but genocide has not become a key concept in scholarship in these fields.[3] In part, this is because academic specialists in colonial American and U.S. history are generally inclined against sweeping indictments. The excessive po-lemics, simplifications, and empirical overreaches in much of the Quincentennial writing made it easy for skeptics to ignore or brush aside.[4] The relative absence of genocide in much of the scholarship in American Indian history can also be explained by the priority given to other agendas, especially the often articulated importance of recovering the agency of Native people against an earlier historiography that suppos-edly portrayed them simply as victims. Indeed, some Native scholars have cautioned that writing Indigenous histories as genocide risks reinforcing pernicious stereotypes of Indians as vanishing and degraded.[5]

Although genocide remains outside most historical narratives, debates about genocide as a general phenomenon in American history and in specific times and places have continued since 1992.[6] Like debates about cases of genocide elsewhere in the world, those about genocide in North America have often become bogged down in what one observer has termed a "merry-go-round of definitional debates." The most authoritative definition is the one codified by the 1948 United Nations Convention on the Prevention and Punishment of the Crime of Genocide. The UN Convention defines genocide as

> any of the following acts committed with intent to destroy, in whole or in part, a national, ethnical, racial or religious group, as such:
>
> (a) Killing members of the group;
> (b) Causing serious bodily or mental harm to members of the group;
> (c) Deliberately inflicting on the group conditions of life calculated to bring about its physical destruction in whole or in part;
> (d) Imposing measures intended to prevent births within the group;
> (e) Forcibly transferring children of the group to another group.

Despite this definition's authoritative status in international law, scholars in genocide studies have proposed numerous competing definitions. Some definitions seek to broaden the kinds of groups that can be the targets of genocide to include political groups. Other definitions narrow the range of genocidal acts by eliminating forms of destruction that do not entail direct killing, while others seek to expand this range by including programs of "ethnocide" or "cultural genocide." There is also substantial disagreement over how to define intent. Some scholars insist on a relatively narrow le-gal definition of specific intent, while others propose broader definitions such as "sus-tained purposeful action." Still others argue that the crucial issue is the consequences of actions or programs regardless of the specific intention behind them. There are also disputes about defining the agent(s) of genocide. Some scholars contend that for destruction to be truly genocidal it must be directed by the state. Others, however, argue that destruction undertaken by a society or elements within a society qualifies as genocide even if the state is not the instigator or directly involved. Finally, there is the issue of the threshold for genocide. Under the UN Convention on genocide, intent to destroy a group "in part" is sufficient, but what exactly does this mean? Some analysts define the threshold as "substantial numbers," but that hardly solves the problem. Indeed, frustration with the inability of genocide studies to agree on a definition of its central term has led to declarations that the debate about genocide is "futile" and calls for the term to be abandoned.[7]

Although arguments about defining genocide in the Americas have paralleled those in genocide studies more generally, the American debate has some unique features. One is that whether we are talking about the entire Western Hemisphere since 1492, the United States including its colonial antecedents, or just the United States, whatever happened unfolded unevenly across vast spaces over a very long period of time. In contrast, well-known twentieth-century genocides occurred much more rapidly and with sustained totality. Does what happened in the Americas have to conform to twentieth-century genocides in order to be considered genocide, or can we conceive of a range of genocidal processes and practices with differential effects on Native communities? A related issue is how to define the targeted group in a situation in which Indians are conceived of as a racial group but have distinctive identities as separate nations and communities. Can the targeting of individual nations or communities be considered genocidal, or is it necessary to demonstrate an intent to destroy Indians as a collective entity? Another issue, unique to the United States, is how to define the state, since it includes the federal and state governments. Are the actions of a particular state sufficient to satisfy those who require state intention for genocide, or is federal government involvement necessary? Finally, there is the question of how to assess the role of disease in depopulation. In making the argument for widespread genocide in the Americas, Quincentennial writers placed substantial weight on the staggering population losses suffered by Indigenous people after 1492. Drawing on scholarship arguing that the pre-Columbian population of the Western Hemisphere was as high as 75 million (with 10–12 million north of Mexico) and that virgin soil epidemics reduced these populations by 70 percent or more, Quincentennial writers argued that the sheer numbers who died (50–60 million for all of the Americas; 7–8 million for North America) are overwhelming and compel recognition as genocide when measured against the death toll for commonly accepted cases of genocide in the twentieth century. Ironically, however, an emphasis on a very high number for initial depopulation provides an opening for a counterposition. Since Europeans who brought pathogens to the Western Hemisphere did not do so with the intention of killing Indigenous people, it can be argued that the Columbian demographic catastrophe was an unfortunate accident of history and not genocidal. To rebut this position, some writers have provided examples of Europeans intentionally inflicting Indians with disease (usually through blankets infected with smallpox) and argued for their typicality. But the evidence marshaled thus far has failed to dislodge a scholarly consensus that the intentional infliction of disease was rare. Recently, scholars have shifted the emphasis on disease in the Americas away from virgin soil epidemics and emphasized how Native people's vulnerability to pathogens and their poor health generally was a consequence of colonialism as it developed over time. These scholars do not necessarily describe colonial processes as genocidal, but by showing how colonial projects (e.g., the enslavement of Indian people) created conditions that favored the spread of pathogens and enhanced their lethality, they make clear that massive population losses cannot be dismissed as accidental and, for those inclined to emphasize consequences over specific intent, allow for an argument that certain projects sustained over time with consistently lethal results should be seen as genocidal.[8]

A recent development in the American genocide debate centers on the question of whether *ethnic cleansing* is a more apt term than *genocide*. In *Ethnic Cleansing: The Crime That Should Haunt America* (2014), Gary Anderson surveys the entirety of U.S. history including its colonial antecedents and argues that the crime of ethnic cleansing best characterizes this history. Anderson also insists that genocide does not apply to any of the history since "policies of mass murder on a scale similar to events in central Europe, Cambodia, or Rwanda were never implemented." Benjamin Madley, author of *An American Genocide: The United States and the California Indian Catastrophe* (2016), has rebutted Anderson by arguing that a sustained genocide occurred in at least one place in the United States: California during the Gold Rush from the early 1850s into the 1870s. Because the case for genocide in California is particularly strong, this latest wrinkle in the debate could conceivably be resolved by an agreement that Madley is right about California but that Anderson is right about the rest of U.S. history. Given the history of the American genocide debate, however, it is doubtful that a consensus will emerge. It is safe to predict that the debate will continue.[9]

Because of the debate's intractability, I often thought while working on this book of avoiding the question of genocide altogether and simply analyzing "forces of destruction" regardless of whether they should be considered genocidal. In the end, though, I could not escape the sense that genocide is an integral part of the history I have written about. Genocide was not present all the time, and so to answer the question of genocide for this part of American history with an absolute "yes" would be simplistic. But replying with an absolute "no" would overlook a great deal. Not only would it fail to take seriously Indians' own views on the matter, it would miss many other overlooked dimensions of this history. It would fail to fully reckon with the fact that government officials consistently used genocidal threats to secure consent, and it would continue to ignore the fact that the United States adopted a policy of exterminating Indians who resisted its demands. Dismissing genocide might also prevent us from fathoming the depths of Indian removal. At one time, I thought ethnic cleansing was probably the best term for the U.S. policy of Indian removal, but as I began to grasp the full impact of removal as it was pursued for more than twenty years (from the 1830s into the 1850s), as I came to a better understanding of the demographic catastrophes it inflicted on so many nations, and as I realized that these catastrophes were the direct result of a policy that was continued by government officials who knew what was happening, I could not escape the conviction that what I was witnessing had to be considered genocide.

Appendix 2
Population Estimates by Nation

The tables below provide the best possible estimates for Native populations over time. As anyone familiar with the sources and methods of Native American demographic history can attest, population estimates are often based on limited observation and in most cases have to be considered rough. In addition, there are questions about who is being counted. Some of the sources for the southern nations, for example, make it clear whether or not enslaved people are included in population figures, but this is not always the case. Similarly, in situations of extensive intermarriage between Indians and non-Indians, it is often impossible to tell whether estimates include people of mixed ancestry, some of whom might identify, for example, as mixed-blood, French, or white. Despite these problems, however, I am confident that the estimates provide a fairly accurate picture of specific populations at particular points in time and, more important, that they reveal general trends over time.

CADDOS (KADOHADACHOS ONLY)

Year	Population
1680	8,000[a]
1803	500–600[b]

continued

CADDOS (KADOHADACHOS ONLY) *continued*

Year	Population
1835	500[c]

a LaVere, *Caddo Chiefdoms,* 76.
b Smith, *Caddo Indians,* 85.
c Ibid., 161.

CATAWBAS

Year	Population	Notes
1755	1,500[a]	
1763	500[a]	
1800	400–500[b]	
1825	110[c]	
1839	88[d]	
1850	110[e]	Includes 76 living with eastern Cherokees

a Merrell, *Indians' New World,* 195.
b Ibid., 229.
c Ibid., 357, n. 13.
d Hudson, *Catawba Nation,* 64.
e Ibid., 66, n. 13.

CHEROKEES

Year	Population	Notes
1745	9,000[a]	
1760	7,200[a]	
1775	8,500[a]	
1790	7,500[a]	

continued

CHEROKEES *continued*

Year	Population	Notes
1825	18,000–20,000	14,000 east of the Mississippi;[b] 4,000–6,000 west of the Mississippi[c]
1832	26,600–28,600	22,600 east of the Mississippi;[d] 4,000–6,000 west of the Mississippi[c]
1839	21,400–23,400	1,400 east of the Mississippi;[e] 16,000 survivors of the Trail of Tears west of the Mississippi;[f] 4,000–6,000 "Old Settlers," already west of the Mississippi[c]
1860	18,532	16,332 west of the Mississippi;[g] 2,200 east of the Mississippi[h]

a Wood, "Changing Population," 60.
b 13,783 in 1824 census east of Mississippi in Kelton, *Cherokee Medicine,* 211.
c Thornton, *Cherokees,* 48–49.
d 2,200 removed between 1832 and early 1838 in Foreman, *Indian Removal,* 242–43, 252–63, 273–78, 280–85; 19,000 in the East before the major removals of 1838 based on figure of 17,000 awaiting removal in May 1838, reported in Foreman, *Indian Removal,* 290, but which is based on counts of those departing several months later and so does not take account of the 2,000 who died in the concentration camps (Chapter 8); 1,400 who avoided removal in Finger, *Eastern Band of Cherokees,* 29.
e Finger, *Eastern Band of Cherokees,* 29.
f Based on reports documenting numbers arriving in the West (Chapter 8): 2,000 between 1830 and early 1838; 1,900–2,000 who left in June 1838; 12,100 who left in the fall of 1838.
g Doran, "Population Statistics," 501. Includes 2,511 slaves.
h *RCIA, 1855,* 575.

CHICKASAWS

Year	Population	Notes
1775	2,300[a]	
1790	3,100[a]	
1825	3,600[b]	
1842	5,000[c]	Not including enslaved people
1860	4,260[d]	Not including enslaved people

a Wood, "Changing Population," 95.
b McKenney, "Statement," insert after 14.
c *RCIA, 1842,* 448.
d Doran, "Population Statistics," 501.

CHOCTAWS

Year	Population	Notes
1775	14,000[a]	
1790	14,700[a]	
1825	21,000[b]	
1831	19,554[c]	
1838	17,700	15,500 west of the Mississippi;[d] 2,200 east of the Mississippi and Louisiana[e]
1860	18,200	16,015 west of the Mississippi (including 2,349 slaves);[f] 2,200 east of the Mississippi and Louisiana[e]

a Wood, "Changing Population," 99.
b McKenney, "Statement," insert after 14.
c *CSEI,* 3:131.
d Based on 18,000 removed and 2,500 death toll in Green, "Expansion of European Colonization," 522.
e Based on 2,261 in 1855 in Kidwell, *Choctaws and Missionaries,* 169.
f Doran, "Population Statistics," 501.

CREEKS

Year	Population	Notes
1745	12,000[a]	
1760	13,000[a]	
1775	14,000[a]	
1790	15,000[a]	
1825	20,000[b]	
1833	25,153	22,694 east of the Mississippi (including 902 enslaved people);[c] 2,459 west of the Mississippi[d]
1838	19,000–21,500	17,000–19,000 who survived removal;[e] 2,000–2,500 already west of the Mississippi[f]
1842	20,000[g]	
1860	15,082[h]	Includes 1,532 enslaved people

a Wood, "Changing Population," 61.
b McKenney, "Statement," insert after 14.
c Foreman, *Indian Removal*, 11.
d Haveman, *Rivers of Sand*, 170.
e Based on subtracting the cumulative death toll from the preremoval population (Chapter 8).
f Based on 1833 figure, with possibility of a decline because of disease (Chapter 8).
g *RCIA, 1842*, 449.
h Doran, "Population Statistics," 501.

DAKOTAS (EASTERN SIOUX)

Year	Population
1803	3,000–6,000[a]
1830	6,700[b]
1849	6,300[c]

a Lewis and Clark 1804 estimate of 3,200 and Zebulon Pike 1805 estimate of 5,775 in DeMallie, "Sioux until 1850," 748.
b Tanner, *Atlas*, 149.
c DeMallie, "Sioux until 1850," 748.

DELAWARES (INCLUDES MUNSEES)

Year	Population	Notes
1600	10,000[a]	
1700	3,000[a]	
1768	3,500[b]	
1818	3,680–3,880[c]	600 west of the Mississippi; 2,000 in Indiana; 80 in Ohio; 1,000–1,200 in Canada
1821	1,900–2,000[d]	West of the Mississippi only
1829	3,000[e]	West of the Mississippi only
1845	1,059[f]	Kansas only
1860	1,008[g]	Kansas only

a Goddard, "Delaware," 214.
b Tanner, *Atlas*, 66.
c 600 in Missouri in Aron, *American Confluence*, 81; 2,000 along the White River and 1,000–1,200 in Canada in Weslager, *Delaware Indians*, 352–53; 80 in Ohio in Morse, *Report*, 362.
d 1,346 moved west in 1821 in Weslager, *Delaware Indians*, 361, plus 600 already there.
e U.S. House, *Letter from the Secretary of War . . . in Relation to Our Indian Affairs*, 93–94.
f *RCIA, 1845*, 539.
g *RCIA, 1860*, 326.

HAUDENOSAUNEES (SIX NATIONS, IROQUOIS)

Year	Population	Notes
1630	20,000[a]	
1640	10,000[a]	
1680	9,000–12,000[b]	
1700	6,000–7,000[c]	
1738	8,800[d]	
1775	9,000[e]	
1783	7,500–8,000[f]	6,000 in New York; 1,500–2,000 in Canada

continued

HAUDENOSAUNEES (SIX NATIONS, IROQUOIS) *continued*

Year	Population	Notes
1830	6,860[g]	4,350 in New York; 2,500 in Canada
1855	3,953[h]	New York only

a Richter, *Ordeal of the Longhouse*, 59.
b U.S. Bureau of Education, *Are the Indians Dying Out?*, 20–21.
c Richter, *Ordeal of the Longhouse*, 188.
d U.S. Bureau of Education, *Are the Indians Dying Out?*, 22.
e Tanner, *Atlas*, 66; U.S. Bureau of Education, *Are the Indians Dying Out?*, 23–24.
f U.S. Bureau of Education, *Are the Indians Dying Out?*, 24–25.
g Tanner, *Atlas*, 132. 350 from Tanner's figure of 4,700 Haudenosaunees in the U.S. subtracted and included under Ohio Senecas.
h U.S. Bureau of Education, *Are the Indians Dying Out?*, 27.

HO-CHUNKS (WINNEBAGOS)

Year	Population	Notes
1768	1,500[a]	
1822	5,800[b]	
1830	5,000[c]	700 in Illinois; 4,300 in Wisconsin
1859	3,000–3,500[d]	

a Tanner, *Atlas*, 66.
b Morse, *Report*, 362.
c Tanner, *Atlas*, 139.
d Based on 2,256 in Minnesota in *RCIA, 1859*, 479; 100 living with Otoe-Missourias in Kansas in *RCIA, 1848*, 459; "several hundred" in Wisconsin in *RCIA, 1856*, 590–91. Lurie, "Winnebago," 702, states that in 1874 there were 860 in Wisconsin; even if there had been a decline since the 1850s, the 1850s number could not have been much over 1,000.

ILLINOIS CONFEDERACY (INCLUDING PEORIAS, KASKASKIAS, CAHOKIAS, AND OTHERS)

Year	Population
1680	10,500–20,000[a]
1700	6,000[b]
1736	2,500[b]
1768	2,200[c]
1822	36[d]

a 10,500 in Blasingham, "Depopulation of the Illinois Indians," 372; 20,000 in Morrissey, *Empire by Collaboration*, 63.
b Blasingham, "Depopulation of the Illinois Indians," 372.
c Tanner, *Atlas*, 66.
d Morse, *Report*, 363.

IOWAYS

Year	Population
1760	1,000–1,500[a]
1822	1,000–1,500[a]
1848	669[b]
1861	305[c]

a Blaine, *Ioway Indians*, 46–47, 136.
b *RCIA, 1848*, 482.
c *RCIA, 1861*, 663.

KANZAS

Year	Population
1702	1,500[a]
1806	1,565[a]
1837	1,471[b]

continued

KANZAS *continued*

Year	Population
1841	1,606[c]
1860	803[d]

a Bailey and Young, "Kansa," 472.
b *RCIA, 1837*, 598.
c *RCIA, 1841*, 268.
d *RCIA, 1860*, 337.

KICKAPOOS (INCLUDING MASCOUTENS)

Year	Population	Notes
1768	2,000[a]	
1819	2,200[b]	
1832	1,950[c]	750 east of the Mississippi; 1,200 west of the Mississippi
1845	1,716	516 in Kansas;[d] 1,200 in Texas, Mexico, Oklahoma[e]
1860	1,500	325 in Kansas;[f] 1,200 in Oklahoma[e]

a Tanner, *Atlas*, 66.
b Ibid., 139.
c Gibson, *Kickapoos*, 109.
d *RCIA, 1845*, 540.
e Based on assumption of stable population of those already west of the Mississippi in 1832.
f *RCIA, 1860*, 324.

LUMBEES

Year	Population
1860	1,400[a]

a Based on 1860 U.S. census tally of 1,462 "free persons of color/colored" in Robeson County in Lowery, *Lumbee Indians*, 23.

MENOMINEES

Year	Population
1757	1,100[a]
1759	800[a]
1768	800[b]
1822	3,900[c]
1830	3,000–4,000[d]
1843	2,500[e]
1852	2,002[f]
1855	1,900[g]

a Beck, *Siege and Survival*, 207.
b Tanner, *Atlas*, 66.
c Morse, *Report*, 362.
d Tanner, *Atlas*, 143.
e *RCIA, 1843*, 433.
f Beck, *Siege and Survival*, 182.
g *RCIA, 1855*, 575.

MIAMIS (INCLUDING WEAS AND PIANKASHAWS)

Year	Population	Notes
1650	4,000–5,600[a]	
1736	3,000[a]	
1768	4,000[b]	
1822	1,400[c]	
1830	1,000[d]	
1839	700[e]	
1846 (before removal)	639[f]	
1846 (after removal)	623	323 in Kansas;[g] 300 in Indiana[h]
1849	550	250 in Kansas;[i] 300 in Indiana[h]
1859	466	166 in Kansas;[j] 300 in Indiana[h]

a Callender, "Miami," 688.
b Tanner, *Atlas,* 66.
c Morse, *Report,* 363.
d Tanner, *Atlas,* 136.
e Foreman, *Last Trek,* 126.
f 339 moved to Kansas in Bowes, *Land Too Good,* 76; 300 remained in Indiana in Anson,
    Miami Indians, 226.
g 323 arrived in Kansas in Bowes, *Land Too Good,* 76.
h Anson, *Miami Indians,* 226.
i *RCIA, 1849,* 1096.
j *RCIA, 1859,* 166.

NEW ENGLAND INDIANS

Year	Population	Notes
1675	30,000[a]	
1776	3,500[b]	
1780	2,100[c]	Southern New England only
1822	2,526[d]	
1825	1,447[c]	Massachusetts and Connecticut only
1835	1,020[c]	Massachusetts and Connecticut only

continued

NEW ENGLAND INDIANS *continued*

| 1850 | 1,212[c] | Massachusetts and Connecticut only |
| 1865 | 1,829[c] | Massachusetts and Connecticut only |

a Fisher and Silverman, *Ninigret,* 108, 170, n. 56.

b Based on 2,100 for southern New England in 1780 in Mandell, *Tribe, Race, History,* 4, plus an additional 400 before Revolutionary War losses; an additional 1,000 in northern New England based on Snow, "Eastern Abenaki," 145, which gives a figure of 175–200 for the Penobscots in Maine in the 1770s; Erickson, "Maliseet-Passamaquoddy," 126, which suggests a similar number for the Passamaquoddies; and, despite absence of data for the western Abenakis, an assumption of several hundred.

c Mandell, *Tribe, Race, History,* 4.

d Morse, *Report,* 361.

NORTH CAROLINA (EAST OF THE MOUNTAINS)

Year	Population
1775	500[a]
1790	300[a]

a Wood, "Changing Population," 60.

OJIBWES (CHIPPEWAS)

Year	Population	Notes
1768	8,000[a]	Includes Canada
1830	15,200[b]	7,600 in Michigan lower peninsula; 3,800 in northern Wisconsin and Michigan Upper Peninsula; 3,800 in Minnesota
1861	15,538[c]	

a Tanner, *Atlas,* 66.

b Ibid., 133, 146, 149. Two-thirds of the 11,500 combined Ojibwe and Ottawa population in Michigan's lower peninsula estimated as Ojibwe.

c Based on figures for Mackinac, Chippewas of the Mississippi, and Chippewas of Lake Superior in *RCIA, 1861,* 820–22 (two-thirds of the 4,930 Ottawas and Chippewas reported at Mackinac Agency estimated as Ojibwe); and 1,200 for Red Lake and Pembina bands in *RCIA, 1850,* 89.

OMAHAS

Year	Population
1780	2,800[a]
1805	900[b]
1820	2,000[c]
1834	1,400[a]
1844	1,300[d]
1855	800[e]

a Liberty, Wood, and Irwin, "Omaha," 415.
b Moulton, *Journals of the Lewis and Clark Expedition*, 3:398.
c Wishart, *Unspeakable Sadness*, 73.
d *RCIA, 1844*, 442.
e *RCIA, 1855*, 406.

OSAGES

Year	Population
1805	6,300[a]
1825	5,200[b]
1842	5,000–6,000[c]
1850	4,500[d]
1857	3,500[e]

a Moulton, *Journals of the Lewis and Clark Expedition*, 3:390, 92.
b McKenney, "Statement," insert after 14.
c Based on comments in Bailey, "Osage," 493.
d *RCIA, 1850*, 66.
e *RCIA, 1857*, 494.

OTOE-MISSOURIAS

Year	Population
1829	1,200[a]
1835	964[a]
1840	943[b]
1860	500[c]

a Schweitzer, "Otoe and Missouria," 454.
b *RCIA, 1840*, 319.
c *RCIA, 1860*, 321.

OTTAWAS (ODAWAS)

Year	Population	Notes
1768	5,000[a]	
1830	4,400[b]	3,900 in Michigan; 500 in Ohio
1840	340[c]	Kansas only
1860	1,913[d]	207 in Kansas; 1,706 in Michigan

a Tanner, *Atlas,* 66.
b Ibid., 133, 136. One-third of the 11,500 combined Ojibwe and Ottawa population in Michigan's lower peninsula estimated as Ottawa.
c *RCIA, 1840*, 320.
d *RCIA, 1860*, 335; *RCIA, 1861*, 821–22.

PETITES NATIONS OF LOUISIANA

Year	Population
1825	1,000[a]

a McKenney, "Statement," insert after 14, gives a total of 1,313 for Louisiana Indians, including 450 Caddos listed separately.

POTAWATOMIS

Year	Population	Notes
1768	3,000[a]	
1830	10,400[b]	Includes some multiethnic Potawatomi, Ojibwe, and Ottawa communities in Wisconsin
1848	3,235[c]	Kansas (from an estimated 4,000–5,000 moved west, 1836–1845)
1860	5,405[d]	2,405 in Kansas; 3,000 east of Missisippi, mostly in Canada

a Tanner, *Atlas*, 66.
b Ibid., 135, 136, 139, 146.
c *RCIA, 1848*, 447.
d *RCIA, 1860*, 332 (Kansas); east of Mississippi based on migration of 2,000+ to Canada to avoid removal and several hundred uncounted in Wisconsin in Clifton, "Potawatomi," 739–40.

QUAPAWS

Year	Population
1680	5,000[a]
1700	2,000[a]
1803	600[b]
1826	455[c]
1834	476[d]
1844	400[e]
1857	400[f]

a DuVal, *Native Ground*, 78.
b Ibid., 190.
c Baird, *Quapaw Indians*, 69.
d Young and Hoffman, "Quapaw," 501.
e *RCIA, 1844*, 459.
f *RCIA, 1857*, 494.

SAUKS AND MESQUAKIES (FOXES)

Year	Population	Notes
1670	2,000[a]	Mesquakies only
1732	140[a]	Mesquakies only
1768	3,500[b]	1,500 Mesquakies; 2,000 Sauks
1800	6,000[c]	
1830	6,500[d]	
1832	6,000[e]	
1838	4,546[f]	
1849	3,000[g]	
1853	2,153[h]	
1857	1,367[i]	
1860	1,280[j]	

a Edmunds and Peyser, *Fox Wars,* 10, 221.
b Tanner, *Atlas,* 66.
c Hagan, *Sac and Fox Indians,* 7.
d Tanner, *Atlas,* 141.
e Based on 1830 figure minus 500 deaths during Black Hawk War (Chapter 9).
f *RCIA, 1838,* 492.
g *RCIA, 1849,* 1094.
h *RCIA, 1853,* 342.
i *RCIA, 1857,* 472.
j *RCIA, 1860,* 334 (includes most Sac and Fox of Missouri).

SEMINOLES

Year	Population	Notes
1775	1,500[a]	
1790	2,000[a]	
1825	5,000[b]	
1832	5,000–6,000[c]	
1843	4,000–4,100	3,625 in Oklahoma;[d] 360 in Florida;[e] 150 in Texas[f]

continued

SEMINOLES *continued*

Year	Population	Notes
1860	2,780	2,630 in Oklahoma (not including Black Seminoles);[g] 150 in Florida[h]

a Wood, "Changing Population," 60.
b McKenney, "Statement," insert after 14.
c Wright, *Creeks and Seminoles*, 288.
d Based on 2,833 in March 1842 census in Foreman, *Indian Removal*, 380; 792 removed who reached Oklahoma between June 1842 and July 1843 in Foreman, *Five Civilized Tribes*, 225, 228, 236.
e 360 still in Florida in 1849 in Foreman, *Five Civilized Tribes*, 248.
f Based on the removal of 152 Seminoles in 1834 in Foreman, *Indian Removal*, 323.
g Doran, "Population Statistics," 501.
h Missall and Missall, *Seminole Wars*, 221.

SENECAS IN OHIO (ALSO REFERRED TO AS WESTERN HAUDENOSAUNEES AND MINGOS)

Year	Population	Notes
1768	600[a]	
1822	551[b]	
1830	500[c]	
1831	500[d]	Ohio
1832	470[e]	Oklahoma
1840	286[f]	Oklahoma
1857	300[g]	Oklahoma

a Tanner, *Atlas*, 66.
b Morse, *Report*, 362.
c 300 on Sandusky River and 200 among Lewistown Shawnees in Tanner, *Atlas*, 136.
d 340 Senecas on Sandusky River removed in late 1831 and 160 part of Lewistown Shawnees removed in late 1832 in Foreman, *Last Trek*, 67, 81.
e Based on 30 who died during journey west in Chapter 9.
f 175 in the Seneca community and half of the 222 in the separate "Seneca and Shawnee" community in *RCIA, 1840*, 315.
g 175 in the Seneca community and half of the 250 in the separate "Seneca and Shawnee" community in *RCIA, 1857*, 493.

SHAWNEES

Year	Population	Notes
1670	2,000–4,000[a]	
1768	1,800[b]	
1822	2,183[c]	1,383 west of the Mississippi; 800 east of the Mississippi
1853	1,755	930 in Kansas;[d] 125 on Neosho Reservation in Oklahoma;[e] 700 on Canadian River in Oklahoma[f]

a Lakomäki, *Gathering Together*, 24.
b Tanner, *Atlas*, 66.
c Morse, *Report*, 362, 366.
d *RCIA, 1853*, 271.
e Half of the 250 "Seneca and Shawnees" in *RCIA, 1857*, 493.
f LaVere, *Contrary Neighbors*, 94.

SUSQUEHANNOCKS

Year	Population
1650	5,000[a]
1698	250[a]

a Jennings, "Susquehannock," 362–63.

VIRGINIA (EAST OF THE MOUNTAINS)

Year	Population
1775	400[a]
1790	200[a]
1825	47[b]

a Wood, "Changing Population," 60.
b Morse, *Report*, 364.

WYANDOTS

Year	Population	Notes
1768	1,000[a]	
1822	542[b]	
1830	527[c]	Ohio
1845	550[d]	Kansas
1853	553[e]	Kansas

a Tanner, *Atlas*, 66.
b Morse, *Report*, 362.
c Tanner, *Atlas*, 136.
d *RCIA, 1845*, 560.
e *RCIA, 1853*, 271.

Notes

ABBREVIATIONS

ASPIA   *American State Papers: Indian Affairs,* 2 vols. (Washington, D.C.: Gales and Seaton, 1832)

CSEI   *Correspondence on the Subject of the Emigration of Indians,* 23d Cong., 2d Sess. (1835), S. Doc. 512, 5 vols., serial 244–248

JCC   *Journals of the Continental Congress, 1774–1789,* 34 vols. (Washington, D.C.: G.P.O., 1904–1937)

IALT   Charles J. Kappler, ed., *Indian Affairs: Laws and Treaties,* vol. 2: *Treaties* (Washington, D.C.: G.P.O., 1904)

RCIA   *Report of the Commissioner of Indian Affairs, 1834–1861,* in *United States Congressional Serial Set*

TPUS   *Territorial Papers of the United States,* 28 vols. (Washington, D.C.: G.P.O., 1934–1956; Washington, D.C.: National Archives and Records Service, 1958–1975)

INTRODUCTION

1. Tocqueville, *Democracy in America,* 324.
2. Ibid., 339. Although Tocqueville wrote with feeling about the Choctaws and deplored U.S. treatment of them and other Indians, he generally regarded empire as a necessity for western democracies, a view developed most fully through his writings advocating French colonialism in Algeria. See Jennifer Pitts, Introduction to Tocqueville, *Writings on Empire and Slavery,* xi–xvii.

3. Pierson, *Tocqueville and Beaumont,* 598.
4. I use "zone of removal" instead of "Indian country" or "Indian Territory," designations created under U.S. law beginning in 1834. U.S. officials' ideas about the territory where they might move Indians predate 1834 and did not entirely conform to the legal designations. For the 1834 legislation and its failure to protect Native people from the consequences of western expansion, see Unrau, *Rise and Fall of Indian Country.*
5. Veracini, "Introducing Settler Colonial Studies," 1; My use of the term "means of elimination" builds on the foundational concept of settler colonialism's "logic of elimination" in Wolfe, "Settler Colonialism," 387. See also Veracini, *Settler Colonialism.* For a recent historical overview of American expansion using settler colonialism as its framework, see Hixson, *American Settler Colonialism.* For an important warning against mistaking settler colonialism's logic of elimination for a description of reality, which would erase Indigenous "struggles for sovereignty," see Den Ouden and O'Brien, "Introduction," 8.
6. Deer, *Beginning and End of Rape,* 13.
7. Jennings, *Invasion of America;* White, *Middle Ground,* ix.
8. For examples, see Calloway, *One Vast Winter Count;* DuVal, *Native Ground;* Barr, *Peace Came;* Hämäläinen, *Comanche Empire;* Witgen, *Infinity of Nations;* Reid, *Sea Is My Country.*
9. Vizenor, "Aesthetics of Survivance."
10. Mann, *Dark Side of Democracy.*

CHAPTER 1. TRAJECTORIES

1. Saunders, ed., *Colonial Records of North Carolina,* 10:778. For the meaning of "Virginians," see Ostler, "Indigenous Consciousness," 601–2.
2. Works showing intertribal conflict and intratribal division in war involving colonists are cited throughout the notes. Examples of the autonomy and power of Native nations include Calloway, *One Vast Winter Count;* DuVal, *Native Ground;* Barr, *Peace Came;* Hämäläinen, *Comanche Empire;* Witgen, *Infinity of Nations.* For the "middle ground," see White, *Middle Ground.*
3. For scholarship challenging the virgin soil epidemic thesis proposed by Crosby, "Virgin Soil Epidemics," see Cameron, Kelton, and Swedlund, eds., *Beyond Germs;* Jones, "Population, Health, and Public Welfare."
4. For the de Soto expedition and its impact, see Ethridge, *Chicaza to Chickasaw,* 11–88; Kelton, *Epidemics and Enslavement,* 59–73.
5. For the precontact estimate of 567,000, which includes east Texas but not Virginia, Maryland, or Kentucky, see Thornton, "Demographic History," 52. For the 1685 estimate of 191,000, which includes Virginia, see Wood, "Changing Population," 61–62. Ubelaker, "Population Size," 695, provides a lower estimate of 204,000 for the precontact South; assuming Wood's 1685 estimate is close, Ubelaker's figure has to be too low. For the Timucuas, see Milanich, "Timucua," 219, 225–27; Worth, *Timucuan Chiefdoms,* 8–26. For the Powhatans and coastal Virginian Algonquians, see Turner, "Reexamination," 45–64 (1607 population, 56); Rountree, *Pocahontas's People,* 30–143

("great mortality," "far greater," 64, 1697 population, 104); Gleach, *Powhatan's World*, 123–98; Cave, *Lethal Encounters*, esp. 171, which summarizes factors affecting the decline of Virginia Indians. For the Chesapeake and Potomac, see Rice, *Nature and History*, 130–34.

6. Kelton, *Epidemics and Enslavement*, 101–59 (50 people, 128); Ethridge, *Chicaza to Chickasaw*, 89–115, 149–68; Wood, "Changing Population," 61–62. On the colonial slave trade, see also Gallay, *Indian Slave Trade*; Snyder, *Slavery in Indian Country*. For guns in the trade, see Silverman, *Thundersticks*, 56–91.

7. Kelton, *Epidemics and Enslavement*, 160–220; Ethridge, *Chicaza to Chickasaw*, 232–54; Wood, "Changing Population," 61–62; Worth, "Yamasee," 252; Usner, *Indians, Settlers, and Slaves*, 65–76 ("treat us," 71); Milne, *Natchez Country*, 175–205; Galloway and Jackson, "Natchez and Neighboring Groups," 610; Feest, "Nanticokes and Neighboring Tribes," 246–47.

8. Thwaites, ed., *Jesuit Relations*, 1:177 ("as thickly planted," "diminished," pleurisy, quinsy), 3:105 ("French poison," "corrupts the body"); Upton, *Micmacs and Colonists*, 18–21; Miller, "Aboriginal Micmac Population," 117–27; Miller, "Decline of Nova Scotia Micmac Population," 118 (50,000 estimate); Snow, *Archaeology of New England*, 36 (12,000 estimate). For the Mi'kmaqs and the "common pot," see Brooks, *Common Pot*, 6–7.

9. For the 1616 epidemic, see Thornton, *American Indian Holocaust*, 71; Jones, *Rationalizing Epidemics*, 29; Marr and Cathey, "New Hypothesis," 281–86. For trade networks and alliances, see Salisbury, *Manitou and Providence*, 141–202; Fisher and Silverman, *Ninigret*, 27–30; Trigger, *Natives and Newcomers*, 175–81; Richter, *Ordeal of the Longhouse*, 53–57.

10. Snow and Lanphear, "European Contact," 23–24; Jones, *Rationalizing Epidemics*, 31–32; Richter, *Ordeal of the Longhouse*, 58–59; Trigger, *Natives and Newcomers*, 230–31, 234.

11. Trigger, *Natives and Newcomers*, 259–71; Richter, *Ordeal of the Longhouse*, 33–38, 60–62; Silverman, *Thundersticks*, 35–38. For an account of Huron migrations, which notes tensions and violence with Ottawas, see Sturtevant, "'Inseparable Companions.'"

12. Cave, *Pequot War*, 58–61, 71–72, 75 (qtns.), 99–100, 104–9, 147–51, 158–61. For captive and enslaved Pequots, see Newell, *Brethren by Nature*, 38–53. Oberg, *Uncas*, 72, 139–41, emphasizes Pequot survival and the reestablishment of their nation.

13. Meuwese, *Brothers in Arms*, 241–48; Lipman, *Saltwater Frontier*, 145–53, 158–60; David de Vries narrative in Jameson, ed., *Narratives of New Netherland*, 228.

14. Drinnon, *Facing West*, 102 ("the English"); Drake, *Book of the Indians*, 64 (Miantonomi qtns.). For recent accounts of the origins of the war, see Richter, *Facing East*, 90–103; Brooks, *Our Beloved Kin*, 118–37 ("English threat," 137).

15. Brooks, *Our Beloved Kin*, 227–31 ("a gratuity," 231); Schultz and Tougias, *King Philip's War*, 5 (casualties); Newell, *Brethren by Nature*, 158 (captives and slaves); DeLucia, *Memory Lands*, 49–53 ("great distress," 50), 133, 214–16. See also Drake, *King Philip's War*, which misreads Native–colonial alliances as having created a "covalent society" (p. 17) torn apart by civil war; Lepore, *Name of War*, for national perceptions; DeLucia, *Memory Lands*, for local memories.

16. For colonial populations, see U.S. Bureau of the Census, *Historical Statistics,* 1168. For Indians in Massachusetts see Mandell, *Behind the Frontier,* esp. 48–163. O'Brien, *Dispossession by Degrees,* details the process of dispossession in one Native community and provides information about epidemics in 1745–1746 and 1759 (p. 189). For conflict between Abenakis and English colonists, see Calloway, *Western Abenakis,* 76–159; for Mi'kmaqs and the same, see Faragher, *Great and Noble Scheme,* 157–67. The best estimate of the New England population on the eve of King Philip's War is in Fisher and Silverman, *Ninigret,* 108, 170, n. 56. For the 1770s New England population, see Appendix 2.

17. Richter, *Ordeal of the Longhouse,* esp. 145, 162–88, 264–67; Shannon, *Iroquois Diplomacy,* 47–77. For population figures, see Appendix 2.

18. Thwaites, ed., *Jesuit Relations,* 59:145 (Marquette qtns.). For an influential statement of an Iroquois "shatter zone," see White, *Middle Ground,* 1–14. For a new interpretation of Ohio Valley Indian movements, see Sleeper-Smith, *Indigenous Prosperity,* 69–81. For Shawnee migrations, see Warren, *Worlds the Shawnees Made,* 90–92, 113–14, 131–32; Lakomäki, *Gathering Together,* 13 ("greatest Travellers"), 26–29. Warren, *Worlds the Shawnees Made,* 61, states that the Shawnees probably suffered a major population collapse in the early seventeenth century from epidemic disease, but this observation relies on the questionable assumption of the validity of the virgin soil epidemic theory. For the Grand Village of Kaskaskia, see Morrissey, *Empire by Collaboration,* 40. For Delaware migrations, see Schutt, *Peoples of the River Valleys,* 7–81; for population, see Goddard, "Delaware," 214; for perceptions of disease, see Weslager, *Delaware Indians,* 152 ("wanted to get rid"). Population figures for Shawnees and Delawares are in Appendix 2.

19. Warren, *Worlds the Shawnees Made,* 98–99, 104–5, 168–78; Lakomäki, *Gathering Together,* 27–30, 42–48, 56–57; Hinderaker, *Elusive Empires,* 25–28, 105–8, 119–28 ("can go," 127); Merrell, *Into the American Woods,* 292 ("Fraud"). For the Susquehannock population, see Appendix 2.

20. For Ohio Valley Indians' relative freedom from epidemic disease, see Sleeper-Smith, *Indigenous Prosperity,* 47. For the Shawnees' play-off strategy, see Hinderaker, *Elusive Empires,* 29–30. For a Shawnee strategy of dispersal and alliance building, see Spero, "'Stout, Bold, Cunning.'" For the lack of epidemics during this period for Shawnees, Potawatomis, and Kickapoos, see Tanner, ed., *Atlas,* 169–74. For the 1714 epidemic at Ouiatenon, see [Claude de] Ramezay to the French Minister, Nov. 3, 1715, in Thwaites, ed., *Collections of the State Historical Society of Wisconsin,* 16:322–23. For the 1732 illness, see Peyser, "It Was Not Smallpox," 159–69 (qtn., 159). For Shawnee and Miami populations, see Appendix 2.

21. Blasingham, "Depopulation of the Illinois Indians," 361–412; Morrissey, *Empire by Collaboration,* 17–23, 29–35, 79, 88–91, 111. For smallpox among the Quapaws, see Young and Hoffman, "Quapaw," 499; in Louisiana, see Usner, *Indians, Settlers, and Slaves* 22. For the Illinois population, see Appendix 2.

22. Skinner, *Upper Country,* 137, provides a French estimate from 1736 that the combined number of warriors in these nations was 1,400. Using a ratio of one warrior for every six people would mean a population of 8,400, but this is far too low, and Skinner's

sense that this figure represented a decline of 80–85 percent since contact appears to be based only on accounts of sporadic disease and war. There is some evidence that the Ho-Chunks endured a significant population loss sometime after 1634, though their population was evidently growing in the early 1700s. See Beider, *Native American Communities*, 55–58. It is noteworthy that a recent history of the Ojibwes, Witgen, *Infinity of Nations*, says very little about disease. Similarly, McDonnell, *Masters of Empire*, notes the devastating impact of smallpox in the Northeast in the 1630s and suggests that it may have spread to the Ottawas, but if so, its impact was blunted because Ottawa villages were less densely populated and more dispersed. But for the likelihood of two smallpox epidemics hitting the Menominees in the late 1600s, see Beck, *Siege and Survival*, 32.

23. Edmunds and Peyser, *Fox Wars*, 156 (1730 casualties), 221 (1732 population); Rush-forth, *Bonds of Alliance*, 199–220; Morrissey, *Empire by Collaboration*, 113 ("devils," "nothing human"). For population figures, see Appendix 2.

24. George Croghan to Governor [James] Hamilton, May 14, 1754, *Pennsylvania Archives* 2 (1853): 144 ("imagine"); Post, "Two Journals," 216 ("French and English"). The most comprehensive history of the Seven Years' War is Anderson, *Crucible of War*. For the coming of the war to the Ohio Valley, see McConnell, *Country Between*, 5–112. Mc-Donnell, *Masters of Empire*, 124–67, considers the coming of the war, which he terms the First Anglo-Indian War, from the perspective of the Ottawas of Michilimackinac.

25. Preston, *Braddock's Defeat*, 116 (qtn.), 149–50 (Indians allied with the French), 277 (death toll). For Indian raids, see Ward, *Breaking the Backcountry*, 60–70.

26. On scalp bounties in Pennsylvania and Virginia, see Barr, "'This Land Is Ours and Not Yours,'" 36. For Kittanning, see Armstrong, "Col. John Armstrong's Account." For negotiations, see Hinderaker, *Elusive Empires*, 142–44.

27. The most recent study of the Anglo-Cherokee War is Tortora, *Carolina in Crisis* ("Chain of Friendship," 19). On rape, see Adair, *History of the American Indians*, 246 ("forcibly violated," "and in the most").

28. Grant, "Successful Expedition," 306–7 (Cherokee casualties); Hatley, *Dividing Paths*, 133 ("stuffed earth"); Dowd, *Groundless*, 132 ("daily committed"); Kelton, *Cherokee Medicine*, 124–34 ("to put every soul," 132; "old-acorns," "will barely," 133); Grant, "Journal of Lieutenant-Colonel James Grant," 25–36 ("about 5,000," 35). For popula-tion decline, see Appendix 2.

29. Duffy, *Epidemics*, 94–95 (smallpox in Charleston); Merrell, *Indians' New World*, 192–95 (Catawba smallpox); Dowd, *Groundless*, 48–57 ("viral retribution," 49; "infested," 54); Anderson, *Crucible of War*, 199 ("seeds"); Bougainville, *Adventure in the Wilderness*, 204 ("great unrest," "the great loss"); "Examination of Cornelius Vanslyke," July 21, 1767 ("great number they lost," "English poisoning"); Pouchot, *Memoir upon the Late War*, 1:92 ("almost entirely"); Blackbird, *History*, 10 ("Lodge after lodge"). For Ca-tawba and Menominee population losses, see Appendix 2.

30. White, *Middle Ground*, 256.

31. Dowd, *War under Heaven*, 54–89; Croghan, "George Croghan's Journal, April 3, 1759 to April [30], 1763," 429 ("Much displast," "Sett So Little"); Thomas Hutchins in Hanna, *Wilderness Trail*, 2:367 ("to kill game"); George Croghan to Sir William

Johnson, Dec. 10, 1762, Johnson to Lords of Trade, Aug. 20, 1762, in Johnson, *Papers,* 3:964 ("stopping ye Sale," "we intend"), 3:866 ("not only," "we should hem").

32. Cave, *Prophets of the Great Spirit,* 14–41 ("wipe them," 15); Dowd, *War under Heaven,* 90–131 ("As to those," 104).

33. For the seizures of forts and sieges, see Nester, *"Haughty Conquerors,"* 73–106. For Indian attacks on settlements, see Merritt, *At the Crossroads,* 272–80; Ward, *Breaking the Backcountry,* 225–26.

34. Fenn, "Biological Warfare," 1552–80 ("Could it not," 1555; "try to inocculate," "try Every," 1556); Heckewelder, *Narrative of the Mission,* 68 ("the doctrine").

35. Fenn, "Biological Warfare," 1554–57 ("gave them," "have the desired," 1554); Thomas Gage to Henry Bouquet, Sept. 2, 1764, Michigan Pioneer and Historical Society, *Historical Collections,* 19:272. For the Bouquet and Bradstreet expeditions, see Anderson, *Crucible of War,* 618–25; Nester, *"Haughty Conquerors,"* 201–21.

36. For the events from Conestoga Town to Philadelphia, see Kenny, *Peaceable Kingdom,* 130–43, 149–55, 162; Spero, *Frontier Country,* 152–58. For the attempt to locate the Moravians in New York, see Kenny, *Peaceable Kingdom,* 148 ("a number"); for deaths in the barracks, see Heckewelder, *Narrative of the Mission,* 88; for the return to Friedenshütten, see Wheeler and Hahn-Bruckart, "On an Eighteenth-Century Trail of Tears," 44–88 ("extreme weather," "several," 45). For Penn and the Contestogas, see Merrell, *Into the American Woods,* 122 ("live in true Friendship").

37. Kiernan, *Blood and Soil,* 245 ("clearly explained"); Pennsylvania House of Representatives, *Votes and Proceedings,* 314 ("Who ever"); Weld, ed., *Benjamin Franklin,* 324 ("barbarous Men"); "The Apology of the Paxton Volunteers," in Dunbar, ed., *Paxton Papers,* 195 ("were in Confederacy," "justly exposed"). Silver, *Our Savage Neighbors,* 163–68, discusses Hamilton's authorization of scalp bounties; for authorization of bounties in 1764, see Young, "Note on Scalp Bounties," 212.

38. Richter, *Facing East,* 190 ("parallel campaigns"). For Native ideas about race, see Richter, *Facing East,* 181–82; Shoemaker, "How Indians Got to Be Red," 625–44; Silverman, *Red Brethren,* 39–41, 64–65. For racial views of Pennsylvania frontiersmen in the early 1760s, see Merritt, *At the Crossroads,* 291–92; Spero, *Frontier Country,* 159–60.

39. Killbuck in Johnson, *Papers,* 11:618; McConnell, *Country Between,* 195 ("were immediately").

40. William Johnson to General Thomas Gage, Feb. 19, 1764, in Johnson, *Papers,* 4:332 ("A Free fair," "That we will"); Croghan, "Croghan's Journal, May 15—September 26, 1765," 1:157 ("smoked out," "he may know"). For the Proclamation of 1763 and its impact, see Calloway, *Scratch of a Pen,* 92–98. For the Fort Niagara negotiations, see McConnell, *Country Between,* 198–99; McDonnell, *Masters of Empire,* 232–36; Anderson, *Crucible of War,* 620. For the 1765 negotiations, see Dowd, *War under Heaven,* 213–17, 229–31.

41. Dowd, *War under Heaven,* 216 (qtns.).

42. George Washington to William Crawford, Sept. 21, 1767, in Butterfield, ed., *Washington—Crawford Letters,* 3. See also Calloway, *Indian World of George Washington,* 181–88.

CHAPTER 2. WARS OF REVOLUTION AND INDEPENDENCE

1. Strang, "Michael Cresap," 106–35 ("tomahawk right," 110); [Croghan], "Extracts of an Abstract from Mr. Croghan's Journal," May 22, 1766, 322 ("as soon," "promote," "several of their People," "Murdered on the Frontiers"); Thomas Gage to Lord Shelburne, Aug. 24, 1767, Alvord, ed., *Collections of the Illinois State Historical Library*, 11:595 ("destroy[ed]"); George Croghan to Sir William Johnson, Oct. 18, 1767, Alvord, ed., *Collections of the Illinois State Historical Library*, 16:88. For the Stump/Ironcutter murders and reaction, see Preston, *Texture of Contact*, 238, 256–57; Downes, *Council Fires*, 138–40.

2. Davis, *Where There Are Mountains*, 95 ("a great deal"); Hatley, *Dividing Paths*, 184–85 ("no man," 185); Kelton, *Cherokee Medicine*, 146 ("We are tired"); Perdue, "Cherokee Relations with the Iroquois," 145; Saunt, *New Order*, 48 ("People Cattle," "supply their Women"); Lord Egremont to Governor [Arthur] Dobbs, Mar. 16, 1763, Saunders, ed., *Colonial Records of North Carolina*, 6:974–76 ("the English," "inculcated," 974).

3. Taylor, *Divided Ground*, 40–42, 47–48; Hinderaker, *Elusive Empires*, 166.

4. Jones, *License for Empire*, 88–92; Shannon, *Iroquois Diplomacy*, 167–68; Calloway, *Pen and Ink Witchcraft*, 65–80; Campbell, *Speculators in Empire*, 139–66; Taylor, *Divided Ground*, 42–44 ("massive and unprecedented," 44); Hinderaker, *Elusive Empires*, 169 ("unite and attack").

5. Hillsborough to Sir William Johnson, Jan. 4, 1769, O'Callaghan, ed., *Documents Relative to the Colonial History of the State of New York*, 8:144–45 (qtns., 145); McConnell, *Country Between*, 253; De Vorsey, Jr., *The Indian Boundary*. For Virginia speculators, see Holton, *Forced Founders*, 9–13, 26–28.

6. Thomas Gage to Earl of Hillsborough, Nov. 12, 1770, Gage to Hillsborough, Oct. 7, 1772, Davies, ed., *Documents*, 2:253; 5:203 (qtns.). For the confederacy, see Dowd, *Spirited Resistance*, 42–43. For Boone, see Faragher, *Daniel Boone*, 76–77.

7. Weslager, *Delaware Indians*, 253–54; McConnell, *Country Between*, 265–68; Dowd, *Spirited Resistance*, 43–44; Hatley, *Dividing Paths*, 155–62, 206.

8. Faragher, *Daniel Boone*, 92–95; Strang, "Michael Cresap," 126 (qtn.); Griffin, *American Leviathan*, 109–11.

9. Hinderaker, *Elusive Empires*, 170–72; McConnell, *Country Between*, 268–70; Griffin, *American Leviathan*, 104–8; Holton, *Forced Founders*, 33–34. On Cresap's commission, see Jacob, *Biographical Sketch*, 68.

10. Dunmore to [John Connolly], June 20, 1774, *Pennsylvania Archives* 4 (1853): 522–23 ("make as many," "reduce the Savages," 523); *Maryland Journal*, Sept. 7, 1774, in Thwaites and Kellogg, eds., *Documentary History*, 155 ("several"); Griffin, *American Leviathan*, 116–20; Calloway, *Shawnees*, 53–57 ("kill all our women," 56).

11. Sosin, *Whitehall*, 245; Griffin, *America's Revolution*, 113–14; Rana, *Two Faces*, 73–79; Holton, *Forced Founders*, 32–33, 35–36 ("worst grievance," 36).

12. Holton, *Forced Founders*, 36–38, makes a persuasive case for speculators as leaders of Virginia's move toward independence, though for John Connolly, a Loyalist speculator, see MacGregor, "Ordeal of John Connolly." For Pennsylvania speculators, see Oaks, "Impact of British Western Policy." My understanding of frontiersmen's views on

independence is informed by Faragher, *Daniel Boone,* 141–43; Hinderaker, *Elusive Empires,* 212–14. The clearest link between western issues and the coming of the Revolution is the empire's need to fund a western standing army to enforce the Proclamation of 1763, which led to the colonial taxation crisis. See Gould, *Among the Powers,* 100–108.

13. *JCC,* 5:511 ("injuries and usurpations"), 513 ("endeavoured to bring"). For Jefferson's language providing a "rationale for extermination," see Drinnon, *Facing West,* 97–98. For violence against Indians as foundational to American nationalism, see Smith-Rosenberg, *This Violent Empire;* Parkinson, *Common Cause.*

14. "Stuart's Account," in Saunders, ed., *Colonial Records of North Carolina,* 10:764.

15. Kelton, "Remembering Cherokee Mortality," 207–8 ("very uneasie"); Calloway, *American Revolution,* 26 ("were alarmed"); Calloway, *Western Abenakis,* 205 ("expressed much concern," "strange," "*Englishmen* kill").

16. Calloway, *American Revolution,* 194–97; Kelton, *Cherokee Medicine,* 155; Grenier, *First Way,* 151–52.

17. Thomas Jefferson to Edmund Pendelton, Aug. 13, 1776, in Boyd et al., eds., *Papers of Thomas Jefferson,* 1:491–94 ("beyond the Missisipi"); Calloway, *American Revolution,* 197–98; Grenier, *First Way,* 152–53; O'Donnell, *Southern Indians,* 43–48; Hatley, *Dividing Paths,* 194–97; Kelton, *Cherokee Medicine,* 156–59; Rockwell, ed., "Parallel and Combined Expeditions," 213 ("marched," "rushed in," "contrary"); Swain, "Historical Sketch." On the three prisoners sold, see "Rutherford's Expedition," 93.

18. Calloway, *American Revolution,* 198–99; Boulware, *Deconstructing,* 159–60; John Stuart to Lord George Germain, Nov. 24, 1776, in Davies, ed., *Documents,* 12:253–54 ("fled with their wives"); Thornton, *Cherokees,* 38; Mooney, "Myths of the Cherokee," 53 ("More than").

19. Hatley, *Dividing Paths,* 219–27 ("surrounded," 223; "Real People," 222; "Virginians," 225; "dyed their hands," 226); Calloway, *American Revolution,* 198–209 ("There was no withstanding," 204; "we are now," 209); Dowd, *Spirited Resistance,* 54–56; Grenier, *First Way,* 159–60; O'Donnell, *Southern Indians,* 108 (29 killed); Boulware, *Deconstructing,* 161–64; Kelton, *Cherokee Medicine,* 164 ("they were willing," "if only one," "shun the smallpox").

20. Braund, *Deerskins and Duffels,* 167–68; Piker, *Okfuskee,* 70; Corkran, *Creek Frontier,* 288–325; DuVal, *Independence Lost,* 78–90, 165–66.

21. O'Brien, *Choctaws,* 51; O'Donnell, *Southern Indians,* 197, 221–31; White, *Roots of Dependency,* 86; DuVal, *Independence Lost,* 92–95, 160–65, 182–85.

22. Hinderaker, *Elusive Empires,* 209–10; Hurt, *Ohio Frontier,* 65; Patrick Henry to George Morgan, Mar. 12, 1777, in Henry, ed., *Patrick Henry,* 46 (qtn.).

23. Downes, *Council Fires,* 202–3; Calloway, *American Revolution,* 39, 167–69 (qtn., 167); Griffin, *American Leviathan,* 127–28, 152–53; Hurt, *Ohio Frontier,* 76; Dowd, *Spirited Resistance,* 75–76.

24. Faragher, *Daniel Boone,* 154–66, 174–75, 182–99, 209.

25. Hurt, *Ohio Frontier,* 68–69; Dowd, *Spirited Resistance,* 77.

26. *IALT,* 3–5 ("it is the design," "enemies," 4; "engage to join," 3); Kellogg, ed., *Frontier Advance,* 138–45; Weslager, *Delaware Indians,* 303–6; Downes, *Council Fires,* 216–17 ("wrote down," 217; "so improperly," 216).

27. Downes, *Council Fires*, 217–21 (qtns., 220); Weslager, *Delaware Indians*, 306–7; Hurt, *Ohio Country*, 79–81; Dowd, *Spirited Resistance*, 77–78.

28. Grenier, *First Way*, 155–56; Griffin, *American Leviathan*, 141–43 ("citizens," 143); McDonnell, *Masters of Empire*, 289–90; William Nester, *George Rogers Clark*, 69–88, 95–96, 327 ("see the whole"); White, *Middle Ground*, 368–70 ("French mode," 370); George Rogers Clark to the Inhabitants of Vincennes, July 13, 1778, Clark to George Mason, Nov. 19, 1779, James, ed., *George Rogers Clark Papers*, 50–53, 114–28 ("had instructions," 127–28).

29. Grenier, *First Way*, 156–57; Griffin, *American Leviathan*, 143–45 ("hung the scalps," 145); White, *Middle Ground*, 375–77; Dowd, *Spirited Resistance*, 57–58; Nester, *George Rogers Clark*, 106–11, 118–50, 158–59; Sheehan, "'Famous Hair Buyer General,'" 20; Clark to Mason, Nov. 19, 1779, in James, ed, *George Rogers Clark Papers*, 148–49 ("the Warriers," "one for Peace," "has your great," 148; "next thing," "Your Women," 149).

30. Dowd, *Spirited Resistance*, 58; Calloway, *American Revolution*, 41; Nester, *George Rogers Clark*, 167–70 (qtn., 167).

31. Dowd, *Spirited Resistance*, 59.

32. Thomas Jefferson to George Rogers Clark, Jan. 1, 1780, in Boyd et al., eds., *Papers of Thomas Jefferson*, 4:258–59 ("against those tribes," 258; "should be," 259); Nester, *George Rogers Clark*, 177–78, 190–97 ("bashed in," 197); West, "Clark's 1780 Shawnee Expedition," 190–91 (casualties); Lakomäki, *Gathering Together*, 112–13 ("Our Women," "are left," 113).

33. Calloway, *American Revolution*, 38; Dowd, *Spirited Resistance*, 80–83; Weslager, *Delaware Indians*, 312–15; Hurt, *Ohio Country*, 85–86; Butterfield, "Expedition against the Delawares," 376–80 (qtns., 379–80).

34. Griffin, *American Leviathan*, 159–60, 165–67.

35. Merritt, *At the Crossroads*, 93–96; Loskiel, *History of the Mission*, pt. 3, 113, 160–61; Heckewelder, *Narrative of the Mission*, 215–20, 232–49 ("many cruel Acts," "murdering" "who were placed," 217; "they had found," 219–20); Bliss, ed., *Diary of David Zeisberger*, 1:4–6 ("two powerful," "jaws toward," "you are in danger," 1:4; "at once," "they would rather," 1:6). Heckewelder, *Narrative of the Mission*, 240, identifies Pomoacan's two spirits.

36. Heckewelder, *Narrative of the Mission*, 313–19 (qtns., 314); Sadosky, "Rethinking the Gnadenhutten Massacre," 199; Silver, *Our Savage Neighbors*, 268–70, 272; Mann, *George Washington's War*, 157–59; Mann, *Dark Side of Democracy*. For an argument that the militia did not intend to kill the Moravian Indians at the outset but that a minority bullied the majority into indiscriminate slaughter, see Harper, "Looking the Other Way," 630–36.

37. Heckewelder, *Narrative of the Mission*, 320–24; Loskiel, *History of the Mission*, pt. 3, 179–81 ("prepare themselves," 179; "slaughter-houses," 180; "penetrated," 181); Sadosky, "Rethinking the Gnadenhutten Massacre," 199–200; Mann, *George Washington's War*, 160–63.

38. Mann, *George Washington's War*, 165; Calloway, *American Revolution*, 39; Dowd, *Spirited Resistance*, 88 ("extermenate"); Downes, *Council Fires*, 273–74; Heckewelder, *Narrative of the Mission*, 338–42 ("Williamson," 338; "do the same," "the believing," 339; "*No quarters*," 342; "are all alike!," 339).

39. Violence continued in the Ohio Valley into 1783, as Shawnees killed seventy-seven militiamen at Blue Licks in Kentucky and Clark responded with an operation against the Shawnees in which he burned six towns and killed ten. After the British peace agreement with the Americans, however, conflict subsided. See Nester, *George Rogers Clark*, 238–39, 244–46, 249–51; Faragher, *Daniel Boone*, 217–24; Griffin, *American Leviathan*, 178–79.

40. For number of Six Nations warriors, see Fenton, *Great Law*, 579. For peaceful coexistence between Haudenosaunees and settlers, see Preston, *Texture of Contact*, 178–215.

41. Shannon, *Iroquois Diplomacy*, 178–80; *JCC*, 2:182 ("family quarrel," "You Indians"); Graymont, *Iroquois in the American Revolution*, 98 ("intention"). For more on U.S.-Haudenosaunee diplomacy, see Sadosky, *Revolutionary Negotiations*, 85–86.

42. Graymont, *Iroquois in the American Revolution*, 58 ("We are unwilling"), 108–11; Taylor, *Divided Ground*, 86–91; Calloway, *American Revolution*, 122–23; Shannon, *Iroquois Diplomacy*, 188.

43. Graymont, *Iroquois in the American Revolution*, 117–39, 142–43, 146–47; Glatthaar and Martin, *Forgotten Allies*, 168–69; Shannon, *Iroquois Diplomacy*, 189; Tiro, "A 'Civil' War," 150–53 (qtn., 152).

44. Graymont, *Iroquois in the American Revolution*, 158–72; Mancall, *Valley of Opportunity*, 136–37; Taylor, *Divided Ground*, 93; Grenier, *First Way*, 162–66; Dowd, *Groundless*, 175–77.

45. Calloway, *American Revolution*, 124–25 ("Principal Place," 124); "Governor Clinton's Orders to Colonel Cantine," Sept. 6, 1778, Clinton, *Public Papers*, 3:742; Taylor, *William Cooper's Town*, 61 ("several small children," "what cruel deaths").

46. Graymont, *Iroquois in the American Revolution*, 184–89; Mancall, *Valley of Opportunity*, 137–38. For Washington's support of the invasion of Iroquoia after Cherry Creek, see George Washington to Horatio Gates, Mar. 6, 1779, in Sparks, ed., *Writings of George Washington*, 6:187.

47. Mintz, *Seeds of Empire*, 76, 89; Graymont, *Iroquois in the American Revolution*, 194; Shannon, *Iroquois Diplomacy*, 192; George Washington to Major General Sullivan, May 31, 1779, Lengel, ed., *Papers of George Washington*, 20:716–19 ("The total destruction," 716–18); Calloway, *American Revolution*, 132–33 ("extirpate us").

48. Graymont, *Iroquois in the American Revolution*, 196 ("violate the chastity," "the savages"); Calloway, *American Revolution*, 53 ("put to death"). Mann, *George Washington's War*, 31–32, refers to "brutal gang rapes."

49. Graymont, *Iroquois in the American Revolution*, 206 (troop strength); Norris, "Journal," 225–26 ("bones scattered," "Patriotic Toasts," 225; "Civilization or death," 226); Halsey, *Old New York Frontier*, 279 ("determination," "it is their intention"). Population figures from Appendix 2.

50. Graymont, *Iroquois in the American Revolution*, 212–18; Lee, *Barbarians and Brothers*, 213, 220; Mann, *George Washington's War*, 94; Hubley, "Journal," 157–58 ("We lost"); Calloway, *American Revolution*, 139 ("several hundred"), 156; Barr, *Unconquered*, 162 ("scores," "abject poverty"). For debates about strategy, in which Haudenosaunee women fully participated, see Pearsall, "Recentering Indian Women," 63.

51. Graymont, *Iroquois in the American Revolution*, 223–40, 245–51; Taylor, *Divided Ground*, 101, 106 ("between two Hells"); Tiro, *People of the Standing Stone*, 56–57;

Glatthaar and Martin, *Forgotten Allies,* 270; Speech of Cornplanter, Half-Town and Great-Tree, Dec. 1, 1790, *ASPIA,* 1:140 ("town destroyer," "to this day"). Fenton, *Great Law,* 117, notes that Indians first called Washington "Town Destroyer" during the Seven Years' War.

52. Parker, ed., *Code of Handsome Lake,* 45.

53. Silverman, *Red Brethren,* 108 (qtn.). On false face masks, see Calloway, *American Revolution,* 53.

54. Fenn, *Pox Americana,* 73, 108, 114–15, 266–67; Taylor, *Divided Ground,* 101; Calloway, *American Revolution,* 58, 139. Kelton, *Cherokee Medicine,* 137–45, 161–65, argues that rumors of a serious outbreak of smallpox among the Cherokees in 1780 lack support in the documentary record.

55. Shannon, *Iroquois Diplomacy,* 193, cites Taylor, *Divided Ground,* 108, for a decline in the New York Haudenosaunee population from 9,000 to 6,000, who in turn cites Graymont, *Iroquois in the American Revolution,* 259–91, but Graymont does not offer such figures. My estimate of 1,500 to 2,000 Haudenosaunees migrating to Canada directly after the Clinton-Sullivan invasion is based on the 1,720 reported in Canada in 1791 in U.S. Bureau of Education, *Are the Indians Dying Out?,* 509. For the Cherokees, see Wood, "Changing Population," 60.

56. Calloway, *American Revolution,* 85–103 ("till these troubles," 92; "inflicted," 103); Silverman, *Red Brethren,* 118–20; O'Brien, *Dispossession by Degrees,* 199; Mandell, *Behind the Frontier,* 167 ("either died"); Fisher, *Indian Great Awakening,* 179.

57. Merrell, *Indians' New World,* 215–21.

58. For Gnadenhütten as genocidal, see Griffin, *American Leviathan,* 167; Dowd, *Spirited Resistance,* 86; Mann, *George Washington's War,* 151; Knouff, *Soldiers' Revolution,* 185; Nash, *Unknown American Revolution,* 377–78; Hixson, *American Settler Colonialism,* 60; Taylor, *American Revolutions,* 262. Studies of the massacre—Harper, "Looking the Other Way," 622; and Sadosky, "Rethinking the Gnadenhutten Massacre," 188—do not address the question of genocide. Their criticism of historians who have seen the massacre as a straightforward manifestation of an attitude of "Indian hating" on the frontier may seem to undercut characterizing the massacre as genocidal, although their identification of a variety of political and social factors that led to violence could be read as specifying the route to genocide.

59. Along similar lines, Harper, *Unsettling the West,* 122, emphasizes that the Williamson militia was sponsored by the state of Pennsylvania and that its actions were modeled on campaigns undertaken by the Continental Army.

60. William Irvine to Benjamin Lincoln, Apr. 16, 1783, in Butterfield, ed., *Washington–Irvine Correspondence,* 187 ("nothing short"); Parkinson, *Common Cause,* 537–53, 546–48; Spero, *Frontier Country,* 239–40; Dowd, *Groundless,* 196–98 (Franklin qtns., 198).

CHAPTER 3. JUST AND LAWFUL WARS

1. Drake, *Biography and History,* 108 ("the late contest," "like a raging whirlwind"); Mt. Pleasant, "After the Whirlwind."

2. Mancall, *Valley of Opportunity,* 147 ("white man"); Taylor, *Divided Ground,* 122–28 ("genteel mansion," 127; "better and more," 126).

3. Mt. Pleasant, "After the Whirlwind," 23, 30–31, 39 (qtns.), 45–48, 54–59; Taylor, *Divided Ground,* 120.

4. Tiro, *People of the Standing Stone,* 66–69; Silverman, *Red Brethren,* 121–22; Taylor, *Divided Ground,* 134.

5. Hatley, *Dividing Paths,* 231–36 ("self-isolation," 233; "fools ignorant," 236); Mooney, "Myths of the Cherokee," 209 ("were exceedingly," "little boy"); Everett, *Texas Cherokees,* 10 ("in the territory"); Thornton, *Cherokees,* 44.

6. Bliss, ed., *Diary of David Zeisberger,* 1:86 (qtn.); Bowes, "Gnadenhutten Effect," 101, 104–7; Sabathy-Judd, ed., *Moravians in Upper Canada,* xxi; Schutt, *Peoples of the River Valleys,* 173, 176–77; Tanner, ed., *Atlas,* 83–86.

7. Braund, *Deerskins and Duffels,* 170–74; Saunt, *New Order,* 67–79; Calloway, *American Revolution,* 232–37; DuVal, *Independence Lost,* 246–62, 295–98; White, *Roots of Dependency,* 89–90; O'Brien, *Choctaws,* 85.

8. George Washington to Jacob Reed, Nov. 3, 1784, Ford, ed., *Writings of George Washington,* 10:415–21 ("rage for speculating," 416–17; "scarce a valuable," 417); Alden, *George Washington,* 93 ("most successful"). Population figures are from Slaughter, *Whiskey Rebellion,* 65; Rohrbough, *Trans-Appalachian Frontier,* 25; Friis, "Series of Population Maps."

9. Jefferson used the phrase "empire of liberty" in a letter to George Rogers Clark, Dec. 25, 1780, Boyd et al., eds., *Papers of Thomas Jefferson,* 4:237; and the phrase "empire for liberty" in a letter to James Madison, Apr. 27, 1809, Looney, ed., *Papers of Thomas Jefferson,* 1:169. For a concise statement of Jefferson's views on European vs. American conditions, see his letter to James Madison, Oct. 28, 1785, Boyd et al., eds., *Papers of Thomas Jefferson,* 8:681–83. For Jefferson's ideas about "republican empire," see Onuf, *Jefferson's Empire,* 53–79. For the idea that an "infinite supply of land . . . meant an infinite supply of virtue," see Pocock, *Machiavellian Moment,* 535. For the West as a "safety valve" for class conflict, see Smith, *Virgin Land,* 234–45. For race and whiteness, see Roediger, *Wages of Whiteness.* Most literature on racialization of Indians emphasizes formal theories holding that although Indians were at a primitive stage of development they were capable of advancement to higher stages. See Berkhofer, *White Man's Indian,* 38–49; Wallace, *Jefferson and the Indians,* 95–96; Griffin, *American Leviathan,* 29–31, 254–55. Despite formal theories, however, I am impressed by the extent to which public officials in their actual dealings with Indians regarded them for all intents and purposes as inherently inferior.

10. George Rogers Clark to Benjamin Harrison, May 22, 1783, James, ed., *George Rogers Clark Papers,* 236–38 ("that we," "present moment," "Reduce them"); George Washington to President of Congress, June 17, 1783, Ford, ed., *Writings of George Washington,* 10:269 ("appearance," "enable us"). For policy during this period, I have relied especially on Horsman, *Expansion and American Indian Policy.*

11. Benjamin Harrison to George Rogers Clark, July 2, 1783, James, ed., *George Rogers Clark Papers,* 245–46 ("distress'd situation," 245); George Washington to James Duane,

Sept. 7, 1783, Ford, ed., *Writings of George Washington*, 10:303–12 ("be compelled," 305; "policy and oeconomy," 311).

12. *JCC*, 25:681–95 (qtns., 686).

13. Taylor, *Divided Ground*, 151–65 (Lee qtns., 159; land sale figures, 165); Cornplanter, Half-Town, and Great-Tree to the Great Councillor of the Thirteen Fires, Dec. 9, 1790, *ASPIA*, 1:206–8 ("you could crush," "they therefore," 206). See also Shannon, *Iroquois Diplomacy*, 193–96; Nichols, *Red Gentlemen*, 27–31; Sadosky, *Revolutionary Negotiations*, 130–38.

14. Horsman, *Expansion and American Indian Policy*, 20 ("we claim"); Calloway, *Shawnees*, 78–79 ("take up," 79). The border established by the Treaty of Fort McIntosh was roughly the same as the one under the 1795 Greenville Treaty, shown in Fig. 10.

15. Lakomäki, *Gathering Together*, 118–19 ("go on," "enter into," 118); "General Butler's Journal," in Craig, ed., *The Olden Time*, 2:517–31 ("acknowledge the United States," "when we say," "God gave us," 522; "obstinate nation," 523–24; "destruction," "dashed it," "take pity," 524); Calloway, *Shawnees*, 5, 79–83.

16. Downes, "Creek–American Relations," 143–46, 151–52, 157; Horsman, *Expansion and American Indian Policy*, 28 ("confiscated"); McLoughlin, *Cherokee Renascence*, 21–22; Cotterill, *Southern Indians*, 66–70; Royce, *Cherokee Nation*, 5–6, 25–30; O'Brien, *Choctaws*, 50–69 ("You see," 61).

17. "Transactions with Indians at Sandusky," Michigan Pioneer and Historical Society, *Historical Collections*, 20:174–83 ("our Interests," 179; "ever be done," 180; "encroaching," 182); White, *Middle Ground*, 413; Lakomäki, *Gathering Together*, 116–17; Downes, *Council Fires*, 282–84 ("to defend," 283).

18. Dowd, *Spirited Resistance*, 93–95 ("make everything," 93–94); Downes, *Council Fires*, 299 ("solemnly renewed"), 300 ("before Christian Nations," "we were," "not Still," "that Unanimity"); White, *Middle Ground*, 421, 441–43; Kelsay, *Joseph Brant*, 402–4; *ASPIA*, 1:8–9 ("a lasting reconciliation," "a set of people," "partial treaties," "void," "cession of our lands," 8; "having managed," "peace and tranquility," "to order," "obliged to defend," 9).

19. Heckewelder, *Narrative of the Mission*, 379–84 ("highly offensive," "spake to us," 379; "they did kill," 381; "Our forefathers," "They gave," "satisfised," "must have," 384; "they have extirpated," 383).

20. *JCC*, 32:334–43 ("equal footing," 339; "The utmost," 340–41). For a celebratory assessment of the Northwest Ordinance, see Bailyn, "Central Themes," 20. For the drafting of the ordinance and its relationship to the land ordinances of 1784 and 1785, see Onuf, *Statehood and Union*, 44–59.

21. "Report of Secretary at War on Indian Affairs," July 21, 1787, "Report of Committee on Indian Affairs," Aug. 9, 1787, *JCC*, 33:385–91, 477–81 ("general treaty," 391; "appear that," "United States may," "fix a stain," "small sum," "may cost," 389; "the finances," 388; "language of superiority," "treat with the Indians," 479; "convince them," 479–80).

22. For arguments for a substantial policy shift, see Prucha, *Great Father*, 1:49; Banner, *How the Indians Lost Their Land*, 130–35 ("the Indian right," "official recognition,"

132; "right to refuse," 135). More accurately, Horsman, *Expansion and American Indian Policy,* 42, characterizes the shift from a policy of "overt dictation" as a superficial one requiring the U.S. to "go through the motions of formal purchase of Indian rights." Horsman (p. 94) also points out that the Senate rejected the Putnam treaty because it "proved too much for the government to swallow." For Knox on the conditions for war, see "Report of Secretary at War on Indian Hostilities," July 10, 1787, *JCC,* 32:327–32 ("if after," 330). For a criticism of the tendency to rely on policymakers' statements to define policy, see Wolfe, "Against the Intentional Fallacy."

23. Horsman, *Expansion and American Indian Policy,* 46–47; Nichols, *Red Gentlemen,* 91–92, 100–103; Downes, *Council Fires,* 421–25; Governor St. Clair to General Knox, Oct. 26, 1788, Smith, ed., *St. Clair Papers,* 2:92–95 ("kill them all," 93); Calloway, ed., *Revolution and Confederation,* 481 ("to have pity," "let the Ohio"); Denny, *Military Journal,* 129 ("The United States," "but if").

24. For the Fort Harmer Treaty, see *IALT,* 18–23. For the United Indian Nations' perspectives on the treaty, see *Minutes of Debates,* 11 ("pen and ink," "speak things"). For confederationist military operations, see Faragher, *Daniel Boone,* 266; William McClery to Governor of Virginia, Apr. 25, 1789, *ASPIA,* 1:84; Downes, *Council Fires,* 310–12; Aron, *How the West Was Lost,* 49–50.

25. Report from H. Knox . . . Relative to the Northwestern Indians," June 15, 1789, Gen. Knox to President of the United States, July 7, 1789, *ASPIA,* 1:12–14, 52–54 ("forming treaties," "raising an army," "establish . . . its character," 13; "exterminating a part," "imparted our knowledge," "the civilization," "the human character," "incapable of melioration," "entirely contradicted," 53).

26. Benjamin Wilson, George Jackson, and William Robinson to the President of the United States, Feb. 2, 1790, *ASPIA,* 1:87 ("to take"). For Shays' Rebellion's impact on the Constitution, see Condon, *Shays's Rebellion,* 119–27; Rossiter, ed., *Federalist Papers,* 84 ("improper or wicked"). For the Whiskey Rebellion, see Bouton, *Taming Democracy,* 219–24; Slaughter, *Whiskey Rebellion* (13,000 troops, 212). For elite attitudes toward frontiersmen as "white savages," Franklin's term for the Paxton Boys, see Nichols, *Red Gentlemen,* 65, 130, 200. For efforts to evict squatters, see Hinderaker, *Elusive Empires,* 239–40; Griffin, *American Leviathan,* 202–3; Harmar to Secretary of War, July 12, 1786, May 14, 1787, Smith, ed., *St. Clair Papers,* 2:14–15, 19–22. For "expansion with honor," see Berkhofer, *White Man's Indian,* 145.

Nichols, *Red Gentlemen,* 10, points out that Knox and like-minded officials "often opposed western expansion, fearing that the opening of new lands to white settlers would depopulate the eastern states and flood the west with ungovernable frontiersmen," but this does not mean that there was not a national consensus for expansion; the only question was the pace and regulation of expansion. Ellis, *American Creation,* 139, contends that Knox and Washington envisioned "a series of Indian enclaves or homelands east of the Mississippi whose political and geographic integrity would be protected by federal law," but there is no evidence for this wishful bit of hagiography.

27. Ablavsky, "Savage Constitution," 1035 ("state encroachments," "wars and Treaties"), 1064 ("the savage tribes"), 1050 ("provide for"), 1058 ("majority of the people," "with-

out money," "chastise"), 1088 ("the wheels"); Sadosky, *Revolutionary Negotiations,* 120–21, 139–40.

28. President Washington to Governor St. Clair, Oct. 6, 1789, St. Clair to Major Hamtramck, Jan. 23, 1790, Smith, ed., *St. Clair Papers,* 2:125–26, 130–32 ("reasonable terms," 125; "continue their incursions," "to punish," 126); Gamelin's Journal, *ASPIA,* 1:93–94 ("I do now," "displeased," "menacing," "bad effect," "took upon," 93; "doubt," 94); Sword, *President Washington's Indian War,* 84–85; Sugden, *Blue Jacket,* 95–97.

29. Summary Statement of the Situation of the Frontiers by the Secretary of War, May 27, 1790, Smith, ed., *St. Clair Papers,* 2:146–47 ("depredations," "the banditti," 146); Secretary of War to General Harmar, June 7, 1790, *ASPIA,* 1:97–98 ("extirpate," 97).

30. Kiernan, "Is 'Genocide' an Anachronistic Concept?," 534 ("utter destruction"), 531 ("concept of genocide").

31. Grimsley, "'Rebels' and 'Redskins.'"

32. Locke, *Two Treatises,* 226; Vattel, *Law of Nations,* 100 ("people of Europe"), 35–36 ("those nations"), 305 ("right to join"). For Vattel's influence on U.S. founders, see Kiernan, *Blood and Soil,* 311; Cumfer, *Separate Peoples,* 42; Witt, *Lincoln's Code,* 16–19, 28, 44; Hunter, "Vattel in Revolutionary America." For the doctrine of discovery, see Miller, *Native America.* My discussion of "just and lawful war" and genocide draws on Ostler, "'Just and Lawful War.'"

33. Sword, *President Washington's Indian War,* 96–116, 120–22 ("herd of elephants," 96); Calloway, *Victory with No Name,* 66–68; Sugden, *Blue Jacket,* 99–105; Denny, *Military Journal,* 145–47 ("reconnoitre the country," 145; "the army," 146–47); Court of Inquiry of General Harmar, Sept. 16, 1791, *American State Papers: Military Affairs,* 1:20–36 ("to endeavor," 21; "surprise any parties," 25); Governor St. Clair to the Secretary of War, Nov. 6, 1790, *ASPIA,* 1:104 ("the savages"). Harmar to Knox, Nov. 4, 1790, *ASPIA,* 1:104, claimed that "not less than 100 or 120 warriors were slain." For a more accurate count, see Eid, "'Slaughter Was Reciprocal,'" 62.

34. H. Knox to Brigadier General Charles Scott, Mar. 9, 1791, Report of Brigadier General Scott, June 28, 1791, *ASPIA,* 1:129–32 ("assault the said towns," 130; "discovered the enemy," "destroyed all," 131; "no act," "inveterate habit," 132); letter to Colonel A. McKee, June 26, 1791, Michigan Pioneer and Historical Society, *Historical Collections,* 24:273 ("literally skinned"); Sword, *President Washington's War,* 138–41; Calloway, *Victory with No Name,* 75. For the rationale for taking captives, see Sleeper-Smith, *Indigenous Prosperity,* 243–46. For a followup operation led by Lieutenant Colonel James Wilkinson against the same towns Scott targeted, which resulted in the killing of ten men and the destruction of some crops and buildings in August, see Sword, *President Washington's War,* 155–56.

35. For Wea efforts to secure the prisoners' freedom and their eventual release, see Sword, *President Washington's War,* 142, 215–17; Buell, comp., *Memoirs of Rufus Putnam,* 297–98 (qtn., 298). For the possibility that the prisoners were raped and for how the women's names provide a window into their environment, see Sleeper-Smith, *Indigenous Prosperity,* 267–70. The list of names is in *ASPIA,* 1:133.

36. Sugden, *Blue Jacket*, 113–27; Sword, *President Washington's Indian War*, 171–91 (21 confederation men killed; Calloway, *Victory with No Name*, 83–92, 108–28 (qtn., 112; over 600 troops killed, 127; estimates of Indians killed, 128).

37. *Minutes of Debates*, 20 (qtn.); Tanner, "The Glaize"; Sugden, *Blue Jacket*, 128–30; Dowd, *Spirited Resistance*, 103–15.

38. Sugden, *Blue Jacket*, 134–38 ("Americans wanted," 137; "We do not," 138); Dowd, *Spirited Resistance*, 103–4; Taylor, *Divided Ground*, 270–72, 277.

39. Quaife, ed., *Indian Captivity*, 115–17, 127 ("Many scalps," 116; "first landing," "increasing strength," "Long-knives," 127); Dowd, *Spirited Resistance*, 99–109; Tanner, "Coocoochee."

40. Coates, ed., "Narrative of an Embassy," 61–131 ("have brought," 125; "white people," "have taken," "Civilize," "Big Knives," 126). For an analysis of Aupaumut's narrative, see Brooks, *Common Pot*, 143–49.

41. H. Knox, Statement Relative to the Frontier Northwest of Ohio, Dec. 26, 1791, *ASPIA*, 1:197–98 ("late disasters," 198; "Miami and Wabash," "banditti," "continued," "were treated," "outrages," "became necessary," 197; "offers of peace," "adequate military force," 198).

42. Calloway, *Victory with No Name*, 142–43; Nichols, *Red Gentlemen*, 164; Bergman, *American National State*, 55–56; U.S. Bureau of the Census, *Historical Statistics . . . Supplement*, 301.

43. "Notes on Cabinet Opinions," Feb. 26, 1793, Boyd et al., eds., *Papers of Thomas Jefferson*, 25:271 (qtns.). Works that describe diplomacy as a "peace offensive" include Prucha, *Great Father*, 1:65; Nichols, *Red Gentlemen*, 140.

44. H. Knox to Benjamin Lincoln, Beverley Randolph, and Timothy Pickering, Apr. 26, 1793, *ASPIA*, 1:340–42. The government sponsored other diplomatic initiatives in 1792. One, involving dispatching traders Peter Pond and William Steedman to Detroit, failed because the emissaries never reached their destination. Another, undertaken by Brigadier General Rufus Putnam, resulted in a peace treaty with several leaders at Vincennes, but the signers were not affiliated with the United Indian Nations, and in any case, as noted above, the Senate refused the ratify the treaty. Another, involving Haudenosaunees and Hendrick Aupaumut, also came to nothing. Accounts of these initiatives are in Horsman, *Expansion and American Indian Policy*, 90–94; Nichols, *Red Gentlemen*, 142–45.

45. Wyandots et al. to Commissioners of the United States, July 27, Aug. 13, 1793, "Speech of the Commissioners of the United States to the Deputies of the Confederated Indian Nations," July 31, 1793, Commissioners of the United States to the Chiefs and Warriors of the Indian Nations, Aug. 16, 1793, *ASPIA*, 1:352–54, 356–57 ("through fear," "Money," "no consideration," 356; "agree that the Ohio," "the negotiation," 357); Lincoln, "Journal of a Treaty Held in 1793" ("seem to expect," 166); Jefferson to Thomas Pinckney, Nov. 27, 1793, in Boyd et al., eds., *Papers of Thomas Jefferson*, 27:450 ("we expected").

46. Knox to Wayne, Sept. 3, 1793, and May 16, 1794, in Knopf, ed., *Anthony Wayne*, 270–72, 327–32 ("audacious savages," 271; "severe strokes," 329). On Wayne's movements, see Sword, *President Washington's Indian War*, 232–37, 249–57. Grenier, *First*

Way, 199–200, emphasizes Wayne's use of rangers and scouts, identified in Gaff, *Bayonets in the Wilderness,* 220, as Choctaws and Chickasaws.

47. Sugden, *Blue Jacket,* 162–68; Sword, *President Washington's Indian War,* 272–78.

48. Howard, ed., "Battle of Fallen Timbers," 39 (qtn.); Sugden, *Blue Jacket,* 170–80; Sword, *President Washington's Indian War,* 282–306.

49. Drake, *Life of Tecumseh,* 95 ("we saw"); Bliss, ed., *Diary of David Zeisberger,* 2:378 ("fight," "so that"). For British considerations, see Taylor, *Divided Ground,* 287.

50. Heckewelder, *History, Manners, and Customs,* 192 ("he had all the cunning"); *ASPIA,* 1:564–83 ("the massacre," 568; "we have now," 573); *IALT,* 39–45 ("quietly to enjoy," without any," 42). For confederation decisionmaking after Fallen Timbers, see Sugden, *Blue Jacket,* 181–200.

51. Calloway, *American Revolution,* 209–11 ("stand up," 210; "peace," 211); Cumfer, *Separate Peoples,* 51; Wilkins, *Cherokee Tragedy,* 18–21; Downes, "Cherokee–American Relations," 46–51; Brown, *Old Frontiers,* 272–79, 293–97.

52. The only primary source for Sevier's attack on Cherokees at Flint Creek is a letter from Sevier to the Privy Council of Franklin, Jan. 12, 1789. The letter appeared in the *Charleston* (South Carolina) *City Gazette or Daily Advertiser,* Apr. 21, 1789; *Augusta* (Georgia) *Chronicle and Gazette of the State,* May 2, 1789. It was reprinted in Williams, *History of the Lost State of Franklin,* 223–24, and cited in Brown, *Old Frontiers,* 297–98. Although there is every reason to believe Sevier could have undertaken such a massacre and no obvious reason why he or anyone else would have exaggerated or fabricated it, unlike other militia actions, including the killing of Old Tassel, which was widely reported and is corroborated in other sources, Sevier's attack at Flint Creek is not mentioned in other contemporary sources.

53. Brown, *Old Frontiers,* 309–13; Cumfer, *Separate Peoples,* 57–64; Horsman, *Expansion and American Indian Policy,* 73–75.

54. Downes, "Creek–American Relations," 170–72; Alexander McGillivray to Richard Winn, Andrew Pickens, and George Mathews, Sept. 15, 1788, *ASPIA,* 1:30 ("are taking refuge," "acts of hostility," "professions," "deceitful snares").

55. Dowd, *Spirited Resistance,* 94, 100–102, 104 ("a dangerous confederacy," 94); Horsman, *Expansion and American Indian Policy,* 71–73; Nichols, *Red Gentlemen,* 118–23, 155; Downes, "Creek–American Relations," 182–84.

56. "Information by Richard Finnelson," enclosed in Governor Blount to the Secretary of War, Sept. 26, 1792, Blount to Secretary of War, Oct. 10, 1792, *APSIA,* 1:288–91, 293–94 (qtns., 290). For Bloody Fellow, see Brown, "Eastern Cherokee Chiefs," 24–26. For the events, see Finger, *Tennessee Frontiers,* 138–39.

57. For Native losses at Buchanan's Station, see *ASPIA,* 1:331. For conflict, see Finger, *Tennessee Frontiers,* 144. For settler demands and Knox's response, see "Report of Committee of Congress: Territorial Defense," Apr. 8, 1794, Secretary of War to the President, Apr. 11, 1794, *TPUS,* 4:335–37 ("repeated depredations," 335; "the protection," "the operations," 336); Knox to William Blount, Dec. 29, 1794, *ASPIA,* 1:634–35 ("direct offensive," 635). For settlers killed, see Opal, *Avenging the People,* 93.

58. James Ore to Governor Blount, Sept. 24, 1794, *ASPIA,* 1:632 (qtns.); Cumfer, *Separate Peoples,* 67; Brown, *Old Frontiers,* 421–27.

59. Henry Knox to William Blount, Dec. 29, 1794, James Robertson to Governor Blount, Oct. 8, 1794, *ASPIA,* 1:633–35 ("not authorized," 634; "information that," 633; "all reasonable," 635).

60. William Blount to Double-Head and other Chiefs and Warriors, Nov. 1, 1794, *ASPIA,* 1:534 ("war will cost"); Boulware, *Deconstructing,* 173–75; Brown, *Old Frontiers,* 429–38 ("walk together," 438); McLoughlin, *Cherokee Renascence,* 25; Horsman, *Expansion and American Indian Policy,* 78–79. For Blount's Cherokee name, see Cumfer, *Separate Peoples,* 57.

61. Furstenberg, "Significance of the Trans-Appalachian West," 650.

62. On the substantial tensions between federal authority and western settlers and the challenges of establishing national authority over a huge and complex geography, see Furstenberg, "Significance of the Trans-Appalachian West," 659–65. For the U.S. commitment to sustained military action against Indians in the West as crucial to fostering closer relations between common people on the frontier and the federal government, see Griffin, *American Leviathan,* 240–53.

63. For an analysis of how resistance can camouflage genocidal intent in the Far West, see Madley, "California and Oregon's Modoc Indians."

64. Rana, *Two Faces,* 11.

65. Cayton, "'Noble Actors,'" 239 ("an atmosphere," "sincerity," "good faith,"); Calloway, *Pen and Ink Witchcraft,* 112 ("façade of civility"); Mann, "Greenville Treaty," 194 ("browbeaten peoples").

CHAPTER 4. SURVIVAL AND NEW THREATS

1. Sugden, *Blue Jacket,* 209–10.

2. Howard, ed., "Battle of Fallen Timbers," 39 ("Canoes were loaded"); Sword, *President Washington's Indian War,* 98 ("nothing but").

3. For Cherokees, see Mooney, "Myths of the Cherokee," 53. For Ohio Valley Indians, see Sleeper-Smith, *Indigenous Prosperity,* 263–64; Tanner, "The Glaize," 16; A. McKee to Sir John Johnson, Jan. 28, 1792, Michigan Pioneer and Historical Society, *Historical Collections,* 24:366 (qtn.).

4. Tanner, "The Glaize"; Cumfer, *Separate Peoples,* 70–71; Snyder, *Slavery in Indian Country,* 107 (qtns.); Sleeper-Smith, *Indian Women and French Men,* 19, 35–39; Anson, *Miami Indians,* 111; Cayton, *Frontier Indiana,* 144–45; White, *Middle Ground,* 448–52; Calloway, *White People, Indians, and Highlanders,* 150–56; Perdue, *Cherokee Women,* 81–83; McLoughlin, *Cherokee Renascence,* 31; Ethridge, *Creek Country,* 111–15; Wright, *Creeks and Seminoles,* 85. At the same time, however, many Native women in the Great Lakes who married French traders eventually became part of what Murphy, *Great Lakes Creoles,* describes as "creole" communities of people with mixed ancestry living in towns like Prairie du Chien who increasingly were categorized and identified as "white." For the Miami and Wea population, see Appendix 2.

5. Faragher, *Daniel Boone,* 156, 197; Ingersoll, *To Intermix,* 108–11; Saunt, *New Order,* 51, 122–35; Ethridge, *Creek Country,* 115–17.

6. Mandell, *Tribe, Race, History,* 4, 42–59.

7. Cayton, *Frontier Indiana,* 200; Calloway, *Shawnees,* 116, 126; Edmunds, *Shawnee Prophet,* 31–32; Schutt, *Peoples of the River Valleys,* 180; Bowes, *Land Too Good,* 84, 91–92; Rafert, *Miami Indians,* 63–64; Tanner, ed., *Atlas,* 95; Gibson, *Kickapoos,* 47–51; Bowes, *Exiles and Pioneers,* 24–26; Lakomäki, *Gathering Together,* 166–69; Weslager, *Delaware Indians,* 353; Warren, *Shawnees and Their Neighbors,* 75; Clarke, *Chief Bowles,* 8–13.

8. White, *Middle Ground,* 487–91.

9. Braund, *Deerskins and Duffels,* 178; McLoughlin, *Cherokee Renascence,* 62; White, *Roots of Dependency,* 92; Atkinson, *Splendid Land,* 146; Dennis, *Seneca Possessed,* 156–58; Tiro, *People of the Standing Stone,* 85; Taylor, *Divided Ground,* 389; Calloway, *Western Abenakis,* 231 (qtn.).

10. Edmunds, *Shawnee Prophet;,* Warren, *Shawnees and Their Neighbors,* 82; Atkinson, *Splendid Land,* 186 ("plenty of hogs"); White, *Roots of Dependency,* 105; Carson, *Searching,* 73–75; McLoughlin, *Cherokee Renascence,* 64; Perdue, *Cherokee Women,* 122–23; Piker, *Okfuskee,* 123–25; Saunt, *New Order,* 159–61 ("seen much," 160); Ethridge, *Creek Country,* 137–38, 158–66.

11. Sleeper-Smith, *Indian Women and French Men,* 78–84; Rafert, *Miami Indians,* 63–65; Ethridge, *Creek Country,* 153–54 (qtn., 153).

12. McLoughlin, *Cherokee Renascence,* 64–68 (qtn., 65); Perdue, *Cherokee Women,* 126–28; Miles, *Ties That Bind,* 38–39; Braund, *Deerskins and Duffels,* 181–82.

13. Tiro, *People of the Standing Stone,* 107; Dennis, *Seneca Possessed,* 165, 168–69; Saunt, *New Order,* 161; Ethridge, *Creek Country,* 182–84, 187–90; Perdue, *Cherokee Women,* 130–33; McLoughlin, *Cherokee Renascence,* 62–64; Carson, *Searching,* 79 ("considerable spirit"); O'Brien, *Choctaws,* 102 ("learn our women").

14. Mandell, *Tribe, Race, History,* 13–18, 27–32 ("mixed subsistence," 13); Mandell, *Behind the Frontier,* 196–98; Shoemaker, *Native American Whalemen,* 13–14, 21–36, 58–76; Silverman, *Faith and Boundaries,* 185–215 (qtns., 210).

15. Quaife, ed., *Indian Captivity,* 109–10.

16. Carter, *Life and Times,* 160–62 ("fatal poison," 162); Prucha, *Great Father,* 1:90–93, 98–102 ("prevent or restrain," 99).

17. Braund, *Deerskins and Duffels,* 146 ("the liquor"); Cumfer, *Separate Peoples,* 106; Ishii, *Bad Fruits,* 48–49; Parker, ed., *Code of Handsome Lake,* 9 ("dissolute person"), 71 ("with vapor"), 27 ("I will").

18. White, *Roots of Dependency,* 95; Braund, *Deerskins and Duffels,* 177; Ethridge, *Creek Country,* 129.

19. Henry Dearborn to Cherokee Delegation, July 3, 1801, Boyd et al., eds., *Papers of Thomas Jefferson,* 34:510–11 (qtns., 510).

20. Ford, ed., *Works of Thomas Jefferson,* 9:326 ("spirit of peace," "our Indian neighbors"), 9:333 ("extensive country").

21. Thomas Jefferson to Andrew Jackson, Feb. 16, 1803, Lipscomb, ed., *Writings of Thomas Jefferson,* 10:357–60 (qtns., 359); Wallace, *Jefferson and the Indians,* 239.

22. Hotchkiss, comp., *Codification of the Statute Law of Georgia,* 85–86 (qtn., 85); Hudson, *Creek Paths,* 46; Horsman, *Expansion and American Indian Policy,* 123.

23. *ASPIA,* 1:669–81 ("it is like," 675; Wilkinson qtns., 678); Green, *Politics of Indian Removal,* 38–39; Horsman, *Expansion and American Indian Policy,* 123–24; Hudson, *Creek Paths,* 46–48.

24. Horsman, *Expansion and American Indian Policy,* 128–32; Ethridge, *Creek Country,* 199–201; Hudson, *Creek Paths,* 50–53, 63–64; *IALT,* 58–59, 85–86.

25. Horsman, *Expansion and American Indian Policy,* 125–28, 136–37 ("brought to reason," "an inducement," 125; "very great," 126); McLoughlin, *Cherokee Renascence,* 92–108.

26. Owens, *Mr. Jefferson's Hammer.*

27. "Harrison's Address to Indian Council," Aug. 12, 1802, Esarey, ed., *Messages and Letters,* 1:52–55 ("ardent wish," 53); "Notes of Speech at an Indian Council," Sept. 15, 1802, Clanin, ed., "Papers of William Henry Harrison," reel 1, 392 ("the Land was made").

28. Thomas Jefferson to William H. Harrison, Feb. 27, 1803, Lipscomb, ed., *Writings of Thomas Jefferson,* 10:370 ("run in debt," "become willing"); White, *Middle Ground,* 496; Owens, *Mr. Jefferson's Hammer,* 78–81; Horsman, *Expansion and American Indian Policy,* 144–46; Carter, *Life and Times,* 170–71; Rafert, *Miami Indians,* 69; Wallace, *Jefferson and the Indians,* 227; *IALT,* 64–65 ("quantity of salt," 65).

29. Secretary of War to Harrison, May 24, 1805, Jefferson to Harrison, Apr. 28, 1805, Esarey, ed., *Messages and Papers,* 1:130 ("the transaction"), 126–28 ("defective," "liberality," 128); Wallace, *Jefferson and the Indians,* 228–31; Owens, *Mr. Jefferson's Hammer,* 84–85, 100–105; Weslager, *Delaware Indians,* 332–33, 339; Carter, *Life and Times,* 175–76.

30. For Lalawethika's early life and first vision, see Edmunds, *Shawnee Prophet,* 28–34 ("abounding in game," 33); Dowd, *Spirited Resistance,* 126 ("liquor resembling," "seized with").

31. Edmunds, *Shawnee Prophet,* 34–38 (qtns., 39).

32. Cave, *Prophets of the Great Spirit,* 69 ("opened the sky"). For Beata, see Fur, *Nation of Women,* 151–52 (Beata qtns., 152). For The Trout, see Dowd, *Spirited Resistance,* 127–31; for Main Poc, see Edmunds, *Potawatomis,* 166. For Tecumseh, see Edmunds, *Tecumseh;* Sugden, *Tecumseh.*

33. Edmunds, *Shawnee Prophet,* 43–46; Dowd, *Spirited Resistance,* 136–37; Gipson, ed., *Moravian Mission,* 131 (qtn.); Olmstead, *Blackcoats,* 116.

34. Edmunds, *Shawnee Prophet,* 47–69; Sugden, *Blue Jacket,* 239; Jortner, *Gods of Prophetstown,* 6–10.

35. For forts, see Tanner, ed., *Atlas,* 98–99. For population figures, see Hurt, *Ohio Frontier,* 262; Cayton, *Frontier Indiana,* 267.

36. Jefferson to Secretary of War Henry Dearborn, Aug. 28, 1807, Lipscomb, ed., *Writings of Thomas Jefferson,* 11:342–46 ("a transient enthusiasm," 342; "we should immediately," 343; "chiefs of the several," "we have no," 344; "we are constrained," "we will never," "they will kill," 345). Some scholars have quoted Jefferson's language and seen it as indicative of a general American disposition. See Drinnon, *Facing West,* 96; Kiernan, *Blood and Soil,* 318–20; Madley, "Reexamining the American Genocide Debate," 109. Wallace, *Jefferson and the Indians,* 239, quotes Jefferson, but in passing and not as a policy statement. Jefferson's statement is absent from standard accounts of policy

such as Prucha, *Great Father;* Horsman, *Expansion and American Indian Policy;* Sheehan, *Seeds of Extinction.*

37. Edmunds, *Shawnee Prophet,* 80–81; Owens, *Mr. Jefferson's Hammer,* 200–204; *IALT,*
101–5.

38. Heckewelder, *Narrative of the Mission,* 409 (qtn.); Edmunds, *Shawnee Prophet,* 81–86;
Sugden, *Tecumseh,* 185–88.

39. Edmunds, *Shawnee Prophet,* 82 ("his people," "he smelt them"), 88–90; Harrison to
the Prophet, July 19, 1810, Esarey, ed., *Messages and Letters,* 1:447–48 ("17 fires," "purchased land," "instantly be restored," "carry your complaints," 448).

40. "Tecumseh's Speech to Governor Harrison," Aug. 20, 1810, Esarey, ed., *Messages and
Letters,* 1:463–67 ("recollect that the time," 464–65; "no harm," "the person," "can you
blame," "you have taken," "distinctions of Indian tribes," 465; "the white people,"
"when Jesus Christ," "you kill'd many," "small pox," 467). Gibson, *Kickapoos,* does
not mention an outbreak of smallpox among the Kickapoos, though it is possible that
an undocumented outbreak did occur; whether Harrison or U.S. officials actually infected annuity goods with smallpox is impossible to say. For the killing of Moluntha,
see Calloway, *Shawnees,* 83–84.

41. Cayton, *Frontier Indiana,* 218, notes Tecumseh's mentions of "murders, insults, and
coerced land cessions," but without providing details; Edmunds, *Shawnee Prophet,* 90,
notes Tecumseh's reference to Gnadenhütten, but only as an example of "American
mistreatment of Indians"; Sugden, *Tecumseh,* 199, mentions in passing Tecumseh's reference to Gnadenhütten as well as pointing out that some Kickapoos thought smallpox was due to annuity distribution, though without making it clear that Tecumseh
directly accused Harrison of biological warfare; Jortner, *Gods of Prophetstown,* 176,
notes Tecumseh's reference to the "white people's" killing of Christ, but his summary
of the speech gives no indication of the other allegations.

42. For citations for quotations from previous chapters, see relevant notes. For Aupaumut, see *Panoplist,* 270–72 ("your villages," 272); Wheeler, *To Live upon Hope,* 243.

43. Harrison to Secretary of War, Aug. 22, 1810, "Tecumseh's Speech to Governor Harrison," Aug. 21, 1810, Esarey, ed., *Messages and Letters,* 1:461 ("with the most," "sprung
up"), 1:469 ("it will be"). For Winamac, see Edmunds, *Shawnee Prophet,* 90.

44. Harrison to Secretary of War, Aug. 22, 1810, Esarey, ed., *Messages and Letters,* 1:463.

CHAPTER 5. WARS OF 1812

1. James Madison to the Senate and House of Representatives of the United States,
June 1, 1812, Williams, comp., *Addresses and Messages,* 1:293–98 (qtns., 297).

2. Sugden, *Tecumseh,* 205–9, 212–13, 217–18; Dowd, *Spirited Resistance,* 143–44 (qtn.).

3. Sugden, *Tecumseh,* 211–12; Edmunds, *Tecumseh,* 137–38.

4. Wood, *Empire of Liberty,* 674–75; Harrison to Secretary of War, Oct. 5 and 10, 1810,
April 23, 1811, Esarey, ed., *Messages and Letters,* 1:474, 475, 508.

5. Jortner, *Gods of Prophetstown,* 181; Edmunds, *Shawnee Prophet,* 99–101; Sugden, *Tecumseh,* 217–19; Harrison to Secretary of War, July 2, 1811, Secretary of War to Harrison, July 17 and 20, 1811, Esarey, ed., *Messages and Letters,* 1:526–28, 535–37 ("If some

decisive," 526; "earnest desire," 536). For an interpretation emphasizing Miami opposition to Prophetstown and the ways Miamis influenced American perceptions of Tenskwatawa and Tecumseh, see Bottiger, *Borderland of Fear*.

6. Harrison to Secretary of War, Aug. 6, 1811, Esarey, ed., *Messages and Letters*, 1:542–46 (qtn., 545). Sugden, *Tecumseh*, 223, quotes Tecumseh on his intention to visit Washington but observes only that Tecumseh had "committed a tactical blunder" in revealing his plans to travel south. See also Owens, *Mr. Jefferson's Hammer*, 213.

7. "Field Report Harrison's Army," Esarey, ed., *Messages and Letters*, 1:597–98; Edmunds, *Shawnee Prophet*, 105–11. For the first position, see Sugden, *Tecumseh*, 228–33; Edmunds, *Shawnee Prophet*, 111–12. For the alternative perspective, see Cave, *Prophets of the Great Spirit*, 118–21.

8. Edmunds, *Shawnee Prophet*, 111–15; Sugden, *Tecumseh*, 231–36, 258.

9. For the view that Tippecanoe sent a message, see Grenier, *First Way*, 208–9; for the view that it damaged Tenskwatawa, see Edmunds, *Shawnee Prophet*, 115–16; Sugden, *Tecumseh*, 257. For revisionist perspectives, see Cave, *Prophets of the Great Spirit*, 123–29; Owens, *Mr. Jefferson's Hammer*, 222–23 (qtn., 222); Jortner, *Gods of Prophetstown*, 196–98. Figures for settlers killed are from Sugden, *Tecumseh*, 261.

10. Sugden, *Tecumseh*, 237, 241–43; Edmunds, *Tecumseh*, 146–48; Carson, *Searching*, 49.

11. Dowd, *Spirited Resistance*, 145; Sugden, *Tecumseh*, 243–51; Edmunds, *Tecumseh*, 148–51; Green, *Politics of Indian Removal*, 39–41; Hudson, *Creek Paths*, 84–94; Martin, *Sacred Revolt*, 120–24; Waselkov, *Conquering Spirit*, 77–80, 82, 90. Dowd, "Thinking outside the Circle," provides good reasons to doubt that the comet or the earthquake was a decisive factor in Creek acceptance of Tecumseh's message.

12. Sugden, *Tecumseh*, 252 (qtn.); Warren, *Shawnees and Their Neighbors*, 80.

13. Hunter, *Manners and Customs*, 47–56 ("in long, eloquent," 51; "are threatened," 53–54); Sugden, *Tecumseh*, 253–55. Scholars are divided about the authenticity of the Hunter account. Edmunds, *Tecumseh*, 218–19, argues that there is little corroborating evidence to support the account of Tecumseh's visit to the Osage, although Sugden, "Early Pan-Indianism," argues for its authenticity on the grounds that Tecumseh told Harrison in August 1811 of his plan to visit the Osages. The content of Tecumseh's speech, in which he related an Indigenous consciousness of genocide in a way consistent with other sources of which Hunter would have been unaware, also supports the account's authenticity.

14. Sugden, *Tecumseh*, 255–56.

15. Edmunds, *Shawnee Prophet*, 120–21; Sugden, *Tecumseh*, 265–66.

16. Taylor, *Civil War of 1812*, 132–40 (qtn., 137).

17. Edmunds, *Shawnee Prophet*, 125, 127–28 (qtns., 127); Edmunds, *Tecumseh*, 168–80; Edmunds, *Potawatomis*, 186–87; Sugden, *Tecumseh*, 279, 282, 285, 287, 291–93, 297–304, 313; Taylor, *Civil War of 1812*, 152–66; Tanner, ed., *Atlas*, 108.

18. Edmunds, *Shawnee Prophet*, 129–32; Sugden, *Tecumseh*, 314–18; Tanner, ed., *Atlas*, 109–10; Grenier, *First Way*, 210; Jortner, *Gods of Prophetstown*, 213–14; Owens, *Mr. Jefferson's Hammer*, 223–25; Anson, *Miami Indians*, 166–70; John B. Campbell to William Henry Harrison, Dec. 25, 1812, Esarey, ed., *Messages and Letters*, 2:253–62.

19. A standard history of the War of 1812, Hickey, *War of 1812*, 86, gives only very brief notice to these attacks. Other works cited in previous notes narrate these attacks without recognizing their significance. The best assessment of the attacks and the general position of the confederacy in the Northwest is in Dowd, *Spirited Resistance*, 184–85.

20. Edmunds, *Shawnee Prophet*, 133–42; Sugden, *Tecumseh*, 321–23, 327–39, 357–75; Owens, *Mr. Jefferson's Hammer*, 225–30; Taylor, *Civil War of 1812*, 212–13, 242–45; Starkey, *European and Native American Warfare*, 161–63.

21. Sabathy-Judd, ed., *Moravians in Upper Canada*, xxv, 513–14 ("disappeared," 513); Bowes, "Gnadenhutten Effect," 115; Eustace, *1812*, 158 ("thrown their children").

22. Grenier, *First Way*, 211; Edmunds, *Shawnee Prophet*, 159–61; Tanner, ed., *Atlas*, 119–20; Davis, *Frontier Illinois*, 149–52; Aron, *American Confluence*, 157–58; Buckley, *William Clark*, 102–7.

23. Anson, *Miami Indians*, 170; Edmunds, *Shawnee Prophet*, 143–44.

24. Braund, "Red Sticks."

25. Waselkov, *Conquering Spirit*, 88–89; Eustace, *1812*, 159 ("the virtuous mother"); *Nashville Clarion*, n.d., in *Niles' Weekly Register*, Sept. 26, 1812, 52–53 ("to exact," "when all," 53); Saunt, *New Order*, 250–52, 254–58.

26. Dowd, *Spirited Resistance*, 172–81; McLoughlin, *Cherokee Renascence*, 179–89.

27. Saunt, *New Order*, 34–37, 205–13; Miller, *Coacoochee's Bones*, 7–11; Sattler, "Remnants, Renegades, and Runaways"; Mahon and Weisman, "Florida's Seminole and Miccosukee Peoples"; Kokomoor, "Re-assessment of Seminoles, Africans, and Slavery"; Nugent, *Habits of Empire*, 107–14.

28. Saunt, *New Order*, 236–46 (qtn., 245), Nugent, *Habits of Empire*, 113–16.

29. Waselkov, *Conquering Spirit*, 96–102, 110–15, 127–35, 190–93; Owsley, *Struggle for the Gulf Borderlands*, 25–26, 30–32, 35–39.

30. *Niles' Weekly Register*, Dec. 18, 1813 (qtn.). Waselkov, *Conquering Spirit*, 195–96, concludes that Red Sticks killed several noncombatants and that scalping was widespread. He also notes that although some women were disemboweled, reports of large numbers of mutilated bodies made by burial parties were probably inflated. He suggests that many bodies had been dismembered by animals.

31. Rogin, *Fathers and Children*, 148 ("exterminate"); Andrew Jackson to Willie Blount, Dec. 29, 1814, Bassett, ed., *Correspondence of Andrew Jackson*, 1:416–20 ("to carry," 417); Scott, comp., *Laws of the State of Tennessee*, 2:103 ("repel the invasion"). On the threat of invasion providing legal justification for Tennessee's actions, see Willie Blount to Brigadier General Thomas Flournoy, Oct. 15, 1813, *ASPIA*, 1:856; for Madison and the Tennessee militia, see James Madison to [Secretary of War] General [John A.] Armstrong, Oct. 11, 1813, Rives and Fendall, eds., *Letters and Other Writings*, 391–92; Skeen, *Citizen Soldiers*, 160. On the mobilization of the Georgia and Mississippi militias, see Owsley, *Struggle for the Gulf Borderlands*, 43–45, 51–52.

32. Thomas Jefferson to Baron Alexander von Humboldt, Dec. 6, 1813, Lipscomb, ed., *Writings of Thomas Jefferson*, 14:23 ("cruel massacres," "committed"); *Niles' Weekly Register*, Dec. 18, 1813 ("reconcile ourselves," "to the wilds," "become extinct," "compelled").

33. Jackson to Brave Tennesseans, Sept. 24, 1813, Moser et al., eds., *Papers of Andrew Jackson*, 2:428–29 ("Brave Tennesseans," "the savage foe," 428); Jackson to Willie Blount,

Nov. 4 and 15, 1813, Bassett, ed., *Correspondence of Andrew Jackson,* 1:341 ("We have retaliated"), 1:348–50 ("Not an Indian," 1:350); Waselkov, *Conquering Spirit,* 163; Remini, *Andrew Jackson and His Indian Wars,* 62–67.

34. Waselkov, *Conquering Spirit,* 163–64; Robert Grierson to Jackson, Nov. 13, 1813, Jackson to Grierson, Nov. 17, 1813, John Cocke to Jackson, Nov. 27, 1813, Moser et al., eds., *Papers of Andrew Jackson,* 2:451–52, 456–57, 462 ("panic struck," 451; "remember Ft. Mims," 457; "64 warriors," 462). For a refutation of the common idea that Jackson felt "grief and rage," see Remini, *Andrew Jackson and His Indian Wars,* 67–69 ("grief and rage," 68).

35. Remini, *Andrew Jackson and His Indian Wars,* 69–75; Waselkov, *Conquering Spirit,* 145 (qtns.), 164–66.

36. Waselkov, *Conquering Spirit,* 167–70; Dowd, *Spirited Resistance,* 186–87.

37. Waselkov, *Conquering Spirit,* 170, Remini, *Andrew Jackson and His Indian Wars,* 75; Martin, *Sacred Revolt,* 161; Piker, *Okfuskee,* 201; Owsley, *Struggle for the Gulf Borderlands,* 81–82.

38. Jackson to Thomas Pinckney, Mar. 28, 1814, Moser et al., eds., *Papers of Andrew Jackson,* 3:52–53 (1st and 2nd qtns.); Remini, *Andrew Jackson and His Indians Wars,* 75–79; Waselkov, *Conquering Spirit,* 170–71; Owsley, *Struggle for the Gulf Borderlands,* 79–81; Grenier, *First Way,* 218–19; Kanon, "'A Slow Laborious Slaughter'"; McLoughlin, *Cherokee Renascence,* 193–94; Wilkins, *Cherokee Tragedy,* 75–79; Halbert and Ball, *Creek War,* 276–77 ("the Tennessee soldiers"); O'Brien, *In Bitterness,* 151 ("the river").

39. On Red Stick military activities in the months after Tohopeka, see Waselkov, *Conquering Spirit,* 325–26, n. 24. For Weatherford's surrender, see Remini, *Andrew Jackson and His Indian Wars,* 82–83 (qtn., 83).

40. The number killed is close to the 1,800 warriors given in Martin, *Sacred Revolt,* 163, though Martin also adds "several hundred" women and children to this toll, and lower than the 3,000 killed stated by Remini, *Andrew Jackson and His Indian Wars,* 80, a figure relying on Green, *Politics of Indian Removal,* 42, whose sources are unclear. The best estimate for Creek population in the 1790s is 15,000 (see Appendix 2); an estimate of 15,000–17,000 in the early 1810s assumes an upward trajectory.

41. Jackson to Willie Blount, Mar. 31, 1814, Bassett, ed., *Correspondence of Andrew Jackson,* 1:489–92 ("lament[ed]," 492); Halbert and Ball, *Creek War,* 277 ("for barbarity," "the boy").

42. Waselkov, *Conquering Spirit,* 171–73; Martin, *Sacred Revolt,* 163 ("have been reduced"); Andrew Jackson to John Armstrong, Aug. 10, 1814, Bassett, ed., *Correspondence of Andrew Jackson,* 2:24–26 ("embrace the proffered," 25); Saunt, *New Order,* 276–82 ("on the spontaneous," 276; "famine is now," "have seen," 282); Ethridge, *Creek Country,* 240–41.

43. Remini, *Andrew Jackson and His Indian Wars,* 83–85, 87–93; Hudson, *Creek Paths,* 117; Jackson to Big Warrior, Aug. 7, 1814, Moser et al., eds., *Papers of Andrew Jackson,* 3:109–11; Owsley, *Struggle for the Gulf Borderlands,* 86–91; Rogin, *Fathers and Children,* 157–59 (qtn., 159). Rogin, 344, n. 106, identifies the author of this statement as Chief Tustunnugga (a title rather than a proper name, with the variant spelling Tustanagee),

whom I infer from the context was Big Warrior. For the 1814 Fort Jackson Treaty, see *IALT,* 107–10.

44. Owens, *Mr. Jefferson's Hammer,* 235–37, 243–44.

45. The category I have identified here does not include an event like the Gnaden-hütten massacre, which had significant social sanction, though not governmental authorization.

46. Kanon, "'Slow Laborious Slaughter,'" 9, cites a letter from Coffee to Sam Houston saying that Jackson offered the Red Sticks a chance to surrender perhaps midway through the fighting, but the letter was written in 1828 and lacks corroboration in contemporaneous reports.

47. Remini, *Andrew Jackson and His Indian Wars,* 64–65, 214–15; Rogin, *Fathers and Children,* 188–89.

CHAPTER 6. NONVANISHING INDIANS ON THE EVE OF REMOVAL

1. Dippie, *Vanishing American,* 8–11 (qtn., 8); Berkhofer, *White Man's Indian,* 88; O'Brien, *Firsting and Lasting.*

2. Appendix 2.

3. Mandell, *Tribe, Race, History,* 4, 6–7, 35–38, 42–47, 105–6; Doughton, "Unseen Neighbors," 208–9; Silverman, *Faith and Boundaries,* 185–241, 285; Campisi, *Mashpee Indians,* 96, 99–100. For the decline of Native slavery in New England, see Newell, *Brethren by Nature,* 246–54.

4. Jarvis, *Brothertown Nation,* 91–92, 99–114; Silverman, *Red Brethren,* 122; Calloway, *Western Abenakis,* 224–35.

5. Population figures, Appendix 2. See also Rountree and Davidson, *Eastern Shore Indians,* 193; Blu, *Lumbee Problem,* 46; Lowery, *Lumbee Indians,* 4–8.

6. Population figures, Appendix 2. For the reduction of the Haudenosaunee land base, see Hauptman, *Seven Generations,* 1–2.

7. Population figures, Appendix 2. Lakomäki, *Gathering Together,* 166–70, 175–78, provides an overview of Shawnee migrations. For Delaware migrations, see Weslager, *Delaware Indians,* 352–53; Schutt, *Peoples of the River Valleys,* 182–85.

8. For conditions of two representative northwestern Ohio Indian communities, the Wapakoneta Shawnees and Wyandots in the 1820s, see Calloway, *Shawnees,* 117–25; Buss, *Winning the West,* 79–89.

9. Based on figures in Appendix 2. For the factors behind the Illinois population decline, see Morrissey, 232–36. For the cumulative impact on the Miamis of repeated losses of relatively small numbers as a result of U.S. military operations, see Mann, "Fractal Massacres." For economic and environmental conditions and strategies in this region, see Rafert, *Miami Indians,* 77–87; Weslager, *Delaware Indians,* 334–38; Sleeper-Smith, *Indian Women and French Men,* 89–97, 118–19; Kay, "Fur Trade," 280–83; Child, *Holding Our World Together,* 31–49; Murphy, *Gathering of Rivers,* 79–109, 137–56; Murphy, "'Their Women Quite Industrious Miners,'" 41.

10. Population figures in Appendix 2. For confirmation of an increasing Creek population after 1814, see Paredes and Plante, "Reexamination of Creek Population Trends."

11. Economic conditions are described in Perdue, *Cherokee Women*, 135–58; McLoughlin, *Cherokee Renascence*, 277–301; White, *Roots of Dependency*, 105, 108–9, 127–28, 132–33; Carson, "Native Americans"; Green, *Politics of Indian Removal*, 56–57, 72; Atkinson, *Splendid Land*, 183–89, 200. Kelton, *Cherokee Medicine*, 181–82, directly addresses factors behind Cherokee population expansion. For the growth of slavery among the southern nations, see Krauthamer, *Black Slaves, Indian Masters*, 17–38; Miles, *Ties That Bind*, 33–43.

12. Based on figures in Appendix 2. Using data in *Handbook of North American Indians*, Ubelaker, "North American Indian Population Size," 292, estimates that the Native population in 1800 in the Northeast, including Canada, was 117,000 and that it was 60,000 for the Southeast, including Louisiana and east Texas, for a total of 177,000. Because Ubelaker's figures include Native communities outside of the eastern United States, it is difficult to tell how close these estimates are to mine, but my sense is that his methodology applied only to the eastern United States would yield somewhat higher estimates. The important point is that there are strong grounds for confidence in a general population increase from the 1770s to the 1820s.

13. Andrew Jackson, "Second Annual Message to Congress," Dec. 7, 1830, Williams, comp., *Addresses and Messages*, 2:745. For scholarship that sees removal emerging because of the "failure" of the civilization policy, see below, n. 28.

14. George Washington to President of Congress, June 17, 1783, Ford, ed., *Writings of George Washington*, 10:269 ("remove into"); Sheehan, *Seeds of Extinction*, 245 ("alternative").

15. McLoughlin, *Cherokee Renascence*, 128–64 ("there never will," 128; "settle on our lands," 132; "farming and Industrey," "throw away," 150; "committing treason," 162); Thomas Jefferson to the Chiefs of the Upper Cherokees, May 4, 1808, Lipscomb, ed., *Writings of Thomas Jefferson*, 16:435 ("settle on our lands").

16. Miles, "'Circular Reasoning,'" 226–27 ("power of motherhood," 227; "would be like," 226); Culioa McTown et al. to Commissioners, July 2, 1817, *ASPIA*, 2:142–43 ("not yet civilized," "return[ing]," 143); McLoughlin, *Cherokee Renascence*, 228–39; *IALT*, 140–44.

17. Miles, "'Circular Reasoning,'" 228–31 ("our neighboring white people," "for the sake," "driven away," 229; "the thought," "to a savage state," 231); McLoughlin, *Cherokee Renascence*, 239–59, 302–8 ("necessary for their wants," 255); *IALT*, 177–81. For the Georgia Compact, see *TPUS*, 5:144 ("reasonable terms").

18. Andrew Jackson and Thomas Hinds to the Chiefs and Warriors of the Choctaw Nation, Oct. 10 and 15, 1820, *ASPIA*, 2:235–37 ("friendly assistance," "are in a distressed condition," "your father," "Choctaw children," "a country beyond," "may live," 235; "'Without a change," "the Choctaw nation," 236), 239–40 ("the patience," "evil counsel," "may be a measure," 240); *IALT*, 191–95; Kidwell, *Choctaws and Missionaries*, 46–49; Wells, "Federal Indian Policy," 198–202; DeRosier, *Removal of the Choctaw*, 53–69, 80–96. Choctaws who went to Arkansas moved to southeastern Oklahoma after an 1825 treaty ceded most of the nation's Arkansas lands. See *IALT*, 211–14.

19. Jefferson to Chiefs of the Chickasaw Nation, Mar. 7, 1805, Lipscomb, ed., *Writings of Thomas Jefferson*, 16:412 ("we would prefer"); "Journal of the Proceedings . . . ,"

Oct. 15–Nov. 1, 1826, *ASPIA*, 2:718–27 ("see your nation," 720; "industry is spreading," "bring forth," "assistance of our father," "red brothers," "headstrong obstinacy," 722; "If calamity," 724); Atkinson, *Splendid Land*, 221–25; Gibson, *Chickasaws*, 147–49.

20. Duncan G. Campbell and James Meriwether to "Friends and Brothers," Dec. 9, 1824, Little Prince et al., to "Friends and Brothers," Dec. 11, 1824, *ASPIA*, 2:569–71 ("has not sent," "the most earnest," 569; "would secure," 570; "The proposal," 571); *IALT*, 214–17, 264–68; Green, *Politics of Indian Removal*, 57–59, 78–125; Hudson, *Creek Paths*, 141–44, 149–50. On the migration of Creeks to Oklahoma in the late 1820s, see Debo, *Road to Disappearance*, 96–97.

21. Dennis, *Seneca Possessed*, 184–89, 224; Tiro, *People of the Standing Stone*, 134–35 ("to an extensive," 134; "sundry individuals," 135); Hauptman, *Tonawanda Senecas' Heroic Battle*, 14–19, 23–28 ("retarding the progress," 16; "your great Father," 24; "the terrors," 28). For the Treaty of Canandaigua, see *IALT*, 34–37 ("never claim," "free use," 35).

22. Bontrager, "'From a Nation of Drunkards,'" 612; Warren, *Shawnees and Their Neighbors*, 47, 56–58; Lakomäki, *Gathering Together*, 154; Calloway, *Shawnees*, 156–57; C. Vandeventer to Lewis Cass, June 29, 1818, *ASPIA*, 2:175–76 (qtn., 175). For the Fort Meigs Treaty, see *IALT*, 145–55; Bowes, *Land Too Good*, 123, points out that a supplemental treaty in 1818 returned lands granted to individuals to "communal ownership."

23. Finley, *History of the Wyandott Mission*, 294 ("President would make"); Buss, *Winning the West*, 81–82; Warren, *Shawnees and Their Neighbors*, 57–63; Lakomäki, *Gathering Together*, 155–56; Calloway, *Shawnees*, 157–58; Lewis Cass to John C. Calhoun, Sept. 18, 1818, *ASPIA*, 2:177 ("proposition to remove," "received by them").

24. Edmunds, *Shawnee Prophet*, 143–83; Warren, *Shawnees and Their Neighbors*, 64–65; Lakomäki, *Gathering Together*, 161–63; Calloway, *Shawnees*, 158–61.

25. Bontrager, "'From a Nation of Drunkards,'" 627–28; Buss, *Winning the West*, 84–90; Finley, *History of the Wyandott Mission*, 294 (qtns.).

26. Tiro, "View from Piqua Agency," 50–53 ("sickness, hunger," 53); Weslager, *Delaware Indians*, 351–53, 361 ("much reluctance," "personal safety," 352; 1,346 Delawares moved west by 1821, 361); Bowes, *Land Too Good*, 104; Schutt, *Peoples of the River Valleys*, 182; Gibson, *Kickapoos*, 78–83 ("raise a warrior force," 80); Bowes, *Exiles and Pioneers*, 40–41; Herring, *Kenekuk*, 20–21; *IALT*, 170–71, 182–84. Gibson, *Kickapoos*, 83, provides a figure of 2,000 for the Kickapoos who went west after the 1817 treaty, but assuming a population of 2,200 for the entire Kickapoo population in 1819 (Appendix 2), Gibson's figure must be too high, since at least 600 Kickapoos remained east of the Mississippi.

27. Bowes, *Land Too Good*, 67–69 ("You must remove," 67); Rafert, *Miami Indians*, 90–94 ("that we should stay," "It is yourselves," "for you make," 92); Edmunds, *Potawatomis*, 228–29.

28. Sheehan, *Seeds of Extinction*, esp. 119–25, 213–18, 243; Prucha, *Great Father*, 1:136–42, 198–200; Horsman, *Expansion and American Indian Policy*, 108–13, 172–73; Onuf, *Jefferson's Empire*, 18–52. These scholars explain the policy's failure as due to some combination of unrealistic assumptions: Jefferson and other humanitarians had an overly optimistic assessment of Indians' ability and/or willingness to embrace American civilization; they naively thought that government agents and missionaries could protect

Indians from civilization's vices; and they failed to anticipate the opposition of white Americans to Indian–white intermarriage, especially when it involved a Native man marrying a white woman. On the latter point, Gaul, "Introduction," 11, observes that white women marrying Native men undermined the gendered foundations of white supremacy by denying white men's capacity to "preserve . . . an ideal of themselves as elevating, idealizing, and protecting white women." For conflicting ideas about "amalgamation" through intermarriage, see Guyatt, *Bind Us Apart*, 133–58.

29. Silverman, *Red Brethren*, 158–60; Thomas Jefferson to Captain Hendrick, the Delawares, Mahicans, and Munries, Dec. 21, 1808, Lipscomb, ed., *Writings of Thomas Jefferson*, 16:450–54 ("the increase," "lived by hunting," "you have been," "diseases and death," "wars," 451; "learn to cultivate," "spin and weave," "raise many," "double your numbers," "your children," "live under," "unite yourselves," "you will mix," 452). For Jefferson's guarantee of land to Aupaumut's community, see Jefferson deposition, Dec. 21, 1808, in Thornbrough, ed., *Letter Book*, 53–54.

30. Silverman, *Red Brethren*, 158 (qtn.). For Anglo American methods of agriculture at New Stockbridge, see Ronda and Ronda, "'As They Were Faithful,'" 51–52.

31. Jefferson's failure to recognize the Stockbridge Indians' actual conditions cautions against uncritical acceptance of his theoretical statements about racial equality. Although in *Notes on the State of Virginia* (1785) Jefferson famously defended North America's Indigenous inhabitants against the charges of European thinkers, the Comte du Buffon among others, that deficiencies in the North American environment promoted human degeneracy, and while in this context he stated that "I believe the Indian . . . to be in body and mind equal to the whiteman" (see Jefferson to Marquis de Chastellux, June 7, 1785, Boyd et al., eds., *Papers of Thomas Jefferson*, 8:186), in practice, as underscored here, he did not accord Indians full racial equality.

32. For an overview of the federal government's civilization efforts into the 1820s, see Prucha, *Great Father*, 1:142–58. For a recent study of the Choctaw Academy, see Snyder, *Great Crossings*.

33. Remini, *Andrew Jackson and His Indian Wars*, 108–19; Andrew Jackson to James Monroe, Mar. 4, 1817, Bassett, ed., *Correspondence of Andrew Jackson*, 2:277–82 ("absurdity," 279; "independent nation[s]," "possessory right," "regulate all the concerns," 280).

34. 21 U.S. 543 (1823) at 574, 587, 590; Echo-Hawk, *In the Courts of the Conqueror*, 4 ("ten worst"), 484, n. 58 (comment on the decision's racism); Williams, *American Indian in Western Legal Thought*, 316–17. See also Wilkins and Lomawaima, *Uneven Ground*, 52–58; Robertson, *Conquest by Law;* Banner, *How the Indians Lost Their Land*, 178–88; Miller, *Native America*, 50–53; Newcomb, *Pagans in the Promised Land*, 89–102; Watson, *Buying America from the Indians*.

35. James Monroe, "Eighth Annual Message to Congress," Dec. 7, 1824, Williams, comp., *Addresses and Messages of the Presidents*, 1:476–77 ("condition of the aborigines," "unless the tribes," "with the extension," 476; "revolting to humanity," "inducements," "vast territory," "schools," 477). For Monroe's views, see also Guyatt, *Bind Us Apart*, 287–88, who discusses the evolution of Indian removal in relationship to similar plans for the colonization of blacks to Africa.

36. J. C. Calhoun to the President of the United States, January 24, 1825, *ASPIA*, 2:542–44 ("small remnants," 542; "climate and nature," "collected," "greater facility," 543; "permanent home," 544).

37. McLoughlin, *Cherokee Renascence*, 350–67, 388–401, 411–12, 424; Young, "Cherokee Nation"; Perdue and Green, *Cherokee Nation*, 38–41, 54–58; Miles, *Ties That Bind*, 100–114.

38. Georgia General Assembly, *Acts*, 249 ("solemnly warn[ed]," "the lands"); *Niles' Weekly Register*, Dec. 29, 1827, 274 ("ought not"); John Quincy Adams, "Fourth Annual Message to Congress," Dec. 2, 1828, Williams, comp., *Addresses and Messages of the Presidents*, 1:627 ("unexpectedly found," "do justice," "their rights"). For McKenney, see Viola, *Thomas L. McKenney*. For Adams's ambivalence toward removal, see Parsons, "'A Perpetual Harrow upon My Feelings,'" 358–59.

39. Rogin, *Fathers and Children*, 4 ("major policy aim"); Andrew Jackson, "First Annual Message to Congress," Dec. 8, 1829, Williams, comp., *Addresses and Messages*, 1:709–10 ("surrounded by whites," "doom[ed]," "humanity and national honor," 710; "a foreign," 709).

40. U.S. House, *Memorial of John Ross;* Tracy, ed., *Memoir of the Life of Jeremiah Evarts*, 324 (qtn.); McLoughlin, *Cherokee Renascence*, 425, 430. For Cherokee arguments in the memorial and other texts in the late 1820s and early 1830s, see Denson, *Demanding the Cherokee Nation*, 27–38; Konkle, *Writing Indian Nations*, 49–61, 71–78.

41. Andrew, *From Revivals to Removal*, 184–93, 205–6; Konkle, *Writing Indian Nations*, 63–68; Evarts, *Essays on the Present Crisis*, 7 ("the title"), 84 (*"force becomes right"*), 100 ("60,000 souls," "be attended").

42. "Circular Addressed to Benevolent Ladies of the U. States," *Christian Advocate and Journal, and Zion's Herald* (New York), Dec. 25, 1829, 65–66 ("as by solemn," "such measures," "final extinction," 65); Hershberger, "Mobilizing Women" ("first national," 25); Miles, "'Circular Reasoning,'" 232–36 ("impress . . . the urgency," 232).

43. Satz, *American Indian Policy*, 14–18; Konkle, *Writing Indian Nations*, 68–71; Cass, "Removal of the Indians" ("the only means," 66; "'as long,'" 86; "rude and barbarous," 93). Guyatt, *Bind Us Apart*, 302–3, points out that although McKenney and McCoy supported removal legislation, they ultimately wanted a more robust program of "colonization," which would have involved territorial status and institution-building.

44. Prucha, *Great Father*, 1:200–201, 204–6; Satz, *American Indian Policy*, 19–31; *Register of Debates in Congress*, 21st Cong., 1st sess., 1830, 6, pt. 1:309–20, 325–39 (qtn., 328).

45. Prucha, *Great Father*, 1:206. On the three-fifths clause, see Howe, *What Hath God Wrought*, 352.

46. *Register of Debates in Congress*, 21st Cong., 1st sess., 1830, 6, pt. 1:316 ("unwarrantable pretensions"), 1:309 (amendment for federal protection); Andrew, *From Revivals to Removal*, 180.

47. Ford, *Settler Sovereignty*, 183.

48. U.S. House, *Memorial of a Delegation*, 1–8 ("flocked in thousands," "by violence," "forced the natives," "our country again," 4; "peaceable," "One was," 5; "forced an Indian," "stop [Cherokees]," "proceeded to destroy," 7); Mooney, "Myths of the Cherokee," 118 (Georgia couple's house); *IALT*, 179 ("white people").

49. Ford, *Settler Sovereignty,* 189–91 ("the right to punish," 191); Garrison, *Legal Ideology,* 111–22; U.S. House, *Memorial of a Delegation,* 7 ("breathe a spirit).

50. "Address to the People of the United States," 446.

51. Nehah Micco et al. to Secretary of War, Apr. 8, 1831, *CSEI,* 2:424–25 ("Our aged fathers," "the worst evil," 424); Harvey, *History of the Shawnee Indians,* 145 ("dreaded," "if they would," "intimations," "alas," "what a mistake"); Hauptman, *Tonawanda Senecas' Heroic Battle,* 39 ("white man").

CHAPTER 7. WEST OF THE MISSISSIPPI

1. Thomas Jefferson to John Breckinridge, Aug. 12, 1803, Lipscomb, ed., *Writings of Thomas Jefferson,* 10:407–11 (qtn., 410).

2. Thomas Jefferson, "First Inaugural Address," Washington, ed., *Writings of Thomas Jefferson,* 8:3.

3. Thomas Jefferson to Robert Smith, July 13, 1804, Jackson, ed., *Letters,* 1:200 (qtn.); Rollings, *Osage;* DuVal, *Native Ground,* 103–27. Fenn, *Pox Americana,* 219–20, notes that there is no evidence that the Osages were hit by the smallpox epidemic that struck most Missouri River nations in the early 1780s. For the Osage population, see Appendix 2.

4. James Wilkinson to Henry Dearborn, Sept. 22, 1805, *TPUS,* 13:229 (qtns.); Aron, *American Confluence,* 136; Rollings, *Osage,* 180, 220. For the Chouteaus, see Hyde, *Empires, Nations, and Families,* 30–42.

5. Thomas Jefferson, speech to the Osages, July 12, 1804, Lipscomb, ed., *Writings of Thomas Jefferson,* 16:405–10 (qtn., 406); DuVal, *Native Ground,* 183–84; Din and Nasatir, *Imperial Osages,* 359–60.

6. For the St. Louis peace agreement, see "A Treaty between the Tribes of Indians . . .," Oct. 13, 1805, *TPUS,* 13:245–47 ("firm peace," 246); Wallace, *Jefferson and the Indians,* 253. For the Potawatomi attacks, see Rollings, *Osage,* 221; Edmunds, *Potawatomis,* 157. For Pike and Osage attacks on Americans, see DuVal, *Native Ground,* 200–201; Schake, *La Charrette,* 148 ("a large number," "an unknown fever," "this evil").

7. Wallace, *Jefferson and the Indians,* 268–71; Rollings, *Osage,* 224–30; Bowes, *Land Too Good,* 96; DuVal, *Native Ground,* 201–5; William Clark to Secretary of War, Sept. 23, 1808, *TPUS,* 14:224–28 ("chearfully approved," 225); *IALT,* 95–99; Buckley, *William Clark,* 75–77 ("if he was," 77).

8. Carver, *Three Years Travel,* 29 (qtn.); Hagan, *Sac and Fox Indians,* 5–7, 12–13 (population, 7).

9. Wallace, *Prelude to Disaster,* 13–21; Hagan, *Sac and Fox Indians,* 18–29; *IALT,* 74–77.

10. DuVal, *Native Ground,* 205–6, argues that at the moment the Osages wished to cultivate peaceful trading relations with Americans and that they had more to fear from nations moving in from the East than from Americans.

11. For the Red Sticks' efforts to recruit Caddos, see Sugden, *Tecumseh,* 351. For Caddo history, see LaVere, *Caddo Chiefdoms;* Smith, *Caddo Indians.* For the Caddos' defense against the de Soto expedition and their maintenance of a relatively high population

through the mid-1600s, see Barr, "There's No Such Thing as 'Prehistory,'" 211–17. Population figures are in Appendix 2.

12. Smith, *Caddo Indians*, 85 (qtns.), 96–97, 101, 105–6; LaVere, *Caddo Chiefdoms*, 131–34.
13. Buckley, *William Clark*, 99–102; Aron, *American Confluence*, 156; Hagan, *Sac and Fox Indians*, 56, 58; William Clark to Secretary of War, Aug. 20, 1814, *TPUS*, 14:786–87 (qtn., 786).
14. Buckley, *William Clark*, 102–12; Aron, *American Confluence*, 157–58; Hagan, *Sac and Fox Indians*, 61–66, 77–82; Fisher, "Treaties of Portage Des Sioux" ("say you wish," 502); Jackson, ed., *Black Hawk*, 86–87 ("touched the goose quill," "not knowing," 87).
15. The only evidence of significant Indian losses during this period comes from a settler reminiscence written almost fifty years later, which relates that sometime in 1813 Missouri rangers surprised a band of unidentified Indians playing stickball near the confluence of Bonne Femme Creek and the Missouri River and killed forty-nine. See Persinger, *Life of Jacob Persinger*, 17. In the absence of corroborating evidence for this event, however, it is unclear that it actually happened.
16. Warren, *History of the Ojibway People*, 265 ("When I go"); Anderson, *Kinsmen*, 90–91 ("dying with hunger," 91); Smith, *Caddo Indians*, 102; LaVere, *Caddo Chiefdoms*, 135.
17. Population figures are from Buckley, *William Clark*, 125; U.S. Bureau of the Census, *Historical Statistics*, 30. For the general trans-Appalachian population explosion, see Belich, *Replenishing the Earth*, 91–93.
18. Population figures in Appendix 2; for the events, see Weslager, *Delaware Indians*, 361–63; Aron, *American Confluence*, 162–64; Faragher, "'More Motley than Mackinaw,'" 317; Warren, *Shawnees and Their Neighbors*, 83–87.
19. Rollings, *Osage*, 238–40; LaVere, *Contrary Neighbors*, 48–49; Eaton, "Legend of the Battle of Claremore Mound"; DuVal, *Native Ground*, 208–10; McLoughlin, *Cherokee Renascence*, 217 (Tolluntuskee qtns.); John C. Calhoun to William Clark, May 8, 1818, *TPUS*, 15:390–91 ("it seems fair," "the President," 391).
20. DuVal, *Native Ground*, 216–17 ("the gift," 217); Buckley, *William Clark*, 129–30; Rollings, *Osage*, 240, 244–49, 268, 274 ("Twenty or Twenty Five," 268). For Osage–Pawnee conflict, see also White, *Roots of Dependency*, 153. For Osage–Comanche conflict prior to the 1830s, see also Hämäläinen, *Comanche Empire*, 111, 154. For Osage–Wichita conflict, see also Smith, *Wichita Indians*, 103, 105, 118.
21. Rollings, *Osage*, 250–55; Buckley, *William Clark*, 168–69 (qtn., 169); *IALT*, 217–21.
22. Rollings, *Osage*, 261–62, 266–67, 272–73; DuVal, *Native Ground*, 224.
23. Rollings, *Osage*, 267; Bowes, *Exiles and Pioneers*, 132.
24. DuVal, *Native Ground*, 67–82, 128–41, 148–49, 190; population figures in Appendix 2.
25. Baird, *Quapaw Indians*, 51–55; DuVal, *Native Ground*, 216, 230 (qtn.).
26. Baird, *Quapaw Indians*, 55–60, 69; Buckley, *William Clark*, 132; *IALT*, 95–96, 160.
27. "Petition to Congress by Inhabitants of Arkansas County," Nov. 2, 1818, "Petition to the President by the Territorial Assembly," Feb. 11, 1820, *TPUS*, 19:10–12, 143–45 ("unnecessarily lavishing," 12); Baird, *Quapaw Indians*, 57, 61–70; DuVal, *Native Ground*, 230–33; Thompson, "History of the Quapaw," 369 ("Since you have"); *IALT*, 210–11.

28. Young and Hoffman, "Quapaw," 504; Baird, *Quapaw Indians*, 71–79; DuVal, *Native Ground*, 233–34.

29. Smith, *Caddo Indians*, 106–11, 115 (qtns., 110); LaVere, *Caddo Chiefdoms*, 135–40, 144–45; Carter, *Caddo Indians*, 252–54. Population figure includes only Kadohadacho communities in Louisiana and not the related Hasinais and Nadacos in Texas.

30. Smith, *Caddo Indians*, 117, 119–24; LaVere, *Caddo Chiefdoms*, 146–49; Carter, *Caddo Indians*, 264–65, 269–73 ("starving," "get all we can," 272); *IALT*, 432–34.

31. J. C. Calhoun to James Monroe, Jan. 24, 1825, *ASPIA*, 2:542; Klopotek, *Recognition Odysseys*, 43 ("have not been reclaimed"); Usner, *American Indians*, 95–127. For the *petites nations* population, see Appendix 2.

32. Hagan, *Sac and Fox Indians*, 102; Anderson, *Kinsmen*, 103–14; Warren, *History of the Ojibway People*, 381–85.

33. For the Ioways, see Blaine, *Ioway Indians*, 139–40. Blaine, 130, also reports that Sauks slaughtered almost all the inhabitants of a large Iowa village in the mid-1820s, though the source for this, Stevens, *Black Hawk War*, 69, is clearly unreliable, stating that the entire Ioway nation was annihilated. For the Omahas, see Wishart, *Unspeakable Sadness*, 7, 77; O'Shea, *Archaeology and Ethnohistory*, 37; Boughter, *Betraying the Omaha Nation*, 25. For Dakota–Sauk and Mesquakie conflict, see Anderson, *Kinsmen*, 106–7, 121; Jackson, ed., *Black Hawk*, 92 ("about knee-high"). Population figures in Appendix 2.

34. Thomas McKenney to Secretary of War, Nov. 30, 1825, *ASPIA*, 2:585 ("long and bloody"); Redix, *Murder of Joe White*, 23 ("in running marks"); Abele, "Grand Council and Treaty," 130–66 ("poisoned," 165); Hagan, *Sac and Fox Indians*, 96–99; Buckley, *William Clark*, 172–75; Witgen, *Infinity of Nations*, 347–48.

35. Cass, "Policy and Practice," 401; *IALT*, 253.

36. Anderson, *Kinsmen*, 124, 133 ("get skins," "wish to push," 133); Hagan, *Sac and Fox Indians*, 117; Foreman, *Last Trek*, 137; Buckley, *William Clark*, 202–3. On the abolition of the factory system, see Prucha, *Great Father*, 1:129–34.

37. Blaine, *Ioway Indians*, 140–42, 158–61, 197–98; Olson, *Ioway in Missouri*, 84–88, 92–94, 100–102, 111–12; *IALT*, 208–9.

38. Blaine, *Ioway Indians*, 161–71 ("bones of their fathers," 165); Olson, *Ioway in Missouri*, 112–13, 118–19; Edmunds, *Potawatomis*, 246–47, 250–51; Aron, *American Confluence*, 229–31; *IALT*, 468–70.

39. Bowes, *Exiles and Pioneers*, 49, 133; Bowes, *Land Too Good*, 107; Gibson, *Kickapoos*, 109; *IALT*, 262–64, 304–5, 365–67. On the shift in U.S. Indian policy in Missouri to one of ethnic cleansing, see Faragher, "'More Motley than Mackinaw,'" 320.

40. Unrau, *Kansa Indians*, 103–5, 145–50, 157–58 ("malignant disease," 149; "had less than," 147); *IALT*, 222–25. Population figures in Appendix 2.

41. Hofstadter, *American Political Tradition*, 71 ("expectant capitalists"); Thorne, *Many Hands*, 188–94, 200–205 ("whiskey capital," 203); Wishart, *Unspeakable Sadness*, 61–62, 73, 76–80, ("stalked," 76); Boughter, *Betraying the Omaha Nation*, 25–27, 34–35.

42. McCoy, *History of Baptist Indian Missions*, 441 (qtns.). Mann, *Tainted Gift*, 49, accepts McCoy's explanation. For the relevance of social conditions to the severity of

a smallpox epidemic that hit the upper Missouri River in 1837, see Jones, *Rationalizing Epidemics,* 105–6. For population figures, see Appendix 2.

43. Baird, *Quapaw Indians,* 51, 69, 78–79; Smith, *Caddo Indians,* 85, 120; Nuttall, *Journal of Travels,* 193 (qtns.). For population figures, see Appendix 2.

44. Child, *Holding Our World Together,* 19–27. Population figures are in Appendix 2. Earlier estimates for the Ojibwe population do not provide a specific estimate for the Minnesota population, but, as observed in Chapter 6, Native populations in the upper Great Lakes were generally increasing in the early nineteenth century under conditions similar to those in Minnesota.

45. Trask, *Black Hawk,* 33–34, 59–60 (though Trask overstates the adverse impact of alcohol); Murphy, *Gathering of Rivers,* 79–99, 105–6, 131–32, 137–65; Jackson, ed., *Black Hawk,* 101–2 ("party," 101; "took out," 101–2). Population figures are in Appendix 2.

46. Trask, *Black Hawk,* 46–47, 61–62, 65, 68–69; Murphy, *Gathering of Rivers,* 101–3, 109–17.

CHAPTER 8. REMOVAL AND THE SOUTHERN INDIAN NATIONS

1. Based on figures in Appendix 2, but not including an estimated 3,000–3,500 Indians on the eastern seaboard with little land. Federal planners did not include them in planning for removal. See John C. Calhoun to President of the United States, Jan. 24, 1825, *ASPIA,* 2:542–43. For accounts of problems with the planning and execution of Indian removal from the perspective of scholars concerned with questions of U.S. state capacity, see Rockwell, *Indian Affairs and the Administrative State,* 159–87; Frymer, *Building an American Empire,* 113–23.

2. For the growth of cotton production and slavery in the American South, see Beckert, *Empire of Cotton,* 105–20; Bruchey, comp. and ed., *Cotton,* 14, 16 (statistics). For the domestic slave trade, see Deyle, *Carry Me Back.* For the impact of Haiti, see Clavin, *Touissant Louverture and the American Civil War,* 11–19 ("second Haitian Revolution," 17); Sinha, *Slave's Cause,* 53–59.

3. Remini, *Andrew Jackson and His Indian Wars,* 242–43.

4. Remini, *Andrew Jackson and His Indian Wars,* 243–46; Gibson, *Chickasaws,* 156–58; Paige, Bumpers, and Littlefield, *Chickasaw Removal,* 25–29; St. Jean, *Remaining Chickasaw,* 10; Atkinson, *Splendid Land,* 227; *CSEI,* 2:240–44 ("country beyond," "for the happiness," 241; "an act of usurpation," 243); *IALT,* 1035–40 ("a country," "null and void," 1036).

5. DeRosier, *Removal of the Choctaw,* 118–23 ("some good men," 118); Akers, *Living in the Land of Death,* 89–92; Kidwell, *Choctaws and Missionaries,* 139–41; Halbert, "Story of the Treaty of Dancing Rabbit," 373–87 ("gave vent," 385); Dillard, "Treaty of Dancing Rabbit Creek," 99–103 ("we love," 103); Akers, "Removing the Heart," 66–69 ("Land of Death," 69).

6. DeRosier, *Removal of the Choctaw,* 123–26; Remini, *Andrew Jackson and His Indian Wars,* 248–49; Dillard, "Treaty of Dancing Rabbit Creek," 103–6 ("brutal bluntness,"

"had no choice," "the President," 103; "be the ruin," 104); *IALT,* 310–17; White, *Roots of Dependency,* 142–43 ("shock and despair," 143).

7. A government official conducted a census in 1831 showing 19,554 Choctaws, including 248 slaves, although some slaves were omitted. See *CSEI,* 3:131. Doran, "Negro Slaves," 346, documents 512 slaves in the Choctaw Nation prior to removal.

8. Foreman, *Indian Removal,* 51–53; DeRosier, *Removal of the Choctaw,* 143–44; Wright, "Removal of the Choctaws," 113–15; *Religious Intelligencer* 16 (Jan. 7, 1832): 506 (qtn.). I infer the advantage of waiting until the harvest is over. Neither Choctaws nor Americans understood in 1831 that mosquitoes transmitted the parasite that causes malaria, nor was malaria identified as a specific disease; nonetheless, the Choctaws' desire that there "must be one frost before they take to the Mississippi swamp" noted in F. W. Armstrong to J. H. Eaton, July 1, 1831, *CSEI,* 1:369, likely documents an observed association between swamps, mosquitoes, and disease.

9. Pierson, *Tocqueville and Beaumont,* 597–98 (qtns.). Adair, *History of the American Indians,* 310, notes the Choctaws' use of dogs in hunting bears; Pesantubbee, *Choctaw Women,* 153, points out that Choctaws "sacrificed" the deceased's favorite horse or dog to accompany the deceased to the next world.

10. Foreman, *Indian Removal,* 53–65; DeRosier, *Removal of the Choctaw,* 144–47; Wright, "Removal of the Choctaws," 116–19; J. Brown to General George Gibson, Dec. 15 and 22, 1831, Jan. 11, 1832, in *CSEI,* 1:427–30 ("our poor emigrants," 427; "frosted," "sustain themselves," 428).

11. Foreman, *Indian Removal,* 76–96; DeRosier, *Removal of the Choctaw,* 153–58; Wright, "Removal of the Choctaws," 120–23; Mann, *Tainted Gift,* 30–38; *Foreign Missionary Chronicle* 1 (June 1833): 45–46 (qtn., 46). For the intention to leave early, see F. W. Armstrong to Lewis Cass, April 20, 1832, *CSEI,* 3:303. On the 1832 epidemic and its spread, see Rosenberg, *Cholera Years,* 21–24, 36–37.

12. Foreman, *Indian Removal,* 97–99; Akers, *Living in the Land of Death,* 112–14; G. J. Raines to Gibson, Sept. 12, Oct. 20, 1833, *CSEI,* 1:849–51 ("diseases," 851); report dated Dec. 27, 1833 in *Missionary Herald* 30 (April 1834): 142 ("not a single child," "the mortality"). For springs and drinking water, see report dated Oct. 2, 1833 in *Missionary Herald* 30 (January 1834): 21. For a discussion of the meanings of fevers and ague, see Valenčius, *Health of the Country,* 79–82. For Choctaws returning to Mississippi, see Snyder, *Great Crossings,* 161.

13. Foreman, *Indian Removal,* 99–101; DeRosier, *Removal of the Choctaw,* 160–62; J. F. Lane to George Gibson, Sept. 24, 1833, in *CSEI,* 1:745 (qtn.).

14. Foreman, *Indian Removal,* 221, gives a figure of 400–500; Akers, "Removing the Heart," 74, states that more than 1,000 died. For the 1837–1838 smallpox epidemic on the upper Missouri, see Fenn, *Encounters at the Heart of the World,* 311–25.

15. For the nonvaccination of the Choctaws in 1832, see Mann, *Tainted Gift,* 26–27. For the problems limiting vaccination of the removed tribes in the West, see Pearson, "Lewis Cass and the Politics of Disease," 25. For McCoy's role in lobbying for the 1832 Indian Vaccination Act, see Trimble, "The 1832 Inoculation Program," 260–61. Pearson, "Lewis Cass and the Politics of Disease," argues that government officials

withheld vaccination from some Indian nations as a means of colonial management. This may be true in some cases, but neglect seems to be the salient issue for the Choctaws. For vaccinating Indians to protect whites, see Dowd, *Groundless*, 232; Isenberg, "Empire of Remedy," 103.

16. *IALT,* 313; Foreman, *Indian Removal,* 102–4; DeRosier, *Removal of the Choctaw,* 135–36; Peterson, "Three Efforts at Development," 144–46 (qtn., 144–45); Kidwell, "Choctaw Struggle," 64–78; Matte, *They Say the Wind,* 51–61. For Choctaws remaining in the East, see Appendix 2.

17. Thornton, *American Indian Holocaust,* 114, gives the 6,000 figure, relying on Allen, "Medical Practices," 62, who cites Cushman, *History of the Choctaw, Chickasaw, and Natchez,* 94, which provides Byington as the authority that 6,000 died "en route" from a total population of 40,000. A figure of 2,500 is provided by Green, "Expansion of European Colonization," 522.

18. Paige, Bumpers, and Littlefield, *Chickasaw Removal,* 35–66, 89–137; Gibson, *Chickasaws,* 159–62, 170–76; Foreman, *Indian Removal,* 204–25; *IALT,* 356–62, 486–88. For the death toll from smallpox, see *RCIA, 1838,* 511. Over the next several years, the Chickasaw leadership encouraged the few hundred Chickasaws who remained in the East to join them. By 1850, almost all Chickasaws had relocated. See Paige, Bumpers, and Littlefield, *Chickasaw Removal,* 143–64.

19. J. J. Abert to Lewis Cass, June 2, 1833, *CSEI,* 4:422–24 ("starvation," 423); Nehah Micco et al. to Secretary of War, Apr. 8, 1831, *CSEI,* 2:424–25 ("compelled to refuse," "our Father," "the land," "the bones," "the unhealthiness," 424). For the western Creeks in the late 1820s and early 1830s, see Haveman, *Rivers of Sand,* 80, 169–70. Population figures are in Appendix 2.

20. Green, *Politics of Indian Removal,* 145–73 (qtn., 148); Haveman, *Rivers of Sand,* 94–97; *IALT,* 341–43.

21. Rogin, *Fathers and Children,* 221–22; Foreman, *Indian Removal,* 111–18, 123–25; Ellisor, *Second Creek War,* 82–139; Haveman, "'Last Evening I Saw the Sun Set,'" 64–70.

22. Haveman, *Rivers of Sand,* 133–35; F. S. Key to Lewis Cass, Nov. 11, 1833, *CSEI,* 4:664–66 ("are already," 665); R. J. Meigs journal, Aug. 9, 1834, U.S. Senate, *Message of the President of the United States . . . Transmitting Documents Relating to Frauds,* 169 ("the earthquakes").

23. Haveman, *Rivers of Sand,* 120–27 (630 leaving in December 1834, 121; 20 deserters, 127; "destitute of clothing," 121); Foreman, *Indian Removal,* 126–28 (469 arriving in March 1835, 128).

24. Haveman, *Rivers of Sand,* 133, 140–48, 176–77, 180–83; Foreman, *Indian Removal,* 141, 145–47; Ellisor, *Second Creek War,* 182–99; John Page to Brigadier General George Gibson, May 20, 1836, *American State Papers: Military Affairs,* 6:771–72 ("whip the white people," 772).

25. Haveman, *Rivers of Sand,* 184–99 (339 missing or dead, 198); Foreman, *Indian Removal,* 152–60; Ellisor, *Second Creek War,* 228–63; Lewis Cass to Thomas S. Jesup, May 19, 1836, U.S. House, *Letter from the Secretary of War Transmitting Certain Orders,* 42–44 ("unconditional submission," 42; "determine . . . who are hostile," 43).

26. Haveman, *Rivers of Sand*, 200–233 ("fire carriers," 203; "impossible to pass through," "denied a proper," 223; "leaving bloody," 230; 188 died, 231); Martin, *Sacred Revolt*, 36 ("represent"); Foreman, *Indian Removal*, 160–65, 177–79.

27. Haveman, *Rivers of Sand*, 242–50, 260–61 (71 escaped, 9 died, 248); Ellisor, "'Like So Many Wolves,'" 7, 15–20, 23; Foreman, *Indian Removal*, 188–90 ("sick and help-less," 190); John E. Wool to Lewis Cass, Sept. 18, 1836, U.S. House, *Message from the President of the United States Transmitting the Proceedings of the Court of Inquiry*, 55–56 ("humanity revolts," "hunted and dragged," 55); *Army and Navy Chronicle* 4 (May 11, 1837): 301 ("sap of the timber").

28. Haveman, *Rivers of Sand*, 234–42, 250–54 ("his head litterally," 238; 93 dead, 250; additional 84, 253); Ellisor, *Second Creek War*, 354–59; Foreman, *Indian Removal*, 179–85 ("the men wished," 181). On the rape of Creek women during removal, see also Sullivan, *Indian Legends*, 2.

29. Haveman, *Rivers of Sand*, 258–60; Foreman, *Indian Removal*, 186–88; *Niles' National Register*, Nov. 11, 1837: 163 (qtns.); Jim Boy and David Barnett to Commissioners, Nov. 22, 1838, U.S. Senate, *Message from the President of the United States Transmitting Treaties*, 470.

30. Ellisor, *Second Creek War*, 360–61, 366–69, 384–86, 391–92 ("search-and-destroy," 366; "men, women, and children," 368); Wright, *Creeks and Seminoles*, 270–72, 297–98.

31. The 3,500 figure was provided in 1842 by H. S. Alexander to Ethan Allen Hitchcock, as reported in Foreman, ed., *Traveler in Indian Territory*, 120. McCoy, *Annual Register of Indian Affairs*, 276, relies on "the authority of an officer of Government" in attributing the 3,500 deaths to "bilious fevers." For population figures see Appendix 2.

32. 30 U.S. 1 (1831) at 2. For "perfect settler sovereignty," see Ford, *Settler Sovereignty*, 183. For Ross's reaction to the decision, see Perdue and Green, *Cherokee Nation*, 82–83 ("conclusively adverse," 83).

33. Perdue and Green, *Cherokee Nation*, 84–85; Wilkins, *Cherokee Tragedy*, 225–28, 230–35.

34. 31 U.S. 515 (1832) at 515.

35. Many scholars recognize a shift in Marshall's views from *Johnson v. M'Intosh* through *Cherokee Nation* to *Worcester*, though there is a tendency to overstate it, with some reading the shift as a redemptive moment in an otherwise sorry history. On the other hand, arguments by other scholars for a strong continuity from the *Johnson v. M'Intosh* to the other cases either overlook evidence of a shift or too easily dismiss it as meaningless rhetoric, thus understating the impact of Cherokee political action. Arguments for a shift can be found in Banner, *How the Indians Lost Their Land*, 219–21; Wilkins and Lomawaima, *Uneven Ground*, 58–61; Norgren, *Cherokee Cases*, 118–20; Garrison, *Legal Ideology*, 178–91; Robertson, *Conquest by Law*, 133–35; Echo-Hawk, *In the Courts of the Conqueror*, 108–9. For arguments for continuity, see Miller, *Native America*, 54–55; Wolfe, "Against the Intentional Fallacy," 13–16.

36. Wilkins, *Cherokee Tragedy*, 235 ("a great triumph"); Perdue and Green, *Cherokee Nation*, 88 ("Rejoicings Dances"); Garrison, *Legal Ideology*, 193–94 ("the decision," 194; "John Marshall," 193).

37. Perdue and Green, *Cherokee Nation*, 94–101; Wilkins, *Cherokee Tragedy*, 236–38, 242–49; Satz, *American Indian Policy*, 52–53; McLoughlin, *Cherokee Renascence*, 445–47;

Garrison, *Legal Ideology*, 194–96; Howe, *What Hath God Wrought*, 412–13. Worcester and Butler were pardoned by Georgia governor Wilson Lumpkin at the initiative of the Jackson administration. Because of an entirely separate issue, South Carolina's nullification of a federal tariff, Jackson did not want to release the missionaries, as this might cause Georgia to support South Carolina, nor did he want to defend Georgia's detention of the missionaries, as this would make it appear that he supported Georgia's "nullification" of the Supreme Court. Having Lumpkin issue a pardon solved the problem.

38. Wilkins, *Cherokee Tragedy*, 225, 251–52 ("fortunate drawers," 251); Perdue and Green, *Cherokee Nation*, 99–100; Foreman, *Indian Removal*, 248–49; *Cherokee Phoenix* quoted in *Boston Recorder*, Aug. 21, 1833 ("called for a drink," "laid hold," "no Indian testimony"); *Missionary Herald* 29 (December 1833): 459 ("past two," "obtaining the various," "anxiety and despondency"); Ben F. Currey to Elbert Herring, June 28, 1833, *CSEI*, 4:446 ("their suffering").

39. Perdue and Green, *Cherokee Nation*, 103–6; Wilkins, *Cherokee Tragedy*, 260–63 (qtn., 261).

40. Perdue and Green, *Cherokee Nation*, 106–7, 110–13 ("Devil's Horn," 111); Wilkins, *Cherokee Tragedy*, 266–69, 272–92; Calloway, *Pen and Ink Witchcraft*, 140–47 ("deceptive to the world," 146); J. F. Schermerhorn to Lewis Cass, Mar. 3, 1836, U.S. Senate, *Report from the Secretary of War . . . in Relation to the Cherokee Treaty of 1835*, 532–39; *IALT*, 439–49.

41. *IALT*, 446; John E. Wool to Lewis Cass, July 25, 1836, U.S. Senate, *Report from the Secretary of War . . . in Relation to the Cherokee Treaty of 1835*, 627-29 (qtn., 628); Hauptman, "General John E. Wool." Hauptman contests the interpretation of Wool as a "humanitarian," an interpretation based on his expressions of sympathy for the Cherokees when settlers violated the New Echota Treaty by taking up Cherokee lands prior to their eviction. Instead, Hauptman argues, Wool's goal was to maintain the "exact letter of the Treaty of New Echota" and thereby obtain "wholesale removal of the Cherokees, and the prevention of an armed Cherokee resistance" (p. 24).

42. Winfield Scott, Address to Cherokees, May 10, 1838, U.S. House, *Removal of the Cherokees*, 11–12 ("President," 11; "has sent me," 11–12; "are approaching," "hopeless," "render resistance," "a general war," "destruction," 12).

43. "Address to the People of the United States," 447.

44. On Choctaw/Creek reports to Cherokees, see John Ross to "Dear Nephew," Apr. 10 [?], 1838, Moulton, ed., *Papers of Chief John Ross*, 1:627–28. Foreman, *Indian Removal*, 242–43, 252–63, 273–78, 280–85, details the journeys and numbers for emigrating parties in March 1832 (550, with an additional 108 enslaved blacks), March 1834 (524), March 1837 (466), October 1837 (365), and March 1838 (250), the latter three consisting primarily of Cherokees associated with the Treaty Party. The only mention of enslaved people is for the 1832 party; it is unclear if enslaved people were included in the other counts or not. All of these groups, except the October 1837 group, took a water route—down the Tennessee to the Ohio, down the Ohio to the Mississippi, down the Mississippi to the Arkansas, and then up the Arkansas. The October 1837 group took an overland route through Tennessee, Kentucky, southern Illinois, and southern Missouri.

45. Foreman, *Indian Removal,* 290, gives a figure of 17,000 awaiting removal in May 1838, based on counts of the removal parties upon departure (some in June, most in the fall). This figure, however, neglects to consider the estimated 2,000 who perished in the removal camps during the summer before removal (see below). Since an additional 1,400 or so avoided being forced west and remained in North Carolina, Georgia, and Tennessee (see Finger, *Eastern Band of Cherokees,* 29), a solid estimate for the eastern Cherokee population in 1838 would be 20,000–21,000.

46. Wilkins, *Cherokee Tragedy,* 319 ("in a humane"); Perdue and Green, *Cherokee Nation,* 123–24 ("soldiers came"); Foreman, *Indian Removal,* 288 ("multitudes were allowed," "plunderers"); Mooney, "Myths of the Cherokee," 130–31 ("silver pendants," "fought through the civil war," 130); Butrick, *Cherokee Removal,* 2 ("use[d] the same," "seeing his children," "whipped a hundred").

47. Mooney, "Myths of the Cherokee," 132 ("subsisted on roots"); Neely, "Acculturation and Persistence," 157–58; Finger, *Eastern Band of Cherokees,* 10–11, 16–21, 28–29; Elizur Butler to David Greene, June 15, 1838, American Board of Commissioners of Foreign Missions, Papers ("completely . . . swept"). For references to Cherokee removal as ethnic cleansing, see Perdue and Green, *Cherokee Nation,* 42; Calloway, *Pen and Ink Witchcraft,* 121; Kiernan, *Blood and Soil,* 330.

48. Foreman, *Indian Removal,* 291–99 (qtn., 299). Foreman states (p. 293) that there were no deaths in the first party, though it appears that this is based not on positive evidence but rather on the absence of a report of deaths; the party began with 800 and lost at least 300, with only 100 reported as having escaped.

49. Perdue and Green, *Cherokee Nation,* 127–29 (qtns., 128); Foreman, *Indian Removal,* 299–300.

50. Butler to Greene, July 12, Aug. 2 ("infant children"), Sept. 14 ("remitting fevers"), 1838, American Board of Commissioners for Foreign Missions, Papers; Butrick, *Cherokee Removal,* 10 ("young married woman," "fear," "yield"), 14 ("abus[ed] her," "was fighting away"). For rape as an attack on tribal sovereignty, see Deer, *Beginning and the End of Rape,* 13.

51. Butler to Greene, Oct. 10, 1838, Butler to Mr. Parham, Mar. 1, 1839, American Board of Commissioners of Foreign Missions, Papers. Butler's figure was based on an estimated 16 deaths per day in all the camps, an estimate consistent with his and Butrick's observations.

52. Foreman, *Indian Removal,* 303–12 ("destitute of shoes," "50 of them," 308; "exceedingly cold," "thinly clad," "very uncomfortable," "great numbers," "fact that," "makes it," 309); Butler to Parham, Mar. 1, 1839, Foreman, *Indian Removal,* 310–12. U.S. House, *Removal of the Cherokees West of the Mississippi,* 9–10, provides the number who died for eight of the parties. Of a total of 7,552 at departure for these eight parties, 404 died along the way. Assuming a similar death rate in the other parties, the death toll for all fourteen parties would have been 739. My sense that desertion does not account for the difference between an estimate of 700 and the total decline of 1,800 receives some confirmation from the fact that the few mentions of desertions from these parties suggest small numbers and that some deserters later joined other parties.

It is also noteworthy that a month after arriving in the West, Jesse Bushyhead wrote that there had been 82 deaths in his party, a much larger number than in the official report for his party, which gives 38 deaths (Foreman, *Indian Removal*, 309, 311), suggesting the possibility of a consistent undercount in the official reports.

53. Butler to Parham, Mar. 1, 1839, provides an estimate of 4,000 for the 1838–1839 removals, with an additional 400–500 who perished in North Carolina. Prucha, *Great Father*, 1:241, n. 58, warns against "uncritically" accepting "greatly exaggerated figures" like Butler's, which he rejects on the basis of the reports of the fourteen parties that emigrated in fall-winter 1838–1839, but this overlooks the fact that Butler's estimate included 2,000 who had perished in the camps. Thornton, "Cherokee Population Losses," 293–94, accepts the 4,000 figure though further argues that a consideration of Cherokee losses should include "what population size would have been had removal not occurred." This yields a "total mortality figure of 8,000" by 1840 (p. 298). This makes an important point, but summaries of Thornton's argument in his own *American Indian Holocaust*, 118; and Stannard, *American Holocaust*, 124, give 8,000 as a figure for actual mortality. My figure of 22,000–23,000 eastern Cherokees in 1832 is based on a population of 20,000–21,000 in May 1838 plus the 2,000 moved between 1832 and late 1837, all noted above.

54. Wright, *Creeks and Seminoles*, 197–213; Saunt, *New Order*, 286–90 (casualty figures at Negro Fort, 288); Nugent, *Habits of Empire*, 120–29; Remini, *Andrew Jackson and His Indian Wars*, 130–62; Missall and Missall, *Seminole Wars*, 25–51 (casualty figures for the village on Econfina Creek, 41).

55. Missall and Missall, *Seminole Wars*, 52–66, 81–84; Mahon, *History of the Second Seminole War*, 44–49, 74–75; Covington, *Seminoles of Florida*, 52–54; "Treaty with the Florida Indians," Dec. 15, 1823, *ASPIA*, 2:429–42 (qtns., 437); *IALT*, 344–45. After the 1832 treaty, 276 Seminoles on the Apalachicola River agreed to move west, though 49 of them died from disease before their departure in late 1834. See Foreman, *Indian Removal*, 322–23.

56. Missall and Missall, *Seminole Wars*, 87–89; Mahon, *History of the Second Seminole War*, 89–92; Davis, "Seminole Council" ("Great Spirit," "from the lands," 338; "I did not touch," 346; "At Payne's Landing," "I was there," 344; "you must go," 348). For Osceola's ancestry and biography, see Wickman, *Osceola's Legacy*, 1–14.

57. Missall and Missall, *Seminole Wars*, 89–97 (qtn., 90); Mahon, *Second Seminole War*, 95–106; Covington, *Seminoles of Florida*, 78–82; Porter, "The Negro Abraham," 18; Roberts, "Dade Massacre" (leaders of Seminole war party, 131, n. 14).

58. Hicks quoted in Wright, *Creeks and Seminoles*, 62. Population figures in Appendix 2.

59. For Black Seminole attitudes, see Littlefield, *Africans and Seminoles*, 10–13; Mulroy, *Seminole Freedmen*, 44; Rivers, *Rebels and Runaways*, 131. Miller, *Coacoochee's Bones*, 66–68, reasonably argues that blacks made a "significant contribution" to Seminole resistance but were not the "driving force."

60. Silverman, *Thundersticks*, 200; Sprague, *Origin, Progress, and Conclusion*, 318 (qtn.). Population figures are from U.S. Bureau of the Census, *Population of States and Counties*, 4.

61. Missall and Missall, *Seminole Wars,* 104–17 ("most distinguished officer," 104); Mahon, *Second Seminole War,* 138–62. For accounts of illness, identified primarily as "fever," among U.S. forces, see *Army and Navy Chronicle* 3 (Sept. 1, 1836): 139; *Niles' Weekly Register* 15 (Sept. 17, 1836): 35. A comprehensive report on causes of death among Florida troops lists "congestive fever," diarrhea, and dysentery. See [U.S. War Department] *Record of Officers and Soldiers Killed.*

62. Foreman, *Indian Removal,* 332–40 ("though with great," 333; "Every soul," 335–36; "Numbers very low," 336); Miller, *Coachoochee's Bones,* 13–15; Farnham, *Travels,* 1:132.

63. Missall and Missall, *Seminole Wars,* 125–29; Mahon, *Second Seminole War,* 190–204, 207–9, 225; Miller, *Coacoochee's Bones,* 39; Foreman, *Indian Removal,* 342–47.

64. Missall and Missall, *Seminole Wars,* 133–41; Mahon, *Second Seminole War,* 209–18; Miller, *Coacoochee's Bones,* 19, 40; Foreman, *Indian Removal,* 348–51.

65. Missall and Missall, *Seminole Wars,* 142–45; Mahon, *Second Seminole War,* 225–34; Silverman, *Thundersticks,* 208–12; Carrier, "Trade and Plunder Networks," 173–75; [Smith], *Sketches of the Seminole War,* 86 (qtns.).

66. Missall and Missall, *Seminole Wars,* 146–47 (Jesup qtn., 146); Mahon, *Second Seminole War,* 235–36, 240–43. For Seminoles' economic adaptations, see Covington, *Seminoles of Florida,* 100–101; Weisman, "Nativism, Resistance, and Ethnogenesis"; Weisman, *Unconquered People,* 110–13.

67. J. R. Poinsett to Major General Thomas S. Jesup, Mar. 1, 1838, U.S. House, *Letter from the Secretary of War Transmitting a Copy of His Answer to the Letter of General Jesup,* 1–2 ("settled policy," 1; "put it out," 2); Missall and Missall, *Seminole Wars,* 147–50; Foreman, *Indian Removal,* 361–62.

68. Jumper and West, *Seminole Legend,* 4 ("more and more"); Shire, *Threshold of Manifest Destiny,* 118 ("If the officers").

69. Foreman, *Indian Removal,* 364–70 ("suffered very much," 369; "a number," 370); Porter, "The Negro Abraham," 28-29; Lancaster, *Removal Aftershock,* 30 (smallpox).

70. Missall and Missall, *Seminole Wars,* 171–73; Covington, "Cuban Bloodhounds"; *Tallahassee Floridian,* quoted in *Niles' National Register,* Mar. 28, 1840: 51; Campbell, "Seminoles" ("deep and lasting," 274, n. 76).

71. Missall and Missall, *Seminole Wars,* 182–86, 192, 197; Mahon, *Second Seminole War,* 276, 278–80, 283–84, 300–301, 304–5; Covington, *Seminoles of Florida,* 98–105; Sprague, *Origin, Progress, and Conclusion,* 274 (qtn.), 281. Chakaika's people are often referred to as the "Spanish Indians," with some arguing that they descended from Florida Indian communities predating the arrival of Europeans. For a useful discussion of this question which observes that Seminoles themselves saw and still regard Chakaika as one of their own, see Weisman, *Unconquered People,* 80–83.

72. Mahon, *Second Seminole War,* 298–300, 302; Missall and Missall, *Seminole Wars,* 193–97; Miller, *Coacoochee's Bones,* 42, 45; Sprague, *Origin, Progress, and Conclusion,* 297 (qtn.); Foreman, *Indian Removal,* 378–80.

73. Missall and Missall, *Seminole Wars,* 200–202; Mahon, *Second Seminole War,* 307–10. Reports of these removals say nothing about the death toll. Had it been high, it presumably would have found its way into the historical record, but it is impossible to know for sure.

74. For U.S. troop numbers and casualties, see Mahon, *Second Seminole War,* 225, 325. Estimates for the number of blacks who escaped slavery and joined the Seminoles in 1835 and 1836 range from 400 to 1,000. The proportion of fighting men is impossible to know. See Rivers, *Rebels and Runaways,* 137. Wright, *Creeks and Seminoles,* 259, estimates that 800–1,000 Creeks (including 200 warriors) fled to Florida after the Creek War. How many of them fought with Seminoles is unclear.

75. Missall and Missall, *Seminole Wars,* xvii ("moral failure"); Prucha, *Sword of the Republic,* 269 ("embarrassing affair"); Remini, *Andrew Jackson and His Indian Wars,* 276 ("idiotic war").

76. For the 1842 census, see Foreman, *Indian Removal,* 380; Miller, *Coacoochee's Bones,* 49. My estimate of 150 Seminoles in Texas is based on the removal of 152 Seminoles under the leadership of John Blunt from the Apalachicola River in 1834 to the Trinity River. See Foreman, *Indian Removal,* 323.

77. Bruchey, comp. and ed., *Cotton,* 16.

CHAPTER 9. REMOVAL AND THE NORTHERN INDIAN NATIONS

1. Andrew Jackson, "Second Annual Message to Congress," Dec. 7, 1830, and "Third Annual Message to Congress," Dec. 6, 1831, Williams, comp., *Addresses and Messages,* 2:745 ("benevolent policy," "pursue happiness," "advance rapidly"), 2:762 ("the time," "extinguish the Indian title").

2. Harvard professor Edward Everett, an influential advocate for removal, saw western lands as a "safety-valve to the great social steam-engine." See [Everett], *Orations and Speeches,* 244.

3. Lewis Cass to Thomas L. McKenney, Mar. 11, 1830, U.S. Office of Indian Affairs, Letters Received (qtn.). Stockwell, *Other Trail of Tears,* 197, notes that Ohio's two Senators, Benjamin Ruggles and Jacob Burnett, both Whigs, opposed the Indian Removal Act, though there is no evidence that they opposed removal of Ohio's Indians. One of the many petitions by white women against the Indian Removal Act (see Chapter 6) originated in Steubenville, Ohio. See U.S. House, *Memorial of the Ladies,* 1–2. But there is no evidence of local opposition to removal once it was under way. For settler sentiment for removal, see Buley, *Old Northwest,* 2:126.

4. Gilley, *Longhouse Fragmented,* 73–74, 79–84 ("Our Great Father," "red children," "the game," 73); John McElvain to S.S. Hamilton, Jan. 13, 1831, John McElvain to Lewis Cass, Nov. 15, 1831, *CSEI,* 2:390–91, 684–85 ("restless and unsettled," 390; "operate to the prejudice," 684); *IALT,* 325–27.

5. Foreman, *Last Trek,* 67–71; Klopfenstein, "Removal of the Indians from Ohio," 33; Stockwell, *Other Trail of Tears,* 207–12; Henry C. Brish to William Clark, Dec. 13, 1831, *CSEI,* 2:705 ("had their feet"); Brish to Clark, May 8, June 12, July 6 and 16, 1832, *CSEI,* 5:116–20 ("too ill," 116). My estimate of the death toll is similar to Stockwell, *Other Trail of Tears,* 211, who states that "at least" thirty died. Other than a report by William Clark to Secretary of War, Aug. 13, 1832, *CSEI,* 3:427–28, indicating that some children remained ill, there is no documentation about the condition of the Senecas in the months after their removal.

6. Buchman, "James B. Gardiner," 83–84; Harvey, *History of the Shawnee Indians,* 193–98 (qtns., 193). For the temperance program, see Warren, *Shawnees and Their Neighbors,* 63–64.

7. *IALT,* 331–34; Harvey, *History of the Shawnee Indians,* 196 ("much divided"), 197 (other qtns.). For Black Hoof's death, see Warren, *Shawnees and Their Neighbors,* 66.

8. *IALT,* 327–31, 335–39; James B. Gardiner to George B. Gibson, June 20, 1832, *CSEI,* 1:689–92 ("their native modesty," "some of their," "like the white man," 690); "Journal of Occurrences Kept by the Conductors of the 'Lewistown Detachment' of Emigrating Ohio Indians," *CSEI,* 4:78 ("remain here"); Gardiner to Lewis Cass, Feb. 25, 1833, Gardiner to William Clark, Oct. 25, 1832, *CSEI,* 4:111–18. On the delay of the Hog Creek Shawnees, see Klopfenstein, "Westward Ho," 30.

9. James B. Gardiner to George Gibson, Oct. 8, 1832, *CSEI,* 1:704–6; James B. Gardiner to Lewis Cass, Oct. 21, 1832, *CSEI,* 3:504–6 ("fearful accounts," 505); Foreman, *Last Trek,* 81–85; "Journal of Occurrences," *CSEI,* 4:78–84. The agent at the Shawnee agency reported the arrival of 74 Ottawas and 334 Wapakoneta Shawnees, a decline from the 100 Ottawas and 366 Wapakoneta Shawnees that Gardiner reported as having begun the journey (he gave a figure of 450 for the Wapakoneta and Hog Creek Shawnees, but, as noted above, 84 Hog Creek Shawnees delayed their journey until spring 1833). See Richard W. Cummins to Lewis Cass, Dec. 22, 1832, *CSEI,* 3:566–67; James B. Gardiner to William Clark, Oct. 25, 1832, *CSEI,* 4:117–18. Because reports on the Wapakoneta Shawnees and the Ottawas did not document many deaths, there remains a possibility that the figures are inaccurate.

10. Foreman, *Last Trek,* 89–92; Stockwell, *Other Trail of Tears,* 259–80; *IALT,* 392–94; Bauman, ed., "Removal of the Indians"; Bauman, "Kansas, Canada, or Starvation." Bauman, "Kansas, Canada, or Starvation," 298, states that half of the Ottawas moved to Kansas in the late 1830s died on the way, but he provides no evidence. The removal agent for the 1838 removal congratulated himself that only one person had perished. See Stockwell, *Other Trail of Tears,* 279. Nonetheless, given the discrepancy in the counts (noted in Foreman, *Last Trek,* 91), a higher death toll seems possible.

11. John McElvain to Secretary of War, May 22, 1831, James B. Gardiner to P. G. Randolph, July 8, 1831, *CSEI,* 2:459–60, 510–11 ("urged them," "mortified and surprised," 459; "a delegation," 510). For the Wyandot population, see Appendix 2.

12. J. B. Gardiner to Lewis Cass, Oct. 26, 1831, *CSEI,* 2:629; Oliphant, ed., "Report of the Wyandot Exploring Delegation" (qtn., 256); Klopfenstein, "Removal of the Wyandots," 121–22; Buss, *Winning the West,* 74–75, 90–92.

13. Klopfenstein, "Removal of the Wyandots," 123–31; Smith, ed., "Unsuccessful Negotiation," 305–31; *IALT,* 460–61, 534–37.

14. Klopfenstein, "Removal of the Wyandots," 131–36 ("mark[ing] the graves," 132); Foreman, *Last Trek,* 95–98; *RCIA, 1844,* 448–49 ("about one hundred," "fatigue in removing," 449). For the number who left Ohio in 1843, see *RCIA, 1843,* 262. For the number in Kansas in 1845, see *RCIA, 1845,* 560. For contemporary understandings of "miasma," see Valenčius, *Health of the Country,* 114–17.

15. Rinehart, "Miami Resistance and Resilience," 141–54 ("total extinction," 146; "miserable despicable country," 151; "had to be hunted down," 151–52; "clod of dirt," 152);

Birzer, "Jean Baptiste Richardville," 103–4; Anson, *Miami Indians,* 198–206, 213–28; Bowes, *Land Too Good,* 70–76; Sleeper-Smith, *Indian Women and French Men,* 116 ("hiding in plain view"). The relevant treaties are in *IALT,* 425–28, 519–24, 531–34. For the Miami population, see Appendix 2.

16. Cass to McKenney, Mar. 11, 1830. For the treaties and lead rush, see Chapter 7. For the Winnebago Uprising and its aftermath, see Jung, *Black Hawk War,* 41–46; Hall, *Uncommon Defense,* 80–82; Lonetree, "Visualizing Native Survivance," 16; *IALT,* 300–303. Population figures are in Appendix 2.

17. Wallace, *Prelude to Disaster,* 27 ("they had never"), 30 ("remind the Black Hawk," "denied that any mention," "must have inserted").

18. Jung, *Black Hawk War,* 54 (qtn.). I have inferred Keokuk's strategy from Colbert, "'The Hinge,'" 56–58; Hall, *Uncommon Defense,* 98–102. According to Tanner, ed., *Atlas,* 151, about 1,000 Sauks and Mesquakies crossed the Mississippi into Illinois in April 1832. For Menominee losses in conflict with Sauks and Mesquakies, see Beck, *Siege and Survival,* 109.

19. Trask, *Black Hawk,* 88–96 ("a sufficient number," 90); John Reynolds to William Clark, May 26, 1831, Edmund P. Gaines to John Reynolds, May 29, 1831, Whitney, ed., *Black Hawk War . . . Part 1,* 13 ("to protect," "remove"), 22–23 ("repel," "invasion," 22; "necessary," "proper," 23). For the size of Black Hawk's band, see Jung, *Black Hawk War,* 60; for the size of Gaines's force, see Whitney, ed., *Black Hawk War . . . Part 1,* 66.

20. "Memorandum of Talks between Edmund P. Gaines and the Sauk," June 4, 5, and 7, 1831, Whitney, ed., *Black Hawk War . . . Part 1,* 27–31 ("the humane disposition," "your great Father," "remain on the lands," "you must," 27; "his Braves," 28; "the Great Spirit," "that if their Chiefs," "had not sanctioned").

21. Jackson, ed., *Black Hawk,* 112 ("take a stick"); "Memorandum of Talks," Whitney, ed., *Black Hawk War . . . Part 1,* 30 ("rose & said," "must move"); Kugel and Murphy, "Introduction: Searching for Cornfields," xiii.

22. Jung, *Black Hawk War,* 62–64 ("a force," 64); Trask, *Black Hawk,* 100–106 ("fifteen or twenty," 102); Jackson, ed., *Black Hawk,* 114 ("remained," "multitude of *pale faces*"); "Articles of Agreement and Capitulation between the United States and the Sauk and Fox," June 30, 1831, Whitney, ed., *Black Hawk War . . . Part 1,* 85–88.

23. Jung, *Black Hawk War,* 65–66; Trask, *Black Hawk,* 136–40, 144–50; Jackson, ed., *Black Hawk,* 116 (qtn.).

24. Jung, *Black Hawk War,* 35–37, 61 (qtn., 61); Trask, *Black Hawk,* 124–36. Jung, *Black Hawk War,* 61, points out that "there is little doubt that [Wabokieshiek's] advice to Black Hawk was based on the ninth article of the Treaty of Ghent." For this article, see *U.S. Statutes at Large* 8 (1814): 222–23.

25. "Fort Armstrong Council," Apr. 13, 1832, Atkinson to Edmund P. Gaines, Apr. 18, 1832, Henry Gratiot to Henry Atkinson, Apr. 27, 1832 (two letters), Atkinson to Alexander Macomb, Apr. 27, 1832, Whitney, ed., *Black Hawk War . . . Part 1,* 251–54, 271–72, 317–19 ("the band," "strike . . . one white man," 251; "acquaintance with the Indians," "strike as soon," 271; "must be checked," 319; "his heart is bad," "will fight," 318). Similar to Gratiot's report, Keokuk reported, based on information he received from two

emissaries to Black Hawk's band, that "the Indians are decidedly hostile, that they will go up Rock River to get among the swamps, and that their object is mischief but in what way he is not able to say," a statement that registers Black Hawk's defiance but not an intention to initiate hostilities. "Answer of Black Hawk and His Band to Henry Atkinson," Apr. 26, 1832, Whitney, ed., *Black Hawk War . . . Part 1*, 314.

26. Trask, *Black Hawk*, 156–59 ("temperament," 157); Jung, *Black Hawk War*, 75–76 ("exaggerated the danger"); Eby, *"That Disgraceful Affair,"* 93–96. For Reynolds's mobilization of the Illinois militia, see John Reynolds to Lewis Cass, Apr. 17, 1832, Whitney, ed., *Black Hawk War . . . Part 1*, 270.

27. For military mobilization, see Jung, *Black Hawk War*, 79–83; Trask, *Black Hawk*, 161–62, 174–78. Trask (p. 177) points out that although Reynolds's mobilization of Illinois volunteers did not initially have federal authorization, on May 5, higher officials ordered Atkinson to "call on the Illinois militia for assistance."

28. Jung, *Black Hawk War*, 83–84; Trask, *Black Hawk*, 180–81; Jackson, ed., *Black Hawk*, 121–23.

29. Trask, *Black Hawk*, 144–53, 159–62, 175–89; Jung, *Black Hawk War*, 65–67, 73–89; Lewis Cass to Henry Atkinson, May 31, 1832, Whitney, ed., *Black Hawk War . . . Part 1*, 493–94, ("commencement of hostilities," 493); Jackson, ed., *Black Hawk*, 128 ("avenge the murder").

30. Jung, *Black Hawk War*, 94–97, 108–14, 120–24; Trask, *Black Hawk*, 194–204, 220–23; Edmunds, *Potawatomis*, 237.

31. Henry Atkinson to Alexander Macomb, June 15, 1832, William Clark to Cass, June 8, 1832, Whitney, ed., *Black Hawk War . . . Part 1*, 589 ("the Sacs elude"), 549–50 ("War of *Extermination*," 550).

32. Jung, *Black Hawk War*, 104, 114–17; Hall, *Uncommon Defense*, 111–12, 145–67.

33. Trask, *Black Hawk*, 239–61, 279–81; Jung, *Black Hawk War*, 127–56; Jackson, ed., *Black Hawk*, 133–36 ("sufficient time," 134; "forced to dig," 133).

34. Jackson, ed., *Black Hawk*, 136–37 ("save our women," 137); Trask, *Black Hawk*, 277–79 ("decoy," 278); Jung, *Black Hawk War*, 159, 165–66. For the size of Black Hawk's band on Aug. 1, I have used Jung's figure of 500 for Aug. 2 (p. 170) and added his estimate of 60 who left with Black Hawk the night of the 1st (p. 166).

35. Trask, *Black Hawk*, 281–89 ("taking deliberate aim," "kill the nits," 286); Jung, *Black Hawk War*, 166–74; "Zachary Taylor: Report on the Battle of the Bad Axe," Aug. 5, 1832, Whitney, ed., *Black Hawk War . . . Part 2*, 942–43 ("killed every Indian," 942).

36. Hall, *Uncommon Defense*, 197–202; Jung, *Black Hawk War*, 172, 175–82.

37. Prucha, *Sword of the Republic*, 211 ("misunderstandings"); Jung, *Black Hawk War*, 86 ("rash members"); Nichols, *Warrior Nations*, 79 ("blundered"); Trask, *Black Hawk*, 290–91 ("citizen-soldiers," 290; "revolutionary rage," "love of freedom," 291). For a similar interpretation to Trask's, see Eby, *"That Disgraceful Affair,"* 19.

38. Lewis Cass to Winfield Scott, June 15, 1832, Whitney, ed., *Black Hawk War . . . Part 1*, 592.

39. Hagan, *Sac and Fox Indians*, 195–201 ("the power," 196); Jung, *Black Hawk War*, 186–98; *IALT*, 349–51 ("partly as," 349).

40. Hall, *Uncommon Defense*, 211–13, 222–30 ("been organized," 223; "hunted us," 230); *IALT*, 345–48; Lonetree, "Visualizing Native Survivance," 17; Saler, *Settler's Empire*, 232–33; Paquette, "Wisconsin Winnebagoes," 401–2 ("survivors simply fled"). Paquette's statement (p. 401) that "one quarter of the tribe fell victims [sic]" is too high for the entire Ho-Chunk Nation, though it is plausible for Ho-Chunks in the Prairie du Chien area. Paquette stated that the outbreak occurred in 1834, but in January 1838 the famous painter George Catlin, who was at Prairie du Chien in 1836, dated it to that year. See *New England Farmer, and Gardner's Journal* 16 (Jan. 31, 1838): 240. The origins of this epidemic are unclear. It was apparently unrelated to the epidemic that began on the upper Missouri River and hit the removed Choctaws and Chickasaws (see Chapter 8).

41. *IALT*, 498–500 ("eight months," 498); Lonetree, "Visualizing Native Survivance," 17–18 ("if they did not"); Lurie, "Winnebago," 699 ("under duress," "eight years," "fugitive existence"); De La Ronde, "Personal Narrative," 363 ("Throwing themselves," "to kill them," "had pity").

42. *RCIA, 1840*, 229 ("dysentery"); *RCIA, 1841*, 417 ("bloodshed and murder"); *RCIA, 1846*, 250 ("considerable sickness"); *RCIA, 1845*, 418 ("want of food"); *RCIA, 1843*, 263 (returned to Wisconsin); Pluth, "Failed Watab Treaty" ("fit for nothing," 6; "retard the settlement," 14); *RCIA, 1852*, 342 ("covered with swamps"); *IALT*, 565–67, 690–93 ("permanent home," 691).

43. For population figures, see Appendix 2.

44. Herring, *Kenekuk*, 52, 71–83 ("disobey the directions," 52; "you will be shortly," 72); Gibson, *Kickapoos*, 109–13 (population figures, 109); Stull, *Kiikaapoa*, 71–74; *IALT*, 365–67 ("permanent residence," 365); population, Appendix 2.

45. Edmunds, *Potawatomis*, 240–52 ("ignored or forgotten," 241); Clifton, *Prairie People*, 234–45, 283–84, 287–92; Bowes, *Land Too Good*, 154–61 ("treated with," "wicked and designing," 155). For the 1832 and 1833 treaties, see *IALT*, 353–55, 367–70, 372–75, 402–15. For the Potawatomi population, see Appendix 2.

46. Edmunds, *Potawatomis*, 252–54, 274; Clifton, *Prairie People*, 292–94, 329–42.

47. Edmunds, *Potawatomis*, 264–67 (qtns., 267); Bowes, *Exiles and Pioneers*, 73–78.

48. Edmunds, *Potawatomis*, 267–68; Bowes, *Exiles and Pioneers*, 78–79; Sleeper-Smith, *Indian Women and French Men*, 131–33; Dunn, *True Indian Stories*, 241–50; Pokagon, *O-gî-mäw-kwě Mit-i-gwä-kî*, 79–83 ("gathered up," 81; "the whole country," "old trapper," 82; "trapped," "driven far westward," 83); Willard and Campbell, eds., *Potawatomi Trail of Death*. For the emergence of typhoid fever in this region in the 1840s and 1850s, see Ackerknecht, *Malaria*, 8–9.

49. *RCIA, 1845*, 459, reported that 5,779 Potawatomis and closely affiliated Ottawas and Ojibwes had been removed west. My estimate is based on the assumption that a considerable majority of this population was Potawatomi. For the Pokagon community, see Sleeper-Smith, *Indian Women and French Men*, 102–7; Clifton, *Pokagons*, 45–51, 65–72; Bowes, *Land Too Good*, 177–81.

50. Clifton, *Prairie People*, 279, 282–85, 301–9 ("adaptive strategy," 279; "voluntary," 285).

51. Karamanski, *Blackbird's Song*, 71–88 ("heart-rending," "where the bones," 74; "advance," 75); Gray, *Yankee West*, 73–75; Bowes, *Land Too Good*, 185–86; *IALT*, 450–56

("select a suitable place," "final settlement," 453). For the Ottawa population, see Appendix 2.

52. Karamanski, *Blackbird's Song,* 146–53; Bowes, *Land Too Good,* 187–210 ("paralyzed," 207; "fear of being," 206–7; "Instead of darkness," "we find," 210); *IALT,* 725–31.

53. Silverman, *Red Brethren,* 161–70, 188–92 ("we have hardly," 190–91; "no longer," 191); Tiro, *People of the Standing Stone,* 144–53. The estimate for the Oneida, Stockbridge, and Brothertown populations in the late 1830s is based on 700 for 1830 in Tanner, ed., *Atlas,* 146, plus 200 Oneidas who had migrated since then.

54. Silverman, *Red Brethren,* 191–95, 206–7 ("bought lots," 207); Jarvis, *Brothertown Nation,* 221–26.

55. Oberly, *Nation of Statesmen,* 59–91 ("murder and drunkenness," 68); Silverman, *Red Brethren,* 198–206 ("good white men," 203; "faithless and bad," 203); Hauptman and McLester, *Chief Daniel Bread,* 111–16.

56. Keesing, *Menomini Indians,* 130–42; Beck, *Siege and Survival,* 108–16, 142–46, 166–82; *IALT,* 319–23, 377–82, 463–66, 572–74, 626–27. For the Menominee population, see Appendix 2.

57. Redix, *Murder of Joe White,* 32–44; Child, *Holding Our World Together,* 51–54 (qtn., 54); Clifton, "Wisconsin Death March," 7–17; *IALT,* 461–62, 491–93, 542–45. This estimate does not include 7,000–8,000 Ojibwes in the lower peninsula of Michigan. See Appendix 2.

58. Child, *Holding Our World Together,* 66–68; Clifton, "Wisconsin Death March," 20–23; White, "Regional Context," 162–68, 170, 176–77, 185, 187–90.

59. Child, *Holding Our World Together,* 68–71; Clifton, "Wisconsin Death March," 23–25; White, "Regional Context," 192–95 (qtns., 195).

60. White, "Regional Context," 194 ("highly exaggerated," "low diet"); Child, *Holding Our World Together,* 73 ("our Great Father," "the children," "poison them").

61. Redix, *Murder of Joe White,* 56–57; Child, *Holding Our World Together,* 75–77; White, "Regional Context," 246–48, 252–54 ("Great Grand Father," 246; other qtns., 247); *IALT,* 648–52. For the date of Bizhiki's death, see *American Phrenological Journal* 22 (1855): 113.

62. Everett, "On the State of the Indians" (qtns., 37). In Secretary of War Calhoun's 1825 outline for removal, he wrote that "the arrangement for the removal, it is presumed, is not intended to comprehend the small remnants of tribes in Maine, Massachusetts, Connecticut, [and] Rhode Island," as these Indians "were so few in number that it is believed very little expense or difficulty will be found in their removal." This presumed that these "remnants" would be moved, but it left them out of subsequent planning, with the result that they dropped off the radar. See Calhoun to President of the United States, Jan. 24, 1825, *ASPIA,* 2:542–43 (qtn., 542). For the New England population, see Appendix 2.

63. Hauptman, *Tonawanda Senecas' Heroic Battle;* population figures in Appendix 2.

64. Tiro, *People of the Standing Stone,* 158–63; Hauptman, *Tonawanda Senecas' Heroic Battle,* 40–44; Jarvis, *Brothertown Nation,* 221; *IALT,* 502–16.

65. Hauptman, *Tonawanda Senecas' Heroic Battle,* 66–68, 127–28 (qtns., 127–28); Hauptman, *Conspiracy of Interests,* 191–209; Big Kettle et al. to Samuel Prentiss, Feb. 28, 1838, Society of Friends, *Case of the Seneca Indians,* 113–21; *IALT,* 537–42.

66. Hauptman, *Tonawanda Senecas' Heroic Battle,* 68–112; *IALT,* 504 (qtn.), 767–71.

67. Mt. Pleasant, "After the Whirlwind," 180; Foreman, *Last Trek,* 333–34; *Niles' National Register,* Aug. 21, 1847; *RCIA, 1846,* 215–16; *RCIA, 1847,* 891; Society of Friends, *Proceedings of the Joint Committee,* 159–60.

68. For population figures, see Appendix 2.

69. *Atkinson's Saturday Evening Post* (Philadelphia), June 15, 1833: 620.

70. Jackson, ed., *Black Hawk,* 149–50.

CHAPTER 10. DESTRUCTION AND SURVIVAL
IN THE ZONE OF REMOVAL

1. Tocqueville, *Democracy in America,* 324 ("plunged," "the nation"), 336 ("same white population," "will again").

2. Hämäläinen, *Comanche Empire* (population figures, 102, 179; "nomadic empire," 283). Hämäläinen (p. 173) notes that the Wichitas and Comanches fought over trade in the 1770s but in the 1810s were incorporated into a set of trading alliances that Comanches largely controlled. For peace between the Kiowas and Comanches in 1806, see Rand, *Kiowa Humanity,* 36. For the Kiowa population, see Levy, "Kiowa," 920; for the Wichita population, see Newcomb, "Wichita," 563. For Choctaws' understanding of the West as a "land of death," see Chapter 8.

3. LaVere, *Contrary Neighbors,* 71, 78–79; Baird, *Peter Pitchlynn,* 50, 56; *IALT,* 435–39; Foreman, ed., "Journal of the Proceedings" ("brothers," 414; "if there be any killing," 415).

4. For Comanche raiding and trade between Comanches and relocated eastern Indians, see Hämäläinen, *Comanche Empire,* 152–54, 215, 220–30.

5. LaVere, *Contrary Neighbors,* 100–104; Gibson, "Indian Territory United Nations" (qtns., 404). For bison shortages, see Hämäläinen, *Comanche Empire,* 296–97; Flores, "Bison Ecology."

6. LaVere, *Contrary Neighbors,* 104–11; Miller, *Coacoochee's Bones,* 98–103; Foreman, ed., "Journal of Elijah Hicks" (Coocoochee qtns., 80; Hicks qtn., 88); *IALT,* 554–57. For Texas's "genocidal war" against the Comanches, see Hämäläinen, *Comanche Empire,* 215; see also the account of Texas Indian policy in Anderson, *Conquest of Texas,* 172–211.

7. Hämäläinen, *Comanche Empire,* 305–12; LaVere, *Contrary Neighbors,* 145–53; Anderson, *Conquest of Texas,* 259–326 (qtn., 260); *IALT,* 706–14. For Choctaw and Chickasaw complaints about Delaware, Kickapoo, and Shawnee raids, see *RCIA, 1841,* 264; *RCIA, 1847,* 885.

8. Population figures are in Appendix 2.

9. For Osage–Pawnee conflict, see *RCIA, 1854,* 333 ("constantly at war"); *RCIA, 1841,* 344; *RCIA, 1844,* 438; Parks, *Darkest Period,* 28–29. For Osage conflict with Sauks and Mesquakies and Comanches, see *RCIA, 1854,* 298; *RCIA, 1858,* 489. For Osage trade with Comanches and Kiowas, see *RCIA, 1848,* 541–42; *RCIA, 1854,* 298 ("*bad medicine*").

10. Ioways and Sauks and Mesquakies sometimes got the better of their enemies. In 1848, for example, Ioways killed several Pawnees, including women and children, who were

making their way back to the Plains after a visit to a government agency at Council Bluffs. Six years later, Sauks and Mesquakies held off a much larger force of Comanches, Kiowas, and Osages and killed sixteen, while losing only six of their own men. *RCIA, 1848*, 440; *RCIA, 1854*, 298; Hagan, *Sac and Fox Indians*, 226–27.

11. For bison shortages in the central and northern Plains, see Isenberg, *Destruction of the Bison*, 103–13; West, *Way to the West*, 53–54. For the growing population of the western Sioux, see Bray, "Teton Sioux Population History." For attacks on Omahas, see *RCIA, 1843*, 401 ("lost some thirty"); *RCIA, 1855*, 406 ("frantic with fear"); *RCIA, 1859*, 481 ("principally of the aged"); Boughter, *Betraying the Omaha Nation*, 48–75 (1846 attack, 53–54); Wishart, *Unspeakable Sadness*, 86–87, 117. For attacks on the Otoe-Missourias, see *RCIA, 1845*, 537; *RCIA, 1847*, 742, 832; *RCIA, 1853*, 347; *RCIA, 1858*, 454; Wishart, *Unspeakable Sadness*, 90, 116.

12. These observations are based on reports from U.S. agents in *RCIA* for the 1850s.

13. McLoughlin, *After the Trail of Tears*, 15–17, 41–58 ("I have signed," 15); Wilkins, *Cherokee Tragedy*, 329–39; *IALT*, 561–65 ("general amnesty," "offenses and crimes," 561).

14. For the feeling between the two factions in 1838, see the recollection of a government agent in *RCIA, 1847*, 886 ("rival[ed] the other"). For the 1839 settlement, see Foreman, *Five Civilized Tribes*, 166–67.

15. *RCIA, 1855*, 491 ("compelled to merge"); Lancaster, *Removal Aftershock*, 41, 56, 80–83, 96, 104–5, 108–15 ("vital interests," 104); Miller, *Coacoochee's Bones*, 121–71; *IALT*, 756–63.

16. Warren, *Shawnees and Their Neighbors*, 98–109, 129–50 (qtn., 99); Lakomäki, *Gathering Together*, 206–14; Bowes, *Exiles and Pioneers*, 166–78; Gibson, *Kickapoos*, 110–14.

17. Oliphant, ed., "Report of the Wyandot Exploring Delegation," 257 ("removed from the temptations"); Unrau, *White Man's Wicked Water*, 41–49, 73 ("inundated with whiskey," seventy "whiskey shops," 41); Leader, "Pottawatomies and Alcohol" ("whiskey capital," 158); Boughter, *Betraying the Omaha Nation*, 46 ("as freely"); Parks, *Darkest Period*, 97 ("whiskey pipeline"); *RCIA, 1858*, 477 ("prairie bars," "in jugs, bottles," "concealed in the woods"). For 1832 federal legislation prohibiting "ardent spirits" in Indian country, see Prucha, *Great Father*, 1:101.

18. Lewis Cass to the Chiefs of the Creek Tribe, Jan. 16, 1832, *CSEI*, 1:743 ("bad white men," "ardent spirits," "tempt or debauch"); Unrau, *White Man's Wicked Water*, 37–38, 55–70, 87–88 ("surrounded by white squatters," 62). For the inability of the federal government to legislate for the states, see Prucha, *Great Father*, 1:334.

19. Akers, *Living in the Land of Death*, 117–19.

20. *RCIA, 1844*, 446 ("rows"), 441 ("broils"); *RCIA, 1851*, 343 ("drunkenness and other diseases"). Unrau, *White Man's Wicked Water*, 52, quotes a report from 1842 that 500 men from "prairie tribes" had been killed in alcohol-related violence over the previous two years, but the report defines those tribes as Plains Indians west of the zone of removal. See *RCIA, 1842*, 433–34 ("prairie tribes," 434).

21. Unrau, *White Man's Wicked Water*, 45–46; *RCIA, 1853*, 314 (qtns.).

22. Unrau, *White Man's Wicked Water*, 39 ("whiskey is bad," "the whites first"); *RCIA, 1845*, 531 ("whiskey trade," "gradually wearing away"); Ishii, *Bad Fruits*, 93–109 ("fountains of deadly evil," 106).

23. *RCIA, 1842*, 446; *RCIA, 1851*, 352; *RCIA, 1849*, 1116; *RCIA, 1846*, 302; *RCIA, 1844*, 471 ("destroy . . . whiskey"); *RCIA, 1857*, 461 ("punishing, by fine"); *RCIA, 1848*, 449 ("old men," "with stripes"); Warren, *Shawnees and Their Neighbors*, 149.

24. Snyder, *Great Crossings*, 274–83; Kidwell, *Choctaws in Oklahoma*, 9–10; McLoughlin, *After the Trail of Tears*, 88–95; Lakomäki, *Gathering Together*, 218 (qtn.). For mission schools in the zone of removal, see Prucha, *Great Father*, 1:290–92.

25. St. Jean, *Remaining Chickasaw*, 17, 43–44; Gibson, *Chickasaws*, 192–97; May, "Oil Springs." For the Chickasaw slave population, see Doran, "Negro Slaves," 346.

26. Chang, *Color of the Land*, 27–31; Akers, *Living in the Land of Death*, 126–27; Kidwell, *Choctaws in Oklahoma*, 6–8; McLoughlin, *After the Trail of Tears*, 67–72, 125, 129–30; Miles, *Ties That Bind*, 163–65. For slave populations, see Doran, "Negro Slaves," 347. For the Seminole economy, see Miller, *Coacoochee's Bones*, 88–105; Lancaster, *Removal Aftershock*, 65; Foreman, *Five Civilized Tribes*, 244–46.

27. Lakomäki, *Gathering Together*, 207–8 ("more opulent," 207); Bowes, *Exiles and Pioneers*, 108–17; Gilley, *Longhouse Fragmented*, 95–96; Dippie, *Vanishing American*, 41 ("the Indian disappears").

28. For floods, see *RCIA, 1844*, 444, 458; *RCIA, 1845*, 514, 531. For drought, see *RCIA, 1851*, 367, 384; *RCIA, 1854*, 314 ("perish from famine"); *RCIA, 1855*, 454, 471, 494; *RCIA, 1856*, 671; *RCIA, 1858*, 489; *RCIA, 1859*, 406; *RCIA, 1860*, 242, 325, 332 ("where game," 325).

29. *IALT*, 304 ("permanent residence"), 558 ("home forever"), 336 ("as long"); Gates, *Fifty Million Acres*, 19–22; Miner and Unrau, *End of Indian Kansas*, 12–19; Herring, *Enduring Indians of Kansas*, 48–49, 88–90; Bowes, *Exiles and Pioneers*, 189–92; Oertel, *Bleeding Borders*, 22; Parks, *Darkest Period*, 64.

30. Cass, "Removal of the Indians," 109.

31. Prucha, "Indian Removal," provides citations to historians of the arid lands argument and refutes them (qtn., 322).

32. *Congressional Globe (Appendix)*, 33rd Cong., 1st Sess. (1854), 154 ("Where shall"); Gates, *Fifty Million Acres*, 16–18; Herring, *Enduring Indians of Kansas*, 46–48, 88–89; Lakomäki, *Gathering Together*, 214–16 ("thrown . . . into," 214; "fearful," 214–15); Weslager, *Delaware Indians*, 404–5; Wishart, *Unspeakable Sadness*, 102; Boughter, *Betraying the Omaha Nation*, 61–67; *IALT*, 608–26, 628–46, 677–81, 796–803, 824–28. The Osages did not cede lands until 1865, but they too faced a squatter invasion in the late 1850s. See *IALT*, 878–83; Burns, *History of the Osage People*, 250–53.

33. On malnutrition, coerced migration, and social disruption as general factors contributing to the poor health of Native Americans, see Jones, *Rationalizing Epidemics*, 4. For psychological stress, see Miles, *Ties That Bind*, 163.

34. For the Sauks and Mesquakies, see *RCIA, 1851*, 328–29; *RCIA, 1852*, 381. My figure of 500 is based on 2,660 for the 1851 population in *RCIA, 1851*, 326, and 2,173 for the 1853 population in *RCIA, 1853*, 342. For the Ioways, Otoe-Missourias, and Omahas, see *RCIA, 1851*, 357 ("made some ravages"), 361. For Osage disease, see Burns, *History of the Osage People*, 240–41; Edwards, "Disruption and Disease"; *RCIA, 1852*, 396; *RCIA, 1855*, 495 ("could procure"). For the Kanzas, see Parks, *Darkest Period*, 91–93. For the Kickapoos, see *RCIA, 1857*, 450. For the Cherokees, see *RCIA, 1852*, 400 ("dreadful scourge").

35. Population estimates are in Appendix 2. For Treaty Party Cherokees in Arkansas, see Dale, "Arkansas and the Cherokees," 102–3. For Cherokees and the California Gold Rush and the 1850s as a "golden age," see Smithers, *Cherokee Diaspora,* 133–36. For accounts of disease, see *RCIA, 1852,* 400; *RCIA, 1857,* 499 ("fevers," "deaths"); *RCIA, 1858,* 493 ("malarious," "among the more").

36. Population figures in Appendix 2. For the Third Seminole War and background, see Missall and Missall, *Seminole Wars,* 209–22; Littlefield, "Third Seminole War."

37. For population figures, see Appendix 2.

38. For population figures, see Appendix 2. Clifton, *Prairie People,* 352, argues that declining Potawatomi numbers in this period were due to people moving from the reservation, but agents' reports of conditions in the late 1850s contradict this assessment.

39. *RCIA, 1840,* 323 ("fast progressing," "south of Missouri"); *RCIA, 1841,* 270–75 ("country of distress," 273; "the poorest," 274); *IALT,* 546–49 ("tract of land," 546); Hagan, *Sac and Fox Indians,* 219–22.

40. Hagan, *Sac and Fox Indians,* 223–26; *IALT,* 546 ("a permanent"); *RCIA, 1846,* 299; *RCIA, 1841,* 274–75 ("have pity"). Population figures are in Appendix 2.

41. Observations about conditions are based on government agents' reports in *RCIA* and correspond to observations in Hagan, *Sac and Fox Indians,* 205–9, 223–24. For population figures, see Appendix 2.

42. Figures for the Quapaws are in Appendix 2.

43. For a discussion of Osage disease and approaches for dealing with it, see Edwards, "Disruption and Disease." Population figures are in Appendix 2.

44. Watts, "How Bloody Was Bleeding Kansas?"; *RCIA, 1855,* 434 (qtn.).

45. Parks, *Darkest Period,* provides a thorough analysis of Kanza history, although his account of the 1846 treaty (p. 14) does not connect it to the need to acquire land to consolidate Potawatomis on the Osage River in Kansas and in Council Bluffs, Iowa, on a single reservation, as discussed in Chapter 9. An exception to the general neglect of Indians in Bleeding Kansas is Oertel, *Bleeding Borders.*

46. Hagan, *Sac and Fox Indians,* 230. For similar turnover of agents for the Kanzas, see Unrau, *Kansa Indians,* 167. For the Manypenny quotation, see *RCIA, 1854,* 219.

47. Prucha, *Great Father,* 1:302–9 ("military despotism," 306; "introduce discord," 308); Guyatt, *Bind Us Apart,* 317–18; Frymer, *Building an American Empire,* 126–27.

CHAPTER 11. THE NAME OF REMOVAL

1. Thorpe, "Jim Thorpe Family . . . Part 1"; Thorpe, "Jim Thorpe Family . . . Part 2"; Wheeler, *Jim Thorpe,* 99–113 (qtn., 113); *New York Times,* Aug. 25, 1912: 4.

2. Based on information in previous chapters; figures for the North include Indians who were removed but eventually returned (i.e., Ojibwes lured to Sandy Lake and a few Haudenosaunees). They do not include Indians on the eastern seaboard.

3. Unruh, *Plains Across,* 85, 345.

4. Based on information in previous chapters; the 1,200 figure includes 400 Ojibwes who lost their lives in the Sandy Lake Tragedy, but it does not include possible deaths

resulting from the Ho-Chunk removal of 1833, including those from the 1834 small-pox outbreak. Nor does it include deaths that likely occurred in the West just after removal for many other communities.

5. Humphreys, *Malaria*, 8–11. Focusing on the Arkansas and Missouri frontiers, Valenčius, *Health of the Country*, 79, notes that it is likely that other fevers, notably dengue, yellow fever, and typhoid fever, were also present, but that malaria was the most prominent. Although Drake, *Systematic Treatise* was written before the discovery of mosquitoes as transmitters of the malaria parasite, the data he gathered established that "from north to south . . . the number of deaths from autumnal fever . . . constantly increases" (p. 137).

6. From data in Appendix 2. Because of the complexities of the Shawnee, Delaware, and Kickapoo removals and migrations, they are not included in this summary. Figures for the southern nations include those already living in the West prior to the removals.

7. Cass, "Removal of the Indians" ("some mental," "an appropriation," 119; "upon the face," "a more wretched," 71); "Address to the People of the United States," 446 ("if we are compelled").

8. For a defense of Jackson as a "sincere if unsentimental paternalist," see Wilentz, *Andrew Jackson*, 68.

9. Nehah Micco et al. to Secretary of War, Apr. 8, 1831, *CSEI*, 2:424.

10. Perdue and Green, *Cherokee Nation*, 42; Kiernan, *Blood and Soil*, 330; Calloway, *Pen and Ink Witchcraft*, 121; Anderson, *Ethnic Cleansing*, 151.

11. Naimark, *Fires of Hatred*, 4. See also Lieberman, "'Ethnic Cleansing' versus Genocide?," 45.

12. The figures for the ethnic cleansing of Bosniaks are from Zwierzchowski and Tabeau, "The 1992–1995 War," 15. For the concept of "partial genocide," see Melson, *Revolution and Genocide*, 27–29; for a recent example of its application to Bosnia, see Murray, *Disrupting Pathways*, 107.

13. Works that characterize removal's consequences as genocidal include Stannard, *American Holocaust*, 121–24; Churchill, *Little Matter of Genocide*, 144; Hixson, *American Settler Colonialism*, 82; Dunbar-Ortiz, *Indigenous Peoples' History*, 8–9, 112–14. Anderson, *Ethnic Cleansing* makes a strong distinction between ethnic cleansing and genocide and sees the latter as inapplicable to the entire history of U.S. actions toward Americans Indians, including removal.

14. Keesing, *Menomoni Indians*, 153–60; Hosmer, *American Indians*, 27; Beck, *Siege and Survival*. Although Menominees were removed within Wisconsin in 1852 (see Chapter 9), I have considered them as a nonremoved nation. For Menominee population figures, see Appendix 2.

15. Witgen, *Infinity of Nations*, 357; Child, *Holding Our World Together*, 64–65. For the Ojibwe population, see Appendix 2. Estimates for the Ottawas are lacking, but given the similarity in conditions for them and the Ojibwes (there were many mixed Ottawa-Ojibwe communities), they likely did not see a drop in their numbers.

16. For population figures, see Appendix 2. For Oneida economic strategies, see Tiro, *People of the Standing Stone*, 175–86 ("INDIAN WAR DANCE," 181; "Indian Minstrel

Company," 184). For the reduction of the Haudenosaunee land base, see Hauptman, *Seven Generations,* 1–2.

17. Finger, *Eastern Band of Cherokees,* 29–40 (1,100 population, 29); Neely, "Acculturation and Persistence," 156–58; James Mooney, "Myths of the Cherokee," 162–63 ("firmly resisted," 163).

18. Finger, *Eastern Band of Cherokees,* 61–63; Neely, "Acculturation and Persistence," 156, 160; Thomas, *Explanation of the Fund,* 12–13; Lanman, *Letters from the Alleghany Mountains,* 111 (qtn.); Smithers, *Cherokee Diaspora,* 129–32. Population figures for the eastern Cherokee are in Appendix 2.

19. Blu, *Lumbee Problem,* 36–50; Lowery, *Lumbee Indians,* 4–8, 11–14; Evans, "North Carolina Lumbees," 49–51 ("'tied mule,'" "white farmer," "give up," 51; "completely landless," 50). For the Lumbee population in 1860, see Appendix 2.

20. Satz, "Mississippi Choctaw," 3–17 ("forced to eke," 14); Kidwell, "Choctaw Struggle," 64–80; Kniffen, Gregory, and Stokes, *Historic Tribes of Louisiana,* 94–96; Usner, *American Indians,* 116–17, 127 ("refuse to abandon," 116; "illustrate that," 127). For population figures, see Appendix 2.

21. John C. Calhoun to President of the United States, Jan. 24, 1825, *ASPIA,* 2:542 ("not intended"); Mandell, 204 ("the land"); *RCIA, 1851,* 269 ("relieved from").

22. Brain, Roth, and DeReuse, "Tunica, Biloxi, and Ofo," 590, 593; Campisi, "Houma," 637; Hudson, *Catawba Nation,* 64–66; Rountree, "Indians of Virginia," 28–36; Conkey, Boissevain, and Goddard, "Indians of Southern New England and Long Island," 4; Erikson, "Maliseet-Passamaquoddy," 125–26; Snow, "Eastern Abenaki," 145.

23. Stanton, "Southern Louisiana Survivors," 98; Usner, *American Indians,* 111; Mandell, *Tribe, Race, Nation,* 10–35, 146–67; Shoemaker, *Native American Whalemen,* 13–14.

24. For "redbone," see Klopotek, *Recognition Odysseys,* 55. For discrimination and racialization, see Rountree, "Indians of Virginia," 36; Mandell, *Tribe, Race, Nation,* 199; Plane and Button, "Massachusetts Indian Enfranchisement Act," 185–86.

25. Mandell, *Tribe, Race, History,* 96–103; O'Connell, "Introduction," xxxiv–xxxvii; Campisi, *Mashpee Indians,* 99–108 (qtn., 101).

26. Hudson, *Catawba Nation,* 64–66; Mandell, *Tribe, Race, History,* 4. Because of the mobility of Indians in New England in the mid-1800s, noted in DeLucia, *Memory Lands,* 252, it is likely that the figures in Appendix 2 are an undercount.

27. O'Brien, *Firsting and Lasting,* xiii–xiv, 108–17 ("considerable settlement," 109; "last male," "only surviving female," 113; "writing Indians out of existence," subtitle of the book).

CONCLUSION

1. *Minutes of Debates in Council,* 6–8.

2. Quinney, "Speech on Stockbridge Traditionary History," 315 ("extinction . . . of my tribe," "is inevitable"), 317–19 (other qtns.). For Quinney's life, see Oberly, *Nation of Statesmen,* 12–13, 52–85.

3. Thomas McKenney and John Tipton quoted in Guyatt, *Providence,* 197; Everett, "On the State of the Indians," 34.

4. Kent and Deardorff, eds., "John Adlum," 468–71. I have discussed Adlum's conversation with Logan in Ostler, "Indigenous Consciousness of Genocide," 609–11.
5. Anderson, *Conquest of Texas;* Hämäläinen, *Comanche Empire,* 303 (Comanche population); Boyd, *Coming of the Spirit of Pestilence;* Whaley, *Oregon and the Collapse of Illahee,* 200 ("Extermination"); Ostler, *Lakotas and the Black Hills,* 44–45.

APPENDIX 1. THE QUESTION OF GENOCIDE IN U.S. HISTORY

1. This appendix draws on Ostler, "Genocide and American Indian History."
2. Lemkin, *Axis Rule;* Stannard, *American Holocaust;* Churchill, *Little Matter of Genocide.* For an insightful criticism of Stannard's and Churchill's approach, see MacDonald, *Identity Politics,* 74–89. In the runup to the Quincentennial, Thornton, *American Indian Holocaust,* also deployed the Holocaust analogy, although he offered a more measured assessment of genocide. Some activists and writers used *genocide* in the 1970s, but the term did not gain traction then. For early uses, see First International Indian Treaty Council at Standing Rock Indian Country, "Declaration of Continuing Independence"; Norton, *When Our Worlds Cried.*
3. Works reflecting the Stannard/Churchill approach in Indigenous Studies include LaDuke, *All Our Relations;* Cook-Lynn, *Anti-Indianism;* Mann, *Tainted Gift;* Dunbar-Ortiz, *Indigenous Peoples' History.* For the influence of this perspective in genocide studies, see Jones, *Genocide,* 72–76. For examples of gesturing to genocide, see Blackhawk, *Violence over the Land,* 75, who writes of "genocidal ambitions"; Hämäläinen, *Comanche Empire,* 215, who describes Texas's war against the Comanches in the late 1830s as "genocidal." As an indication of the larger absence of genocide in mainstream scholarship in U.S. history, there is no mention of genocide in perhaps the field's best textbook, Foner, *Give Me Liberty!* Authoritative overviews of the field of American Indian history barely mention the subject. See Deloria and Salisbury, eds., *Blackwell Companion to American Indian History;* Hoxie, ed., *Oxford Handbook of American Indian History.*
4. For a strikingly brief dismissal of using the concept of genocide to describe what happened in early American history, see Axtell, *Beyond 1492,* 261–63.
5. Bauer, *We Were All Like Migrant Workers,* 9.
6. For arguments that genocide is applicable to at least some parts of American history, see Kiernan, *Blood and Soil,* 213–48, 310–63; Cave, "Genocide in the Americas"; Cave, *Lethal Encounters;* Madley, "Reexamining the American Genocide Debate"; Hixson, *American Settler Colonialism.* For arguments that genocide is not applicable to this history, see Katz, "Pequot War Reconsidered"; Lewy, "Were American Indians the Victims of Genocide?"; Anderson, *Ethnic Cleansing.*
7. For a comprehensive catalog of definitions, see Strauss, "Contested Meanings" ("sustained purposeful action," 352; "substantial numbers," 367). For "ethnocide" and "cultural genocide," see Novic, *Concept of Cultural Genocide.* For the definitional problem, see Stone, "Introduction," 2 ("merry-go-round"); Weiss-Wendt, "Problems in Comparative Genocide Scholarship," 44 ("futile"); Boghossian, "Concept of Genocide." For the UN Convention definition, see Jones, *Genocide,* 12–13.

8. For problems of defining genocide when considering the issue in North America, see Rensink, "Genocide of Native Americans"; Alvarez, *Native America and the Question of Genocide,* 164–67.

9. Anderson, *Ethnic Cleansing* (qtn., 4); Anderson, "Native Peoples of the American West"; Madley, *American Genocide;* Madley, "Understanding Genocide in California." Commenting on Anderson vs. Madley, Jacobs, "Genocide or Ethnic Cleansing," suggests that *settler colonialism* is a better term, but this seems unlikely to resolve the matter, since it leaves open the question of how to categorize the range of settler colonialism's means of elimination and impacts.

Bibliography

Abele, Charles A. "The Grand Indian Council and Treaty at Prairie du Chien, 1825."
 Ph.D. diss., Loyola University, 1969.
Ablavsky, George. "The Savage Constitution." *Duke Law Journal* 63 (February
 2014): 999–1089.
Ackerknecht, Erwin H. *Malaria in the Upper Mississippi Valley, 1760–1900*. Balti-
 more, Md.: Johns Hopkins University Press, 1945.
Adair, James. *The History of the American Indians*. London: Edward and Charles
 Dilly, 1775.
"Address to the People of the United States by the General Council of the Chero-
 kee Nation, July 1830." In *Memoir of the Life of Jeremiah Evarts*, ed. E. C. Tracy,
 442–48. Boston, Mass.: Crocker and Brewster, 1845.
Akers, Donna L. *Living in the Land of Death: The Choctaw Nation, 1830–1860*. East
 Lansing: Michigan State University Press, 2004.
———. "Removing the Heart of the Choctaw People: Indian Removal from a
 Native Perspective."*American Indian Culture and Research Journal* 23:3 (1999):
 63–76.
Alden, John Richard. *George Washington: A Biography*. Baton Rouge: Louisiana State
 University Press, 1984.
Allen, Virginia R. "Medical Practices and Health in the Choctaw Nation, 1831–
 1885." *Chronicles of Oklahoma* 48 (Spring 1970): 60–73.
Alvarez, Alex. *Native America and the Question of Genocide*. Lanham, Md.: Rowman
 and Littlefield, 2014.

Alvord, Clarence Walworth, ed. *Collections of the Illinois State Historical Library.* Vols. 11, 16. Springfield: Illinois State Historical Society, 1916, 1921.

American Board of Commissioners for Foreign Missions. Papers. Houghton Library, Harvard University. Cherokee Mission (ABC 18.3.1). Vol. 10. Microfilm edition. Roll 744.

American Phrenological Journal 22 (1855).

American State Papers: Indian Affairs. 2 vols.

American State Papers: Military Affairs. Vol. 1.

American State Papers: Military Affairs. Vol. 6.

Anderson, Fred. *Crucible of War: The Seven Years' War and the Fate of Empire in British North America, 1754–1766.* New York: Alfred A. Knopf, 2000.

Anderson, Gary Clayton. *The Conquest of Texas: Ethnic Cleansing in the Promised Land.* Norman: University of Oklahoma Press, 2005.

———. *Ethnic Cleansing and the Indian: The Crime That Should Haunt America.* Norman: University of Oklahoma Press, 2014.

———. *Kinsmen of Another Kind: Dakota–White Relations in the Upper Mississippi Valley, 1650–1862.* Lincoln: University of Nebraska Press, 1984.

———. "The Native Peoples of the American West: Genocide or Ethnic Cleansing?" *Western Historical Quarterly* 47 (Winter 2016): 407–33.

Andrew, John A., III. *From Revivals to Removal: Jeremiah Evarts, the Cherokee Nation, and the Search for the Soul of America.* Athens: University of Georgia Press, 1992.

Anson Bert. *The Miami Indians.* Norman: University of Oklahoma Press, 1970.

Armstrong, John. "Col. John Armstrong's Account of Expedition against Kittanning, 1756." *Pennsylvania Archives* 2 (1853): 767–75.

Army and Navy Chronicle 3 (Sept. 1, 1836).

Army and Navy Chronicle 4 (May 11, 1837).

Aron, Stephen. *American Confluence: The Missouri Frontier from Borderland to Border State.* Bloomington: Indiana University Press, 2006.

———. *How the West Was Lost: The Transformation of Kentucky from Daniel Boone to Henry Clay.* Baltimore, Md.: Johns Hopkins University Press, 1996.

Atkinson, James R. *Splendid Land, Splendid People: The Chickasaw Indians to Removal.* Tuscaloosa: University of Alabama Press, 2004.

Atkinson's Saturday Evening Post (Philadelphia), June 15, 1833.

Augusta (Georgia) Chronicle and Gazette of the State, May 2, 1789.

Axtell, James. *Beyond 1492: Encounters in Colonial North America.* New York: Oxford University Press, 1992.

Bailey, Garrick A. "Osage." In *Handbook of North American Indians,* Vol. 13: *Plains,* ed. Raymond J. DeMallie, 476–96. Washington, D.C.: Smithsonian Institution Press, 2001.

Bailey, Garrick A., and Gloria A. Young. "Kansa." In *Handbook of North American Indians,* Vol. 13: *Plains,* ed. Raymond J. DeMallie, 462–75. Washington, D.C.: Smithsonian Institution Press, 2001.

Bailyn, Bernard. "The Central Themes of the American Revolution: An Interpretation." In *Essays on the American Revolution,* ed. Stephen G. Kurtz and James H. Hutson, 3–31. Chapel Hill: University of North Carolina Press, 1973.

Baird, W. David. *Peter Pitchlynn: Chief of the Choctaws.* Norman: University of Oklahoma Press, 1972.

———. *The Quapaw Indians: A History of the Downstream People.* Norman: University of Oklahoma Press, 1980.

Banner, Stuart. *How the Indians Lost Their Land: Law and Power on the Frontier.* Cambridge: Harvard University Press, 2005.

Barber, John W., and Elizabeth G. Barber. *Historical, Poetical and Pictorial American Scenes.* New Haven, Conn.: J. W. Barber, 1850.

Barr, Daniel P. "'This Land Is Ours and Not Yours': The Western Delawares and the Seven Years' War in the Upper Ohio Valley, 1755–1758." In *The Boundaries Between Us: Natives and Newcomers Along the Frontiers of the Old Northwest Territory, 1750–1850,* ed. Daniel P. Barr, 25–43. Kent, Ohio: Kent State University Press, 2006.

———. *Unconquered: The Iroquois League at War in Colonial America.* Westport, Conn.: Praeger, 2006.

Barr, Juliana. *Peace Came in the Form of a Woman: Indians and Spaniards in the Texas Borderlands.* Chapel Hill: University of North Carolina Press, 2007.

———. "There's No Such Thing as 'Prehistory': What the Longue Durée of Caddo and Pueblo History Tells Us about Colonial America." *William and Mary Quarterly,* 3d ser., 74 (April 2017): 203–40.

Bassett, John Spencer, ed. *Correspondence of Andrew Jackson.* 7 vols. Washington, D.C.: Carnegie Institution, 1926–1935.

Bauer, William J., Jr. *We Were All Like Migrant Workers Here: Work, Community, and Memory on California's Round Valley Reservation, 1850–1941.* Chapel Hill: University of North Carolina Press, 2009.

Bauman, Robert F. "Kansas, Canada, or Starvation." *Michigan History* 36 (September 1952): 287–99.

Bauman, Robert F., ed. "The Removal of the Indians from the Maumee Valley: A Selection from the Dresden W. H. Howard Papers." *Northwest Ohio Quarterly* 29 (Winter 1957–1958): 10–25.

Beck, David R. M. *Siege and Survival: History of the Menominee Indians, 1634–1856.* Lincoln: University of Nebraska Press, 2002.

Beckert, Sven. *Empire of Cotton: A Global History.* New York: Alfred A. Knopf, 2015.

Beider, Robert E. *Native American Communities in Wisconsin, 1600–1960: A Study of Tradition and Change.* Madison: University of Wisconsin Press, 1995.

Belich, James. *Replenishing the Earth: The Settler Revolution and the Rise of the Anglo-World, 1783–1939.* New York: Oxford University Press, 2009.

Bergman, William H. *The American National State and the Early West.* Cambridge: Cambridge University Press, 2012.

Berkhofer, Robert F., Jr. *The White Man's Indian: Images of the American Indian from Columbus to the Present.* New York: Alfred A. Knopf, 1978.

Birzer, Bradley J. "Jean Baptiste Richardville: Miami Métis." In *Enduring Nations: Native Americans in the Midwest,* ed. R. David Edmunds, 94–108. Urbana: University of Illinois Press, 2008.

Blackbird, Andrew J. *History of the Ottawa and Chippewa Indians of Michigan.* Ypsilanti, Mich: Ypsilantian Job Printing House, 1887.

Blackhawk, Ned. *Violence over the Land: Indians and Empires in the Early American West.* Cambridge, Mass.: Harvard University Press, 2006.

Blaine, Martha Royce. *The Ioway Indians.* Norman: University of Oklahoma Press, 1979.

Blasingham, Emily L. "The Depopulation of the Illinois Indians, Part 2, Concluded." *Ethnohistory* 3 (Autumn 1956): 361–412.

Bliss, Eugene F., ed. *Diary of David Zeisberger: A Moravian Missionary among the Indians of Ohio.* 2 vols. Cincinnati, Ohio: R. Clarke & Co., 1885.

Blu, Karen I. *The Lumbee Problem: The Making of an American Indian People.* Cambridge: Cambridge University Press, 1980.

Boghossian, Paul. "The Concept of Genocide." *Journal of Genocide Research* 12 (March–June 2010): 69–80.

Bontrager, Shannon. "'From a Nation of Drunkards, We Have Become a Sober People': The Wyandot Experience in the Ohio Valley during the Early Republic." *Journal of the Early Republic* 32 (Winter 2012): 603–32.

Boston Recorder, Aug. 21, 1833.

Bottiger, Patrick. *The Borderland of Fear: Vincennes, Prophetstown, and the Invasion of the Miami Homeland.* Lincoln: University of Nebraska Press, 2016.

Bougainville, Louis Antoine de. *Adventure in the Wilderness: The American Journals of Louis Antoine de Bougainville, 1756–1760.* Trans. and ed. Edward P. Hamilton. Norman: University of Oklahoma Press, 1964.

Boughter, Judith A. *Betraying the Omaha Nation, 1790–1916.* Norman: University of Oklahoma Press, 1998.

Boulware, Tyler. *Deconstructing the Cherokee Nation: Town, Region, and Nation among Eighteenth-Century Cherokees.* Gainesville: University Press of Florida, 2011.

Bouton, Terry. *Taming Democracy: "The People," The Founders, and the Troubled Ending of the American Revolution.* New York: Oxford University Press, 2007.

Bowes, John P. *Exiles and Pioneers: Eastern Indians in the Trans-Mississippi West.* Cambridge: Cambridge University Press, 2007.

————. "The Gnadenhutten Effect: Moravian Converts and the Search for Safety in the Canadian Borderlands." *Michigan Historical Review* 34 (Spring 2008): 101–17.

————. *Land Too Good for Indians: Northern Indian Removal.* Norman: University of Oklahoma Press, 2016.

Boyd, Julian P., et al., eds. *The Papers of Thomas Jefferson.* 60 vols. projected. Princeton, N.J.: Princeton University Press, 1950–.

Boyd, Robert T. *The Coming of the Spirit of Pestilence: Introduced Infectious Disease, 1774–1874.* Seattle: University of Washington Press, 1999.

Brain, Jeffrey P., George Roth, and Willem J. de Reuse. "Tunica, Biloxi, and Ofo." In *Handbook of North American Indians,* Vol. 14: *Southeast,* ed. Raymond D. Fogelson, 586–97. Washington, D.C.: Smithsonian Institution Press, 2004.

Braund, Kathryn E. Holland. *Deerskins and Duffels: The Creek Indian Trade with Anglo-America, 1685–1815.* Lincoln: University of Nebraska Press, 1993.

————. "Red Sticks." In *Tohopeka: Rethinking the Creek War and the War of 1812,* ed. Kathryn E. Holland Braund, 84–104. Tuscaloosa: University of Alabama Press, 2012.

Bray, Kingsley. "Teton Sioux Population History, 1655–1881." *Nebraska History* 75 (Summer 1994): 165–88.

Bray, William. "Observations on the Indian Method of Picture Writing." *Archaeologia* 6:22 (1782): 159–62.

Brooks, Lisa. *The Common Pot: The Recovery of Native Space in the Northeast.* Minneapolis: University of Minnesota Press, 2008.

————. *Our Beloved Kin: A New History of King Philip's War.* New Haven, Conn.: Yale University Press, 2018.

Brown, John P. "Eastern Cherokee Chiefs." *Chronicles of Oklahoma* 16 (March 1938): 3–35.

————. *Old Frontiers: The Story of the Cherokee Indians from the Earliest Times to the Date of Their Removal to the West, 1838.* Kingsport, Tenn.: Southern Publishers, 1938.

Bruchey, Stuart, comp. and ed. *Cotton and the Growth of the American Economy: 1790–1860.* New York: Harcourt, Brace & World, 1967.

Buchman, Randall L. "James B. Gardiner." In *Encyclopedia of American Indian Removal,* Vol. 1, ed. Daniel F. Littlefield, Jr., and James W. Parins, 83–84. Santa Barbara, Calif.: Greenwood, 2011.

Buckley, Jay H. *William Clark: Indian Diplomat.* Norman: University of Oklahoma Press, 2008.

Buell, Rowena, comp. *The Memoirs of Rufus Putnam and Certain Official Papers and Correspondence.* Boston, Mass.: Houghton, Mifflin, 1903.

Buley, R. Carlyle. *The Old Northwest: Pioneer Period, 1815–1840.* 2 vols. Bloomington: Indiana University Press, 1950.

Burns, Louis F. *A History of the Osage People.* Tuscaloosa: University of Alabama Press, 2004.

Buss, James Joseph. *Winning the West with Words: Language and Conquest in the Lower Great Lakes.* Norman: University of Oklahoma Press, 2011.

Butrick, Daniel S. *Cherokee Removal: The Journal of Rev. Daniel S. Butrick, May 19, 1838–April 1, 1839.* Park Hill, Okla.: Trail of Tears Association, 1998.

Butterfield, C. W. "Expedition against the Delawares." In *Frontier Retreat on the Upper Ohio, 1779–1781,* Collections of the State Historical Society of Wisconsin, Vol. 24, ed. and with an introduction by Louise Phelps Kellogg, 376–81. Madison: State Historical Society of Wisconsin, 1917.

Butterfield, C. W., ed. *The Washington–Crawford Letters.* Cincinnati, Ohio: Robert Clarke, 1877.

———. *Washington–Irvine Correspondence.* Madison, Wis.: David Atwood, 1882.

Callender, Charles. "Miami." In *Handbook of North American Indians,* Vol. 15: *Northeast,* ed. Bruce Trigger, 681–89. Washington, D.C.: Smithsonian Institution Press, 1978.

Calloway, Colin G. *The American Revolution in Indian Country: Crisis and Diversity in Native American Communities.* Cambridge: Cambridge University Press, 1995.

———. *The Indian World of George Washington: The First President, The First Americans, and the Birth of the Nation.* New York: Oxford University Press, 2018.

———. *One Vast Winter Count: The Native American West before Lewis and Clark.* Lincoln: University of Nebraska Press, 2003.

———. *Pen and Ink Witchcraft: Treaties and Treaty Making in American Indian History.* New York: Oxford University Press, 2013.

———. *The Scratch of a Pen: 1763 and the Transformation of North America.* New York: Oxford University Press, 2006.

———. *The Shawnees and the War for America.* New York: Viking, 2007.

———. *The Victory with No Name: The Native American Defeat of the First American Army.* New York: Oxford University Press, 2015.

———. *The Western Abenakis of Vermont, 1600–1800: War, Migration, and the Survival of an Indian People.* Norman: University of Oklahoma Press, 1990.

———. *White People, Indians, and Highlanders: Tribal Peoples and Colonial Encounters in Scotland and America.* New York: Oxford University Press, 2008.

Calloway, Colin G., ed. *Revolution and Confederation.* Vol. 8 of *Early American Documents: Treaties and Laws, 1607–1789,* ed. Alden T. Vaughan. Bethesda, Md.: University Publications of America, 1994.

Cameron, Catherine M., Paul Kelton, and Alan C. Swedlund, eds. *Beyond Germs: Native Depopulation in North America.* Tucson: University of Arizona Press, 2015.

Campbell, John. "The Seminoles, the 'Bloodhound War,' and Abolitionism, 1796–1865." *Journal of Southern History* 72 (May 2006): 259–302.

Campbell, William J. *Speculators in Empire: Iroquoia and the 1768 Treaty of Fort Stanwix.* Norman: University of Oklahoma Press, 2012.

Campisi, Jack. "Houma." In *Handbook of North American Indians,* Vol. 14: *Southeast,* ed. Raymond D. Fogelson, 632–41. Washington, D.C.: Smithsonian Institution Press, 2004.

———. *The Mashpee Indians: Tribe on Trial.* Syracuse, N.Y.: Syracuse University Press, 1991.

Carrier, Toni. "Trade and Plunder Networks in the Second Seminole War." Master's thesis, University of South Florida, 2005.

Carson, James Taylor. "Native Americans, the Market Revolution, and Culture Change: The Choctaw Cattle Economy, 1690–1830." In *Pre-Removal Choctaw History: Exploring New Paths,* ed. Greg O'Brien, 183–99. Norman: University of Oklahoma Press, 2008.

———. *Searching for the Bright Path: The Mississippi Choctaws from Prehistory to Removal.* Lincoln: University of Nebraska Press, 1999.

Carter, Cecile Elkins. *Caddo Indians: Where We Come From.* Norman: University of Oklahoma Press, 1995.

Carter, Clarence Edwin, and John Porter Bloom, eds. *Territorial Papers of the United States.* 28 vols. Washington, D.C.: G.P.O., 1934–1956; Washington, D.C.: National Archives and Records Service, 1958–1975.

Carter, Harvey Lewis. *The Life and Times of Little Turtle: First Sagamore of the Wabash.* Urbana: University of Illinois Press, 1987.

Carver, Jonathan. *Three Years Travel throughout the Interior Parts of North America.* Boston, Mass.: West and Greenleaf, 1802.

Cass, Lewis. "Policy and Practice of the United States and Great Britain in their Treatment of Indians." *North American Review* 24 (April 1827): 365–442.

———. "Removal of the Indians." *North American Review* 30 (January 1830): 62–121.

Cave, Alfred A. "Genocide in the Americas." In *The Historiography of Genocide,* ed. Dan Stone, 273–95. New York: Palgrave Macmillan, 2008.

———. *Lethal Encounters: Englishmen and Indians in Colonial Virginia.* Lincoln: University of Nebraska Press, 2013.

———. *The Pequot War.* Amherst: University of Massachusetts Press, 1996.

———. *Prophets of the Great Spirit: Native American Revitalization Movements in Eastern North America.* Lincoln: University of Nebraska Press, 2006.

Cayton, Andrew R. L. *Frontier Indiana.* Bloomington: Indiana University Press, 1996.

———. "'Noble Actors' upon 'the Theatre of Honour': Power and Civility in the Treaty of Greenville." In *Contact Points: American Frontiers from the Mohawk Valley to the Mississippi, 1750–1830,* ed. Andrew R. L. Cayton and Fredrika J. Teute, 235–69. Chapel Hill: University of North Carolina Press, 1998.

Chang, David A. *The Color of the Land: Race, Nation, and the Politics of Landowner-ship in Oklahoma, 1832–1929.* Chapel Hill: University of North Carolina Press, 2010.

Charleston (South Carolina) City Gazette or Daily Advertiser, April 21, 1789.

Child, Brenda J. *Holding Our World Together: Ojibwe Women and the Survival of Community.* New York: Viking, 2012.

Churchill, Ward. *A Little Matter of Genocide: Holocaust and Denial in the Americas, 1492 to the Present.* San Francisco: City Lights Books, 1997.

"Circular Addressed to Benevolent Ladies of the U. States." *Christian Advocate and Journal, and Zion's Herald* (New York), Dec. 25, 1829: 65–66.

Clanin, Douglas E., ed. "The Papers of William Henry Harrison, 1800–1815." India-napolis: Indiana Historical Society, 1999 (microfilm).

Clarke, Mary Whatley. *Chief Bowles and the Texas Cherokees.* Norman: University of Oklahoma Press, 1971.

Clavin, Matthew J. *Touissant Louverture and the American Civil War: The Promise and Peril of a Second Haitian Revolution.* Philadelphia: University of Pennsylva-nia Press, 2012.

Clifton, James A. *The Pokagons, 1683–1983: Catholic Potawatomi Indians of the St. Joseph River Valley.* Lanham, Md.: University Press of America, 1984.

———. "Potawatomi." In *Handbook of North American Indians,* Vol. 15: *Northeast,* ed. Bruce Trigger, 725–42. Washington, D.C.: Smithsonian Institution Press, 1978.

———. *The Prairie People: Continuity and Change in Potawatomi Indian Culture, 1665–1965.* Lawrence: Regents Press of Kansas, 1977.

———. "Wisconsin Death March: Explaining the Extremes in Old Northwest Indian Removal." *Transactions of the Wisconsin Academy of Sciences, Arts, and Letters* 75 (1987): 1–39.

Clinton, George. *Public Papers of George Clinton.* Vol. 3. Albany, N.Y.: James B. Lyon, 1900.

Coates, B. H., ed. "A Narrative of an Embassy to the Western Indians from the Original Manuscript of Hendrick Aupaumut." *Memoirs of the Historical Society of Pennsylvania.* Vol. 2, pt. 1, 61–131. Philadelphia: Carey, Lea & Carey, 1827.

Coe, Charles H. *Red Patriots: The Story of the Seminoles.* Cincinnati: Editor Publish-ing Co., 1898.

Colbert, Thomas Burnell. "'The Hinge on Which All Affairs of the Sauk and Fox Indians Turn': Keokuk and the United States Government." In *Enduring Na-tions: Native Americans in the Midwest,* ed. R. David Edmunds, 54–71. Urbana: University of Illinois Press, 2008.

Condon, Sean. *Shays's Rebellion: Authority and Distress in Post-Revolutionary America.* Baltimore, Md.: Johns Hopkins University Press, 2015.

Congressional Globe (Appendix). 33d Cong., 1st sess., 1854.

Conkey, Laura E., Ethel Boissevain, and Ives Goddard. "Indians of Southern New England and Long Island: Late Period." In *Handbook of North American Indians,* Vol. 15: *Northeast,* ed. Bruce Trigger, 177–89. Washington, D.C.: Smithsonian Institution Press, 1978.

Continental Congress. *Journals of the Continental Congress, 1774–1789.* Ed.Worthington C. Ford et al. 34 vols. Washington, D.C.: G.P.O., 1904–1937.

Cook-Lynn, Elizabeth. *Anti-Indianism in Modern America: A Voice from Tatekeya's Earth.* Urbana: University of Illinois Press, 2001.

Corkran, David H. *The Creek Frontier, 1540–1783.* Norman: University of Oklahoma Press, 1967.

Cotterill, R. S. *The Southern Indians: The Story of the Civilized Tribes before Removal.* Norman: University of Oklahoma Press, 1954.

Covington, James W. "Cuban Bloodhounds and the Seminoles." *Florida Historical Quarterly* 33 (October 1954): 111–19.

———. *The Seminoles of Florida.* Gainesville: University Press of Florida, 1993.

Craig, Neville B., ed. *The Olden Time.* Vol. 2. Pittsburgh, Penn.: Wright and Charlton, 1848.

Croghan, George. "Croghan's Journal, May 15–September 26, 1765." In *Early Western Travels, 1748–1846,* Vol. 1, ed. Reuben Gold Thwaites, 126–66. Cleveland: Arthur H. Clark, 1904.

———. "Extracts of an Abstract from Mr. Croghan's Journal," May 22, 1766. In *Minutes of the Provincial Council of Pennsylvania,* Vol. 9, 322. Harrisburg, Penn.: Theo. Fenn, 1852.

———. "George Croghan's Journal, April 3, 1759 to April [30], 1763. *Pennsylvania Magazine of History and Biography* 71 (October 1947): 305–444.

Crosby, Alfred. "Virgin Soil Epidemics as a Factor in the Aboriginal Depopulation in America." *William and Mary Quarterly,* 3d ser., 33 (April 1976): 289–99.

Cumfer, Cynthia. *Separate Peoples, One Land: The Minds of Cherokees, Blacks, and Whites on the Tennessee Frontier.* Chapel Hill: University of North Carolina Press, 2007.

Cushman, H. B. *History of the Choctaw, Chickasaw, and Natchez Indians.* Greenville, Tex.: Headlight Printing, 1899.

Dale, Edward E. "Arkansas and the Cherokees." *Arkansas Historical Quarterly* 8 (Summer 1949): 95–114.

Davies, K. G., ed. *Documents of the American Revolution, 1770–1783 (Colonial Office Series).* 21 vols. Dublin: Irish University Press, 1972–1981.

Davis, Donald Edward. *Where There Are Mountains: An Environmental History of the Southern Appalachians.* Athens: University of Georgia Press, 2000.

Davis, James E. *Frontier Illinois.* Bloomington: Indiana University Press, 1998.

Davis, T. Frederick. "The Seminole Council, October 23–25, 1834." *Florida Histori-cal Society Quarterly* 7 (April 1929): 330–56.

Debo, Angie. *The Road to Disappearance: A History of the Creek Indians.* Norman: University of Oklahoma Press, 1941.

Deer, Sarah. *The Beginning and End of Rape: Confronting Sexual Violence in Native America.* Minneapolis: University of Minnesota Press, 2015.

De La Ronde, John T. "Personal Narrative." In *Report and Collections of the State Historical Society of Wisconsin for the Years 1873, 1874, 1875, and 1876,* 345–65. Madison, Wis.: E. B. Bolens, 1876.

Deloria, Philip J., and Neal Salisbury, eds. *Blackwell Companion to American Indian History.* Malden, Mass.: Blackwell, 2002.

DeLucia, Christine M. *Memory Lands: King Philip's War and the Place of Violence in the Northeast.* New Haven, Conn.: Yale University Press, 2018.

DeMallie, Raymond J. "Sioux until 1850." In *Handbook of North American Indians,* Vol. 13: *Plains,* ed. Raymond J. DeMallie, 718–60. Washington, D.C.: Smithso-nian Institution Press, 2001.

Dennis, Matthew. *Seneca Possessed: Indians, Witchcraft, and Power in the Early American Republic.* Philadelphia: University of Pennsylvania Press, 2010.

Denny, Ebenezer. *Military Journal of Major Ebenezer Denny, an Officer in the Revolu-tionary and Indian Wars.* Philadelphia: J. B. Lippincott, 1859.

Den Ouden, Amy E., and Jean M. O'Brien. "Introduction." In *Recognition, Sov-ereignty Struggles, and Indigenous Rights in the United States: A Sourcebook,* ed. Amy E. Den Ouden and Jean M. O'Brien, 1–34. Chapel Hill: University of North Carolina Press, 2013.

Denson, Andrew. *Demanding the Cherokee Nation: Indian Autonomy and American Culture, 1830–1900.* Lincoln: University of Nebraska Press, 2004.

DeRosier, Arthur H., Jr. *The Removal of the Choctaw Indians.* Knoxville: University of Tennessee Press, 1970.

De Vorsey, Louis, Jr. *The Indian Boundary in the Southern Colonies, 1763–1775.* Chapel Hill: University of North Carolina Press, 1966.

Deyle, Steven. *Carry Me Back: The Domestic Slave Trade in American Life.* New York: Oxford University Press, 2005.

Dillard, Anthony Winston. "The Treaty of Dancing Rabbit Creek between the United States and the Choctaw Indians in 1830." *Transactions of the Alabama Historical Society* 3 (1899): 99–106.

Din, Gilbert C., and A. P. Nasatir. *The Imperial Osages: Spanish–Indian Diplomacy in the Mississippi Valley.* Norman: University of Oklahoma Press, 1983.

Dippie, Brian W. *The Vanishing American: White Attitudes and U.S. Indian Policy.* Lawrence: University Press of Kansas, 1982.

Doran, Michael F. "Negro Slaves of the Five Civilized Tribes." *Annals of the Associa-tion of American Geographers* 68 (September 1978): 335–50.

———. "Population Statistics of Nineteenth Century Indian Territory." *Chronicles of Oklahoma* 53 (Winter 1975–1976): 492–515.

Doughton, Thomas L. "Unseen Neighbors: Native Americans of Central Massachusetts: A People Who Had 'Vanished.'" In *After King Philip's War: Presence and Persistence in Indian New England,* ed. Colin G. Calloway, 207–30. Hanover, N.H.: University Press of New England, 1997.

Dowd, Gregory Evans. *Groundless: Rumors, Legends, and Hoaxes on the Early American Frontier.* Baltimore, Md.: Johns Hopkins University Press, 2015.

———. *A Spirited Resistance: The North American Indian Struggle for Unity, 1745–1815.* Baltimore, Md.: Johns Hopkins University Press, 1992.

———. "Thinking Outside the Circle: Tecumseh's 1811 Mission." In *Tohopeka: Rethinking the Creek War and the War of 1812,* ed. Kathryn E. Holland Braund, 30–52. Tuscaloosa: University of Alabama Press, 2012.

———. *War under Heaven: Pontiac, the Indian Nations, and the British Empire.* Baltimore, Md.: Johns Hopkins University Press, 2002.

Downes, Randolph C. "Cherokee–American Relations in the Upper Tennessee Valley, 1776–1791." *East Tennessee Historical Society Publications* 8 (1936): 35–53.

———. *Council Fires on the Upper Ohio: A Narrative of Indian Affairs in the Upper Ohio Valley until 1795.* Pittsburgh, Penn.: University of Pittsburgh Press, 1968.

———. "Creek–American Relations, 1782–1790." *Georgia Historical Quarterly* 21 (June 1937): 142–84.

Drake, Benjamin. *Life of Tecumseh and of His Brother the Prophet.* Cincinnati, Ohio: Anderson, Gates, and Wright, 1858.

Drake, Daniel. *A Systematic Treatise, Historical, Etiological, and Practical on the Principal Diseases of the Interior Valley of North America.* Vol. 1. Cincinnati, Ohio: Winthrop B. Smith, 1850.

Drake, James D. *King Philip's War: Civil War in New England, 1675–1676.* Amherst: University of Massachusetts Press, 1999.

Drake, Samuel G. *Biography and History of the Indians of North America.* 5th ed. Boston, Mass.: Antiquarian Institute, 1836.

———. *The Book of the Indians of North America.* Boston, Mass.: Antiquarian Bookstore, 1833.

Drinnon, Richard. *Facing West: The Metaphysics of Indian-Hating and Empire-Building.* 1980. Rpt., New York: Schocken, 1990.

Duffy, John. *Epidemics in Colonial America.* Baton Rouge: Louisiana State University Press, 1953.

Dunbar, John R., ed. *The Paxton Papers.* The Hague: Martinus Nijhoff, 1957.

Dunbar-Ortiz, Roxanne. *An Indigenous Peoples' History of the United States.* Boston, Mass.: Beacon Press, 2014.

Dunn, Jacob Piatt. *True Indian Stories with Glossary of Indiana Indian Names.* Indianapolis, Ind.: Sentinel Printing, 1909.

DuVal, Kathleen. *Independence Lost: Lives on the Edge of the American Revolution.* New York: Random House, 2015.

———. *The Native Ground: Indians and Colonists in the Heart of the Continent.* Philadelphia: University of Pennsylvania Press, 2006.

Eaton, Rachel Caroline. "The Legend of the Battle of Claremore Mound." *Chronicles of Oklahoma* 8 (December 1930): 369–76.

Eby, Cecil. *"That Disgraceful Affair": The Black Hawk War.* New York: W. W. Norton, 1973.

Echo-Hawk, Walter R. *In the Courts of the Conqueror: The 10 Worst Indian Law Cases Ever Decided.* Golden, Colo.: Fulcrum, 2010.

Edmunds, R. David. *The Potawatomis: Keepers of the Fire.* Norman: University of Oklahoma Press, 1978.

———. *The Shawnee Prophet.* Lincoln: University of Nebraska Press, 1983.

———. *Tecumseh and the Quest for Indian Leadership.* Rev. ed. New York: Pearson Longman, 2007.

Edmunds, R. David, and Joseph L. Peyser. *The Fox Wars: The Mesquakie Challenge to New France.* Norman: University of Oklahoma Press, 1993.

Edwards, Tai S. "Disruption and Disease: The Osage Struggle to Survive in the Nineteenth-Century Trans-Missouri West." *Kansas History: A Journal of the Central Plains* 36 (Winter 2013–2014): 218–33.

Eid, Leroy V. "'The Slaughter Was Reciprocal': Josiah Harmar's Two Defeats, 1790." *Northwest Ohio Quarterly* 65 (Spring 1993): 51–67.

Ellis, Joseph J. *American Creation: Triumphs and Tragedies in the Founding of the Republic.* New York: Alfred A. Knopf, 2007.

Ellisor, John T. "'Like So Many Wolves': Creek Removal in the Cherokee Country, 1835–1838." *Journal of East Tennessee History* 71 (1999): 1–24.

———. *The Second Creek War: Interethnic Conflict and Collusion on a Collapsing Frontier.* Lincoln: University of Nebraska Press, 2010.

Erickson, Vincent O. "Maliseet-Passamaquoddy." In *Handbook of North American Indians,* Vol. 15: *Northeast,* ed. Bruce Trigger, 123–36. Washington, D.C.: Smithsonian Institution Press, 1978.

Esarey, Logan, ed. *Messages and Letters of William Henry Harrison.* 2 vols. Indianapolis: Indiana Historical Commission, 1922.

Ethridge, Robbie. *Creek Country: The Creek Indians and Their World.* Chapel Hill: University of North Carolina Press, 2003.

———. *From Chicaza to Chickasaw: The European Invasion and the Transformation of the Mississippian World, 1540–1715.* Chapel Hill: University of North Carolina Press, 2010.

Eustace, Nicole. *1812: War and the Passions of Patriotism.* Philadelphia: University of Pennsylvania Press, 2012.

Evans, W. McKee. "The North Carolina Lumbees: From Assimilation to Revitalization." In *Southeastern Indians since the Removal Era,* ed. Walter L. Williams, 49–71. Athens: University of Georgia Press, 1979.

Evarts, Jeremiah. *Essays on the Present Crisis in the Condition of the American Indians; First Published in the National Intelligencer, under the Signature of William Penn.* Boston, Mass.: Perkins & Marvin, 1829.

Everett, Dianna. *The Texas Cherokees: A People between Two Fires, 1819–1840.* Norman: University of Oklahoma Press, 1990.

Everett, Edward. "On the State of the Indians." *North American Review* 16 (January 1823): 30–45.

———. *Orations and Speeches on Various Occasions.* Boston, Mass.: American Stationers' Company, 1836.

"Examination of Cornelius Vanslyke," July 21, 1767. Special Collections, William L. Clement Library, University of Michigan, Ann Arbor.

Faragher, John Mack. *Daniel Boone: The Life and Legend of an American Pioneer.* New York: Henry Holt, 1992.

———. *A Great and Noble Scheme: The Tragic Story of the Expulsion of the French Acadians from Their American Homeland.* New York: W. W. Norton, 2005.

———. "'More Motley than Mackinaw': From Ethnic Mixing to Ethnic Cleansing on the Frontier of the Lower Missouri, 1783–1833." In *Contact Points: American Frontiers from the Mohawk Valley to the Mississippi, 1750–1830,* ed. Andrew R. L. Cayton and Fredrika J. Teute, 304–26. Chapel Hill: University of North Carolina Press, 1988.

Farnham, Thomas J. *Travels in the Great Western Prairies.* 2 vols. London: Richard Bentley, 1843.

Feest, Christian F. "Nanticoke and Neighboring Tribes." In *Handbook of North American Indians,* Vol. 15: *Northeast,* ed. Bruce Trigger, 240–52. Washington, D.C.: Smithsonian Institution Press, 1978.

Fenn, Elizabeth A. "Biological Warfare in Eighteenth-Century North America: Beyond Jeffrey Amherst." *Journal of American History* 86 (March 2000): 1552–80.

———. *Encounters at the Heart of the World: A History of the Mandan People.* New York: Hill and Wang, 2014.

———. *Pox Americana: The Great Smallpox Epidemic of 1775–82.* New York: Hill and Wang, 2001.

Fenton, William N. *The Great Law and the Longhouse: A Political History of the Iroquois Confederacy.* Norman: University of Oklahoma Press, 1998.

Finger, John R. *The Eastern Band of Cherokees, 1819–1900.* Knoxville: University of Tennessee Press, 1984.

———. *Tennessee Frontiers: Three Regions in Transition.* Bloomington: Indiana University Press, 2001.

Finley, James B. *History of the Wyandott Mission at Upper Sandusky, Ohio, under the Direction of the Methodist Episcopal Church.* Cincinnati, Ohio: J. F. Wright and L. Swormstedt, 1840.

First International Indian Treaty Council at Standing Rock Indian Country. "Declaration of Continuing Independence," June 1974. https://www.iitc.org/about-iitc/the-declaration-of-continuing-independence-june-1974/ (accessed Feb. 7, 2018).

Fisher, Julie A., and David J. Silverman. *Ninigret, Sachem of the Niantics and Narragansetts: Diplomacy, War, and the Balance of Power in Seventeenth-Century New England and Indian Country.* Ithaca, N.Y.: Cornell University Press, 2014.

Fisher, Linford D. *The Indian Great Awakening: Religion and the Shaping of Native Cultures in Early America.* New York: Oxford University Press, 2012.

Fisher, Robert L. "The Treaties of Portage Des Sioux." *Mississippi Valley Historical Review* 19 (March 1933): 495–508.

Flores, Dan. "Bison Ecology, Bison Diplomacy: The Southern Plains from 1800 to 1850." *Journal of American History* 78 (September 1991): 465–85.

Foner, Eric. *Give Me Liberty!: An American History.* 5th ed. New York: W. W. Norton, 2017.

Ford, Lisa. *Settler Sovereignty: Jurisdiction and Indigenous People in America and Australia, 1788–1836.* Cambridge: Harvard University Press, 2010.

Ford, Paul Leicester, ed. *The Works of Thomas Jefferson.* 12 vols. New York: G. P. Putnam's Sons, 1904–1905.

Ford, Worthington Chauncey, ed. *The Writings of George Washington.* 12 vols. New York: G. P. Putnam's Sons, 1889–1893.

Foreign Missionary Chronicle 1 (June 1833).

Foreman, Grant. *The Five Civilized Tribes: Cherokee, Chickasaw, Choctaw, Creek, Seminole.* Norman: University of Oklahoma Press, 1934.

———. *Indian Removal: The Emigration of the Five Civilized Tribes of Indians.* Norman: University of Oklahoma Press, 1932.

———. *The Last Trek of the Indians.* Chicago: University of Chicago Press, 1946.

Foreman, Grant, ed. "The Journal of Elijah Hicks." *Chronicles of Oklahoma* 13 (March 1935): 68–99.

———. "The Journal of the Proceedings at Our First Treaty with the Wild Indians, 1835." *Chronicles of Oklahoma* 14 (December 1936): 393–418.

———. *A Traveler in Indian Territory: The Journal of Ethan Allen Hitchcock, Late Major-General in the United States Army.* Cedar Rapids, Iowa: Torch Press, 1930.

Friis, Herman R. "A Series of Population Maps of the Colonies and the United States, 1625–1790." *Geographical Review* 30 (July 1940): 463–70.

Frymer, Paul. *Building an American Empire: The Era of Territorial and Political Expansion.* Princeton, N.J.: Princeton University Press, 2017.

Fur, Gunlög. *A Nation of Women: Gender and Colonial Encounters among the Delaware Indians.* Philadelphia: University of Pennsylvania Press, 2009.

Furstenberg, François. "The Significance of the Trans-Appalachian Frontier in Atlantic History." *American Historical Review* 113 (June 2008): 647–77.

Gaff, Alan D. *Bayonets in the Wilderness: Anthony Wayne's Legion in the Old Northwest.* Norman: University of Oklahoma Press, 2004.

Gallay, Alan. *The Indian Slave Trade: The Rise of the English Empire in the American South, 1670–1717.* New Haven, Conn.: Yale University Press, 2002.

Galloway, Patricia, and Jason Baird Jackson. "Natchez and Neighboring Groups." In *Handbook of North American Indians,* Vol. 14: *Southeast,* ed. Raymond D. Fogelson, 598–615. Washington, D.C.: Smithsonian Institution Press, 2004.

Garrison, Tim Alan. *The Legal Ideology of Removal: The Southern Judiciary and the Sovereignty of Native American Nations.* Athens: University of Georgia Press, 2002.

Gates, Paul Wallace. *Fifty Million Acres: Conflict over Kansas Land Policy, 1854–1890.* Ithaca, N.Y.: Cornell University Press, 1954.

Gaul, Theresa Strouth. "Introduction." In *To Marry an Indian: The Marriage of Harriett Gold and Elias Boudinot in Letters, 1823–1839,* ed. Theresa Strouth Gaul, 1–76. Chapel Hill: University of North Carolina Press, 2005.

Georgia General Assembly. *Acts of the Official Assembly of the State of Georgia, 1827.* Milledgeville, Ga.: Camak & Ragland, 1827.

Gibson, Arrell M. *The Chickasaws.* Norman: University of Oklahoma Press, 1971.

———. "An Indian Territory United Nations: The Creek Council of 1845." *Chronicles of Oklahoma* 39 (Winter 1961–1962): 398–413.

———. *The Kickapoos: Lords of the Middle Border.* Norman: University of Oklahoma Press, 1963.

Gilley, Brian Joseph. *A Longhouse Fragmented: Ohio Iroquois Autonomy in the Nineteenth Century.* Albany: State University of New York Press, 2014.

Gipson, Lawrence Henry, ed. *The Moravian Indian Mission on the White River: Diaries and Letters May 5, 1799, to November 12, 1806.* Indianapolis: Indiana Historical Bureau, 1938.

Glatthaar, Joseph T., and James Kirby Martin. *Forgotten Allies: The Oneida Indians and the American Revolution.* New York: Hill and Wang, 2006.

Gleach, Frederick W. *Powhatan's World and Colonial Virginia: A Conflict of Cultures.* Lincoln: University of Nebraska Press, 1997.

Goddard, Ives. "Delaware." In *Handbook of North American Indians,* Vol. 15: *Northeast,* ed. Bruce Trigger, 213–39. Washington, D.C.: Smithsonian Institution Press, 1978.

Gould, Eliga H. *Among the Powers of the Earth: The American Revolution and the Making of a New World Empire.* Cambridge, Mass.: Harvard University Press, 2012.

Grant, James. "Journal of Lieutenant-Colonel James Grant, Commanding an Expedition against the Cherokee Indians, June–July 1761." *Florida Historical Society Quarterly* 12 (July 1933): 25–36.

———. "Successful Expedition against the Cherokees." *Gentleman's Magazine* 30 (July 1760): 306–7.

Gray, Susan E. *The Yankee West: Community Life on the Michigan Frontier.* Chapel
    Hill: University of North Carolina Press, 1996.

Graymont, Barbara. *The Iroquois in the American Revolution.* Syracuse, N.Y.: Syra-
    cuse University Press, 1972.

Green, Michael D. "The Expansion of European Colonization to the Mississippi
    Valley, 1780–1880." In *The Cambridge History of the Native Peoples of the Ameri-
    cas,* Vol. 1: *North America, Part 1,* ed. Bruce Trigger and Wilcomb E. Washburn,
    461–538. Cambridge: Cambridge University Press, 1996.

———. *The Politics of Indian Removal: Creek Government and Society in Crisis.*
    Lincoln: University of Nebraska Press, 1982.

Grenier, John. *The First Way of War: American War Making on the Frontier, 1607–
    1814.* Cambridge: Cambridge University Press, 2005.

Griffin, Patrick. *American Leviathan: Empire, Nation, and Revolutionary Frontier.*
    New York: Hill and Wang, 2007.

———. *America's Revolution.* New York: Oxford University Press, 2012.

Grimsley. Mark. "'Rebels' and 'Redskins': U.S. Military Conduct toward White
    Southerners and Native Americans in Comparative Perspective." In *Civilians
    in the Path of War,* ed. Mark Grimsley and Clifford J. Rogers, 137–61. Lincoln:
    University of Nebraska Press, 2002.

Guyatt, Nicholas. *Bind Us Apart: How Enlightened Americans Invented Racial Segre-
    gation.* New York: Basic Books, 2016.

———. *Providence and the Invention of the United States, 1607–1876.* Cambridge:
    Cambridge University Press, 2007.

Hagan, William T. *The Sac and Fox Indians.* Norman: University of Oklahoma
    Press, 1958.

Halbert, H. S. "Story of the Treaty of Dancing Rabbit." *Publications of the Missis-
    sippi Historical Society* 6 (1902): 373–402.

Halbert, H. S., and T. H. Ball. *The Creek War of 1813 and 1814.* Edited and with
    an introduction by Frank L. Owsley, Jr. 1895. Rpt., Tuscaloosa: University of
    Alabama Press, 1969.

Hall, John W. *Uncommon Defense: Indian Allies in the Black Hawk War.* Cambridge:
    Harvard University Press, 2009.

Halsey, Francis Whiting. *The Old New York Frontier: Its Wars with Indians and
    Tories, Its Missionary Schools, Pioneers and Land Titles, 1614–1800.* New York:
    Charles Scribner's Sons, 1901.

Hämäläinen, Pekka. *The Comanche Empire.* New Haven, Conn.: Yale University
    Press, 2008.

Hanna, Charles A. *The Wilderness Trail.* Vol. 2. New York: G. P. Putnam's Sons, 1911.

Harper, Rob. "Looking the Other Way: The Gnadenhutten Massacre and the
    Contextual Interpretation of Violence." *William and Mary Quarterly,* 3rd ser., 64
    (July 2007): 621–44.

———. *Unsettling the West: Violence and State Building in the Ohio Valley.* Philadelphia: University of Pennsylvania Press, 2018.

Harvey, Henry. *History of the Shawnee Indians from the Year 1681 to 1854, Inclusive.* Cincinnati, Ohio: Ephraim Morgan & Sons, 1855.

Hatley, Tom. *The Dividing Paths: Cherokees and South Carolinians through the Era of Revolution.* New York: Oxford University Press, 1993.

Hauptman, Laurence M. *Conspiracy of Interests: Iroquois Dispossession and the Rise of New York State.* Syracuse, N.Y.: Syracuse University Press, 1999.

———. "General John E. Wool in Cherokee Country, 1836–1837: A Reinterpretation." *Georgia Historical Quarterly* 85 (Spring 2001): 1–26.

———. *Seven Generations of Iroquois Leadership: The Six Nations since 1800.* Syracuse, N.Y.: Syracuse University Press, 2008.

———. *The Tonawanda Senecas' Heroic Battle against Removal: Conservative Activist Indians.* Albany: State University of New York Press, 2011.

Hauptman, Laurence M., and L. Gordon McLester III. *Chief Daniel Bread and the Oneida Nation of Indians of Wisconsin.* Norman: University of Oklahoma Press, 2002.

Haveman, Christopher D. "'Last Evening I Saw the Sun Set for the Last Time': The 1832 Treaty of Washington and the Transfer of the Creeks' Alabama Lands to White Ownership." *Native South* 5 (2012): 61–94.

———. *Rivers of Sand: Creek Indian Emigration, Relocation, and Ethnic Cleansing in the American South.* Lincoln: University of Nebraska Press, 2016.

Heckewelder, John. *History, Manners, and Customs of the Indian Nations Who Once Inhabited Pennsylvania and the Neighbouring States.* Rev. ed. Philadelphia: Historical Society of Pennsylvania, 1876.

———. *A Narrative of the Mission of the United Brethren among the Delaware and Mohegan Indians from Its Commencement in the Year 1740 to the Close of the Year 1808.* Philadelphia: McCarty & Davis, 1820.

Henry, William Wirt, ed. *Patrick Henry: Life, Correspondence and Speeches.* Vol. 3. New York Charles Scribner's Sons, 1891.

Herring, Joseph B. *The Enduring Indians of Kansas: A Century and a Half of Acculturation.* Lawrence: University Press of Kansas, 1990.

———. *Kenekuk, the Kickapoo Prophet.* Lawrence: University Press of Kansas, 1988.

Hershberger, Mary. "Mobilizing Women, Anticipating Abolition: The Struggle against Indian Removal in the 1830s." *Journal of American History* 86 (June 1999): 15–40.

Hickey, Donald R. *The War of 1812: A Forgotten Conflict.* Urbana: University of Illinois Press, 1989.

Hinderaker, Eric. *Elusive Empires: Constructing Colonialism in the Ohio Valley, 1673–1800.* Cambridge: Cambridge University Press, 1997.

Hixson, Walter L. *American Settler Colonialism: A History.* New York: Palgrave Macmillan, 2013.

Hofstadter, Richard. *The American Political Tradition and the Men Who Made It.* 1948. Rpt., New York: Vintage, 1973.

Holton, Woody. *Forced Founders: Indians, Debtors, Slaves, and the Making of the American Revolution in Virginia.* Chapel Hill: University of North Carolina Press, 1999.

Horsman, Reginald. *Expansion and American Indian Policy, 1783–1812.* East Lansing: Michigan State University Press, 1967.

Hosmer, Brian C. *American Indians in the Marketplace: Persistence and Innovation among the Menominees and Metlakatlans, 1870–1920.* Lawrence: University Press of Kansas, 1999.

Hotchkiss, William A., comp. *A Codification of the Statute Law of Georgia.* 2nd ed. Augusta, Ga.: Charles E. Grenville, 1848.

Howard, Dresden W. H., ed. "The Battle of Fallen Timbers as Told by Chief Kin-Jo-I-No." *Northwest Ohio Quarterly* 20 (January 1948): 37–49.

Howe, Daniel Walker. *What Hath God Wrought: The Transformation of America, 1815–1848.* New York: Oxford University Press, 2007.

Hoxie, Frederick E., ed. *The Oxford Handbook of American Indian History.* New York: Oxford University Press, 2016.

Hubley, Adam. "Journal of Lieut.-Col. Adam Hubley." In *Journals of the Military Expedition of Major General John Sullivan against the Six Nations of Indians in 1779,* compiled by Frederick Cook, 145–67. Auburn, N.Y.: Knapp, Peck & Thomson, 1887.

Hudson, Angela Pulley. *Creek Paths and Federal Roads: Indians, Settlers, and Slaves and the Making of the American South.* Chapel Hill: University of North Carolina Press, 2010.

Hudson, Charles M. *The Catawba Nation.* Athens: University of Georgia Press, 1970.

Humphreys, Margaret. *Malaria: Poverty, Race, and Public Health in the United States.* Baltimore, Md.: Johns Hopkins University Press, 2001.

Hunter, Ian. "Vattel in Revolutionary America: From the Rules of War to the Rules of Law." In *Between Indigenous and Settler Governance,* ed. Lisa Ford and Tim Rowse, 13–22. Abingdon, UK: Routledge, 2013.

Hunter, John D. *Manners and Customs of Several Indian Tribes Located West of the Mississippi.* Philadelphia: J. Maxwell, 1823.

Hurt, R. Douglas. *The Ohio Frontier: Crucible of the Old Northwest, 1720–1830.* Bloomington: Indiana University Press, 1996.

Hyde, Anne F. *Empires, Nations, and Families: A History of the North American West, 1800–1860.* Lincoln: University of Nebraska Press, 2011.

Ingersoll, Thomas N. *To Intermix with Our White Brothers: Indian Mixed Bloods in the United States from Earliest Times to the Indian Removals.* Albuquerque: University of New Mexico Press, 2005.

Isenberg, Andrew C. *The Destruction of the Bison: An Environmental History, 1750–1920.* Cambridge: Cambridge University Press, 2000.

———. "An Empire of Remedy: Vaccination, Natives, and Narratives in the North American West." *Pacific Historical Review* 86 (February 2017): 84–113.

Ishii, Izumi. *Bad Fruits of the Civilized Tree: Alcohol and the Sovereignty of the Cherokee Nation.* Lincoln: University of Nebraska Press, 2008.

Jackson, Donald, ed. *Black Hawk: An Autobiography.* Urbana: University of Illinois Press, 1955.

———. *Letters of the Lewis and Clark Expedition with Related Documents, 1783–1854.* 2nd ed. 2 vols. Urbana: University of Illinois Press, 1978.

Jacob, John J. *A Biographical Sketch of the Life of the Late Captain Michael Cresap.* Cincinnati, Ohio: Jno. F. Uhlhorn, 1866.

Jacobs, Margaret. "Genocide or Ethnic Cleansing? Are These Our Only Choices?" *Western Historical Quarterly* 47 (Winter 2016): 444–48.

James, James Alton, ed. *George Rogers Clark Papers, 1771–1781.* Collections of the Illinois State Historical Library. Vol. 8. Springfield: Illinois State Historical Library, 1912.

Jameson, J. Franklin, ed. *Narratives of New Netherland, 1609–1664.* New York: Scribner's, 1909.

Jarvis, Brad D. E. *The Brothertown Nation of Indians: Land Ownership and Nationalism in Early America, 1740–1840.* Lincoln: University of Nebraska Press, 2010.

Jennings, Francis. *The Invasion of America: Indians, Colonialism, and the Cant of Conquest.* New York: W. W. Norton, 1976.

———. "Susquehannock." In *Handbook of North American Indians,* Vol. 15: *Northeast,* ed. Bruce Trigger, 362–67. Washington, D.C.: Smithsonian Institution Press, 1978.

Johnson, William, Sir. *The Papers of Sir William Johnson.* 14 vols. Albany: University of the State of New York, 1921–1965.

Jones, Adam. *Genocide: A Comprehensive Introduction.* New York: Routledge, 2006.

Jones, David S. "Population, Health, and Public Welfare." In *The Oxford Handbook of American Indian History,* ed. Frederick E. Hoxie, 413–31. New York: Oxford University Press, 2016.

———. *Rationalizing Epidemics: Meanings and Uses of American Indian Mortality since 1600.* Cambridge: Harvard University Press, 2004.

Jones, Dorothy V. *License for Empire: Colonialism by Treaty in Early America.* Chicago: University of Chicago Press, 1982.

Jortner, Adam. *The Gods of Prophetstown: The Battle of Tippecanoe and the Holy War for the American Frontier.* New York: Oxford University Press, 2011.

Jumper, Betty Mae Tiger, and Patsy West. *A Seminole Legend: The Life of Betty Mae Tiger Jumper.* Gainesville: University Press of Florida, 2001.

Jung, Patrick J. *The Black Hawk War of 1832*. Norman: University of Oklahoma Press, 2007.

Kanon, Thomas. "'A Slow Laborious Slaughter': The Battle of Horseshoe Bend." *Tennessee Historical Quaterly* 58 (March 1999): 2–15.

Kappler, Charles J., ed. *Indian Affairs: Laws and Treaties*. Vol. 2: *Treaties*. Washington, D.C.: G.P.O., 1904.

Karamanski, Theodore J. *Blackbird's Song: Andrew J. Blackbird and the Odawa People*. East Lansing: Michigan State University Press, 2012.

Katz, Steven T. "The Pequot War Reconsidered." *New England Quarterly* 64 (June 1991): 206–24.

Kay, Jeanne. "The Fur Trade and Native American Population Growth." *Ethnohistory* 31 (Autumn 1984): 265–87.

Keesing, Felix M. *The Menomini Indians of Wisconsin: A Study of Three Centuries of Cultural Contact and Change*. Madison: University of Wisconsin Press, 1987.

Kellogg, Louise Phelps, ed. *Frontier Advance on the Upper Ohio, 1778–1779*. Collections of the State Historical Society of Wisconsin. Vol. 23. Madison: State Historical Society of Wisconsin, 1916.

Kelsay, Isabel Thompson. *Joseph Brant, 1743–1807: Man of Two Worlds*. Syracuse, N.Y.: Syracuse University Press, 1984.

Kelton, Paul. *Cherokee Medicine, Colonial Germs: An Indigenous Nation's Fight against Smallpox, 1518–1824*. Norman: University of Oklahoma Press, 2015.

———. *Epidemics and Enslavement: Biological Catastrophe in the Native Southeast, 1492–1715*. Lincoln: University of Nebraska Press, 2007.

———. "Remembering Cherokee Mortality during the American Revolution." In *Beyond Germs: Native Depopulation in North America*, ed. Catherine M. Cameron, Paul Kelton, and Alan C. Swedlund, 198–221. Tucson: University of Arizona Press, 2015.

Kenny, Kevin. *Peaceable Kingdom Lost: The Paxton Boys and the Destruction of William Penn's Holy Experiment*. New York: Oxford University Press, 2009.

Kent, Donald H., and Merle H. Deardorff, eds. "John Adlum on the Allegheny: Memoirs for the Year 1794: Part 2." *Pennsylvania Magazine of History and Biography* 84 (October 1960): 435–80.

Kidwell, Clara Sue. "The Choctaw Struggle for Land and Identity in Mississippi, 1830–1918," In *After Removal: The Choctaw in Mississippi*, ed. Samuel J. Wells and Roseanna Tubby, 64–93. Jackson: University Press of Mississippi, 1986.

———. *Choctaws and Missionaries in Mississippi, 1818–1918*. Norman: University of Oklahoma Press, 1995.

———. *The Choctaws in Oklahoma: From Tribe to Nation, 1855–1970*. Norman: University of Oklahoma Press, 2007.

Kiernan, Ben. *Blood and Soil: A World History of Genocide and Extermination from Sparta to Darfur*. New Haven, Conn.: Yale University Press, 2007.

———. "Is 'Genocide' an Anachronistic Concept for the Study of Early Modern Mass Killing?" *History* 99 (July 2014): 530–48.

Klopfenstein, Carl G. "The Removal of the Indians from Ohio." In *The Historical Indian in Ohio: A Conference to Commemorate the Bicentennial of the American Revolution,* ed. Randall Buchman, 28–38. Columbus: Ohio Historical Society, 1976.

———. "The Removal of the Wyandots from Ohio." *Ohio Historical Quarterly* 66 (April 1957): 119–36.

———. "Westward Ho: Removal of Ohio Shawnees, 1832–1833." *Bulletin of the Historical and Philosophical Society of Ohio* 15 (January 1957): 3–31.

Klopotek, Brian. *Recognition Odysseys: Indigeneity, Race, and Federal Tribal Recognition Policy in Three Louisiana Indian Communities.* Durham, N.C.: Duke University Press, 2011.

Kniffen, Fred B., Hiram F. Gregory, and George A. Stokes. *The Historic Indian Tribes of Louisiana: From 1542 to the Present.* Baton Rouge: Louisiana State University Press, 1987.

Knopf, Richard C., ed. *Anthony Wayne: A Name in Arms: Soldier, Diplomat, Defender of Expansion Westward of a Nation: The Wayne-Knox-Pickering-McHenry Correspondence.* Pittsburgh, Penn.: University of Pittsburgh Press, 1960.

Knouff, Gregory T. *The Soldiers' Revolution: Pennsylvanians in Arms and the Forging of Early American Identity.* University Park: Pennsylvania State University Press, 2004.

Konkle, Maureen. *Writing Indian Nations: Native Intellectuals and the Politics of Historiography, 1827–1863.* Chapel Hill: University of North Carolina Press, 2004.

Kokomoor, Kevin. "A Re-assessment of Seminoles, Africans, and Slavery on the Florida Frontier." *Florida Historical Quarterly* 88 (Fall 2009): 209-36.

Krauthamer, Barbara. *Black Slaves, Indian Masters: Slavery, Emancipation and Citizenship in the Native American South.* Chapel Hill: University of North Carolina Press, 2013.

Kugel, Rebecca, and Lucy Eldersveld Murphy. "Introduction: Searching for Cornfields—and Sugar Groves." In *Native Women's History in Eastern North America before 1900: A Guide to Research and Writing,* ed. Rebecca Kugel and Lucy Eldersveld Murphy, xiii–xxxvi. Lincoln: University of Nebraska Press, 2007.

LaDuke, Winona. *All Our Relations: Native Struggles for Land and Life.* Cambridge, Mass.: South End Press, 1999.

Lakomäki, Sami. *Gathering Together: The Shawnee People through Diaspora and Nationhood, 1600–1870.* New Haven, Conn.: Yale University Press, 2014.

Lancaster, Jane F. *Removal Aftershock: The Seminoles' Struggles to Survive in the West, 1836–1866.* Knoxville: University of Tennessee Press, 1994.

Lanman, Charles. *Letters from the Alleghany Mountains.* New York: George P. Putnam, 1849.

LaVere, David. *The Caddo Chiefdoms: Caddo Economics and Politics, 700–1835.* Lincoln: University of Nebraska Press, 1998.

———. *Contrary Neighbors: Southern Plains and Removed Indians in Indian Territory.* Norman: University of Oklahoma Press, 2000.

Leader, Jeanne P. "The Pottawatomies and Alcohol: An Illustration of the Illegal Trade." *Kansas History* 2 (Autumn 1979): 157–65.

Lee, Wayne E. *Barbarians and Brothers: Anglo-American Warfare, 1500–1865.* New York: Oxford University Press, 2011.

Lemkin, Raphaël. *Axis Rule in Occupied Europe: Laws and Occupation, Analysis of Government Proposal for Redress.* Washington, D.C.: Carnegie Endowment for International Peace, 1944.

Lengel, Edward G., ed. *The Papers of George Washington: Revolutionary War Series.* Vol. 20. Charlottesville: University of Virginia Press, 2010.

Lepore, Jill. *The Name of War: King Philip's War and the Origins of American Identity.* New York: Alfred A. Knopf, 1998.

Levy, Jerrold E. "Kiowa." In *Handbook of North American Indians,* Vol. 13: *Plains,* ed. Raymond J. DeMallie, 907–25. Washington, D.C.: Smithsonian Institution Press, 2001.

Lewy, Guenter. "Were American Indians the Victims of Genocide?" *Commentary* 118 (September 2004): 55–63.

Liberty, Margot P., W. Raymond Wood, and Lee Irwin. "Omaha." In *Handbook of North American Indians,* Vol. 13: *Plains,* ed. Raymond J. DeMallie, 399–415. Washington, D.C.: Smithsonian Institution Press, 2001.

Lieberman, Benjamin. "'Ethnic Cleansing' versus Genocide?" In *The Oxford Handbook of Genocide Studies,* ed. Donald Bloxham and A. Dirk Moses, 42–60. New York: Oxford University Press, 2010.

Lincoln, Benjamin. "Journal of a Treaty Held in 1793, with the Indian Tribes North-West of the Ohio, by Commissioners of the United States." *Collections of the Massachusetts Historical Society* 5 (1836): 109–76.

Lipman, Andrew. *The Saltwater Frontier: Indians and the Contest for the American Coast.* New Haven, Conn.: Yale University Press, 2015.

Lipscomb, Andrew A., ed. *The Writings of Thomas Jefferson.* 20 vols. Washington, D.C.: Thomas Jefferson Memorial Association, 1903–1904.

Littlefield, Daniel F., Jr. *Africans and Seminoles: From Removal to Emancipation.* Westport, Conn.: Greenwood Press, 1977.

———. "Third Seminole War." In *Encyclopedia of American Indian Removal,* Vol. 1, ed. Daniel F. Littlefield, Jr., and James W. Parins, 234–36. Santa Barbara, Calif.: Greenwood, 2011.

Locke, John. *Two Treatises of Government.* 1690. Rpt., London: A. Millar et al., 1764.

Lonetree, Amy. "Visualizing Native Survivance: Encounters with My Ho-Chunk Ancestors in the Family Photographs of Charles Van Schaick." In *People of the*

Big Voice: Photographs of Ho-Chunk Families by Charles Van Schaick, 1879–1942,
ed. Tom Jones et al., 13–22. Madison: Wisconsin Historical Society Press, 2011.

Looney, J. Jefferson, ed. *The Papers of Thomas Jefferson: Retirement Series.* 23 vols.
projected. Princeton, N.J.: Princeton University Press, 2004–.

Loskiel, George Henry. *History of the Mission of the United Brethren among the Indians of North America.* London: John Stockdale, 1794.

Lowery, Malinda Maynor. *Lumbee Indians in the Jim Crow South: Race, Identity, and the Making of a Nation.* Chapel Hill: University of North Carolina Press, 2010.

Lurie, Nancy Oestreich. "Winnebago." In *Handbook of North American Indians,*
Vol. 15: *Northeast,* ed. Bruce Trigger, 690–707. Washington, D.C.: Smithsonian
Institution Press, 1978.

MacDonald, David B. *Identity Politics in the Age of Genocide: The Holocaust and Historical Representation.* New York: Routledge, 2008.

MacGregor, Doug. "The Ordeal of John Connolly: The Pursuit of Wealth through
Loyalism." In *The Other Loyalists: Ordinary People, Royalism, and the Revolution in the Middle Colonies, 1763–1787,* ed. Joseph E. Tiedemann, Eugene R.
Fingerhut, and Robert W. Venables, 161–78. Albany: State University of New
York Press, 2009.

Madley, Benjamin. *An American Genocide: The United States and the California Indian Catastrophe.* New Haven, Conn.: Yale University Press, 2016.

———. "California and Oregon's Modoc Indians: How Indigenous Resistance
Camouflages Genocide in Colonial Histories." In *Colonial Genocide in Indigenous North America,* ed. Alexander Laban Hinton, Andrew Woolford, and Jeff
Benvenuto, 95–130. Durham, N.C.: Duke University Press, 2014.

———. "Reexamining the American Genocide Debate: Meaning, Historiography,
and New Methods." *American Historical Review* 120 (February 2015): 98–139.

———. "Understanding Genocide in California under United States Rule,
1846–1873." *Western Historical Quarterly* 47 (Winter 2016): 449–61.

Mahon, John K. *History of the Second Seminole War, 1835–1842.* Rev. ed. Gainesville:
University Press of Florida, 1985.

Mahon, John K., and Brent R. Weisman. "Florida's Seminole and Miccosukee
Peoples." In *The New History of Florida,* ed. Michael Gannon, 183–206. Gainesville: University Press of Florida, 2012.

Mancall, Peter C. *Valley of Opportunity: Economic Culture along the Upper Susquehanna, 1700–1800.* Ithaca, N.Y.: Cornell University Press, 1991.

Mandell, Daniel R. *Behind the Frontier: Indians in Eighteenth-Century Eastern Massachusetts.* Lincoln: University of Nebraska Press, 1996.

———. *Tribe, Race, History: Native Americans in Southern New England, 1780–1880.*
Baltimore, Md.: Johns Hopkins University Press, 2008.

Mann, Barbara Alice. "Fractal Massacres in the Old Northwest: The Example of the
Miamis." *Journal of Genocide Research* 15 (June 2013): 167–82.

———. *George Washington's War on Native America.* Westport, Conn.: Praeger, 2005.

———. "The Greenville Treaty of 1795: Pen-and-Ink Witchcraft in the Struggle for the Old Northwest." In *Enduring Legacies: Native American Treaties and Contemporary Controversies,* ed. Bruce Elliott Johansen, 135–201. Westport, Conn.: Praeger, 2004.

———. *The Tainted Gift: The Disease Method of Frontier Expansion.* Santa Barbara, Calif.: Praeger, 2009.

Mann, Michael. *The Dark Side of Democracy: Explaining Ethnic Cleansing.* Cambridge: Cambridge University Press, 2005.

Marr, John S., and John T. Cathey. "New Hypothesis for Cause of Epidemic among Native Americans, New England, 1616–1619." *Historical Review* 16 (February 2010): 281–86.

Martin, Joel. *Sacred Revolt: The Muskogees' Struggle for a New World.* Boston, Mass.: Beacon Press, 1991.

Matte, Jacqueline Anderson. *They Say the Wind Is Red: The Alabama Choctaw—Lost in Their Own Land.* Montgomery, Ala.: New South Books, 2002.

May, Jon D. "Oil Springs." *Encyclopedia of Oklahoma History and Culture.* www.okhistory.org (accessed Nov. 9, 2017).

McConnell, Michael N. *A Country Between: The Upper Ohio Valley and Its Peoples, 1724–1774.* Lincoln: University of Nebraska Press, 1992.

McCoy, Isaac. *The Annual Register of Indian Affairs within the Indian (or Western) Territory.* Washington, D.C.: Peter Force, 1838.

———. *History of Baptist Indian Missions: Embracing Remarks on the Former and Present Condition of the Aboriginal Tribes; Their Settlement within the Indian Territory and Their Future Prospects.* Washington, D.C.: William M. Morrison, 1840.

McDonnell, Michael A. *Masters of Empire: Great Lakes Indians and the Making of America.* New York: Hill and Wang, 2015.

McKenney, Thomas L. "Statement Showing the Names and Numbers of the Different Tribes of Indians. . . ." In U.S. Senate, *Message from the President of the United States, Transmitting Sundry Documents in Relation to the Various Tribes of Indians within the United States.* 18th Cong., 2nd sess., 1824–1825. S. Doc. 21, serial 109.

McLoughlin, William G. *After the Trail of Tears: The Cherokees' Struggle for Sovereignty, 1839–1880.* Chapel Hill: University of North Carolina Press, 1993.

———. *Cherokee Renascence in the New Republic.* Princeton, N.J.: Princeton University Press, 1986.

Melson, Robert. *Revolution and Genocide: On the Origins of the Armenian Genocide and the Holocaust.* Chicago: University of Chicago Press, 1992.

Merrell, James H. *The Indians' New World: Catawbas and their Neighbors from Euro-pean Contact through the Era of Removal.* New York: W. W. Norton, 1989.

———. *Into the American Woods: Negotiators on the Pennsylvania Frontier.* New York: W. W. Norton, 1999.

Merritt, Jane T. *At the Crossroads: Indians and Empires on a Mid-Atlantic Frontier, 1700–1763.* Chapel Hill: University of North Carolina Press, 2003.

Meuwese, Mark. *Brothers in Arms, Partners in Trade: Dutch–Indigenous Alliances in the Atlantic World, 1595–1674.* Leiden: Brill, 2012.

Michigan Pioneer and Historical Society. *Historical Collections: Collections and Researches Made by the Michigan Pioneer and Historical Society.* Vol. 19. Lansing, Mich.: Robert Smith, 1892.

———. *Historical Collections: Collections and Researches Made by the Michigan Pio-neer and Historical Society.* Vol. 20. Lansing, Mich.: Robert Smith, 1892.

———. *Historical Collections: Collections and Researches Made by the Michigan Pio-neer and Historical Society.* Vol. 24. Lansing, Mich.: Robert Smith, 1895.

Milanich, Jerald T. "Timucua." In *Handbook of North American Indians,* Vol. 14: *Southeast,* ed. Raymond D. Fogelson, 219–28. Washington, D.C.: Smithsonian Institution Press, 2004.

Miles, Tiya. "'Circular Reasoning': Recentering Cherokee Women in the Anti-removal Campaigns." *American Quarterly* 61 (June 2009): 221–43.

———. *Ties That Bind: The Story of an Afro-Cherokee Family in Slavery and Free-dom.* Berkeley: University of California Press, 2005.

Miller, Robert J. *Native America, Discovered and Conquered: Thomas Jefferson, Lewis and Clark, and Manifest Destiny.* Lincoln: University of Nebraska Press, 2008.

Miller, Susan A. *Coacoochee's Bones: A Seminole Saga.* Lawrence: University Press of Kansas, 2003.

Miller, Virginia P. "Aboriginal Micmac Population: A Review of the Evidence." *Ethnohistory* 23 (Spring 1976): 117–27.

———. "The Decline of Nova Scotia Micmac Population, A.D. 1600–1850." *Cul-ture* 2:3 (1982): 107–20.

Milne, George Edward. *Natchez Country: Indians, Colonists, and the Landscapes of Race in French Louisiana.* Athens: University of Georgia Press, 2015.

Miner, Craig, and William E. Unrau. *The End of Indian Kansas: A Study in Cultural Revolution, 1854–1871.* Lawrence: University Press of Kansas, 1978.

Mintz, Max M. *Seeds of Empire: The American Revolutionary Conquest of the Iroquois.* New York: New York University Press, 1999.

Minutes of Debates in Council on the Banks of the Ottawa River, . . . November, 1791. Philadelphia: William Young, 1792.

Missall, John, and Mary Lou Missall. *The Seminole Wars: America's Longest Indian Conflict.* Gainesville: University Press of Florida, 2004.

The Missionary Herald 29 (December 1833).

The Missionary Herald 30 (January 1834).

The Missionary Herald 30 (April 1834).

Mooney, James. "Myths of the Cherokee." In *Nineteenth Annual Report of the Bureau of American Ethnology, 1897–1898*, Pt. 1. Washington, D.C.: G.P.O., 1900.

Morrissey, Robert Michael. *Empire by Collaboration: Indians, Colonists, and Governments in Colonial Illinois Country.* Philadelphia: University of Pennsylvania Press, 2015.

Morse, Jedidiah. *A Report to the Secretary of War of the United States on Indian Affairs.* Washington, D.C.: S. Converse, 1822.

Moser, Harold D., et al., eds. *The Papers of Andrew Jackson.* 17 vols. projected. Knoxville: University of Tennessee Press, 1980–.

Moulton, Gary E., ed. *The Journals of the Lewis and Clark Expedition.* 13 vols. Lincoln: University of Nebraska Press, 1983–2004.

———. *The Papers of Chief John Ross.* 2 vols. Norman: University of Oklahoma Press, 1985.

Mt. Pleasant, Alyssa. "After the Whirlwind: Maintaining a Haudenosaunee Place at Buffalo Creek, 1780–1825." Ph.D. diss., Cornell University, 2007.

Mulroy, Kevin. *The Seminole Freedmen: A History.* Norman: University of Oklahoma Press, 2007.

Murphy, Lucy Eldersveld. *A Gathering of Rivers: Indians, Métis, and Mining in the Western Great Lakes, 1737–1832.* Lincoln: University of Nebraska Press, 2000.

———. *Great Lakes Creoles: A French-Indian Community on the Northern Borderlands, Prairie du Chien, 1750–1860.* Cambridge: Cambridge University Press, 2014.

———. "'Their Women Quite Industrious Miners': Native American Lead Mining in the Upper Mississippi Valley, 1788–1832." In *Enduring Nations: Native Americans in the Midwest,* ed. R. David Edmunds, 36–53. Urbana: University of Illinois Press, 2008.

Murray, Elisabeth Hope. *Disrupting Pathways to Genocide: The Process of Ideological Radicalization.* New York: Palgrave Macmillan, 2015.

Naimark, Norman M. *Fires of Hatred: Ethnic Cleansing in Twentieth-Century Europe.* Cambridge, Mass.: Harvard University Press, 2001.

Nash, Gary B. *The Unknown American Revolution: The Unruly Birth of Democracy and the Struggle to Create America.* New York: Viking, 2005.

Neely, Sharlotte. "Acculturation and Persistence among North Carolina's Eastern Band of Cherokees." In *Southeastern Indians since the Removal Era,* ed. Walter L. Williams, 154–73. Athens: University of Georgia Press, 1979.

Nester, William R. *George Rogers Clark: "I Glory in War."* Norman: University of Oklahoma Press, 2012.

————. *"Haughty Conquerors": Amherst and the Great Indian Uprising of 1763.* Westport, Conn.: Praeger, 2000.

Newcomb, Steven T. *Pagans in the Promised Land: Decoding the Doctrine of Christian Discovery.* Golden, Colo.: Fulcrum, 2008.

Newcomb, William W., Jr. "Wichita." In *Handbook of North American Indians,* Vol. 13: *Plains,* ed. Raymond J. DeMallie, 548–66. Washington, D.C.: Smithsonian Institution Press, 2001.

Newell, Margaret Ellen. *Brethren by Nature: New England Indians, Colonists, and the Origins of American Slavery.* Ithaca, N.Y.: Cornell University Press, 2015.

New England Farmer, and Gardner's Journal 16 (Jan. 31, 1838).

New York Times, Aug. 25, 1912: 4.

Nichols, David Andrew. *Red Gentlemen and White Savages: Indians, Federalists, and the Search for Order on the American Frontier.* Charlottesville: University of Virginia Press, 2008.

Nichols, Roger L. *Warrior Nations: The United States and Indian Peoples.* Norman: University of Oklahoma Press, 2013.

Niles' National Register, Nov. 11, 1837: 163.

Niles' National Register, March 28, 1840: 51.

Niles' National Register, Aug. 21, 1847: 389.

Niles' Weekly Register, Sept. 26, 1812: 52-53.

Niles' Weekly Register, Dec. 18, 1813: 370.

Niles' Weekly Register, Dec. 29, 1827: 274.

Niles' Weekly Register, Sept. 17, 1836: 35.

Norgren, Jill. *The Cherokee Cases: Two Landmark Federal Decisions in the Fight for Sovereignty.* Norman: University of Oklahoma Press, 2003.

Norris, James. "Journal of Major James Norris." In *Journals of the Military Expedition of Major General John Sullivan against the Six Nations of Indians in 1779,* compiled by Frederick Cook, 223–39. Auburn, N.Y.: Knapp, Peck & Thomson, 1887.

Norton, Jack. *When Our Worlds Cried: Genocide in Northwestern California.* San Francisco: Indian Historian Press, 1979.

Novic, Elisa. *The Concept of Cultural Genocide: An International Law Perspective.* New York: Oxford University Press, 2016.

Nugent, Walter. *Habits of Empire: A History of American Expansion.* New York: Alfred A. Knopf, 2008.

Nuttall, Thomas. *A Journal of Travels into the Arkansas Territory during the Year 1819.* Ed. Savoie Lottinville. 1821. Rpt., Norman: University of Oklahoma Press, 1990.

Oaks, Robert F. "The Impact of British Western Policy on the Coming of the American Revolution in Pennsylvania." *Pennsylvania Magazine of History and Biography* 101 (April 1977): 171–89.

Oberg, Michael Leroy. *Uncas: First of the Mohegans.* Ithaca, N.Y.: Cornell University Press, 2003.

Oberly, James W. *A Nation of Statesmen: The Political Culture of the Stockbridge-Munsee Mohicans, 1815–1972.* Norman: University of Oklahoma Press, 2005.

O'Brien, Greg. *Choctaws in a Revolutionary Age, 1750–1830.* Lincoln: University of Nebraska Press, 2002.

O'Brien, Jean M. *Dispossession by Degrees: Indian Land and Identity in Natick, Massachusetts, 1650–1790.* Cambridge: Cambridge University Press, 1997.

———. *Firsting and Lasting: Writing Indians out of Existence in New England.* Minneapolis: University of Minnesota Press, 2010.

O'Brien, Sean Michael. *In Bitterness and in Tears: Andrew Jackson's Destruction of the Creeks and Seminoles.* Westport, Conn.: Praeger, 2003.

O'Callaghan, E. B., ed. *Documents Relative to the Colonial History of the State of New York.* Vol. 8. Albany, N.Y.: Weed, Parsons and Co., 1857.

O'Connell, Barry. "Introduction." In *On Our Own Ground: The Complete Writings of William Apess, a Pequot,* ed. Barry O'Connell, xiii–lxxvii. Amherst: University of Massachusetts Press, 1992.

O'Donnell, James H., III. *Southern Indians in the American Revolution.* Knoxville: University of Tennessee Press, 1973.

Oertel, Kristen Tegtmeier. *Bleeding Borders: Race, Gender, and Violence in Pre–Civil War Kansas.* Baton Rouge: Louisiana State University Press, 2009.

Oliphant, J. Orin, ed. "The Report of the Wyandot Exploring Delegation, 1831." *Kansas History* 14 (August 1947): 248–62.

Olmstead, Earl P. *Blackcoats among the Delaware: David Zeisberger on the Ohio Frontier.* Kent, Ohio: Kent State University Press, 1991.

Olson, Greg., *The Ioway in Missouri.* Columbia: University of Missouri Press, 2008.

Onuf, Peter S. *Jefferson's Empire: The Language of American Nationhood.* Charlottesville: University of Virginia Press, 2000.

———. *Statehood and Union: A History of the Northwest Ordinance.* Bloomington: Indiana University Press, 1987.

Opal, J. M. *Avenging the People: Andrew Jackson, the Rule of Law, and the American Nation.* New York: Oxford University Press, 2017.

O'Shea, John M., and John Ludwickson. *Archaeology and Ethnohistory of the Omaha Indians: The Big Village Site.* Lincoln: University of Nebraska Press, 1992.

Ostler, Jeffrey. "Genocide and American Indian History." In *Oxford Research Encylopedias: American History,* ed. Jon Butler. New York: Oxford University Press, 2015. http://americanhistory.oxfordre.com/view/10.1093/acrefore/9780199329175.001.0001/acrefore-9780199329175-e-3 (accessed Feb. 28, 2018).

————. "'Just and Lawful War' as Genocidal War in the (U.S.) Northwest Ordinance and Northwest Territory." *Journal of Genocide Research* 18 (February 2016): 1–20.

————. *The Lakotas and the Black Hills: The Struggle for Sacred Ground.* New York: Viking, 2010.

————. "'To Extirpate the Indians:' An Indigenous Consciousness of Genocide in the Ohio Valley and Lower Great Lakes, 1750s–1810." *William and Mary Quarterly,* 3rd ser., 72 (October 2015): 587–622.

Owens, Robert M. *Mr. Jefferson's Hammer: William Henry Harrison and the Origins of American Indian Policy.* Norman: University of Oklahoma Press, 2007.

Owsley, Frank Lawrence, Jr. *Struggle for the Gulf Borderlands: The Creek War and the Battle of New Orleans, 1812–1815.* Gainesville: University Press of Florida, 1981.

Paige, Amanda L., Fuller L. Bumpers, and Daniel F. Littlefield, Jr. *Chickasaw Removal.* Ada, Okla.: Chickasaw Press, 2010.

Panoplist; or, The Christian's Armory 1 (November 1805).

Paquette, Moses. "The Wisconsin Winnebagoes." *Collections of the State Historical Society of Wisconsin.* Vol. 12, 399–433. Madison, Wis.: Democrat Printing, 1892.

Paredes, J. Anthony, and Kenneth J. Plante. "A Reexamination of Creek Population Trends: 1738–1832." *American Indian Culture and Research Journal* 6:4 (1983): 3–28.

Parker, Arthur C., ed. *The Code of Handsome Lake, the Seneca Prophet.* New York State Museum Bulletin 163 (1912).

Parkinson, Robert G. *The Common Cause: Creating Race and Nation in the American Revolution.* Chapel Hill: University of North Carolina Press, 2016.

Parks, Ronald D. *The Darkest Period: The Kanza Indians and Their Last Homeland, 1846–1873.* Norman: University of Oklahoma Press, 2014.

Parsons, Lynn Hudson. "'A Perpetual Harrow upon My Feelings': John Quincy Adams and the American Indian." *New England Quarterly* 46 (September 1973): 339–79.

Pearsall, Sarah M. "Recentering Indian Women in the American Revolution." In *Why You Can't Teach United States History without American Indians,* ed. Susan Sleeper-Smith et al., 57–70. Chapel Hill: University of North Carolina Press, 2015.

Pearson, J. Diane. "Lewis Cass and the Politics of Disease: The Indian Vaccination Act of 1832." *Wicazo Sa Review* 18 (Fall 2003): 9–35.

Pennsylvania Archives 2 (1853).

Pennsylvania Archives 4 (1853).

Pennsylvania House of Representatives. *Votes and Proceedings of the House of Representatives of the Province of Pennsylvania.* Vol. 5. Philadelphia: Henry Miller, 1775.

Perdue, Theda. "Cherokee Relations with the Iroquois in the Eighteenth Century." In *Beyond the Covenant Chain: The Iroquois and Their Neighbors in Indian North America, 1600–1800*, ed. Daniel K. Richter and James H. Merrell, 135–49. Syracuse, N.Y.: Syracuse University Press, 1987.

———. *Cherokee Women: Gender and Culture Change, 1700–1835.* Lincoln: University of Nebraska Press, 1998.

Perdue, Theda, and Michael D. Green. *The Cherokee Nation and the Trail of Tears.* New York: Viking, 2007.

Persinger, Jacob. *The Life of Jacob Persinger.* Sturgeon, Mo.: Moody & M'Michael, 1861.

Pesantubbee, Michelene E. *Choctaw Women in a Chaotic World: The Clash of Cultures in the Colonial Southeast.* Albuquerque: University of New Mexico Press, 2005.

Peterson, John H., Jr. "Three Efforts at Development among the Choctaws of Mississippi." In *Southeastern Indians since the Removal Era*, ed. Walter L. Williams, 142–53. Athens: University of Georgia Press, 1979.

Peyser, Joseph L. "It Was Not Smallpox: The Miami Deaths of 1732 Reexamined." *Indiana Magazine of History* 81 (June 1985): 159–69.

Pierson, George Wilson. *Tocqueville and Beaumont in America.* New York: Oxford University Press, 1938.

Piker, Joshua. *Okfuskee: A Creek Indian Town in Colonial America.* Cambridge: Harvard University Press, 2004.

Pitts, Jennifer. Introduction to Alexis de Tocqueville, *Writings on Empire and Slavery.* Trans. and ed. Jennifer Pitts, ix–xxxviii. Baltimore, Md.: Johns Hopkins University Press, 2001.

Plane, Ann Marie, and Gregory Button. "The Massachusetts Indian Enfranchisement Act: Ethnic Contest in Historical Context, 1849–1869." In *After King Philip's War: Presence and Persistence in Indian New England*, ed. Colin G. Calloway, 178–206. Hanover, N.H.: University Press of New England, 1997.

Pluth, Edward J. "The Failed Watab Treaty of 1853." *Minnesota History* 57 (Spring 2000): 2–22.

Pocock, J. G. A. *The Machiavellian Moment: Florentine Political Thought and the Atlantic Republican Tradition.* Princeton, N.J.: Princeton University Press, 1975.

Pokagon, [Simon]. *O-gî-mäw-kwĕ Mit-i-gwä-kî (Queen of the Woods).* 3rd ed. Hartford, Mich.: C. H. Engle, 1901.

Porter, Kenneth Wiggins. "The Negro Abraham." *Florida Historical Quarterly* 25 (July 1946): 1–43.

Post, Charles Frederick. "Two Journals of Western Tours." In *Early Western Travels, 1748–1846*, Vol. 1, ed. Reuben Gold Thwaites, 177–291. Cleveland, Ohio: Arthur Clark, 1904.

Pouchot, [Pierre]. *Memoir upon the Late War in North America between the French and English, 1755–1760.* Vol. 1. Ed. and trans. Franklin B. Hough. Roxbury, Mass.: W. Elliot Woodward, 1866.

Preston, David L. *Braddock's Defeat: The Battle of the Monongahela and the Road to Revolution.* New York: Oxford University Press, 2015.

———. *The Texture of Contact: European and Indian Settler Communities on the Frontiers of Iroquoia, 1667–1783.* Lincoln: University of Nebraska Press, 2009.

Prucha, Francis Paul. *The Great Father: The United States Government and the American Indians.* 2 vols. Lincoln: University of Nebraska Press, 1984.

———. "Indian Removal and the Great American Desert." *Indiana Magazine of History* 59 (December 1963): 299–322.

———. *The Sword of the Republic: The United States Army on the Frontier, 1783–1846.* New York: Macmillan, 1969.

Quaife, Milo Milton, ed. *The Indian Captivity of O. M. Spencer.* Chicago: R. R. Donnelley & Sons, 1917.

Quinney, John W. "Speech on Stockbridge Traditionary History." *Report and Collections of the State Historical Society of Wisconsin.* Vol. 4, 313–20. Madison, Wisc.: James Ross, 1859.

Rafert, Stewart. *The Miami Indians of Indiana: A Persistent People, 1654–1994.* Indianapolis: Indiana Historical Society, 1996.

Rana, Aziz. *The Two Faces of American Freedom.* Cambridge: Harvard University Press, 2010.

Rand, Jacki Thompson. *Kiowa Humanity and the Invasion of the State.* Lincoln: University of Nebraska Press, 2008.

Redix, Erik M. *The Murder of Joe White: Ojibwe Leadership and Colonialism in Wisconsin.* East Lansing: Michigan State University Press, 2014.

Register of Debates in Congress. 21st Cong., 1st sess., 1830, 6, pt. 1.

Reid, Joshua L. *The Sea Is My Country: The Maritime World of the Makahs.* New Haven, Conn.: Yale University Press, 2015.

Religious Intelligencer 16 (Jan. 7, 1832).

Remini, Robert V. *Andrew Jackson and His Indian Wars.* New York: Viking, 2001.

Rensink, Brenden. "Genocide of Native Americans: Historical Facts and Historiographical Debates." In *Genocide of Indigenous Peoples,* ed. Samuel Totten and Robert K. Hitchcock, 15–36. New Brunswick, N.J.: Transaction, 2011.

Rice, James D. *Nature and History in the Potomac Country: From Hunter-Gatherers to the Age of Jefferson.* Baltimore, Md.: Johns Hopkins University Press, 2009.

Richter, Daniel K. *Facing East from Indian Country: A Native History of Early America.* Cambridge: Harvard University Press, 2001.

———. *The Ordeal of the Longhouse: The Peoples of the Iroquois League in the Era of European Colonization.* Chapel Hill: University of North Carolina Press, 1992.

Rinehart, Melissa. "Miami Resistance and Resilience during the Removal Era." In *Contested Territories: Native Americans and Non-Natives in the Lower Great Lakes, 1700–1850,* ed. Charles Beatty-Medina and Melissa Rinehart, 137–65. East Lansing: Michigan State University Press, 2012.

Rivers, Larry Eugene. *Rebels and Runaways: Slave Resistance in Nineteenth-Century Florida.* Urbana: University of Illinois Press, 2012.

Rives, William C., and Philip R. Fendall, eds. *Letters and Other Writings of James Madison.* Vol. 3. Philadelphia: J. B. Lippincott, 1867.

Roberts, Albert Hubbard. "The Dade Massacre." *Florida Historical Quarterly* 5 (January 1927): 123–38.

Robertson, Lindsay G. *Conquest by Law: How the Discovery of America Dispossessed Indigenous Peoples of Their Lands.* New York: Oxford University Press, 2005.

Rockwell, E. F., ed. "Parallel and Combined Expeditions against the Cherokee Indians in South and in North Carolina, in 1776." *Historical Magazine,* 2nd ser., 2 (October 1867): 212–20.

Rockwell, Stephen J. *Indian Affairs and the Administrative State in the Nineteenth Century.* Cambridge: Cambridge University Press, 2010.

Roediger, David R. *The Wages of Whiteness: Race and the Making of the American Working Class.* Rev. ed. New York: Verso, 2007.

Rogin, Michael Paul. *Fathers and Children: Andrew Jackson and the Subjugation of the American Indian.* New York: Knopf, 1975.

Rohrbough, Malcolm J. *The Trans-Appalachian Frontier: People, Societies, and Institutions, 1775–1850.* New York: Oxford University Press, 1978.

Rollings, Willard H. *The Osage: An Ethnohistorical Study of Hegemony on the Prairie-Plains.* Columbia: University of Missouri Press, 1992.

Ronda, Jeanne, and James P. Ronda. "'As They Were Faithful': Chief Hendrick Aupaumut and the Struggle for Stockbridge Survival, 1757–1830." *American Indian Culture and Research Journal* 3:3 (1979): 43–55.

Rosenberg, Charles E. *The Cholera Years: The United States in 1832, 1849, and 1866.* Chicago: University of Chicago Press, 1962.

Rossiter, Clinton, ed. *The Federalist Papers.* New York: New American Library, 1961.

Rountree, Helen C. "The Indians of Virginia: A Third Race in a Biracial State." In *Southeastern Indians since the Removal Era,* ed. Walter L. Williams, 27–48. Athens: University of Georgia Press, 1979.

———. *Pocahontas's People: The Powhatan Indians of Virginia through Four Centuries.* Norman: University of Oklahoma Press, 1990.

Rountree, Helen C., and Thomas E. Davidson. *Eastern Shore Indians of Virginia and Maryland.* Charlottesville: University of Virginia Press, 1997.

Royce, Charles C. *The Cherokee Nation of Indians.* 1887. Rpt., Chicago: Aldine Publishing, 1975.

Rushforth, Brett. *Bonds of Alliance: Indigenous and Atlantic Slaveries in New France.* Chapel Hill: University of North Carolina Press, 2012.

"Rutherford's Expedition against the Cherokees." *University Magazine* (University of North Carolina), new ser., 7 (February 1888): 89–95.

Sabathy-Judd, Linda, ed. *Moravians in Upper Canada: The Diary of the Indian Mission of Fairfield on the Thames, 1792–1813.* Toronto: Champlain Society, 1999.

Sadosky, Leonard. "Rethinking the Gnadenhutten Massacre: The Contest for Power in the Public World of the Revolutionary Pennsylvania Frontier." In *The Sixty Years' War for the Great Lakes, 1754–1814,* ed. David Curtis Skaggs and Larry L. Nelson, 187–213. Lansing: Michigan State University Press, 2001.

———. *Revolutionary Negotiations: Indians, Empires, and Diplomats in the Founding of America.* Charlottesville: University of Virginia Press, 2009.

St. Jean, Wendy. *Remaining Chickasaw in Indian Territory, 1830s–1907.* Tuscaloosa: University of Alabama Press, 2011.

Saler, Bethel. *The Settler's Empire: Colonialism and State Formation in America's Old Northwest.* Philadelphia: University of Pennsylvania Press, 2015.

Salisbury, Neal. *Manitou and Providence: Indians, Europeans, and the Making of New England, 1500–1643.* New York: Oxford University Press, 1982.

Sattler, Richard A. "Remnants, Renegades, and Runaways: Seminole Ethnogenesis Reconsidered." In *History, Power and Identity,* ed. Jonathan D. Hill, 36–69. Iowa City: University of Iowa Press, 1996.

Satz, Ronald N. *American Indian Policy in the Jacksonian Era.* Lincoln: University of Nebraska Press, 1974.

———. "The Mississippi Choctaw: From the Removal Treaty to the Federal Agency." In *After Removal: The Choctaw in Mississippi,* ed. Samuel J. Wells and Roseanna Tubby, 3–32. Jackson: University Press of Mississippi, 1986.

Saunders, William L., ed. *The Colonial Records of North Carolina.* Vols. 6, 10. Raleigh, N.C.: Josephus Daniels, 1888, 1890.

Saunt, Claudio. *A New Order of Things: Property, Power, and the Transformation of the Creek Indians, 1733–1816.* Cambridge: Cambridge University Press, 1999.

Schake, Lowell M. *La Charrette: A History of the Village Gateway to the American Frontier Visited by Lewis and Clark, Daniel Book, and Zebulon Pike.* Lincoln, Neb.: iUniverse Star, 2005.

Schultz, Eric B., and Michael J. Tougias. *King Philip's War: The History and Legacy of America's Forgotten Conflict.* Woodstock, Vt.: Countryman Press, 1999.

Schutt, Amy C. *Peoples of the River Valleys: The Odyssey of the Delaware Indians.* Philadelphia: University of Pennsylvania Press, 2007.

Schweitzer, Marjorie M. "Otoe and Missouria." In *Handbook of North American Indians,* Vol. 13: *Plains,* ed. Raymond J. DeMallie, 447–61. Washington, D.C.: Smithsonian Institution Press, 2001.

Scott, Edward, comp. *Laws of the State of Tennessee.* Vol. 2. Knoxville, Tenn.: Heiskell & Brown, 1821.

Shannon, Timothy J. *Iroquois Diplomacy on the Early American Frontier.* New York: Viking, 2008.

Sheehan, Bernard W. "'The Famous Hair Buyer General': Henry Hamilton, George Rogers Clark, and the American Indian." *Indiana Magazine of History* 79 (March 1983): 1–28.

———. *Seeds of Extinction: Jeffersonian Philanthropy and the American Indian.* Chapel Hill: University of North Carolina Press, 1973.

Shire, Laurel Clark. *The Threshold of Manifest Destiny: Gender and National Expansion in Florida.* Philadelphia: University of Pennsylvania Press, 2016.

Shoemaker, Nancy. "How Indians Got to Be Red." *American Historical Review* 102 (June 1997): 625–44.

———. *Native American Whalemen and the World: Indigenous Encounters and the Contingency of Race.* Chapel Hill: University of North Carolina Press, 2015.

Silver, Peter. *Our Savage Neighbors: How Indian War Transformed Early America.* New York: W. W. Norton, 2008.

Silverman, David J. *Faith and Boundaries: Colonists, Christianity, and Community among the Wampanoag Indians of Martha's Vineyard, 1600–1871.* Cambridge: Cambridge University Press, 2005.

———. *Red Brethren: The Brothertown and Stockbridge Indians and the Problem of Race in Early America.* Ithaca, N.Y.: Cornell University Press, 2010.

———. *Thundersticks: Firearms and the Violent Transformation of Native America.* Cambridge, Mass.: Harvard University Press, 2016.

Sinha, Manisha. *The Slave's Cause: A History of Abolition.* New Haven, Conn.: Yale University Press, 2016.

Skeen, Carl Edward. *Citizen Soldiers in the War of 1812.* Lexington: University Press of Kentucky, 1999.

Skinner, Claiborne A. *The Upper Country: French Enterprise in the Colonial Great Lakes.* Baltimore, Md.: Johns Hopkins University Press, 2008.

Slaughter, Thomas P. *The Whiskey Rebellion: Frontier Epilogue to the American Revolution.* New York: Oxford University Press, 1986.

Sleeper-Smith, Susan. *Indian Women and French Men: Rethinking Cultural Encounter in the Western Great Lakes.* Amherst: University of Massachusetts Press, 2001.

———. *Indigenous Prosperity and American Conquest: Indian Women of the Ohio River Valley, 1690–1792.* Chapel Hill: University of North Carolina Press, 2018.

Smith, Dwight L., ed. "An Unsuccessful Negotiation for Removal of the Wyandot Indians from Ohio, 1834." *Ohio State Archaeological and Historical Quarterly* 58 (1949): 305–31.

Smith, F. Todd. *The Caddo Indians: Tribes at the Convergence of Empires, 1542–1854.* College Station: Texas A & M University Press, 1995.

————. *The Wichita Indians: Traders of Texas and the Southern Plains, 1540–1845.* College Station: Texas A & M University Press, 2000.

Smith, Henry Nash. *Virgin Land: The American West as Symbol and Myth.* Cambridge: Harvard University Press, 1950.

Smith, William Henry, ed. *The St. Clair Papers: The Life and Public Services of Arthur St. Clair.* 2 vols. Cincinnati, Ohio: Robert Clarke & Co., 1882.

[Smith, W. W.] *Sketch of the Seminole War and Sketches of a Campaign by a Lieutenant, of the Left Wing.* Charleston, S.C.: Dan Dowling, 1836.

Smith-Rosenberg, Carroll. *This Violent Empire: The Birth of an American National Identity.* Chapel Hill: University of North Carolina Press, 2010.

Smithers, Gregory D. *The Cherokee Diaspora: An Indigenous History of Migration, Resettlement, and Identity.* New Haven, Conn.: Yale University Press, 2015.

Snow, Dean R. *The Archaeology of New England.* New York: Academic Press, 1980.

————. "Eastern Abenaki." In *Handbook of North American Indians,* Vol. 15: *Northeast,* ed. Bruce Trigger, 137–47. Washington, D.C.: Smithsonian Institution Press, 1978.

Snow, Dean R., and Kim M. Lanphear. "European Contact and Indian Depopulation in the Northeast: The Timing of the First Epidemics." *Ethnohistory* 35 (Winter 1988): 15–33.

Snyder, Christina. *Great Crossings: Indians, Settlers, and Slaves in the Age of Jackson.* New York: Oxford University Press, 2017.

————. *Slavery in Indian Country: The Changing Face of Captivity in Early America.* Cambridge: Harvard University Press, 2010.

Society of Friends. *The Case of the Seneca Indians in the State of New York, Illustrated by the Facts.* Philadelphia: Merrihew and Thompson, 1840.

————. *Proceedings of the Joint Committee Appointed by the Society of Friends . . . for Promoting the Civilization and Improving the Condition of the Seneca Nation of Indians.* Baltimore, Md.: William Wooddy, 1847.

Sosin, Jack M. *Whitehall and the Wilderness: The Middle West in British Colonial Policy, 1760–1775.* Lincoln: University of Nebraska Press, 1961.

Sparks, Jared, ed. *The Writings of George Washington.* Vol. 6. Boston, Mass.: Russell, Odiorne, and Metcalf, 1834.

Spero, Laura. "'Stout, Bold, Cunning and the Greatest Travellers in America': The Colonial Shawnee Diaspora." Ph.D. diss., University of Pennsylvania, 2010.

Spero, Patrick. *Frontier Country: The Politics of War in Early Pennsylvania.* Philadelphia: University of Pennsylvania Press, 2016.

Sprague, John T. *The Origin, Progress, and Conclusion of the Florida War.* New York: D. Appleton, 1848.

Stannard, David E. *American Holocaust: The Conquest of the New World.* New York: Oxford University Press, 1992.

Stanton, Max E. "Southern Louisiana Survivors: The Houma Indians." In *Southeastern Indians since the Removal Era,* ed. Walter L. Williams, 90–109. Athens: University of Georgia Press, 1979.

Starkey, Armstrong. *European and Native American Warfare, 1675–1815.* Norman: University of Oklahoma Press, 1998.

Stevens, Frank E. *The Black Hawk War, Including a Review of Black Hawk's Life.* Chicago: Frank E. Stevens, 1903.

Stockwell, Mary. *The Other Trail of Tears: The Removal of the Ohio Indians.* Yardley, Penn.: Westholme, 2014.

Stone, Dan. "Introduction." In *The Historiography of Genocide,* ed. Dan Stone, 1–6. New York: Palgrave Macmillan, 2008.

Strang, Cameron B. "Michael Cresap and the Promulgation of Settler Land-Claiming Methods in the Backcountry, 1765–1774." *Virginia Magazine of History and Biography* 118:2 (2010): 106–35.

Strauss, Scott. "Contested Meanings and Conflicting Imperatives: A Conceptual Analysis of Genocide." *Journal of Genocide Research* 3 (November 2001): 349–75.

Stull, Donald D. *Kiikaapoa: The Kansas Kickapoo.* Horton, Kan.: Kickapoo Tribal Press, 1984.

Sturtevant, Andrew. "'Inseparable Companions' and Irreconcilable Enemies: The Hurons and Odawas of French Détroit." *Ethnohistory* 60 (Spring 2013): 219–43.

Sugden, John. *Blue Jacket: Warrior of the Shawnees.* Lincoln: University of Nebraska Press, 2000.

———. "Early Pan-Indianism: Tecumseh's Tour of the Indian Country, 1811–1812." *American Indian Quarterly* 10 (Autumn 1986): 273–304.

———. *Tecumseh: A Life.* New York: Henry Holt, 1997.

Sullivan, Elizabeth. *Indian Legends of the Trail of Tears and Other Creek Stories.* Tulsa, Okla.: Giant Services, 1974.

Swain, D. L. "Historical Sketch of the Indian War of 1776." *Historical Magazine,* 2nd ser., 2 (November 1867): 273–75.

Sword, Wiley. *President Washington's Indian War: The Struggle for the Old Northwest, 1790–1795.* Norman: University of Oklahoma Press, 1985.

Tanner, Helen Hornbeck, ed. *Atlas of Great Lakes Indian History.* Norman: University of Oklahoma Press, 1987.

———. "Coocoochee: Mohawk Medicine Woman." *American Indian Culture and Research Journal* 3:3 (1979): 23–41.

———. "The Glaize in 1792: A Composite Indian Community." *Ethnohistory* 25 (Winter 1978): 15–39.

Taylor, Alan. *American Revolutions: A Continental History, 1750–1804.* New York: W. W. Norton, 2016.

———. *The Civil War of 1812: American Citizens, British Subjects, Irish Rebels, and Indian Allies.* New York: Alfred A. Knopf, 2010.

———. *The Divided Ground: Indians, Settlers, and the Northern Borderland of the American Revolution.* New York: Alfred A. Knopf, 2006.

———. *William Cooper's Town: Power and Persuasion on the Frontier of the Early American Republic.* New York: Alfred A. Knopf, 1995.

Thomas, William H. *Explanation of the Fund Held in Trust by the United States for the North Carolina Cherokees.* Washington, D.C.: Lemuel Towers, 1858.

Thompson, Vern E. "A History of the Quapaw." *Chronicles of Oklahoma* 33 (Autumn 1955): 360–83.

Thornbrough, Gayle, ed. *Letter Book of the Indian Agency at Fort Wayne, 1809–1815.* Indianapolis: Indiana Historical Society, 1961.

Thorne, Tanis C. *The Many Hands of My Relations: French and Indians on the Lower Missouri.* Columbia: University of Missouri Press, 1996.

Thornton, Russell. *American Indian Holocaust and Survival: A Population History since 1492.* Norman: University of Oklahoma Press, 1987.

———. "Cherokee Population Losses during the Trail of Tears: A New Perspective and a New Estimate." *Ethnohistory* 31 (Autumn 1984): 289–300.

———. *The Cherokees: A Population History.* Lincoln: University of Nebraska Press, 1990.

———. "Demographic History." In *Handbook of North American Indians,* Vol. 14: *Southeast,* ed. Raymond D. Fogelson, 48–52. Washington, D.C.: Smithsonian Institution Press, 2004.

Thorpe, Grace F. "The Jim Thorpe Family: From Wisconsin to Indian Territory, Part 1." *Chronicles of Oklahoma* 59 (Spring 1981): 91–105.

———. "The Jim Thorpe Family: From Wisconsin to Indian Territory, Part 2." *Chronicles of Oklahoma* 59 (Summer 1981): 179–201.

Thwaites, Reuben Gold, ed. *Collections of the State Historical Society of Wisconsin.* Vol. 16. Madison: The Society, 1902.

———. *The Jesuit Relations and Allied Documents: Travels and Explorations of the Jesuit Missionaries in New France, 1610–1791.* 73 vols. Cleveland: Burrows Brothers, 1896–1901.

Thwaites, Reuben Gold, and Louise Phelps Kellogg, eds. *Documentary History of Dunmore's War, 1774.* Madison: Wisconsin Historical Society, 1905.

Tiro, Karim M. "A 'Civil' War: Rethinking Iroquois Participation in the American Revolution." *Explorations in Early American Culture* 4 (2000): 148–65.

———. *The People of the Standing Stone: The Oneida Nation from the Revolution through the Era of Removal.* Amherst: University of Massachusetts Press, 2011.

———. "The View from Piqua Agency: The War of 1812, the White River Delawares, and the Origins of Indian Removal." *Journal of the Early Republic* 35 (Spring 2015): 25–54.

Tocqueville, Alexis de. *Democracy in America.* Ed. J. P. Mayer. Trans. George Lawrence. New York: Perennial, 1988.

Tortora, Daniel J. *Carolina in Crisis: Cherokees, Colonists, and Slaves in the American Southeast, 1756–1763.* Chapel Hill: University of North Carolina Press, 2015.

Tracy, E. C., ed. *Memoir of the Life of Jeremiah Evarts.* Boston, Mass.: Crocker and Brewster, 1845.

Trask, Kerry A. *Black Hawk: The Battle for the Heart of America.* New York: Henry Holt, 2007.

Trigger, Bruce G. *Natives and Newcomers: Canada's "Heroic Age" Reconsidered.* Kingston, Ont.: McGill-Queen's University Press, 1985.

Trimble, Michael K. "The 1832 Inoculation Program on the Missouri River." In *Disease and Demography in the Americas,* ed. John W. Verano and Douglas H. Ubelaker, 257–64. Washington, D.C.: Smithsonian Institution Press, 1992.

Turner, E. Randolph. "A Reexamination of Powhatan Territorial Boundaries and Population, ca. 1607 A.D." *Quarterly Bulletin of the Archeological Society of Virginia* 37 (June 1982): 45–64.

Ubelaker, Douglas H. "North American Indian Population Size, A.D. 1500 to 1985." *American Journal of Physical Anthropology* 77 (November 1988): 289–94.

———. "Population Size, Contact to Nadir." In *Handbook of North American Indians,* Vol. 3: *Environment, Origins, and Population,* ed. Douglas H. Ubelaker, 694–701. Washington, D.C.: Smithsonian Institution Press, 2006.

U.S. Bureau of the Census. *Historical Statistics of the United States: Colonial Times to 1970.* Washington, D.C.: G.P.O., 1975.

———. *Historical Statistics of the United States, 1789–1945: A Supplement to the Statistical Abstract of the United States.* Washington, D.C.: G.P.O., 1949.

———. *Population of States and Counties of the United States: 1790 to 1990.* Washington, D.C.: G.P.O., 1996.

U.S. Bureau of Education. *Are The Indians Dying Out?: Preliminary Observations Relating to Indian Civilization and Education.* Washington, D.C.: G.P.O., 1877.

U.S. Congress. House. *Letter from the Secretary of War . . . in Relation to Our Indian Affairs Generally.* 20th Cong., 2nd sess., 1828–1829. H. Doc. 117. Serial 186.

———. *Letter from the Secretary of War Transmitting a Copy of His Answer to the Letter of General Jesup.* 25th Cong., 2nd sess., 1838. H. Doc. 272. Serial 328.

———. *Letter from the Secretary of War Transmitting Certain Orders Issued by the Department Respecting Calls for Volunteers or Militiamen.* 24th Cong., 2nd sess., 1837. H. Doc. 140. Serial 303.

———. *Memorial of a Delegation from the Cherokee Indians.* 21st Cong., 2nd sess., 1831. H. Doc. 57. Serial 208.

———. *Memorial of John Ross and Others.* 20th Cong., 2nd sess., 1829. H. Doc. 145. Serial 187.

———. *Memorial of the Ladies of Steubenville, Ohio, against the Forcible Removal of the Indians without the Limits of the United States.* 21st Cong., 1st sess., 1830. H. Rept. 208. Serial 200.

———. *Message from the President of the United States Transmitting the Proceedings of the Court of Inquiry in the Case of Brevet Brigadier General Wool.* 25th Cong., 1st sess., 1837. H. Doc. 46. Serial 311.

———. *Removal of the Cherokees.* 25th Cong., 2nd sess., 1837–1838. H. Doc. 453. Serial 331.

———. *Removal of the Cherokees West of the Mississippi.* 27th Cong., 2nd sess., 1842. H. Rept. 1098. Serial 411.

———. *Report of the Commissioner of Indian Affairs, 1848.* 30th Cong., 2nd sess., 1848. H. Ex. Doc. 1. Serial 537.

U.S. Congress. Senate. *Annual Report of the Commissioner of Indian Affairs, 1849.* 31st Cong., 1st sess., 1849. S. Ex. Doc. 1. Serial 550.

———. *Correspondence on the Subject of the Emigration of Indians.* 23rd Cong., 2nd sess., 1835. S. Doc. 512. 5 vols. Serial 244–248.

———. *Message from the President of the United States Transmitting Treaties with the Creek, Osage, and Iowa Indians.* 25th Cong. 3rd sess., 1839. S. Ex. Doc. H.

———. *Message of the President of the United States . . . Transmitting Documents Relating to Frauds, etc., in the Sale of Indian Reservations of Land.* 24th Cong., 1st sess., 1836. S. Doc. 425. Serial 284.

———. *Report from the Office of Indian Affairs, 1834.* 23rd Cong., 2nd sess., 1834. S. Doc. 1. Serial 266.

———. *Report from the Office of Indian Affairs, 1836.* 24th Cong., 2nd sess., 1836. S. Doc. 1. Serial 297.

———. *Report from the Secretary of War . . . in Relation to the Cherokee Treaty of 1835.* 25th Cong., 2nd sess., 1838. S. Doc. 120. Serial 315.

———. *Report of the Commissioner of Indian Affairs, 1835.* 24th Cong., 1st sess., 1835. S. Doc. 1. Serial 279.

———. *Report of the Commissioner of Indian Affairs, 1837.* 25th Cong., 2nd sess., 1837. S. Doc. 1. Serial 314.

———. *Report of the Commissioner of Indian Affairs, 1838.* 25th Cong., 3rd sess., 1838. S. Doc. 1. Serial 338.

———. *Report of the Commissioner of Indian Affairs, 1839.* 26th Cong., 1st sess., 1839. S. Doc. 1. Serial 354.

———. *Report of the Commissioner of Indian Affairs, 1840.* 26th Cong., 2nd sess., 1840. S. Doc. 1. Serial 375.

———. *Report of the Commissioner of Indian Affairs, 1841.* 27th Cong., 2nd sess., 1841. S. Doc. 1. Serial 395.

———. *Report of the Commissioner of Indian Affairs, 1842.* 27th Cong., 3rd sess., 1842. S. Doc. 1. Serial 413.

———. *Report of the Commissioner of Indian Affairs, 1843.* 28th Cong., 1st sess., 1843. S. Doc. 1. Serial 431.

————. *Report of the Commissioner of Indian Affairs, 1844.* 28th Cong., 2nd sess., 1844. S. Doc. 1. Serial 449.

————. *Report of the Commissioner of Indian Affairs, 1845.* 29th Cong., 1st sess., 1845. S. Doc. 1. Serial 470.

————. *Report of the Commissioner of Indian Affairs, 1846.* 29th Cong., 2nd sess., 1846. S. Doc. 1. Serial 493.

————. *Report of the Commissioner of Indian Affairs, 1847.* 30th Cong., 1st sess., 1847. S. Ex. Doc. 1. Serial 503.

————. *Report of the Commissioner of Indian Affairs, 1850.* 31st Cong., 2nd sess., 1850. S. Ex. Doc. 1. Serial 587.

————. *Report of the Commissioner of Indian Affairs, 1851.* 32nd Cong., 1st sess., 1851. S. Ex. Doc. 1. Serial 613.

————. *Report of the Commissioner of Indian Affairs, 1852.* 32nd Cong., 2nd sess., 1852. S. Ex. Doc. 1. Serial 658.

————. *Report of the Commissioner of Indian Affairs, 1853.* 33rd Cong., 1st sess., 1853. S. Ex. Doc. 1. Serial 690.

————. *Report of the Commissioner of Indian Affairs, 1854.* 33rd Cong., 2nd sess., 1854. S. Ex. Doc. 1. Serial 746.

————. *Report of the Commissioner of Indian Affairs, 1855.* 34th Cong., 1st sess., 1855. S. Ex. Doc. 1. Serial 810.

————. *Report of the Commissioner of Indian Affairs, 1856.* 34th Cong., 3rd sess., 1856. S. Ex. Doc. 5. Serial 875.

————. *Report of the Commissioner of Indian Affairs, 1857.* 35th Cong., 1st sess., 1857. S. Ex. Doc. 11. Serial 919.

————. *Report of the Commissioner of Indian Affairs, 1858.* 35th Cong., 2nd sess., 1858. S. Ex. Doc. 1. Serial 974.

————. *Report of the Commissioner of Indian Affairs, 1859.* 36th Cong., 1st sess., 1859. S. Ex. Doc. 1. Serial 1023.

————. *Report of the Commissioner of Indian Affairs, 1860.* 36th Cong., 2nd sess., 1860. S. Ex. Doc. 1. Serial 1078.

————. *Report of the Commissioner of Indian Affairs, 1861.* 37th Cong., 2nd sess., 1861. S. Doc. 1. Serial 1117.

U.S. Office of Indian Affairs. Letters Received by the Office of Indian Affairs, 1824–1800. National Archives Record Group 75. Microfilm M234, roll 427.

U.S. Statutes at Large 8 (1814): 218–23. *Treaty with Great Britain.*

[U.S. War Department]. *Record of Officers and Soldiers Killed in Battle and Died in Service during the Florida War.* Washington, D.C.: G.P.O., 1882.

Unrau, William E. *The Kansa Indians: A History of the Wind People, 1673–1873.* Norman: University of Oklahoma Press, 1971.

————. *The Rise and Fall of Indian Country, 1825–1855.* Lawrence: University Press of Kansas, 2007.

———. *The White Man's Wicked Water: The Alcohol Trade and Prohibition in Indian Country, 1802–1892.* Lawrence: University Press of Kansas, 1996.

Unruh, John D., Jr. *The Plains Across: The Overland Emigrants and the Trans-Mississippi West, 1840–60.* Urbana: University of Illinois Press, 1982.

Upton, L. F. S. *Micmacs and Colonists: Indian–White Relations in the Maritime Provinces, 1713–1867.* Vancouver: University of British Columbia Press, 1979.

Usner, Daniel H., Jr. *American Indians in the Lower Mississippi Valley: Social and Economic Histories.* Lincoln: University of Nebraska Press, 1998.

———. *Indians, Settlers, and Slaves in a Frontier Exchange Economy: The Lower Mississippi Valley before 1783.* Chapel Hill: University of North Carolina Press, 1992.

Valenčius, Conevery Bolton. *The Health of the Country: How American Settlers Understood Themselves and Their Land.* New York: Basic Books, 2002.

Vattel, Emmerich de. *The Law of Nations, or Principles of the Law of Nature.* 1758. Rpt., London: G. G. and J. Robinson, 1797.

Veracini, Lorenzo. "Introducing Settler Colonial Studies." *Settler Colonial Studies* 1:1 (2011): 1–12.

———. *Settler Colonialism: A Theoretical Overview.* New York: Palgrave Macmillan, 2010.

Viola, Herman J. *Thomas L. McKenney: Architect of America's Early Indian Policy: 1816–1830.* Chicago, Ill.: Sage Books, 1974.

Vizenor, Gerald. "Aesthetics of Survivance." In *Survivance: Narratives of Native Presence,* ed. Gerald Vizenor, 1–23. Lincoln: University of Nebraska Press, 2008.

Wallace, Anthony F. C. *Jefferson and the Indians: The Tragic Fate of the First Americans.* Cambridge, Mass.: Harvard University Press, 1999.

———. *Prelude to Disaster: The Course of Indian–White Relations Which Led to the Black Hawk War of 1832.* Springfield: Illinois State Historical Library, 1970.

Ward, Matthew C. *Breaking the Backcountry: The Seven Years' War in Virginia and Pennsylvania, 1754–1765.* Pittsburgh, Penn.: University of Pittsburgh Press, 2003.

Warren, Stephen. *The Shawnees and Their Neighbors, 1795–1870.* Urbana: University of Illinois Press, 2005.

———. *The Worlds the Shawnees Made: Migration and Violence in Early America.* Chapel Hill: University of North Carolina Press, 2014.

Warren, William W. *History of the Ojibway People.* 2nd ed. Edited and with an introduction by Theresa Schenck. St. Paul: Minnesota Historical Society Press, 2009.

Waselkov, Gregory A. *A Conquering Spirit: Fort Mims and the Red Stick War of 1813–1814.* Tuscaloosa: University of Alabama Press, 2006.

Washington, H. A., ed. *The Writings of Thomas Jefferson.* 9 vols. Washington, D.C.: Taylor and Maury, 1853–1854.

Watson, Blake A. *Buying America from the Indians:* Johnson v. McIntosh *and the History of Native Land Rights.* Norman: University of Oklahoma Press, 2012.

Watts, Dale E. "How Bloody Was Bleeding Kansas?: Political Killings in Kansas Territory, 1854–1861." *Kansas History* 18 (Summer 1995): 116–29.

Weisman, Brent R. "Nativism, Resistance, and Ethnogenesis of the Florida Seminole Indian Identity." *Historical Archaeology* 41:4 (2007): 198–212.

———. *Unconquered People: Florida's Seminole and Miccosukee Indians.* Gainesville: University Press of Florida, 1999.

Weiss-Wendt, Anton. "Problems in Comparative Genocide Scholarship." In *The Historiography of Genocide,* ed. Dan Stone, 42–70. New York: Palgrave Macmillan, 2008.

Weld, H. Hastings, ed. *Benjamin Franklin: His Autobiography with a Narrative of His Public Life and Services.* New York: Derby & Jackson, 1859.

Wells, Samuel J. "Federal Indian Policy: From Accommodation to Removal." In *The Choctaw before Removal,* ed. Carolyn Keller Reeves, 181–213. Jackson: University Press of Mississippi, 1985.

Weslager, C. A. *The Delaware Indians: A History.* New Brunswick, N.J.: Rutgers University Press, 1972.

West, Elliott. *The Way to the West: Essays on the Central Plains.* Albuquerque: University of New Mexico Press, 1995.

West, Martin. "Clark's 1780 Shawnee Expedition." In *The Life of George Rogers Clark: 1752–1818: Triumphs and Tragedies,* ed. Kenneth C. Carstens and Nancy Son Carstens, 176–97. Westport, Conn.: Praeger, 2004.

Whaley, Gray H. *Oregon and the Collapse of Illahee: U.S. Empire and the Transformation of an Indigenous World, 1792–1859.* Chapel Hill: University of North Carolina Press, 2010.

Wheeler, Rachel. *To Live upon Hope: Mohicans and Missionaries in the Eighteenth-Century Northeast.* Ithaca, N.Y.: Cornell University Press, 2008.

Wheeler, Rachel, and Thomas Hahn-Bruckart. "On an Eighteenth-Century Trail of Tears: The Travel Diary of Johann Jacob Schmick of the Moravian Indian Congregation's Journey to the Susquehanna, 1765." *Journal of Moravian History* 15:1 (2015): 44–88.

Wheeler, Robert W. *Jim Thorpe: World's Greatest Athlete.* Rev. ed. Norman: University of Oklahoma Press, 1979.

White, Bruce M. "The Regional Context of the Removal Order of 1850." In *Fish in the Lakes, Wild Rice, and Game in Abundance: Testimony on Behalf of Mille Lacs Ojibwe Hunting and Fishing Rights,* ed. James M. McClurken, 141–328. East Lansing: Michigan State University Press, 2000.

White, Richard. *The Middle Ground: Indians, Empires, and Republics in the Great Lakes Region, 1650–1815.* Cambridge: Cambridge University Press, 1991.

———. *The Roots of Dependency: Subsistence, Environment, and Social Change among the Choctaws, Pawnees, and Navajos.* Lincoln: University of Nebraska Press, 1983.

Whitney, Ellen M., ed. *The Black Hawk War, 1831–1832*. Vol. 2: *Letters and Papers, Part 1, April 30, 1831–June 23, 1832*. Collections of the Illinois Historical Library. Vol. 36. Springfield: Illinois State Historical Library, 1973.

———. *The Black Hawk War, 1831–1832*. Vol. 2: *Letters and Papers, Part 2, June 24, 1832–October 14, 1834*. Collections of the Illinois Historical Library. Vol. 37. Springfield: Illinois State Historical Library, 1975.

Wickman, Patricia R. *Osceola's Legacy*. Tuscaloosa: University of Alabama Press, 1991.

Wilentz, Sean. *Andrew Jackson*. New York: Henry Holt, 2005.

Wilkins, David E., and K. Tsianina Lomawaima. *Uneven Ground: American Indian Sovereignty and Federal Law*. Norman: University of Oklahoma Press, 2001.

Wilkins, Thurman. *Cherokee Tragedy: The Ridge Family and the Decimation of a People*. 2nd ed. Norman: University of Oklahoma Press, 1986.

Willard, Shirley, and Susan Campbell, eds. *Potawatomi Trail of Death: 1838 Removal from Indiana to Kansas*. Rochester, Ind.: Fulton County Historical Society, 2003.

Williams, Edwin, comp. *The Addresses and Messages of the Presidents of the United States, 1789 to 1846*. 2 vols. New York: Edward Walker, 1849.

Williams, Robert A., Jr. *The American Indian in Western Legal Thought: The Discourses of Conquest*. New York: Oxford University Press, 1990.

Williams, Samuel Cole. *History of the Lost State of Franklin*. 1923. Rpt., Philadelphia: Porcupine Press, 1974.

Wimer, James. *Events in Indian History*. Lancaster, Penn.: G. Hills, 1841.

Wishart, David J. *An Unspeakable Sadness: The Dispossession of the Nebraska Indians*. Lincoln: University of Nebraska Press, 1994.

Witgen, Michael. *An Infinity of Nations: How the Native New World Shaped Early North America*. Philadelphia: University of Pennsylvania Press, 2012.

Witt, John Fabian. *Lincoln's Code: The Laws of War in American History*. New York: Free Press, 2012.

Wolfe, Patrick. "Against the Intentional Fallacy: Legocentrism and Continuity in the Rhetoric of Indian Dispossession." *American Indian Culture and Research Journal* 36:1 (2012): 1–46.

———. "Settler Colonialism and the Elimination of the Native." *Journal of Genocide Research* 8 (December 2006): 387–409.

Wood, Gordon S. *Empire of Liberty: A History of the Early Republic, 1789–1815*. New York: Oxford University Press, 2009.

Wood, Norman B. *Lives of Famous Indian Chiefs*. Aurora, Ill.: American Indian Historical Publishing Co., 1906.

Wood, Peter H. "The Changing Population of the Colonial South: An Overview by Race and Region, 1685–1790." In *Powhatan's Mantle: Indians in the Colonial Southeast*, rev. ed., ed. Gregory A. Waselkov, Peter H. Wood, and Tom Hatley, 57–132. Lincoln: University of Nebraska Press, 2006.

Worth, John E. *The Timucuan Chiefdoms of Spanish Florida.* Vol. 2: *Resistance and Destruction.* Gainesville: University Press of Florida, 1998.

———. "Yamasee." In *Handbook of North American Indians,* Vol. 14: *Southeast,* ed. Raymond D. Fogelson, 245–53. Washington, D.C.: Smithsonian Institution Press, 2004.

Wright, J. Leitch, Jr. *Creeks and Seminoles: The Destruction and Regeneration of the Muscogulge People.* Lincoln: University of Nebraska Press, 1986.

Wright, Muriel H. "The Removal of the Choctaws to the Indian Territory, 1830–1833." *Chronicles of Oklahoma* 6 (June 1928): 103–28.

Young, Gloria A., and Michael P. Hoffman. "Quapaw." In *Handbook of North American Indians,* Vol. 13: *Plains,* ed. Raymond J. DeMallie, 497–514. Washington, D.C.: Smithsonian Institution Press, 2001.

Young, Henry J. "A Note on Scalp Bounties in Pennsylvania." *Pennsylvania History* 24 (July 1957): 207–18.

Young, Mary. "The Cherokee Nation: Mirror of the Republic." *American Quarterly* 33 (Winter 1981): 502–24.

Zwierzchowski, Jan, and Ewa Tabeau. "The 1992–1995 War in Bosnia and Herzegovina: Census-Based Multiple System Estimation of Casualties' Undercount." Paper presented at the International Research Workshop on "The Global Costs of Conflict," Berlin, February 1–2, 2010. https://pdfs.semanticscholar.org/7760/022b84647f680b26d3d628f34afb70ce8122.pdf (accessed March 6, 2018).

Acknowledgments

It's sobering to realize how long it's been since I began thinking about this book. George W. Bush was president, and it was only his first term. When I began, I had some poorly formed ideas. Fortunately, I found patient people willing to converse and comment. I benefited from talking with Scott Straus at a forum on genocide at the University of Washington in March 2004. The Yale Genocide Studies Program, under the direction of Ben Kiernan, generously invited me to present what amounted to a rough draft of a grant proposal in November 2005. Johnny Faragher's comment was particularly helpful. At the European Association of American Studies conference in Nicosia in spring 2006, I appreciated encouragement from Arnold Krupat. The University of Oregon Humanities Center's conference "Witnessing Genocide" in April 2007 provided another important venue for me to work things out.

As I continued to feel my way along, I had the good fortune to spend several weeks at the Newberry Library in fall 2010. I'm indebted to Diane Dillon for arrangements and to the scholarly community there at that time, especially Juliana Barr and Jeani O'Brien, with whom I had a small glass of wine on one or two occasions. That spring I presented an early piece of this book at the "Bloody Days" conference at the McNeil Center in Philadelphia. I'm indebted to David Silverman for his comment on my paper there. I also benefited from participation in the symposium "Why You Can't Teach American History without Indians" at the Newberry Library in May 2013. Fred Hoxie's comment on my paper was very valuable, as was the general discussion. Since then, I've continued to benefit from comments on conference papers, including one by Andrew Woolford at the June 2013 conference of the International

Association of Genocide Scholars in Siena and another by Ned Blackhawk at the July 2014 meeting of the same organization in Winnipeg. Many of my colleagues at the University of Oregon attended a particularly inept work-in-progress talk I gave at the Oregon Humanities Center in May 2013. Their forbearance on this and other occasions were acts of mercy. John McCole, Ellen Herman, and David Luebke, who served as heads of the History Department at the University of Oregon, supported my work, as did department managers Martina Armstrong and Lauren Pinchin and their staffs. I didn't inflict this manuscript on my wife, Rosemarie, but her example of clear, clean writing was always before me as I stumbled along. She is heroic, and I'm happy to be getting old with her.

When I first approached Chris Rogers at Yale University Press, he promised to enlist top scholars to review my manuscript, and he did not disappoint. Criticisms and suggestions from Colin Calloway, Johnny Faragher, and at least one other anonymous reviewer were invaluable, as was the extraordinarily helpful reading I received from Chris himself. I was also fortunate that John Bowes, Joe Fracchia, and Paul Kelton were willing to read portions or all of the manuscript. This book is hardly perfect, but you should have seen it before these readers intervened! As I was finishing a final draft, Brett Rushforth provided a careful reading of the first chapter. Along the way, several experts responded to specific questions. I would like to thank James Buss, Cynthia Cumfer, Gregory Dowd, Tom Hatley, Christopher Haveman, Mike Moore of the Tennessee Division of Archaeology, Nancy Sherbert of the Kansas State Historical Society, Karim Tiro, Douglas Ubelaker, and Peter Wood.

I would have despaired of completing this book had it not been for generous support that allowed me to devote my full time to the project for significant periods. The University of Oregon is not a wealthy institution at least where the humanities are concerned, but under the direction of Steve Shankman, Barbara Altman, Paul Peppis, and Julia Heydon, the Oregon Humanities Center has done an incredible job of supporting research in the humanities, including the humanistic social sciences. I benefited especially from my time as an OHC fellow in spring 2008 and spring 2013. I also received invaluable external support from the National Endowment for the Humanities in the form of a summer fellowship in 2012 and a full-year fellowship in 2015–2016. Perhaps now more than ever the NEH's mission to "achieve a better understanding of the past" is essential. I can only hope that this book contributes to that mission.

Some of what I've learned about American Indian history has come from books, but I've probably learned even more from practitioners through conversation and friendship. I'm especially grateful to Juliana Barr, Colin Calloway, Brenda Child, Shari Huhndorf, Karl Jacoby, Brian Klopotek, Tsianina Lomawaima, Amy Lonetree, Ben Madley, Mark Meuwese, Jeani O'Brien, Beth Piatote, Josh Piker, Jacki Rand, Josh Reid, Jim Rice, Neal Salisbury, Nancy Shoemaker, and Susan Sleeper-Smith.

I've also learned a great deal from graduate students I've had the opportunity to work with as I was thinking about and writing this book. Torrie Hester, Nathan Jessen, Matthew Kruer, Patrick Lozar, Nick Rosenthal, and Gray Whaley have gone on from Oregon to do great things elsewhere. Quinn Akina, Marc Carpenter, Patience Collier, Feather Crawford, Tara Keegan, Annie Reiva, Christopher Smith, and Ian Urrea are doing great things now. They inspire me and give me hope.

Index

Figures are indicated by "f" following the page number.

Abenakis, 18, 121, 128, 185, 186

Abraham (Black Seminole), 276, 281, 285f

Adams, John Quincy, 197, 208

Adams–Onís Treaty (1818), 274

Adlum, John, 379–80

African Americans: Black Seminoles, 166, 249, 276–77, 284, 445n59, 447n74; incorporation into Native communities, 125–26, 166, 185–86, 189, 249

agriculture: in Native economy, 129–30, 130f

Alabama: asserting sovereignty over Creek Nation, 257

alcoholism and alcohol trade: alcohol-related violence, 339, 454n20; Council Bluffs as center of trade, 239–40, 338; destructiveness of, 337–40; as disease, 5, 22, 240, 347; factors promoting, 5, 339; federal laws applying only to reservations, 338–39; increase after removal of tribes, 338; indebtedness and, 133–34; Indian attempts to control, 132–33, 340; Santa Fe Trail as whiskey pipeline, 338; temperance movements in Native communities, 133, 292, 340

American Board of Commissioners for Foreign Missions, 193

American Fur Company, 235

American Revolution: Cherokees and southern colonies, 55–58; Creeks, Choctaws, and Chickasaws during, 59; Delawares as guides and fighters against British, 61–62; as "family quarrel" with Britain, 70, 74, 75; genocide during, 78–80; Gnaden-hütten massacre (1782), 65–69, 68f; independence as crisis for Native communities, 54–55; invasion of Ohio Valley (1777–1780), 59–65; land speculators' interests and, 53–54, 413n12; as "most destructive" war for Native nations, 74–78; movement of western boundaries as incentive for, 42–43; Native communities allied